Readers' Acclaim for Oberon Grimoire for the Appre.

"GRIMOIRE FOR THE APPRENTICE WIZARD is a landmark book. It's a combination history book, motivational book, self-help book and magickal primer all wrapped up in one.

"This is not a fictional Merlin story. The type of wizard described in this book is achievable. The concepts taught are the same ones that successful people all over the world have used to become captains of industry, company presidents and good parents. That's why I purchased copies for my grandchildren. (That way they will keep their hands off my copy!)" —**James Sawyer**, FL

"The GRIMOIRE provides a set of tools designed to allow young minds the opportunity to find their own way through the labyrinth of their imagination. I highly ... highly recommend this book to both new and old readers alike. It is refreshing to see an author who not only claims the intention to provide an open philosophy that still honours its history and practice, but who succeeds in doing so." —**Griffin**, CA

"The GRIMOIRE is so extensive that I highly recommend it to anyone on the Magickal Path, of any age—for it contains amazing amounts of reference material and sound psychism. It is incredibly well illustrated with diagrams, charts, magickal alphabets, herbal drawings, pictures and accessible depictions of some otherwise abstract concepts (including modern quantum physics)."—**Lady Pythia**, OH

"This is a phenomenal book. The author has put forth a fantastic compilation of knowledge for the aspiring wizard or avid reader. The text reads easy while at the same time provides a depth of information and practicing magick can be read over and over. I will never part with this compendium of magickal knowledge." —**Gabriel Moorhouse**

"Author Oberon Zell-Ravenheart clearly knows his stuff, and has a rare gift for sharing his decades of experience with the friendly ease of a true Wizard who knows how much to reveal, and where best to direct attention for one's development.

"This book will be devoured by the questing neophyte. The best part is how much fun this book is. This book will be seen on both virtual and actual bookshelves, and I am sure it will crop up on the pages of Gaiman, Moore, and yes, even at Hogwarts. I can hardly wait for the trading cards!!" —**Raven Marquez**, CA

"This book is jammed full of information and interesting tidbits, and it is laid out masterfully with borders and tables and charts. Our kids pick it up and thumb through it all the time, and I have read it cover to cover. Anyplace you open the book is something really interesting for young and old. Worth every penny and will be around the house for a long, long time." —**Ann**, a writer, Mom, & IT Director

"This is a book of everything you ever wanted to know about magick but didn't know whom to ask. Parents, buy this book for your son or daughter. Read it along with them so you'll know as much as they do. If enough kids apprentice themselves to the good Grey Council, we can have genuine hope for the future of the planet." —**Barbara Ardinger**

"There really is no better book then this. It is a window into many time, places and cultures, and lets you build your own practice, with or without spirituality. I recommend this book for everyone who is interested in growing and increasing their knowledge." —**Marina K. Payne**, OR

"This is one of the most incredible books I've read on magick. It covers the basics accurately and completely, giving the reader a realistic foundation to work upon. There is no idealism but hints at fantasy and imagination—traits of a true Wizard. This work is perfect for anyone at any level of magickal study. Cheers to you, Oberon." —**OakRaven**, MT

"Pure genius! If you only bought one book on Wizardry, buy this one! If you are looking for a superb book on the art and science of becoming a modern day wizard, look no further. For in the book as well as the school you have found the lost treasure. It's a Keepsake!" —**Terry Mook**, PA

"I don't think a day has gone by since that I haven't read and studied from this amazing work. It's not only a fascinating read, but for many, this book will open a door that previously stood closed: the door to magick and wizardry as ways of life.

"The GRIMOIRE is also the main text for the Grey School of Wizardry, an on-line school of wizardry for children and adults. The best news of all? A sequel to the book is in process!" —**Susan "Moonwriter" Pesznecker**, OR

"As a member of the magickal community, I purchased this book solely on the author's name alone. Oberon Zell-Ravenheart is like saying Dumbledore within Hogwarts.

"The book was highly researched, well written, and easily understandable. It is a unique way to do a book of this nature. I recommend this book to anyone and everyone. No matter what religion you are, you will find this book interesting.

"Also, as a member of The Grey School of Wizardry, yes you read that right, Dumbledore—er—ah—I mean Headmaster Oberon Zell-Ravenheart creates a warm and inviting environment for all who wish to truly begin their path to becoming a Wizard." —**Myrddin**, CT

"Even though the GRIMOIRE was meant for teenagers, it is not written that way. The GRIMOIRE has tons of information about all different aspects of Wizardry, which any age could use. Oberon Zell-Ravenheart wrote the book as if he was sitting there in front of you giving you the lessons. You can tell he cares about the student and knows what he is talking about. Very few authors manage to write this way.

"I highly recommend the GRIMOIRE and the Grey School. I look forward to Zell-Ravenheart's next book. Excellent work, Oberon Zell-Ravenheart!" —**Solaris**, NC

"This book on Wizardry is a highly-prized and much needed book of mentorship, training and fun on the path of the young Wizard! This book is the product of a man and Wizard who is on the edge of Paganism today. For anyone wishing to find their way to Hogwarts, this book is the roadmap!

"Along with this book comes the added bonus of the Grey School of Wizardry, where Professor Ravenheart is currently the Headmaster. See you at Platform 9¾!" —**Oracle**, FL

"If you only bought one magick book, GRIMOIRE FOR THE APPRENTICE WIZARD would be the one!"—**Lilyth Rose**, CA

COMPANION FOR THE APPRENTICE WIZARD
EDITED BY ALLY PELTIER AND ABBY WILLOWROOT
TYPESET AND FORMATTED BY OBERON ZELL-RAVENHEART
COVER ILLUSTRATION AND DESIGN: JEAN WILLIAM NAUMANN
PRINTED IN THE U.S.A. BY BOOK-MART PRESS

To order this title, please call toll-free 1-800-CAREER-1 (NJ and Canada: 201-848-0310) to order using VISA or MasterCard, or for further information on books from Career Press.

The Career Press, Inc., 3 Tice Road, PO Box 687,
Franklin Lakes, NJ 07417
www.careerpress.com
www.newpagebooks.com

Library of Congress Cataloging-in-Publication Data

Zell-Ravenheart, Oberon, 1942-
    Companion for the apprentice wizard / by Oberon Zell-Ravenheart.
        p. cm.
    Includes bibliographical references and index.
    ISBN 1-56414-835-1 (pbk.)
        1. Magic. 2. Wizards. I. Title.

BF1611.Z44 2006
133.43′3—dc22

2005057654

Companion for the Apprentice Wizard

Oberon Zell-Ravenheart
and the Faculty of the
Grey School of Wizardry

NEW PAGE BOOKS
A division of The Career Press, Inc.
Franklin Lakes, NJ

Foreword: The Companion and the Grey School
By Jesse Wolf Hardin, The Grey Council of Wizards

My dear friend Oberon Zell-Ravenheart is the Arch Wizard, the leading living elder of a noble magickal tradition dating back long before the likes of Merlin, back to those primitive medicine men and women who were the first to enlist power, the first to thirst for the taste of the unknown. But ours has always been a "profession" with few written records, with the knowledge of the ages passed on mostly orally from a master to his or her apprentice. With the publication of his *Grimoire For The Apprentice Wizard*, we were provided with the first credible, contemporary handbook of wizardry, and the beliefs and practices that form its very foundation. In this *Companion* volume, you have the second in a continuing series of supplemental texts provide exercises and assignments to increase your understanding, awareness, responsibility, power, and personal magickal abilities.

You'll find herein hands-on practices, delightful challenges, and yet moretools for changing our selves and our realities. In these pages are diagrams for fascinating magickal objects and ritual items that you can construct yourself, alongside hints on how join in being a conscious co-creator of an evolving universe! The emphasis, more than ever, is not just on learning, but on *doing*. There have always been a considerable number of people interested in reading about the ways of magick, but it's the most special of you who are willing to commit to the day to day work of a responsive, magickal life.

Most of us grow up and then grow old in societies where hardly anyone says what they really feel or does what they say they're going to do, where we're exposed to untruths, and often find ourselves surrounded by the artificial...from the imitation leather on our sandals to fake smiles and plastic trees.

A lot of what you'll read about Wizardry elsewhere is filled with "fluff-bunny," feel-good illusions. On the other hand, we're each and every one of us given a chance in life to be our authentic selves, even if at a cost. We're all born into a miraculous world filled with very real things to care about, including ourselves, each other, and the rest of the inspirited living planet, Gaia. We're also presented with opportunities—like those in this book you now hold in your hands—whether we find them through diligent research or have them seemingly dropped by the spirits into our very laps. There are cartoon wizards and weekend "wannabes," as well as genuine wizards doing amazing things. Your life is your chance, and perhaps even your calling, to "make it real:"to make real magick, and to better this wondrous world.

Believe it. You are gifted with the mental, spiritual, physical, and extrasensory potential you need to fulfill your deepest purpose; and to accomplish the miraculous. The term "mysteries" derives from the Greek "musterion," a word that meant not the unknown so much as "that which is known only by certain initiates and adepts." As a student of these writings you can count yourself among the select, the intimates of mysteries and unravelers of secrets...keepers not so much of faith as an insatiable curiosity, the endless urge to discover.

These days I host a number of students and apprentices of all ages here at our wilderness sanctuary, an ancient ceremonial center and true place of power. But bear in mind that all of our teachings, and all my five published books including *Gaia Eros* (New Page, 2004), are the product of forty-some years of devoted exploration and disciplined study. This lifetime of training began when I was a young solitaire, finding that my hyper-awareness and spooky intuition had put me on a lonely trail. With no-one understanding how I felt or being comfortable with my powers, I ended up running away from military school at the tender age of thirteen. And thus began my unending quest for wisdom and purpose. Not that they were particularly hard on me there, but what I hungered to know and experience couldn't be found in any state-approved curriculum. In the days before there was a Grey School of Wizardry, there was simply no place that taught the awareness, practices, responsibility and magick associated with this calling and art.

I had to sift through the fluff and nonsense of thousands of so-called "great books" to find in them those rare passages that illuminated what I knew instinctually to be truths. And without a gathering of wise elders to turn to, I was forced to spend years searching them out one at a time, hitchhiking hundreds of miles to try to meet and talk with the visionaries of my time: the hip Buddhist Alan Watts, radical poet Gary Snyder, native medicine man Rolling Thunder, Taos Indian spiritual leader Teles Goodmorning, and the priests and priestesses of numerous esoteric traditions. I studied Eastern mysticism, Wicca, primitive magick and applied shamanism, with most of what I know nonetheless coming directly from instructive nature and my many encounters with the forces and spirits I found there.

While I have no regrets for the difficult path I took, you are blessed to have the Grey School, somewhere you can go for understanding as well as information, affirmation, advice, training and support.

And you're fortunate to have this book—a true "Companion" in your continuing, insistent quest for vision, sacred purpose, meaningful service, wisdom and power. In this, you need never feel alone.

As always, some of the words or concepts you read here may be difficult for you at first. I'm sure you'll find that it's well worth your effort. Oberon will never talk down to you, because he knows you're able to rise to any challenge. And you have another advantage in that he is one of you: a playful and blissful youth at heart, even now with his flowing white beard.

Perhaps, like you, he was a bit of an ancient Medicine Man from the day he was born.

Join Oberon, myself and the rest of the Grey Council and School in committing to the lifelong effort to learn, to distinguish ourselves, to be "excellent to each other," to help Mother Earth, and to be the caring and courageous wizards we are surely meant to be!

Make it so, I say.

—Jesse Wolf Hardin
The Earthen Spirituality Project
Gila Wildlands, New Mexico

Prologue: The Third Wish
By Oberon Zell-Ravenheart

When I was a kid, I discovered the legend of the "Three Magic Wishes." In just about every culture, there are stories about a magick wish-bringer that grants three wishes. It may be the genie of the magic lamp, as in the tale of Aladdin. Or the magic fish in the Grimm Fairy tale. Often it is a ring—from Solomon's to Tolkein's. In W.W. Jacobs' famous short story (1902), it's a monkey's paw. And in a recent movie, it's a magick wishing powder.

Sometimes the offer comes from the gods (as Hera, Athena and Aphrodite presented their respective bribes to Paris, resulting in the Trojan War). And in Christian mythology, the deal is invariably offered by the Devil—starting with the temptation of Jesus (Mark 1:13; Luke 4:2). The Medieval tale of Dr. Faustus and Mephistopheles has given rise to modern literary and movie treatments of this theme, such as "Phantom of the Paradise," Terry Pratchett's "Eric," and "Bedazzled" with Elizabeth Hurley and Brendan Frazer.

In the Bible, Satan offers Jesus first Wealth; then Power; and finally, Fame. Jesus rejects them all, saying, "Get thee behind me, Satan!" But these three objectives remain the primary obsessions of humanity, and the basis of most people's wishes and pursuits (including those of many preachers and politicians claiming to follow Jesus!).

"Nine rings were given to the race of Men, who above all things desire Power." (*Lord of the Rings*) In at least two film treatments that I've seen ("The Man Who Could Work Miracles" and "Bruce Almighty" with Jim Carey), Godlike powers are temporarily granted to a mortal man, with humorously devastating results.

Every version of this story is a "wisdom tale," and the obvious lesson is always: "Be careful what you wish for; you may receive it!" Invariably, the protagonist totally screws up the first two wishes (if not the entire set), by wishing for wealth, fame and power—and getting them; but with terrible consequences.

In some versions of the story, however, a second and deeper lesson is conveyed, as the protagonist considers more carefully the third and final wish, and finally gets it right: instead of wishing for himself, he wishes for others. And that turns the curse of the three wishes into a blessing.

The purpose of such stories, of course, is to get us all thinking about our own goals, aspirations, and the work of our lives by which we each attempt to manifest what we wish for. This is what magick is all about—manifesting our wishes.

So when I came upon these stories as a kid, I began thinking about that final wish, deciding that it should be my first rather than last. And what I eventually came up with was a wish of ultimate magickal empowerment: "I wish for the full awakening of the psychic potential of every person in the world"—not just for myself. I figgered that there were far more good people than bad people in the world, and this would give us the edge.

Now, every magick-user knows that you can't just make a wish and then go off and forget about it. You have to conjure it into manifestation by focusing everything in your life and thoughts to that end; to "Make It So!" I came up with this wish about 50 years ago, and virtually everything I have done in my entire life over the past half-century has been wrapped around its manifestation.

In the early '70s, I expanded my original wish into a Vision of the awakening of planetary consciousness —of Gaea Herself. This Sacred Mission Statement became "...to evolve a network of information, mythology and experience to awaken the Divine within and to provide a context and stimulus for reawakening Gaea and reuniting Her children through tribal community dedicated to responsible stewardship and the evolution of consciousness."

And I have refined that original wish and a lifetime of work into a single word: "Awaken!"

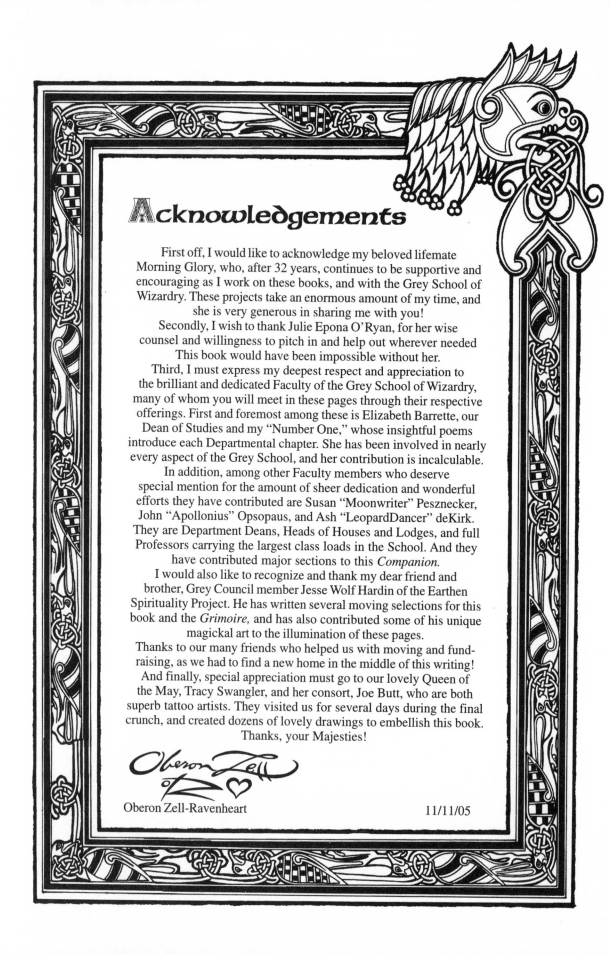

Acknowledgements

First off, I would like to acknowledge my beloved lifemate Morning Glory, who, after 32 years, continues to be supportive and encouraging as I work on these books, and with the Grey School of Wizardry. These projects take an enormous amount of my time, and she is very generous in sharing me with you!

Secondly, I wish to thank Julie Epona O'Ryan, for her wise counsel and willingness to pitch in and help out wherever needed This book would have been impossible without her.

Third, I must express my deepest respect and appreciation to the brilliant and dedicated Faculty of the Grey School of Wizardry, many of whom you will meet in these pages through their respective offerings. First and foremost among these is Elizabeth Barrette, our Dean of Studies and my "Number One," whose insightful poems introduce each Departmental chapter. She has been involved in nearly every aspect of the Grey School, and her contribution is incalculable.

In addition, among other Faculty members who deserve special mention for the amount of sheer dedication and wonderful efforts they have contributed are Susan "Moonwriter" Pesznecker, John "Apollonius" Opsopaus, and Ash "LeopardDancer" deKirk. They are Department Deans, Heads of Houses and Lodges, and full Professors carrying the largest class loads in the School. And they have contributed major sections to this *Companion.*

I would also like to recognize and thank my dear friend and brother, Grey Council member Jesse Wolf Hardin of the Earthen Spirituality Project. He has written several moving selections for this book and the *Grimoire,* and has also contributed some of his unique magickal art to the illumination of these pages.

Thanks to our many friends who helped us with moving and fund-raising, as we had to find a new home in the middle of this writing!

And finally, special appreciation must go to our lovely Queen of the May, Tracy Swangler, and her consort, Joe Butt, who are both superb tattoo artists. They visited us for several days during the final crunch, and created dozens of lovely drawings to embellish this book. Thanks, your Majesties!

Oberon Zell

Oberon Zell-Ravenheart   11/11/05

Table of Contents

Preface: "Once upon a time..."

Y FAVORITE PAINTING IS AN ORIGINAL piece that hangs on the living room wall in the home of Chaz and Debi LeFaye, Headmistress of the Academy of Ancient Arts near Lake Tahoe, NorCalifia. The 33" x 47" painting is by James C. Christiansen, and titled "Once Upon a Time..." As a grey Wizard and storyteller, I obviously identify very much with the central figure. And so, with Chaz and Debi's permission, I am reproducing it here.

Once upon a time...

...in September of 1961, actually; two young students met at the beginning of their freshmen year at a small college in the middle of rural Missouri. Their names were Lance Christie and Tim Zell, and each of them had grown up in the '50s feeling that they must be a different species from their parents and the people around them. Today, we would call them "changelings," from an old word meaning a Faerie child who has been somehow slipped into a family of "mortals." Each had left home on a quest to seek out others of their Kind.

Both were avid readers of science-fiction novels and comic books, and had been particularly taken by the recurrent theme of the emergence of a new stage in human evolution (*Homo Novus*, or "New Man," as this was called in the tales). They thought of themselves as mutant forerunners of a new kind of future humanity, which would have full use of all the powers of mind described in the stories.

One of their favorite such myths were Zenna Henderson's stories of "The People"—orphans of a destroyed and beloved homeworld whose refugee ancestors had crashed on Earth long ago in lifeboats when their mother ship exploded in orbit. Scattered and out of touch with others of their kind, they be-

came feared and persecuted for their "unearthly" powers and abilities. Those who survived learned to hide their differences, becoming secretive and paranoid. The moving stories tell of how various individuals find each other, generations later...

From their first meeting, Tim and Lance recognized each other as Kindred. Over the following months, they came together in many late-night discussion sessions, planning how they might find and contact others like themselves, and what they might do when they found them. They considered forming a club, a community, a foundation, a school, an institute—even a movement, if there were enough of them.

To learn about how to create such groups, Tim briefly joined one of the campus fraternities; and Lance and several other "misfits" founded an alternative "Animal House" fraternity called *Mu Omicron Alpha*—MOA (a Moa was a large flightless bird of New Zealand—now extinct).

Stranger than Fiction

And then, in October of 1961, a novel called *Stranger in a Strange Land* by Robert A. Heinlein arrived in Lance's mailbox as the Science Fiction Book Club selection of the month. He finally got around to reading it the following March, and, as he said, "was seized with an ecstatic sense of recognition." Lance turned the book over to Tim on April 4, saying that this one book dealt with much of what they had been thinking and talking about, and had brilliantly articulated many of their own coalescing thoughts.

The novel tells the tale of Valentine Michael Smith, a human born on the planet Mars as the sole survivor of a crashed first expedition, and raised by the ancient and wise race of Martians. Upon being brought back to Earth twenty years later by the next expedition, Michael (and with him, the reader) is able to view all of humanity's ingrained culture and cherished institutions from the unique perspective of an outsider. And, gathering others around him, he begins to create alternatives...

To foster this fledgling community of awakened souls, Michael establishes the Church of All Worlds, bringing them under the protection of the First Amendment to the U.S. Constitution: "Congress shall make no law respecting the establishment of religion; nor prohibiting the free exercise thereof."

As Mars is a cold, dry world, water is considered the most precious substance in the universe; and in the story, drinking *(grokking)* and sharing water becomes a metaphor for the deepest understandings and commitments. To share water and become a "water brother" with someone is to form a lifelong bond deeper than blood or marriage. And on April 7, 1962, Lance and Tim did just that, pledging to begin living a new dream, and bringing others into it. They gave the name *Atl* to the water-brotherhood they founded, as that was the Aztec word meaning both "water," and "ancient home of our ancestors."

Right about the same time, Marvel Comics introduced "The X-Men," a group of young mutants with assorted uncanny powers and abilities who are located and brought together by a wise mentor, Professor Charles Xavier, to become students in his "School for Gifted Youngsters." This idea also became an inspiration to those young water-brothers of the '60s. Indeed, Tim went on to earn a teaching certificate and work for many years in public and private schools—as a teacher and a counselor. But it took over forty years for that Vision to become fully realized, in an online School of Wizardry.

In the interim, a real-life Church of All Worlds was created, flourished for four decades, and was eventually torn apart through internal conflicts, dissension, and power struggles. Its demise freed up the energies of those involved for other projects. Tim had long ago taken on other identities—for a long time as Otter; and much later, as Oberon. Yes, that's me over there in the pointy hat! During this long journey, I had become a Wizard.

And now I am also the Headmaster of the Grey school of Wizardry…the wheel has turned full cycle.

The Grey School of Wizardry

So what, I can hear you asking, *is* the "Grey School of Wizardry"? Well, like everything else in my life as a Wizard, this too is a story…

When I began writing the *Grimoire,* I had no intention of starting an actual school of Wizardry. I figured that I'd design the *Grimoire* itself as a course of study, and then simply refer readers to various websites and online schools of Wizardry where they could go for further teachings. Since I'd taken particular pains to design a book that would be accessible to teenagers (particularly Harry Potter fans), I also wanted to make sure that sites I would be referring my readers to would be teen-friendly as well.

But at the time of that writing, as I soon discovered, there didn't seem to be any online websites or chat groups dedicated to serious Wizardry or Magick that were suitable for teens, and that weren't specifically *Pagan* or *Wiccan*-oriented. Paganism and Wicca are *religious* orientations, whereas Magick and Wizardry are *studies* and *practices* that are independent of any particular religion. And I felt this was an important distinction that I wanted to keep. Moreover, all of the serious websites and on-line schools that offered

magickal studies at all were for adults only—operating at a college level, and not admitting anyone under 18. And they were very expensive.

When I get an idea for something I really think should exist, but doesn't yet, I often take it as a "Mission Impossible" assignment to make it so. This was such an assignment. So I recruited a brilliant Web Wizard (Steven Day) and assembled a Faculty of qualified and dedicated teachers, and together we created a special "Grey School of Wizardry" website at www.GreySchool.com.

The earliest age of admission is 11, and the classes are designed for junior high and high school level (though we have students of all ages—clear up into their 70s!). I took on the responsibility of being Headmaster, and the *Grimoire* became the basic foundational textbook, with many of its lessons being incorporated into classes. Like the *Grimoire,* the Grey School is graduated in seven "year-levels," culminating in a Certificate of Journeyman Wizard.

Just as writing the *Grimoire* had taken all of 2003, creating the Grey School of Wizardry occupied the entirety of 2004. And no sooner had we gotten all the systems in place than my Publisher commissioned another book—this one! It is clear now that we have begun something that just won't quit. After this *Companion* book, there'll have to be a *Grimoire for the Journeyman Wizard.* And it'll have to have a Companion. And then a Grimoire (and a Companion) for the Master Wizard, and the Adept. And the Grey School will have to evolve to develop a college-level program for Journeyman Wizards to become Masters, and a graduate-school program for Masters to become Adepts.

Here's what one of our Grey School students has to say about this Vision:

> *Just Imagine:*
> *Ten years from now. Over a thousand have graduated to Journeymen Wizard, and another thousand Apprentices continue in training. The pendants we wear are no longer merely logos of the school we attend, but the symbol of our Order. And our symbol is not just recognizable to those whom we call brother and sister, but to the greater world, both Magickal and Mundane. We are respected as honored and reliable sources of wisdom, guidance and hope to the communities we live in. We are recognized in congress, the military, in covens and conclaves, and through our deeds we are recognized as an organization devoted to helping influence the evolution of the world.*
> —Stacy "WillowRune" Robinson

I think I am going to be very busy for quite awhile. The good thing is that I am enjoying wonderful company on this magickal adventure! So, to paraphrase Bilbo Baggins: "May we all live happily ever after, to the end of our days!"

Introduction

Booking Passage

There is no Frigate like a Book,
to take us Lands away,
Nor any Coursers like a Page
of prancing Poetry...
   – Emily Dickenson

The world holds no boundary a book cannot breach,
And rare is the mystery that no page may teach.
Power fills the written word, opening its wings,
For knowledge is a bird that loud in silence sings.

This is the teacher at whose aged feet I sit,
The classroom that I choose when I have choice of it.
I have learned little that does not lie in some book –
And that, I have sought to place there myself. Go look.

—Elizabeth Barrette

 ELCOME BACK, MY FRIENDS, TO THE wonderful world of Wizardry!

My previous book, *Grimoire for the Apprentice Wizard,* provided a general introduction to Wizardry in its many forms and aspects. I put into it everything that I and the Grey Council thought you should know to have a functional foundation in what is truly the world's oldest and best-documented profession—that of the Wizard. We all set out to create the book we wished we could have gotten hold of when we first set foot on our magickal journey—and I believe that we succeeded. I hope you will have already picked that book up and have it available, because I will be referring to it frequently, and I prefer not to repeat myself.

Now, in this companion volume, I will focus not so much on lessons and teachings, as with the *Grimoire,* but rather on practical exercises derived from them to develop your psychic and magickal skills, plus instructions, diagrams, and templates for many things to make and do. This kind of book is properly called a *Practicum,* because it is all about the practical applications of teachings. I wanted to call it *Practicum for the Apprentice Wizard,* but my Publisher didn't think readers would pick up on such a title, so they decided on *Companion.* Members of the Grey Council whom you've already met in the *Grimoire* have contributed to this volume as well, and many new contributors are from the Faculty of the Grey School of Wizardry, of which I am Headmaster.

Much of this material is based on classes developed for the Grey School. Each of the sixteen Departments in the Grey School—and in this book—is keyed to a particular color.

Color-Coded Wizardry

Throughout history and legend a number of "Schools," Orders, and specialized practices of magick and Wizardry have been designated. Many of these have distinguished themselves by colors. Much as the students of Hogwarts are entered into the respective Houses of Gryffindor (red), Ravenclaw (blue), Hufflepuff (yellow) or Slytherin (green), the work and teachings of these schools have focused on such color-coded categories of practice.

Wizards following those schools have consequently adopted those colors also, so we have Red Wizards, Green Wizards, White Wizards, Black Wizards (these tend to be Sorcerers), etc. Grey Wizards (or, as some call themselves, "Rainbow Wizards") are non-specialized, being adept in many areas. Some Witches have also adopted color identifications – particularly White and Green. And similar colors are also accorded to Faeries.

In J.R.R. Tolkein's *Lord of the Rings,* each of the five great Wizards (known in Elven as the *Istari*) of Middle Earth was identified by a color. After Gandalf the Grey destroyed the Balrog, he became Gandalf the White, replacing Saruman the White who had been seduced by the Dark Lord Sauron (black). Another Wizard of Middle Earth was Radagast the Brown, who had a special affinity with animals. The remaining two Istari are never mentioned in the trilogy, but they are identified in other books. Their names are Pallando and Alatar, and they are both blue.

We see the same concept in the academic world, where the gowns traditionally worn by university professors are colored according to their areas of major studies. This system originated in the 12th and 13th centuries, when the first universities were chartered by the Roman Catholic Church. Most of what they taught was religious studies, and teachers and students were mainly clergy. Thus the academic cap, gown, and hood originated in the clerical dress of that period.

At the Council of Oxford in 1222, Stephen Langton, Archbishop of Canterbury in England, decreed that all clergy within his jurisdiction should wear the *cappa clausa* ("closed cape"), a closed, flowing gown then in fashion. Because Oxford and Cambridge were in his province, the clerks at both universities complied with the decree. Over the years English clergy adopted other styles, but professors—many of whom were also Wizards—kept the *cappa clausa*, and it eventually became exclusively academic.

The Intercollegiate Code provides a standardized correspondence of 27 gown colors with academic disciplines. Some of these (there are many more) are:

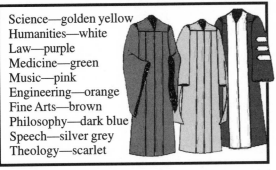

Science—golden yellow
Humanities—white
Law—purple
Medicine—green
Music—pink
Engineering—orange
Fine Arts—brown
Philosophy—dark blue
Speech—silver grey
Theology—scarlet

In the same way, as students begin their 2nd year of apprenticeship in the Grey School of Wizardry, they will be asked to consider which colors of Wizardry they feel most connected with. These colors are used to designate Departmental Majors. They will also appear on the student's Diploma certifying them as a Journeyman Wizard, which will be awarded upon graduation. Students are encouraged to create a Tabard (a simple over-the-shoulder draping that Wizards wear when doing particular kinds of magick) and other magickal garb of their chosen colors. Students may also work with those colors in various forms of magick such as candle-burning, chromotherapy, altar cloths, choices of gemstones in personal jewelry, etc.

You may notice that there are four more colors here than those I listed in the *Grimoire*, and I'd like to explain this. The twelve traditional Colors of Magick are: **aqua** (Metapsychics, or "mind magicks"), **blue** (Healing), **green** (Wortcunning, or Herbalism), **yellow** (Divination), **red** (Alchemy and Magickal Sciences), **orange** (Performance and Conjury), **brown** (Beast Mastery), **violet** (Cosmology and Metaphysics), **clear** (Mathemagicks), **white** (Ceremonial Magick), **grey** (Lore), and **black** (Sorcery and the "Dark Arts"). These are included as chapters in this book.

However, there is a secret 13th Color of Magick which is not generally spoken of in the "outer court," or among apprentices. This color is **pink**, and its inner Mysteries are explored at the Journeyman level. However, after much debate among the Faculty, we decided to introduce this area of magick in the Grey School through the Department of Lifeways, and so I am also including such a chapter in this *Companion*. In this context, it will address your relationships with other people.

The other three colors presented in the Grey School and this book are not exactly colors of magick *per se,* but more areas of Wizardly studies, which we considered useful to include. Each of these, in their own way, draws upon and utilizes many of the other colored magicks. These Departments are: Wizardry (**indigo**), Nature Studies (**silver**), and Magickal Practice (**gold**).

Consider all these colors to be areas of specialization, such as Majors in college. Just as a student may graduate from college with a Major in, say, Botany, and become known as a Botanist; an apprentice in Wizardry may complete their apprenticeship specializing in Wortcunning, and become known as a Green Wizard.

Notes on Style

Here are a few notes about my writing style. First, you will notice that when I refer to some important historical person, I will often list after their name their dates of birth and death, like: (1475-1520). If such dates are obviously during the *common era* of our Western civil calendar (in which the current year I am writing is 2005), I will often leave them at that.

If they are very early on, however—such as in Roman times, I may specify "common era" by noting "CE" after the date—as in "376 CE." This means the same as when other writers use "AD" (for *anno domini*—"year of our Lord" in Latin—referring to the "Christian Era"). In the same way, for dates *before* the common era, I will add "BCE," just as others might use "BC" (for "before Christ"). You will find this same usage in many magickal and scientific writings, so I thought an explanation would be in order.

Sometimes we just don't have precise records of a person's year of birth or death, so the following customary notes have been adopted: "c." stands for *circa,* meaning "about." "fl." means "flourished," indicating the time during which someone was most famous. "b." and "d." means "born" and "died." For Kings, Queens, Emperors, and Popes, "r." indicates the period of their reign.

Since this *Companion* will be introducing you to many new words and concepts, I will include simple phonetic keys to pronunciation for words that might be somewhat obscure. Here is an example: (pro-NUN-see-AY-shun). The syllable (SIL-a-bull) in all capital letters is the one which gets the emphasis (EM-fa-sis). (There is a joke about "Putting the em-FAH-sis on the wrong sil-AH-bull"...)

And since many magickal terms come from older languages than English (especially Latin and Greek), I will frequently include a little translation when I first introduce such words, such as *polyhedron* (Gr. "many-sided"). I will also draw your attention to such words by writing them in *italics* the first time they appear.

Department I: Wizardry (indigo)

So You Want to Be a Wizard?

So you want to study magic
Such as makes the world go 'round?
Well, you've barely skimmed the surface
Of what you've already found!

So you want to be a Wizard
And to learn the ancient lore?
Let me tell you, little seeker,
That I've heard that song before!

> *But you don't understand...*
> *You still can't understand*

This is not all spells and sparkle,
Never mind what minstrels say;
It's a duty and a privilege
That will plague you night and day.

First, there's nothing I can teach you
That does not come from within,
So go see the world, then come back,
And perhaps I'll let you in.

> *But you don't understand...*
> *You still can't understand*

So you whisper to the shadows
And you listen to the light
And you walk across the fire
To go dancing with the night.

So you ride down wild rivers
'Til they tumble into seas
And you share your tears with snowstorms
'Til you think your cheeks will freeze.

> *But you don't understand...*
> *You still can't understand*

So you hike through winding canyons
And you crawl through dripping caves

And you sneak through cemeteries
To lie dreaming on the graves.

So you drive yourself up mountains
Over desert, plain, and fen
And you fling yourself from clifftops
Then you do it all again.

> *But you don't understand...*
> *You still can't understand*

So you drop your expectations
And give up the quest at last
And the present and the future
Seem as ghostly as the past

So you see the stars a-whirling
In the heavens overhead,
And you hear a hundred voices
And you wonder if you're dead.

> *But you don't understand...*
> *You still can't understand*

Oh, then suddenly you feel it
Like an arrow in the heart –
Piercing secrets, bringing power –
And you know it's time to start.

So you climb up to my tower
As you did so long before,
And you marvel for a moment
Then walk through the open door.

> *But you don't understand...*
> *You still can't understand*

So I greet you as a student
And you hear the words I say:
For to get the most of knowledge,
You must give it all away;

For to get the most of power,
You must keep your honor whole;
And to make the most of magic,
You must let it share your soul.

> *But you don't understand...*
> *You still can't understand*

You have faced Earth, Air, and Water
Flame and Spirit both as well
For the whole wide world has
    taught you
And you've learned much– I can tell.

There's a place far down inside you
Where there waits a hidden prize.
Let me be your magic mirror:
See yourself through my own eyes.

> *But you don't understand...*
> *You still can't understand*

Now you see the deepest secret:
That a Wizard serves all life,
Taking up the hand of magic
Like a husband or a wife.

Feel the power bloom within you,
Filling all your mortal span:
Wizard, from this moment onward,
Do whatever good you can.

> *So now you understand...*
> *At last you understand.*

—Elizabeth Barrette

1. Introduction

IZARDRY IS ABOUT WISDOM. JUST AS Artistry is the applied craft of an Artist, Wizardry is the applied craft of a Wizard.

What is it that distinguishes wisdom from foolishness? Simple. Wisdom is about seeing the larger picture, and considering the consequences of every word and deed. Foolishness is what happens when we pursue our own narrow self-interest and ignore any con-sideration of consequences. To see sterling examples of this, just observe most politicians in action!

The color associated with Wizardry in general is Indigo, which relates to perception, imagination, illusion, and the ability to see patterns. Indigo shading to ultraviolet is often called "the color of magick." This is a popular color for Wizard's robes—often emblazoned with stars, moons, and other astronomical symbols.

In this Department, we will explore perceptions and illusions, and make a few of the clever little toys that have been invented over the centuries to take advantage of the way our eyes and brains work to create the world we see. You will learn how our perceptions can be manipulated, and how to create such illusions!

But before we get to that part, you need to create and begin keeping your Magickal Journal. Grey School Professor Susan "Moonwriter" Pesznecker, Dean of Cosmology & Metaphysics, will teach this important first lesson.

2. Your Magickal Journal
By Susan "Moonwriter" Pesznecker (indigo)

The History of Journal-Keeping

Some of the first records—and perhaps the first journals—were written on scrolls. A scroll is a rolled up piece of parchment, papyrus, or paper that is used for writing.

Parchment is made from calf, sheep, or goat skin, while papyrus was made from the stems of the papyrus plant. Papyrus was first used in Ancient Egypt around 3000 BCE but by 1000 BCE, people from West Asia began buying it from the Egyptians. Up until then, the West Asians had only used clay tablets; they found that papyrus was much more convenient!

To make papyrus, the plant stems were cut lengthwise and soaked in water until they began to rot. Several layers of these strips were laid on top of each other in different directions, then pounded while wet, smashing the stems together into a single sheet.

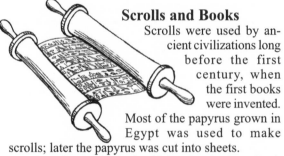

Scrolls and Books

Scrolls were used by ancient civilizations long before the first century, when the first books were invented. Most of the papyrus grown in Egypt was used to make scrolls; later the papyrus was cut into sheets.

A *codex* (Latin for book) is a handwritten book dating from the Middle Ages. The codex was an improvement over the scroll because it could be opened flat at any page, allowing easier reading and writing on both sides of the page. The codex also made it easier to organize documents in a library because it could be stood upright on shelves.

History suggests that as soon as there were materials to write on, people began keeping journals. Journals have served many important roles in history and exploration. When ships struck out across the oceans, the Ship's Log or Captain's Log was its most valuable possession and the log-keeper the most valuable crewmember, second only to the captain. These logs provided details of the journey that would later be evaluated by monarchs and scientists back home. Without a journal, much of the journey's importance would have been lost.

In the same way that explorers' journals marked and recorded their adventures, your magickal journal will track your journey as a Wizard. Through it, you will be able to look back at your progress, from one class to another and one year to another. You'll be able to chart your discoveries, recall rituals or holidays, or note insights from your professors. You'll use it to detail those "ah ha" moments that are dear to the heart of magick.

In short, through your Journal and a set of related tools, you will learn. And grow.

Just for fun

Make your own scroll! You'll need a piece of paper, a 10-inch piece of ribbon, and a wooden spoon or thick dowel. Starting with the short end, wrap the paper tightly around the dowel. When it's all wound up, tie it securely in place with the ribbon. Set it aside for a week, then untie the ribbon and remove from the wooden center. You'll have a nice rolled up scroll on which to write charms, draw secret maps, or note the moon phases!

Your Magickal Journal

Choosing a Magickal Journal

As an apprentice Wizard, one of the most important things you will do is keep a magickal journal. Why is the magickal journal so important?

- Writing about your new skills and abilities will help you to track your progress.
- By writing the details of spells, rituals, and other projects, you will be able to refer back to and reuse them.
- By recording dates, moon phases, weather information, etc., you may be able to make connections between your abilities and various magickal or natural correspondences.
- Discipline is an important part of Wizardry. Writing in your journal requires self-discipline, and that alone is a good reason for doing it.

What Kind of Journal Should I Use?

First and foremost, you should pick a method of journaling that is easy for you, so you'll be more likely to use it often and to enjoy doing so. Many apprentice Wizards choose a traditional paper journal, either lined or unlined. Some prefer a loose-leaf binder, which allows you to add and rearrange pages.

Your journal should be big enough to use comfortably, but small enough to fit into a backpack or other carrying case. It may be hard or soft-covered; hard-covered journals tend to hold up longer than soft ones.

Nowadays it's easy to find journals with decorative covers. You may want to search for a journal that matches an area of wizardly interest, your magickal name, a spirit animal or totem, etc. You might choose a color that reflects your magickal interests, such as green for Wortcunning, or black for Dark Arts. If you're ambitious and artistic, you might even choose to decorate your own!

Technologically adept Wizards might choose a computer or laptop for keeping their magickal journal, setting it up in a word-processing document. If you use a computer for your journal, you will probably still choose to carry a small spiral notebook with you, so that you can write down ideas when you're away from your computer.

Dedicating Your Journal

Some Wizards conduct a ritual to consecrate and/or dedicate their Journal. Or, they might create a blessing to write on the inside of the front cover. Both ritual and blessing might ask that the journal serve as a tool of wisdom, guidance, and focus. For example:

Guard my words and keep them safe,
Here within this treasured place.

Keeping Your Journal Safe

A magickal journal is a personal and private thing. No one should look into your journal without your permission. Some Wizards even believe that no one should *ever* look into another person's magickal journal, and that to do so diminishes its power.

When you aren't using your journal, keep it in a safe place so that it doesn't fall into mundane hands. You may wish to wrap it in a cloth that corresponds with your main area of study (see the Introduction for color associations). Keep it on a shelf, in a drawer, or in its own box.

Using Your Magickal Journal

What should I write?

The answer is simple: write whatever you want and whatever seems relevant to your Wizardly growth. Every entry should include:
- Date
- Time
- Weather
- Location (where are you writing from, or where did the ritual/spell/event take place?)
- Your main topic or idea

Additional entries may include (according to your interests):
- The moon phase or zodiacal position
- What's happening in your Wizardly studies
- What's happening in your mundane life: family, friends, work, school, trips, etc.
- What's happening in the mundane world
- Your dreams, and any thoughts about them
- Your feelings, moods, or insights about any topic
- Favorite quotes or insights
- Poems, stories, sketches, maps, diagrams, or other creative works
- Magickal works such as rituals, spells, talismans, or alphabets
- Magickal books, films, or other sources of learning
- Future plans or goals

As your journal grows, you may want to consider these questions:
- Do you see any relationships between events in the natural world (weather, moon phase, day/night, season, etc.) and your own inner world?
- Do you see any patterns or progress in your studies?
- Can you see emotional or spiritual growth in your entries?

Some Wizards like to set certain times—Solstices, Equinoxes, the start or end of the month, etc.—at which they review their journal entries. This helps them chart their progress and evaluate their Wizarding life.

You can also draw in your journal. Diagrams, sketches, maps, and other illustrations will add to your written entries.

When should I write in my journal?

At first, try to write every day. This will get you into a disciplined routine, and routines and discipline are helpful to beginning Wizards! As you become more experienced, you will write as often as you feel the need to.

You'll also want to make an entry whenever something important happens to you as a Wizard, for example, when you attend a community celebration of magickal folks, or if you master a new skill.

Making Your Journal a Thing of Beauty

Inks, Pens, and Archival Materials

Some Wizards choose to use ballpoint (rather than "gel") ink in their journals, as it doesn't bleed or run when damp. Others prefer gel inks. Both gel and ballpoint pens are available with archival-quality inks, which remain stable over decades.

An advantage of gel pens is their availability in a wide variety of colors, which can allow your writing to correspond with specific magickal colors. (For example, a healing spell could be written in blue, or an herbal charm in green). Gel pens also come in metallic and glitter varieties. The metallics are quite stable. Glitter pens can be fun, but the glitter eventually wears off when the journal pages rub together.

Pencil entries are best avoided, as they smudge and fade quickly.

Some Wizards reserve a special pen for important

entries. I have a sterling silver fountain pen that I use to write anything that I consider "special," or important.

Others enjoy using a quill pen that is dipped into a well or bottle of ink. This is fun and is definitely a most Wizardly activity. However if you try this, make sure you do so in a safe place, one in which a spill wouldn't be disastrous. Most of these inks are permanent! I have included a magickal ink recipe in my Alchemy lesson in Chapter 9.

Calligraphy

Artistic Wizards might use colored pencils or pens to decorate their pages, creating "illuminated" journals. Or they might adorn the pages with calligraphy. Calligraphy (from the Greek "beauty"+"writing") is the art of decorative writing. A particular style of calligraphy is described as a "hand."

Calligraphy

Calligraphy is an art. As handwritten communication becomes more rare, calligraphy has become reserved for special occasions and events, most notably the addressing of wedding invitations and announcements.

It is possible to buy books and kits that teach the basics of calligraphy or illumination. Several web sites teach calligraphy. If you are lucky enough to have a group from the Society of Creative Anachronism nearby, you may find a teacher of calligraphy among its ranks.

Applying What You've Learned

Here are some projects you can do to develop your skills:

- Make a journal entry using a specific color or type of ink.
- Find someone who can teach you calligraphy; or pick up a book on calligraphy at a stationary store. Practice until you can write all of the letters of one alphabet easily. Then, use your skills to make an entry in your magickal journal.
- Use skills of illumination and/or calligraphy to create a greeting card for a friend or family member.

3. Awareness for Wizards

By Jesse Wolf Hardin (silver)

For the Wizard every moment is a decisive moment, and we treat everything we do and don't do as a deliberate decision. We're never witless victims, so we can never whine! This is what makes us different from the mundanes, more so than our other skills, the ways we dress or believe. In fact, the defining trait for a Wizard is heightened awareness. The most amazing of our magickal abilities can only serve us or our purpose well when we are totally aware– aware of the full extent of our abilities as well as any possible limitations, aware of the present situation and context, aware of the conscious intent and magickal energies of others.... and aware of the intentional as well as unintentional effects of our spells, prayers and actions.

We have the most evolved ability to think and reason of any creature on this planet, but Wizards also need to develop a kind of ancient animal awareness housed not only in the mind but in flesh and bone, and in our very genetic makeup. It was common to our ancient tribal ancestors, and in the primates we evolved from. You can see it in the alertness of a cat when it is hunting a bird or mouse, just as it once glinted in the eye of prehistoric saber-tooth tigers.

This quality is most noticeable in us when we are surprised by a new and dangerous situation, when everything around us seems suddenly clear and in focus, when we become aware of every movement and sound and seem able to anticipate what will happen next. This kind of thing occurs without any commentary or abstract thought going on in our minds, just as when there's a rustling at our feet we know to jump out of the way without first thinking the word "snake."

This is what the Buddhists call *presence*, being aware of the vital present moment. The Wizard and spiritual warrior combines this heightened presence with purposeful action and considered response, in order to help shape events and thus consciously co-create our world. Only the totally aware can make the right choices.... and for the Wizard every single act, no matter how big or small, is a conscious choice.

While everyone is born with some capacity for awareness, most mundanes will grow up without exercising their inner abilities, or else actually decide to be less aware in order to get away with less responsibility. On the contrary, Wizards embrace responsibility and spend their entire lives strengthening their abilities and deepening their awareness through deliberate practice. When a baby is growing up, it has to practice walking over and over again before finally getting good at it.

The fastest runners are athletes who practice diligently, people who push themselves to do their best and expand their abilities on a daily basis. It's no different for Wizards who must practice their awareness skills every moment they aren't asleep, for so long as they breathe! And the rewards and delights come alive, for those most aware of life.

Try these simple awareness exercises:

- Always be aware of which way the sun comes up and sets, even in a strange town or when it is cloudy. Whether the moon is waning, waxing or full. The direction that water flows from where you stand and the nearest above ground creek, plus the direction of the wind no matter how lightly it touches your cheek.

• Nature is the best place to practice awareness—even in a wooded backyard or park—but it isn't the only place. Practice awareness every moment that you are not asleep, practice when hanging out and practice in school.

• Attention is a gift we give to ourselves every time we pay close attention to what's around us. When walking down the sidewalk, notice what grass or plants grow on either side. Notice the designs where the cement has cracked, and the dandelions that poke their heads up through them. Notice the different sounds of the vehicles coming and going even if you find it unpleasant, and notice and enjoy the diverse songs of the birds even while you're busy talking.

• Focus on perceiving the world through one physical sense at a time, in order to increase its strength. One way to do this is to blindfold yourself, and then try to find a friend just by the sounds he makes, or find an orange placed near you in the grass by sense of smell alone. Another is to have someone give you bites of food with your eyes closed so you can guess what you are eating. It's not as easy as you might think!

• Wherever you are, notice the locations of edible plants and life-sustaining drinking water. Look out for any sources of potential threats– from dangerous traffic to fallen power lines to sullen faces, icy walkways and suspicious places.

Mother Earth, the inspirited source of all insight and magick, is there for us when we need her. We have only to stop, seek and listen. Art by Jesse Wolf Hardin

• If you know others who are into developing their powers, you can make a game of challenging each other. Have one friend walk through a room when no one is expecting a test, then ask the others what they noticed. Who just passed through, what was he or she wearing? What else did he or she do? Was there anything in his hand? How did others in the room respond or interact with her? Were there any clues as to his intention or purpose?

• Watch the people around you. What do their body postures communicate, and do they tell a different story than the person's facial expressions? Based on their clothes, hair and posture, what do they want us to think about them, and what do they think about themselves? Are their energies focused inward uncertainly, or do they project their energies? If they are projecting, what is it that they are trying to effect, direct,

change or create? How aware does each person seem to be of the other, and in what ways are they connecting or relating? Try to identify the source of fear in the room and in each person, and the source of gifting and love.

• Practice sensing the presence of resident energies and entities, especially the spirit of place. Once you get attuned to feeling the unseen, it becomes like a game of "Hot and Cold." The closer you get to real power the more it feels significant, tingly and impossible to ignore, and when you pass by or make a turn in the wrong direction the sensation subsides.

• Notice what is hard, and deliberately get stronger from it. Notice what takes skill and learn from it. Notice the benefits of commitments, and consciously commit to the whole and right.

• Notice what makes you feel comfortable and what makes you uncomfortable. Remember that comfort can be the bigger disadvantage to a Wizard. Our greatest opportunities for power lie through those doors that most disrupt and discomfort us, by those we're at first afraid to open.

• Always notice the effect you have on people, as well as on the environment around you. What impact does your attitude or example, your attention or neglect, your ideas and actions have on the people you come into contact with? Are they better informed or inspired? How does the way you live directly or indirectly impact Gaia's other magickal life forms—the land, water and air—for better or worse? Constantly shift your perception and actions to best benefit others and the world.

• Practice focusing and intensifying your intentions, and then watch what happens. What did you intend, pray or wish for so hard that it seemed to come true? Which friends, ideas, conversations, activities, types of TV shows, or personal habits seem to distract your attention and dilute your intentions, lessening or preventing the desired magickal results?

• At the end of every day, try to remember the details of everything that happened, how things looked, acted and felt, and write the details down in your Journal. Record not only what you noticed, but how you responded and what effects or results you inevitably brought about.

4. Perceptions and Illusions

By Oberon (grey)

As I explained in the Grimoire, a large part of Wizardry is learning to see things in ways others don't. A fun way that Wizards through the ages have developed to demonstrate and hone this ability is the art of Optical Illusions.

Many illusions are of matters of *perspective* ("looking through"), where our mind automatically links size with distance, so that if one object appears smaller than another, we perceive it as being further away. And if something seems to be far away, we expect it to look smaller. We take this phenomenon so for granted today that it's hard to believe that perspective wasn't employed by artists until the Renaissance! Medieval art commonly shows distant figures the same size as those in the foreground, as our minds know them to really be. If you have a friend stand at a distance away from you, you can close one eye and hold up your hand so that it appears you can grab him between your thumb and forefinger! But we know this is just an illusion, and our mind compensates, so we perceive him at his correct size. And that's how those Medieval artists would have drawn him!

Here is an amusing drawing made by William Hogarth in 1754, to admonish and teach people how to draw in perspective. Hogarth said: "Who makes a design without the knowledge of perspective will be liable to such absurdities as shown in this frontispiece."

Peter Jackson used the principle of perspective to good advantage in making *The Lord of the Rings,* when he created "forced perspective" camera angles to make the Hobbits appear much smaller than the actors actually were. He would just have Frodo or Bilbo stand a little further away than Gandalf or Aragorn, so the Hobbits seemed smaller in comparison. To perfect the illusion, Jackson had the props and sets shown with the Hobbits made proportionately larger.

Another example is the "moon illusion," one of the most famous of all optical illusions. The full moon, when just above the horizon, appears to be much larger than when it is overhead. Yet the moon, 238,000 miles away from the Earth, always subtends the same angle wherever it is in the sky—roughly half a degree. It seems larger near the horizon because our minds perceive the horizon as being further away than the sky overhead.

"Terra Subterranea" by Roger Shephard (above) is an illusion based on false perspective. Which figure is really larger—the scared little man running in front, or the giant mean bully chasing him? Actually, both figures are identical in every way—including size!

Another form of Optical illusions is based on *ambiguity* ("both wandering"—having two or more possible meanings). Ambiguous images show more than one thing at the same time. These are really the most amazing forms of hidden images! What you

see depends on the way you look at it. These are also called *metamorphic* images. The little face on the preceding page is a classic example. Look; then look again—what do you see?

Do you see the mother, father, *and* daughter by G.H. Fisher?

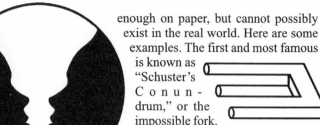

Or how about this one to the left; is it a swan or a squirrel?

In the famous example to the right, the effect is created by a reversal of background vs. foreground, depending on whether you are seeing the images as the black part, or the white. Can you see both the vase *and* the faces?

What is the image above?

There are images that look completely different if you just turn them to the side. Would you trust this man on the right?

There are images that actually play tricks with your mind! Hold this page a foot or so away, and stare at the center point of the circles below while moving your head backwards and forwards. S ee what happens!

Then there are images that look real

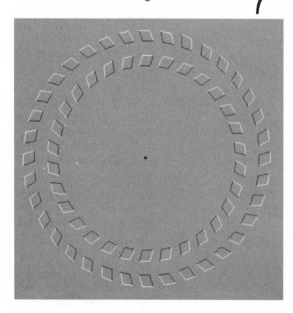

enough on paper, but cannot possibly exist in the real world. Here are some examples. The first and most famous is known as "Schuster's Conundrum," or the impossible fork.

There are endless variations on it, such as this elephant, by Roger Shepard, called "L-Egs-istential Quandry." How many legs *does* that elephant have?

Many, many more such optical illusions— quite a few of them in full color—may be seen at the "Amazing Art" website: http:// members.lycos.nl/ amazingart

Watchbird

There is another optical illusion effect that has many uses. It is based on rendering a 3-D image in concavity (hollow) rather than the normal convexity (bulging) of real objects. Because we expect real things to be convex, these types fool us easily. Such illusions are very ancient indeed—I have seen them painted on cave walls in France by Cro-Magnon artists of 20,000 years ago! In the long passages, animals were painted as if they were processing towards the cave entrance to be born. Some were painted on flat surfaces. Others were cleverly painted over natural lumps and bulges in the rock wall. But the most amazing were painted into hollows in the stone—and as you moved past them, the light from the flickering oil lamps would cast shadows inside these hollows that made the figures truly seem to come alive!

This technique has become most popular today in the form of hollow-cast insides of face-masks, realistically painted as if they were normally convex. Framed like ordinary portraits, they appear to turn and follow you around the room in a very spooky way!

I have designed a little paper model you can copy onto card stock and cut out to illustrate this illusion. I call it "The Watchbird Watching You!" Before you cut it out, use the back edge of a dull table knife and a ruler to "score" along the dotted fold lines. Use white milk glue for this and all other cutouts.

After you assemble it,

place it on a shelf at eye-level, close one eye, and move back and forth in front of it. The bird's head will appear to turn, and its eyes will follow you wherever you go! But the illusion disappears when you look at it with both eyes. Can you figure out why?

By the way, the effect is greatly enhanced if you set the Watchbird into a clear glass vase or fishbowl with rounded sides.

5. Optical Animations

In the early 19th century, several scientists and inventors made the discovery that a series of still images can be used to create the effect of a continuous moving picture. This happens because the brain naturally retains images the eyes see for a moment to ensure that the world does not go black every time you blink!

This is known as the *Phi phenomenon,* or, more commonly, the "persistence of vision." First noted in 1820 by Peter Mark Roget, this refers to the length of time the *retina* (the light-sensitive projection screen" at the back of our eyes) retains an image. If we see a light flash every tenth of a second or less, we perceive it as continuous. The impression of each flash of light remains, or persists, in the retina for at least 1/10 of a second. Because of this persistence, we can't tell where one flash ends and the next begins. Instead, we perceive a continuous light.

This phenomenon is the basis for all animations and movie films. A series of progressively changing images must be presented to the eye at the rate of at least 10 per second, and a blank space must fall between each image, so that they do not blur into each other. The brain then forms a mental bridge between the two images, and it appears that the static images are actually moving. (Have you ever looked closely at a piece of movie film to see all the individual images? It takes 24 frames of film per second to convince your eye that something is moving on a projection screen!)

Animated optical toys based on this phenomenon were given names from the Greek that end in *trope* for "turning" or *scope* for "viewing."

Thaumatrope

In 1824, English physician Dr. John Ayrton Paris invented a simple device to demonstrate the Phi Phenomenon to the British Royal College of Physicians. It consisted of a disc with pictures on both sides, and two pieces of string attached to it. When the disc was spun between the strings, the images on the back and front appeared to blend together to form a single picture. Two years later, he began selling these as the first animated toys in London. He called it a *Thaumatrope (THOM-a-trope)* (Greek: "wonder turner"). Popular images included birds and mice in cages, circus performers, and fights between dogs and cats. Thaumatro-

pes were the first of many optical toys, simple devices that continued to provide animated entertainment until the development of modern cinema.

You can easily make your own Thaumatropes from the designs I've provided in the back of this book.. Just copy these images at 150%, then glue one of a pair of images onto a piece of cardboard, like the kind on the back of a notepad. Cut out the circle of the cardboard and image, then cut out and glue the other image on the backside of the disc. (*Important:* one side has to be upside-down from the other!) When the glue is dry, punch a hole on each side where shown. Then run about 8 inches of string through each hole and tie off the ends. Or you can loop and fasten long rubber bands through these holes. I also recommend coloring in the canary yellow, and the tree leaves green.

To use your Thaumatrope, hold both loops of the strings or rubber bands around your index fingers, then twist the disc around and around a number of turns. Pull your fingers apart to increase or decrease tension, and make the disc spin continually. As it does, you will see the images on both sides blend into one. The dead tree will become fully-leafed; the bird will be in the cage; and the word will spell "Magick."

Which it is. *Thaumaturgy* ("wonder working") is the Greek word for practical magick!

Now try making your own Thaumatrope drawings. Get creative! Draw a horse on one side and a man on the other to make the man appear to be riding the horse. Draw a juggler on one side and balls in the air on the other; a bald man's head on one side and a wig on the other; a fish and a fisherman. Have fun creating "half images" that make interesting "wholes" when you spin your thaumatrope.

Phenakistiscope

The next step in the development of animation was the *Phenakistiscope* (FEE-na-KISS-ti-skope). It was invented in 1830 by Joseph Antoine Ferdinand Plateau in Belgium and independently by Professor Simon Ritter von Stampfer of the Polytechnical Institute, Austria, in 1832.

Plateau called his invention the *Phenakistiscope* ("spindle viewer") and Von Stampfer called his the *Stroboscope* ("twisting-around viewer"). In 1833, Ackerman was selling these discs in London under the name "Fantascope"—my own favorite. But it was also called: *Phantamascope, Kaleidorama,* or Magic Disc. Today the all-but-unpronounceable spelling "phenakistiscope" is unfortunately preferred.

The Phenakistiscope was a disc on which a series of 8-16 cartoon images in slightly different positions were drawn around the outer edge, with small slits cut out between the images. Common images included abstract patterns or performers such as jugglers or acrobats. The disc could be mounted on a spindle and viewed through the slots with the images facing a mirror. When it was spun, a person looking through the slits from the back of the disc would see a continuous moving image reflected in the mirror.

Von Stampfer's Stroboscope places a stationary second disc with a wedge-shaped window slot in front of the spinning disk, so you can view the animation without using a mirror.

To make your own Fantascope, just copy the discs in the back of this book onto card stock and cut them out—including the pie-shaped "doors" on one of the discs. Using a pushpin through the center, fasten the disk with the window to the end of a wooden dowel, and tape it into place so that when you hold the dowel horizontal, the window is at the bottom, as shown here.

Then use the same pushpin to affix the disc with the little pictures of the dancing couple like a pinwheel, with the pictures facing the window so they will show through.

To view the effect, look at the window side, and spin the disc with the pictures until the speed causes them to run together. You will see the first type of animation ever invented!

With a strobe light, you can even view the movement directly without using the disc with the wedge-shaped window.

Now, try making your own. Just divide a circle into 12 or 16 equal wedges—like cutting a pizza— and draw your own little animated cartoon!

"Between the Worlds"

Now, here is the real lesson in Wizardry that the Fantascope can reveal:

All that we perceive as "The Real World" manifests to our senses and our scientific instruments as vibrations of various frequencies. Whether we are talking about the vibrational frequencies of elemental atoms, those of the electromagnetic energy spectrum, or those of sound, *everything*—matter, energy, time and space—exists at and as a vibrational frequency. And we, whose senses are designed to "lock into" particular ranges of these frequencies, such as the ranges of visible light and of audible sound, have built-in mechanisms in our brains and senses to smooth over the discontinuity between vibrations, so we perceive them (and the world) as continuous.

In effect, we are like the tuners of a radio or TV, which can range up and down the dial to select from countless frequencies to receive whatever station or channel we wish. The difference is that our own internal "tuners" are programmed for only certain frequencies, and all others are simply "tuned out."

The Fantascope demonstrates this quite elegantly, as its small number of images and variable speed of rotation lend themselves easily to experiments.

Consider now—if all we perceive is the part of the frequency cycle that matches our receptors, what about the spaces between? The Fantascope has gaps between the images that we fail to perceive due to our inherent "persistence of vision." What if we add another series of images in those gaps, but at a different phase rate of frequency? Take, for instance, Plateau's 16-image disc of the pirouetting dancer (drawn in 1832). To view it as a continuous image, the disc must be spun at the rate of one revolution per second, which presents 16 image frames per second to our eye. Our retina holds that image just long enough for the next one to come along.

But let's insert (as I have done here) another series of four Fairies equally spaced *between* those 16 frames. Cut this one out, and affix it to the dowel with a pushpin, just as you did with the dancers. This time, however, you will have to hold the dowl with the window disc in your other hand, so that the window is now at the top.

Spinning the disk at one revolution per second, the dancer gracefully pirouettes in place. However, if we spin the disk faster, at the rate of *four* revolutions per second, the images of the dancer then blur and disappear (phase out), while the images of the Fairy now match our visual reception of 16 frames per second, and suddenly, we see the Fairy!

How many other worlds, parallel universes, alternate dimensions, might exist *in between* the phases of the vibrations we see and hear? "Between the worlds" lie the realms of Faerie, the Dreaming, the Afterworlds —and possibly the sources of many of the weird phenomena that have been reported throughout history.

"Ah, what senses do we lack, not to see and hear a world all around us?" (Frank Herbert, *Dune*)

Zoetrope

The *Zoetrope* (ZOE-uh-trope) was invented in 1834 in England by William George Horner, who called it the *Daedalum* ("ingenious wheel"). It didn't become popular until decades later, when it was patented and marketed as a toy by manufacturers in France (1860), England and America (1867). The American developer, William Lincoln, re-named it the *Zoetrope* ("life turner").

The Zoetrope worked on the same principles as the fantascope, but the pictures were drawn on a strip which could be set around the bottom third of a metal drum, with the slits now cut in the upper section of the drum. The drum was mounted on a spindle so that it could be spun, and viewers looking through the slits would see the cartoon strip form a single moving image.

The zoetrope's speed is variable. The faster the drum is spun, the smoother and more continuous the image is perceived. When the Zoetrope slows down so that each image is seen for a tenth of a second or more, the illusion of movement begins to break down.

Praxinoscope

The problem with the Zoetrope is that the small slots do not let enough light through. In 1878, Emile Reynaud in Paris made an adaptation with mirrors instead of slots. He called this the *Praxinoscope* (prax-IN-o-skope), or "practical viewer." It used a drum, just as the Zoetrope had, with the images drawn on a band placed around the inside of the cylinder. However, rather than having slits through which the images were viewed, the cartoon strip was reflected in mirrors set between the outer edge of the drum and the central spindle. A candle set above illuminated the images more clearly.

The Praxinoscope Theater also had surrounding images to make the experience more complete. The drum was set into a wooden box, with a hole in the lid

through which the viewer saw a background scene that set the images on the cartoon strip into context.

All these early animation devices were called "Philosophical Toys" in the Victorian era. They were the forerunners that inspired the creation of moving pictures, as the Zoetrope strips were simply extended to become movie film. This involved drawing hundreds or thousands of such images and printing them on a transparent ribbon, which could then be reeled in front of a bright light to project the animation on a screen, as in hand shadow pictures. And when it finally became possible to take photographs fast enough to simulate a moving image, the modern cinema was born!

Most modern film projectors run at a rate of 24 frames, or pictures, per second. VCRs record and play tapes at a rate of 30 frames per second. But the old silent movie projectors ran at only 16-18 frames per second. They were so slow they seemed to flicker!

This brings us to our next lesson, "Magick in Animated Movies," which will be presented by our Grey School Dean of Studies, Elizabeth Barrette:

6. Wizards and Magick in Animated Movies

By Elizabeth Barrette (grey)
(Adapted from "It's a Magical World: Sacred Themes in Disney Animation," *PanGaia,* Autumn 2000.)

Many movies tell stories that concern magick and Wizards. The goal of this lesson is to explore such portrayals in animation. As an Apprentice, you should study not just the practical aspects of spellcasting but the underlying ideas. Other lessons will delve into serious ethical and technical concerns; this one deals with creativity and interpretation. The idea is for you to start thinking about Wizards and magic, and what they mean to you.

Here is a list of thirteen movies that feature Wizards and magickal events. They are listed here in the order of their release. Watch each movie and write an entry about it in your Magickal Journal. (These movies should be easy to find for rent, for sale, or on broadcast.) As in Wizardry, not all of the questions have a "right" answer. Just write what you think!

The Movies

Alakazam the Great

(Taiji Tonomura, 1961, G) is the oldest movie recommended in this class. It may look a little unpolished if you're used to modern movies, but it has a lot of charm. The story concerns a mischievous monkey named Alakazam. Not content with being king, he wants magickal power as well—so he steals it. Since it turns out to be more than he can handle, Alakazam spends the rest of the movie learning the appropriate uses of power.

The Sword and the Stone

(Disney, 1963, G) Adapted from the novel of the same name by T. H. White, this is a whimsical rendition of the often dark Arthurian legend. It follows young Arthur at a crucial time in his life. This film contains some of the most insightful observations about magick in any animated movie. Merlin explains, "Don't get any silly ideas that magick will solve all your problems—it won't."

One highlight is a set of sequences featuring transformation/shapeshifting magick during which Arthur spends time as a bird, a squirrel, and a fish (thus experiencing all three realms of the ancient Celts: Land, Sea, and Sky). The epic shapeshifting duel between Merlin and Mad Madame Mim is loads of fun, yet carries a serious message about ethics in magick: Merlin uses his wits to vanquish his opponent (who cheats without apology) without breaking the rules himself.

Magick and science can work together, too; wise old Merlin is a master of both. This film repeatedly emphasizes the importance of brains over brawn; in the end, it isn't muscle that allows Arthur to pull the sword from the stone, but rather his innate purity of heart that makes him worthy of the throne.

Wizards

(Ralph Bakshi, 1977, PG) tackles a theme rare in animation and fantasy, but a mainstay of science fiction: the post-apocalyptic future after a nucle-

ar war. Enchanted creatures such as Fairies arise from the wholesome lands, while nasty mutants arise from the nuclear wastelands. Twin Wizards—or really, one Wizard and one Sorcerer—battle for the fate of the world. Avatar and Blackwolf use very different methods, both magickal and mundane, to achieve their goals.

The Hobbit

(Rankin/Bass, 1980, U) Based on the J.R.R. Tolkien book of the same name, this movie tells of a quiet little guy, Bilbo Baggins, who gets swept up in somebody else's adventure due to the meddling of his Wizard friend, Gandalf the Grey. In the company of thirteen Dwarves, they set off to reclaim stolen treasure —nearly getting killed by Trolls, Goblins, Elves, and giant spiders along the way. Bilbo finds a magick ring that seems helpful at first but later causes much trouble. The climaxes include vanquishing the dragon Smaug, and a battle over the disposition of the recovered treasure. Bilbo has a charmingly succinct opinion of adventures: "Nasty, uncomfortable things; make you late for dinner!"

The Last Unicorn

(Rankin/Bass, 1982, PG) Based on the novel by Peter S. Beagle, this is a hauntingly beautiful story. One carefree Unicorn suddenly discovers that she is the last of her kind. She sets off to find the others, only to realize that few people can see her true self anymore. Captured by the creepy Mommy Fortuna, the Unicorn escapes with the aid of Schmendrick, a magician who aptly demonstrates Isaac Bonewits' observation that "sincerity is no substitute for competence." Together they travel to the castle of King Haggard, whose Red Bull keeps the unicorns trapped in the sea. Transformed into a human for disguise, the Unicorn almost forgets her mission, and ultimately pays a high price to save her people.

The Lion King

(Disney, 1994, G) explores the concept of sacred kingship, in which a king is magickally connected to his land. Fleeing from tragedy, the young hero Simba makes friends with Timon and Pumbaa, following their "Hakuna Matata" (No Worries) philosophy, which marks his adolescence and time away from responsibility. Simba doesn't want to return to the Pridelands. Rafiki, like any good sha-

man, confronts the reluctant hero, but it is when Simba's father appears to him in a vision that he finally understands what he must do. Simba returns to his home, only to find the land unfertile and desolate, ruined by the rule of an unfit king. With Simba's victory, the rains come; the land is restored by the return of the rightful king.

Fantasia 2000 (Disney, 1999, G) continues a tradition begun with the original *Fantasia* in 1940, illustrating musical scores. Indeed, "The Sorcerer's Apprentice" by Paul Dukas appears in both. In this story, Mickey Mouse borrows his master's enchanted hat while the Wizard is sleeping, in

hopes of making his chores easier; but the magick proves harder to master than he expected. Another gem is "Firebird Suite," the 1919 version by Igor Stravinsky. An elk stag breathes on an icicle, creating a female spirit – the Sprite – whose magic soon covers the land with life. But she awakens the terrible Firebird in the mountain, who almost destroys her forever. This story says a lot about the sources and applications of magick.

Spirited Away (Disney Home Entertainment; Hayao Miyazaki, 2001, PG) follows a young girl as her family moves to a new home. But a shortcut leads them into a strange, magickal realm—where Chihiro's parents soon get themselves trapped. It turns out to be a vacation spot for the spirit world, and Chihiro must make a place for herself there so that she can discover how to free her parents. Rich in Japanese symbolism, this movie explores themes of trust, devotion, and familial obligation.

7. The Journey
By Moonwriter (indigo)

You're studying Wizardry, you're learning new skills, you're keeping your records, and you're slowly be-

ginning to acquire tools and clothing that make you look like a Wizard.

But of course, there's more to it than that.

Wizardry is a journey, and every day spent walking the Wizard's path will be different than the one before it.

In these lessons we've talked a lot about the nuts and bolts of that journey, the ways that you can use a journal and various materials to support your work.

But all trappings aside, the real work happens inside of you. The journey is your own.

Please read the following stories carefully and think about the symbolism within them, what those symbols might mean to you, and how the stories might parallel your work as an apprentice Wizard.

Story 1

As the mists part, the skiff glides silently toward shore, poled by two sun-tanned men wearing rough breechclouts. We land on a sandy shore and they regard me silently as I leave the boat, stepping into water up to my ankles that surprises me with its amniotic warmth.

I leave the boat and begin walking up the beach. A time of testing begins for me here. Several women stand on the beach and acknowledge me, unsmiling but not unfriendly. They gesture towards a path that leads into the trees. As I take to the path, I can feel them following me. The sun is overhead, the breeze smells of berries, and the trees and grass seem an extraordinary shade of green. I feel as if I have stepped into some other place, a place that I have only dreamed of 'til now.

After a few minutes walk, the path ends in a clearing. To one side stands a simple structure of stone and wood. I am gestured toward the structure, and made to understand that I must enter alone.

I step into darkness. It takes a moment to adjust my eyes, then I move through the entryway and into the main room. A hearth blazes to one side, and next to it stands a woman. She is unlike any woman I have ever seen, and yet she seems to be every woman I have ever seen. Her hair is black, edged with streaks of silver white. Her eyes are gray and gaze upon me unflinchingly. She is robed in swirls of diaphanous blue. A moonstone hangs around her neck, and above it, a silver torque with runic carvings. In her right hand she holds a stave, its beam simple and its top crowned with a gleaming piece of quartz. I see a tattoo on her right wrist, a tattoo of the waxing crescent moon, in the same blue as her gown. Around her waist, a satin cord holds a leather pouch, which bulges with a collection that I cannot imagine.

To one side of the room is a small circular table. It is covered with a forest green cloth that glitters as if with flecks of gold. The table is set in a fashion that almost looks random and yet implies order. I see candles, shells, a chalice full of water, a gleaming obsidian knife, and more wonders that I cannot count. Behind the table the wall is lined with shelves, and those shelves with bottles of every shape, size, and color, some containing liquid, some appearing full of dried leaves or seeds. A set of weights and a scale sit nearby, as does a leather journal and quill.

To the other side of the fire is a moderate-sized table, with two chairs. The table is simply set with a blue cloth. On one side of the table is a tray of fruit, a loaf of rough bread, and a flagon of what looks to be wine. On the other side is a book. A magnificent book. A tome, perhaps. It is of leather, with burnished silver hinges. It seems to glow, or perhaps tremble, from whatever is captured within. On its surface is inscribed a host of symbols, inscrutable to my untrained eye. I am suddenly aware of my simple brown garment, and my empty hands.

The woman smiles, and gestures toward the bread and fruit. "Come," she says. "You must be hungry. Let us eat first. Then we will begin."

Story 2

The boy walks into the hills alone. He is roughly dressed in a jerkin and cape, with stout boots and a warm hat. On his back, a pack holds a few potatoes, a knife, rope, blanket, and firemaking materials. He climbs with the help of a carved stave of alder and carries a waterskin.

The apprentice is open to learning, feeling, and applying what they are given for the good of the world.
Art by Jesse Wolf Hardin

He finds a spot high on side of the mountain. This'll do for the night, he says to himself. He clears a spot for a fire, setting it in front of a cliff edge so that the heat will reflect back against it.

Checking his waterskin, he finds it nearly full. Taking out the knife, he walks from the clearing into the trees and cuts several fir boughs, which he carries back to the cliff and uses to form a bed. He knows that if he sleeps on the bare ground, it will be much too cold; the boughs will provide a crude sort of mattress. That task done, he sets to gathering fuel for his fire, using downed wood and murmuring a thanks to the forest as he does so. In no time at all, he has a substantial pile.

The boy is on quest. He is charged to stay on the mountainside until the vision comes. He seeks his spirit animal, and even more importantly, he seeks his new name. To get one, he needs the other. He is young for this ritual—just turned 14—but he had

asked to go, and it had been allowed. He knows that many expect him to fail, that they believe he won't be strong enough to endure alone until the visions find him. He knows differently. Completely at home in the outdoors, the boy knows how to read the skies, tell the weather, and hear the rhythms of the Earth. He can find food and water, can make a warm camp, and can hear the animals coming before they hear him. He feels well suited and ready for the task ahead.

As sunset approaches, the boy builds a teepee fire within a ring of stones. Using the sunset to judge the West direction, he sets stones around the fire ring at the cardinal points. As the sun falls behind the mountains, he murmurs an evening blessing, calls honors to all four elemental directions, thanks the powers for the gift of fire, and then kindles a blaze. The fire catches quickly, crackling loudly against the cooling air. As the fire burns, the boy pushes a potato into the embers to roast.

Night falls slowly, the colors of sunset ebbing from the land. The boy settles against the cliff side, snug in the fire's reflected warmth, the potato eaten and followed by a satisfying drink of water. He gazes into the fire, clears his mind, and lets the images come.

Spirits of the west, the water of life, the water in my skin, nourishing me. Spirits of the west, bathe my soul.
Spirits of the north, those of Earth and rock and soaring cliffs and green forests, protect me through this night, shield me.
Spirits of the east, those of air and clouds, spirits of the wind that blows cold or sweet, that freshens the world, let me breathe deep in your wisdom.
Spirits of the south, place of fire, dance within my heart and heat my eyes with vision.

He sits quietly, starting into the flames, watching the sparks lifting into the air, hearing the crackle of wood, smelling the acrid smoke, feeling the heat against his face. As the night chills he draws the blanket around his shoulders. Later, he sleeps.

The next morning, the boy wakes to a cold, clear sunrise. Morning color splays over the granite rocks on which he stands. While no vision had come to him, he had slept well, and dreamed. Now his mind feels clear in the sweet morning air. He smiles, and sets about poking up the fire. Taking a piece of charcoal from the fire's edge, he draws a single long, straight mark on both arms. The first evening had passed.

Tonight, he thinks. Tonight.

Whistling, he begins his day.

Department II: Nature (silver)

EnteleKinesis

Destiny is a force imposed from without.
Entelechy is a force arising from within,
the outward manifestation of an inner will,
the inevitable expression of essence

It is the destiny of a prince to become a king.
It is the entelechy of an acorn to become an oak tree.

Grow or die. Evolve,
or face extinction.

The soul shapes itself, makes itself
in its own image. The end result
grows organically, naturally,
indelibly from the beginning.

The spark becomes the bonfire.
The seed becomes the tree.

Yet we who are human can go beyond even this,
can tap that primal magick to recreate ourselves;
we can learn to evolve consciously.

You cannot change who you were
or who you could become
directly; you can only affect who you are.
You cannot make changes against your own nature –

an oak will never be a willow,
nor a willow be a rose.

But you can shape the reach of your branches
to best encompass the light, to shelter the small lives
that thrive beneath and within you. Every moment
is another chance to do better
with what you have at hand.

Over the slow motion of years,
the spiral timepiece of your life unwinds;

you emerge, blos-
som, bear
fruit,
move ever and more
fully into the realm
of your wisdom.

You grow not into a mold but into a motion,
into an effortless eternal unfolding of self from soul.

Each movement draws you closer to your own conclusion.
The bed does not create the river.
The river carves the bed, flowing out and down
to the ocean as it follows its own nature.

As we each create being and each other, we make
a world to move through, a stage to stand on,
a frame for the final flawless involvement
of our lives.

Karma is only an excuse for foolishness
and absolvement from responsibility.
Entelechy comprises an ultimate acceptance of shape,
not as a path imposed from without
but as a pattern exposed from within.

Entelekinesis composes the process
of moving from one to the other,
becoming ever more fully
a loyalist unto oneself.

Believe in your own excellence, in the perfection of
your pattern
for putting together a perfect you
and do not make way for waves or vagaries. Keep one eye
always on that inner compass, and its unshakeable faith
will guide you to your own emergence

entelekinesis.

—Elizabeth Barrette

1. Introduction

ELCOME TO THE WORLD OF NATURE! Nature Studies includes all aspects of metaphysics and mysticism that relate to Nature and Her Mysteries. This is such an important aspect of Wizardry that Wizards have also been called "Natural Philosophers."

In this Department, you will acquire an essential understanding of the ways of Nature, and become comfortable and experienced with all aspects of the Natural World. You will be given wise counsel for hiking, exploring, camping, gardening, and enjoying instructive adventures in the many realms of Nature—in both wilderness and urban settings. You will also study ecology, and learn of the ways in which Natural systems are currently threatened—and how to defend them.

The color associated with this Department is Silver, representing the feminine energies of intuition, insight, dreams, psychic gifts and divination. Silver represents the color of the Moon, the secrets of Nature, women's Mysteries and magicks, and Witchcraft.

Consider….
1. The source of Nature is spirit.
2. Nature is not a random accident. It has meaning, significance, and purpose.

3. Certain aspects of Nature are invisible.
4. Nature is a part of a greater whole, which is beyond time and space.
5. Nature's beauty has intrinsic value.
6. That which preserves the beauty and harmony of Nature is good. That which destroys it is bad.
7. All animals, plants, and landscapes are sacred.
8. All creatures have an equal right to self-fulfillment.
9. The inner world is a part of Nature.
10. We should celebrate the creation with song, dance, art, poetry, and stories.
11. Science is an indispensable tool for gaining knowledge about Nature.

(Larry Cates; http://portalproductions.com/spiritNature)

The first lesson in this Department comes from Grey Council member Jesse Wolf Hardin:

2. Gaia, the Living Earth

By Jesse Wolf Hardin (silver)

Sitting at the center of my home altar is a stunning forest-colored sculpture of a serene and beautiful woman of power: Gaia! She both graces and calls attention to our information table when I'm out giving conference or festival presentations. The artist and arch wizard Oberon has sculpted her as a well-muscled figure sitting poised and cross-legged, with facial features belonging to no single race. She emanates not only the power of a protective mother but also the sensuality of a young maiden. Engraved on her legs are the shapes of a number of fish and shellfish inhabiting oceans both ancient and contemporary. Gaia's equally green arms bear the outlines of primeval plant life and the giant sequoias that are lately in danger of being cut down by logging corporations in Northern California. Her beautiful hair is plaited into spiraling DNA-like braids diverse species of wildlife ascend her braided tresses with the oldest and simplest life forms at the bottom. The higher up on her head the more recent and complex the animal form, and sharing the highest point on her crown is both the telepathic whale and a young human child who holds in her tiny hands a small blue ball representing the planet we are each charged to learn from and care for. She is Gaia the Earth Mother, the Goddess embodied in the ground we walk on as well as the many other creatures and plants we live and travel among.

Depending on where one lives she may be called Cybele, Mami Aruru, Nu Kwa or Terra. She is known as Assaya in Yoruba, Kunapipi to the Aborigine, the Hindu say Prithivi and to the indigenous people of Peru she is Pachamama, from whose body we sprout and grow like arms or legs! It is from the ancient Greeks that we get the name "Gaia," (popularly pronounced such that it rhymes with "Maya"). According to them she was created from light and love out of the encompassing chaos and her first born was Ouranos, the heavens. Fertilized by the energies of Eros, she symbolizes life itself. Like Oberon's sculpture, Gaian consciousness is spreading once again among the most empathic and aware, and just as humanity seems to need the wisdom and alliance of ancient Gaia the most!

The earliest carvings of the Earth Mother date back from 30,000 to over 100,000 years ago, and are among the oldest evidence of human ritual and art. To quote Homer, Gaia is "the eldest of all, and mother of all the Gods." It is she who inspires the founders and informs the practitioners of every nature-based spiritual or magickal practice including Wizardry and Wicca, pantheism and Neo-Paganism, deep ecology and Druidry. No matter what we call ourselves, Gaia is the source of our beings and the venue for our visions. She is the force all seekers can turn to for encouragement and direction, and her dreams can bring clarity, focus and power to every form of spiritual and magickal practice. And for everyone, even those who deny or dishonor her, she is the lap and cauldron we tumble back into when we die—the very flesh and the prayer from which we arise.

The entire universe is purposeful, creative and inspirited. However we think of the Goddess, God or Gods, it's a force of unity that includes everything there is and all that will ever be. But for those of us born of the Earth, the nearest expression of that divinity is always the planet itself. We have only to reach out and touch the soil or hug a tree to be in contact with the God/Goddess, and all the power of the universe is available to us through the natural world and our own inner magical natures. We don't live on top of Gaia as if she were just a stage for our activities. We are each an extension of her, her sensory organs and magical agents, and we each have a special part to play as her learners and teachers, musicians and artists, warriors and lovers.

Early cultures taught that we had to keep our part of our sacred pact with the Earth Mother, and that if we blew it we'd end up sealing our own doom. Clearly, neglecting her or our connection and duties to her has brought about both the dis-ease of civilization and an environmental crisis of terrifying proportions. At the same time, everything we need is available right here right now, a gift of Spirit through Gaia. We're each blessed to be able to turn to wild nature for the visions and lessons we need to be the Seekers, heroes and heroines of our time.

Some Basic Practices:

• Practice envisioning the Earth as a luminous living being capable in her own way of feeling satisfaction, joy and pain...Gaia! The more you do this, the less likely it will be that you will ever act in ways that hurt her, and the more attention you'll pay to her needs, instructions, blessings and lessons.

• Try drawing her the way she appears to you, and don't worry about how perfect it is. It should be more visionary than realistic.

• Now envision your physical being as a bodily extension of Gaia, as one of her organs of sensation and perception. Whenever you are tempted to do something that dishonors or disrespects your inspirited body like bingeing or starving yourself, drinking too much booze or doing the kinds of drugs that you know are harmful, keep in mind that what you to yourself you are simultaneously doing to her.

• Draw yourself as a part of Gaia, and then do another drawing of yourself with the spirit of Gaia inside you.

• Honor, but don't worship Gaia. You are born with the ability to represent the worst of what Gaia does, and with the capacity to be the best of what she puts forth.

• Build an altar dedicated to the Earth Mother in your most special space. Include powerful found objects that represent each of the clans of Gaia (such as feathers for the bird clan, rocks from the mineral clan, a container of water to stand for her rivers and seas, bits of fur or antler for the four-leggeds and so on). Add other items collected on days when you went through major trials, in order to remind you of your hard-earned lessons as you become ever-more the willful wizard.

• Position a single item in the center of your altar, to represent the entirety of Gaia in the form you can most relate to. This can be a framed drawing, or a collage of natural images that you cut out of magazines and paste together into a circular globe or the outline of a woman. A sculpture works well too, and besides buying Oberon's or some other figure you can also get clay and work up your own. You can also press natural found materials like shells, fossils, wood or crystals into the clay. If all you can make is the most basic shape, be happy. It will then look most like

the ancient Willendorf and other Earth Mother finds.

• Don't be a pushy missionary shoving Gaian gospel down anyone's throat. Nonetheless, you can still reach out at the perfect moment to better help other voluntary seekers to sense and tap the energy of Gaia both around them and within them. It's good for the people you touch in this way, and good for the Earth that all life depends on.

• Choose a language that allows you to inspire people outside your community. Instead of using the term "Gaia," you can substitute "Mother Earth." Very few people will take offense at that. This ups the chances that you will be heard, and that the people you are talking to will be helped.

• Practice feeling the pain of what is out of balance both within you and around you in the world. This is one way Gaia senses an imbalance and can begin to slowly make the necessary magical and evolutionary corrections.

• Practice owning who you are as a special gifted being, finding satisfaction in both the gifts receive and those you give to others. Gaia feels satisfaction through us!

• Practice feeling joy without embarrassment or constraint, and sense how much that tickles and pleasures the whole of sentient Gaia!

• Create a song or chant that honors Gaia and connects you to the All.

• Include at least brief preliminary acknowledgment of Gaia as the source of all Spirits, entities and lessons in every ritual you do and circle you cast.

• Write and perform both private and public rituals focusing on the Earth Mother and aimed at awakening a sense of the immanence of Gaia in everyone attending.

• For every prayer that you ask of Gaia, pledge some act or effort in turn.

3. Becoming One with Nature
by Abby Willowroot (silver)

Becoming One with Nature is the process of becoming mindful of the many cycles that are all around us and inside us. It is learning to value small miracles and fleeting moments. It is experiencing the world without a need to "capture" the experience. Becoming aware of the natural world as it presents itself in your everyday life is a habit that once developed, will serve you well. Your skills of perception will sharpen in direct proportion to how often you exercise them. Instincts and abilities long forgotten or never used will awaken and become strong and reliable. A Wizard is only as good as his abilities to perceive the subtleties of the world around him.

Each morning you arise and begin your journey of being anew. The way you wake up has a lot to do with how you will move through the day. Learning to interact with life in a more positive, healing and magick-al way is a daily challenge, and one that requires be-ginning each day in a mindful way. Setting your men-tal alarm clock to go off half an hour before your reg-ular alarm will insure the day starts in a positive way, waking without stress, accompanied by insights or images from the dream state. Telling your brain what time to wake you is a great way to move into con-scious flow. It also serves to put you in control of your sleep and dream cycles.

Along the Wizard's journey there are many op-portunities for learning, but none are as important as learning Nature's mysteries and secrets. These form the foundation on which all else is built. Within each day there are countless opportunities to learn some-thing new from Nature, even for those who live in cit-ies. Looking at the sky throughout the day, every day, will help make you wise in the ways of weather. Pay-ing attention to the feel of the air on your skin will teach you to sense the coming rain an hour before it arrives. Always looking carefully at a tree you pass every day will teach you to see subtle changes in Na-ture. Practice speaking psychically with animals you encounter. These are all simple things to do that yield powerful insights for a Wizard.

All around us the world is in a state of change. Some changes are stressful, others open us to a re-newal of our dreams, ideals and possibilities. Long-held habits and beliefs change as we learn new more holistic ways of being and using our powers. We are living in a time of Renaissance, a time of intellectual, artistic flowering, a time of unlimited possibilities. It is also a time of huge environmental challenges and climatic changes. The Wizards now in training will be enormously important as their skills and ethics have a powerful influence on future events. Because we are at such a precarious juncture in human history, the ability to become one with Nature is an especially es-sential skill for all Wizards.

Mysticism, spirituality and self-expression are mingling with cultural influences from around the world. Wizards, shamans, priestesses, monks, tribal elders and people of all belief traditions are coming together and seeking solutions to common concerns and global changes. For the first time in history we are being exposed to the teachings and healing practices of many cultures. Our eyes are opening to both an-cient mysteries and future technology. We are discov-ering that our shared genetic heritage and cultural dif-ferences have the power to enrich and unite us beyond borders. Paradoxically, the richness of these resources only deepens the mysteries of life and the mechanics of power. The need for skilled practitioners of the metaphysical arts has never been more essential.

The voice of Mother Earth is speaking to all of us. Sometimes on the breeze, sometimes in meditation or ritual, sometimes in laughter, we hear Her message.

Those who dance under the moon in celebration of the Goddess often sing "We all come from the God-dess and to Her we shall return; like a drop of rain, flowing to the ocean…" These words remind us that our connection with the Earth is the constant thread that binds our lives together and unites our fate.

Green Witches, Wizards and tribal healers are working around the world to heal the environment and rekindle awareness of the sacred spirits of Nature. Cultural icons like Sting, Bono, and Al Gore have worked tirelessly to share the message of our inter-connectedness and the fragility of the environment. Even business visionaries like Ted Turner and Bill & Melinda Gates have poured tremendous resources into environmental and health programs for people and the planet, because they understand that we all are con-nected. Powerful, positive forces for change are on the move. As Wizards we draw our powers from the Universe and the Earth. We are challenged to use our powers in ways that heal and embrace our home plan-et. All of our skill begins with our developing a deeper understanding of Nature, our fellow creatures and ourselves.

As a Wizard, you are a powerful shaper of the future. The deeper your understanding of Nature and the natural laws of the Universe, the stronger your ability to shape the future. We are approaching a time when the skills of wise Wizards will be crucial to re-storing balance in our world. Learning Nature's les-sons, both simple and complex, will make you ready. Everyday, learn at least one new thing about the natu-ral world by observing. Practicing this simple exercise will heighten your powers of perception, and so your skill as a Wizard.

Deep in every cell of your body there are genetic memories. Tapping into conscious contact with these memories becomes second nature when you live in contact with wild Nature. It is crucial for every Wiz-ard to open the doors of perception and have access to the powerful wisdom these memories contain. Learn to know Nature and you will learn to know yourself—your true, unlimited self.

It can be tempting to speed past Nature studies and move onto the glitzier aspects of Wizardry, but no true power is possible without a strong foundation in understanding the workings of Nature.

4. The Amateur Naturalist

By Moonwriter (indigo)

What is a naturalist? A naturalist is someone who stud-ies and interacts with the natural world around them. Through observation and interactions, the naturalist begins to understand the web of life, and to sees how everything is tied together. In the words of our Grey

School motto, *Omnia vivunt, omnia inter se conexa:*. "Everything is alive; everything is interconnected" (Cicero).

What You'll Need

You can read about Nature, watch shows about it on TV, and even visit it at the local zoo. But nothing compares to actually going out into the natural world and learning to watch what takes place around you.

In order to complete the activities in this lesson, you'll need the following equipment, most of which you probably already have in your home:

Blank journal
Ballpoint pens
Pencils
3-4 dark crayons
Red cellophane
Empty egg carton
Old telephone book
Plain white 8"x11" paper
Fine point permanent marker
Colored pencils (if you want to add color to your sketches)
Large and small zip-lock freezer bags (one can hold your journal)
Bottle of liquid paper/white-out
Small containers: empty film canisters, Altoids boxes, etc.
Empty jars with tight lids
Glass jar with lid, very small holes poked in the top (for a critter home)
Flashlight
Magnifying glass
Pocketknife or multitool
Tweezers
Garden clippers (optional, but very handy)
Scissors
Cotton string
Clear "scotch" tape
Tape measure (as least 3 feet long)
White glue (such as Elmer's)
A glue stick
A folded newspaper
Camera (—could be anything from a disposable camera to one that is digital)

Some good Nature guide-books are essential. I particularly recommend the following:

A Practical Guide for the Amateur Naturalist, by Gerald Durrell. This book is easy to find used on-line for as little as two or three dollars (check Amazon.com or Powells.com for good used prices). It's a marvelous resource, full of splendid pictures and detailed instructions.

Boy Scout Handbook and *Boy Scout Fieldbook*, both published by the Boy Scouts of America (www.scoutstuff.org)

Also, you may want to acquire field books appropriate for your area; this might include books about birds, flowers, rocks, mammals, etc.

NOTE: Much "field book" information these days can be found on-line. However, it's really nice to have 1-2 field books that you can keep with you. The small "Golden Pocket Guides" by Herbert Zim are wonderful for this and are very inexpensive: on Amazon.com, I found used copies for as low as $.69 each!

Ethics and Assumptions

The dictionary defines wilderness as "an unsettled, uncultivated region left to its wild condition and characterized by vastness, wildness, and unchecked profusion."

My favorite definition of wilderness is, "A place where man is a visitor, and is not expected to remain."

When you step outside of your home and into the outdoors, you take the first step into the wilderness. Granted, your back yard probably isn't a wild space (although it may be, if you're lucky!), but every step away from your front door brings you closer to wild spaces.

When you enter the outdoors, you enter a sacred space, a place that is bound by the turning of the great seasonal wheel, a place of life and death, and a place of creation. In everything you do, remember that you walk on sacred ground, and that the Earth and stars are the place of your birth. I mean this literally: every atom that forms our bodies was borne from the life and death of stars, the atoms flying through the infinity of space, entering our atmosphere, and settling to the Earth, where they became available for life-forming processes. As astronomer and cosmologist Carl Sagan said, "We are made of star stuff."

Being a naturalist requires certain ethical rules and regulations:

1. Never collect a plant or flower unless you are collecting from an abundant site.
2. Always collect the smallest possible specimen.
3. There are times when photography should be used in place of collecting. **You should never collect endangered species, disturb any animal home, or remove any remnant of American Indian culture.** A photo will allow you to treasure these discoveries without disturbing them.
4. Follow the "Leave No Trace" method of collecting. When you leave an area, there should be no evidence of your presence.
5. As an apprentice Wizard, you should always respect the integrity and sanctity of the natural world. When entering a place or removing a specimen, you should first get some sense of whether this is acceptable to

the ecosystem you're working in. After finishing your work, give thanks to the energies of the place. You may wish to offer a blessing or carry out a simple ritual.

Safety

When working in the outdoors, plan ahead for safety. Have everything you need at hand, and make sure that potential dangers—sharp tools, flames, etc.—are considered and managed. As with anything in Wizardry, safety can be considered in terms of the four elements: Earth, Air, Fire, and Water.

Earth

Using a hiking stave will help you keep your balance on hikes and can be a useful tool as well.

To make a stave, choose a long stick that is about 2" in diameter and at least as tall as your shoulder. Use a pocketknife to peel the bark, if desired. Staves can be decorated in any number of ways, or left plain. Attach a strap to the top part to support your wrist, as in the picture.

Air

Before heading into the outdoors or holding an outdoor ritual, you may want to consider the weather. Keeping one eye on the heavens will help you avoid weather "surprises" and will keep you safe and comfortable. Learn to "read" the sky and cloud patterns through observation and notes in your journal. Practicing your skills of divination and augury will also improve your weather predicting abilities.

Here's a great site for current and extended weather predictions: http://www.wunderground.com

Fire

If you use any sort of flame (candles, alcohol burners, campfires, etc.) in the outdoors, make sure to work on fireproof surfaces.

Paper should never be anywhere near flames! Also make sure that there is nothing hanging near the flames that could catch fire.

Don't wear robes, stoles, or anything with loose sleeves that could brush the flames and catch fire.

If you're a young apprentice, make sure an adult is nearby when you are using matches.

Campfires should be built in established fire rings or barbecue pits. Make sure that the surrounding area is clear of flammable materials and overhanging branches.

Never, never, NEVER leave any sort of flames unattended.

Never look directly at the sun through a pair of binoculars or a telescope. Permanent blindness may be the result!

Water

When in the outdoors, don't drink water directly from a stream, lake, pond, river, or any body of water. The water may be contaminated with germs that can make you very sick. Before drinking, the water must be treated in one of the following ways:

Filtration—using a modern backpacker's water filter
Boiling (a heavy, rolling boil) for 1-2 minutes
Chemical treatment with potable iodine tablets (from camping supply stores) or by adding 2 drops of chlorine bleach per quart of water

5. Journaling and Collecting

How To Start and Use a Nature Journal

The naturalist's greatest tool is his journal. It's where he writes about his journeys, observations, and discoveries. It's where he records the sense of wonder that steals over him as he watches a butterfly hatch from a cocoon, or enjoys a lunar eclipse.

Your journal should be small enough to tuck into a kit or pocket on your Nature adventures. It might be a simple spiral-bound notepad or a fancy hardbound blank book. Ideally, at least some of the pages should be blank, to allow for drawing sketches, maps, etc.

In addition to written notes, your naturalist journal should also include sketches, maps, charts, graphs, and anything else that seems appropriate. You may want to glue photographs or other materials onto its pages.

Use your journal to keep track of hikes, campouts, stargazing, or family outdoor adventures. Add a quick sketch of an interesting butterfly or a gorgeous rainbow, or draw a map of your herb garden. Paste in a photograph from a favorite outing. However you use your journal, have fun with it!

Here is a list of ideas to help you get started in recording your observations:
Where are you?
What day is it?
What's the weather like?
What is the moon phase?

Using as many different adjectives as you can, describe the area you are in. Adjectives are descriptive words that tell which, how many or what kind of, words like brown, magnificent and soft.

What living creatures are you aware of?
What energies or presences are you aware of?
How do things smell?
What sounds do you hear? You may wish to

sit very still and close your eyes while you listen carefully. Afterwards, write or draw about what you heard.

Come back to the same spot at different times of the day or evening. What is different? What is the same? Come back to the same spot under different weather conditions. What is different? What is the same?

How many different kinds of plants can you find? Draw them! What features do the plants have in common? How do they differ?

Sit quietly in your outdoor spot and write a poem about the natural world around you. Remember, poetry can rhyme, but it doesn't always have to. Who says that your words even have to be in straight lines? If you're writing about a flower, try writing the words in the shape of a flower. Try a haiku, this form of Japanese poetry consists of three lines: the first line has five syllables, the second has seven, and the third has five.

You may be moved to sit and write a story.

Or, you may be impressed with the magickal feeling of the place, and may be prompted to outline a ritual, or draft a prayer or blessing.

Observation

To *observe* is to become aware of something through careful and directed attention. *Observation* means taking that careful attention and using it to note or record various occurrences or phenomena. If you're observant, you're alert, and quick to perceive or notice things.

Observation doesn't come naturally to many of us. In our busy, everyday lives, we tend to focus on whatever we're concerned with at the moment, so we often don't really see everything that's going on around us. Fortunately, the skills of observation—like all of the other magickal skills you're learning in your apprenticeship—can be practiced, and learned.

As a backyard naturalist, you'll learn that good observation is all about two things: patience and repetition.

If you want to really see what goes on in a natural setting, you must be willing to spend a great deal of time and patience to do so. The best results are often gathered by finding a natural area and sitting motionless and silently, watching to see and hear what happens around you. As the wildlife becomes accustomed to your presence, they'll be less and less shy.

As for repetition, in order to understand the behavior of plants, animals, the weather, etc., you must watch them over and over again. This allows you to see things you may not have seen before, and also will allow you to see responses to the turning of the great seasonal wheel.

As you practice observation, you'll find yourself looking at the natural world with renewed curiosity and understanding. You will also find yourself appreciating the magickal qualities of Nature, and may find ideas to incorporate into ritual and observances. Nature is also a grand source of materials for regalia and magickal tools: tree limbs, downed wood, sea shells, stones, herbs, dried plants, pinecones, and more may find their way into your magickal practices, your wortcunning, or your altars.

Collecting and mounting plant specimens

Collect plants early in the morning, while they are in their highest color and full of natural oils. If possible, place them gently into a plastic bag—this will help prevent wilting.

Once collected, keep plants in a dark place and out of direct sunlight. Get them into the plant press as quickly as possible, and no longer than 3-4 hours after they are collected.

Professional botanists often use a *vasculum* like this to keep plants safe and intact until they can get them into a plant press. As you collect each plant specimen, make a descriptive note about it in your journal. This will help you identify each plant later, which is especially important if you're collecting several at one time. You may also want to sketch or describe the area where you found the plant. Was it found in the shade? The sun? Growing between rocks or under a tree?

Dry the plants using a plant press (see below). When placing your specimens in the press, arrange them carefully, for the way you position them will be the way they dry permanently.

To mount your dried specimens, position them on a large piece of plain white paper.

In the lower right corner, label the plant specimen as follows, using permanent ink:

Plant's common name
Genus and species (optional)
Where the plant was found
Description
Date the plant was found
Naturalist's name

A completed label might look like this:

Western columbine
Aquilegia Canadensis
Found in a sunny clearing
    at the edge of a forest.
Short plant (about 10" tall).
Yellow flowers with red spikes.
August 6, 2006
Ima Naturalist

You can put each completed pages into a sheet protector for additional protection. Finished pages may be stored in a notebook, piled flat in a box, or framed and hung on the wall.

Using a plant press

A plant press is used to flatten and dry plant specimens so that they can be mounted and saved.

Newsprint is a soft, absorbent type of paper. Every plant press is filled with newsprint pages. Plants are placed between the pages and the stack is bound or pressed together tightly for days to weeks, until the plants are completely dried.

The simplest type of plant press is made by layering plants between sheets of paper and then pressing the sheets between several heavy books. Another simple press uses a telephone book. A phone book's pages are already made of newsprint, so plants may simply be slipped between the pages. The phone book is then put in a safe place with several heavy books set on top of it. Check your plants weekly, removing when they are completely dry.

Collecting and labeling rocks

Minerals have specific chemical compositions and a unique crystal structure. Rocks are made from a combination of two or more minerals. For example, quartz is a mineral. Granite is a rock, composed of the minerals quartz and orthoclase or microcline.

The three types of rock are:

Igneous: Igneous rocks are composed of interlocking mineral crystals; and are created by cooling magma (the melted rock within the Earth's core). One of the best examples of an igneous rock is basalt, the most common rock found in the Earth's crust. In fact, most of the ocean floor is made of basalt, as is most of the northwestern United States. Granite is another important igneous rock. Most of the Sierra Nevada mountain chain is made of granite.

Hint: An easy way to remember how igneous rocks form is to remember that the word "igneous" is like "ignite." Those fiery words make you think of the hot, fiery, melted rock that creates igneous rock.

Metamorphic: Metamorphic rocks are formed when movements of the Earth's crust create huge extremes of pressure and temperature, changing existing rocks into new varieties. Gneiss (pronounced "nice") is a metamorphic rock formed by the crushing and melting of granite. Marble is another type of metamorphic rock.

Sedimentary: Sedimentary rocks are formed when particles of rocks (sediment, in all sizes) are layered and compressed to form a new rock. Sedimentary rocks often form underwater. Limestone is an example of sedimentary rock.

When you collect rocks, wrap each one in newspaper or place in a plastic baggie. This will keep them from being scratched or chipped.

Before wrapping, make a journal note of when and where you found each rock, and of the rock's description. Assign each rock a number. Write the same number on the corner or a piece of paper; tear the number off and wrap it up with the rock. That way you won't have any trouble about correctly identifying each rock later on.

When you return home, wash each rock carefully to remove dirt, mud, etc. Allow the rock to dry.

Now, decide which surface is the rock's "top" and which is its "bottom," in terms of how you want to display it in your collection. Take a bottle of liquid paper and dab a pea-sized spot on the bottom surface of the rock. Allow the dot to dry thoroughly. Then with a ballpoint pen or a very fine permanent marker, write the rock's identification number on the white spot.

Finally, set up an organized page in your journal to start a list of your rock specimens and their numbers. Here you can place final information about where you found the rock, the terrain, etc. You may also want to add a sketch of the specimen or its surrounding terrain. Leave a little bit of additional space for future notes.

An egg carton makes an excellent storage container for rock and mineral specimens. The compartments not only hold specimens but will keep them from rubbing together. Labels for each rock can be written or glued inside the upper surface of the carton, as a key to the rocks it contains.

Some people like to display rocks in small open white boxes. A piece of felt or cotton batting in the bottom of the box will help hold the specimen in place and will keep the surface unscratched.

Collecting rocks can reward the naturalist with a true sense of wonder. Rock-forming processes have been active for billions of years. Today, in the Guadalupe Mountains of western Texas, one can stand on limestone that was once a coral reef in a tropical sea about 250 million years ago. In Vermont's Green Mountains one can see schist, a metamorphic rock, that was once the muddy edge of a shallow sea. Half Dome in Yosemite Valley, Calif., which now stands nearly 8,800 feet above sea level, is composed of quartz monzonite and granite, igneous rocks that solidified several thousands of feet below the Earth's surface.

Rocks can be wonderful magickal talismans. Whenever a friend or family member of mine travels, I ask them to bring me a rock from their destination. Likewise, I pick up rocks whenever I travel. As a result, I have rocks from all over the world, including granite from the tops of the Sierra Nevadas, pahoehoe lava from Hawaii, a vial of sand from the Maine coast, and pebbles from Russia, Sweden, and the Arctic. Many of these have found their way into various rituals at different times.

Finding North, South, East, and West

Being able to find the four compass directions—also known as the ordinal directions—can be important when you're drawing a map, when you want to create directions so that you can return to a place, or when you want to do ritual and "call the quarters."

The simplest way to find directions is with a compass. With a standard orienteering compass, the red (magnetized) needle will always point north. Hold the compass in front of you, level with the ground. Now turn slowly until both you and the red needle are pointing in the same direction. You are now facing north! South will then be directly behind you, with east to your right and west to your left.

The next simplest way to find directions is by using the sun. The sun always rises in the east and always sets in the west. At noon, it is in the middle between east and west. By determining where the sun is, you can estimate the other ordinal directions.

For example, if it's about 4 PM, and the sun is settling close to one of the horizons, what direction is that? (Answer: west. The sun always sets in the west.) If you face the setting sun, where is north? (Answer: to your right. If you face the setting sun, you face west, and so north would be to your right.)

To find north at night, just find the North Star. Locate the Big Dipper (*Ursa Major*, the Great Bear) and imagine a line running up through (from the bottom of the dipper towards the top, no matter how the constellation is situated) the two 'pointer' stars that make up the outer edge of the dipper itself. Now look to a point about five times the distance

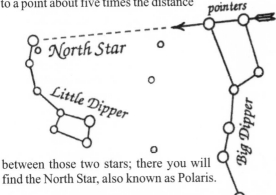

between those two stars; there you will find the North Star, also known as Polaris.

The Cricket Thermometer (Oberon)

When you hear the chirping of a cricket, you can immediately calculate the temperature quite accurately. Count the number of chirps in 15 seconds and add 40. The result will be the Fahrenheit temperature. This is known as Dolbear's Law; A. E. Dolbear (1837-1910) was a physics professor at Tufts College.

The chirping sound that crickets make is called *stridulation,* from the Latin *stridulus,* meaning "squeaky." Crickets make this sound by rubbing together little "teeth" on their wings. Only male crickets chirp, but only the females can hear the sounds!

Telling distance to a lightning flash (Oberon)

If you are outdoors, and a storm comes up, you should seek protected shelter immediately—especially if you see lightning! Cloud-to-ground lightning can kill or injure by direct or indirect means. The lightning current can branch off to a person from a tree, fence, pole, or other tall object. In addition, flashes may conduct their current through the ground to a person after the flash strikes a nearby tall object. The current may also travel through power or phone lines, or plumbing pipes to a person who is in contact with an electric appliance, telephone, or plumbing fixture. Similarly, objects can be struck directly, and this may result in an explosion, burn, or total destruction.

So don't be an isolated tall object, and don't be near anything else that may be an isolated tall object! The best defense is to avoid exposure to lightning when a thunderstorm occurs. Know where safe shelter is located and leave enough time to reach it before the lightning threat is overhead.

You can tell the distance to lightning strikes by the 'flash-to-bang' method. When you see a flash, start counting the seconds until you hear the thunder. At sea level, sound travels at a speed of about 761 mph, or 1,100 feet/second. This comes to about a mile in five seconds. Safe shelter must be reached before a flash is 2-3 miles away, which is 10-15 seconds flash-to-bang.

Hiking Safety

1. File a "trip plan." Let someone know where you're going, who you're with, when you're leaving, and when you'll return. Some people like to carry a cell phone for safety.

2. Follow the "Rule of Four." Always have at least four people in your group when hiking or camping. That way, if someone is injured, one person can stay with the injured person while two others hike out to get help.
3. Carry the "10 Outdoor Essentials." Carry them for all outings, in all weather. You never know when they might save your life.

Food
Flashlight
Pocketknife
First Aid kit
Extra clothing
Map and compass
Lighters and fire starters
Rain gear or space blanket*
Sunscreen and/or sun protection
Water and canteen or water bottle

*A space blanket is a lightweight sheet of aluminized fabric that can be wrapped around the hiker or used as a tarp shelter. A plastic "painter's drop cloth,"available at home and hardware stores for $2-3, also works well.

Other useful items to carry:
Rope or string
Insect repellant
Chapstick
A warm cap or hat
Plastic whistle (not metal, which sticks to the lips in sub-freezing temperatures)

Create your own workroom or "museum"

You may choose to set aside space for a naturalist workroom, museum, or both.

Your workroom space should include a large worktable, shelves, and storage spaces. You'll need access to a sink and a stove. The "Techniques and Equipment" chapter in your text has hundreds of ideas for investigations and experiments to conduct in a workroom, as well as the equipment needed and how to set everything up.

Your natural history museum can be as simple as a shoebox, and as complicated as you'd care to make it. Most naturalists enjoy displaying the results of their fieldwork. You may wish to set aside a shelf or table-top in which to store and display your specimens, your field books, or a particularly nice page of your journal.

Keep your eye open for creative ways to store and display your materials:

Cigar boxes and other small sturdy boxes are excellent for both storage and display.

You may be able to find small bookshelves or cabinets at garage and tag sales, and for very low prices. A simple shelf can be made from boards and cinder blocks. Many stores offer inexpensive plastic shelves and boxes.

6. Survival Fire-Making
By Oberon (grey)

When you go camping, you should always carry a pocketknife and couple of Bic lighters. These are worth their weight in gold, and far more productive than matches. However, just in case you should somehow find yourself out in the wilderness without one, a good Wizard should also know how to make fire from nothing. This is, after, our oldest magick!

Marking a spark is easy; the trick is getting a fire from the spark! You will need special tinder: bone-dry, finely-divided organic material that will catch the spark, ignite readily, and blaze into hot flame. In addition to the pre-made fire-starters that Moonwriter describes below, you can use mouse nests, birch bark curls, dry weed tops, cedar bark, scraped lint from cloth or cardboard, charred cloth, or cotton insulation from your jacket or sleeping bag.

Fire Starters (Moonwriter)

Fire starters are an important part of your emergency kit. A good fire starter lights quickly and burns long and hot enough to help get a fire going. Here are two easy "recipes":

1. Roll up 2-4 sheets of newspaper "the long way" to create a long, not-too-tight roll. Tie white cotton string around the roll every 2 inches, knotting the string tightly and leaving long ends. Use scissors to cut the newspaper roll between the strings. Melt paraffin in a tin can placed in a saucepan of hot water. Holding the string ends, dip the pieces of newspaper roll into the melted paraffin, allowing it to soak in for several minutes. Remove from paraffin and allow the fire starter to dry and harden on waxed paper.
2. Collect laundry lint from your clothes dryer. (Natural fiber lint—wool, cotton, linen—works best.) Fill the holes in a cardboard egg carton with the lint. Melt paraffin and pour the melted wax over the lint. Allow to cool and harden, then use scissors to cut the sections apart, leaving you with 12 fire starters.
3. An old stub of candle also makes a good fire starter.

To use any of the above, place one in your fire pit. Arrange small pieces of twigs and straw around the starter, then light. As the fire catches, begin adding more wood to the fire, increasing the size of the wood and adding carefully, so as not to smother the blaze.

(Oberon) Blowing on the flames will help it catch—especially if you can come up with a hollow pipe, reed or tube of some kind to blow through. Once the tinder gets burning, you're pretty much set. Now, all you have to do is add fuel at just the right rate to keep the fire going the way you want it to be. You should place each new log carefully—there is a whole art form to this! Make sure you have handy a poking stick to help you rearrange the logs as they burn and fall.

Flint & Steel: Flint, quartz, or other very hard rock will spark when you strike it a glancing blow from your steel pocketknife. Catch the spark in your tinder, then hold it in your cupped hands and blow gently on the bright spot from below until it bursts into flames. Learn to recognize flint, and if you come across a piece when you are hiking, stick it into your pocket.

Lens: A magnifying glass can be used to focus the Sun's rays onto tinder and ignite it. You can even use eyeglasses, binoculars or a camera lens. If you are out in the winter, you can make a fire-starting lens out of ice! Just find a frozen pool, stream, puddle—or even pour a little water into a dish and let it freeze. Break off a piece of ice that is about half an inch to an inch thick, and 2-3 inches in diameter. Place it between your bare palms, and rotate them back and forth until the ice melts into a lens shape. Then all you need is for the Sun to shine!

Fire-Drill: Without a flint, steel, or magnifying glass, you can always make a fire-drill on the spot. This requires four pieces: **Hearth, Spindle, Bow** and **Bearing.** You can shape these with your knife, or even a sharp stone.

Fig. 1

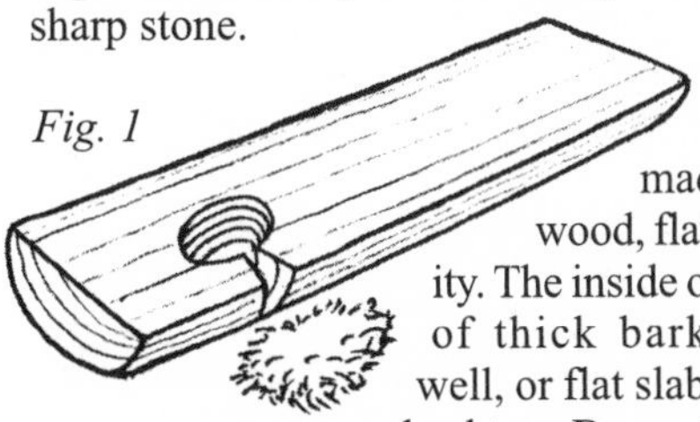

The **Hearth** piece must be made of dry, dead wood, flattened for stability. The inside of a piece of thick bark works well, or flat slabs from a dead tree. Bore a 1" round hole partway into it, very close to the edge, with a keyhole notch to the edge to allow hot coals to fall into your tinder. (Fig. 1)

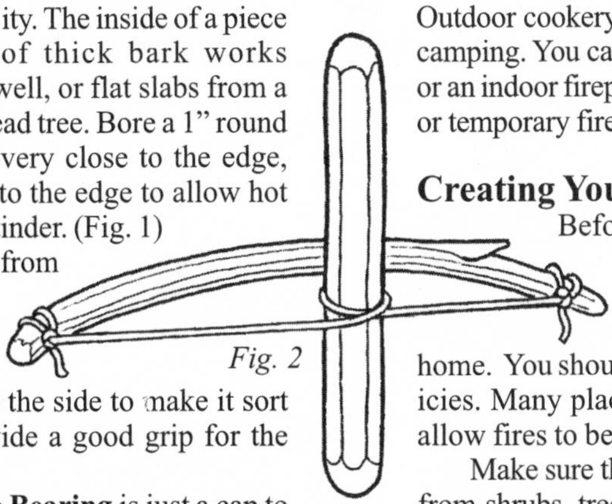

Shape a **Spindle** from a straight stick about a foot long and an inch thick. Round both ends, and scrape the side to make it sort of octagonal (to provide a good grip for the thong). (Fig. 2)

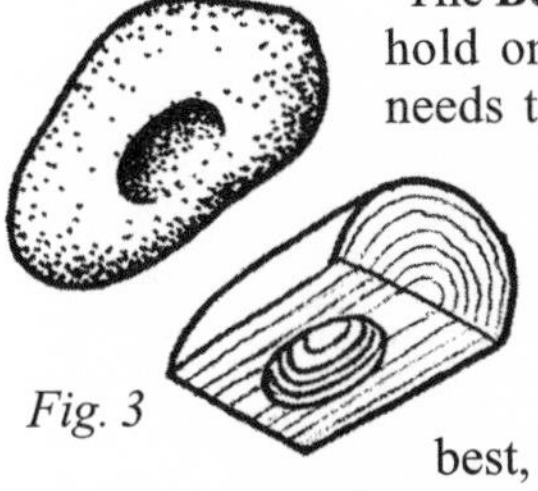

Fig. 2

The **Bearing** is just a cap to hold on the top of the spindle. It needs to fit into the palm of your hand, and have a 1" hollow for the spindle. You can shape a bearing from wood, bone, or a smooth pitted stone, but bone or stone is best, if you can find it, as a wooden bearing may heat up too much. (Fig. 3)

Fig. 3

The **Bow** is made from a curved branch, about 2" long, strung with a thong like an archery bow. A shoelace makes a perfect thong if you don't have any other cord; in an emergency you can braid a thong from cloth

strips, unraveled webbing, or even tough grass or bark fibers. String it taut, and then twist the spindle into the thong. (Fig. 2)

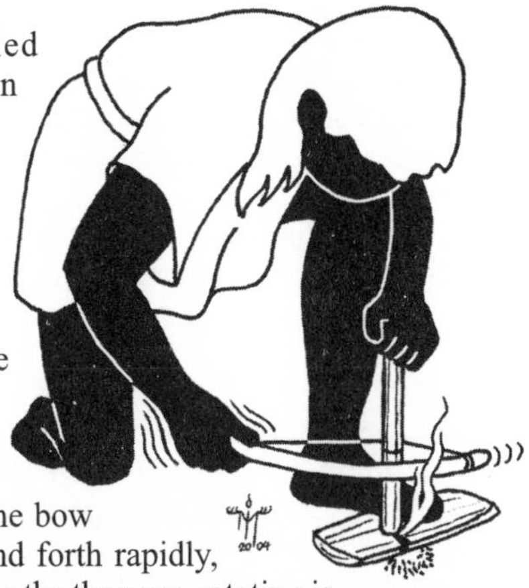

Assemble your drill, holding the hearth in place with your foot, and move the bow smoothly back and forth rapidly, keeping tension on the thong so rotation is continuous. Soon you will see smoke curling up from the hearth. Dump the glowing coal into your tinder, and blow on it to make it catch.

> **NOTE:** *Never leave a fire burning unattended—*or even smoking! Make sure that the last person to go to bed puts out the fire completely, with sprinkled water and dirt, until there are no glowing coals or smoke.

7. Outdoor Cookery
By Moonwriter (indigo)

Outdoor cookery can be fun, and not just when you're camping. You can also practice in an outdoor barbecue or an indoor fireplace. You can even create a permanent or temporary fire pit in your own yard!

Creating Your Own Backyard Fire Pit

Before doing this, you should obtain permission if you're using someone else's yard, such as your landlord, roommates, or parents if you live at home. You should also investigate your local fire policies. Many places do not allow "open burning" but allow fires to be built for cooking purposes.

Make sure that your fire pit is built at least ten feet from shrubs, trees, and any houses or structures, with nothing overhanging the spot. When using the pit, always keep a shovel, a pail of water, and a hose close by.

To build a permanent fire pit, remove the turf and plants from an area 3-4 feet in diameter. Encircle the pit with large stones or bricks and you're set!

To build a temporary fire pit, mark out a four-foot circle on the grass. Using a sharp, square-edged shovel, dig down about three inches, then force the shovel blade sideways, allowing you to slice off the layer of turf. Repeat until all of the turf has been removed from the marked-off area. Set the slices of turf in a shady spot and cover with a wet towel.

Build your fire in the center of the denuded area.

After you're done with the fire, allow it to burn down completely. Later that same day, shovel away and dispose of cold wood and ashes (add the ashes to your compost pile). Hose down or otherwise cool the spot, then replace the strips of sod that you cut away earlier. Water well. The sod should reattach itself in 2–3 weeks. Make sure to water it occasionally during that time.

Stick Cookery

Many foods can be cooked on a stick. You'll need a good thick stick, about as big around as your little finger. Peel the stick with your pocketknife and trim one end to a point. For a great hot dog stick, choose a stick with a "fork" on one end.

Second, you'll either need a charcoal fire or a wood fire that has burned down, leaving a bed of hot coals. Coals are necessary to provide steady, even heat. Flames aren't suitable for stick cookery; they create too much heat and can burn the outside of the food before the inside is even warm.

Foods can either be impaled on a roasting stick or wrapped around it. The most common impaled foods are hot dogs and "kebabs"—chunks of meat, fruit, and vegetable. Roast all of these slowly over coals until hot and nicely browned.

For a special treat, prepare "angels on horseback:" slice a hot dog lengthwise, creating a pocket. Push slices of cheese into the pocket. Now, wrap the hotdog with a piece of raw bacon; use toothpicks to fasten the bacon around the hotdog. Roast slowly over coals until the bacon is cooked.

Marshmallows and cubes of pound cake are also good choices for stick-roasting. Heat them slowly over coals, so that they puff and toast a golden color. If a marshmallow catches on fire, don't wave it around! Hot marshmallows are a mass of burning molten sugar, and can cause serious burns if they're flipped onto someone's skin. Burning marshmallows should be dropped off into the fire as a special treat for the elemental salamanders residing within.

For mock angel food cake, dip cubes of pound cake in sweetened condensed milk and roll in coconut. Impale on a stick and roast until done.

A roasting stick can also be used for biscuit cookery. You should use a thicker stick for this—about the size of your thumb. Combine biscuit mix with water or milk (according to directions) in a small bowl, mixing to form a thick dough. On a clean, flat surface, roll the dough out into a "snake" a little larger than the diameter of your thumb. Wrap the dough snake around the end of your roasting stick, pinching

it slightly to make it hold on. Now roast the biscuit twist s-l-o-w-l-y over hot coals, turning often so it cooks evenly. It's important to roast it slowly enough for the inside to cook through—a good exercise in patience for aspiring Wizards! The twist is done when it is puffed and golden brown. Serve with butter and jam.

Foil Cookery

Foil dinner cookery starts with a bed of coals—either charcoal or a wood fire that has burned down well. You'll also need a roll of heavy-duty foil, some over mitts, and a pair of tongs. If you're cooking in a campfire, a camp shovel can be used instead of tongs.

Just about anything that can be baked in the over can be cooked in foil over hot coals. The most common recipe is the traditional foil dinner. Start with a 16-18 inch double-thick square of heavy-duty aluminum foil. Into the center, put 1/4 pound crumbled raw ground beef. Add half of a potato (peeled and cut into cubes) and a handful of vegetables: your choice of sliced onion, celery, mushrooms, peppers, carrots, etc. Top with 2-3 large spoonfuls of undiluted canned cream of mushroom soup and 1-2 spoonfuls of water. Now, carefully fold and seal the foil, forming an airtight packet. Place the packet on the coals. Roast for about 40-45 minutes, turning every 10-15 minutes with tongs or camp shovel. If your ears are magickally sensitive, you may be able to hear the contents sizzling as they cook!

Open the packet carefully—if not quite done, seal it up again and cook for another 10 minutes.

Once you have this basic recipe down, you can vary the contents. Try diced ham with sweet potatoes and pineapple, ground pork with apples and onions, or chicken with Yukon gold potatoes, leeks, and sweet onion. Different "cream of" soups will also add different flavors, as will herbs and seasonings.

Corn on the cob is easy to cook in foil. Before cooking, soak the corn (with its leaves and husk still in place) in cold water for at least 30 minutes. Drain the corn and wrap—still wet, and still with leaves and husk left on—tightly in foil. Roast in the coals for about 30 minutes, turning every 5-10 minutes. Serve with butter, salt, and pepper. For a variation on this, place the soaked corn—in its husk—directly on the coals and roast as above.

Baked potatoes are another foil staple. Scrub potatoes clean and poke 4-5 deep holes in each one. Wrap tightly with foil and stuff them into a bed of coals. Roast for 30-40 minutes, turning every 5-10 minutes. When you can stick a knife in and the potato feels soft, it's done. Serve with salt, butter, sour cream, and fresh chives.

For a special foil dessert, try Banana Dreamboats. Partially peel a banana, and cut a slit along its length. Insert chocolate chips and miniature marshmallows into the slit Wrap the stuffed banana in foil, making sure that the slit stays "on top." Roast

on the coals for 20 minutes or so. Don't turn it—you don't want the chocolate and marshmallow to leak out. Serve with a spoon.

Baked apples are another tasty foil-cooked treat. With the apple standing upright, use a melon-baller to remove the core from the top side of the apple—make sure to leave the bottom intact. Use a knife to remove about 1 inch of peel from the top of the apple. *(illos)* Stuff the empty cavity with brown sugar, raisins, nuts, and butter. Add about 1/2 teaspoon of water. Set the apple upright on a square of foil; gather the foil up to tightly enclose the apple while keeping it upright. Bury the apply in hot coals and roast for 15-20 minutes.

There are a few principles to keep in mind for success with foil cookery. First, the foil packet *must* be folded airtight, so that the juices inside cannot leak out. Second, foil packets must be turned every 10 minutes or so, and turned carefully so that they don't tear.

If you have a fireplace in your home, making foil dinners is a fun activity on a cold winter evening! You can also cook them in the oven: bake at 350 for about 40 minutes.

Onion and Orange Cups

Onion Cups: Cut a large onion in half around its equator. Remove some of the center, leaving a 3/4 inch shell all around. Fill the cavity with seasoned ground beef.

Using long tongs, set the onion cup directly on the coals, wedging it in so that it doesn't tip over. Leave it there until the meat looks cooked and smells heavenly! (*Note:* if you're worried about ashes getting into the meat, place a piece of foil on top of it.

For orange cups, cut an orange in half and scoop out most of the pulp, leaving the peel intact to form the cup. (Save the scooped-out orange for a salad or for tomorrow's breakfast.) Prepare yellow or white cake mix. Pour the cake mix into the orange cups, then cook the orange cups on hot coals as directed for Onion Cups. You'll have a tasty orangey cupcake when you're done!

Cooking Bacon and Eggs in a Paper Bag

This is a fun one, and will amaze people who've never seen it done. You'll need a lunch-size individual brown paper bag, three pieces of bacon, 1-2 eggs, and a roasting stick. You'll also need a bed of coals—no flames, please!

Open the bag. Lay the bacon slices in the bottom of the bag, cutting them if necessary so that they completely cover the bag's bottom. (It's okay if some of the bacon extends up the sides of the bag.) Fold the top of the bag over to seal, and secure the paper bag to the end of the roasting stick—use twist-ties, metal clips, or whatever you can think of to do this.

Now, hold the bag over the hot coals. The beginning can be a little tricky: you want the bag and the bacon within to warm up slowly without catching on fire. Ideally, as the bag and bacon heat up, the bacon will release its fat and the bag will slowly become soaked with bacon grease.

Once the bag is heating up and has become grease-soaked, and the bacon has started to cook, remove the bag from the heat, open it, and add the cracked eggs to the bag, placing them right on top of the bacon. Do not drain any fat from the bag! Close the top, put the bag back on the stick, and continue cooking. From this point, your job is to slowly cook the bacon and egg until it's done. Keep the bag far enough away from the coals so that it doesn't catch fire.

Check the bacon and egg every 5 minutes or so. When it's done, set the bag on a plate, cut the top away, add salt and pepper, and eat directly from the bag.

Cooking on a Flat Rock

This is yet another fun way to do camp cooking. It takes some trial and error, but it's well worth your time to learn. Rocks are the oldest known cooking surface, used during ancient times long before metal and metal pans were invented.

You'll need to find a large, flat rock—something about 12-14" square and maybe 4-5 inches thick. Don't pick a rock from a creek or riverbed, as these often contain trapped water and may explode when heated!

Clean your rock carefully with soap and water, then apply a thin coat of vegetable oil on what will be the top (cooking) surface.

To use your rock, you'll need hot coals—either charcoal or a burned-down campfire. Use a rake or shovel to create a thick bed of coals, then set the rock—cooking side up—directly on the coals, adjusting it so that the cooking surface is flat. Wait for 30-40 minutes for the rock to heat up. One way to tell that it's hot enough is to drip some water onto the cooking surface. If the water hisses into steam or dances around, the rock is ready to use.

Once the rock is hot, you can use it just as you would a frying pan or skillet. Oil the rock a little more before using, then place bacon, eggs, pancakes, hamburgers, etc., directly on the rock's surface. Cook food until done. After use, allow the fire and rock to cool overnight. Scrub the rock clean, oil lightly, wrap in a clean towel, and put away for future use.

8. The Dandelion and the Ant: Plant and Animal Guides for the Urban Wizard

© 1996 by Elizabeth Barrette (grey)

These lessons on totem spirits in the city environment began as a guest presentation for the Urban Pagan Study Group in 1996. Since then it has grown in length and complexity. It speaks to a burgeoning branch of Paganism...that of the city Witches.

Pagans often find it difficult to fit into city life. Some of us take to it naturally, but most feel as if we lose a part of ourselves, a vital connection to the cycles of life. Yet Nature holds as much power over the urban world as the wilds – remember Earthquakes in San Francisco, heat waves in Los Angeles, hurricanes in Tampa. Even the cement and metal of the "concrete jungle" come from the Earth.

No matter how challenging the situation, life figures out how to colonize every available niche. Tree roots buckle the sidewalks. Scavengers scamper through the alleys. Green leaves and hungry bellies find ways to survive even the urban environment. Adaptability is a virtue. Persistence pays off. Consider what these inhabitants of the concrete jungle can teach us.

Plant Guides

Bluegrass: *"Just look at what you can accomplish when you stick together."* You never see just one grass plant. Grass is gregarious. Teamwork creates a plush green lawn on which to rest your weary feet – and walking on this plant won't kill it. Grass teaches us the value of cooperation and resilience.

Dandelion: *"You can't get all of us."* Dandelion's power is persistence. If you rip off the leaves, the roots remain. If you dig out the roots, the seeds remain. Dandelion's resourcefulness reminds us to dig in, hunker down, hang on. Our words and actions spread out like seeds, taking root in far places.

Forsythia: *"Don't be afraid to start over."* One of the few plants to grow equally well as a hedge or as an individual shrub, Forsythia cuts through the muddy grays of late winter with its display of brilliant yellow blossoms. It readily spreads by shoot or seed, and regrows even if pruned back to the ground. Look here for regeneration.

Ginkgo: *"Think before you act! Plan ahead. Consider the consequences."* This ancient tree gives magnificent shade – but if you plant a female, she drops vile-smelling fruit all over the place come fall. Ginkgo's power comes from great age and experience, a warning to make all decisions with care.

Privet Hedge: *"Good fences make good neighbors."* This ubiquitous landscaping plant appears as a tidy wall of greenery. Privet persists in mediocre soil and withstands the onslaught of smog. It excels at setting boundaries. If you need help with shielding, look here.

Tree of Heaven: *"What a mess! No problem, I can fix it."* Urban developers *hate* this tree; nursery owners often refuse to sell it; yet still it crops up in planting programs time and again, quickly making a perceived nuisance of itself. Tree of Heaven only grows in disturbed, damaged soil: it's a patch plant. It also acts like a canary in a coal mine, warning of trouble. Tree of Heaven's power is transformation; it thrives in poor conditions, improving them and then making way for other species.

Animal Guides

Ant: *"It's all alike down here."* Ant's power is insignificance. She is too small to notice, so she doesn't get bothered much. Her world centers on such a tiny scale that the differences a city imposes don't affect her much; she doesn't notice them either. Ant can point you towards the levels that civilization doesn't alter; if you fall through the cracks, she can show you how to make yourself at home there.

Peregrine Falcon: *"Never give up."* Threatened with extinction just a few decades ago, this fierce and beautiful bird of prey has made an amazing recovery. It has overcome habitat loss, pesticides, and other major changes. When you feel helpless against the forces arrayed against you, remember that you too can soar above them.

Pigeon: *"An artificial cliff – what a great place for a nest!"* Pigeon, on the other hand, welcomes the changes. A difference that makes no difference is no difference to Pigeon. If you're a techno-Pagan, look here for inspiration. Pigeon's power is finding artificial niches that fit better than the natural originals.

Rat: *"What do you mean, garbage? Give me that."* This industrious glutton reminds us to look for hidden uses instead of throwing things away. Like Tree of Heaven, Rat transforms trash into treasure. Rat's power is resourcefulness: he can live anywhere, eat anything, use everything. If you want to break a wasteful consumerist habit like buying disposable goods, turn here for inspiration.

Sparrow: *"No crumb is too small."* Darting and dodging among the crowd, Sparrow grabs the scraps that others leave behind. This little bird can make use of nesting sites too tight for other birds, and hide in the densest brush or clutter to escape predators. Sparrow teaches thriftiness and the ability to evade danger by remaining inconspicuous.

Squirrel: *"Save a little something for a rainy day."* Frisky and irrepressible, this mammal is a fixture of parks and city yards – anywhere there's a tree and a patch of ground. Here we get the slang term "squirrel away" for savings. Watch Squirrel burying nuts for winter, and you'll see why. Need help building your own hoard? Ask Squirrel!

Honoring Urban Guides

You can work with urban totems directly or indirectly. The indirect method is easier and more discreet. Set up an altar in your bedroom, and decorate it with symbols of your animal or plant guides. Photos or artwork depicting the totem are always appropriate. You might also include a physical representation, such as a leaf from a plant or a spoonful of Earth from an anthill. Use your altar as a focus when you meditate on your guide.

The direct method involves doing something to improve the urban habitat. If you have a yard – or even just a balcony – to call your own, you can create a "pocket garden" to attract wildlife. Put out a birdfeeder. Grow guardian plants or ones that appeal to your animal guides. At minimum, offer water; that alone attracts wildlife, because fresh water is hard to find. Then see who shows up.

If you don't have space of your own, look for public resources. You can feed birds or squirrels, and enjoy the plants, in a nearby park. Ask about volunteer opportunities; sometimes you can help plant trees or maintain flowerbeds. Some cities even have a "community garden" program where you can plant things in a small plot shared with other urban gardeners.

Conclusion

No, these plants and animals aren't particularly glamorous. Yes, they have rotten reputations in some places. But look at Eagle and Bear and Redwood Tree, then compare their current situation with the urbanites. Dandelion, Ant, and crew have all learned to adapt. These survivors thrive in the urban environment, often reaching far beyond their accomplishments in any natural setting. They may seem insignificant, but their power touches every city on Earth. The next time you feel out of place in the urban world, reach out to one of them. They each have something to teach you.

Quest

If you live in town, survey your neighborhood; if you live in the country, visit a nearby town for this project. How many different plants and animals can you find? Do they have a strong magickal aura? Discuss your findings in a journal entry.

Department III: Practice (gold)

Staff of Sun, Wand of Song

Fire's child
Bright and wild
Standing tall and strong
Warm and golden
None beholden
Staff of sun and wand of song

Family royal
Friendship loyal
Leading toward the light
Wanton stranger
Hints of danger
Keep the torch within your sight!

—Elizabeth Barrette

1. Introduction

WELCOME TO THE WORLD OF MAGICK-AL Practice! In this Department you will acquire the essential *accoutrements* (equipment), both physical and conceptual, to make your magick effective: your tools, regalia, and sanctum sanctorum, as well as signs, symbols, spells and charms.

The color associated with this department is Gold, reflecting the masculine energies of strength, leadership, and vitality. Gold represents the color of the Sun, the sign of Leo, adolescence, joy, fruitfulness and nobility. Men of magick often prefer tools, amulets and jewelry made of gold, bronze, or brass.

Magickal Practice is divided into two main sections. This first part concerns accoutrements and regalia; and the second part is all about spells and charms. To practice Wizardry, and to make use of the lessons offered here and in the *Grimoire,* you will first need to assemble your Wizard's tool-kit. Grey School Professor Moonwriter presents the following lessons:

Part 1—Accoutrements

Your Wizard's Tool Kit
By Moonwriter (indigo)

A Wizard must always be prepared for anything. As an apprentice Wizard, you should assemble a Kit—a sort of toolbox that you will keep on hand for use as needed.

You'll need a sturdy pack or satchel, such as a backpack or cosmetic case. Soft-bodied toolboxes—especially those with a lot of compartments—also work well. Many camera cases are good too, especially those with moveable dividers. Whatever size or shape it takes, it should be portable enough for you to take on outings, and big enough to carry the things you'll need.

Some Wizards use their Kit to store magickal supplies and materials. Here are some useful supplies and materials for your Kit:

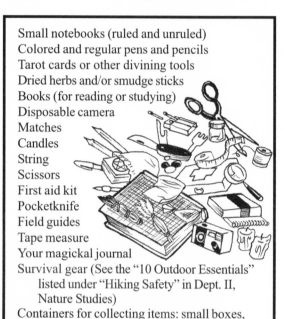

Small notebooks (ruled and unruled)
Colored and regular pens and pencils
Tarot cards or other divining tools
Dried herbs and/or smudge sticks
Books (for reading or studying)
Disposable camera
Matches
Candles
String
Scissors
First aid kit
Pocketknife
Field guides
Tape measure
Your magickal journal
Survival gear (See the "10 Outdoor Essentials" listed under "Hiking Safety" in Dept. II, Nature Studies)
Containers for collecting items: small boxes, plastic bags, etc.
Packet of cornmeal (for Earth offerings)*

*Dean of Studies Elizabeth Barrett writes, "I use cornmeal for Native American tasks. But left to my own devices, I'm more likely to offer something of immediate use to the Earth: birdseed, fertilizer, and native wildflower seed are personal favorites. Enterprising Wizards may roll seeds and fertilizer into a ball protected by a layer of clay, which will dissolve gradually in the rain."

This is only a partial list. You will come up with your own ideas, and you will add to and change your Kit as you grow in Wizardry. For example, if you become interested in nature studies, you might emphasize field guides and collecting materials in your Kit. If you're into performance magick, your Kit might include sleight-of-hand conjuries, or some ritual poetry books to peruse when you have the time. If divination is your forte, you might keep Tarot cards or runes in your Kit.

Have fun building your Kit, and watching it grow with you!

Your Wizardly Accoutrements

As you progress in Wizardry, you'll begin to acquire the "accoutrements" of a Wizard.

Now let's be clear about one thing: it's possible to be a Wizard without ever owning a cape or wielding a staff! But it's easy (and fun!) to look and feel the part. Like anything that becomes a profession, skill, or hobby, the work of Wizarding becomes more fun and interesting when you have some of the trappings that go with it. Also, there are some situations where a good tool or the proper attire will actually help you in your efforts.

Here are some of the things you might think about for your Wizardly space:

Record-keeping

For record keeping, you'll need journals, pens, pencils, a glue stick, etc. You may want to acquire special boxes, notebooks, chests, or even a filing cabinet in which to keep your writings and projects, and the tidbits that you cut out of magazines, newspapers, etc.

Clothing and Tools

As you work at becoming a Wizard, you may want to dress the part. Many Wizards like to make all of their own clothing and tools, and the *Grimoire* has sections on making your own magickal tools and attire. A visit to the fabric store will reward you with fabrics and patterns to make cloaks, tunics, dresses, and other arcane or ritual clothing.

Some Wizards prefer to buy their tools and attire. Many communities have shops that sell magickal items. Renaissance and Pagan fairs and festivals are also good places to pick up items, as are fantasy conventions, costuming conventions, and party/costume/theatre stores.

The month of October is a great time to find magickal items, as the mundane world prepares for Halloween. You might find clothing, make-up, magickal effects, light sticks, special candles, and more. At this time, fabric stores go all-out in featuring bolts of magickal fabrics and patterns for all sorts of wizardly garb.

There are a number of on-line magickal shops, too. Several reputable on-line businesses sell Wizard caps and cloaks. Before buying, do your research to make sure that the items are well made, and check the return policies. Some Wizards recommend against buying a magickal tool sight-unseen; that is, they recommend that you see and hold the tool before buying it. As an apprentice Wizard, this is probably a good rule to follow.

Books and Magazines

No *sanctum sanctorum* is complete without a magickal library, and as your Wizarding interests grow and develop, there will undoubtedly be many books you'll want to acquire. One of the cheapest ways to do this is through the purchase of used ("experienced") books. Powells.com and Amazon.com are two reputable web sites that sell used books, often for pennies on the dollar.

Another great source is ABE Books, a network of about 10,000 used-book stores around the country.

You may also want to invest in magick-oriented journals and magazines, or in DVDs that feature magickal themes.

Miscellaneous Items

There's no end to the items that a Wizard can use! Candles, statuary, herbs, smudging equipment, altar cloths, chalices, oil diffusers, scrying mirrors, divination materials, tools for working on magickal items, crystals, small vials and boxes, clocks, calendars, tarot cards, artwork, jewelry, calligraphy materials, parchments, fountain pens, and astronomical devices are things that you might need at one time or another.

Larger items might include bookshelves, filing cabinets, a desk, a jewelry box, and other pieces that will help you with your Wizardly workings.

Again, many of these can be made, or purchased cheaply. You might also keep a wish list, so that if someone wants to get you a gift you can offer a suggestion.

Bringing the Elements into your Magickal Space

Since the Elements influence every aspect of our magickal lives, you will benefit from making them a part of your home and your magickal space.

Earth: Earth grounds us and gives us our center. Use natural stoneware or earthenware on your table. Set stones, rocks, and crystals around your home. Use natural sea salt in your kitchen.

Air: Air is energizing, and improves the clarity of the mind. To bring air into your home, open the windows. Burn candles, incense, or essential oils. Hang wind chimes and banners outside your windows. Hang mobiles inside your home.

Fire: Fire is energy in its purest form. To bring in fire, burn candles and smudges. If you have a fireplace, keep a fire burning as a gathering point and a place to meditate. Hang prism-creating crystals in the windows. Cook with fiery spices and peppers.

Water: Water calms, soothes, and heals. One of the best ways to bring water into your space is with a small tabletop fountain. Or, try setting out a bowl of water, with flower petals or floating candles on its surface. Seashells, sea glass, and pieces of coral make lovely displays.

Spirit: Spirit supports our energy and emotions, connects us to the world, and inspires us to greater things. For spirit, you may wish to incorporate photographs of your loved ones, or items of family memorabilia. Choose things with great personal meaning.

Task

Select a blank page in your magickal journal. On the page, make a list of at least 10 things that you hope to acquire for your Wizardly works. For each one, note (a) whether you could make it, and how you would do so, and (b) if you needed to purchase it, how you could do so cheaply.

You can use this as a way to plan and track your Wizardly belongings. Some Wizards like to keep a record of when and where they obtain (or made) each item.

3. Regalia

Your Wizard's Clothing
by Oberon (grey)

I wrote a whole section in the *Grimoire* on how to create your Wizardly *regalia* (costume); see pp. 112-116. I'm not going to repeat any of that here, but I would like to add a few items I didn't really describe in detail, or explain how to make. These are your pointy hat, your traveling cloak, and your boots.

Your Pointy Hat

The tall pointy hats traditionally associated with Wizards and Witches have been around for quite awhile. According to Historians at Berlin's Museum for Pre- and Early History, oracular Wizards of ancient Bronze-Age Europe wore conical hats of gold intricately embellished with astrological symbols that helped them to predict the movement of the sun and stars.

Such figures, referred to as "king-priests," were held to have supernatural powers because of their ability to accurately predict the correct time for sowing, planting and harvesting crops.

"They would have been regarded as Lords of Time who had access to a divine knowledge that

enabled them to look into the future," says Wilfried Menghin, director of the Berlin Museum, which has been carrying out detailed research on a 3,000-year-old 30" high Bronze Age cone of beaten gold that was discovered in Switzerland in 1995 and purchased by the museum the following year.

Mr. Menghin and his researchers discovered that the 1,739 sun and half-moon symbols decorating the Berlin cone's surface make up a scientific code which corresponds almost exactly to the "Metonic cycle" discovered by the Greek astronomer Meton in 432 BCE—about 500 years after the cone was made—which explains the relationship between moon and sun years. "The symbols on the hat are a logarithmic table which enables the movements of the sun and the moon to be calculated in advance," Mr. Menghin said. "They suggest that Bronze Age Wizards would have been able to make long-term, empirical astrological observations."

Another conical hat, found near the German town of Schifferstadt in 1835, had a chin-strap attached to it. Studded with sun and moon symbols, it is the earliest example found and dates back to 1,300 BCE.

Other German archaeologists have suggested that the gold-hatted king-priests were to be found across much of prehistoric Europe. Professor Sabine Gerloff, a German archaeologist from Erlangen University, has found evidence that five similar golden cones were exhumed by peat diggers in Ireland during the 17th and 18th centuries.

(The above is from *The Berlin News Telegraph* of 3/17/2002: "Mysterious gold cones 'hats of ancient wizards'" by Tony Paterson)

In the Gobi Desert, West of China, a 2,200-year-old mummy of a Caucasian woman (left) was found wearing a tall black pointy hat just like those traditionally worn by Witches!

Witch and Wizard hats have become so popular for costumes that you can now pick up perfectly fine ones at any costume store—especially around Halloween. However, if you'd like to make your own, Simplicity pattern # 9887-A shows a fine Wizard's hat with a brim.

Your Traveling Cloak

A Traveling Cloak is meant to also serve as a bedroll when you find yourself sleeping out on the moors. In shape, it's much like an oversized Tabard, only with rounded corners. Gandalf wears one in *The Fellowship of the Ring*. To make yours, you will need 36" wide blanket material in a dark color that will make it hard to see at night (olive green, dark grey, indigo,

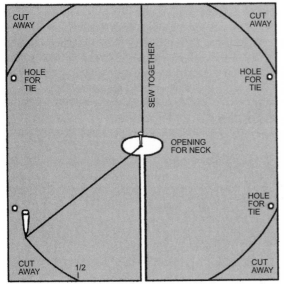

brown, or black are common choices). You might even find a camouflage pattern!

Measure from the top of your shoulder to the top of your foot, and double that length for each of two pieces. Then sew them together halfway up the length. The part that's sewn together will be the back, and the free sections will hang down in front—like your Tabard.

At the center point, cut a short (3"-4") slit to each side to make a "T" for your neck. Hem the cut edges, and let the lapels fall into place. Later, you can add a cloak clasp to hold the front together.

Now, lay your cloak our full and even on the floor to make a large rectangle. Put a flat piece of wood under the center point, and stick a push-pin into the middle of it, right where the "T" comes togeth-er. Take a long piece of string, and make a loop in one end to go over the pushpin. Stretch the string down the length of the front slit, and make another loop at the bottom front of the cloak. Put a marking pen in that loop, and, holding the strong taut, use it as a compass to draw a curve at the bottom front and back of your cloak (you should have someone else hold the center board and pushpin so it doesn't slip…). Start at a point halfway between the center and the outside edge. (see diagram above)

Cut away the leftover cloth and hem the edges. If you want to add a hood, you use these pieces to make one, using the pattern shown in the *Grimoire* (p. 116).

The final touch of your traveling cloak is to attach 12" cords halfway up the sides at front and back, so they can be tied together, making armholes. When you use your cloak as a bedroll, just untie these cords and you'll have a cozy blanket!

Your Boots

Of course, you could also make your own boots, if you have skills in leather-working. But this is trickier than I have room to explain here. Personally, I recommend just buying yourself a suitable pair. The best affordable ones I know of are available from Museum Replicas Ltd. (www.Museum Replicas.com) Look under "Men's Cloth-ing; Shoes, Boots, Sandals." The most "Wizardly" of these are the lace-up suede low or high boots, which are what Gandalf wears in the *Lord of the Rings* mov-ies. These are available with or without fringe, in black or brown. They are very comfortable, and the price is quite reasonable. I love mine!

Your Magickal Shawl

By Moonwriter (imndigo)

The *Grimoire for the Apprentice Wizard* gives instruc-tions for making an apprentice's tabard, a garment that drapes over your shoulders and hangs down over your chest. The tabard is color-coded to the wearer's mag-ickal attributes, according to the 16-color system established in the Intro-duction.

Some Wizards—especially girls and women—may prefer to make a magickal shawl instead of a tabard. A shawl can be color-coordinated in the same way as a tabard. It can be worn over any cloth-ing—magickal or not—and is very easy to put on. It can be used as ritual attire, or can simply be slipped over your shoul-ders when you sit down to write in your magickal journal.

Making a shawl is very inexpensive, and can be done very quickly. Since shawls are so easy to make, you may end up making more than one to use for various purposes or for different colors of magick.

To sew a shawl, you will need these things:
A piece of cloth 30-36" wide and aslong as your outstretched arms from fingertip to fingertip
Matching thread
A sewing machine
An iron

In choosing your cloth, you will probably select a color that reflects your magickal interests. You may also want to look for specific patterns. For example, I have a wortcunning shawl that is green with acorns and oak leaves scattered over it. And I have a cosmology shawl of violet-indigo satin, scattered with moons and stars.

Before starting, wash your fabric according to the directions that were on the end of the fabric bolt when you purchased it. Dry in the dryer, also according to directions. This process is called "pre-shrinking" and is an important part of any kind of sewing.

After pre-shrinking, use your scissors to trim away any fraying edges.

Making your shawl is as simple as "finishing" all four sides. By finishing, I mean turning and hemming the edges so that there is no fraying or unraveling.

Start by turning all four edges—one at a time—over ¼" toward the fabric's "wrong side," and then ironing each fold into a crease. Use straight pins to hold the fold in place. You can turn and sew these edges in any order.

When that's done, use your sewing machine to sew all the way around the perimeter of the shawl, sewing the folded edges down by sewing just barely inside of the fold. Make sure to sew on the fabric's "wrong side." And don't worry if this isn't perfect—it's not going to show!

Once that is done, you're going to fold each edge in one more time to make the actual hem.

Start with *one* of the long sides of the shawl. Fold the previously sewn edge over another 5/8" and pin with straight pins. As before, make sure to fold the fabric toward the wrong side. Use your sewing machine to sew the fold closed, with your needle set ½" from the fabric's edge. Repeat this with the other long side. After both long sides are hemmed, hem the two short sides—one at a time—in the same way.

When all four sides are done, remove any remaining pins and iron all four hems flat and smooth, ironing from the 'wrong side" of the fabric. If using satin or other "exotic" fabrics, use a cool iron so that you don't burn the material.

That's it—you now have a shawl!

Your Altar Cloth
By Moonwriter (indigo)

An altar cloth is simply a piece of decorative cloth used as the base for an altar. Altar cloths may also be used for other magickal work, such as a place to lay out Tarot cards or a scrying mirror.

As with other magickal attire and regalia, your altar cloth will likely be color-coordinated to match your magickal interests or intentions. You may choose

to make more than one.

For a very simple altar cloth, choose a two or three foot square of material in a color or pattern that meets your magickal needs. Choose the size according to the space available for it—it can be as big or as small as it needs to be.

Prewash the fabric as previously directed for the shawl.

Trim the edges, then hem the cloth as described for the shawl, either sewing the hem or using fusible webbing. (*Note:* remember to turn the hem edge toward the "wrong side" of the fabric.)

4. A Portable Altar
By Oberon (grey)

If you are traveling a lot, or away from home, you might want to make a portable altar to take with you and set up wherever you are. A common way to do this is with a hard-sided briefcase. Find a large print of a favorite painting (calendars are great sources!) that symbolizes the essence of your magick to you, and affix it to the inside of the lid. You might even want to get a large enough clear plastic cover that you can slip several prints behind it, and then put the one in front that you want to see for any particular occasion.

Then get three pieces of foam, and cut them slightly larger than the exact dimensions of the inside of the briefcase. Two of these should be 1" thick. The other should be the same thickness as the remaining depth of the briefcase, so that all three will fit together snugly in the case. Place one of the 1" layers of foam into the bottom of the briefcase.

Finally, you will need a thin piece of stiff material cut to the same size, which will sit on top to prove a hard flat surface for your altar setup. Heavy cardboard works fine, or you can use 1/8" wood or Formica paneling.

Now collect a set of small objects to represent the four Elements. If you have special magickal tools—such as Wand, Athamé, Chalice, Thurible, and Pentacle—include these as well (many people get special sets of miniature implements just for this purpose). A pair of votive candles or candlesticks for tapers (white and black) are also good to include, as well as incense, spare candles, and a lighter.

Then there are special objects—such as little figurines of deities, totems, personal treasures, photos, charms, etc. Whatever you like.

When you have assembled teverything you want to have on your portable altar, arrange them all in place in the bottom of the briefcase, with the lid open behind, to see how it all looks set up. You might want to leave some things out, or bring in others.

Then lay all the pieces you want to include on top of the thick piece of foam, arranged as a puzzle, with space between each piece. With a marking pen, draw a tight line around each object. Take away the pieces, and cut out the holes you've marked, using a very sharp knife and scissors. If the objects are as deep as the foam, then cut the holes all the way through. But if they are shallow (like your Wand, Athamé, or candles), just cut the hole deep enough to receive them. (Don't bother making holes for completely flat objects like feathers, incense sticks, or photos; these will go on top of the foam.) Then place the cutout foam into the case on top of the other piece.

You can make this especially magickal by getting a very thin piece of stretchy velvet fabric, and covering the entire piece of cut-out foam, tucking the edges down around the inside of the case. Leave it loose enough that the objects will press the fabric down into the cutouts. You might want to use the same kind of fabric to also cover the remaining piece of foam, which will serve as a lid over the cutout section.

Also get a nice altar cloth the right size to cover the inside of the briefcase and hang out over the sides.

To pack your portable altar for travel, insert all the pieces into their proper holes. Then place the remaining piece of foam over the objects, add any flat objects, fold your altar cloth and lay it over everything, place the stiff surface board on top, and close the lid. You now have a wonderful portable altar you can set up for your magick, anywhere, any time!

(Whiskerwind, Prefect of the Flames Lodge in the Grey School, adds the following:)

Another idea is you could also use a small box, like a cigar box and paint it or glue pictures on it and glue or Velcro miniature-sized altar pieces to it (many people get special sets of miniature implements just for this purpose).

The lid becomes the bottom of the altar

and the top of the altar is the box part like a diorama. How you decorate it is your personal choice. Even a small "Altoids" box can become a "pocket altar!"

These kinds of altars are used in Mexico a lot and other "Latino" cultures. They look really cool. You could also use them at home, where you can easily close them up for privacy if one doesn't want them in plain sight.

5. Crafting Magic Wands
By Abby Willowroot (silver)

Wand making requires a commitment to tapping your inner resources and making yourself open to new experiences and challenges. Expanding your perception of your skills and allowing the energy of the Universe to flow through you is a powerful and healing experience. A wand is not just a static object; it is a dynamic living thing, a tool for channeling powerful energies. From the moment you begin working to make a wand that intention and power is there within the materials.

The materials that can be used in making a wand are limitless. Of course there are traditional materials such as wood and metal, but there are also alternative materials. We live in the 21st century, and while it can be romantic to look to the past for wizardly regalia, it is also perfectly appropriate to look to the present and the future. A Wizard of the 13th century is not necessarily more real or powerful than a Wizard of this century. Traditions are important but they should never limit you. Be open to expanded possibilities in any endeavor.

Preparing yourself to create a magical tool is the most important part of the creative process. It involves a commitment to trusting the Universe and your own perceptions. Skill is important, but it is the least essential part of creating a powerful metaphysical tool— intention and focus are the most important parts. To set the metaphysical groundwork, begin by meditating on what you are going to bring into being. Focusing on the wand's intangible aspects like feel, elemental energy, expected use, and your intentions are the essence of the wand. How it looks, how long it is, or if it has stones and symbols are all external, and secondary to the core essence of the wand.

When you have a clear sense of the wand you will create, begin selecting materials. Keep yourself open to changing your initial ideas about what the wand will be. Often when we have something wonderful in mind, the Universe offers us something even better.

Never hurry the process—your wand will take as long as it takes. There is no set time limit on crafting a magical tool. The more patient you are, the fewer frustrations you will experience along the way, just as it is in life. If you come to a place where you are not sure what to do next, do nothing. Put the wand down and walk away, asking the cosmos what comes next. In a while you will know exactly how to proceed. This time could be an hour or a week; just flow with it and don't push the river. Your wand will be with you for a long time. It is worth taking the time necessary for the wand to evolve magically and powerfully.

Metal wands can be made from tubing available at hardware stores. Copper, brass, or chrome pipe can be bought in any length, and the store will cut it for you. Traditionally, many wizards recommend a wand be the same length as the distance from your elbow to your fingertips. Although this is often recommended, it is not a hard and fast rule. Choose a length that suits you.

Useful tools for making metal wands are a soldering iron, lead free solder and flux, sandpaper, steel wool, epoxy glue, and end caps that fit the tubing.

Wooden wands can be made from fallen or harvested branches, or wood dowels. My preference is for fallen branches, since I prefer not to amputate a living tree unnecessarily. The wood can be carved while wet or dry, as there are advantages to both methods. For a Harry Potter type wand, it is best to begin with a long dowel and sand the length of the wood to create the shape. The hilt end can be carved and then sanded as well.

Useful tools for making wooden wands are a Number 11 exacto knife, a pack of extra blades, several different grades of sandpaper, emery paper, steel wool, oil for the wood, stain, wax, and epoxy glue.

Glass or acrylic wands can be made from lengths of glass or acrylic rod. Hollow glass rods can be filled with well-dried natural materials like acorns, seeds, pebbles, gemstones or fried corn. A harvest wand can be made by securing a sheaf of wheat or grass inside a hollow glass rod and anchoring it with a Fimo base. For this type of wand, never add anything else inside the tube as it will damage the grain stalks. Lead free solder and a soldering iron can be used to ornament these types of wands.

Leather-wrapped wands can be made by stretching soft leather over a wood shaft. There are two different types: those where the leather is wound around the length of the wand, and those with the leather wrapped around the wand once and stitched with either one or two side seams. The leather can be embellished with symbols, designs, fringes, beads, or charms and talismans.

These are the most common, basic types of wands. The type you choose to make will depend on your own taste, beliefs and preferences. Remember, you are making a magical tool for your own use, so trust your own inner knowing. Wizards often have a number of wands that they use for different purposes, so let your wand come clearly into its own focus. Do not try to pack everything you can think of into it. Since you are

creating it in an organic way, the wand will soon assert its own nature as it nears completion. Let it be what it is. Also remember that shiny isn't always better than muted, big isn't always better than small, and fancy isn't always better than simple.

6. Make a light-up Magick Wand

By Oberon (grey)

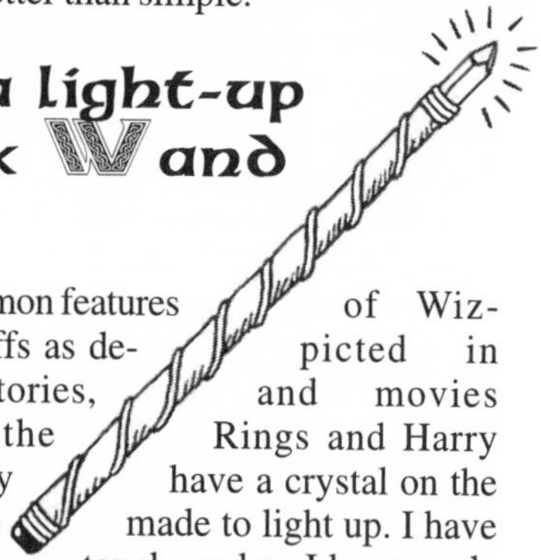

One of the most common features of Wizards' wands and staffs as depicted in popular imagery, stories, and movies (such as Lord of the Rings and Harry Potter) is that they have a crystal on the end which can be made to light up. I have always liked this touch, and so I have made mine to do likewise. And you can, too.

To make a light-up magick wand, you will need a stick with a base at least 5/8" in diameter, so you will be able to drill out a hole for a small AAA battery. The tip will need a crystal of the same diameter as the end of the stick. You can pick one of these up at almost any New Age or metaphysical store.

Then you will need a light. A bright white LED works best for a wand, as it will last practically forever, and it comes with wires attached. Try and get one with wires about 2' long, if you can. You will also need a small penlight spring and probably some more wires.

Fig. 1

You can get all this from Radio Shack.

And you will also need a screw-on metal cap from a small flavor extract bottle. It must fit tightly over the base end of the wand, which should be trimmed to a diameter of 5/8". (Fig. 1)

The most important thing, however, is getting a branch with a vine twisted around it, making a spiral groove the entire length of the wand when you trim out the bark. This is where you will run the wires from the battery to the lighted end. The stick should be no less than 5/8" in diameter, as straight as possible, and as long as the distance from the inside of your bent elbow to the tip of your middle finger (a *cubit,* in ancient terms). If the otherwise perfect branch you find is curved, you can straighten it out by soaking it in hot water for an hour or so, and then C-clamping it to a length of 2"x4" and drying it in the oven at about 200°F. (Fig. 2)

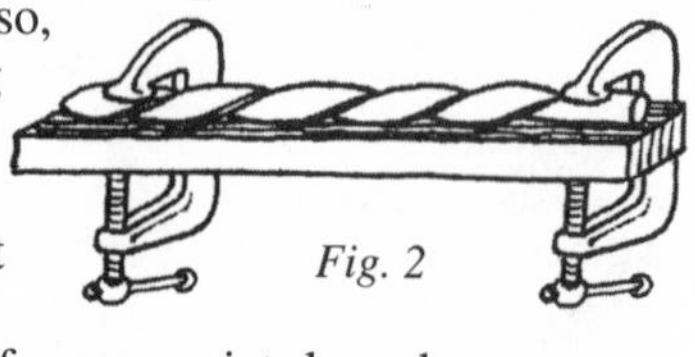

Fig. 2

Good prospects for appropriate branches are prunings from grapevines, or other naturally twisty vines. Here's a photo of one I'm working on. (Fig. 3) For

Fig. 3

details on cutting, preparing, and consecrating your wand, see the *Grimoire,* pp. 104-105.

After you have carefully trimmed away the bark, and sanded your wand smooth as silk, buff it with a 50:50 blend of olive oil and beeswax that have been melted together under low heat. Add a few drops of essential oil to the mix. Then dip a corner of soft cloth in the oil/beeswax mixture, and rub it into the wood to a fine polish

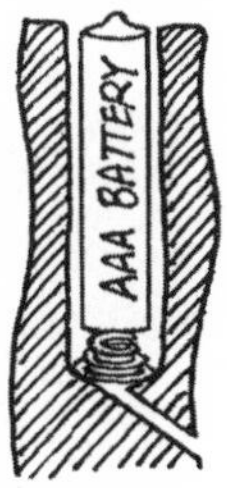

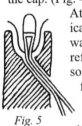

Fig. 4

You must now drill a hold in the base big enough for the battery to slip in and out easily without sticking. Make sure the hole is only ¼" deeper than the battery, so that the spring will push it up against the cap. (Fig. 4)

At the other end, drill a conical hole nearly as wide as the wand, for the LED. This will be used for a reflector, which you make by smearing some tacky glue (rubber cement works fine) into the hole. Then press a small piece of aluminum foil into the hollow with a pencil eraser and smooth it out. When the glue is dry, carefully trim away the excess foil. (Fig. 5)

Fig. 5

Then drill two small holes just large enough for the wires to pass through, at 45° angles connecting the bottoms of the battery and the LED holes to the spiral groove. (Figs. 5-6) You may have to use a Dremel to deepen and augment the natural groove.

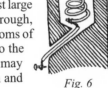

Fig. 6

If the wires on the LED aren't long enough to reach all the way to the base of the wand, you will need to add more length. Twist the ends tightly in a line, solder the connection, and then paint over it with rubber cement to insulate it. (Fig. 7)

Fig. 7

Wrap a short piece of #12 guage bare copper wire around the base end to match the ridges in the screw-on cap. Secure it in place by bending the ends of the wire and sticking them into tiny holes drilled into the wood. Test to make sure it fits perfectly, then Krazy Glue it, but don't get any glue on the outer surface. (Fig. 1)

Run the wires from the LED through the hole at the bottom of the reflector, then down along the length of the spiral groove. Terminate the end of one wire at the copper wire for the screw-on cap, and solder it, Then cement it into place with Krazy Glue. (Fig. 1) Make sure the bare wire is exposed at the terminal, with no glue or insulation covering it.

As for the other wire from the LED, you will need to bring it to the surface of the wand about 3" from the base. You may do this by drilling a little perpendicular hole through the groove to the opposite side, or

just bring a bit of wire out of the groove. You will need to make this into a terminal, which you may do by wrapping the bare end around a tiny brass brad, which can be recessed and soldered over. (Fig. 8)

Fig. 8

Now take another short length of wire and attach one end to the penlight spring by wrapping and soldering it. Insert the spring into the bottom of the battery hole, with the wire running through the 45° hole. Pull it taut, then create another terminal for the end of this wire, about ½" from the other one, and cut off the excess. (Fig. 6)

Test the wiring by installing the battery, and screwing on the metal cap. Place your thumb over both terminals, and the circuit will be completed through your skin; the LED should now light up!

When you've got everything working perfectly, glue the crystal into place over the LED with cleear Krazy Glue Gel, and wrap a bit of silver soldering wire around the connection. Cover the electrical wires by continuing this wire all the way down the groove, and imbed the end into a tiny hole drilled just before the screw-on cap. Run a bead of Krazy Glue all along the wire.

On the cap, Krazy Glue a round cabochon, and wrap a bit of silver wire around it.

Now you have a truly magickal Wizard's wand that actually lights up, just like in the stories!

7. Make a Planetary Hour Calculator

By John "Apollonius" Opsopaus (White)

Planetary magick makes use of the powers of the seven Esoteric Planets in order to perform a magickal operation, such as making a talisman. For example the Power of Venus might be used to bring love into your life, or the Power of Jupiter for prosperity. (See the *Grimoire for the Apprentice Wizard*, 3.VI.5 & 4.VII.3, for the Powers of the Planets.) Such a magickal operation is more effective if it is done at a time when the planet's power is especially strong. Since each day of the week is ruled by a planet, it's a good idea to do a Jupiter operation on Jupiter's day (Thursday). Furthermore, a planet rules each hour of each day, and so it's best to do planetary magick during the hour ruled by the planet. For example, as you will learn, on a Wednesday, Jupiter rules the 4th and 11th hours of the day and the 6th hour of the night. It is better yet to combine the day and hour rulerships, so for example you do a Jupiter operation in a Jupiter hour on Jupiter's day. (As you will see, the planet that rules a day also rules that day's 1st and 8th hours of daylight and 3rd and 10th hours of nighttime.) So knowing these planetary hours is very useful for magick, but how can you determine them? A Planetary Hour Calculator can be very helpful; it will also strengthen your intuitive grasp of the Cycle of Planetary Powers.

Making the Calculator

There are two parts to the Planetary Hour Calculator, the *Planetary Dial* and the *Hour Divider*, which I'll discuss in order. The Planetary Dial has two parts: the *back-plate*, which is engraved with cherubs and the numbers 1 to 12 in two rings, and the *dial*, which is engraved with a *heptagram* (seven-pointed star) and the signs of the planets. Copy the Calculator from the back of this book onto card stock and carefully cut out the back-plate and dial. Next you will have to mount the dial on the back-plate so that the dial turns freely. The easiest way to do this is with one of those two-winged brass paper fasteners you can find in stationary stores. Carefully punch holes in the centers of the dial and the back-plate and enlarge them until they're big enough for the "wings" of the fastener. Push the fastener through the dial and back-plate and bend the wings out flat. An even better way is to use a grommet, which you can buy in a fabric store.

The second half of the Calculator is the Hour Divider. It has two parts, the Hour Grid (which has many lines marked with three columns of numbers) and Hour Ruler (which has the numbers 1 to 12 from left to right). Copy the Grid and Ruler from the back of this book and cut them out. You're ready to go!

Using the Planetary Dial

Notice that the points of the dial are marked with the first letters of the days of week (*M, Tu, W, Th, F, Sa, Su*). Make sure you don't confuse *M* and *W*: the bottoms of the letters are toward the center of the dial. To find the planetary hours for a particular day of the week, turn the dial until the day's point is directed straight up, toward the "1" at the top of the back-plate. Try it! Now you can read the planet associated with each hour of the day and night, as indicated by the planetary symbols. Note that the inner ring (marked with the sun symbol) gives the 12 hours of the day, and the outer ring (marked with the moon symbol) gives the 12 hours of the night. For example, to find out the planetary hours for Wednesday, turn the point marked *"W"* to the top. Then we can see that the first hour of day is Mercury's, the second is the Moon's, the third is Saturn's, and so forth. Similarly, the first hour of night is the Sun's, the second is Venus's, and so on. It is also easy to see, for example, that Jupiter has the 4th and 11th hours of the day and the 6th of the night.

Using the Hour Divider

The planetary hours are not the same length as the ordinary 60-minute hours we see on a clock. Instead, for magickal purposes wizards divide the daylight into twelve equal parts and the nighttime into twelve equal parts. Since the length of night and day changes throughout the year, so also do the lengths of the planetary hours (and so they are sometimes called *uneven hours* or *seasonal hours*). The seasonal change in the hours also depends on your latitude for, as you know, there is a greater change in the length of day and night toward the poles than toward the equator. This might seem very complicated, but with the Hour Divider it's not too hard to do.

The first step is to determine the time of sunrise and sunset at the location where you want to your magickal working on the day you want to do it. You can get this information from an almanac, such as *The Old Farmer's Almanac*, which gives the sunrise and sunset times of each day and instructions for correcting it for your location. There are also Internet sites with this information. *Complete Sun and Moon Data for One Day* <http://aa.usno.navy.mil/data/docs/RS_OneDay.html> provides sunrise and sunset time for any date and location. You can also get a table for an entire year.

Let's work through an example. Suppose you are planning daylight working for Mercury's hour on a particular day, which happens to be Thursday. Using the Planetary Dial, you determine that the fifth and twelfth uneven hours of that day are Mercury's. To determine when they occur, it's necessary to divide by twelve the daylight hours on that day. Suppose you find that at your location on that day the sun rises at 6:50 AM and sets at 8:37 PM.

Look now at the Hour Grid. The thick lines represent clock time, from 4 to 12 and 1 to 9 (bottom to top). The thin lines represent the quarter hours. For daylight hours, the lower half of the grid is AM and the upper half is PM. Therefore, in the lower left corner of the grid find the line for sunrise (or estimate the space between the lines). So for 6:50 AM, we will be a little below the dark line for the lower 7. It doesn't matter where along this line you pick; all that matters is its vertical position, how far it is from the bottom of the grid. Now look at the Hour Ruler. Place the arrow that is to the left of the 1 at the place on the grid for sunrise. Next find the time for sunset in the upper right of the grid. 8:37 PM will be about halfway between the 8:30 and 8:45 lines. Now carefully rotate the ruler

Tables of Magickal Correspondences 5 – Quintads

Western (Druidic, Qabalistic, Alchemical) Magick

ELEMENT	SPIRIT (energy)	AIR (gas)	FIRE (plasma)	WATER (liquid)	EARTH (solid)
DIRECTION (n.h.)	Center / Up	East	South	West	North
DIRECTION (s.h.)	Center / Up	West	North	East	South
SEASON	Winter	Spring	Summer	Autumn	Year's End
MOON PHASE	New	Waxing	Full	Waning	Dark
PROPERTY	Singularity	Vaporous	Combustible	Fluid	Stable
BODILY ELEMENT	Spirit	Breath	Aura	Blood & Fuids	Flesh & Bones
SENSE	Hearing	Smell	Hearing	Taste	Touch
FINGER	Thumb	Index	Middle	Ring	Little
CELTIC VOWEL	Ailm (A)	Onn (O)	Ura (U)	Eadha (E)	Idho (I)
LIFE STAGE	Birth	Initiation	Consummation	Repose	Death
BLOOD PASSAGE (f.)	Nativity	Menarche	Defloration	Parturition	Menopause
GODDESS ASPECT	Nymph (Koré)	Maiden (Artemis)	Lover (Aphrodite)	Mother (Demeter)	Crone (Hecaté)
GOD ASPECT	Boy (Kouros)	Youth (Faunus)	Hero (Tammuz)	Father (Dagda)	Sage (Merlin)
RIDDLE	I am the Womb of every holt.	I am the Blaze on every hill.	I am the Queen of every hive.	I am the Shield to every head.	I am the Tomb to every hope.
SPIRITS	Angels	Syphs	Salamanders	Undines	Gnomes
TETRAMORPH	Sphinx	Man	Lion	Eagle	Ox
ARCHANGEL	Cassiel	Raphael	Michael	Gabriel	Uriel
CONSCIOUSNESS	Enlightenment	Intelligence	Will	Wisdom	Memory
PERSPECTIVE	Holistic	Outward	Future	Inward	Past
QABALA ACTION	Essence	Movement	Expansion	Contraction	Stability

Chinese (Taoist) Magick

ELEMENT	WATER	WOOD	FIRE	METAL	EARTH
DIRECTION	North	East	South	West	Center
SEASON	Winter	Spring	Summer	Autumn	Doyo
CLIMATE	Cold	Windy	Hot	Dry	Wet
PHASE	Storage	Birth	Growth	Harvest	Transformation
PLANET	Mercury	Jupiter	Mars	Venus	Earth
SENSE ORGAN	Ears (Hearing)	Eyes (Sight)	Tongue (Speech)	Nose (Smell)	Mouth (Taste)
TASTE	Salty	Sour	Bitter	Pungent	Sweet
SOUND	Groaning	Shouting	Laughing	Weeping	Singing
FACULTY	Will	Spiritual	Inspirational	Vital	Intellectual
ANIMAL	Tortoise	Dragon	Phoenix	Tiger	Ox
COLOR	Black	Green/Blue	Red	White	Yellow
TSANG ORGAN	Kidney	Liver	Heart	Lung	Spleen/Pancreas
FU ORGAN	Bladder	Gall Bladder	Small Intestines	Large Intestine	Stomach
EMOTION	Fear	Anger	Joy	Grief	Sympathy

Hindu & Tibetan Magick

ELEMENT (Tattwa)	ETHER (Akasha)	AIR (Vayu)	FIRE (Tejas/Agni)	WATER (Apas)	EARTH (Prithivi)
DIRECTION	Center	North	West	East	South
COLOR (Hindu)	Black or Indigo	Vlue	Red	Silver	Yellow
SENSE	Hearing	Touch	Sight	Taste	Smell
ACTION	Walking	Handling	Speaking	Procreation	Evacuation
INNER SOUND	Thunder, drums	Flute	Bees, crickets	Ocean, waterfall	Bell, gong, cymbal
ABSTINENCE	Injury	Untruth	Greed	Sensuality	Theft
OBSERVANCE	Cleanliness	Attention, purity	Body conditioning	Study of self	Contentment
TROUBLES	Possessiveness	Aversion	Desire	Egoism	Ignorance
CENTER (Tibet)	Skull	Perineum	Throat	Heart	Navel
ANIMAL	Lion	Garuda Bird	Turquoise Dragon	Elephant	Horse

until the 12 on the right aligns with the sunset time. You may have to adjust the ruler a little so that it stays on the graph, but double check to make sure that the leftmost arrow point is still in line with the sunrise time, and the rightmost with the sunset time.

Now you can find the clock time for each of the planetary hours by reading them from the ruler. So if you want to do your working in the fifth hour, you look at the position on the grid of the arrows on either side of 5, and you will see that the fifth hour begins at about 11:26 AM, and that it ends at about 12:35 PM. (With practice you will get better at placing the ruler and reading the times.)

Computing the time for a nighttime working is similar, except we must divide by twelve the time from sunset to *the next day's* sunrise. Also, for nighttime hours, the lower half of the grid is PM and the upper half AM. To illustrate, suppose we want to do a nighttime working in the Moon's hour on a particular Sunday. From your Planetary Dial you can see that the sixth uneven hour of the night belongs to the Moon. We look up the time of sunset on Sunday (suppose it's 8:32 PM) and the time of sunrise *the following Monday* (suppose it's 6:55 AM). In this case, we locate *sunset* in the lower left corner of the grid and *sunrise* in the upper right. Position the ruler as before, but in this case put the leftmost arrow (by 1) on the sunset and the rightmost (by 12) on the sunrise. Read off the times for the sixth hour, and you will find it begins at approximately 12:52 AM and ends at about 1:43 AM.

One shortcut is to remember that the first hour of a day is ruled by the same planet as that day. So if you can do your working at dawn, you can skip all the calculations so long as you know the time of sunrise in your location. However, you may have to wait a week to do your magick!

I should mention that the Hour Divider will not work for locations nearer the poles than the 50th parallel, so it will work about as far north as Seattle, for example. (Nearer to the poles the extreme lengths of the days and nights exceed the size of the grid.) Of course you can get computer programs that will compute the planetary hours for you for any location, and they can be very useful, especially if you are in a hurry, but they don't strengthen you mental powers as well as doing it yourself does.

8. Table of Magickal Correspondences—5

By Oberon (grey)

In the *Grimoire,* I listed Tables of Magickal Correspondences for sets of 2 (Dyads), 3 (Triads), 4 (Elements), 7 (Planets/Days and Chakras), 10 (Sephiroth), and 12 (Zodiac), and 13 (Trees). For the Apprentice, these are the most useful. However, I would like to include in this volume a few brief sets of Correspondences for the number 5. See the chart on the preceding page.

Part 2—Workings

Hocus Focus

With such charms my days are filled:
Watch me turn lead into gold.
With each door opened and closed,
This key grows ever more prized.
A wooden bridge, battered boards:
My chewed pencil splinters words.
Call me wizard, of a kind,
For this is my magic wand.
           —Elizabeth Barrette

Now for the second part of this chapter: spells and charms for magickal practice. First, we will learn how to create talismans, amulets, and sigils. Then will come the spells themselves! I know you will want to skip the setup and go straight to the spells, but I caution you to resist doing this. You really need to have the foundations in place, and the walls up, before you try and put the roof on!

1. Making your own Amulets & Talismans

By Abby Willowroot (silver)

Talisman: A magickally charged object or drawing that one makes or acquires, then carries on one's person in order to bring good luck, or as a tool to accomplish a specific purpose. Usually engraved with appropriate symbols, talismans may be made or bought, and any object may be turned into a talisman by magickally charging it.

Amulet: An object charged with power for protection, or to turn aside bad luck, and carried on one's person. Amulets are usually made from found natural objects, such as holy stones, fossils, crystals, shells, meteorites, acorns, bones, etc. However, amulets can also be made or drawn.

    (Oberon, *Grimoire for the Apprentice Wizard*)

Amulets have always held a special place in history. From the most ancient times ornaments were made as special amulets and talisman. Adorning ourselves for magical purposes and drawing the blessings of the gods seems to be an innately necessary practice for our species.

Making an amulet or talisman is a process that takes place between yourself, your visions and the materials, and transforms all three. Remember that you are in co-creation with the materials you select. Creating an amulet or talisman not only changes the materials used, it also changes you. Taking an active part in the process of creating your own magical tools and adornments transforms your spirit with action, while expanding your skills and powers of perception.

Today there is an unlimited array of materials we can use to create personal amulets. Your expressions are only limited by your own imagination. Keeping this is mind, look around your environment. As a Wizard living in the 21st century you can appropriately incorporate any available materials into magical amulets and talisman, anything you find is a part of your world and carries energy.

Metal, oven fired clay, epoxy resins, wood, paper, twine and threads, fabric, and almost any found objects can be combined in pleasing ways.

When choosing the materials you will use, be as open-minded as possible. Focus on what you would like to express through your amulet or talisman and the energies you wish to attract. If you want to create something to draw the powers of fire and electricity you wouldn't use ocean elements, nor would you want to use things that felt too earthy. If you take the time to become clear about the energies you want to work with in a particular amulet the selection of materials will be much easier for you.

Working with found objects is a powerful way of recycling and can make an amulet truly unique. Found objects include; broken jewelry or pottery bits, small toys, ribbons, photographs, gears, and other mechanical parts, computer chips or parts, beads, leather scraps, bottle caps, coins, nuts, seed pods, dried flowers, grasses, pebbles, rusted metal bits, knobs, dials, printed circuits, CDs, and much more.

Gemstones, crystals, glass gems, buttons and other items can be added to amulets, or form the central part of an amulet. Many fine amulets have been made by taking a piece of soft leather and cutting slits for crystal points to poke through. The leather is then sewn up and embellished with runes, magical symbols or other symbols.

Leather can be stretched and shaped by wetting it and stretching it over a form.

Leather Talisman

Materials: soft leather, oven bake clay, crystals, beads, a sharp embroidery needle, carpet thread or embroidery floss, a neck cord.

Form a rounded 2" to 3" teardrop shape with "Sculpey" or Fimo oven fire clay. Press a crystal point into the clay at the bottom of the teardrop. Press glass beads, or gems into the clay above the point, leaving enough clay all around to anchor them in the clay. When

you are pleased with the look, bake the clay on a piece of thick paper on a cookie sheet, in an oven according to package directions. You can also form a flat teardrop, abstract or round shape putting crystals and gems on only one side. If you do this the piece should be at least ¾ " thick.

Clay Gem

Slit

Leather   Stitching

Once the piece has baked and cooled, lay a piece of soft leather over the amulet and cut it just slightly larger than your amulet, leaving enough leather at the top to form a substantial loop for hanging. Dip the leather in warm water and stretch over the amulet, cut a small slit to allow the crystal to poke through. Once the crystal is properly exposed pull the leather taut and make small slits for each of the gemstones to peek through. Pull the leather taut and begin stitching up the sides, if you want fringe, leave the extra leather on the sides to be cut later. If you want to make smooth sides, trim the leather in close to the amulet and sew closed with an overcast stitch. After both sides have been sewn, go back and pull the leather aside so the entire gem or bead surface can be seen. When the leather dries it will stay put. Once the leather dries, condition it with a small amount of saddle soap or oil from your hands. Finish the top loop by sewing it over, onto the top of the amulet, or simply stringing a cord through the loop you have cut. You now have a beautiful and stable amulet that should last for years. The leather can be decorated with a sharpie pen, paint, ribbons or other materials.

Leather amulets can be made without the clay, but using the clay insures that the beads are permanently anchored and stable.

Metal Amulets

Metal amulets can be combined with wood or small metal parts. Wire available at any hardware store includes, copper, nickel, bailing wire and brass. Buy wire that is labeled "soft". Do not buy wire solder, as it contains lead and is toxic to wear. Using several different wire thicknesses will give you a lot of design flexibility. The wires can be woven together or used as

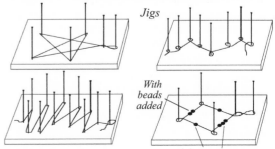

Jigs

With beads added

small accents in the design. Draw a design that has the wire crossing over itself for maximum impact. A design can be woven just like cloth if you like. To create a bending jig for wire, draw a design on a scrap piece of board and hammer headless nails (brads) half way into the places where the wire will bend. When you are ready, wrap the wire around the nails and slide up over the nails. Gently hammer the design on scrap wood with a rubber or rawhide mallet to strengthen and stiffen it. Polish with fine steel wool or emery cloth. (extra fine sandpaper).

If you want to add metal bits or beads to the wire, add them as you string the wire between the jig nails. You can also wind the wire several times around a nail, and if you like, tie them together with a lighter piece of wire, perhaps adding a bead or two.

You can back your design with another material, leather or wood by cutting it to the right size and attached with thin wire or thread.

Whatever you create, keep your imagination active and your options open. Go boldly forth and create!

2. Light Up Your Life with Candle Magic

By Lady MoonDance

Whether you know it or not, chances are that you have, at some point in your life, taken part in candle magic. When was the last time you made a wish and then blew out the candles on your birthday cake? This is candle magic in its simplest form. Likewise, in churches around the world, Catholic to Unitarian Universalist, people perform magic by lighting a candle to help heal a friend, ask for guidance or seek the resolution to a problem. The burning of candles during the winter holidays (Hanukkah, Yule/Winter Solstice, Christmas, Kwanza, and Imbolc/Candlemas), is an act of sympathetic magic meant to draw back the warmth and light of the sun—this popular tradition began in ancient Rome, where candles were exchanged as gifts at Saturnalia. Even in India, the beginning of Winter is marked by the celebration of Divali, another "Festival of Lights," where lamps and candles placed around the home and set afloat on the Ganges River represent renewal and may carry wishes for the year ahead.

From the beginning of time, we have universally recognized the power of a lit flame, whether it is providing life-giving warmth, releasing the savory smell of dinner, illuminating scary stories shared around a campfire, or creating the perfect mood for a romantic meeting. Its glow in the darkness captures our gaze, and we are easily lost in its flicker. This is the power that we seek to harness in candle magic, where we use the candle itself as the focal point for our magical working. The only real difference between performing can-

dle magic and just lighting a candle is one of intent. Your magic can be as simple or as complex as you wish, but everything that you do as you prepare and burn your candle is for the purpose of imbuing it with your desired outcome. However, also remember that in candle magic, everything is optional except the candle (and in a pinch, you can even simply envision that), so feel free to take whatever works for you, and leave the rest behind.

Selecting A Candle

There are many kinds of candles: pure beeswax - which is often rolled in sheets as well as formed, hand-dipped tapers, molded shapes, candles poured into jars or holders. Shaped candles include cats (often used for luck or in working with pets), skulls (which may be used for healing), human figures (often employed for love and relationship workings), and pretty much anything that you can imagine. Feel free to begin exploring these, but don't fall prey to the belief that only a certain kind of candle will work for a particular purpose. In selecting the shape and size, it is often more important to think of how long you want it to burn. A small tea light will easily burn out in a few hours, and a votive in a night or two. Pillars last longer, but you may need to drain off wax or trim them in order to get them to burn down completely. Seven knob candles are specially designed so that one section can be burned each day for a week, and the tall, slim, glass-enclosed candles, called devotional or novena candles, may last even longer. (Any plastic overwrap on these can be removed if necessary, but also consider the energy that may have already have been put into these, or any other candles, when selecting them.) Repeatedly burning a candle, and the act of caring for the candle during that time, can be useful for focusing on long-term goals, or anything that you wish to reinforce, or send extra energy into. You may wish to select a specified number of hours or nights based on your purpose, or to simply allow it to burn until it goes out by itself.

The most important consideration in candle magic is the color. Your selected color contributes the vibrational energy of that hue to your magic, as well as conveying your intention to your subconscious as you work. Below are only a few of the many possible choices and some of their common meanings:

Red - Fire, Love, Passion, Emotions, Courage, Sex, Strength, Power, Anger, Blood, Energy

Pink - Honor, Love, Romance, Femininity, Friendship, Girl Children

Orange - Attraction, Encouragement, Stimulation, Fire, Courage, Autumn

Yellow - Air, Thought, the Mind and Communication, Attraction, Charm, Confidence, Happiness, Joy, Summer

Green - Earth, Fertility, Prosperity, Abundance, Growth, Luck, Healing, Spring

Blue - Water, Success, Material/Earthly Destiny, Patience, Tranquility, Healing, Clarity, Wisdom

Light Blue - the Sky, Peace, Boy Children

Turquoise - Healing, Balance, Water

Purple - Spirituality & Spiritual Destiny, Power, Peace, Royalty

Brown - Earth, Groundedness, Stability, Work, Job Issues and "Mundane" Issues

White - Yang Energy, Light, Purity, Unity, Healing, Spirit & Oneness - Contains & Reflects all Colors, Can Be Used In Place of Any Other Color

Black - Yin Energy, Darkness, The Void & Pure Potential, Banishing, Releasing, Protection & the Ending of Bad Luck or Hexes - Negates all Colors & Energy

Gray - Neutrality, Stalemate, Loss, Neither one thing nor the other, hidden things, indecision

Gold - The "Masculine" aspects of the Divine, the Sun, Prosperity & Abundance

Silver - The Goddess or Lady, the Moon, Prosperity & Abundance

Some candles made especially for magic are created with the bottom half dipped in an outer coating of black, so that the color will burn down and flow over the black. These are generally called reversing candles, as they are used to turn around bad luck or "negative magic" in regards to love (red), money (green) or any other purpose (white). Inversely, candles where the black runs down over the red are meant to cause the ending of a relationship and so should be used with extreme care.

In selecting a candle, remember that it is a focal point for you - your conscious and subconscious energy - so choose the color or colors that work best for you. I often like to go shopping in my favorite mundane stores, places like Target, Michael's and JoAnne's, looking for a candle that "speaks" to me. Likewise, I might choose to hand-pour one, adding or leaving out color, fragrance or herbs, as feels right for the purpose at hand.

Also, remember that a white candle (or sometimes a black one) can be used for any purpose. Try holding a plain colored candle in your hands and imagining what color the perfect candle would be: silver and purple swirls and spirals, the colors of the earth and the sky, green with red polka dots—let your imagination color it for you. Doing so is a wonderful way to begin putting your energy and intent into your candle.

If you are selecting a candle to do magic for a specific person (preferably with their permission), you may want to do so based on their (western) astrological sign. Traditional correspondences, which actually come from the colors associated with the planet that rules each sign, include:

Aries (Mars) Red & More Red (all shades from pink to crimson)

Taurus (Venus) Pink, Mauve, Light Yellow & Pale Blue

Gemini (Mercury) Yellow, Green, Violet

Cancer (The Moon) Sea Green, Silver, White

Leo (The Sun) Yellow, Orange, Gold

Virgo (Mercury) Rust, Navy, Grey

Libra (Venus) Light Blue and Lavender

Scorpio (Pluto/Mars) Dark Reds (Crimson, Burgundy, Maroon)

Sagittarius (Jupiter) Purple, Dark Blue

Capricorn (Saturn) Dark Green, Brown, Dark Gray, Blue, Navy

Aquarius (Uranus/Saturn) Light Yellow, Indigo, Electric Blue

Pisces (Neptune/Jupiter) Pale or Sea Green, Turquoise, Indigo

If this color does not "feel" right for the person, remember to follow your instincts, and go with what does. You can also simply hold the color candle that fits your purpose, and picture in your mind's eye the person you are directing the energy toward.

In doing this or any other magic, always follow your own personal code of magickal ethics in as far as doing magick that affects others. Also, phrases like "for the highest good" and "I ask for this or something better" are good to keep in mind regarding your magickal statements and intentions in any working.

Charging, Decorating and Dressing Your Candle

The simplest way to charge your candle is to hold it in both hand and focus your intent into it, envisioning your desired outcome or speaking your intention. While you are doing so, you may also wish to "dress" it. Yes this sounds strange, but there are no actual clothes involved. "Dressing" is a traditional method for energizing your candle with your intentions. First, select an oil: choose one that contains essential oils or fragrances that fits your intention, or use a basic, unscented oil - even a virgin olive or corn oil from your kitchen will do. Traditionally, you hold the base of the candle in your left (or receptive) hand and the top on in right (or sending) hand. Placing your hands side-by-side in the middle, rub outward with each hand. While visualizing your purpose, you may also wish to rub the oil on the candle according to how you wish the energy to flow, meaning up and out or down and into it, moving swiftly in long strokes, or round and round in slowly, circling spirals. For glass-enclosed candles, pour a few drops of oil into the candle and spread them across the top.

Many other methods can be used to add additional energy to your candles. Carve words, runes, symbols or pictures into them with a toothpick or pen. Decorate the outside of glass-enclosed novenas with images from magazines and catalogs. Using proper care to prevent fires, roll dressed candles in dried herbs or select ones with herbs and other items already inside. Place a few drops of essential oil into the top of your candle each day before lighting it, burn incense nearby or choose candles with scents that reflect your desires.

Candle Layouts

Instead of using only one candle, you can arrange several candles on your altar to reflect your purpose. One traditional arrangement is to use two or more "guardian candles" at the back of your altar or around it (to represent the Lord and Lady, the Directions or other Divine forces,) then place a candle closer to you, or in the middle, that represents the purpose or intent of your working. In front of that candle, you may wish to position a candle for the recipient, often called an "astral candle." In this arrangement, the energy can flow into the protected space, going through the intentional candle and gathering your purpose there, to bring what is desired to rest with the recipient, or astral, candle.

You will find book after book with other layouts, but you may also wish to design your own by simply using the candles to visually represent your purpose:

- **Want to draw something toward you?** Select a candle for that purpose and one for yourself. Burn them for several nights, moving the candles closer together each time. When they are touching, let them burn down. If they blend together as they melt, so much the better.
- **Want to repel something away?** Do the opposite.
- **Want to see yourself surrounded by good fortune?** Select candles representing what you need (money, a new job, love, etc.) and place them around your astral candle.
- **Want stability?** Four candles in a square can represent this, just as the legs of a chair or table do, whereas two candles might represent two people in a relationship and three, the Divine (the three faces of the God or Goddess).

Add other symbols, herbs and items to your altar that you wish, decorating it to create and call to you your desires. Anything you can add that helps you to better focus your energy and symbolize your intent is acceptable.

Pinch, Snuff or Blow?

In most cases, it is considered best to let your candle burn completely down in order to complete the spell. However, you may wish to burn it for only a specified length of time, or a bit at a time, spread out over several night, weeks or months. There are many opinions about the best way to extinguish your flame. Instead of following only one "right way," I prefer to look at where I want the energy of the flame to go at the moment: do I want to seal it in (pinch or snuff it out) or to send it out to the universe (blow it out)? When pinching out a candle, lick your fingers first in order not to get burned. Doing so also mixes your own energy into the spell much more than impersonally using a candlesnuffer. A dramatic ending effect can be achieved by chapping your hands just above the flame. The generated puff of air extinguishes the candle, dispersing the energy of the flame in the process.

When Your Work is Done

Each candle should only be used for the purpose for which it was charged, and any reminders should be buried, even if that just means sending them to the landfill with your garbage. If the spell was for cleansing or release, you may likewise choose to release the remains in a nearby body of flowing water, but be conscious of your impact on the environment in doing so.

In creating candle magic, feel free to be as elaborate is you like, but also remember that sometimes all you really need is a single candle, and a little time spent burning it.

3. Spells for every purpose

Banishing, Binding & Exorcism

BANISHING NEGATIVE THOUGHTS

Anyone can have negative thoughts; it's what you *do* with those thoughts that matters. With magick, you can take those negative thoughts and do something physical with them. Such as: write them on little pieces of rice paper with non-waterproof ink, wad them up, and toss them into running water. Or bury them in the ground at the dark of the moon. Or burn them in a little cauldron. Or toss them into a ritual fire. When you do so, you can recite a little charm, such as

Sticks and stones may break my bones,
But thoughts can never harm me."

Or *"Avante, avante, maleficante!"* (pronounced a-VON-tay, a-VON-tay, MAL-ef-e-KON-tay, which means "get away, get away, all evil!").

THE CHILL-OUT

Write the name of the person who may cause harm to themselves or others three times on a piece of paper. Draw three circles around it. Fold the paper in thirds, and then in thirds again. Tie it up with red string and white string (or thread or yarn). Then fill a paper cup with water. Put the tied-up paper into the water until it sinks to the bottom. Then put the paper cup in the back of the freezer. As you are doing this, say:

Let this person from now on be
Unable to do any harm to me,
Chilled and frozen and gone from my mind.
Now I'll attract someone good and kind.

As long as it's in the freezer, that person can't harm themselves or anyone else.

(—Athena Shaffer & Lilana D'Venus)

CUT 'EM OUT

One way to get someone out of your life is to find a picture of the both of you together, and cut the other person out of it. (—Athena Shaffer)

MIRROR BOX BINDING

Line a box that can be completely closed with foil, shiny side facing inwards, toward the inside of the box. Put a picture of the person who wishes you harm (or name written on paper) inside the box. Then close the box. As long as it remains closed, he can't cause harm to himself or others. (—Athena Shaffer)

SWEEP 'EM OUT

To get rid of an unwanted visitor, put a broom behind a door with the handle facing that person. They don't have to see it, it can be anywhere in the house as long as it's behind a door and the handle pointing toward the general direction of the visitor. By the way, when you move, *do not* take an old broom with you to the new house. It will bring all the problems from the old place into the new. Throw it away and get a new one for the new house. (—Athena Shaffer)

THREE DROPS

A medieval chant to stop someone from harming you. Say three times:

I, (your name) breathe on thee
(name of person wishing you harm).
Three drops of blood I draw from thee:
First from thy heart,
The other from thy liver,
The third from thy vigorous life,
And thou loseth the strife.

(—Athena Shaffer)

Beauty

FOR BEAUTIFUL SKIN

Place a drop of rose oil on the very bottom of a red candle, then light it on your altar. Take a jar of cold cream, drop 7 drops of rose oil in it, and stir it with a White Feather! (Yes, this is messy! Have paper towels handy for easy clean up). Then use this enchanted cold cream to wash your face whenever you need to. (—Athena Shaffer)

TO GROW BEAUTIFUL HAIR

Wash your hair with high-quality keratin shampoo and crème rinse. Massage your scalp thoroughly with fingertips of both hands while you repeat the following three times:

Full and lush shall my hair grow;
Like a river, it will flow.
Longer, faster, make it grow;
In the breezes shall it blow.
By the magick that I know,
As I do will, it will be so!

After washing your hair, pat it partly dry with a towel, then massage in a bit of styling mousse, and brush it out with a boar-bristle brush while again repeating the spell three times. (—Oberon)

Cleansing

RUNNING WATER OFFERING & BLESSING

(For Depression)

I was inspired to do this working by a small bridge across a babbling brook in a nearby park. You could also stand on rocks in the middle of a small stream, or kneel on the bank, perhaps placing your hands down into the water. In this case, a smaller body of water and being able to be close enough to it to hear or feel it flowing are key.

Stand on the bridge or rocks listening to the water, and allow the negative ions to infuse your body. First turn to face downstream. Watching the water flow away from you, speak all the things that you give up, such as:

I give you my depression and anxiety.
I give you my pain.
I give you my sadness.
I give you my tears.
I give you my apathy.

Speak aloud if you can, but feel free to think them to yourself if you prefer. Offer each of these to the water as you say them.

Now go to the other side of the bridge, or turn to face upstream, and welcome all the things you seek:

I welcome healing.
I welcome strength.
I welcome courage.

I welcome happiness and joy.

Thank the stream for its healing and blessings and if you wish, end with *"So mote it be."*

It is best to repeat this meditation frequently, changing the items as appropriate, and it can be incorporated into your daily nature visit and/or mediation time.

(—Lady MoonDance)

RUNNING WATER CLEANSING

An alternative method is to simply turn facing the flow of the stream. Even though you are standing above the water, close your eyes and imagine the energy of the water washing over you, softly flowing all around your body. Spread your arms out wide (either physically, or in your mind's eye) and see yourself standing firm in its midst. As it flows past, see it removing all the dirt and crude from your body, representing the things that you need to get rid of in order to heal. In this version you don't have to name them, and you may even be surprised at some of the things that break off to be washed away. Just as it carries things away from you, it also brings fresh, clean things to you, which become part of you.   (—Lady MoonDance)

Consecration

YOU BELONG TO ME!

This is a spell for the consecration of your magickal tools.

Materials: Tool(s) to be cleansed, salt for Earth, incense (Sandalwood or Patchouli) for Air, lighter and candle for Fire and bowl of Water.

Open the Circle. Call on the Ancients, asking for their assistance, guidance and blessings. Meditate, focusing on what you want to accomplish. Light the candle. With candle's flame, light (and bind) incense. Mix salt in the water (bind).

Pass the tool through the incense, saying:

I bless thee with the power of air.

Pass the tool through candle's flame, saying:

I bless thee with the power of fire.

Dip or sprinkle water/salt mix in/on tool, saying:

I cleanse thee with the power of water,
Renewing thee with the power of Earth.

Raise the tool in the air and declare:

So Mote it Be,
You Belong to Me!

Thank the Ancients for their assistance, guidance and blessings before you close the circle.

(—Adella Moon Dragonstar)

Guidance

GUARDIAN DRAGON

This spell is for conquering your deepest fears and

secrets. Get comfortable, take deep breaths, concentrating on your breathing.

In your mind, envision yourself in a peaceful valley, at the edge of a cliff looking down on the glistening waters below. Throw all cares and worries into the river/ocean, turning your back on them once finished. They're gone from your mind, and no longer exist. In front of you is your Guardian Dragon, waiting for your call. Now that your mind is focused and clear, ask the following:

Show me what I wish to see,
The darkest secrets haunting me.
Give me answer, Knowledge true,
Show me what I have to do.
Balanced mind, soul and self,
Is the key to perfect health.
Help me conquer on the way,
The deepest secret to the day.
The path is long, and splits in two,
Show me Dragon, what to do.

Let your Guardian Dragon show you the way in your mind, or open your eyes and let it show you in your life.

(—Adella Moon Dragonstar)

Divination

DIVINATION POUCH & SPELL

Needed: small purple pouch, mugwort, cloves, rosemary, thyme, lilac, honeysuckle, peppermint, purple marker.

Gather these herbs and place them in a small purple bag/pouch. Using a violet marker draw an eye on the sides of the pouch. Sleep with the pouch under your pillow at night. When you are in need of psychic sight or are doing divinations rub the pouch over the third eye chakra.   (—LeopardDancer)

Dreams, Astral, Nightmares

DREAM SPELL: RELAXING

You will need one incense stick of cherry, jasmine, or patchouli, and something to put it in. With thoughts of the result in your mind, light it and say:

Guardians of the sleeping hours,
Join with me your awesome powers.

Next, with the smoking incense, make the Pentagram over the subject while saying these words:

Earth, Air, Fire, Water and Spirit,
Working together in harmony.
Banish sleeplessness from this soul.
May s/he rest peacefully throughout the night.
So mote it be!

Place the smoking stick of incense into its holder next to the subject's bed. Thank the Guardians for their help.

(—Adella Moon Dragonstar)

Influence

SPELL OF THREES

Only use this to help break or bind a person's bad behavior. Bear in mind that you may have to repeat and the effects will not be instantaneous. For those Dun'marran, one would concentrate on sending this to one's Patron. Do not do this with ill in your heart or it will backfire!

Wind in the north, run through the trees.
Three times three, let them see, let them see.
Sands of the east, rich soils beneath
Three times three, set them free, set them free.
Fires in the south, awaken from sleep.
Three times three, let them see, let them see.
Waters of the west, flow to the sea.
Three times three, set them free, set them free.

(—LeopardDancer)

Love

LOVE CORD SPELL

Needed: three lengths of ribbon or thread of a length you desire in various pleasing colors that make you think of love.

Braid the cords together tightly while thinking of your heart's desire. Firmly tie a knot in the middle then work your way out to the edges with more knots, making a total of seven knots. Wear or carry the cord until you find your love. At such a time return the cord to the elements by burning it and scattering the ashes.   (—LeopardDancer)

FOR A DISTANT LOVED ONE

Spell—incantation, really—to send a message to a loved one from the heart. To be used when the loved one is either away, or you are.

Materials: Tarot: Aces of each suit, and any card that may help in what to say and bring to the message. Picture of the loved one. Wand

Start by sweeping out negative energies, then opening the Circle, chanting a rhyme of your own making, or even the Mystics Rhyme (the Mystic Magick Spell above). Place the picture on a smooth surface, preferably the floor. Surround it with the Aces in their respective directions for their element. (See above). With four other cards, close the circle around the picture, saying and thinking:

I send the power of (card) to you,
So you may (what does it do?)

If need be, use another card to give yourself strength or any other help you need in order to send the message. Tap each card, all eight, with your wand, thinking of the loved one and sending each separate message. Go clockwise, for positivity. After that, hold your wand in your hand, close your eyes, think of the loved one and send the message. Be sure to keep the picture of the loved one in your mind. When finished, tap again, clockwise, saying:

I gave you (power of card)

For each. To make it more powerful, if you wish, you can stare at the picture and think the message to them. As you stare, your wand is touching it.

When you feel you're finished,

So mote it be, or *Blessed be,* or even use *Bide the Wiccan Laws I must, in perfect love and perfect trust.*

Close the circle with the Mystic Magick Spell (or whatever rhyme you wish to use to close the circle.) Be sure to go in the opposite direction to close it.

(—Adella Moon Dragonstar)

MOON SPELL

To see or hear from someone you miss, when the moon is waxing, look up at Her and chant 3 times:

I see the Moon,
the Moon sees me.
The Moon sees someone I long to see.

(Then chant the person's name three times)

As I will, so mote it be.

Note, you say the person's name three times each round, making it 9 times total.   (—Athena Shaffer)

Luck & Good Fortune

FOR GOOD LUCK

(This is from the Koyukon Tribe—but I add the word "good" before Luck because Luck can go either way. I've learned to be more specific!)

Chant 3 times:

Raven who is, Raven who was,
Raven who always will be.
Make prayers to Raven.
Raven, bring us good luck!

(—Athena Shaffer)

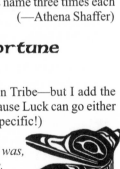

Manifestation

MYSTIC MAGICK

A chant usually used for focus and asking for aide when needed. Repeated at the end three times, each last line different.

Mystic's might, pure delight.
Show me the path which is right.

It may be rough, it may be long,
Mystic Magic, hear my song.
    2: Play my song.
    3: Sing my song.
              (—Adella Moon Dragonstar)

CALL TO POWER

I raise my hands, my heart, my voice
To call upon the forces of life.
Earth, Air, Fire, Water and Spirit
The five elements combine to become one
Triple Goddess, hear the calls
I call the Maiden for a new beginnir
Mother for life
Crone for experience
Goddess bless, Blessed be
Triple Goddess, I call for thee.
Mystic power, so mote it be.
        (—Adella Moon Dragonstar)

CANDLE POWER

Lord and Lady, from above,
give me strength, peace and love.
Give me hope I desire,
from the candle's burning fire.
My mind to peace, from war within,
help me find the peace, my friend.
The blue of flame, my desire,
this spell is done by the burning fire.
        (—Adella Moon DragonStar)

Money, Wealth, Prosperity

FOR MONEY

Put a drop of patchouli oil on the very bottom of a green candle. Light the candle on your altar, along with Gonesh # 6 incense. Chant 3 times (or in groups of three)

Orbiting Jupiter, Trine the Sun,
Bring in Money on the run!

              (—Athena Shaffer)

MONEY POUCH

Needed: green candle, 6 dimes, green pouch, cinnamon.

Ring the coins around the candle and light it. Chant the following three times:

Money grow,
Money flow.
Money shine,
Money mine!

Sprinkle the pouch with cinnamon and (after about 15 minutes) collect the coins one by one and place them in the pouch, while chanting:

Bring me money three times three

Keep the pouch on or near you until you feel the spell has been satisfied.   (—LeopardDancer)

SILVER MONEY SPELL

(This takes a week to do)

Put a bowl somewhere prominent and each day, for seven days, place a dime in the bowl. On the seventh day take the bowl of dimes and a green candle with holder to a proper spell working area. Before you begin in full, imagine yourself as a prosperous person. Know that you have no need to worry about money. Hold the candle in your hands and imagine money coming to you. Know that avenues for gain are opening to you. Place the candle in holder on a flat surface and take up the bowl of dimes. Pour the dimes into your left hand and place each one in a ring around the candle. With each dime chant:

Money flow, money shine.
Money grow, money's mine.

Once all the dimes are ringed around the candle, light the candle. Imagine the power of money flowing from the dimes to the candle's flame and out to you. For ten minutes sit before your money candle while it burns and imagine a life with money to spare. One where bills are quickly paid off. See yourself spending money wisely, making investments and savings for the future. Kill any thoughts of debt, taxes or doubts that the spell will not work. After ten minutes leave the candle to burn out on its own. After it has done so, take the seven dimes and place them back in the bowl. Place the bowl back in its spot and each day continue to place silver coins in the bowl to feed the spell. One or two will suffice.   (—LeopardDancer)

MONEY SPELL

Materials: Green and White candles; God and Goddess candles, incense of Jasmine or Patchouli, Tarot Cards: The World, The Magician (or your self-card), The Sun. Tiger's Eye stone, Balancing Quartz/Smokey Quartz stones. Also, if you wish, Wand.

To Prepare: Arrange these items on your altar, preferably on a Full Moon. Say:

On this night, I call to me,
The Powers of Success, Luck, and Money.
Hail to the Goddess, I summon your assistance.

Light the Goddess Candle.

Hail to the God, I summon your assistance.

Raise hands to the sky, close your eyes and imagine your desired quest. Light the Incense)

As I bring the flame to scent,
So I bring its power to me.

While the incense is still flaming, light the Green Candle.

As I bring the flame to candle,
So I bring its power to me.

Light the White candle.

As I bring the flame to candle,
So I bring its power to me.

Wave still-flaming, pass over all three stones, Left to Right, circular 3 times each. Blow the incense out, placing in a safe place between the Green and White

Candles. Close your eyes, wand hand to the sky for the first sentence. Open them again, saying each as you pinch out each candle. (Don't blow them out, it's considered disrespectful!)

Thank you, Goddess,
I send you home in peace and love.
Thank you, God,
I send you home in peace and love.
On that note, by powers of three,
This spell is done, so mote it be!
(—Adella Moon Dragonstar)

Peace

SWEET AS HONEY SPELL

This is for when you're dealing with someone you never seem to get along with, but have to see on a regular basis—because you're working on a project together, because you share custody of the kids, or whatever.

You will need a down feather; an envelope; honey; and either a picture of you and one of the other person, or your name on one card and his or her name on another card. Dab a bit of honey on each of the pictures or cards, saying:

Sweet as honey let us be,
I to you and you to me;
Both respect and both acclaim,
United by our common aim.

Sandwich the feather between the two, saying:

Soft as down be all our words,
Wisely said and clearly heard;
Let us work in harmony:
This is my will, so mote it be.

Put the "sandwich" into the envelope and close without sealing it. You can put a symbol of the shared project on the envelope. Keep secure until the project has ended.
(—Estara T'shirai)

Protection & Safety

STRENGTH SPELL

When you need a little extra strength try this. For those Dun'marran, one would concentrate on sending this to one's Patron.

Strength of day, strength of night.
Give me strength beyond my sight.
(—LeopardDancer)

PROTECTIVE MIRROR

Here is a spell for consecrating a silver-backed protective mirror. You should recite it while walking deosil around the house, temple or bedroom that you want to protect from negative energies, holding the mirror with its glass side facing outwards. After this you hang it over the door, again glass face outwards.

Silver backed mirror of the art,
Protect me in the Lady's name,
Save me from sorrow, save me from shame,
Send hateful thoughts back whence they came
(Magnified three fold in Her name) [This is optional and only to be used when facing deliberate malignant attack]
Let only love through to my heart!
(—Frederick Lamond)

FEATHER LIGHT

For overall protection, get a small basket from a craft shop. Fill it with feathers. Put it above your front door (or main door that you use). As long as the basket of feathers is there, it will protect you and your household from negativity or bad intentions.
(—Athena Shaffer)

Success

FOR SUCCESS

Light a gold or yellow candle (put a drop of patchouli oil on the very bottom of the candle first) on the altar and Gonesh #6 incense. Take a small box. Take a piece of jade and get spider webs on it. Put it in the box. Then take something that either represents the success you want, or write your intent on a piece of paper. Put it in the box.

Put the box on the altar in front of the candle, and chant 3 times:

Thy iron will, thy patient skill
Within this talisman instill
That I may fare successfully.
As I will, so mote it be!

Then close the box and keep this talisman in a safe place.
(—Athena Shaffer)

NEW YEAR'S SPELL

To be done on either Samhain (Celtic new year) or January 1st.

Materials needed: 12 Months Stones, index card, pen(cil), lighter, candle, flame-proof bowl (preferably cauldron) with water either in it or handy, lighter, candle (preferably white), and stone necklace with a focus-energy-protection-type stone in it.

Before you begin, write the most regretted thoughts of the previous year on the index card.

Set up the mini-altar in a safe place away from flammable objects. As you set up, think about what you desire for the coming year. Place the candle on the mini-altar, the 12-Months Stones surrounding it in a circle. Cast the circle as usual and light the candle. Pass the cleansed stone of the necklace over the fire, saying:

As the new year progresses,
May this stone give me _____.

Fold the card in fours before burning it in the bowl. For safety, you can set the bowl in the sink before you burn it. That way, you can drown the fire with water.

> *By flame of the fire,*
> *The year past is gone.*
> *Bring me what I desire,*
> *As the new year carries on.*

Close the circle, as usual, and clean up the mess.

(—Adella Moon DragonStar)

Success in Studies

CITRINE STUDY SPELL

Needed: two yellow candles and a citrine stone. Anoint both candles and the citrine with lemon oil. Light candles and place citrine between/in front of them so that the candlelight shines on it. Chant the following:

> *Charge the stone with candle light,*
> *To fill my mind with wisdom bright.*
> *To keep my mind alert and clear*
> *So that no bane may interfere*
> *Let what I read be knowledge gained*
> *My curiosity maintained*
> *For all my life to stay with me*
> *As I will, so shall it be.*

Let the candles burn and charge the stone while you study. Keep the stone with you to aid in studying, learning, giving papers, etc. (—LeopardDancer)

Wishing

THE WISHING STAR

In the early evening, as the light of sunset fades, look to the West for the first star to appear (probably the planet Venus). As soon as you see it, kiss the palm of your hand, and hold it up to the star, saying:

> *Star light, star bright,*
> *First star I see tonight,*
> *I wish I may, I wish I might,*
> *Have this wish I wish tonight:*
> (make your wish) (—traditional)

WISHING WELL SPELL

> *I toss a penny in the well*
> *To make a little wishing spell*
> *First I wish that all be well*
> *And now my secret wish I'll tell:*
> (speak your wish into the well, and
> listen to the echo) (—Oberon)

BIRTHDAY CANDLES

Here's what to say before blowing out the candles on your birthday cake:

> *A year has come; a year has passed.*
> *I make my birthday wish at last!*
> *Magick powers, old and new,*
> *Make my birthday wish come true!*
> (make your wish, then blow out all the candles with one breath!) (—Morning Glory Zell-Ravenheart)

4. The Stone of Power

By Francesca DeGrandis

Wizards believe in self-expression and personal exploration, as opposed to the mindless fads, hollow conformity, and clone-like groups that media absurdly equates with self-discovery, uniqueness, and freedom of expression. But where do you find the power to be yourself? The self-confidence, courage, determination? And how do you achieve the calm, fortitude, or whatever traits are needed to face life's *other* challenges? Create a Stone of Power. Instructions are below.

The Stone of Power grants you any type of inner power you need. However, the Stone of Power doesn't just act internally. As a powerful lucky charm, it also affects the world outside. You receive power inside and out. The stone, as you'll see in the spell, gives you, well, *power*—all and every kind. For example, this talisman can bestow good fortune when you're trying out for a new job, entering a sports match, or attempting another daunting or competitive act.

To create your lucky talisman, first look for a stone that strikes your fancy; the reason doesn't matter. Perhaps you like the smooth feel it has as you rub it, or the shape resembles an animal you identify with. You needn't even know why the stone draws you. However, if a rock somehow evokes power in your mind, it could be the ideal selection. But, if the "right" stone doesn't appear, use what's available. As you'll see from the following, all stones are innately Stones of Power; all they need is for you to use the following instructions.

Bless the stone by holding it while reciting, aloud or silently: *"This stone is from the Earth and in it are all of Gaia's powers. In each piece of the Earth is all the power of the Earth. I am a piece of the Earth. All of Gaia's powers are in me. I am strong."*

Now recite this to deepen the magic: *"One stone. One planet. The fires from Gaia's heart that feed the dragon's breath feed this stone. The passing of time fed this stone. The weight of gravity and of the Earth's spinning fed this stone. The water's weeping, water's pouring, water's weight, fed this stone. The stars in the sky fed this stone. And so all these powers I carry when I carry this stone. Gaia is an alchemist, a magician; She has wrought this talisman for me."*

After you've done the above, keep the stone on your altar or, if no other special place is available, wherever you can. You don't have to actually carry the stone for it to work, despite the words recited in the blessing. But keep it on you when you want to remember your new found luck and inner strength or feel it'll help you better draw on them. You can also plug into the power more by reciting a line or two of the ritual over and over like a chant. This can build strength, self-worth, resolution, luck, peace, and the list could go on forever because this talisman is about power and power takes endless forms. *All* the powers of the Earth, remember. In fact, once you've made the stone, any spell you do should have extra kick.

Earth spirituality is practical—along with rites, prayers, and theology, the Witch follows through with sensible measures on the mundane plane. That's part of understanding how to tune into the benefits of your newfound Stone of Power.

Don't think that, having done the spell, you can avoid life's hard work. You may have more luck, confidence, imagine an endless list here now—huzzah!—but you still need to practice before the sports match, write the job résumé, dress attractively for your upcoming date.

It also is essential to understand power—both inner and outer—because that's what this stone is about. It's not called "Stone of *Power*" just to sound impressive. Here's the true nature of power:

1) Everyone wants it. The stone gives it to you easily enough, but you have to understand it to use it to your liking.

2) Power helps you get what you want, for sure, but not by dominating others. For example, don't confuse the focused, often unstoppable drive of the winner with aggression that is out of control, dangerous, and bullying. Gaia's not going to stand at your back supporting efforts to cheat, commit revenge, or otherwise impose your needs or viewpoints on someone. Every atom of the universe is intrinsically honorable. So no matter how much pain, need, or love you have, your rock—and all of Gaia's power that it represents—will only help you when you act ethically. A feeling of empowerment may temporarily come from spiteful gossip and other destructive forces but it'll backfire.

3) However, remember: once you've done the spell, be honorable and all the power of the Earth *will* stand behind you to take care of that pain, need, love. So—oh Goddess, here comes the cliché but it's needed—if at first you don't succeed, try and try again. And again.

4) You also have to *open* to power. This and the previous three items are the true secrets of the stone, and of the adept! If you're not yet able to see positive changes in yourself or your life, you may erroneously think that your attempt to create the power stone failed. Make trial runs, low-risk attempts so you

don't fall on your face, to feel a *bit*—just a bit—of the stone's gift. You can have acquired all the power of Gaia—um, in fact, you did!—but you may need some time and practice to open up to it. Baby steps are that practice, and you're eventually striding through life, big, confident, lucky, blessed.

Here are more ways to open to power: Community service builds inner power: self-respect, confidence, social skills, savvy about moving through the world are only a few examples. As to luck, once you've written the résumé, rehearsed for the dance performance, or practiced asking that special someone for a date, relax. Kick back. Try to not worry. Catch a show. Luck has more chance to work if we at least *try* to trust it's going to work. Frantic tension and power do *not* go hand in hand.

A Stone of Power is an immense asset, which works better and better as your understanding of, and ability to use, power grows. The downside: this learning process never ends. The upside: stick with it, and you'll have enormous, diverse powers for all life's undertakings. If, over time, greater challenges come your way, so can greater ability to meet them. The more you open to power, in all its forms, the better the stone works. Go for it!

5. Unobtrusive Magick for Public Places

By Crow Dragontree (grey)

Have Magick, will travel

By now, I presume that you've created a rather impressive set of Wizard's tools. You've got your wand decked out, a pentacle in Wizardly condition, and a variety of other tools that truly set the mood for magick. I'm also sure that you've read—and perhaps even used—quite a few spells. I can just imagine it—you, lighting candles, creating your magickal space, setting up an altar and creating a Wizardly atmosphere fit for any magickal working. I'll bet you've whipped up some marvelous magick and cast spells with great results. Well done! You've certainly earned a pat on the back.

Have you ever noticed, though, how the great Wizards of legend and myth seem to be able to simply cast powerful spells with a wave of their hand, or a few muttered words? I'll even bet that if you took the staff and pointed hats away from half of the Wizards you've seen in fiction, then dressed them in street clothes, they'd look just like anyone else. No one would really be able to tell when they were casting a spell. It would just look like an off-handed gesture, or something muttered beneath their breath that no one but other Wizards would realize that magick was afoot. Perhaps not even furtive gestures or murmured words would be evident—only a knowing smile, and perhaps a nod and a wink if any other *Wizards Incognito* were around.

Now *that* would be handy! In reality, if you're suddenly given a pop quiz in science class and you'd like to magickally boost your memory, you can't take the time to light up a few candles and set up an altar on your desk! Even if you had the time, you may wish to avoid that kind of attention, not to mention rules against open flames on campus. Similarly, when you're hanging out with your friends after lunch and that guy who's constantly giving you a hard time approaches you with that look on his face, you might want a boost of protection, but don't feel terribly comfortable whipping out your wand and casting a circle. Wouldn't it be nice to be able to cast a spell *unobtrusively*—without anyone else knowing, at any place or time?

As it happens, there is an entire discipline of magick directed at casting practical, portable spells in ways that don't look out of place to nonmagickal folk. This brief part of the *Companion* will give you an opportunity to explore ways in which you can bring magick from your sanctuary and into the rest of your world without seeming terribly unusual.

First, however, there are a few basic concepts we should visit.

Now you see it...

The basic process of unobtrusive magick involves a common, everyday tool, such as candy or a stuffed animal, coupled with the magickal techniques of relaxation and visualization. These last two components are of particular importance and should be developed prior to getting together the props. As such, this section of the lesson will cover exercises to build up your ability to relax and visualize on command.

You might remember the concept of visualization from the *Grimoire for the Apprentice Wizard* (Course 4, Lesson 6, "*The Laws of Magick*") as one of the laws of magick. It can be argued that visualization is used in just about every spell ever conducted in some form or another. Simply by focusing your mind on a particular intent, you engage in some level of visualization. In unobtrusive magick, this little magickal tool becomes incredibly important. Because you won't have many of the tools that help to place you in a magickal frame of mind when you cast an unobtrusive spell, you must be able to use your abilities to concentrate and imagine in order to create change. Visualization is the crux—the all-important central tool—to unobtrusive magick.

I know you probably think you have a great imagination—and you're probably right—but I'm willing to bet that the level of visualization needed for unobtrusive magick might be a bit challenging for you at first. Don't worry, I'm about to give you some exercises that will help you develop that mental muscle!

However, I'd like to clear up a fairly common misconception first. Because "visualization" has the word "visual" stuck in it, most people simply figure that Visualization is merely the ability to imagine *seeing* something. For semantic purists, that very well may be true, but for our purposes, visualization is a multi-sensory experience. When you cast an unobtrusive spell, you'll want to smell, feel, hear, and taste the outcome of your spell! Also bear in mind that visualization may come as more of a strong *sensation* than an actual sensory perception. That is, you may *feel* the smell, sight, taste or sound much more clearly than you may normally smell, see, taste, or hear it.

With these things in mind, let's build up some of the necessary skills. It might be helpful to note at this point that these exercises are very useful for other things than just spellcasting. For example, people who are able to relax in just about any situation are believed to be at a lower risk for stress-related illnesses and are likely to live longer than those who do not exercise relaxation. In addition, visualization exercises not only strengthen the ability to imagine, but to concentrate as well. I wouldn't be a bit surprised if you noticed your schoolwork improving after doing these exercises for a while!

Exercise 1: just relax!

The first thing you'll want to do before casting any unobtrusive spell is relax. I know that might be difficult when you're in a "need-a-spell-fast" situation, but if you practice relaxation regularly, you'll find it easier and easier to relax on command. I'd like you to begin by trying each of these exercises in a quiet, dimly lit place where you won't be disturbed for at least 15-20 minutes. After you're able to do these exercises easily, try them in various places such as in the living room with the television on or on the bus on the way to school. Eventually, you'll be able to relax instantly, just about anywhere.

There are many ways to learn to relax. Perhaps the fastest and most effective is called *Progressive Muscle Relaxation* (PMR). To do this, simply tense all of your muscles, then let them relax. Start with bunching up your toes, then tighten your legs, clench your buttocks, tighten your stomach, flex your biceps and squinch up your face. Now hold it for a few seconds and very, very slowly, relax.

Notice the difference in your muscles and your body as the tension slips away. Feel how much more relaxed you are. As you relax your muscles say something out loud that has a relaxing soothing sound to it. Make that your "relaxation word." Many people simply choose "relax," but others I've worked with have chosen more unique words with a personal meaning to them, such as "home." Whatever word you choose, be sure to use the same word every time. Eventually, after many, many times of doing this exercise, you'll only need to say the word to automatically slip into a state of relaxation wherever you are.

It's my guess, however, that when you decide to do your exercises in public, this one might make you feel a bit silly. PMR is truly something you'll want to practice in private! If you want to practice relaxing in public with something other than your relaxation word and you don't wish to look as if you're having bowel troubles, you might try this next exercise:

Sit back as comfortably as possible and think about your toes. No, I'm serious. Think about your toes. Feel the weight of your toes, the temperature of your toes, the blood pulsing through them and the way they feel in your shoes, if you're wearing them. Now imagine a golden, warm light filling each toe. Feel the warmth of this light in your toes. Now, let that light slowly spread up into your feet, relaxing each little muscle with which it comes in contact.

Allow the light to spread up your feet to your calves, your thighs, your buttocks, across your abdomen, and let it settle in your back at the base of your spine. After a few seconds, allow this relaxing, warm light slowly climb up your spine and spread across your shoulders, relaxing every little muscle on the way. The light then climbs up your neck, over your scalp, and across the muscles in your face—especially your jaw. Feel each of these muscles relax as you imagine this light covering them.

Now that you're fully relaxed, let's start visualizing!

Exercise 2: The Candle

This exercise is intended to build your ability to visualize objects that aren't physically there. As far as visualization goes, this is pretty much the easy part. Start in a dark or dimly lit room with where you can work for at least 15 minutes with no distractions. Take a few deep breaths and do whichever relaxation exercise you prefer. Close your eyes and call to mind a candle. Sometimes it's easiest to start with just imagining the flame, glowing and dancing, with the burning wick barely visible within. Next, imagine the candle itself; try to see its color, size, and every detail right down to the beads of wax dripping down its sides.

Not as easy as you thought, eh? Don't worry, with a bit of practice, you'll be able to visualize a candle and, eventually, anything else you like—even with your eyes open! I typically recommend trying these exercises either daily or every other day until visualization

with your eyes closed in a dim room becomes easy. Then, try it with your eyes open in the dim room. After that, you might wish to experiment with various settings, such as one of those long and boring rides you might have to take with your parents. Just remember that visualization may come more as a *sensation* than as a *vision*.

Exercise 3: The Orange

Once you're able to do Exercise 2 easily and comfortably, try visualizing something that not only has a specific visual dimension, but stimulates the imagination on a variety of sensory levels. An orange is perfect for this!

Once you're relaxed and situated in just the same way as you began Exercise 2, begin to visualize an orange. Imagine its color, the bumpy texture, and the way the light reflects off of its skin. Now, imagine what that texture must feel like as you run your imaginary fingers across its surface. Use your imaginary fingers to peel this orange, and smell the spray coming off of the pulp. Slowly, take an imaginary bite, tasting the sweet citrus taste of the orange. I'll be willing to bet that your mouth will water every time you do this exercise!

Just as in Exercise 2, keep practicing this exercise on a daily basis or every other day, eventually practicing this exercise in a variety of different situations. Try using different items in this exercise to keep things interesting and to exercise that visualization muscle. Just remember to make sure that it stimulates as many senses as possible, so savory foods and drinks do quite well.

Exercise 4: The Applepine

This is an exercise that my daughter recommends to bring visualization to a magickal level. Once you're able to do Exercise 3 consistently and easily, you're ready for what may very well be the ultimate level of visualization. In unobtrusive magick, we visualize items that may not be there and situations that may not have yet happened (such as visualizing a good grade on that test you haven't yet taken). To be able to do this, it is quite helpful to be able to fully visualize a completely fictional item. When just beginning this exercise, however, it might be easier to create a fantasy combination of items with which you are already familiar. For this purpose, my daughter invented the *applepine*. The applepine is a cross between an apple and a pineapple.

Just as in the previous exercises, relax and settle into your dimly lit, interruption free zone. Try to imagine the way the applepine looks. It's shaped something like a squash, with yellow skin covered by green pineapple-like spines. Run your imaginary fingers over the rough, prickly spines. These spines pull off easily to reveal a soft, yellow, pulpy fruit beneath them. Inhale the scent of the applepine—it smells a little bit like coconut. Finally, pop a piece of this imaginary fruit into your mouth, savoring its tart yet sweet flavor.

Like before, once you can fully visualize the applepine, try moving on to other imaginary things that you've never seen before. For some ideas, try just about any object mentioned in Lewis Carrol's classic poem *Jabberwocky* (for example, what the heck would a tumtum tree look like? We know it's good to rest under, but can you climb it?).

Once you've made a bit of headway with your visualization skills, the world of unobtrusive magick will be yours! In the meantime, however, let's look at some of the tools and props to get you underway in the casting of unobtrusive spells.

Candy Magick

The idea of using candy in a magickal way occurred to me when I was in college. I was taking a particularly hard class and a final exam was looming. Although I had studied diligently for the test, I wanted to help my memory by bringing a bit of magick discreetly to the classroom that day. Of course, I couldn't light a bunch of candles around my desk, so I was at a bit of a loss.

A magickally-inclined friend recommended that I dress in yellow and orange—the colors generally associated with mental abilities and communication. While this is certainly an effective means of working magick, it would hardly have been discreet if old Crow came to class dressed like a daisy! As I was explaining this to my friend, she casually offered me a piece of gum. That small gesture, an offhanded offering of Wrigley's Spearmint, struck a chord. Herbs such as spearmint and peppermint have long been associated with mental ability. Why not mint-flavored gum?

Experiments in learning and memory have repeatedly shown that people score better on tests if they take the test while drinking a small cup of coffee—but only if they studied while drinking coffee as well! This is a process called *state dependent learning*. Of course, I don't necessarily recommend taking coffee to your school. Caffeine isn't very good for you. However, this demonstrates a very important function played by our senses of taste and smell. Our olfactory (smell) senses, for example, are the only senses in our possession that are processed by the emotional parts of our brain before our thinking parts get to interpret the sensation. My son, for example, loves the smell of apples and cinnamon. Once that aroma hits the air, he's transported immediately to his grandmother's kitchen, with all of the fun and love that goes with it. Since smell is very closely tied to taste, it is no wonder that something as small, common, and convenient as candy can

be a powerful magickal tool!

The basic method for casting unobtrusive spells with candy is rather simple. First, gather the candy that you want to use for your spells. Place them on your altar. Now relax and visualize. Imagine the energy associated with your spell going into the appropriate candy. That is, if you have a piece of pineapple-flavored candy that you wanted to use in a money spell for a raise in your allowance, visualize "money energy" filling up that piece of candy. Visualize yourself as having the extra money you needed. How will you feel? What will you do? Imagine all of those images filling up your pineapple candy.

To help you decide which flavors to use for which spells, I'm including a short list of some of the most common candy flavors:

Apple— love, healing
Banana— prosperity
Blueberry— protection
Cherry— divination
Chocolate— intuition
Clove *(try Blackjack gum)*— protection and love
Coconut— protection
Coffee— success, energy
Grape— mental powers and money
Horehound *(often found in herbal cough drops)*— mental ability
Lemon— purification, friendship, longevity
Licorice— love, fidelity
Marshmallow— health, love, protection
Mints *(in general)*— learning and memory
Orange— love, money, divination
Pineapple— luck, money
Raspberry— love, protection
Watermelon— health, psychic ability

Of course, this list only provides a flavor of candy possibilities and is far from exhaustive. In her book, *The Supermarket Sorceress*, however, Lexa Rosean provides a rather complete list of magickal correspondences for candy and food.

Once you have your candy "charged," simply wait until you feel that you need to release the magick. When that time comes, pop the charged piece of candy in your mouth. Savor the taste of the candy as you visualize releasing the energy into the universe to fulfill your intent. You'll be casting powerful spells, and all anyone will notice is someone enjoying a piece of candy!

If you cannot or do not eat candy, do not feel left out! You can simply substitute food for the candy in your spells. Focus on an apple to bring you health or eat a handful of grapes while studying to help your understanding and memory. It's certainly healthier than candy, anyway!

The Secretive use of Symbols

Unless you have wizardly confectioners such as Willy Wonka or Bertie Bott at your disposal, you may not have access to magickally-charged candy whenever the need arises. In addition, there are times when popping a bit of candy may be terribly inappropriate—such as in the classroom or at the dinner table.

Fortunately, not all unobtrusive magick relies on the equivalent of a Hallowe'en loot bag. As you're probably already aware, the use of magickal symbols has been a major part of magick for centuries. Today, you can find these symbols in plain view, where no one seems to recognize them. Pentacles, for example, are found just about everywhere as mere decoration, and few recognize them as powerful symbols of protection and magick!

A very popular means of using symbol magick is through the use of runes. In fact, the Germanic runes are probably the most widely used cohesive system of magickal symbols. Indeed, there's an entire set of cut-out runes in this very book, as well as a very effective listing of their divinatory meanings! You might also choose to review pages 234-235 in the *Grimoire for the Apprentice Wizard* for more potential meanings of the runes.

Once you have the divinatory meanings of these runes worked out, their magickal meanings are quite simple to determine. For example, if you're at school and your teacher has landed you with a pop quiz on which you'd really like to do well, you could easily use the rune *Lagaz* to help bring success to your academic pursuit.

But, how can we use these unobtrusively?

Although varying traditions will differ widely upon the ways in which they use these symbols. A few things seem to stay constant:

- You can draw or carve them on an object (sometimes unobtrusive, but not always covert)
- You can use them by simply saying their names (fairly handy if no one notices you mutter under your breath and your hands are full)
- You can trace them in the air (this can be very unobtrusive if you do this in such a manner that no one notices)

The way you use your chosen symbol, really, is dependent upon the resources you have at hand. For example, to use Lagaz in the example above, you could draw the rune on the top of your test paper, but that might be a bit too obvious for your taste. Perhaps you'd prefer to mutter the name of the rune beneath your breath while you're taking the test. Personally, I'd find that rather distracting—it would keep me from concentrating on my test and the teacher may think I'm trying to give away answers! Perhaps tracing the symbol over the test with your finger might work. That leaves no traces and, if you are careful, can be very covert.

One of my favorite ways of doing magick is by tracing a symbol in the air with my wand. Since I can't pull out my magickal tools just anywhere, I manage to work magick with whatever's handy. For example, I boarded a plane a few years ago with a relaxing book to read and hopes for safe travel. As the plane was getting ready for takeoff, I leaned back and propped up my book as if I were reading. Behind the book, where no one could see, I traced the rune *Raidho*, for safe travel. It was not only a safe trip, but a rather enjoyable one as well.

However you do it, be sure to relax and use as much visualization as possible. Imagine very clearly how it will look, feel, or even taste and sound to have your spell come to fruition. Fill your symbol with that imagery, and then let it go.

Developing your own Symbols

Now *this* could be a great deal of fun!

Naturally, you are not bound to using the Germanic runes for this sort of magick. I've developed my entire system of divination and magick around a series of symbols of my own creation to which I have ascribed various meanings. There are considerable advantages to developing your own system of symbols for magickal use. Naturally, this is a marvelous experience for developing and deepening Wizardly skills such as creativity. Symbols that you've developed on your own often have much more personal meaning and, in the process, will have a greater magickal bond with you. While there are no hard and fast rules to developing your own symbols for magickal use, I can offer a few guidelines:

- **Keep them simple:** Simple line drawings are more easily traced in midair or carved into an object than more complex works of art.
- **Start with just a few at first:** When you're first starting, create just a few symbols for the most basic magickal needs (e.g., success, protection, and the like). That way, you need not be encumbered with memorizing many new symbols at once.
- **Give them names:** You can meditate or use some other intuitive or introspective method to give your symbols particular names, so that you can use sounds in your magick as well. It is easier, however, to give them short, easy-to-pronounce names if you plan to use them magickally!

Above all, remember to visualize when creating your symbols. I know I sound like a broken record, but some of the beauty of magickal symbolism is that it reminds the user of their underlying meanings. For example, my own symbol for "secrets" is a crescent. For me, it resembles the Moon, which represents the mystery and hidden wonders of the night. As you design your symbols, try to visualize the intent of your symbol as clearly as possible. Often, a shape may be very clear to you in the visualization. It may be the crescent of the Moon, the triangle of a flame, or the circle of the Sun. In either case, you will find a symbol that will be personally linked to your intent.

Let yourself have a bit of fun with this and let your creativity and imagination go wild. It is *your* magick, after all.

The power of Stuffies

This is a form of unobtrusive magick that my daughter uses rather frequently. Her process is really quite simple. First, she chooses one of her many stuffed animals (we call them "stuffies"), charges it with her intent, then utilizes it through—yes, you've guessed it—visualization.

Here's an example of a spell she recently cast. She had changed schools and, as a girl of her age might be, she was quite nervous. She wanted to cast a spell that would not only provide her protection, but make her feel at home no matter where she would be.

Her first task was to choose an animal that she associated with these attributes. The Turtle seemed an obvious choice. Its hard shell not only provides protection, but also a portable home for all occasions. It's also an animal that appears calm at almost all times. These are nice qualities to have when in a new situation! Next, she charged the Turtle. She did this by cutting a small opening in its side, and adding herbs that are commonly associated with protection, such as anise, cloves, and St. John's Wort. Sewing the Turtle back together, she visualized the energy of protection being sewn up inside.

While she could have probably taken this magick stuffy to school with her, she wanted to be discreet. To this day, the magick turtle remains somewhere in her room, an inconspicuous magickal addition to the household. Wherever she is, if she feels the need for protection or security, she simply envisions the Turtle's shell surrounding and guarding her.

When casting your own spell with stuffies, you'll want to begin with selecting the appropriate animal. You'll want to pick an animal that you personally associate with the intent of the spell. Here's a very brief list of attributes associated with stuffies from my own home that you might find useful:

Alligator— protection, power, stealth
Bear— healing, strength, family care
Butterfly— playfulness, change, beauty
Cow— money, domestic abundance, health
Dog— fidelity, courage

Dragon— power, imagination, information
Lion— leadership, courage, strength
Monkey— cleverness, mischief, agility
Owl— wisdom, secrets, mental and psychic ability
Rabbit— prosperity, swiftness
Swan— beauty, potential, grace
Turtle— security, persistence, the ability to remain calm under stress

In the *Grimoire for the Apprentice Wizard,* Oberon Zell-Ravenheart indicates the attributes of many wonderful animals (pay particular attention to Course 6, Lesson 4: *"Shapeshifting and Borrowing"*). In that same section, Morning Glory Zell-Ravenheart provides a series of "Mottoes of Animals" that may be particularly helpful in choosing an animal to represent your spell.

Now that you've chosen your stuffy, you'll want to charge it with your intent. It's a process I call "preparing the plush." You may make it as complex or as simple as you like. You may desire to set up an altar and stuff it with special herbs, stones, or symbols drawn on paper. On the other hand, perhaps you'd prefer to simply relax on the edge of your bed and visualize your intent filling the stuffy. The only other advice that I will offer here is that, if you choose to use candles in charging the stuffy, be very, very careful. Stuffies often catch fire very easily and that could seriously put a damper on your spell!

Once charged, your stuffy is ready for unobtrusive use. No matter where you are in relation to the stuffy, you may call upon its energy to cast your spell. If you're stuck on that pop quiz at school, imagine the feathers and crown of the owl covering you, helping you to decide on the wisest answers. Wear the fur and muscles of the bear when in need of extra strength or the mane of the lion when you find yourself in a position of leadership. Used wisely and responsibly, their energies can be of immeasurable assistance.

In sum

The wandering Wizards of our favorite stories rarely have an entire physical toolbox of magick on hand. Indeed, it would be rather cumbersome to carry an entire altar around on one's back! With these simple tools and ideas, you have the beginnings of the skills necessary to cast spells in any place, at any time. Bear in mind, however, that these concepts are merely *tools* and the processes I've described only represent the *beginning*. With much practice, creativity, and experimentation, where you take your magick from here is entirely up to you. Keep up the good work!

Department IV:
Metapsychics (aqua)

Believe, O Dreamer

Fire's child
Believe, O Dreamer,
That your dreams are real
For they cast long shadows
In the waking world,
Whether or not you have the eyes
*   to see*
The far horizons of their shade.

Believe, O Dreamer,
What you hear in dreams
For it whispers of a deeper truth
Than daylight's ears could bear.

Believe, O Dreamer,
What your nose knows in dreams
For in this rich dimension
Evil reeks
Like fish washed up by wild tides
And kindness smells of roses.

Believe, O Dreamer,
Those tastes you tongue in dreams
For be they bitter
Or be they sweet, they come to you
With reasons.

Believe, O Dreamer,
The subtle wisdom of your skin
For a hairshirt brings only misery

Where silk brings supple magic
And anyway you can shift your skin
In this pliant region.

Believe, O Dreamer,
The things you do in dreams
For they will change your life
No less
Than any act the sun has seen.

—Elizabeth Barrette

1. Introduction

ELCOME TO THE WORLD OF METAPSY-chics, or "Mind Magicks." This department includes all forms of psychic skills and their development, meditation, dreamwork, and "path-working." Lessons here will draw upon the wisdom of many cultures.

The color of magick for this department is Aqua, representing all mental magicks, such as meditation and psychic attunement. Associated with Friday and the planet Venus, Aqua is an excellent hue for peacefulness and profound reflection.

Meditation is the basis of most of the Eastern disciplines of magick and Wizardry, and is particularly crucial for the Western Wizard who wishes to learn to master and focus the power of the Will. The power of the Will is the force behind effective magick. Properly used, meditation opens the door to individual growth and personal advancement.

2. The very first things you have to learn

by Estara T'shirai (black)

The following practices are essential to all other magickal work. To master them is to have a solid foundation in place for learning any specialization, and to have the means to protect oneself in the meantime.

Keep the following balance in mind:

1. Learn the simple method first. This gives you the "feel" for the practice and what it is intended to do. It also gives you a version to teach to others in need.

2. Learn at least one variation. After you have mastered the simple version, doing at least one variation will give you a sense of what is possible and will encourage you to experiment to find the best methods for you.

3. Study other variations. Getting a sense of how other traditions approach the practice will help you understand what is happening should you come into contact with members of those traditions. The more systems of magic and religion you study, the better you will understand what others are doing and how best to respond.

Also remember that READING IS NOT ENOUGH. These skills must be practiced on a regular basis to be mastered and used effectively.

Meditation

This skill involves moving from your normal waking state into a state of focus and calm. The ability to reach this state is needed in every other magical or spiritual endeavor. It is also beneficial to your mundane life, as its calming influence relieves stress and improves concentration.

Simple Method:

The most common method of meditation taught is the "clear-mind" meditation. Sit comfortably, take a few deep, relaxing breaths, and whisper to yourself, "Clear." Try to completely empty your mind of all thoughts. If you catch yourself thinking, take another deep breath and repeat to yourself, "Clear." It will take quite a bit of practice to be able to completely clear your mind for any length of time, but you should begin to notice improvement after only a few sessions.

If you find the clear-mind meditation maddening rather than helpful, try a single-focus meditation. Sit comfortably, take a few deep, relaxing breaths, and this time, focus on a chosen word, phrase, or image. Use this "mantra" to focus your mind and clear it of other concerns. Thoughts pertaining to the "mantra" are acceptable, but these to should fade as you practice more.

If neither of these appeals, try an action-oriented meditation. This is similar to a single-focus meditation, except that the focus is an activity rather than a word or image. You can use tai chi, yoga, a martial arts kata, spinning thread, or any relatively simple activity to clear and focus your mind. A friend of mine meditates while doing embroidery.

Variations:

Any studied form of standard meditation is acceptable. Only remember that clearing and focusing is not the same thing as zoning out: going into mild trance in front of the television is not meditating.

Awakening the other senses

These activities are meant to train your astral senses, which (unless you have already reawakened them) may be atrophied and inactive in your physical life. These senses are crucial in detecting and performing magic, and in communicating with nonphysical beings.

Simple Method:

Begin by choosing a simple focus object for the sense you want to train. For example, you might select a candleholder for sight, or the chime of a particular bell for hearing, a favorite perfume for smell, a piece of fruit for taste, a feather or a piece of textured fabric for touch.

Study the actual object first, paying close attention to its details. Then, remove the object and try to recreate it in your mind as accurately as you can. For example, look closely at the candleholder, then close your eyes and try to "see" it in your mind.

Variations:

As you become good at this, start to choose more complex objects as the focus. Then, try to focus on more than one sense at a time: for example, try to recapture both the sound and the appearance of the bell. Ultimately, you want to be able to sense an object as clearly

in your mind as if it were actually in front of you.

You will find that your other senses also improve as you practice other exercises in which they are used.

Centering

Centering is simply concentrating all of your focus and energy into your physical body. (You are literally "Contemplating Your Navel.") This is a preliminary step in self-cleansing and grounding, and the practice helps the ability to focus on the individual *chakras* to balance them—all skills coming up later. Centering also collects your energy for you, which may be scattered by activity or lack of focus. Centering is related to meditation, and each skill helps the other.

Simple Method:

Take a few deep, relaxing breaths, and begin to imagine that you are following your own breath inside your body. Each breath carries you deeper into yourself, deeper and deeper, until you find yourself within your center, behind your navel.

Variations:

As this skill improves, it is possible to center using fewer breaths. While in your center, you may imagine that you are surrounded by a vast pool of liquid light. (Such experiences will become more vivid as your other senses awaken.) Take note of the color of this light: it is a personal power color for you, and may be used to help you project and control energy.

Grounding

Grounding connects the energy of your body to the energy of the Earth. This has obvious benefits for followers of an Earth-honoring practice, but it has additional uses as well. One, it serves as an anchor, making you more difficult to move by outside forces. Two, it serves as a source of additional energy in order to conserve or augment your own. Three, it provides a channel with which to send away excess or unwanted energies.

Simple Method:

Sit down and center yourself. Then move further down into yourself until you at the very tip of your spine. From here, imagine that a large taproot is growing down out of you like a tail, and into the Earth. Each breath pushes the root further down into the Earth, plunging all the way in time to the very center of the Earth, her hot crystalline core. Feel the root reach into the heart of this core, flooded by warm, golden, healing energy. Now, use your breath to pull this energy up towards you. As it reaches you, breathe it up through your spine and let it radiate out into the rest of your body until you are entirely filled with the light of the Earth's core. At this time, if needed, you may send unwanted energies back down the root to be recycled by the Earth (see self-cleansing, below).

Variations:

Numerous different effects are possible in grounding. You can actually journey astrally into the center of the earth, by which you will gain other things than energy; you can send down a pillar instead of a root, which emphasizes the anchoring effect; you can send down roots from a standing position, and become a tree with flowers of energy blooming from your arms; you can elongate your astral legs until they touch the core of the earth, which frankly feels odd but is sometimes done. Once you master one method, feel free to experiment with others.

Self-cleansing

This is another skill that improves your personal energy and focus when you are preparing to do serious work. It also clears out pockets of negative energy that may be attached to you, whether due to your own mindset or health or to outside influences. Self-cleansing is also a preliminary step to some of the later exercises.

Simple Method:

Center and ground yourself. Place your hands on the Earth. As you do, breathe deeply and imagine that all sickness and negativity inside you is gathering into a ball in your chest. Take a deep breath in, and as you exhale see that collected negativity cascade down your arms into the earth. Release it all into the ground, and imagine that the Earth takes the energy into herself and cleanses it for her own use elsewhere.

Variations:

The release can be done through your feet if kneeling and touching the ground is too conspicuous for you; it can be flicked out the hands (be sure not to hit anyone!), released into a smoky quartz you keep for this purpose, stomped into the ground, or released by a catch phrase you save for releasing negative energy harmlessly. With practice, a variation can be developed in which you envision another person being cleansed—but be sure to have the person's permission.

If only (or additionally) an external cleansing is required, the body can be smudged (purified by exposure to incense smoke—sage is the most often used for this), or a rattle can be used to break up energy around the body. If you are experienced with moving energy through your hands, you can also sweep energy off of another person with your hands (be sure to cleanse yourself afterward). For these methods, be sure to move smoothly over the body so as not to leave anything behind. You might, for example, make a habit of going up the front of the body and down the back, or of starting at the head and moving consistently toward the feet.

Shielding

For a Guardian, the art of shielding is crucial, and its benefits hopefully are obvious. Depending on the strength and intent of the shield used, it can range from a buffer against irritating coworkers to armor against a magical onslaught.

Simple Method:

Center and cleanse yourself. In your center, see the pool of colored light that represents your personal energy. Imagine that a mist of that color rises within your body, filling you completely. It continues to expand, out your pores, your nose and mouth, until it takes the shape of an egg around your entire body. This egg of light develops a hard shell that keeps out all unwanted energy.

Variations:

Most decent books on magickal practice will give at least one or two methods of shielding—sometimes they will be presented as "quick" forms of circle casting. Shields can be created ahead of time and triggered by catch phrases, stored in objects, molded into different shapes, and decorated with symbols.

Individual chakras, parts of the body, or objects can have their own shields, as can entire areas. Here, more than in any of the other fundamental skills, there is room for individual experiment. In any case, you should cleanse yourself or your object before shielding, to prevent accidentally sealing in negative energies (though this opens up interesting possibilities for combative magic, which is outside the scope of this lesson).

Chakra Balancing

The *chakras* are energy centers located down the spinal cord. Each is believed to govern different functions, encompassing the physical, mental, emotional, and spiritual. Making sure these centers are balanced with each other and filled with clean energy allows everything else to run more smoothly.

Simple Method:

Center yourself, then move down to the base of the spine. From here, you will move into each chakra, measuring the size and brightness of each chakra. They may be envisioned as spheres or wheels. If any are too large or small (racquetball size is good), take note of this and imagine it growing or shrinking to the desired size. Likewise, if any are very dim or murky, imagine them becoming clearer and brighter. It is helpful to use energy obtained by grounding to feed small, dim, or murky chakras.

1. **Base chakra:** the tip of the spine. This governs the impulse for physical survival. It is usually seen as red.
2. **Sacral chakra:** the sexual organs (lower abdomen). This governs sex, obviously, but also basic empathy and "gut reactions." Orange.
3. **Solar plexus:** just that, above the navel but below the chest. This is the seat of the Will. Yellow.
4. **Heart chakra:** the heart. It governs compassion and is the balance point of the chakra system. Green (pink if you prefer).
5. **Throat chakra:** the base of the throat. It governs intellect and communication. Blue.
6. **Third eye:** the forehead, between the brows. It controls the astral senses. Indigo.
7. **Crown:** at the top of the head. It is the link to the spiritual realms and their wisdom. Violet.

Variations:

Stones or candles of the appropriate colors are often used to help balance the chakras. There are whole books devoted to the chakra system for those interested in further study. Particularly recommended is *Wheels of Life,* by Anodea Judith, and its companion: *The Sevenfold Journey.*

3. Meditation

By Donata Ahern (aqua)

The dictionary defines meditation as a relaxed, focused state of mind. For a Wizard, that's only a beginning—it's not the main purpose.

Why would a Wizard want to meditate? There are many benefits to be found in the practice of meditation. The first one you may notice is a state of calmness and relaxation. As you continue your prac-

tice you may find that meditation helps you to handle stress with less upset and anxiety. These are general benefits helpful to anyone, and are easily learned.

The main reason you, as a Wizard, will want to meditate is because it helps you to concentrate and focus your mind. This allows you to access your intuition, with its deep wisdom and connection to the higher or collective consciousness. The focus gained through meditation will help you to direct your energy toward a desired outcome. The discipline of regular meditation strengthens your Will. Magick requires the force of your Will to focus and direct your energy toward your desired positive outcome. When you have a strong Will, your magick becomes more powerful and effective.

Before any meditation you should create sacred space about yourself. This acts as a protection and a container to help focus your energy. You can simply visualize or imagine a circle of white light surrounding you, or you may cast a circle in whatever manner you usually do this.

There are different forms of meditation...

Active meditation involves physical movement. If you practice *Yoga* or *T'ai Chi,* you already know that it requires you to focus your mind. These are forms of active meditation. Another active practice is to *walk* slowly, concentrating on each movement of your body as you take a step, and counting each step as you walk, or repeating a word or phrase with each step.

Another method of active meditation is *twirling.* Imagine that you have a nail or piece of wood in between the big toe and the next toe of your right foot (no pain is involved!). This will act as a stable pivot for you as you twirl around it. Hold up your right hand above your face, and gaze into the center of your palm. This concentration will help to focus you and prevent falling. Now start twirling slowly to the right, keeping your right foot balanced on the imaginary pivot as you gaze at your palm. If you prefer, do this with the left foot and left hand, and pivot to the left. Have a soft chair or couch nearby as you may feel dizzy the first few times you try this! Build up the time you are able to twirl. After about five minutes of twirling, you will be in a state of altered consciousness.

Passive meditation is what is generally meant by 'meditation.' In passive meditation you are seated and not moving about. You can sit in a chair, with your feet on the ground (don't cross your legs or feet), spine straight, or you can sit cross-legged on the floor or a cushion, again with your spine straight. Why is it important to keep the spine straight? You have energy channels that go up your spine, and when it is straight the energy flows more easily. This aids your concentration.

A beginning step in passive meditation is relaxation. A simple way to relax is to focus on each part of your body in turn. You can imagine the sun as a small spotlight focusing on each part of your body as you concentrate on it. Begin with the top of your head. Consciously tighten the area, and then relax it. Repeat this as you move your concentration to your eyebrows, your eyes, your cheeks, your nose, your mouth. Then focus on your neck. Continue in this way, taking your time, moving through your body all the way to your toes. Feel the deep relaxation in your entire body.

Now that you are seated comfortably and relaxed, focus on your breath. Sense it flowing in through your nostrils, and then flowing downwards into your lungs. Feel your abdomen filling like a balloon. As you exhale, breath out any tension or stress you may be feeling. You can continue to simply follow your breath this way for your entire meditation session. You may wish to count your breaths, in and out. In, count 'one', and out, count 'two.' Repeat this with each breath.

As you breathe deeply in and out, you may wish to add something – a word or phrase – to help your concentration. One universal *mantra,* or word, is "Om." You may use "Peace," "Love," "Oneness," or any other word that appeals to you. You may prefer a phrase, such as "We are all One," or several words together, such as "Peace, Love, Light." There are phrases that have been used as mantras for centuries. One of the most general is "Om Mani Padme Hum." Another passive form of mantra meditation is chanting. In this form, you chant your mantra aloud. This can be a word, phrase, or a longer prayer.

Another way to practice passive meditation is to stare at an object, such as a lighted candle, or a mirror, or both at the same time, with the candle in front of the mirror. If you become distracted, simply bring your concentration back to the object.

Contemplation is another form of passive meditation. In contemplation, you choose a word, phrase, or sentence before you start your meditation session. During the session you think about the word, phrase, or sentence you chose and you examine it as much as you can. For example, you may choose to contemplate or meditate on "Do no harm." What does this really mean? How do you avoid all harm? Can you? Does this mean doing 'no harm' to yourself? Is this selfish? How do you feel about eating meat? Or being a soldier and having to kill someone? Other ideas will come up as you meditate. You may choose to mediate on "We are all connected through the Web of Life." What does this mean? Does it include beings other than humans? Animals? Trees? How do my actions affect the whole web? You will find many other words and phrases that are excellent for this purpose.

Calming your mind

In passive meditation you may notice distracting thoughts that interfere with your concentration. Imagine that you are a calm pool. Imagine that a pebble is tossed into the pool, creating ripples that move outward across the surface the surface of the pool. Watch as the ripples disappear. These are your thoughts. Let them move away. Don't make an effort to stop them. You may also imagine a clear blue sky, with your thoughts as clouds that move across it. Again, simply watch the clouds move away.

The result of meditation is a more focused mind, a deeper state of relaxation, and a disciplined and strengthened Will. With these qualities you are able, as a Wizard, to practice magick more effectively! As an example, bless a crystal or candle. Decide what the purpose of this crystal or candle is—for example, to send healing energy. Stand before your altar, or table, with the crystal or candle on it. Focus on your breath. Bring up earth energy into your heart center, and then bring down sky energy, as you were shown above.

Let these energies mingle in your heart center. Hold your hands over the crystal or candle. Feel the power of your intent to place healing energy into the object, which will hold and later release this energy. Breathe in deeply and focus on the energy in your heart center. As you exhale, let the energy flow down your arms, into your hands, and into the crystal or candle. Feel the power and energy in your breath flowing out your hands to bless the object. When you want to send healing energy, focus on the object (if a candle, light it) and consciously send the energy to the one that needs it. You can also have a crystal that you bless the same way, and that you add to whenever you feel happy, confident, and successful. Keep adding to this positive energy that you store in the crystal through your meditation technique. If you feel 'down, or discouraged, go into a light state of meditation, and pull out some of the positive energy stored in the crystal. Hold the crystal for a few minutes of meditation. You'll feel much better afterwards!

At the end of any meditation session, whether active or passive, take a moment to give thanks to the spirits of place, to any deities or other beings you were aware of in meditation. Then ground, sending any excess energy into the earth. This will bring you back to ordinary consciousness and will prevent a 'spacey' feeling. Let the circle of light about you fade away. If you cast a circle, take it down in your usual way. Clean up any burnt out candles or incense you may have used. Go about your day in peace!

Guided Meditation

Here is a Guided Mediation script, by Grey School teacher Holly Ravenweed (indigo). You can have another person read this to you while you meditate, tape record it to listen to, or read through it and do it on your own:

Light a candle (this is helpful, but not absolutely necessary). Sit or lie down in a comfortable spot. Close your eyes and quiet your breathing. Spend a moment noticing the smells and sounds around you. Imagine that it is night. Above your head the full moon shines low and full. It is filled with a beautiful white light that shimmers and glows. You can see this light streaming down towards you. As the light reaches you, you can feel its gentle glow surrounding you. You absorb the light through your skin and it fills your body with a feeling of peace and relaxation. Feel it through all the parts of you—arms, legs, head and body--until it reaches your center and you are full. You can feel your heart beating. Now, your heart is growing strong and sure as you are flooded with love for all of the Earth, her people, her creatures, her plants and waters. You can feel the light of the Moon flowing through you and into the Earth below. You know that you are an important part of creation. You know that what you do and say matters. You know that you are loved. Rest in this peacefulness for a few more minutes. Take your time, and when you are ready to return to where you belong, the light of the Moon will take you there.

4. Practical Metapsychics
(Tricks and Techniques for Mental Mastery)
By Robert Elm (silver)

I have written this lesson to provide my own personal solutions to the major problems that can face one who has difficulty at the outset of this undertaking, instead of just telling you the ancient practices themselves. This way you will be able to apply these tricks and techniques to the other books and texts that you may come into contact with.

These classical techniques have been used all over the world and include the practice of visualization (unfortunately named, because it is in fact much more than just the imagined sense of vision), exercises in direct awareness as opposed to thought or interpretation of experience and the sensing and control of "psycho-spiritual" energies variously called *chi, prana, mana, orgone, vril, magis* as well as many other names.

While these and other important techniques may have variations and are very different from one another,

there are still a few simple exercises that can help you to develop them more quickly and more powerfully.

The multi-sensory experience of your world

The first simple exercise I would like to suggest to you is the practice of focusing upon the multi-sensory experience. It is a simple fact that we experience many senses at one time. The five senses of sight, sound, touch, taste and smell are the most well-known, but what about the sense of your thoughts? What about the sense of imagined sounds and sights? What about the sense of your emotions? What about the sense of balance? Your sense of time? What of your sense of understanding meaning (words are just sounds without meaning, and what would a word be without understanding?)?

These and many more are a part of your total experience. The more of these that you experience at one time, the more natural and real things around you seem to be; that is, the reality tone of your world begins to increase. This is an exercise in awareness, and a very important one. If you want to develop your intuition you need to see the world in a multi-sensory way. The more information you get from direct experience, the better your intuition can answer your questions about reality. The more senses you use, the more information your intuition has to work with.

Experiencing the world in such a way may seem at first to be a difficult matter. But the truth is that looking at the world in this manner is more natural and easier to do than splitting up the senses and focus-

ing only through sight or sound. A simple example is one practiced in many a science class all over the world. Students' noses are plugged up and their eyes are blindfolded as a liquid is given to them to drink. The students must then try to identify what it is they just tasted. It is almost impossible to do so. What most people mean by the sense of taste is a combination of taste, smell, and often a sense of touch as when a strangely textured food is tried for the first time.

I'd like for you to find a nice natural place, one where you feel a sense of beauty, such as a park, a wooded area, a beautiful rock formation—or even a greenhouse if you can't find a place like the ones I describe above. Now, once you have found such a place, sit down and just listen, watch, smell…The key is to just let your experience of the place surprise you and inform your mind without letting one sense to predominate over the others. If you find yourself watching too intently or listening too exclusively, then be sure to relax your control a bit. Let your senses open and just let the world in!

This simple exercise is a very important one. Many visualizations in books on the subject will ask you to visualize a tree or a stone, but the sad truth is that few people know what a tree really looks like or feels like or smells like—so how are you to visualize something to the point where it feels like it is a real thing? But knowing the item you want to visualize is only the start, because when you visualize that thing, you should also imagine with more than just your sense of sight. The more sensory imagination you include in your visualization, the more reality tone your visualized scene will have. So if you are to visualize a golden pyramid, don't just produce an image in your mind; imagine picking it up and feeling its cool weight, imagine its hardness and the sharpness of its corners and edges, imagine tasting it and experiencing its overall metallic taste and smell.

This is also an important thing to consider when you are trying to learn to experience and control psycho-spiritual energy, because often people don't see this energy but can feel it or just sense it in its own way. By learning to experience the world in an open and non-divided way as I am suggesting here, the chances of your experiencing this energy around and within you is dramatically increased. I myself do not see this energy often, but I know that it is there and can sense its presence much more readily than I can see or even feel it. The way that you will be able to experience this force is totally a personal matter.

The power of a question

Multi-sensory experience is, of course, only one of the techniques that will make the beginning a much easier thing to face. There is one way in particular that I would like to share here, and that is the use and power of a question. I am not speaking of the very useful practice of asking a teacher questions, but of the power of a question itself upon the unconscious mind.

When you ask a question you are acknowledging a missing piece to an inner puzzle. By asking a question the subconscious mind will automatically begin to fill in the blank to the best of its ability. I strongly suggest that you not use the following until you have practiced experiencing and thinking of the world in multi-sensory terms, as this practice will intensify the use of your questioning as I am about to describe it to you now.

A question is, as I said above, a mental vacuum that the mind will seek to fill. By asking questions that have multi-sensory descriptions, the imagination is automatically engaged and will produce a visualization without the necessity of a conscious attempt to do so.

Examples:

"What would a brown fuzzy moth sound like if it flew up to your ear as it swirled about the room?"

"What would the cold glistening surface of a golden pyramid taste like?"

"What would a red juicy strawberry feel like as you sink your teeth into its tart/sweet flesh?"

I am sure that at least one of these questions elicited an automatic reaction that made an image of the object asked about to appear in the mind. It should be understood though that the power of a question has not only the power to invoke an image into the mind but to invoke an emotion, mood or desire.

Example:

"What is courage? What does it feel like to have it well up into my chest and warm my heart with fearlessness? What would courage look like if I could see it?"

It is an easy thing to invoke an emotion when you use a question. You may be able to use a statement to do the same thing, but it has the problem that if you are as in this instance not very brave, a part of your mind may say, "That isn't true, I'm a coward."

By using the question, you aren't saying that you are brave or that the fearlessness *is* rising in you as a palpable sensation, but that you are wondering what it would feel like. Of course, if you are attentive, you will realize that you are indeed feeling the courage rise within you as the description says. It is the same way with all the uses of question in this way. Remember, while you are reading the question, the image, emotion or whatever you are trying to invoke into your mind is forming there of its own accord. You only need to be attentive and you won't have any difficulty in catching the invoked mental object. A question can never be a lie, so when you use it there can be no mental friction that stops it from being accepted as true, and the message is easily sent to the subconscious mind to aid you in whatever your task may be.

Desire can easily be intensified by the use of questions. First off, though, why would one want to increase a desire? Desire is the intent of the subconscious mind. Thus if you want to encourage the easier development of a certain mental ability, you can create and intensify the desire using questions to do so.

Example:

"Why would I want to develop automatic writing? Why would I want to be able to feel the pencil in my hand write of its own accord things that I do not consciously know? Why would I want to gain insight into my own inner workings and what my subconscious mind thinks and wants?"

Note the use of multi-sensory language in the above example. Be sure to word as many questions in this way as you can, because the subconscious mind pays closer attention to vibrantly described scenes than abstract ideas. The richer the scenery of the question, the greater the impact it will have upon your subconscious mind. You can cement this practice by thinking of things that you would want to gain from such a practice.

Example:

"What kind of kind of knowledge can I bring up by the practice? Who can I help with Automatic Writing? What stories, what art can be created with it?"

If you continue to add to your list of reasons to automatically write you'll start to feel your mind becoming enthusiastic about the process. But don't stop there, enthusiasm is just the beginning! You want your subconscious mind to get worked up enough to actually do the work by itself. If you can't think of any other reasons to do it, then savor the feeling of what you've decided automatic writing can do for you. Think of all the reasons you thought of in turn, and just feel the drive to do this strengthen. Remember! The reasons that you want to learn automatic writing are much less important than the feeling of wanting to do it. Focus on the emotions that well up when you let your mind go wild and fantasize about what automatic writing can do for you.

This example is just one. By thinking in terms of using a question to develop an ability such as this, you are making the beginning of the endeavor much easier than you can imagine. When your subconscious is on your side in practices such as these, you are working with the main element that will make or break your attempt to succeed at the process. Most if not all the basic exercises of the mind require the cooperation, if not direct aid, of the subconscious mind in order to succeed in the attempt. This is because it is the subconscious mind that does all the real work!

Affirmation

Affirmation is often taught in and of itself to make things happen in one's life as if by magick. I disagree with this approach but I still see the importance of it in the context of developing your mental abilities. I find it extremely useful in conjunction with the previously mentioned technique of using questions to invoke an image, desire or emotion. The reason for this is that once you state the question that invokes the image or feeling, it may quickly fade. But, by stating that the thing invoked by questions is a real thing, that this is so, the image will remain and it will have a greater reality tone than if it was questioned into existence alone.

Using a question will develop the image or emotion or desire and give it shape, while using an affirmation will give it a sense of solidity in the mind, a sense of it being real and existing as a thing instead of just an idea.

An affirmation is performed by stating in positive terms what you want to have happen or exist as if it is already there. It is important to understand that by "positive" it is not meant to infer a value judgment, as in good as opposed to bad, but as in stating only that which is. The words *not, nor, isn't* and others which mean something being said is "negated" are not allowed.

Using the previous example of questioning courage into existence, we can say that after the feeling of courage is there we can make it truly ours by affirming its existence.

Example:

"I feel courage filling my heart and making me strong in the face of all things great and small. Fear is my servant and I am its master. I am now and forever brave."

Affirmations may be used any time that you want to cement a feeling or a desire into place, though in many books you will find affirmations to cause a change in your mental habits or even to cause a magickal change in the world around you. While this is possible, using a question as discussed above before using the affirmation to cement it into place you will find that you need to use much less effort to cause these changes than using affirmation alone.

So what now?

Why learn all these silly things? How is this connected to the ancient techniques that books on mental powers and magick describe? Quite simply, these tricks will help you in getting "over the hump" in your beginning practice of almost any magickal art. If you are not proficient at visualization and get little more than a vague image, then you will find that these three basic techniques will trick or coax the images you desire to form in your mind of their own accord. If you are having particular difficulty with getting one of the more advanced practices, like *psychokinesis,* you can cause a powerful desire to develop in your unconscious mind and use questioning and affirmation to develop a certainty not only that such abilities are possible, but a confidence in your own ability to perform these acts.

5. Creating your Astral Sanctum

By Donata Ahern (aqua)

What is sacred space, or a *sanctum*? It is a place that you set aside for your personal use in your spiritual practice. This special place becomes a focus for your ceremony and meditation. When you go there, wherever it may be, just by that act, you signal to yourself that you are entering other consciousness, and are connecting to your Higher Self. You enter into a place apart from your daily world. This becomes automatic after a while, and you'll find it is a great aid for you. A sacred space will usually have an altar as the central point or focus. An altar helps you to concentrate on what you want to do, whether a ceremony, meditation, or a combination of both.

Your sacred space or sanctum can be an entire room or part of a room, such as your bedroom. Your altar can be set up on a table, or can be on top of a dresser, or even on a shelf or windowsill. It doesn't need to be obvious, so if you share your room with someone else, you can be the only one who knows this is special for you. A lace placemat or a scarf can be your altar cloth, if you wish one. Place objects on your altar that are special for you, and have meaning for you. Crystals are often used on altars for their beauty and their ability to increase and store your energy. Crystals can enhance your ability to enter a light trance. Hold your crystal in your hand, and look into it. If you wish, you may imagine yourself within the crystal,

in another world. This is an enjoyable way to meditate. A simple goddess image for your altar can be a seashell, a small ammonite (a fossil with a spiral on it), or a plant. A simple god image can be anything upright, such as a standing crystal, an antler, a pinecone, or even a small branch. In this way you may have objects on your altar that aren't obvious sacred objects to anyone except yourself. Natural objects like these add to the beauty of your space. The altar and the objects you place on it will hold your energy, and build it up, so that the atmosphere of your space becomes filled with calm, powerful energy. When you are away from your home, if you feel any stress, you need only think of your altar and feel a link to it, and to the energy it holds for you. Use this energy to feel calm again, and ready to deal with the stressful situation.

It's easier to maintain a regular meditation and ceremony practice when you have the things you need ready and convenient, and a place to do it. You can keep candles, matches, and incense in a box on or under the altar, or in a drawer if your altar is on a dresser. Your altar becomes a focus for your energy, and is a reminder of your ongoing connection to the sacred. It is important to be aware of this connection, and if only briefly, to recognize it daily with a meditation and/or ceremony. After all, if you live with family or others, you won't expect to live in harmony with them if you only speak to them once a week and ignore them the rest of the time! In the same way, it's important to make a connection with the Mighty Ones or Spirit daily. Make your sacred space as attractive as possible. When you honor Spirit or the Mighty Ones, you also honor yourself.

You can create sacred space that you can return to regularly in the astral as well as on the physical plane. Why would you want to create an astral sacred space? There are several reasons. First of all, you'll find the exercise that follows very relaxing and calming. This is a big plus all by itself. Even more than that, when you travel on the astral plane you are training your intuitive creative mind to work for you. This opens you to a trust in the wisdom and truth of your intuition, which is important for a wizard. Much of the work of a wizard depends on a developed intuition. The exercise given here is an exercise in creative visualization. It may feel as though you are just imagining it – don't worry about it. You are using your power of visualization, or imaging. This is much more purposeful than imaginative 'daydreaming'. Trust the process. Your imagination is a powerful tool when used in this manner.

This visualization exercise is a form of astral travel. Astral travel allows you to explore other worlds in pathworking and shamanic journeys. When you create an astral sacred space, you have a 'home base' that you can use whenever you do astral journeys. You can leave and return to this sacred place on the astral level, and this adds to your confidence and security. When you learn how to travel your astral sanctum in your imagination, you can go there at any time, and for any length of time. If you are riding on a bus, or standing in a line, you may take a moment and go to your astral sacred space. It is always available to you. As you continue to go to it, you may meet your Guide there. Your Guide will be able to answer questions and help you in many ways. You have a Guide whether or not you are consciously aware of one at this time, so you may wish to ask your Guide to appear and meet you in this sacred space in the astral.

And finally, it's fun to have a secret place all your own! Your sacred space is yours! You create it, and you make it exactly as you wish it to be. It is a haven, a workplace, a resting or vacation spot, with whatever you want for your comfort, convenience, and happiness. Have fun and enjoy your time there!

To create your astral sacred space, go to your physical altar, and bless yourself with the four elements (blessed salt and water, and incense for fire and air). Do this with the intention that you are going to create your astral sacred space. You do this through the power of your imagination, in an active visualization.

Now imagine yourself in a place of nature. This may be somewhere you already know in the real world, or it may be a place you totally imagine and create now. Look around. What do you see? Is it daytime? Is the sky clear and blue? Or is it nighttime? Do you see the moon and stars? Is it warm or cool? What do you hear? You may hear bird songs, small animals scurrying, and the sound of your feet as you softly walk along. What do you smell? If in a woods, perhaps pine scent, or if in a meadow, the lovely scent of wild flowers as you brush gently past them. Take your time with this exercise. Allow yourself to experience each of your senses. Let yourself feel very peaceful and relaxed as you do this.

As you walk along, you come to a bridge over a babbling brook or creek. Crossing over water is a signal to you that you are entering another state of consciousness. Cross this bridge now. Notice its construction—it may be wooden, or stone. Is it old or new? Does it span a ravine? Or is it just above the creek? The bridge may creak as you cross. Look into the brook as you pass over it, and listen to the sound it makes. Notice how large it is, how calm, or how quickly moving. As you step off the bridge on the other side of the brook, you find yourself in a beautiful place of nature. Make this place as beautiful as you can. Include trees,

water, mountains, a beach, whatever you find beautiful. Build a cottage or house if you wish. Take your time with this. Have everything in your home that will add to your enjoyment and comfort. Is there a garden nearby? Do you have a view? If so, what is it? Do you want to have an altar in your home here? If so, imagine that you place something on it from your physical altar at home.

When you are ready, leave your home, and walk outdoors. Even if you've already set up a sacred space in your visualized home, you'll want to create sacred space outdoors, in nature. Walk around until you come to a place that feels comfortable and special to you. This may be a clearing in the woods, or a stone circle, or a natural mound in the meadow. It may overlook water or a beach, or it may be enclosed by trees, or it may be in an open area. Find and create a place that appeals to you. Take your time. When you have found your sacred space within this place of nature, set up your altar and place your objects on it—whatever you choose. Consecrate your altar with the four elements as you did in your physical space. Make the intention that you are dedicating this sacred space, and will return to it regularly. Now spend a few minutes just breathing in and out, totally relaxed and at peace, feeling the harmony and beauty of your sacred space. When you are at your physical altar, make a conscious connection to this astral sanctum, and you will build up your awareness of its existence on the astral. This becomes as real as your physical altar. This will be your primary space for some of your wizardry work. This is a big step forward in your development as a Wizard!

When you are ready, thank the spirits of this place, and walk back across the bridge over the stream. As you step off the bridge you are standing on the earth. Sit down on the earth, breathing any excess energy down into the Earth Mother. Relax deeply into the earth. Feel the grounding energy of Earth. Breathe in and out a few times. Now that you know the way, you may return at any time to this place of nature, and your sacred space. Return now to your physical sacred space, to your altar, where you are seated. Breathe in and out a few more times, and return to normal reality. Open your eyes and find yourself at your physical altar. Thank Spirit or the Mighty Ones for the blessing of your astral sanctum. Put away anything that needs to be put away, be sure your candles are out, and now go on your way, refreshed and at peace.

Bright Blessings!

6. Exploring the bright floor: magick for the dreaming mind

By Elizabeth Barrette (grey)

"Dream-sorrows leave real tears on the pillow, and dream-glories leave real pride in the heart."

The magick of dreams is a legacy of all humans. Some evidence suggests that other mammals also dream. Although modern culture holds little respect for these nightly experiences, most traditional cultures consider them significant or even vital. Shortened or interrupted sleep can interfere with dreaming, which leaves the person feeling sluggish or irritable. It's not just that our bodies need time to rest and recover from the day's activity; our minds also need time to relax and integrate things. So we dream.

Wizards understand the power of dreams. These visions activate our subconscious minds and put us in touch with subtler realities than that of the waking world. Dreamspace is a realm of magick and mystery, where the things we say and do and discover can resonate into our everyday lives. To channel this power effectively, there are many techniques you can explore.

Learning about Dreams

During the night, an average person goes through several periods of dreaming. The first of these usually occurs about an hour and a half after falling asleep. Dreams occur during REM (which stands for Rapid Eye Movement) sleep. Most people seem to dream primarily in visual images, but some report full sensory experiences such as the taste of an apple pie. Expert dreamers can achieve effects often considered impossible by mundane sources.

Aside from the dreaming that occurs in deep sleep, there is the dreamy borderland you pass on the way in and the way out. The *hypnogogic* state lies between waking and sleeping, as you are falling asleep; the *hypnopompic* state lies between sleeping and waking, as you are waking up. In fact the title of this piece comes from a poem I read in college; the author used the metaphor of a department store elevator for describing sleep, with the hypnogogic state as a "bright floor" between the upper level and the dark below, a place that was intensely attractive but also elusive. The poem essentially lamented the author's frustration at always falling past the most interesting place. Rather baffled, I said to my teacher, "But that's where I get *off* every night!" I've found the borderlands between waking and sleeping to be among the most useful for creative pursuits and intuitive discoveries, so I've learned to expand the time I spend there. From there I can move straight into the night dreams and get more out of them too.

There are, of course, many different types of dreams. The main categories are recall dreams, nonsense dreams, and True Dreams. Recall dreams simply replay fragments of recent events, as the mind processes its experiences. Nonsense dreams are bizarre, perhaps even random jumbles of material with no apparent meaning – the ones where you find yourself ice-skating on chocolate only to be chased away by a group of clowns riding ostriches, or some other absurdity. True Dreams are intensely powerful visions, either arising from the deep wells of your own magick or sent from beyond by higher powers. Thesecan be life-changing. More specific types include message dreams (little snippets that convey a particular idea, usually from an outside source), epiphanies (sudden realizations or solutions to problems), puzzle dreams (where you have to figure out the real meaning from the symbolism), creative dreams (after which you wake up with a story or painting in your head), and nightmares (full of anxiety or outright terror). Beginning with puberty, most people also experience some sensual dreams.

The choices we make in dreams and the things we realize there can have very definite effects on our waking lives. Wizards in particular learn to use this magickal space for such things as self-exploration and studying archetypes.

You can learn more about the lore, history, and science of dreams by reading magickal and mundane texts on the topic. An excellent place to start is the book *Teach Yourself to Dream* by David Fontana.

Basic skills

In order to make the best use of your dreams, you need to acquire certain essential skills and habits. Some of these are easy to learn; others may take years to acquire.

1. **Keep a dream journal.** Recording your dreams makes it easier to analyze them and identify long-term patterns. A simple spiral-bound notebook and pencil by your bed will work fine.
2. **Set your intent before climbing into bed.** For instance, you might tell yourself, "I remember all my dreams." You could also choose a theme for the night's dreaming.
3. **Learn to fall asleep eqasily.** If you toss and turn for twenty minutes, you'll wear yourself out and be less receptive to dreaming. Aim for a relaxed, dreamy state of mind as soon as you lie down.
4. **Work on dream recall.** Your dreams don't do much good if you forget them all before you can figure out what they mean. Wring out as much detail as you can and write it down.
5. **When you wake up, lie still for a minute and think about your dreams.** This gives you a better chance of catching them before they slip away.

6. **Create your own dream dictionary.** Someone else's book is a good place to start, but you'll always have things that mean something different to you. Symbolism is crucial in dreamwork, but you need to allow for personal interpretations.

These skills will serve you well in pursuing your dreams. You can enhance your dreaming ability with work in other areas of magick, such as meditation or herbalism. Also, dreamwork can give you an edge in working other types of magick as well.

Techniques of Dream Magick

Most dreamwork involves navigating through or otherwise influencing dreamspace itself. However, there are also things you can do in waking life that relate to dreaming, and thus fall within the same area of expertise. Remember that definitions of magickal concepts can vary from one source to another; people may use different terms to describe the same thing. Also, some of these techniques can be used for malicious as well as beneficial purposes. Some Sorcerers find the subtlety of dreams very appealing, and they may use dreamwork to manipulate their victims or steal power for themselves.

Dreambeaching – waking deliberately from a dream you wish to leave. In order to do this, you need conscious awareness that you are dreaming, and enough Will to yank yourself out of it. This is one effective way of handling nightmares.

Dreamcasting – working magick in dreamspace that resonates into waking life. To use dreamspace as a setting for your magickal activities on purpose, you need full control over your dreams; but sometimes your subconscious mind will take over and work a spell for you, while you sleep. This makes it difficult or impossible for anyone else to catch you working magick and hassle you about it, if you don't live in a magick-friendly environment.

Dreamcatching – intercepting nightmares or other troublesome dreams before they can get into someone's head and cause trouble. Certain herbs and stones have this precious quality, as do various crafted objects. A skilled Wizard can also do it by manipulating dreamspace either while awake or asleep.

Dreamdiving – returning to the same dream after waking once and then going back to sleep. Some dreams naturally recur, and repeat themselves over and over again with little or no variation. However, you can create a similar effect if you are awakened before you're really finished with a dream, by returning to it deliberately.

Dreamfaring – traveling through dreamspace to visit distant places, times, or worlds. Similar to astral travel, this allows you to leave the confines of your own mind and body. It's not uncommon for this to happen spontaneously, but the destination is often random; to control your destination, you need the ability to direct the flow of your dreams.

Dreamfledging – reaching an epiphany of personal growth through actions taken or decisions made in dreamspace, the emotional benefits of which resonate into waking life. This happens to some people naturally, but is one of the goals that dreamworking Wizards seek on purpose.

Dreamkeeping – archiving special dreams so that you remember them in the morning, and indeed, can remember them long-term as well. This also refers to holding the power of a visionary dream so it can affect the waking world. Dream dictionaries and journals are important tools for dreamkeeping.

Dreamseeing – scrying or otherwise divining the unknown through dreams. This is only one of many magickal activities that can be done in dreamspace. To do it deliberately, you must have some ability to influence the events in your dreams; but it's not uncommon for magickal talents to "slip out" in this fashion, even if you are not consciously guiding the action.

Dreamsending – creating a message or a complete dream, and placing it in another person's mind. This is a tricky but useful technique. Though most often employed to exchange simple messages between friends, it can be used by the unscrupulous to plague someone with unpleasant dreams.

Dreamshaping – altering a dream in progress. You must have an awareness that you are dreaming and the Will to affect it. This technique is often used to quell nightmares, although it can be used just for fun. Dreamspace is the original "virtual reality!"

Dreamsharing – partaking of the same dream with someone else. When two people, usually close friends or family members, both take part in a single dream, it's a very intimate experience. This happens occasionally and naturally in modern mundane culture; but in many tribal cultures, it is the norm, and whole families may share a dream together. Another version involves different people having separate parts of a dream that fit together like puzzle pieces once compared in the morning.

Dreamsinging – influencing dreams through music or song, as in a lullaby. This is one of the traditional talents of a Bard. Parents can often do this for young children. A Wizard skilled in dreamwork may also develop this ability. It can grant soothing dreams, dispel nightmares, and aid healing.

Dreamsolving – using the subconscious, fluid reality of dreamspace to process waking challenges and come up with solutions. Most people have had this happen spontaneously a time or two, but to harness its power for real, you need enough control to choose the theme of your dreams.

Dreamspeaking – interpreting dreams for others or yourself. This makes a wonderful specialty for a Wizard. You'll be surprised how fast you can get a reputation for this, and how many otherwise non-magickal people will ask you about it. For this you need intuition plus a broad knowledge of archetypes and symbolism.

Dreamspinning – controlling dreams by choosing a theme to begin with. Just as you can make strong yarn from fluff, you can make a dream from nebulous ideas. Gaining this ability gives you access to many others based on it. One mundane term for this is "dream incubation."

Dreamswimming – navigating through dreamspace in such a way as to be able to bring ideas from there into the waking world, such as stories or pictures. It gets its name because the ideas want to stay in dreamspace, and moving them is like trying to carry stones in a wet paper towel. You have to swim to where they are, gather them, swim up again – and if they drop back down, you have to swim deeper to retrieve them, and then surface. This takes as much finesse as sheer Will.

Dreamwaking – experiencing a dream while aware that it is a dream. Mundanely known as "lucid dreaming," this ability forms the basis of many others. In order to make the most of a dream, you first must know what it is.

Dreamwalking – entering another person's dreams. This can be a joyful intimacy for friends, or a rude intrusion by an enemy. It's also one of the ways in which an expert dreamworker can help someone else resolve their problems.

Dreamwalking is the process of psychically entering another person's dreams or subconscious thoughts. This is best done when the person is sleeping though it is effective, to some degree, anytime the person's conscious mind is blurred or distracted. This is not astral projection. The person doing the walking is still very much inside his own body and aware of his own conscious. It is more like bi-location, in which a person's consciousness can be split and exist in two places and the same moment (Belanger, 2004). Dreamwalking can be a pleasant experience shared between close friends or lovers but it can also be a powerfully negative tool used for spying, manipulation, energy theft, and more. To dreamwalk on someone without his or her consent is a psychic attack and should not be done. —Alexzandria Baker, "The Makings of Metaphysical Kinship"

It takes time to learn dreamwork, for this is a subtle art and a complex science. Everyone dreams, but it takes more than that to make full use of the potential. You can begin studying dreamwork this very night and get significant improvement rather quickly – but it can take a lifetime to master. These skills will continue to grow with you throughout your study of Wizardry.

7. How to do it
by Oberon (grey)

The following lessons will give you practical exercises to develop your abilities in a few of the more dramatic psychic skills. As with any skills involving honing a talent—such as music, dancing, or art—the key element here is practice!

In the *Grimoire,* "Class V: Magickal Talents" (pp. 32-38), I listed a couple dozen of the most important psychic talents and gave a few basic exercises for several of them. Please consult those pages, as I don't intend to repeat them here. Rather, I will offer some additional exercises, focusing particularly on a few that I didn't go into very much in the previous book.

The two most popular talents that most people think of are certainly *Telepathy* and *Psychokinesis.* I discussed both of these at some length in the *Grimoire,* and gave several good starting exercises. Here's a bit more you can do to help develop your skills in these.

Telepathy ("remote feeling")

Direct mind-to-mind communication of thoughts, ideas and images. Telepathy involves "hearing" the thoughts of others inside your head, and/or being able to project your thoughts to others. Far from being a rare "gift," we are discovering that this ability is a natural function of our brains, and may underlie all communication.

In 1996, neuroscientists discovered a curious cluster of neurons in the premotor cortex of the brain that replicate activity going on in the same area of the brain of another person when one is observing their behavior. Because the cells reflected the actions of others, the neuroscientists named them "mirror neurons." Later experiments confirmed that, in addition to mirroring actions, these cells also reflect sensations and emotions.

"Mirror neurons suggest that we pretend to be in another person's mental shoes," says Marco Iacoboni, a neuroscientist at the UCLA School of Medicine. "In fact, with mirror neurons we do not have to pretend, we practically are in another person's mind."

Mirror neurons may help cognitive scientists explain how children develop a theory of mind (ToM), which is a child's understanding that others have minds similar to their own. Over the years, cognitive scientists have come up with a number of theories to explain how ToM develops.

Simulation theory states that we are natural mind readers. We place ourselves in another person's "mental shoes," and use our own mind as a model for theirs.

Vittorio Gallese, a neuroscientist at the University of Parma in Italy, and one of the original discoverers of mirror neurons, contends that when we interact with someone, we do more than just observe the other person's behavior. He believes we create internal representations of their actions, sensations and emotions within ourselves, as if we are the ones that are moving, sensing and feeling.

Many scientists believe that mirror neurons embody the predictions of simulation theory. "We share with others not only the way they normally act or subjectively experience emotions and sensations, but also the neural circuits enabling those same actions, emotions and sensations: the mirror neuron systems," Gallese told *LiveScience*

("Scientists Say Everyone Can Read Minds" By Ker Than. Special to *LiveScience,* 27 April 2005)

Since the foundations of telepathy in the mirror neurons operate at a very basic level, telepathy exercises based on transmitting sensations, feelings, images, and music are a better place to start than trying to communicate words and sentences.

In the back of this book is a page containing three sets of five cards each, designed for use in telepathy exercises and experiments. The first of these, with the star, circle, cross, wavy lines and square, are called Zener Cards, for Dr. Karl Zener of Duke University, who developed them in collaboration with Dr. J.B. Rhine of Harvard in the 1920s. I introduced these in the *Grimoire,* and explained how to use them.

In addition to the standard Zener deck, however, I have also designed two other sets of cards that might work better for some people. One set is based on the Tarot Aces—Wand, Cup, Sword, Pentacle—to which I have added a a Labrys (for Spirit) as a fifth "Ace."

The other set is of emotionally laden symbols: skull, sensuality, butterfly, eye, and swastika. To make use of these, make five copies of the whole page on white card stock, then cut them out into three sets of 25 cards each. Use them exactly the same way as I described in the *Grimoire* for using the standard Zener cards (p. 38).

However, you don't have to rely on these images alone. You can make your own telepathy cards by finding any five different images that evoke distinct feelings for you, then make five copies of each on same-size cards. You might also try using colors—either by coloring in these or other images, or even making cards of differently colored paper, such as red, blue, yellow, green, and purple. The most important thing is that the other person you are "sending" to cannot see the cards you are holding—even from the back side of the deck!

Psychokinesis ("mind moving")

Moving or influencing objects without touching them physically. This is one of the rarest and most difficult psi-talents to manifest and control, but many people can learn to do some of the basic exercises. With practice, you could become more skilled.

In the *Grimoire* (pp. 36-37), I gave some good starter exercises in "PK." I recommend you work with these until you develop some facility. In the back of this book, I have designed a couple of forms of "spinners," which are popular PK exercise devices. Copy these onto card stock, and cut them out. When you can make the spinner turn, stop, and spin in the opposite direction, you might want to try working with dice. Use only one die at first, and concentrate on throwing 6's. Keep a little chart of your scores, and see if you can improve them.

Another good exercise for PK is target tossing. All forms of throwing objects at a target are natural uses for PK, and practice will improve not only your physical skills, but also your psychic PK ability. Consider pitching, bowling, frizbee, basketball, darts, knife-throwing, archery, and even golf.

Shooting a hole-in-one on the golf course is one of the hardest feats in sports—given the size of the ball and hole, and the distance involved, it would seem to be completely impossible. Yet some professional golfers have managed to do this many times. Norman Manley of California holds the world record for the most hole-in-ones at 59! Manley shot his first hole-in-one in 1964, and aced four holes in 1979.

The longest straight-shot hole-in-one in golf history was hit by Robert Mitera on October 7, 1965 at the Miracle Hills Golf Club in Omaha, Nebraska. Mitera used his driver to ace the 10th hole from 444 yards! He couldn't even see the flag from where he teed off, and he only realized what he'd done when he arrived at the green and found his ball in the hole. This inconceivable achievement had to involve PK!

There are countless opportunities every day for you to practice your PK skills in target tossing—the easiest is just tossing wadded-up balls of scrap paper into the wastebasket from across the room. Focus on the target and direct your concentration as you visualize the wad going right in. "Use the Force," just like Luke Skywalker did to get his torpedo into the Death Star vent!

Pyrokinesis ("fire moving")

Starting or controlling fires and flames by force of mind alone. People who can do this are called *Pyrokinetics,* or Fire-starters.

The basic exercises for pyrokinesis use a single lit taper candle in a closed dark room—with no air currents coming from anywhere. Sit comfortably, with the candle on a table at least eight feet away from you, the flame at eye level. Breathe slowly and evenly through your nose, and follow the directions in the above lesson on "Meditation" to enter a light meditative state. Let the flame fill your entire consciousness, and let everything else fade away. Now, visualize the flame rising up higher, then lowering. Make it flare up, and then dim down. Make it flutter and dance. If you're having trouble affecting the flame just by staring at it, try pointing with your finger, projecting your aura out to touch and move the flame. When you get good at this, you can later apply these skills to "shaping" the flames in a campfire, or a fireplace.

Related to Pyrokinesis is "Smoke-Weaving." This is something I have gotten quite good at, and I use it all the time when sitting around a campfire, to keep the smoke out of our eyes! Ordinary stick incense in a nice holder provides the perfect medium for basic exercises in this skill. Use the same dark, still room as above, but now put the lit candle off to the side, behind a screen, so that you don't see the flame. Put your lit incense 8-10 feet directly in from of you, at eye level, so it is illuminated by the candle flame, and clearly visible. It is very important that there be no breeze or other movement of air in the room! As above, breathe slowly and evenly through your nostrils. Then hold up your hand, extending one or more fingers, and "shape" the smoke by projecting the auras of your fingers all the way into the smoke. Make it rise straight up in a thin column, then cut across it to disturb the pillar. Make it spiral, dance, and weave. Separate it into several threads. When you get good at this, you can then apply these skills to shaping, weaving, and dancing with the smoke of a campfire!

8. Telepathy tips
By Elizabeth Barrette (grey)

Here are some basic tips on developing telepathy:

1) Don't read out loud. If you pick up information from another person, wait for them to verbalize it before you start talking about it. They may not have told anyone, or may not realize it themselves.

2) Don't pry. It's rude to go digging in someone else's mind without permission.

3) Don't think out loud, unless you're purposely trying to contact someone. You don't need to broadcast your grocery list, and you definitely do not want to broadcast the rude thing that was the first to pop into your head but you decided not to say out loud.

4) Practice your basic skills of grounding, centering, and shielding. They will help keep your thoughts in your own head, and other people's thoughts out, when you're not actively using your talent.

5) As you practice with telepathy, you'll get better. At first you may have only short range, brief duration, and have a hard time picking out a specific thread of thought from the general babble. Learn to focus and you can hear or send thoughts farther away and more clearly.

6) Don't push yourself too hard. You can give yourself an overstrain headache that will last for hours. Practice for a few minutes at a time and gradually expand from there.

7) If you haven't already taken classes in Metapsychics and Dark Arts, check out the offerings there because the Grey School offers plenty of materials that you may find useful in developing and controlling telepathy.

8) Also check out materials for "The Gentle Art of Verbal Self-Defense" by Suzette Haden Elgin. The exercises for that are pretty much the same as for cultivating telepathy or empathy, and will also help you delicately back out of situations where your telepathy may get you into trouble.

As you master your talent, you'll learn how to apply it for everyone's benefit. Helpful things that can be done with telepathy include enhancing your grasp of a foreign language, finding lost people, sending or receiving messages from friends, communicating with discorporeal beings, and sensing conversational boobytraps so you can avoid them or defuse them.

Department V: Healing (blue)

Patchworking

Know me, see me
Find me, free me
From whatever things
May harm or hinder
Know me, see me
Find me here.

Touch me, feel me
Hold me, heal me
In your arms I can
Forget my sorrow
Touch me, feel me
Hold me near.

Shape me, bend me
Move me, mend me
Wield the power to
Make whole the broken
Shape me, bend me
Move me clear.

—Elizabeth Barrette

1. Introduction

ELCOME TO THE WORLD OF HEALING! This Department is color-coded "blue." Healing refers to all forms of magickal arts and practices devoted to curing diseases, relieving aches and pains, promoting tissue regeneration, restoring vitality and fertility, etc. Throughout history, healers have been the folk doctors, nurses and midwives—especially in rural and "primitive" communities without access to officially licensed physicians and pharmacists.

It is the mission of this Department to achieve a basic foundation in, and comprehension of, various Arts of Healing—one of the hallmarks of Wizardry.

The color of magick associated with this Department is blue for the Element of Water. Blue is the color of emotional work: love, peace, healing and protection. Considered the color of wisdom, thoughtfulness, and celestial regions, blue shares Friday and the planet Venus with green (as in aqua, or blue-green). Blue is identified with the signs of Virgo and Capricorn, the 5th (throat) chakra and the natural sciences. A feeling of youthfulness fills this color. Blue is an excellent hue for peacefulness and profound reflection. Use it also for healing, harmony, creativity, communication and resonance.

> The use of plants for medicines was commonplace throughout Europe during the Middle Ages. Although the early Christian Church discouraged this, preferring faith healing, the Christian monks preserved many Greek medical texts. Monasteries with their herb gardens became the local centres for herbal treatment. Herbal medicine was also practiced by midwives and wise women (i.e. witches) in their local communities. Fear and superstition were rife, and many magical properties were attached to herbal medicine, ultimately leading to the persecution and death of many wise women and herbal healers.
>
> —Gerry M. Thompson, *Atlas of the New Age*

For the rest of this chapter, I cannot possibly improve upon the following lessons by Grey School Faculty members Fred Lamond and Susan Pesznecker (Moonwriter), so here they are:

2. History and Symbols of Healing

By Fred Lamond (blue) and Moonwriter (indigo)

When health "fails," we look for ways to heal or be healed. Healing practices may be roughly divided into two groups:

1. Physical healing: methods that involve actual physical methods or actions—such as herbs, medicines, gems, and massage.

2. Psychic healing: methods in which vital energy is made to flow from one place to another—such as pranic healing, chakra healing, and Reiki.

Healing probably began with the simplest of folk medicine, a combination of magickal and hands-on practices that likely included herbals medicines, poultices, chanting, and the like. For Stone Age humans, one of the most critical leaps was from being a migratory, food-gathering (hunting) community to becoming a permanently-located, food-producing (agricultural) community. Neolithic humans quickly became expert farmers, cultivating hundreds of different plants, including many with primary medicinal qualities. For these ancient peoples, medicine and magic were likely indistinguishable, with herbs seen as having both mysterious and medicinal properties.

The written record of herbalism dates back to at least 3000 B.C.E., with the Sumerians recording the medicinal use of such common plants as laurel, caraway and thyme. Herbalism was a common part of their early rituals and rites up until the time of the Egyptians (2500 B.C.E.), when "rational" medicine began to hold sway over the arcane.

Some of the earliest formal approaches to medicine occurred in India and China. Medicine here relied on elemental "principles" and on ideas of balance within the body. In the fifth century, the *Ayurveda*—a basic Hindu medical encyclopedia—was compiled.

Chinese medicine is an ancient tradition with roots in Shamanic practices, the earliest Chinese practitioners choosing herbs primarily for their ability to banish evil spirits. The first known Chinese herbal dates from about 2700 B.C.E. and lists 365 medicinal plants and applications. Chinese herbalists used their senses and perceptions to diagnose "imbalance," with illness seen as a disharmony or dysynchrony within the whole person. Treatment was aimed at restoring balance by enabling and supporting the body's self-healing mechanisms.

There were few groundbreaking medical advances in ancient Greece, but the Greeks were known for their study of human anatomy as an investigative science. They are also known for the Hippocratic method, which based healing on the systematic observation of the patient. Hippocrates, widely called the father of modern medicine, classified all herbs by fundamental qualities: hot, cold, dry or damp. He advocated a combination of simple herbal medicines, fresh air, rest and proper diet to maintain health.

The Greeks and Romans described herbs according to their elemental energies (Earth, Air, Fire and Water) and their flavors (spicy, bitter, sweet, sour, salty and bland), theories that were also used by their Indian and Chinese contemporaries.

The Roman Empire is known for its attention to health and health maintenance, and for establishing the first modern hospitals. Galen, the famous Roman physician, believed that the body was composed of four humours: blood, phlegm, black bile, and yellow bile. He made early connections between physical health and the measurement of vital signs such as the pulse and respiration.

The Middle Ages (roughly 400-1500 C.E. and usually defined as the period between Greco-Roman culture and the Renaissance) was a dark time for medicine. There was little understanding of how the body actually worked, and living conditions for many—par-

ticularly within cities—were crowded and unsanitary. This was the time of the great plagues, which were directly related to overcrowding, poor sanitation, and the presence of vermin.

During the Middle Ages, the Church discouraged the practice of medicine and herbalism, seeing both as substitutes for or imitations of Christ's omnipotence. Eventually the Church made a more direct effort to suppress these ancient traditions. Fortunately, the crafts were preserved in handwritten manuscripts and via memorized knowledge, passed down through the centuries from teacher to apprentice—often in secrecy.

Known as centers of medieval scholarship, monasteries also became centers of herbal practices and hand-transcription of herbal manuscripts. The monks kept herbs in storerooms called "officinae," giving rise to the Latin *offinalis* suffix that names many herbs today. The same monasteries also became famous for maintaining robust, varietal herb gardens, with medicinal herbs grown among conventional food crops. Monasteries evolved into centers of medical knowledge, their gardens, storerooms and texts providing the raw materials for the sciences of herbalism and botany.

While both men and women practiced herbalism in the Middle Ages, it was mostly men—monks or scholars—who wrote and compiled the enduring works. Women had little access to formal education, but tended to spend more time in actual practice, using herbalism on a daily basis to tend to the needs of family and neighbors. Through these mechanisms, folk medicine thrived, supporting herbal practices that ranged from scientific to "heathen." Among the heathen were the prototypical "wise-women" who furnished generations-old secret herbal remedies along with arcane spells and enchantments. These women became a focus of much of the witch hysteria of the times, and herbalism was increasingly linked to Pagan and Christian superstition, to the detriment of both.

The eleventh century saw the blossoming of medical schools throughout Europe, usually teaching Hippocrates' or Galen's systems. The most famous school was at Salerno—also the location of famous spas and health resorts—and followed Hippocrates' disciplines of diet, exercise, fresh air and judicious use of herbs.

With the Renaissance, the science of medicine began to take huge leaps forward. During this period, political independence from the Church and a renewed interest in the classics led to a blossoming of scientific and medical advances that remains unparalleled in human history. Many of the great medicinal herbals were written, compiled and printed during this time. Andreas Vesalius fine-polished the science of human anatomy. William Harvey explained the circulatory system.

The 16th and 17th centuries saw a public loss of respect for herbalism. The activity of notable physician-scientists, the creation of new medical techniques, and the development of chemistry and other physical sciences led to the dominance of chemical medicine as the preferred system of the 1800s and 1900s. Philippus Paracelsus, a Swiss physician, exemplified this shift. As much alchemist as medical practitioner, Paracelsus renounced Galen's theories as antiquated and advocated for the use of alchemy in medical treatment, including use of copper, sulfur, arsenic, mercury and iron. His work took the spotlight away from herbal practices, and also left many patients with heavy metal-based organic toxicity.

In the 18th century, Edward Jenner suggested the possibility of vaccines. In the 19th, x-rays and antisepsis appeared. With the advent of the twentieth century, plants still provided most materials for medicine, fabric dyes and perfume. Folk medicine continued to both support and rely on the local herbalist. Homeopathy began, grounded in the Hippocratic idea of eliminating disease by assisting the body's own recuperative powers. Homeopathy claimed that microscopic doses of herbal drugs could stimulate the body's self-healing.

Medicine in the modern era has benefited from advances in the sciences of biology, chemistry, and physics. New advances in medical imaging have improved both diagnosis and treatment, as have an increased armament of medications. The science of gene therapy promises to one day correct genetic-based diseases that were previously thought incurable.

Today, a resurgence of interest in natural healing and folk traditions has led to renewed interest in the use of all types of magickal medicine. Many people are making careers in herbalism, naturopathy or other practices that are primarily based on maintaining a healthful lifestyle, rather than treating illness.

Symbols of Healing

The *caduceus* is a mythic symbol of medicine and healing. Mercury's winged staff is the basis of the symbol, indicating harmony from strife. The wings themselves show transcendence. Two snakes—the twins of good and evil—twine around the staff.

You probably know the universal symbol of first aid: the *Red Cross*. Sometimes it's white or green, but the chunky cross is always associated with first aid or safety.

In our modern times, a *bright blue street sign* with a superimposed "H" points the way to the closest hospital.

In the Grey School of Wizardry, an important symbol of healing is *the color blue,* consistent with the healing blue light that flows to us from the Universe. Students who take on healing as an academic major or minor (a decision made in the Second Year) may adopt blue-colored regalia. They may also put together a healer's kit, containing not only simple first aid supplies, but also the magickal materials associated with their particular healing practices.

3. Physical Healing
By Fred Lamond (blue) and Moonwriter (indigo)

Here are a few of the most important methods of natural healing of physical conditions and injuries.

Herbal Healing

Herbalism is the lore and art of understanding and using the magickal, medicinal and other properties of plants—especially herbs, or, in Old English, *worts*. These are aromatic plants whose stems don't produce woody tissue, and that generally die back at the end of each growing season. Herbology, the study of herbs and their uses, is thus often known in the Wizarding world by its ancient name of *Wortcunning*.

Herbal healing makes use of herbs for their medicinal properties. See the following Chapter for a detailed exploration of Wortcunning.

Gem (and Crystal) Therapy

In this type of healing, different gemstones and crystals—each with their own magickal properties and correspondences—are used to support health or healing. Many are believed to affect the energy and "vibrations" within the human body.

In most cases, the most important aspects of the gem or crystal include color and clarity. The color of the stone is usually matched to the correspondence of the afflicted area. Clarity or opacity may be selected to impart different qualities.

Here are some examples of gems commonly used in healing, and their properties:

Amethyst (violet): eases insomnia, protects against illness (when used in an amulet).
Bloodstone (red and green): halts bleedings, eases bruising and trauma.
Carnelian (orange): eases or protects against skin disorders.
Crystal quartz (clear): relieves pain, headache, and fever; supports all types of healing works.
Garnet (red): regulates the heart, treats inflammation.
Lapis Lazuli (blue): Soothes, calms, supports healing rituals.

Malachite (indigo): relaxes the nervous system, promotes sleep and tranquility.

Sapphire (blue): heals the eyes, treats fever.

In one method of gem healing, the stone is placed on the afflicted area for at least one hour daily, and then is worn as a ring, pendant, charm, or amulet in order to affect the vibrations of the patient's body and/or to suffuse the wearer's body with the qualities of the gem.

Gems may also be used during meditation or massage. In a popular type of massage, heavy, heated stones are allowed to rest on the major muscle groups; this is followed by massage.

Aromatherapy

In aromatherapy, herbs, incenses, candles, and essential oils are used for their scents. The scents have the ability to alter the patient's mood, and can influence the level of consciousness.

Aromatherapy may have direct effects, too. For instance, if the patient has a cold, taking a hot bath or shower to which 2-3 drops of juniper or rosemary essential oil has been added can help sinuses and ease breathing.

Aromatherapy is often used with other types of healing. For example, the burning of lavender scents during pranic healing can relax patients, making them more receptive to the healing efforts.

Here are some scent examples:

Bergamot: refreshes, uplifts, soothes grief and depression, eases anxiety and stress.

Geranium: cheers, uplifts, supports strong energies.

Juniper: deeply purifies, cleanses, protects, clears the mind.

Lavender: relaxing, calms, cleanses, purifies. If you only have one essential oil, this is the one to have.

Lemon: stimulating, refreshes, cheers, cleanses, eases stress.

Orange: uplifts, cheers, balances, revitalizes, eases insomnia.

Rosemary: Protects, purifies, refreshes, stimulates the mind.

Sandalwood: relaxes, purifies, balances emotions.

Incense is a "hardened" version of an essential oil. Incense comes in stick and cones. To use, it is placed in a fireproof container and lit. Essential oils may also be used to scent candles.

> *Important safety note: Never leave burning incense or candles unattended, and never light them when you're in a situation where you might fall asleep with them still burning.*

Dietary Therapy

Many illnesses may be treated or improved by certain types of diets. For example, someone with gall bladder problems will feel remarkably better if they eat a low fat diet, while someone with diabetes will do well to avoid large quantities of refined sugar. A person who is overweight or has abnormal cholesterol levels may benefit from a reduced calorie diet.

People experiencing gastrointestinal upset will feel best if they temporarily shift to a simple foods, particularly avoiding those that are high in fat, high in acid (e.g., orange juice), or high in roughage (fruits, vegetables, grains).

Fasting is another type of dietary therapy. During a fast, the intake of food and fluids may be modified in order to detoxify the body, affect weight loss, or to accomplish other goals.

> *Note: Fasting can be dangerous, and should only be used under the guidance of a skilled, experienced healer.*

Many people adhere to diets that restrict certain types of food. A common example is vegetarianism. Consider these definitions:

Vegetarian diet: a diet composed primarily or wholly of vegetables, fruits, grains, nuts, and seeds. Some vegetarians also eat fish.

Lacto-ovo vegetarian diet: same as vegetarian, but also includes eggs and dairy products.

Vegan diet: a strict form of vegetarianism in which only plant products are eaten. Some vegans also refuse to use animal products (e.g., fur, leather) in their daily lives.

4. Eastern, Western, & Alternative Medicine

By Fred Lamond (blue) and Moonwriter (indigo)

Traditional **Western Medicine**—what we think of involving physicians, hospitals, etc.—is a kind of physical healing, with reliance on medications and surgical treatments. Western medicine is often referred to as *allopathic*. Modern medicine can be miraculous and lifesaving, and its use should never be discounted. In fact, there are many times when Western medicine is necessary in order to save lives.

Magickal healing methods can always supplement Western medicine, and can often treat problems that don't respond well to traditional approaches.

For example:

Patients being treated for tension headaches may need analgesics; however, they may also benefit from guided relaxation, aromatherapy, and other magickal healing techniques.

Patients receiving antibiotics for acute sinusitis

may also benefit from hot, steamy baths to which a few drops of juniper or rosemary essential oil has been added. They may also be improved with healing rituals, as well as infusions of sage.

The term **Eastern Medicine** is often used to described alternative (non-western) medical practices. Some well-known Eastern or alternative practices include:

Chiropractice: a system of therapy in which disease is considered to result from abnormal functioning of the nervous system. Treatments involve manipulation of the spinal cord and other body structures.

Homeopathy: a system of treating disease that is based on administering minute doses of a drug or substance that, if given in massive doses, would produce symptoms or would produce the disease itself. The theory behind homeopathy is that exposing the body to minute amounts of a substance increases its recognition of that substance and helps it mount a suitable defense.

Midwifery: midwives are practitioners—usually women—who are trained to care for women before, during, and after childbirth.

Naturopathy: a system of therapy that relies on natural remedies—such as sunlight, diet adjustments, and massage—to treat illness.

Osteopathy: a medical system based on the idea that musculoskeletal disturbances affect other body parts. Osteopathy incorporates many western medical approaches, but also relies heavily on manipulation as a means of restoring the proper musculoskeletal structures.

Traditional Chinese medicine (TCM): includes Chinese herbalism, acupuncture, acupressure, moxibustion, and other techniques.

Acupuncture uses the placement of fine needles along invisible energy meridians that run through the body. The needles work to balance and sometimes redirect the energy flow.

Acupressure is similar to acupuncture, but uses pressure (usually with fingers or thumbs) instead of needles.

In moxibustion, herbs or other substances are burned in a special holder on the skin to produce desired effects.

5. Psychic Healing: A Review of Various Techniques

By Fred Lamond (blue) and Moonwriter (indigo)

In psychic healing, the healer draws vital energy from the Universe and directs its flow into the body of the patient. The healer's Will and intention are critical to the success of psychic healing. At all times you must believe that your patient will improve. You must actually *see* them improving hour by hour, day by day.

Your personal strength and condition are also critical to psychic healing. Without correctly grounding, centering, and channeling the psychic energy, you may become exhausted or ill yourself.

Chakra Healing

The *chakra* system describes a set of seven energy centers within the human body. In order for a person to be in good health, all seven chakras must be functioning properly.

The student of *chakra healing* begins by learning how the system exists and works, including concepts of chakra imbalance and how to both assess and balance one's own chakra energies. The student then learns to interpret excesses, deficits, and balances in one or more chakras, how to deepen one's connection to them, and how to heal and balance the chakras, thus improving health.

Auric Healing

Each person has an *aura*—a bioelectric field that emanates from and surrounds them.

In *auric healing,* the healer changes a patient's condition by surrounding the patient with a specifically chosen colored light that repairs and enriches the patient's aura. In this way, auric healing is also a type of *chromatotherapy.*

Color Healing (Chromatotherapy)

Chromatotherapy is "therapy with colors." Chromatotherapy is all about color and light—after all, colors only exist because of light. Chromatotherapy is based on the idea that each color vibrates at a certain resonance, and thus has a specific biological and psychological effect on living organisms (human, animal, and plant).

The chromatotherapist treats patients by bathing them in colored light, which is pulled down from the heavens. Each color has specific associations. For example, emotional upsets benefit from indigo-colored light, green is felt to be calming, etc.

In another type of chromatotherapy, colored charms or elixirs may also be used to assist in healing.

Reiki

Reiki (RAY-kee) is a Japanese form of healing that is becoming increasingly popular worldwide. It involves the transfer and balance of energy between practitioner and patient to enhance the body's natural ability to heal itself.

Reiki is a holistic, natural, energy healing system that touches on all levels: body, mind, and spirit. Reiki also incorporates elements of other alternative healing practices such as spiritual healing, auras, crystals, chakra balancing, meditation, aromatherapy, naturopathy, and homeopathy.

In most cases, Reiki does not involve actual touching. The practitioner holds his or her hands a few inches or farther away from the patient's body and manipulates the energy field from there.

Pranic Healing

In *pranic healing,* the healer sends energy—*prana*—from her own body to the body of the patient. The goal is to stimulate the affected parts of the body, restoring energy and normal functioning. This type of healing usually involves physical contact, i.e., laying on of hands, therapeutic massage, etc.

In order to avoid depleting one's own energy, the energy sent from healer to patient is usually channeled from a universal source, or is received in response to calling on a matron or patron deity.

Healing at a Distance

Also called "absent healing," this involves sending healing energy to a patient who is not physically present, or who is at a distance. The principles are similar to those for pranic healing, with the energy typically in the form of white light.

6. Foot Massage & Reflexology

By Oberon (grey)

"Rub her feet." –Robert Heinlein,
The Notebooks of Lazarus Long

One of the easiest and most rewarding healing experiences you can give someone is a simple footbath and massage.

The healing art of foot massage is called *Foot Reflexology.* This is a kind of pressure therapy based on the idea that "meridians," or paths of energy, like Ley lines on the Earth, run from the tops of our heads to the bottoms of our feet, encompassing all vital systems along the way. Thus the soles of the feet comprise a kind of microcosm of the entire body, with different areas corresponding to all the organs and glands of the head and torso. Massaging these areas on the feet relieves stress and pain in the corresponding areas of the body, promoting natural balance and revitalization.

Modern Reflexology originated in the 1890s research of Sir Henry Head of London, who coined the term. William Fitzgerald, MD, introduced Reflexology into the US in 1913 as *zone therapy*. He divided the body into ten vertical zones and taught that "bioelectrical energy" flowed through these zones to "reflex points" in the hands and feet. Eunice Ingham, founder of the International Institute of Reflexology, further developed Reflexology in the 1930s-40s by concentrating on the feet. She mapped out the anatomy of the body on the feet to create the first foot charts.

Reflexologists believe that their technique can alleviate a wide variety of stress-related problems, including headaches, premenstrual syndrome, digestive disorders, poor circulation, hypertension, asthma, and chronic pain from arthritis and sciatica.

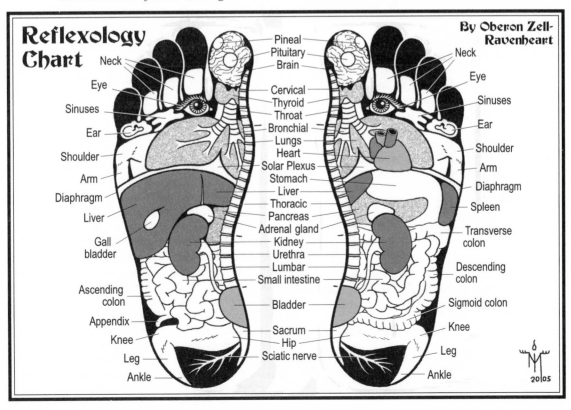

Reflexology Chart — By Oberon Zell-Ravenheart

Left foot labels: Neck, Eye, Sinuses, Ear, Shoulder, Arm, Diaphragm, Liver, Gall bladder, Ascending colon, Appendix, Knee, Leg, Ankle

Center labels: Pineal, Pituitary, Brain, Cervical, Thyroid, Throat, Bronchial, Lungs, Heart, Solar Plexus, Stomach, Liver, Thoracic, Pancreas, Adrenal gland, Kidney, Urethra, Lumbar, Small intestine, Bladder, Sacrum, Hip, Sciatic nerve

Right foot labels: Neck, Eye, Sinuses, Ear, Shoulder, Arm, Diaphragm, Spleen, Transverse colon, Descending colon, Sigmoid colon, Knee, Leg, Ankle

20|05

Have the patient sit in a comfortable chair, take off his or her shoes and socks, and begin with a gentle and loving foot-wash, using a basin of soapy water and a fluffy towel to dry. Then, one foot at a time, using mainly your thumbs, press and rub thoroughly each of the areas shown on these Reflexology charts.

If the patient complains of pain or says "ouch," check the diagram to determine what body part corresponds to the sore area. This could indicate a problem in that organ or a potential for one.

Continue your massage over the tops of the feet, and in the hollows behind the ankles. Take your time, judging by the moans of pleasure from your patient. I guarantee your patients will love you for this!

There's a great interactive foot chart by Barbara & Kevin Kunz at: http://uk.dk.com/static/cs/uk/11/features/reflexology/extract.html

7. Self Healing

By Fred Lamond (blue) and Moonwriter (indigo)

Personal Health Practices

An effective Wizard is a healthy Wizard! Working magick means working with energy, and in order to do this well, you need a body that is strong, fit, and functioning optimally.

Health is not simply the absence of disease. Health is a dynamic, positive state in which the body, mind, and soul are functioning optimally, infusing their owner with a profound sense of well-being and vitality.

The following are recommendations for fostering good health:

1. Maintain normal weight.
2. Eat a diet that includes a wide variety of fresh fruits and vegetables, whole grains, and protein sources such as meat, fish, eggs, dairy, legumes, and soy.
3. Avoid foods that are processed or deep-fried. These tend to be high in sodium, may contain preservatives, and are often loaded with the very dangerous "trans-fatty acids." (Note: Learn to be a label reader! If you find the words "partially hydrogenated" on the ingredient label, trans fats are present and the food should be avoided.)
4. Drink lots of water every day.
5. Sleep at least 7-8 hours every night.
6. Exercise for at least one-half hour on most days of the week.
7. Have a hobby! Research has shown that having enjoyable pastimes is a terrific stress reducer.
8. Spend time with people you care about. (Another stress reducer!)
9. Spend time every day meditating or engaging in spiritual practices.
10. See your dentist and physician as needed for routine medical care and immunizations. Follow their recommendations!

Preventative and Curative Rituals

Before attempting to heal anyone else, you should know how to keep healthy yourself, and to heal yourself when the need arises. The following is a self-healing ritual that you should use daily as a means of strengthening yourself, maintaining health, and prevent illness.

Take at least 30 minutes daily—either when waking up, just before going to sleep, or both—to concentrate on your own body and each of its constituent parts: feet, knees, legs, base, stomach, digestive organs, lungs, heart, etc.

Either lay down in a quiet room or sit, relaxed, in a comfortable chair. Ground, center, (##Oberon—refer them to discussion elsewhere of core energy techniques) and take a few moments to slip into a meditative state. Then, contemplate the parts of your body, moving from head to toe.

Concentrate on each individual part and talk to it as if it were a separate person. Tell it how you appreciate its contribution to your well-being and enjoyment of life, and how you love it. Then be aware of the feelings or sensations relayed back by that part of your body, and be prepared to respond.

If you get a message of illness, injury, or pain from your body, concentrate longer on that part. Put as much energy as you can summon into it, and listen to what it says in return.

When you are ill, you may not always be able to summon from within yourself the energy to heal the part of the body that is ill, and your whole energy pattern may itself be infected by the illness. So when doing curative healing, always ask the help of the loving, healing power of the Universe under whichever name you are accustomed to call it. Imagine an intense ray of blue light coming from the Universe and enveloping you, and then direct a major part of that blue light to the affected part of your body. Repeat this procedure at least twice a day for 30 minutes each time until you are well again. At the same time, use creative visualization: imagine the energy as your own avenging knight, hunting down and killing the marauding germs! This type of guided visualization has been studied with formal research methods and shown to improve the effectiveness of just about every kind of treatment.

If you are sick in bed (or on the couch!) you will have the time to do the curative rituals more frequently. Unlike many allopathic drugs, the blue healing light of the Universe does not have any undesirable side effects, so you need not be afraid of taking too much of it.

> *Note: Try recording your own vital signs (VS) before and after your healing ritual. Do this on at least several occasions. Not only will this help you to become skilled with the practice, but it may also show changes in your own VS that occur as a result of your ritual.*

After the ritual is completed, ground, center, and then sit or stand up slowly.

Examples

Let's imagine that you conduct a self-healing ritual and concentrate on your feet. If they respond with an aching feeling, this may mean that your shoes are too tight or do not give support in the right places, or it may mean that you are spending too much time on your feet.

You may respond by engaging in a meditative ritual that sends healing energy to your feet. However, it also makes sense to take direct supportive measures, like buying some better shoes and trying not to stand for such long periods.

If your stomach feels heavy and discontented, you may have been eating too much, or may have eaten the wrong sort of food. If so, sending healing light or energy to your stomach may help to relieve the symptoms. A cup of infused ginger or peppermint may relieve stomach upset. You would also want to modify your diet so as to avoid further upset.

If you undertake appropriate remedial action, you should feel improved within a day or two. If your symptoms continue, consider seeing your medical practitioner.

This type of preventative ritual should become an easy addition to your daily practices of relaxation and meditation.

8. Healing Others
By Fred Lamond (blue)
and Moonwriter (indigo)

When you have mastered self-healing techniques and are able to keep yourself healthy and fit most of the time, you can begin learning to heal others.

Healing Others in Person

> **IMPORTANT:** *Unless your patient is unconscious and in a state of emergency, you should always ask permission before you do a healing.* **If your patient is unconscious or in a state of emergency, your first action should be to activate the 9-1-1 system and to get emergency medical care to the patient's side as quickly as possible!**

If the patient agrees, then ask, "Can you visualize yourself as healed in body, mind and spirit?" By involving the patient, you activate his own self-healing powers and make him part of his own healing. By adding a patient's intention to yours, the healing will be much more powerful. .

Before you begin, records your patient's vital signs

(VS), as well as observations about his condition.

Now, ground and center. Then, draw at least seven long, slow breaths of vital force from the Universe into your own body. While you do this, remind yourself that the healing energy of the Universe moves to the patient *through* you; it does not come *from* you.

Now, call silently upon the Universe to help you. (Some people may also choose to call on a patron or matron deity that is meaningful to them or that corresponds to their magickal traditions.) When healing others, the Universe helps you act as a channel for the energy it sends you. If you were to try healing with your own energy alone, you might rapidly become exhausted, and you might fall prey to the same symptoms as your patient.

When healing another, open yourself up to the healing energy of the Universe and act as a channel to its blue healing light. Use the energy to envelop your patient in a bubble of blue light, directing most of the light at the part of their body that is sick or in pain. You may also choose to direct the light at a specific location or a specific chakra point in the patient's body. While doing this, direct every force of your conscious Will at the patient's healing, visualizing your success as you do so.

Continue this for as long as you can, or until the patient is feeling noticeably better. For best results, keep the ritual going for as long as thirty minutes. However— particularly since you are a beginning practitioner—you must be careful not to exhaust yourself. If you start to feel tired, it is time to stop.

When you finish, be sure to ground and center. Then, pause for a moment of self-meditation before you leave your place of healing and return to the material plane.

Record post-ritual VS and observations.

If possible, teach your patients to do their own self-healing ritual. Point to or touch each part of the body in turn and tell them to will as much of their energy into that part and talk to it as if it were a separate person. Tell them to practice self-healing at least twice a day on their own, even when you are not there. It cannot hurt, and even for an untrained patient, it may do a lot of good. You may also be able to help them use visualization.

Healing Others at a Distance

To heal another person at a distance you need to establish a psychic link. If you love the other person or know him or her very well, the link will already be there. Otherwise, ask him or her to send you a photograph and a lock of hair. If you are artistic, you might also draw or paint the person on the basis of his/her photograph, or make a clay figure that you will then name with the person's name.

Having established the psychic link, you are prepared to begin. In a quite space, position the link-objects on an altar space front of you. Ground, center, open yourself to the Universe's healing energy, and envelop the link-objects (the mental or physical images of your patient) with the Universe's healing blue light, concentrating especially on those parts that are sick. If after a while you feel spontaneously that the Universe's blue healing light is enveloping your image of the patient directly without passing through you, welcome this development and let it happen.

You may at some time be part of a healing group, where all participants collectively visualize the Universe's healing energy bathing the patient. If so, you will all want to consult with each other before the healing ritual begins, so that you all visualize the healing energy at the same time and in the same way.

Once you have completed the collective healing spell do not discuss it, even with other members of the healing group. Talk dispels the healing energy and can make it ineffective. Only when the healing is complete and your patient is again healthy and fit should you feel free to discuss with others what you did so as to learn lessons for the future. This tradition of remaining silent after doing magickal work is a common tenet of all kinds of magick, not just healing.

9. Wizardly First-Aid & Safety

By Moonwriter (indigo)

We live in a wonderful world, full of adventure. Whether you're exploring the woods, whittling a mag-

ick wand, lighting candles for a ritual, hiking on a sunny day, or taking a dip in the local swimming hole, it's important to always think about safety.

By learning the basics of personal safety and first aid, you will not only keep yourself safe but will also be able to protect those around you, or to come to the aid of those in need.

Two great resources for personal safety and general first aid are the *Boy Scout Handbook* and *Boy Scout Fieldbook*.

Other excellent resources:

The American Red Cross First Aid and Safety Handbook by American Red Cross and Kathleen A. Handal

FastAct Pocket First Aid Guide, by Kurt Duffens and Brad Rickey

First Aid & Safety for Dummies, by Charles B. Inlander, Janet Worsley Norwood, People's Medical Society

Most first aid is completely logical—even if you can't remember exactly what to do in a situation, you can usually figure it out if you calm yourself and think. For example:

If someone is bleeding, the bleeding must be stopped.
If someone has stopped breathing, breathing must be restarted.
If a wound is present, it must be cleaned and protected.
If a person is too cold, he needs to be warmed up.
If a person is too hot, she needs to be cooled down.
If the stomach is upset, the person should eat lightly, if at all.
If bones, joints, or muscles are injured, they should be rested, and movement prevented.

IMPORTANT: *To protect yourself from diseases passed via the blood (most notably HIV-AIDS and some forms of hepatitis), put on latex or rubber gloves before handling bleeding wounds.*

Before applying an ointment or giving any type of medication or herbal preparation, you should always ask patients if they are allergic to the substance. If they are, don't use it!

Medications and herbal preparations must not be given to children under age 18 without first getting their parent's permission.

Physical assessment; vital signs

An important part of your first aid training is the assessment of the injured or ill patient. The term "vital signs" describes a patient's heart rate, breathing rate, temperature, and blood pressure. To take vital signs, you will need a wristwatch (with a second hand) and a thermometer.

Heart rate, or pulse: To take a patient's heart rate, feel the pulse at the wrist, pressing lightly just below the base of the thumb. Count the beats for 15

seconds and multiply it by 4. This will give you the heart rate in beats per minute (bpm).

The healthy adult human has a heart rate of 50-100 bpm. Children's heart rates may be a little faster, and baby's hearts are faster still. Athletes in superior condition may have heart rates in the 40s and 50s—their hearts are in such strong condition that they pump more blood with each beat, and thus work more efficiently.

In some cases, you may have trouble finding a radial (wrist) pulse. In this case, you may need to check a carotid pulse. The carotid artery and pulse are located in the neck, just below the angle of the jawbone. When you find it, press very gently—you don't want to press so hard as to interfere with the blood flow. As with a wrist pulse, count for 15 seconds and multiply by 4.

When checking the heart rate, also note whether the rate is regular or whether there are irregularities.

Respiration: To find the respiratory rate, simply ask the patient to breathe normally, and then watch the rise and fall of their chest. Count the number of breaths in 15 seconds and multiply by 4.

The normal human respiratory rate is 14-20 respirations/minute. Young children and babies breathe more quickly.

You should also note whether respirations are easy or labored, whether the patient coughs, and whether you hear any unusual noises (wheezing, gurgling, etc.).

Temperature: The process here will depend on what kind of thermometer you have available. If it is electronic, follow the directions that come with it.

For adults and older children, a plain mercury thermometer will work to check temperature. Have someone who knows how show you how to "shake down" the thermometer. The patient should hold it under their tongue for 3-4 minutes. After using, shake it down again, then wash in COOL (not hot!) water and dry well.

Normal human temperature (by mouth) is between 97.8-98.6 degrees Fahrenheit. Anything over 100 degrees is considered to be a fever.

When you take vital signs or make observations about your patients, note the time and write everything down. Don't trust your memory! Your notes may be invaluable in helping the patient.

The scary ones: Emergencies

The following emergencies are beyond the scope of what you'll learn here. But you need to at least be aware of them, for your correct actions could save someone's life.

In all cases, the most important aspect of life-threatening emergency care is to call 9-1-1 and bring professional help to the patient. If you must deal with a life-threatening crisis and cannot make the 9-1-1 call yourself, ask someone else to do it immediately.

Stopped breathing

Symptoms: Patient is not breathing. Skin may be pale or bluish-gray. Pulse may be slow, weak, or absent.

Treatment: CALL 9-1-1. If the victim appears to be choking, give the Heimlich maneuver. Administer rescue breathing. Treat for shock.

Arterial bleeding

Symptoms: Bright red blood pumps or spurts from a wound. Patient may be pale and lose consciousness. Pulse may be rapid.

Treatment: CALL 911! Apply direct pressure to the wound. If another rescuer is available, ask them to apply pressure over the closest pressure point between the injury and the heart. Elevate bleeding part above level of heart. Treat for shock.

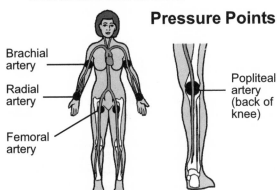

Pressure Points

Brachial artery

Radial artery

Femoral artery

Popliteal artery (back of knee)

Heart attack (also called myocardial infarction, or MI)

Symptoms: Patient complains of pain or pressure in chest, left shoulder, or left arm. May have trouble breathing and break out in a sweat. Respirations and pulse may be rapid. Pulse may be irregular.

Treatment: CALL 9-1-1. Loosen tight clothing. Assist the patient to relax in a semi-reclining position. Keep them quiet. It patient is alert and able to swallow, give 1 aspirin tablet. Treat for shock.

Anaphylactic allergic reaction

Symptoms: Patient experiences sudden massive signs of allergic reaction—itching, swelling, trouble breathing, wheezing, enlargement of lips, development of blotches or hives, etc. Respirations and pulse may be elevated. Temperature may also be elevated.

Treatment: CALL 9-1-1. If patient has an adrenaline syringe/kit, use it. If patient is alert and can swallow, give 50 mg. of Benadryl by mouth. Try to keep patient calm. If patient has trouble breathing, help him to a semi-sitting position. Treat for shock.

Stroke (also called cerebrovascular accident, or CVA)
Symptoms: Patient complains of sudden dizziness severe headache, difficulty speaking or problems moving any part of the body.
Treatment: CALL 9-1-1. Try to keep patient calm. If patient has trouble breathing, help him to a semi-sitting position. Treat for shock.

Shock

Symptoms: Any serious injury or crisis may be accompanied by shock. Patient is pale and sweaty, may be nauseated, and may faint. Respirations may be slow and shallow. Pulse may be rapid and thready.
Treatment: CALL 9-1-1. Lay patient down and elevate legs. *(Note: Persons having trouble breathing should be placed in a reclining position, with legs elevated.)* Keep patient warm.

Simple cuts, abrasions, and bruises

In case of active bleeding, apply pressure until the bleeding stops. Raising the affected part above heart level will also help slow the bleeding, as will using pressure points. When bleeding stops, wash the wound gently with soap and water, then rinse well. Apply antibacterial ointment and a sterile dressing (gauze held in place with tape) or a band-aid.

> Note: "Sterile" means free from germs. Be careful not to touch the sterile part of a dressing or band-aid.

For bruises, apply ice to the bruised area for 20 minutes out of every two hours. After two days, stop the ice and switch to heat applications, this time for 20 minutes out of every 2-3 hours.

Infusions of yarrow and calendula are useful for washing minor wounds. To make the infusion, boil 2 cups of fresh water. Remove from the heat. Add 1-2 teaspoons of crushed dried yarrow or calendula flowers (or 2-4 teaspoons of the chopped fresh flowers). Steep for 10 minutes. Strain, and use the infused liquid to wash the wound. *Make sure the infusion has cooled somewhat before using!*

Stomach upset

If you think that you or someone else has eaten something poisonous, call Poison Control. The US National Poison Control Center may be reached at 1-800-222-1222.

For a mild stomach upset, one or two calcium-based antacids may relieve the symptoms.

Ginger or mint infusions (tea) may also soothe a disgruntled stomach. To make the infusion, boil 2 cups of fresh water. Remove from the heat. For peppermint tea, add 2-3 teaspoons of crushed dried peppermint leaves or 2-4 teaspoons of the chopped fresh leaves; for ginger tea, thinly slice a 1 inch section of fresh ginger root and add to the boiled water. Steep for 5-6 minutes. Strain, and offer a cup of the infusion to the patient. The tea may be sweetened with honey if desired.

If vomiting begins, do not give the patient anything (including water!) by mouth until the vomiting has stopped. At that point, offer tiny bits of ice or sips of plain water. If the patient tolerates that, gradually increase the amount of water, then add broth, soda pop, sweetened herbal tea, or diluted apple juice. Gradually increase the diet, offering grains, fruits, and vegetables LAST. If the patient begins to vomit again, start over at the beginning.

If patient has an upset stomach and complains of stomach or abdominal pain—especially if he or she has a fever—a doctor should be called immediately to be sure it isn't appendicitis.

Burns and sunburn

Burns caused by heat are classified as being first, second, or third degree.

In first-degree burns, the skin is red and unbroken. It may be painful. Sunburn is a good example of a first-degree burn.

In second-degree burns, the skin is red, blistered, and very painful.

In third-degree burns, the skin is broken and very damaged, often with pieces missing. It may look frankly charred, grayish-white, or reddened. Deep tissue and bone may be visible. There may or may not be pain.

Treatment:

For first- and second-degree burns, cool the skin with cold water or water gel burn dressings. Cover with a light sterile dressing. The first-degree burn may peel as it heals; at this stage, application of an unscented lotion may be soothing. Calendula salve is also useful in this situation (refer to an herbal resource for preparation instructions).

For second-degree burns, cover the blistered areas with a sterile dressing. Do not open the blisters! Keep the wounds dressed until they begin to heal, then leave open to the air. Offer ibuprofen or acetaminophen if needed for pain. If second-degree burns cover an area larger than a slice of bread, a physician should be called in.

For third-degree burns, cover the area with sterile bandages, treat for shock, and get the patient to an emergency room. Third-degree burns are a MEDICAL EMERGENCY.

Note: *The idea of applying butter to a heat burn is an Old Wives' Tale, and causes more harm than good.*

For chemical burns, flood the burned area with water. If irritation persists or there is a residual burn, call a doctor for advice. If the eyes are involved, keep the irrigations going continuously and call a doctor for advice.

Disorders of heat regulation: hyper- and hypothermia

"Thermia" is a word that refers to temperature. If you're hyperthermic, you have too much heat and are overheated. If you are hypothermic, you have too little heat and are too cold. Both conditions can be very dangerous if untreated.

Hyperthermia (heat exhaustion and heat stroke) and hypothermia can be prevented by dressing properly for the surroundings, and by avoiding extreme weather conditions.

People who are hypothermic may look confused, speak slowly, lose coordination, and stumble. They may be irritable or cranky. In extreme cases, they may lose consciousness and sink into a coma. Their respirations and pulse may slow, and their temperature may drop.

The fingers, toes, nose, and ears are susceptible to a cold weather injury known as frostbite. Frostbite means that the tissue has actually begun to freeze. Frostbitten tissue may look gray, bluish-white, or black.

Hypothermic victims should be taken to the emergency room immediately. If this is impossible, they should be taken into a warm room. Their cold clothing should be removed and replaced with warm clothing and blankets. They should be given warmed liquids to sip. They should be warmed slowly; if rewarmed too fast, they may go into shock.

Victims with frostbite must be taken to an emergency room immediately. The frostbitten areas should be covered lightly. Under no circumstances should they be rubbed or immersed in water! Both of these actions will increase the tissue destruction.

A person with heat exhaustion has a red, sweaty face, feels weak, and looks wobbly. They are dehydrated and may pass out. Victims of heat exhaustion should be taken to a cool place. As much clothing should be removed as possible, and the patient should be given cool water to sip. A fan may help, as will cool, wet cloths applied to armpits and groin (the same spots as the pressure points).

A severe type of hyperthermia is known as "heat stroke." In heat stroke, the body's cooling mechanisms fail and the body can no longer cool itself. The patient will have hot, dry, pale skin and will collapse. Their temperature will soar to 105 degrees or higher. They may quit breathing and their heart may stop. Heat stroke is a medical emergency. The patient must be cooled or they will die. The patient with heat stroke MUST be taken to an emergency room immediately.

Blisters

Wash and dry the area gently. Heat a needle or the very tip of your pocketknife in a flame briefly to sterilize, then use the sharp point to gently open one edge of blister (the blister's skin is dead, so this won't hurt). Apply antibiotic ointment and a sterile dressing or band-aid.

Sprains and strains

Sprains and strains occur when muscles, tendons, or ligaments are stretched or torn. A person with a strain or sprain will complain of severe pain and won't be able to bear weight or use the limb. There will be dramatic swelling and bruising. (My daughter had a severely sprained ankle once, and it looked like a blue cantaloupe!)

To prevent ankle and knee injuries in the outdoors, wear sturdy shoes or boots, watch where you're walking, and use a hiking stave. Use special care when crossing unstable or rocky slopes.

The patient with a sprain should quit using the injured limb. Treat with the R-I-C-E acronym:

R: Rest. Keep the patient from using the injured part. Immobilize the part if possible.
I: Ice. Apply ice packs to minimize bruising, 20 minutes every two hours.
C: Compression. Wrap an "ACE" bandage gently around the injured part, taking care to simply apply the wrap *without* stretching it.
E: Elevation. Keep the injured part above heart level.

Offer ibuprofen for pain. In severe cases, you may need to treat for shock. If swelling or pain is severe or if the injury isn't significantly better in two days, the patient should see a physician to rule out fracture.

Insect, spider, and tick bites

Become familiar with the venomous creatures in your area. For example, here in Oregon I have to watch out for the usual wasps, as well as scorpions, the diamondback rattlesnake, and black widow, recluse, and hobo spiders. Get into the habit of shaking out gloves, boots, and other outdoor items before putting them on, so that you don't inadvertently stuff your hand or foot into contact with a venomous critter. When camping, keep your sleeping bag rolled during the day so that the openings

Swollen-stinger Scorpion

are covered. Wear garden gloves when working outdoors.

In buggy country, use insect repellant and avoid standing water, as this is where mosquitoes breed and hatch.

Black Widow

Aetes Mosquito

People with severe bee sting allergies should always carry rescue medication (including an adrenaline syringe), and those with them should know where it is and how to use it.

In tick country, keep your skin covered, with pants tucked into socks, shirts tucked into waistbands, etc. Check your skin all over at night before bed, so that any lurking ticks can be spotted.

Wood tic

Insect bites and stings may be soothed with cortisone ointment. If you're out in the middle of nowhere, mud will also work, as will a paste made of water and baking soda. Herbal salves—particularly calendula—may also help, as will cool compresses and ice packs. Yarrow and Calendula washes may be soothing (see instructions given above under "Simple cuts, abrasions, and bruises").

Yellowjacket

If stung by a bee, use the edge of your pocketknife to "flick out" the stinger, then treat as above.

If a person who is allergic to bees is stung, administer their rescue medications immediately, apply an ice pack to the sting, and get them to an emergency room.

To remove a tick, grasp it with tweezers and exert a steady pull until it is dislodged. Treat the site as for any wound. Call a physician to see whether or not any additional action is needed. (Ticks in some areas are associated with disease.)

Poisonous or Irritating Plants

If you live in an area where poison oak, ivy, or sumac abound, learn to recognize them. Everyone should also know what stinging nettles look like. (You'll only blunder into a patch of nettles once!)

Don't eat any wild plant or berry unless you are certain of what it is. Never eat mushrooms in the wild unless a mushroom expert is present and can assure you of their safety.

If you come into contact with a poisonous plant, remove your clothes, get into a warm shower, and wash with lots of soap and water. If you develop a rash, applications of cortisone cream may help, as may cool wet compresses (using plain water or infusions of calendula, yarrow, or witch hazel—as explained above).

If you believe that someone has eaten a dangerous poisonous plant, contact Poison Control at 1-800-222-1222, and follow instructions exactly.

Making a First Aid Kit

Your first aid kit should be small enough to carry on outings. In order for a first aid kit to be useful, it can't be sitting home in the closet!

The kit should be assembled in its own container. Small containers—such as film canisters or Altoid containers—can hold first aid supplies.

Whenever you take the kit with you and use anything from it, be sure to always replace the items when you get home. That way you and your kit will always be ready to go.

A Basic First Aid Kit:

Small bar of soap in a plastic baggie
Latex or rubber gloves
Bandana or large fabric square
Antibacterial ointment (e.g., Neosporin)
1% cortisone ointment (available over the counter)
Band-Aids of various sizes
3" gauze squares
Roll of 1" first aid tape
Moleskin (for blisters)
1 small pair of scissors
1 pair of tweezers
A small pad of paper
Pencils
3-4 plastic baggies (zip-loc)
A small container of sunscreen
A small container of insect repellant
Matches
Aspirin tablets (available OTC)

Optional Items:

Small container of hand sanitizer gel
Burn water gel dressings
Sunburn gels, anesthetic/antiseptic sprays (e.g., Bactine), etc.
3-inch Ace bandage/wrap
Plastic mouth barrier for rescue breathing
SAM splint (i.e., a collapsible, easy to carry splint system)
Space blanket
Fine sewing needle
Diphenhydramine HCl (Benadryl) tablets (available OTC)
Ibuprofen (Motrin) or acetaminophen (Tylenol) tablets (available OTC)
Antacid tablets, e.g. Tums (available OTC)
Water purification tablets
Herbs: dried, salves, etc.
Anything else you care to add

Department VI: Wortcunning (green)

Cornerstones

My life is not one thing, but many things:
It is a barrel of cilantro and summer savory
Spilling over the sides, oaken staves
Sprung from the weight of rich soil and
Straining against the red-rusted hoop.

It is an old cistern filled in my childhood, as the days
Of my life fill future's hollow with history, in which
I plant impossible dreams that somehow flourish
Like the tropical tarragon which refuses to yield

To winter's lash,
ever renewing
itself each spring.

It is a corner of green
notched into a patio,
From which the mint is forever escaping into
The yard, sneaking its peridot toes between
The bricks and creeping past the cornerstones
Engraved: "Love," "Kindness," "Peace," and "Hope."

—Elizabeth Barrette

1. Introduction

ELCOME TO THE WORLD OF Wortcunning! This is the old word used for the knowledge of the secret properties of herbs, and this has always been a particular study of the Wise. Wortcunning includes all aspects of herbal lore and plant magicks. This department also covers practical work—such as gardening and Kitchen Witchery.

It is the mission of this department to equip the student with a solid foundation in the knowledge and mastery of all aspects of herbal lore and plant magicks, from myth to method, including practical applications and folklore. As a long-standing tradition of Wizardry, the Art of Wortcunning equips Wizards with tools beneficial in both the magickal and mundane aspects of daily life. Our concerns include, but are not limited to, knowledge, healing, safety, food as medicine, ecology and living in harmony with the Earth.

The color of magick associated with this department is Green, representing the Element of Earth. Green is the color of vegetation, as in gardening and herbalism, fertility and prosperity. Hope, joy, delight, growth and change are all aspects of green. Forest green is connected with fertility, the body, courage and classical music or wilderness sounds. Ivy green represents the emotional aspects, coping with grief, cliffside ponderings, and hushed music or silence. Pale green, as in the color of new grass, aids the healing process.

2. What is Wortcunning?

By Moonwriter (indigo)

You may already know quite a bit about herbs. Perhaps you cook with them, or enjoy drinking herbal tea. You might have a wreath of dried herbs hanging in your home, or you might bathe with herbal soaps or essential oils. If you have a yard or garden, there's a good chance that it has herbs growing in it, whether wild or intentionally.

What is an herb? The word "herb" is used to refer to a group of aromatic plants that are often used medicinally or in cooking. The scientific meaning is of a plant whose stem doesn't produce woody, persistent tissue and that generally dies back at the end of each growing season.

Herbalism is the lore and art of understanding and using the magickal, medicinal and other properties of plants—especially herbs, or, in Old English, worts. The study of herbs and their uses is often known in the Wizarding world by its ancient name of Wortcunning.

Wortcunning has a long and rich history. Humans have long used herbs for cooking and medicinal uses. Many cultures have incorporated herbs into their religious or spiritual practices, while others have considered herbs and spices more valuable than gold and jewels! After the fall of Rome in the fifth century, the salt and spice trade routes became so valuable that wars were fought over them. One of the most colorful moments in United States history was the "Boston Tea Party," when colonists rebelled against pay-

Boston Tea Party

ing high taxes on their beloved English tea, which they considered a staple of civilized life.

Today you can find herbs just about everywhere you look: in foods, syrups, beverages, dyes, fabric, perfumes, decorative items, toothpastes, candles, gardens, and more. The medicinal herb business has also grown tremendously over the past years, thanks to increasing interest in non-traditional ("Western") medicine.

Herbs have always been an important part of the magickal world, whether in charms, candle work, healing, ritual drinks, or a host of other uses. The colors, oils, and fragrances of herbs can have a powerful affect on mood, attitude, and intention, all important parts of Wizardly actions and spell casting.

Harvesting and Using Herbs—the Basics

The constituent chemicals—and thus the therapeutic properties—of medicinal herbs can be affected by the timing and method of their harvesting. Depending on the plant, the flowers, leaves, stems, roots, bulbs, bark, seeds, and/or sap may be harvested.

In general, the following are true about harvesting herbs:

1. Flowering herbs are best harvested in the morning on a dry day.
2. Roots and barks will have certain seasons in which they are best harvested.
3. Once harvested, herbs should used right away or should be dried quickly, away from sunlight or bright light.
4. Once dry, herbs should be stored in labeled (and dated) glass or ceramic containers in a dark place.
5. Most dried herbs will keep 12-18 months.

3. Wortcunning—a Glossary

By Moonwriter (indigo)

As you begin working with herbs, you will learn a brand new vocabulary. Here are some of the more common terms:

Bezoar: An antidote to a dangerous poison.
Charm: One or more herbs (and sometimes other substances) that are placed within a small container or cloth packet/pouch. The properties of the herbs and the user's intention give the charm its power.
Compress: A pad is soaked in a hot or cold herbal infusion and then applied to the area being treated.
Cream: Herbs are mixed with water, fats, and/or oils to form a creamy mixture.
Decoction: Fresh or dried herbs are added to water

and simmered over low to medium heat for up to an hour.
Drying: The process of removing all moisture from herbs, so that they may be stored for long periods. If even a small amount of moisture remains, the herbs will become moldy and will be worthless (and potentially dangerous).
Elixir: An infusion that cures illness or promotes health or longevity.
Infusion: An infusion is like a tea, but is stronger (more herbs are used and/or the herbs are steeped in the liquid for a longer time). Sometimes other substances—such as sweeteners—are added to infusions.
Infused oils: Herbs are added to a carrier oil and heated gently for a period of time. The oil is then strained and stored in a cool, dark place. In cold infusions, the herbs are allowed to soak in the oil for a long period of time, sometimes up to 2-3 weeks, without heating.
Liniments: These are prepared the same way as tinctures, but rubbing alcohol is used as the base. The result is for EXTERNAL USE ONLY (and bottles should always be labeled so!) Liniments are rubbed into aching muscles and joints.
Ointment: Herbs are combined with fats, waxes (e.g., paraffin, beeswax) and/or oils to make a thick creamy mixture.
Philtre: A "love potion."
Plaster: Same as "poultice."
Poison: Any substance that is toxic to the recipient and is capable of causing illness or death. Some items that are medicinal can become poisonous if taken in unsafe doses or if used incorrectly. Universal signs for poison are the skull and crossbones and the "Mr. Yuk" sticker.
Powders: Dried herbs are processed in a food processor or with a mortar and pestle until they become a fine powder. Empty gelatin capsules are then filled with the powder.
Potion: Any type of liquid brew (i.e., infusion, decoction) intended for drinking by the person it is meant to affect.
Poultice: Whole, chopped, or mashed herbs are heated briefly in water to cause them to wilt. The wilted herbs are then applied to the body part being treated, and are held in place with a wrapping of some sort.
Salve: Same as "ointment."
Skin wash: An infusion that is use to bathe wounds, rashes, etc.
Syrup: Honey or unrefined sugar is added to an herbal infusion or decoction. Syrups are often used for cough preparations or to flavor medicines given to children.

Tea: A tea is made by steeping fresh or dried herbs in a quantity of hot water for a specific period of time.

Therapeutic: If something is therapeutic, it's either treats illness or adds to one's well being.

Tincture: Herbs (fresh or dried) are steeped in alcohol or in a mixture of alcohol and water. Tinctures are usually administered in drops (very small quantities).

Toddy: A traditional mixture in which a hot herbal infusion is mixed with a quantity of alcohol. Lemon juice and honey are also typical additions.

Tonic: An infusion that cures illness or promotes health or longevity. Tonics are often associated with season use, as in the "spring tonic."

4. Using Herbs Safely

By Moonwriter (indigo)

> ### IMPORTANT! BEFORE YOU READ
> ### FURTHER, PLEASE READ THIS!

No one should ingest or recommend a medicinal herb to someone else without first studying all the cautions associated with that herb (see bibliography for suggestions about texts that explain the cautions). If you are experiencing a medical condition, you should see a competent health professional.

In Wizarding terms, herb use is a science, an art, and a magickal practice. It is a science because it uses substances that contain active chemicals and cause specific reactions to take place. The science of herbs requires precision and careful attention to detail. Herb use is also an art, because a good herbalist brings all of her senses into the use of herbs, and learns to make judgments about the patient, the situation, and the best herbal approach.

The use of herbs in magick and ritual makes herbalism an important aspect of magickal practice.

Herbal practices require careful study. If you decide to undertake a serious study of Wortcunning, you will need to study and practice for years in order to have a beginning mastery of the craft.

Many herbs are entirely safe, while others may have harmful side effects. A few can be deadly. In the United States, the use of herbs is not regulated by the Food and Drug Administration (FDA). Safe use relies on the wisdom, care, and integrity of the individual practitioner. As an apprentice Wizard, it is important that you learn the rules for handling and working with herbs.

Let's work through a basic list of safety rules, and their explanations.

1. You're a beginning Wizard. Therefore you should only use herbs in ways that are explained and/or approved by a professional or mentor.

As you become familiar with herbs in your studies, devote space to them in your magickal journal. Makes notes of your herbal "experiments," i.e., what you did, how it worked, etc. By doing this, you will gradually build a working file of herbs that you have learned about and can use safely.

2. Keep track of what you learn.

Every time you use or study a new herb, take notes. Give each herb a separate page in your magickal journal. Write down everything you know or find out about the herb on its very own page. Sketch the herb, if you can. Add your herbal experiments. If you do this with each herb, soon you will understand more about them.

3. Just because it's an herb, doesn't mean it's safe!

Many people feel that just because herbs are natural, they are automatically safe. They think that because herbs are natural, they can't be harmful.

Wrong!

Even herbs can be harmful. For example, the foxglove plant—which has lovely flowers—provides digitalis. Digitalis is used by physicians to treat people with heart conditions…but, used improperly, it is a deadly poison that can kill.

To be safe, all herbs should be treated like a form of medicine. It's also a good idea to have the number for Poison Control at hand.

4. Learn about herbs before you use them.

The *Grimoire* has basic information about herbs. You may also want to invest in one or more books or field guides about herbs. There are also several excellent websites that provide detailed information and often feature photos, as well. See the "Resources" section in the Appendix for suggestions.

5. Before using an herb, be certain of its identity.

Before using an herb, you must be absolutely sure that you know what it is.

The Mother Earth is Our Lady of Plants, bestowing the blessing of magickal and medicinal herbs. Art by Jesse Wolf Hardin.

The best way to be sure that you are using the right kind of herb is to buy it from a reputable dealer, such as a natural health store. This might include buying raw, unprocessed herbs or might extend to buying processed herb tablets, capsules, teas, etc. Before you buy any herbal product make sure that the herb's scientific name, plant part used, date of manufacture, date of expiration, and name and address of the manufacturer are on the label.

Another way to be sure of your herbs is to grow them yourself, using seeds or plant starts from a garden shop that keeps a large stock of herbs.

When learning herbs, go slowly. Start with only one or two, and learn as much as you can about them before moving on to new ones.

Last but not least, it's a good idea to know and use the Latin names of herbs. This is a good way to be sure that you are talking about exactly the same herb as is your teacher or reference material. If you say "mint," you could be referring to any number of plants. If you say Mentha arvensis, other herb users will know that you are speaking about a specific type of peppermint used in Chinese medicine.

6. Before using a pre-made herbal remedy, be certain of its other contents.

Herbal remedies may have other unlabeled medicines or materials mixed in with them. Never take a pre-made herbal remedy without knowing each of its components. Reputable herb companies will list each item on the label.

7. Be aware that herbs can interact with each other and with other non-herbal medications.

When herbs are taken with a prescribed or over-the-counter drug, health problems may occur. Some herbal products contain active ingredients that can produce unexpected side effects. For example, Saw Palmetto contains an estrogen-like chemical, while Gingko biloba can interfere with blood clotting.

If you are taking medication regularly for any reason, you should discuss possible interactions with your doctor before using herbs. Even if your health care provider gives the okay to use herbs while taking prescription medication, do not take the herbs and medication at the same time, as the two may interact.

8. Be prepared!

Before starting your herbal workings, have all of your ingredients ready. Double-check your information and read your instructions through carefully. Make sure that you have thought ahead about safety. Have a paper and pencil ready to record the details of your experiment.

9. When preparing an herb, follow directions exactly.

When working with herbs, more is not better!

Even a safe herb can become toxic when used incorrectly. Follow directions, measure carefully, and follow exact dosage recommendations.

10. Be cautious in administering herbs to pregnant or breast-feeding women, young children (6 and under), and infants.

Fetuses and babies are unable to detoxify harmful chemicals in herbs. Any chemical that enters their bodies presents a serious stress to their systems. Caffeine is a good example of this. The caffeine in a cup of coffee is cleared from an adult body in about five hours, but the proportionate amount of caffeine takes a newborn infant about 80 hours to clear.

However, there are plenty of herbs that are very good for children and babies. A newborn should get the herb through the mother's breast milk. Chamomile is a classic for teething babies, and elderflower is great for babies with a fever. Also, many herbs can be tinctured in vegetable glycerin and given to kids.

Because scientific studies have not been done on many herbs, the student must earnestly study the cautions associated with each and every herb they intend to take or recommend to someone else. The book Herb Contraindications & Drug Interactions by Francis Brinker is a good book to start learning about herbal cautions.

Older people (65+) and people with serious health conditions (particularly liver and kidney problems) should also be careful about the use of herbs.

Never administer or recommend herbs to anyone under age 18 without a parent's permission.

11. Give herbs time to work.

Herbs must be given time to work before either changing the dosage or discontinuing. Your instructor or mentor will advise you in this area.

Like all medicines, herbs work best in a supportive environment. Support herbal effects by maintaining optimal health: sleep well, exercise, and follow the proper diet.

12. If adverse effects occur, stop using the herb immediately.

An adverse effect is anything that is unexpected and that is not a desired effect of the herb that was administered. Examples of adverse effects (also called "side effects") can include nausea, vomiting, rash, diarrhea, agitation, etc.

If an adverse effect occurs, stop using the herb immediately. If the adverse effects persist, a doctor's advice should be sought.

13. Store your herbs well marked and out of children's each.

Make sure your herbs are carefully labeled and dated. This will help you to identify them easily, and will also remind you when an herb is outdated.

Like any medicine, herbs should be stored well out of the reach of children. Store them in a dark place and in tightly closed glass containers. If exposed to light or heat, herbs quickly lose their potency.

14. Never take any essential oil internally.

Essential oils are only for external use in substances such as lotions, creams, and inhalations. They can be dangerous when ingested, and should never be included in preparations that are to be eaten or drank. Keep them well out of the range of children.

15. When you come up against something you don't know, STOP and ask an expert.

> *This may be the most important rule yet. When you don't know something, you have to stop what you're doing and find out what it is that you need to know. The easiest way to do this is to ask an expert herbalist.*

You may not be comfortable asking questions. You might worry about admitting that you don't know all of the answers. But part of studying Wizardry is always being a seeker. No Wizard has all of the answers, and even the greatest Wizard asks many questions.

The ethics of safe herb use requires that you always consider safety first. When in doubt…ASK.

5. Planting a Simple Herb Garden

By Moonwriter (indigo)

If possible, use block planting rather than rows. This is especially effective with herbs, as they fill in spaces very nicely.

Pick a spot that gets at least 6-8 hours of sun each day. The more, the better!

Prepare the soil before you plant. Dig in a bag or two of organic compost, and scatter in a good dose of a timed-release plant food.

If at all possible, "go organic." By avoiding pesticides and herbicides, you will bring earthworms, bugs, bees, and spiders into your garden, which will make the garden and ecosystem healthier.

Here are some suggestions for herbs that are attractive, easy to grow, and have multiple uses):

1. **Lavender**— different varieties grow to different sizes. Lavender shrubs are good focal points of a garden, as well as a bee magnet!
2. **Mint (peppermint, spearmint, etc.)**—can be thuggish and spreads easily by rhizomes. Some people solve this by planting it in a container, which they bury un-

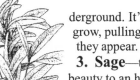

derground. It's also easy to just let it grow, pulling up unwanted plants as they appear.

3. **Sage**—the variegated ones add beauty to an herb space.
4. **Thyme**
5. **Oregano**—honeybees love this!
6. **Calendula**—"pot marigold." This is pretty, brings in bees, and has medicinal uses. The petals are also excellent (and beautiful) in salads.
7. **Chives**
8. **Rosemary**—be careful in picking out the variety. Some stay small and bushy, while other varieties grow huge very quickly. A larger bush can anchor the back or end of a plot. The stems of the larger varieties make good skewers for barbecue.
9. **Lemon balm**
10. **Chamomile**

If you have room, you should also consider parsley, chervil, garlic, and blood sorrel. All are edible and medicinal. The sorrel, with its red-veined leaves, is also very beautiful in a garden.

All of these (except chamomile) are either perennial or self-seeding, so once you've planted them, they'll return year after year.

You may wish to start with small plant starts, rather than seeds. In either case, most herbs are very easy to grow if you simply following the planting instructions that come with them.

Water your herbs every few days, or as needed to keep the soil moist when you stick your finger one inch under the surface of the soil. Mulching your herbs—piling up bark or pine mulch around them—will help them retain water.

Herbs respond well to pruning, getting bushier every time you trim them.

6. A Simple Herb Container Garden

By Moonwriter (indigo)

You don't need a full-sized garden to grow herbs. Many herbs are perfectly happy growing in containers. Here's how to grow a simple outdoor container garden, one that might be able to sit on porch, deck, fire escape, or in a sunny corner of the yard.

Materials:

A large container about two feet across (make sure it has at least 1-2 holes in the bottom)

River rocks (bigger than the holes in the pot's bot-

tom) or pieces of broken pots
A bag of good quality potting soil (regular dirt will not work for this, so buy some at the garden shop)
Some granular plant fertilizer
A small trowel or hand shovel
Either herb "starts" (small plants that are already growing) or seeds. Here are examples:

- For a kitchen garden: sage, thyme, rosemary, mint, oregano, and pansies or violets
- For a tea garden: mint (2-3 varieties), chamomile, lemon balm, pineapple sage, hyssop, and stevia
- For a medicinal garden: peppermint, chamomile, calendula, sage, and garlic

Before planting, choose your location. The herbs mentioned here need at least 6-8 hours of direct sunlight each day. If making a kitchen garden, you may want to have the container close to the kitchen, so that you can snip fresh herbs when you cook.

When ready to plant, move the empty pot to the desired location. Place the rocks or pottery shards over the holes in the pot bottom. Now, fill the pot with potting soil. When it's half full, water it gently—this will help settle the soil. Scatter a couple of tablespoons of granular plant food over the soil. Now, fill the pot the rest of the way, scattering in another couple of tablespoons of granular food.

If using herb starts, set them on top of the potting soil, and move them around to find a pleasing arrangement. Check the information that comes with your plants to get an idea of how tall the plants will be when full-grown.

Use your trowel to plant the herb starts. Gently push the soil down around them to make sure that there are no air holes around the plants. Water thoroughly.

If planting seeds, study the seed packets to find out how large the plants will be when grown. Follow the packet directions for planting depth. Note, though, that in a container, you can plant the seeds more closely than if you were planting in garden rows. Water thoroughly, being careful not wash away the seeds!

Whether planting seeds or starts, start a magickal journal page for your garden. Note the date that you planted the garden. Sketch a layout of what is planted where, so you don't forget!

Now, step back and wait—a good exercise in patience for an apprentice Wizard.

If you planted starts, they'll start to grow in a week or two. As soon as they've increased in size, you can begin cutting off pieces of herb to use. Don't worry: this won't harm the plant. In fact, herbs that are pinched back respond by growing bushier!

If you planted seeds, you will see them sprout in 7-10 days. Follow package directions in thinning them and caring for them. You should have useable herbs inside of two months.

Water enough so that the soil in your container feels just barely damp to a finger pushed an inch under the soil surface.

To harvest and dry your herbs, follow the directions given on page 96. Remember to store in the dark in tight glass jars.

Kitchen creations: Add thyme and parsley to scrambled eggs. Sage and rosemary are wonderful with meats, while oregano is a classic Italian herb. Pansy and violet petals are delicious when added to a salad, and make the salad beautiful to look at! For a special treat, finely chop a combination of fresh kitchen herbs. Take a thick piece of French bread. Spread with butter, and then sprinkle with the chopped herbs. Season with black pepper and add a grating of cheese. Heat under the broiler (young wizards—ask a parent for help!) until melted and bubbly.

Tea creations: To make tea, steep 1-2 teaspoons of dried herb or 2-3 teaspoons of fresh herb in a cup of freshly-boiled water for 5-10 minutes. Strain into a warmed cup and drink. For iced tea, steep the herbs and then strain the results into a refrigerator container, and chill until ready to drink. Try mixing and matching the various herbs to create different tastes. Use tiny pinches of stevia leaf—a powerful sweetener—to sweeten your tea.

Medicinal creations: Steep calendula petals in a quarter cup of almond or vegetable oil to make a soothing skin rub. Mint teas comfort an upset stomach, while chamomile tea is calming to the nerves and helps people sleep. Chamomile and spearmint make a delicious combination. Sage infusions are excellent for those with colds or sore throats--do not give more than 1 cup, 3-4 times per day. Garlic has many medicinal uses: for a sore throat, place unpeeled garlic cloves in a glass pan with 1-2 tablespoons of olive oil. Roast in a 350 degree oven until the cloves are lightly browned and very soft. Allow them to cool, then squeeze the contents out of the peel and eat.

7. Your Edible Garden through the Seasons
By Ellen Evert Hopman (green)

Spring—Violets & Dandelions

Springtime is Violet time. Look for clumps of purple and white Violets in shady gardens and lawns. You can cook the leaves like spinach and place them in salads. Violet leaves are a great source of iron and vitamins A and C.

Violet flowers can be eaten whole: simply put the fresh flowers on an iced cake for a springtime birthday treat or candy them for later use. To candy the flowers, rinse them carefully in cool water and then use tweezers to dip them in beaten egg whites. Place on a clean paper towel and sprinkle sugar over them. Allow the sugared flowers to remain on the towel until dry. Pack carefully with layers of paper towel and a little sugar in an airtight tin.

Violets

Dandelion is an edible plant as well. You can use baby dandelion leaves in salads or steam them as a potherb. The leaves are rich in Vitamin A and the yellow flowers are loaded with Calcium, which benefits the heart. Add the flower petals to a salad (be sure to remove the bitter green sepals and do not eat the stems).

When foraging for greens and flowers on your lawn please be sure you are at least 1000 feet from a road in order to avoid collecting plants that have absorbed pollutants. Always soak wild greens in water to which a few teaspoons of vinegar or salt have been added. Soak for 20 minutes to remove insects and parasites.

Dandelion

VIOLET OR DANDELION JELLY

Fill a glass jar with either Dandelion flowers (remove the sepals and stems) or Blue Violet flowers.

Pour boiling hot water over the flowers until the jar is filled. Allow the jar to sit overnight.

Strain out the flowers and reserve the liquid. To two cups of liquid add the juice of one lemon and a package of powdered pectin. Place the liquid in a non-aluminum pot and bring to a boil. Add a tiny piece of butter (to prevent froth) and four cups of sugar and bring to a boil again. Boil hard for one minute; pour into clean jars and seal.

Foraging for Wild Edibles

Spring is the time to begin foraging for wild edibles. Here are a few Springtime herbal recipes.

NETTLE PANCAKES

Gather young Nettle tips. Be sure to wear rubber gloves to protect yourself from the sting. (A quick rinse of the leaves in cold water removes the acid that causes the stinging).

Chop and then simmer the Nettle leaves with just enough water to cover them, until they are soft.

Fold the Nettles into cooked mashed potatoes.

Add salt and pepper to taste.

Shape with your hands into "pancake" shapes, coat with flour,

Nettle

and fry in olive oil, 5-10 minutes per side, until golden brown. Serve with a dollop of sour cream.

JAPANESE KNOTWEED MUFFINS

Gather young spears of Knotweed, 2-8 inches high. Remove the leaves and chop up. You will need 2 cups of chopped Knotweed.

Sift together 1½ cups flour
1 tsp baking powder
1 tsp baking soda
Add ½ cup of fresh Dandelion petals (be sure to remove the stems and sepals). In a separate bowl, mix one stick of melted butter.
1 cup brown sugar
2 eggs
1 tsp vanilla
1 cup yogurt or sour cream

Knotweed

Fold in the 2 cups of chopped Knotweed. Add to the flour mix and stir well. Pour into muffin tins. Bake at 350 degrees for 15-20 minutes.

FLOWER FRITTERS

Take edible flowers like Dandelions (remove the green sepals and stems), Wisteria flowers or Black Locust tree flowers. Dip in a mixture of egg and milk then into a bowl of breadcrumbs or flour. Fry in olive oil until brown. Blot on a paper towel to remove excess oil, and serve.

TULIP BOWLS

Remove the stamens and pistils from Tulips being careful to keep the flower intact. (The white, pink or peach colored Tulips have the best flavor but the red ones look the most dramatic). Set the Tulip on a bed of lettuce and fill with tuna salad or egg salad. Or take individual Tulip petals and arrange them in a circle on a plate. Fill with tuna or egg salad as elegant "finger food."

Tulip

FLOWER SALADS

Add edible flowers to a salad. You can use Forsythia blossoms, Violet leaves and flowers, Johnny Jump up flowers, Wisteria flowers, Black Locust flowers, Tulip petals, Dandelion flowers (remove the stems and sepals), Norway Maple flowers, Rose petals, and many more.

Late Spring-Early Summer
—Lamb's Quarters & Nettles

Spring and early Summer are the times to find Lamb's Quarters in the garden. This plant got its name because it likes to grow in places where sheep once lived. It is an annual with lance-shaped, toothed leaves near the bottom of the plant and narrow, toothless leaves on top. The leaves are slightly fleshy and nearly white on the underside. The plant can grow to from 1-3 feet in height. Check to see if the leaves have an aromatic, varnish-like smell. If so, you probably have Mexican Tea, which should not be eaten (it is, however, okay to make a tea out of the dried leaves). Lamb's Quarters are an excellent potherb: cook them like spinach, adding a bit of butter and lemon. Native Americans used this plant to treat scurvy. The cold tea is good for diarrhea and the freshly chopped leaves can be used to poultice burns.

Another plant that is found in old fields and neglected areas is Stinging Nettle. You will know if you have this plant because just brushing against it will cause intense itching and red welts on your bare legs and arms. Consider yourself fortunate, however. This plant is one of the healthiest vegetables in the garden. The acid that produces the sting disappears very quickly once the plant is dried or rinsed with cool water in the sink (be sure to wear garden gloves when handling Nettles!)

Nettle

Nettles are hairy plants with tough square, hairy stems, oval hairy leaves and greenish flower clusters. They are perennials and can grow up to four feet in height. They taste exquisite when no more than six inches tall. Rinse and chop the leaves of young plants and add them to soups or make a clear Nettle broth. Nettles are rich in protein, iron and trace minerals. They are anti-histaminic which means they will help relieve allergies. Taken as a tea in wintertime, nettles help warm the body and improve digestion. Steep 2 teaspoons of the dried leaves in a cup of freshly boiled water for 10 minutes. Externally, the cooled tea is used to bathe burns and itchy skin.

June—Day Lillies

By June, orange Day Lilies will grace many gardens. This plant grows in yards and has escaped into the wild in abandoned farms and homesteads. Its leaves are sword-like and its flowers, with petals curved slightly back, face the sun and last for only one day.

Day Lily

Originally from Asia, this plant is grown as a vegetable for Oriental markets. The unopened buds are called "Little Golden Spears" and are delicious sautéed in a little olive oil or butter. The opened flowers are dipped in batter and fried as fritters or added to soups and stews as a thickener. The leaves are chopped and added to salads and the tubers can be cooked like po-

tatoes or sliced and added to salads. As with all wild foods, start by soaking the plants in water with a few teaspoons of vinegar or salt added, for twenty minutes. This will cause any insects or parasites to drop off. Rinse and enjoy.

Day Lilies are also medicinal; in China the root tea has been used as a diuretic and a poultice for mastitis. There is some evidence that the roots have antibacterial properties. The roots also contain colchicine, used in the treatment of gout. It is probably a good idea not to overdo it by eating this plant every day.

Another common plant is Jewel Weed, which has spotted yellow or orange blossoms, tender, succulent stems, and oval leaves. It thrives in damp areas such as moist woods. Its delicate stems can be added to salads in the early spring. Later on the plant is used as a cooked green. Simmer for 10-15 minutes with two changes of water, but do not drink the water.

Medicinally, Jewel Weed has been used as a treatment for Poison Ivy rash. Some people smear the crushed plant directly onto their skin if they think they have been affected. Others make a tea and use it as a wash. Another way is to put the plants into a blender with just enough water to liquefy them and then freeze the resulting mash as ice cubes which can be stored in a plastic baggie in the freezer and used later as needed. The mashed plants have also been used to poultice burns, cuts, insect bites, bruises, nettle rash, and sprains.

Jewelweed

Early Summer— Nasturtiums & Red Clover

Nasturtium

Spicy Nasturtiums will be blooming soon, on trellises and fences. Their red, yellow or orange blossoms climb on stems that are five to ten feet in length. The flowers are larger than the leaves, which are quite round. Pile the fresh blossoms on a slice of whole grain bread that you have slathered with cream cheese or add the flowers to a salad. The flowers are also floated on soups or used to decorate cakes.

The spicy nature of the flowers makes them a warming food for the lungs; eat them freely to break up chest congestion or take ½ teaspoon of the fresh juice, three times a day. The juice of the blossoms can also be used externally to disinfect a wound.

Another welcome flower that will be blooming shortly is the wild clover. A familiar sight in meadows and gardens, wild clover grows from one to two feet in height, with several slightly hairy stems. The leaves,

LambsQuartes

which are green or slightly blotched with white and minutely toothed, appear in clusters of three and have a distinctive "V" marking. The blossoms are rose-colored and may be light or dark. Pick the fresh flowers and float them in soups, add them to salads, or use them to decorate a cake. Try making tea sandwiches for a garden party using freshly buttered squares of white bread (remove the crusts), watercress and clover blossoms. Serve with organic black tea.

Red Clover

Red clover tea is an expectorant and antitussive, making it useful for colds, asthma, bronchitis and other spasmodic coughs. The tea is also a "blood purifier" (stimulates the liver) that has been used as a folk remedy for cancer. Externally the tea is applied to burns, sores and ulcers. Red clover blossoms are often used in herbal cigarettes. Add the dried flowers to other dried medicinal herbs such as catnip and mullein to calm an asthmatic cough.

For tea, steep the flowers for 10-20 minutes using 2 teaspoons of flowers per 1/2 cup of water. Use the tea straight for an external wash or add honey as a sweetener for internal consumption. Adults (or a 150 lb person) can drink ½ cup three times daily, children (or a 75 lbperson) should take ¼ cup or less depending upon body weight, three times a day.

Summer —
Evening Primrose & Yarrow

Evening Primrose

Two edible plants that are common in Summer fields are Evening Primrose and Yarrow.

Evening Primrose grows to a height of 1-5 feet and has clusters of yellowflowers whose four petals open in the early evening and wilt the next day. It begins flowering in June. A biennial (it lives for two years and flowers in the second year), its first year roots can be peeled and boiled for twenty minutes or until soft in two changes of water. Pour off the water each time and do not drink it. The roots taste milder in spring and fall and a little spicier in summer. Serve with butter and salt.

The young leaves of Evening Primrose can also be boiled in two changes of water for about twenty minutes and served with butter.

Native Americans used a poultice of the roots for bruises. The seeds produce oil that is beneficial to the liver and helps skin conditions such as eczema.

Yarrow was called "Medicine Plant" by pioneers. It grows to a height of 1-3 feet and has distinctively flat white clusters of five small flowers. Pick the young leaves off your lawn when they are no more than 1 or 2 inches long and add them to salads (after soaking in water to which a few teaspoons of salt or vinegar have been added for about twenty minutes, to remove parasites). The feathery leaves become highly aromatic as the summer progresses and eventually are too bitter to eat. Once the herb has flowered it can be picked and dried for tea. Yarrow tea is used for fevers and colds and has a special affinity for the intestinal tract. It is a classic for stomach flu, especially when combined with peppermint leaves and elder flowers. Some may find the taste unpleasantly strong, do not drink the tea more than once or twice.

The Latin name for this plant is *Achillea millefolium;* Achillea after the Greek hero Achilles and millefolium because its leaves are segmented into thousands of tiny sections. Achilles bled to death in the Trojan War and Yarrow has styptic properties, meaning it stops bleeding when applied fresh as a poultice.

Yarrow

Summer —Mints

Wild and cultivated mints thrive in the shady gardens, wet meadows and stream banks. Wild mint grows from 6 to 25 inches tall; has fine backward bending hairs and tiny clusters of whitish or light purple flowers that appear where the opposite leaves join the stem. In common with other mint species, wild mint has a strong aromatic smell, and squared stems. Some mints have flowers on terminal spikes, rather than at the leaf axils. Your nose will tell you if you have found mint.

The simplest way to enjoy mint is to steep the fresh or dried leaves in freshly boiled water that has been removed from the stove, for 5 - 10 minutes. Add a drizzle of honey as a sweetener. All mints are excellent for colds, fevers, sore throats, gas, indigestion, and stomach cramps. Add crumbled dried mint leaves or chopped fresh leaves to a fruit salad. Mint can also be sprinkled on carrots, spinach, green beans or potatoes. Add mint to iced tea and use the fresh leaves to decorate cakes and ice cream desserts.

TO MAKE MINT JELLY:

Cut up 3 pounds of apples; do not peel (the peel is where most of the pectin is)

Put the fruit into a large pot and barely cover with water

Cover and cook over a low heat 3 - 15 minutes, until the juice runs freely

Strain through a colander

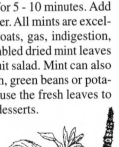

Spearmint

Pour the liquid through several layers of cheesecloth or into a damp jelly bag

Allow to drip for at least an hour to yield at least 4 cups of juice

Boil the 4 cups of juice for 5 minutes

Add ¾ c. sugar for each c. of juice

Put in 1 cup chopped mint stems and leaves for every cup of juice Boil 10 - 30 minutes until jelling begins. While the jelly boils you can add a few drops of green food coloring [To test for the jellying point: Take a cold metal spoon and scoop up some of the boiling liquid. Tilt the spoon and if the jelly runs off in sheets rather than separate drops, it is done. Or put a few drops on a plate and place it in the freezer to see if it jells when cool. Voila!]

Skim off the foam and pour into hot, sterilized jars. Seal with metal lids or paraffin and store.

Late Summer –
Milkweed & Burdock

If you are lucky enough to live near a fallow field look out for milkweed, which is coming into bud at this time. A great favorite of Monarch butterflies, its leaves are slightly downy and opposite, wide and about 8 inches long. The rounded *Milkweed* clusters of pinkish-purple flowers form in July and August. The stem contains white latex, which is immediately visible if you break off a leaf. By fall the plant, which attains a height of 2-4 feet, has produced large warty seedpods, which eventually dry out, split open, and release hundreds of downy seed tassels, which can be used to stuff toys and pillows. The fluff is waterproof and was once used to fill life preservers.

The GREEN flower buds and immature seed pods can be eaten before they open, boiled with several changes of water, and served with little olive oil and soy sauce, or butter. Be sure to drop the buds into water that is already boiling, not cold water, to avoid any bitter taste. The open flower clusters can be dipped in boiling water for one minute then dipped again in batter and fried as fritters. DO NOT EAT ANY OTHER PART OF THE PLANT. Burdock is a common weed that inhabits fallow fields and disturbed areas locally. This plant makes those annoying little brown burrs in the fall that stick to your pants and to your dog. It has large rhubarb-like leaves and thistle-like flowers that are about an inch in diameter and pinkish-maroon in color. The plant blooms in late summer and early fall. The leaves can be used externally as a wash for skin *Burdock* eruptions such as hives or eczema and to poultice burns and ulcers. DO NOT EAT THE LEAVES! Burdock is a biennial (it lives for two years, blooming in the second summer). The root of a first year plant can be boiled to make a tea that "cleans the blood" by stimulating the liver. Simmer one teaspoon of root per cup

of water, for about 20 minutes. In the Orient the root is considered a vegetable. Boil the root of a first year plant for 30 minutes in two changes of water and serve with butter. Excellent!

Herbal Teas

Amongst the flowers that bloom in your garden may be a few that are suitable for herbal teas. For example Bee Balm (Monarda), which was a classic, purple, red or pink Victorian garden flower and is a great favorite of hummingbirds and bees. Bee Balm grows to about 3 feet in height and like Mint, it has square, hairy stems and opposite, ovate and serrate leaves. You can steep the leaves and flowers in freshly boiled water (use 2 teaspoons of the fresh herb or 1 teaspoon of the dried herb) for about 10 minutes. Bee Balm makes a soothing tea for stomach upsets and indigestion. The flavor is similar to "Earl Grey" tea.

Creeping thyme is another common plant in our region that can be found in gardens and on lawns. Its leaves are tiny, only 3/8 inch long, and the plant attains a height of no more than six inches. The flowers, which are clustered at the tip of each branch, can be any color from white to purple. Traditional European herbalists used Thyme for coughs and colds and stomach aches. Steep 2 teaspoons of the fresh herb or 1 teaspoon of the dried her per cup of freshly boiled water for about 10 minutes.

According to folk tradition thyme is a very grounding herb. Plant some in an area where you like to sit and meditate, to bring peace and balance to your senses.

Blueberry is another common plant in the Valley. Everyone knows about eating its fruits but did you know you could make a tea from its leaves and fruits? Gather the leaves when the berries are still green and steep 2 teaspoons of the fresh leaf in one cup of freshly boiled water for 20 minutes. Native Americans used the leaf tea as a "blood cleanser". Drink blueberry leaf tea for a few days only. You can also simmer 1 teaspoon of dried blueberries in one cup of water for 20 minutes in a pot with a very tight lid (to preserve the volatile oils) and drink up to 2 cups a day for as long as you like.

Late Summer –
Blackberries

It's Blackberry time! Look for stands of wild Blackberries at the edges of forested areas and in abandoned fields.

Blackberries have thorns, leaves in groups of three to seven leaflets, and green or reddish stems that can grow as high as six feet. Look for small, white, five-petaled flowers in June, and black fruits in late July and early August. The fruits are high in bio-flavinoids that help to build the immune system - everyone should eat highly pigmented berries, fruits and vegetables as

Blackberries

long as they are available in summer (red apples, red berries, red grapes, red cabbage, plums, tomatoes, red peppers, etc). The fresh, young leaves and tender stem tips can be eaten in salads. The leaves can be dried to make a tea that helps with diarrhea. The tea of the root is also a traditional remedy for diarrhea and dysentery. Use 2 teaspoons of the dried leaves per cup of freshly boiled water. Steep for up to 20 minutes and drink about a cup a day. Or simmer 1 teaspoon of the chopped root per cup of water for 20 minutes in a pot with a tight lid. Cool and drink one or two cups a day.

Blackberry jelly, jam, and wine all help with loose bowels and diarrhea. Gourmet chefs will enjoy making Blackberry vinegar. Place the berries in a clean glass jar and cover with vinegar. Allow them to stand for three days and then strain carefully through a sieve. (Raspberry vinegar is also a gourmet delicacy).

Fresh Blackberry leaves can be mashed in the blender and applied as a poultice to burns and ulcers. Add just enough water to the leaves so you can make a mush. Pour the green mush into a bowl and add just enough powdered slippery elm bark, or whole grain flour, to thicken it slightly. Spread the mix on a clean cloth and apply to a burn. Keep the plant matter against the skin for an hour and then discard.

I winter you can cover the dried leaves with just enough boiling water to soften them and apply to scalds and burns.

Late Summer–Fall
—Eat the Trees!

Maple

When thinking about edible herbs in the garden don't forget the trees! In the late summer we all enjoy the fruits of the trees such as apples and cherries, mulberries, pears and peaches. But trees are edible in other seasons as well.

In the spring you can harvest very young tree leaves and use them in salads. Look for immature Maple leaves that still have a rosy blush on them. Tiny Beech leaves and the new growth on Hawthorn trees are also edible. Something I always look forward to in spring is the new growth on the Hemlock trees (No, they are not poisonous, the Greek philosopher Socrates was killed by drinking the juice of Water Hemlock, a field herb, not Hemlock trees!).

Hemlocks have very small pinecones and very small needles (only 3/8 to 5/8 of an inch long). The bark is cinnamon brown and deeply furrowed. *Hemlock* Look for the pale green new growth at the tips of Hemlock branches. It has a delicate, lemony flavor and is loaded with Vitamin C. You can make a tea of the branch tips or add them to salads or just graze off the tree. As the summer progresses the new growth turns dark green and is too tough to eat.

Another spring favorite is sap from Birch trees, which can be tapped just like the Maples. No need to boil down the sap, just drink it fresh from the tree. All the Birches except the white Birch have a very nice wintergreen flavor. In the spring you can *Birtch* gather some branches and cut them into 1-inch sections and put them in the pot. Cover with cold water, put on a tight lid and simmer for 20 minutes. Use honey or Maple syrup as a sweetener and try adding a few slices of freshly chopped ginger root or the bark of the root of a young Sassafras tree, for added flavor.

White Pines have blue-green needles that grow in bundles of five and are 2½ to 5 inches in length. The bark is grayish, furrowed, and thickly ridged. These trees make a very nice lemony tea. You can use the needles and twigs all year *White pine* round, just place them in a pot of fresh cold water, cover tightly, and simmer for 20 minutes. The tea can be enjoyed in the dead of winter and makes a nice soothing remedy for colds, being slightly antiseptic and full of Vitamin C.

8. A Word About Wild Mushrooms
By Oberon (grey) & Moonwriter (indigo)

What we see as "mushrooms" are only the fruiting bodies of vast networks of fungi that extend underground—sometimes over many acres. Fungi are one of the five great Kingdoms of life on Earth; in order of their appearance in the evolutionary record, these are: Monera, Protista, Plantae, Fungi, and Animalia. There are thousands of kinds of wild mushrooms; many are poisonous and some are so deadly that even a single bite can kill you.

A tiny handful of mushroom species, however, are both prized delicacies and easily *Puffballs* identifiable, as they in no way resemble any of the dangerous varieties. In North America, these are white puffballs, golden chanterelles, and morels. In Europe, truffles are the great prize fungi. All are exquisitely delicious—sliced and fried in butter, mixed with other vegetables in a stirfry, or used in various recipes.

Morels

Chanterelle

Once you have learned to identify these very few unmistakable fungi, you will be able to go on wonderful treasure hunts in the places where they grow wild. But mushroom hunting should always be learned from one who is well experienced, not on your own!

If you are interested in exploring this exotic realm, get yourself a good guidebook—and find a good guide to take you into the woods and fields for your first season. An excellent book is the *National Audubon Society Field Guide to North American Mushrooms,* which covers 703 species in detail, with color photos.

The ones to avoid entirely are the gilled mushrooms, or "toadstools" —those with the typical "mushroom" shape, like the ones you buy in the grocery store. While there are many edible varieties of these, the few poisonous and even deadly ones are of this type also, and they can be nearly impossible to distinguish from the harmless ones. The best rule is to never, ever harvest any type of gilled mushrooms!

Deadly Mushrooms: Amanita, Death's cap, Destroying Angel

The following was adapted from the website of the California Poison Control System. After you read it, please visit their website at the link provided. (The US National Poison Control Center may be reached at 1-800-222-1222)

About Mushroom Poisoning in the US

More than 9,000 cases of mushroom ingestions are reported to the American Association of Poison Control Centers annually. Even though only about 100 types of mushrooms are responsible for most cases of mushroom poisoning, and less than a dozen species are considered deadly, there are approximately 5,000 varieties to sort them from in the United States. If a mushroom is at all poisonous, it will be more dangerous to young children, old people and those already battling illness. Even mushrooms usually considered "safe" have caused death in very young children and very ill adults. Then there are a number of mushrooms that can cause death in healthy adults.

Mushroom Identification

A biologist trained in the study of mushrooms is called a "mycologist." To make a positive identification, a mycologist looks at many factors, such as the color, gills, spores, stalks and base portion of the mushroom. The spores must be examined under a microscope to detect differences. He or she must also consider whether the mushroom being examined was growing in the woods, on a lawn or on a tree. The process is so involved that it is impossible to identify a mushroom from a description over the telephone. It is truly a very difficult and time-consuming art that demands precision and accuracy, as well as many years of study.

(© CPCS and Regents, University of California. 2000; http://www.calpoison.org/public/mushrooms.html)

9. A Simple Herbology Work Using Mint

By Moonwriter (indigo)

The mint family includes many varieties—peppermint and spearmint are two—that are easy to grow and quite safe to work with.

Medicinally, mint is excellent for treating indigestion or an upset stomach.

Magickally, mint is thought to be associated with intelligence, eloquence, divination, study, self-improvement, breaking negative habits, communication, and wisdom. (Note: These are only partial descriptions, to give you an idea of how mint is used.)

To grow and harvest mint:

Method 1: Plant mint in a sunny corner of your garden and water every few days. As it grows, pinch or snip off pieces just above sets of leaves; this will give you some herb to work with and will also encourage the plant to become bushier. Always pinch and/or collect mint early in the morning for best flavor. To dry, place the stems and leaves on a plate and set on a shelf *away from direct light* until the leaves are completely dry and brittle, i.e., several days. When dry, strip the leaves from the stems. Discard the stems. Put the leaves in a clean glass (or plastic) container and store in a dark cupboard.

Method 2 (faster method, but not as fun): Buy a bunch of mint at your local grocery or farmer's market. Dry and process as in Method #1.

Method 3: (fastest method) Buy already-processed and dried mint from a local health food store or botanica.

Peppermint

To prepare a mint infusion (tea):

In a non-aluminum saucepan, bring 1 cup of freshly drawn cold water to a rapid boil.

When water boils, remove the pan from the heat. Stir in 2 teaspoons of crushed dried mint leaves.

Put a lid on the pot, and allow to sit, off the heat, for 5-10 minutes (the longer it sits, the stronger it will be).

Strain the liquid into a warmed teacup. Flavor as desired with honey or raw sugar.

Congratulations! You have made an herbal infusion! Now sit in a quiet place, and enjoy your mint tea. The next time your stomach is a little upset—perhaps you ate too fast, ate too much, or ate something that

didn't agree with you—prepare the mint infusion and sip it slowly. It will calm your stomach.

10. Potions and Lotions

Here are a few formulae for magickal herbal potions, lotions, oils, powders and charms.

A Wisdom and Memory Charm (Moonwriter)

You will need:

A sprig of rosemary (for memory)
1 teaspoon of dried blueberries (also for memory)
1 bay leaf (for wisdom)
6" circle of fabric (the colors and pattern should correspond with your magickal intentions)
12" of embroidery floss (also of a corresponding color)

Hold the herbs and berries in your dominant hand. Ask them to share their strengths and powers with you as you approach your exams, assignment, or other task. Be as specific as you can.

Place the herbs and berries in the calico, and bring up the edges to make a little hobo-style bundle. Tie this with the embroidery floss.

Sleep with the bundle under your pillow. In the morning, write down notes of any dreams you recall.

Carry the charm until the task is completed. Then, open the charm and place the herbs and berries in a mug. Pour boiling water over them and steep for 5 minutes. Flavor with honey. Drink, and contemplate your magickal workings. Blessed be!

A potion to provide Protection and Wisdom (Moonwriter)

½ tsp. dried peppermint (for memory)
½ tsp. dried sage (for protection and wisdom)
¼ tsp. dried hyssop or anise-hyssop (for luck)
Moonwater (water that sat out and charged under the full moon)
Pinch dried stevia (optional, for sweet taste)

Bring 1 C. of fresh cold mineral water and 2 T. moonwater to a boil.

Once the water boils, turn off the heat, then add the dried herbs. Allow the mixture to infuse for 5 minutes.

Pre-warm a special tea cup or mug with hot water. Strain the infusion into the cup.

Holding the cup in both hands, bring the cup up under your face, and breath out onto the surface of the tea, sending your intent into it. Then breathe in the steam from the tea, receiving its essence into your being. Drink the tea slowly, while focusing your intent on the coming examinations and the desired outcome.

Grieving Oil (Estara T'shirai)

6 drops cypress
6 drops lavender
1 drop chamomile
1 pinch marjoram

School Oil (Estara T'shirai)

Lavender
Chamomile
Rue
Aids focus and relieves anxiety.

Self-Love Sachet (Estara T'shirai)

Anise
Lavender
Parsley
Rose
Uva ursi
Marjoram
Orris root
Rose quartz
A few drops Venus oil

Tie all these ingredients into pink and/or sea green cloths.

Forgiveness Powder (Estara T'shirai)

Rosemary
Marjoram
Lavender
Meadowsweet
Vervain
Peppermint

Use when you need help letting something go so you can get on with your life.

11. Final Thoughts

By Moonwriter (indigo)

You have learned that Wortcunning is serious business, and that it carries great responsibility.

As a student of Wizardry, you are ethically bound to use all of your care and wisdom to make sure that you handle and administer herbs safely.

As you become more skilled in the uses of herbs, you will find it exciting to talk with fellow Wizards and herbalists about your experiments. In doing so, it is important that you only pass on information that you know to be absolutely correct and safe.

If you're not certain about an herbal preparation, don't recommend it to others. Also, if someone else passes on their information to you, ask enough questions and request enough information to satisfy yourself that what they're describing is safe.

Don't worry that you may offend anyone by questioning what they tell you. If they are practicing ethically, they will understand and respect your concern. They will also be anxious to show you that their words are valid and can be trusted.

Department VII: Divination (yellow)

Capnomancy

shapes in the smoke
make faces, form images
that speak their meanings
to my mind

in the folds of blue and gray
I see the future
and the past:

all that passes through the air
leaves a shiver of itself behind,
a swirl of furling currents

in the spirit of the world

I have learned, have taught myself
through long trying
to read those skirling words
written by the simple presence
of my subject

in the shift of smoke
I have seen the end of the world
and the beginning—smoke
themselves, but brighter
than any rainbow

come, ask your question;
the smoke will answer,
and I will tell you
what it knows

—Elizabeth Barrette

1. Introduction

ELCOME TO THE WORLD OF DIVINA-tion! This is the art of foretelling or predicting the future—discovering things that are lost, hidden or secret. Although not all seers were Wizards, all Wizards are expected to be seers. Many ancient peoples were completely obsessed with divination, and would hardly make a move without consulting diviners, seers, oracles or prophets. Unusual occurrences, such as disturbing dreams and *omens,* were also given divinatory meanings—this is where we get our word *ominous.* Over the ages, seers have devised many techniques of divination—called the *Mantic Arts* (from *mantis,* meaning "diviner"). These arts include such systems as runes, oghams, scrying, Tarot, dowsing, palmistry, dream interpretation, augury, and numerous other methods.

The color of magick for this department is Yellow, which represents the Element of Air. Yellow is associated with mental work: meditation, will, intellect, divination and communication. Another version of gold, yellow is the color of friendship, goodness and faith. Yellow (or sometimes a very light yellow-green) is associated with Wednesday, the planet Mercury, the sign of Taurus and the 3rd (Solar Plexus) Chakra. Golden yellow is the color of charm, trust, Summer, bright sounds like laughter, and upbeat music. Pastel yellow tends more towards Spring, psychic endeavors and creativity. Yellow is a terrific color to improve balance, self-esteem, charisma, divination and creativity. Use it also for strength of will, vitality, purpose and effectiveness.

Hundreds of systems of divination have been devised over the ages. See the *Grimoire* (pp. 227-228) for a list of some of the most popular. In this chapter we will explore just a few of these, with enough information that you can practice them yourself. Future books in this series will delve more deeply into the subject, with more complex systems.

2. The Prophet's Mission
By Jesse Wolf Hardin (silver)

Wizards, shamans and holy priestesses of many different faiths have been prophesying the future for tens of thousands of years. Some of these foretellings have been heeded, with entire movements forming of magickal folks hoping to prevent or lessen a potential tragedy beforehand. Make no mistake; the value of prophecy lies in the degree to which we can make use of the information and Vision that we are given!

For all of life's surprises and sudden turns, everything that happens does so in relationship to every other being, energy and occurrence. This can be shown in many ways, including the new science of turbulence, mapping a process that was recently considered not only chaotic but also utterly unpredictable. Accurate prophecies arise not so much from out of body revelations as from increased recognition of these kinds of patterns of relationships: of expansion and contraction, gifting and need, cause and effect. While trance work can get one out of their mind and dramatically broaden perception, the specific ability we are talking about is more of a genetically encoded, bodily sensing of the endless interconnections and purposeful direction of what was, what is, and what may one day be!

Some people are born with a greater gift for prophecy than others. These gifted folks have hold of an advantage, for sure, but they bear an increased burden as well. With foreknowledge comes responsibility—the ability and necessity to respond. Both the depth of such gifts and their implications have always guaranteed that the prophet would be a rare individual, both respected by the community or tribe and also kept at a comfortable distance. Everyone, however, is born with some capacity to see into the future and act on what they see—a skill that we can strengthen through practice and then put to use for both our good and the good of the greater whole. Inside you, there is a visionary seeking to recognize and internalize all the available mysteries of the universe!

We can increase our prophetic skills through intense focus and constant advances in perceptual and empathic recognition. Since all things and events form patterns, all patterns can be depended upon to leave traces or tokens of significance. These traces are what we call "signs," and "reading" the future is not only revelation but a reading of this complex text of unfolding life. Signs are tracks— whether left behind by animals, by unfolding human processes, or by manifest Spirit. If we look closely we can learn not only the character of that which left them, but also the direction it proceeds from, and the direction it is heading: its likely origins, and its probable destination. All signs convey meaning, as much as we are able and willing to grasp.

An omen is a sign of what has yet to happen. When these signs are less than clear, we call it "foreshadowing." When one is consciously aware of the signs influencing them, there is a mating of informed presaging and inexplicable premonition. Connections are inevitably made at a subconscious level, so that we are able to "follow the dots" from where we are to where things are going. It is Spirit, the animating force of Nature that speaks... not a booming tenor ringing from out of the sky, but as a celebration of the spiraling   s e l f - knowledge and self-direction of the universe heard from

within us more than from without.

Contrary to what we may have been told, omens are intrinsically neither "good" nor "bad." Whether unfolding events are fortunate or unfortunate, benevolent or harmful, depends not only on our situation, attitude and perspective, but also on our ability to employ the raw energies and incumbent lessons of whatever comes to pass. An omen is a prognosis and prescription, as well as a warning of any difficulties to come. Truly, signs and omens are not only indications, but also suggestions. Every sign is a call for intentional relationship and response, containing important information on how best to proceed. And every omen is more than a warning— it's an opportunity to intentionally and compassionately influence future events!

Omens are real, but they're also easily imagined or misinterpreted. One who is afraid will read into every omen the imminent arrival of that which they fear. One who is unsure will tend to interpret all kinds of omens as fortunate, as they look for the assurance they need to go on. And how we relate and respond even to the real omens in our lives is still up to us. An omen is a reminder of choice, and every moment is a decisive moment.

By tapping the prophetic powers we're born with, we evolve our personal medicine and leave both victimhood and blind obedience behind, pursuing our destiny rather then giving in to fate. "Fate" is something we claim to suffer or bear, while "destiny" is that which we help to bring about. Fate is what we accept, destiny something we rise for, follow and assist. It is embracing all that we are and all that we can be... in alignment and cooperation with the intentions and forces of

CVM DEO.

Earth and Spirit. It is our original directive, as well as our personal potential to fulfill our terrestrial, magickal and spiritual opportunities and assignments.

We should feel emboldened, knowing beyond question that we are each born with the heart and power necessary to complete these assignments. No matter how unenlightened or unnatural one's surroundings, we are inevitably afforded the crucial moments, venues and teachers required to develop the most needed skills. And we're each entrusted with the essential and fundamental lessons, whether we choose to make full use of them or not. Destiny is our personal Gaian song, but it is still up to us whether or not we get up and put our hearts into the ongoing dance. How well we fulfill our individual role in this cosmic, rhythmic choreography depends on our intention and follow-through, informed by the past and present experiences of this living world, and empowered by the advantage and hope that grounded prophecy provides.

- Think back and try to remember what things that have happened in your life were ones you felt you knew were going to happen beforehand?
- Pay attention to when your mind is making an educated calculation and "guess," and when your prediction is a "feeling."
- When you can't think of any good reason for something to happen, but feel sure that it's going to happen anyway, that's when you can be most certain that you are tapping your prophetic abilities and not just your intelligence.
- When you have a prophecy, get into a habit of both journaling about it and sharing it with your most trusted and allied friends. This not only keeps us honest with ourselves, but it's also a record to refer to later as things continue to evolve and unfold.
- Try to prophecy about things that will happen in the coming months, instead of events that might occur long after you are dead and gone.
- It's best to only warn people about something you envision when there is something they can possibly do about it.
- Don't feel bad if a prophecy doesn't seem to come true. When we are proven wrong, it should be inspiration to continue practicing and fine-tuning our prophetic abilities.
- There will be times when our prophecy was real but misdefined. It may occur in a different time frame than we anticipated, or it may come in another form that we will only recognize af-

ter the fact ("Oh, so THAT was what my vision was trying to show me!").
- Beware of the effects of the "Cassandra Syndrome" (speaking Truth, but not being believed). Your prophecies are all the more important when very few people believe you.
- Try to sense the future of not only yourself and the people you know, but also of other life forms, the living landscape of Gaia the Earth, and the universe beyond this sacred globe.
- For each prophesied event, consider what could be done to improve it benefits and lessen the dangers... and then take it upon yourself to do those things!

3. Framing the Question
By Donata Ahern (aqua)

Be sure to ask *May I, Can I, Should I*, whenever you use any divination system. This is the ethical use of these techniques as amagickal tools. *May I, Can I, Should I*, has the following meaning:

May I means: Do I have permission to divine this question or situation? *Can I* means: Do I have the ability to successfully divine in this area and am I ready? *Should I* means: It is appropriate, proper and suitable for me to divine in this area? If you get a 'NO' for any of these questions, don't dowse.

Go to your quiet spot with your tools. You will need to ask some practice questions that have no emotional attachment for you, such as: Is my vitamin C level OK? You don't emotionally care if it's a little high or low. There are many areas that you might play with. Pick areas that you are not emotionally concerned with, or for which you don't already know the answer. Do this every day for 5 to 10 minutes.

Asking the Question
You need to be careful about the wording of the questions you ask. An example might be: Does my car need gas? The answer would be "YES," even if the gas tank is full. You have a gasoline car which runs on what we call gas, so of course it needs gas. Divinatio takes every word in a question by its literal meaning.

Rule #1: You need to be very specific about what you want to know. This includes what, where, when and sometimes instructional information relating to the question.

Rule #2: Use only words, phrases and conditions

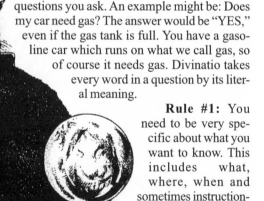

that you have set up with the particular tool, and for which there is an agreed-on method of response.

Rule #3: Make the question a definite request for information that exists somewhere. Don't ask for an opinion. For example: If I ask you: Are you strong? Your answer would be based on what you think I meant by the word "strong"—strong physically, mentally, emotionally, etc. Now apply rules 1, 2, and 3 (what, when and a reference to something). Are you strong enough, right now, to pick up this one-gallon carton of milk? Now, could you give me a correct answer to that question?

Framing the Question (Q.)

When you wish to explore a new area, try the following. Ask several different questions looking for agreement or confusing/unclear answers. Confusing answers clue you that undiscovered information is influencing your answer.

For dowsing, for example, here are some misleading Q's: (Look at their literal meaning) Q. Is there water in the [designate the area]? The answer is YES. (There is water everywhere.) Q. Is there a water source, less than 300 feet deep, that could supply 5 GPM (gallons-per-minute)? The answer is Yes. (especially in a hard rain storm). The next Q. may give you a clue that something is wrong. Q. Could this water source allow a well to supply 5 GPM of potable (drinkable) water to the surface, year around? If the answer is NO, you then know something was wrong with the first Q's. By asking multiple Q's, you can often find problems, and learn what you will need to develop clear Q's.

Always use questions that have worked well before, and test new ones. Test them, as above, by asking the question several different ways to see if you get an appropriate answer each time. This makes you carefully think about what the words actually mean and if you have left out anything in the question. It may be helpful to ask a question two different ways.

Don't be too serious. Relax and allow your intuition to flow. Always dowse for the best good for yourself and others.

4. Eternity's Gamble: Basic Forms of Divination

By LeopardDancer (grey)

Dice Divination

Divination using dice, also known as *cleromancy,* is an ancient and relatively simple form. The earliest types of dice were made from the knucklebones of certain animals. Dice where also made from clay. These were the forerunners of today's dice. The Tibetans practiced it under the name *Sho-Mo.* Though an ancient form of

divination most forms used today were likely created in the 19th and 20th centuries and are mostly used for entertainment value.

A message received from the dice is said to come true within nine days. And dice casting must never be done on Mondays or Wednesdays. All types of modern dice-casting are 'tongue in cheek' and should never be taken as absolutely true.

One Die

When using a single die make a circle like the one below. Cast the die onto the circle. Both the number and letter having a meaning that is then combined to get your answer. Ask no question, let the dice be your guide

A - next year
B - money
C - travel
D - domestics
E - present
F - health
G - love, marriage
H - legal matters
I - present state of mind
J - career
K - friends
L - enemies

1 - generally favorable
2 - success depends on friends
3 - excellent chance for success
4 - disappointment and trouble
5 - good intentions
6 - uncertainty

Two Dice

When casting two die add the pips together after they are rolled. This form is more a yes/no oracle much like the "Magic 8-Ball" toy.

2 - yes	**3** - no	**4** - take care
5 - be wise	**6** - good luck	**7** - of course
8 - have faith	**9** - be patient	**10** - certainly
11 - doubtful	**12** - a chance	

Three Dice

This is by far the most common form of dice casting. Three dice are cast and the number of pips added up. The total corresponds to your answer. Three dice divination is not used to answer specific questions. Rather, the dice will reveal the message you need to know.

3 - pleasant surprises in the future.
4 - a period of bad luck is about to begin.
5 - plans will come to fruition
6 - a loss of some kind
7 - difficulties in business
8 - look out for gossips

9 - romance takes an unexpected turn
10 - birth of a new child or of a project
11 - a parting of sorts
12 - a message of importance will arrive
13 - grief will visit soon
14 - a new friend to be found
15 - start no new projects for a few days
16 - a journey will have positive results
17 - change in plans is necessary
18 - forthcoming events will be successful and joyful

20 -sided Die

Here a 20 sided die, coming from the role-play gaming (RPG) world, is rolled and the number that appears refers to your answer.

1 - family difficulties
2 - look closely at things, they are not often as they seem
3 - pleasant surprises await you
4 - grief is coming
5 - a wish will be granted
6 - bad luck coming
7 - relationship difficulties coming
8 - look out for gossips or criticism without just cause
9 - a marriage soon
10 - a birth soon
11 - illness coming
12 - important message will be received soon
13 - sorrow is imminent
14 - valuable assistance will be granted
15 - a new friend to be found
16 - a pleasant journey to come
17 - avoid temptation
18 - heed outside advice
19 - profitable events
20 - good news coming

Coin Divination

Coin divination may be used in a few different ways. We've all played "heads or tails," right? Simply assign yes to one side, and no to the other. Hold the coin in your fist while concentrating on your answer. Then flip the coin up and see if it lands heads or tails.

Another method involves using about 20 coins, though it can be any even number from 10 up. Pennies work best for this, as they are easily obtained. Collect 20 pennies and find a small pouch to keep them in. When you have a question, hold the pouch in your hand while concentrating on it. Then reach in and pull out a handful of coins. If you pull out an even number then the answer is yes. An odd number is no.

Stone Divination

There are many, many different ways to use stones for divination purposes. Most are elaborate types of divination, but there are a few simple methods. You may

use a style similar to the coin one in the last lesson. Gather 10+ stones of an equal size and put them in a pouch. The small glass beads used in fish tanks work quite well. And they are very pretty too! Again, hold the pouch in your hand while concentrating on the question. Reach in and pull out a handful. An even amount is positive. A negative number means no.

You may also take two similar stones and paint one black and one white. Or find similar sized stones of those colors. Keep them in a pouch. Hold the pouch while thinking of your question. Reach in and pull out one stone. Black is no, white is yes.

Water Divination

Place a flower petal in the bottom of a bowl. Slowly fill the bowl up with water, while concentrating on your question. If it floats then your answer is yes. If it doesn't then the answer is no. If it floats then sinks, no answer is possible at the time.

Similarly, you can take three small scraps of paper and write yes on one, no on another and leave the last blank. Place all three in the bottom of the bowl. Slowly fill the bowl with water, all the while concentrating on your question. The first slip that rises to the top is your answer, blank being that no answer is available at the moment.

Flower Divination

Here are two more methods I'm sure you are all familiar with. The 'she loves me, she loves me not' trick works just as well with yes/no questions. Hold a daisy in your hand and concentrate on your question. Then pluck the petals, saying with each petal, 'yes,' 'no,' 'yes,' etc. The last petal plucked will be your answer.

Then there's the dandelion trick. Take a fluffy dandelion and hold it in your hand while concentrating on your question. Then blow the seeds away. If all leave then the answer is yes. If most leave then the answer is yes, but you won't see results just yet. If most are left then the answer is no.

5. Make a Divination Box
by Oberon (grey)

Most forms of divination begin with a ran-dom

distribution of elements, and then attempt to make some magickal sense out of them by finding patterns. When we flip a coin to get "heads" or "tails" it is random. In *cartomancy* (card reading), the first thing we do is shuffle the deck. Dice, runestones, knuckle bones, yarrow stalks. and oracle stones are "thrown" by scattering them. Some systems use a set background template, like a dartboard, where various sections are assigned meanings, and whatever falls within certain sections attains the significance or meaning of that section.

In the mundane world, it's sort of like deciding where to take a vacation by closing your eyes and sticking a pin into a map! Wherever the pin lands is assigned the definition of "Holiday destination." Horoscopes are charted that way, with the positions of the planets and stars falling into various "houses." Tarot card readings are "laid out" according to a particular spread design.

Here's a simple divination system you can create yourself:

Find a shallow 8-1/2"x11" box, or box lid, like the ones notepaper comes in. Take a piece of paper the same size and fold it into four sections. In the upper right section, write the word "YES." In the upper left, write "MAYBE." In the lower left, write "NO." And in the last section, write "DUNNO." Unfold the paper and place it in the box so you can see the writing. Next, on another piece of paper, write some simple question for which an answer could be "yes" or "no." Find a special small stone or crystal you particularly fancy. To do a reading, hold that stone cupped in your hands and shake it up good while you repeat the question over and over. Then, say the following:

> *O mighty Fates*
> *The pact is sealed*
> *Now let this fortune*
> *Be revealed!*

Now, toss the stone into the box, aiming for the center point. Whatever space it lands in gives you your answer.

If you'd like to add an extra dimension of probability to this reading, use a die instead of a stone. The higher the number, the higher the probability for that answer.

Practically all systems of magickal divination are based on this simple principle; some systems are just a lot more elaborate and complex than others. You could divide that paper into as many sections as you want, in any shapes you want, and write anything you want in the sections. And you could use dice instead of stones, with the numbers giving added "weight and meaning" to the sections they land in. No matter how complex you make it, the principle is the same.

6. Jokers Wild: Playing Card Divination

By LeopardDancer (grey)

Playing card divination *(cartomancy)* is similar to Tarot card divination, but simplified and much easier to do at a whim.

History

There are several theories regarding the origins of modern playing cards. One says they came from China, during the 7th to 10th centuries, where the Chinese 'money cards' strongly resemble modern card styles. The 'money cards,' engraved on copper and silver, were comprised of four numbered suits. Indian cards from a similar era as the Chinese 'money cards' were also broken into four suits: scepters, swords, cups and rings. A really unusual theory has chess and cards evolving from divinatory practices of primitive peoples, but there is not much support for this idea. Another theory of playing card origins has Marco Polo bringing the concepts back to Europe with him after his travels to China.

Another theory has them originating in Egypt, where a card game comprised of 4 numbered suits was played. These suits were swords, polo sticks, cups and coins. Each suit consisted of 10 numbered cards and three 'court cards,' the same as today's kings, queens and jacks. The Crusaders and the Romany (Gypsies) are other possible contenders for the origins of modern cards. An Arab origin theory is linked to the Saracen invasion of Sicily and the Moorish conquest of Spain. Indeed, the Spanish and Italian words for cards (*naipes,* naibi) share a linguistic Arab root. Though, in all likelihood they come from as many different sources as their cousins, the tarot cards. And like the tarot cards, playing cards can be elaborately decorated.

Cards are mentioned as early as 1299 in Italy, 1370 in Spain, and 1380 in Germany. The earliest European decks to resemble ours today featured 52 cards in 4 suits, 10 numbered cards per suit and a king and two marshals per suit. The French in particular, used playing cards as a divination tool. In fact, Napoleon planned (and believed he won) several key battles using the prophetic power of playing cards.

It is the French 52 card deck that is used worldwide today. The deck consists of an Ace, a King, a Queen and a Jack (once called Knave) and numbers 2-10 per suit. The suits themselves have different names and different symbols in various countries. The English adopted the French symbols, but changed the names. The French *pique* or pike looked like a spade to the English, the *carreau* or square was tipped over to become the diamond, the *trefle* or trefoil became the English club, and the *coeur* or heart remained the same.

Reading the Cards

One of the great things about playing card divination is that wherever you are you can buy a cheap deck of playing cards and have an instant divination tool. However, if you plan to make playing cards a major divination tool, you should have a deck that has meaning for you personally and either keep it under your pillow or, more traditionally, wrapped in black silk and placed on a high shelf, when they are not in use. Another great thing about playing cards as your divination tools is that they can also be used for mundane games as well as card tricks!

You may read playing cards for yourself or for others. You may use them for simple questions and for in-depth answers. If you are reading for someone else shuffle the deck a few times yourself and then have the questioner to do the same. The questioner then cuts the deck three times (traditionally using the left hand, associated with intuition) and then you will shuffle the deck once more and deal the cards. Or you may have the questioner spread the facedown cards in a circle and draw randomly for a reading.

Card Meanings

Playing card meanings are not set in stone. They may be adapted for individual use without changing the underlying significance. Meanings are not direct parallel to tarot but are definitely shaded by the tarot Minor Arcana.

If you should choose to include the Joker cards, they may be suggestive of unexpected factors or of fate, such as the blank rune in a Runecaster's bag. However, Jokers do not have to be used and this is an individual choice of the reader. For myself, I choose not to use them as I do not use the blank rune.

Pairs and sets have special significance when reading playing cards. Four of a same number means a greatly amplified result, whether positive or negative. Three of the same signifies harmony of different forces. Two of a kind represent either conflict, reconciliation or connections, depending on the suits involved. If the court or face cards show up in excess then the focus is usually persons rather than situations.

Diamonds

Diamonds correspond to the Pentacles in Tarot. This is the suit of Earth and represents the information garnered from our five senses and from common sense. Diamonds refer to practical things.

Ace- a new financial or practical matter, change of home, a home related project, or an upsurge of prosperity.

Two- balance between two aspects of life or between areas of responsibility, a mutually beneficial partnership, domestic issues resolved through exerting effort, extra source of income.

Three- a venture with firm roots or a strong grounding, addition to the family in some way(usually through birth), extra commitments or 'burdens' that will end up having long term advantages.

Four- limitations in the practical sphere where one must decide to either gamble and risk it or to be content with what one has already, choices for the home or regarding kids may not be easy, stress importance of patience regarding property or finance issues that seem to have no immediate resolutions.

Five- temporary practical or monetary problems may foster a feeling of isolation. Look for a new source of advice or help. Don't abandon your plans but modify them where necessary.

Six- documents and small print are important. Keep a tight rein on finances and avoid too many commitments. Reflect and conserve energy rather than taking action. Family matters may take over for awhile.

Seven- harmony in domestic and financial matters. Long term plans are favored at this time. Put trust in your dreams and intuition as well as your common sense. Children or animals may bring joy.

Eight- a new practical or money-making skill may be discovered. Family or financial situations may change abruptly. Channel any restlessness into tangible improvements.

Nine- put personal interests first. Success lies through speculation and expanding horizons. Independent thoughts and actions are favored.

Ten- success financially or happiness in the home. Completion of plans or practical matters; or a new permanent domestic commitment.

Jack- a practical, reliable younger person whose common sense, helpful attitude and responsibility with money make them seem wise beyond their years. Unvarying comfort and support through good times and bad.

Queen- a practical organized older woman or one in a long term relationship; her skills lie in making others feel at home in any setting and in sorting out problems; a good ally and a caring mother figure.

King- though sometimes considered dull, this king is reliable in all areas; he has near infinite patience, and tends to show affection through deeds rather than words.

Hearts

This suit corresponds to the Cups or chalices of Tarot. They are tied to the Element of Water and usually signify love, emotion, intuition, relationships of all sorts, those in love or people who are in their twenties/thirties.

Ace- an important new relationship or friendship; a new beginning emotionally; a sudden burst of insight that should be trusted; unexpected happiness or a new start after an emotional setback; unreturned love.

Two- a love match, a deep commitment of love or marriage, growing friendship or a mending of old quarrels. The coming together of two different aspects of ones life.

Three- rivalry in love or friendship. Emotional conflicts in which two people seek sympathy or favor. Stress caused by others emotional pressure or blackmail.

Four- choices involving the emotions. General feelings of restlessness and emotional dissatisfaction. Another person's commitments may be in question.

Five- misunderstandings; a need to communicate from the heart; accepting the reality of things as they are now rather than yearning for the impossible; passions that may not be wise.

Six- harmony and quite contentment, whether in friendship or love. The positive influences of loyal friends; accepting that differences of attitude in others are not conducive to fostering loving or friendly relationships. Reconciliation, especially with older people.

Seven- intuition, dreams, and telepathic communication. Trust your true instincts and inner voice. Communication will be spiritual and deep with those close to you. May find that colleagues, coworkers and acquaintances share the same wavelength as you and are eager to cooperate.

Eight- movement to a new phase in a relationship. Be aware of jealousy, the need to end potentially destructive relationships or attachments or to end emotional blackmail. Maybe enjoy a holiday with loved ones.

Nine- emotional independence; self confidence. Very lucky card. Harbinger of happiness in chosen area of life whither love or personal venture or what have you.

Ten- emotional happiness and fulfillment through others. Giving emotionally to others and deriving satisfaction from others. Happy marriage or relationships.

Jack- a young person, an emotionally vulnerable older person or and incurable romantic of any age who seeks perfection in love. The original 'knight in shining armor' who may love sentiment and romance more than the real life person.

Queen- a mature woman, any woman in a permanet relationship or a woman who nurtures others and provides an ear and a shoulder to cry on. They can become overwhelmed by other's sorrows and emotional needs that she may lose her own identity. May hold others back from full emotional independence without realizing it.

King- an older man who has charisma and the ability to make everyone feel as if they are special and worth something. If faithful he is a great romantic and very gentle, but he can be easily tempted with flattery. Alternatively, may be a social worker type who cares for the troubles of the world but find his own emotions difficult to handle or control.

Clubs

Clubs correspond to the Tarot Wands or staves. They are associated with the Element of Fire and in readings they speak to ambitions, success, career, health, travel, expansion, business ventures, communication, mature people, and coworkers/colleagues.

Ace- a new beginning in a career, a new ambition, original ideas, a new perspective or an opportunity to travel. A new channel of communications. A desire to be free from a restricting situation.

Two- a time to deliberate on possible options or paths. Plans involving others may seem restrictive. There is a need to balance the demands of career and health, especially when exhaustion or stress is a major factor. Approach possible business ventures or partners with caution.

Three- decisions about travel and an opportunity to broaden horizons. Business or work commitments and opportunities may increase and will demand extra energy and input. Communication will involve several people.

Four- move forward despite the constraints placed by others, though this can be frustrating. The ability to win trust is vital and clear communication is essential, even if this slows things down. Written communications may be more valuable than verbal in clarifying oneself and ones position.

Five- a time to argue one's case and to stand one's ground in matters outside the home. Care should be taken healthwise to avoid accidents through exhaustion and carelessness as well as stress from over involvement in problems caused or created by others. Rivals may be less open to communication or compromise. May sure to get the credit you deserve for your input and ideas.

Six- a tranquil period at work; the opportunity should be taken for a short break from responsibility and to spend time relaxing and resting; health should be stable or should show improvement. This is a time for creativity and networking to make contacts for future en devours.

Seven- personal success and satisfaction. High levels of energy and creativity. Ideals are important and there may be principles for which you will need to fight. Ultimate happiness comes from seeing beyond immediate returns to a long term goal.

Eight- a sudden upsurge of energy, enterprise, changes in career, travel or lifestyle. A time to 'seize the day.' Perhaps even striking out on your own in some way.

Nine- responsibilities may seem overwhelming with too much to do and very little time in which to do it. Many of these burdens can and should be delegated. Self-doubt and loss of confidence make things seem worse than they really are. Press ahead with courage and conviction.

Ten- successful completion of a goal; a chance to change direction and learn new skills, perhaps regarding communication. A dream, an ideal, or overriding ambition will be realized in the near future. Look for personal happiness, self-confidence and independence.

Jack- an energetic young person or someone who is constantly dashing from one thing to another. This jack is inclined to lose interest in something if things do not go well and they tend to be absorbed in their work or interests to the exclusion of other people. He or she is a great communicator, but can be rather blunt with the truth.

Queen- a mature woman who is independent whether she is in a permanent relationship or not. She is a good organizer, is energetic and is able to combine many different strands of life. This may, however, lead to exhaustion. She is tactful and persuasive and gets what she wants will still managing to keep everyone happy.

King- a successful, ambitious man, who is an innovator and a powerful communicator. They do tend to be insensitive to the needs and feelings of others, usually because they are impatient to finish a task. He can generally find a way around any difficulty. This king is idealistic and will not compromise on matters of principle.

Spades

Spades are the equivalent of Tarot's Swords and represent the Element of Air. They represent limitations, challenges, traditions, formal learning, justice, assessment, older people and aging.

Ace- a new beginning after difficulty or sorrow. A new form of learning. A sudden recourse to justice. A new challenge that can open doors.

Two- two alternatives that may not seem attractive, but between which a choice must be made. The need to use logic when there may be conflict between people or life aspects. Deciding the truth of two bits of information.

Three- malice or rivalry that can only be solved by reason. Accepting challenges or overcoming obstacles that may involve time and effort, but will lead to success. Assimilating facts that seem to have no immediate use, but may become useful later.

Four- limitations and obstacles come mainly from inner fears based on past experiences. Injustices may be keenly felt, but unless they can be resolved, should be set aside. Moving forward may involve losses, however unfair.

Five- be sure of facts to avoid mistakes, hidden spite and less than honest dealings by others. Disillusionment that others may not have high standards should not cause you to abandon your plans, though you may need to be less open with your intentions.

Six- formal justice may prove surprisingly helpful. A calm period after turbulence or self-doubt. Relationships that have been difficult may show improvement.

Seven- intuition helps when logic and expert opinion fall. Maximize any advantages and do not draw back from possible conflict.

Eight- change is possible if you leave the past behind you and look to the future with hope. Talk through your worries and fears and you may find that the future holds many possibilities you had not considered. New contacts and avenues will prove useful.

Nine- courage and determination can overcome anything thrown your way. Fears of failure and rejection are unfounded. Battles are better fought in truth than in your head. You know more than you think you do.

Ten- better times are ahead. May indicate a natural ending to which there will follow a new beginning. Optimism is the key here.

Jack- a young person or an immature older person who can hurt others thoughtlessly or purposefully. Usually very clever and humorous which can manifest as sarcasm and witty criticism. Tend to be distrustful of people and of life in general though there are usually reasons behind such beliefs.

Queen- known as the Queen of Sorrows, this is a critical, disappointed mature woman, the gossiping neighbor, disapproving mother-in-law. This queen, however, can be surprisingly loyal and forceful of defending her own. She is often possessive out of fear of being left alone.

King- this is the disapproving authority figure, the harsh judge, the critical father, the one whose own vast store of knowledge makes him intolerant of others mistakes. A perfectionist who fears his own vulnerability and so prefers isolation.

Divination spreads

There are several ways to read the playing cards and one can adapt any Tarot spread to use these cards with. You may choose a single card reading or to use several cards in a spread. Three such spreads are a *three-card spread,* the *Horseshoe spread* and the *Celtic Cross spread.*

A *single-card spread* is used to give an overview of a situation. In a *three-card spread,* three cards are randomly drawn and laid from left to right. These are read the same way they are laid. The first card (on the far left) is the past card, the one in the middle is the present and the one to the far right is the future. This spread can be applied to any situation to provide an indication of the influences that have caused the situation (past card), the influences currently predominant (present) and the likely outcome of the matter (future).

A *Horseshoe spread* is similar to the three-card spread but seven cards are laid out from left to right. This is used most often for a single situation or question. The first card represents the past and the influences that gave rise to the current situation. The second card revolves around present circumstances. The third represents the questioner's hopes and fears about the question involved. The fourth card deals with the obstacles and problems the questioner must deal with in regards to the situation. The fifth card represents the people and environment around the questioner. The

sixth is the future and fresh events that will affect the situation. The seventh and last card represents the most likely outcome of the situation based on the other cards.

The *Celtic Cross spread* is used in many forms of divination such as Tarot and Runecasting. This spread may be used to address specific issues or to do in-depth readings.

1 - the Present. The predominating events, issues, attitudes and influences around the question or situation.

2 - the Cross. Current obstacles, problems, conflicts and oppositions that the questioner must deal with.

3 - the Root. The basis or cause of the current situation.

4 - the Past. Events or influences from the recent past that are just now starting to fade away.

5 - the Crown. The best that can be achieved from the current situation.

6 - the Future. Future events and fresh influences about to come into play.

7 - the Questioner. How the questioner relates to the situation in question.

8 - the House. How people around the questioner affect and view the matters at hand.

9 - the Hopes and Fears. Questioner's hopes and fears regarding the question or current situation.

10 - the Outcome. The long-term outcome of the situation or the lesson that can be learned from it.

7. Tasseomancy: Tea Leaf Reading

by Oberon & Moonwriter

Tea was first used in China, over 5,000 years ago—as both a refreshing beverage and a soothing medicine. It was imported to England in the mid-17th century as a luxury drink. Until 1885, most tea came from China (hence the expression: "Not for all the tea in China!"), but after that date, India and Ceylon got into the act, and soon became the largest suppliers of tea to the Western world.

Tea was so valuable in Victorian times that it was often kept locked in little boxes to prevent the servants from sampling it! This is when tea-leaf reading, or *Tasseomancy,* became a popular form of divination

"Cup-Tossing" by N.J. Crowley

among upper-class ladies. It is customarily shared only among close friends.

Reading tea leaves

For each guest, place 1 tsp of dried mint leaves into a teacup. Cover with freshly-boiled water and allow to steep for five minutes. Either have your guests drink the tea, or pour the water off carefully, leaving the leaves and a bit of liquid. Each person then covers their cup with their hand and swirls the cup several times. Then, guests should exchange teacups and "read" the leaves. The clumps form the symbols, including shapes, letters or numbers.

Unfortunately, just as with Dream interpretation, there are several entirely different tables of interpretations for the images formed by the leaves. Here are some of the most common arrangements and interpretations:

Airplane: an impending journey
Anchor: an unpleasant situation
Apple: prosperity, achievement
Arrow: bad news in love
Axe: possible danger or difficulty to you or a friend
Ball: desire to travel
Bell: good news
Bird: good luck, good news
Boat: a visit from a friend
Book (closed): a question needing investigation
Book (open): the answer to a question
Candle: a light for the future, help from friends
Cat: deceit, a false friend
Circle: success
Coin: prosperity
Dog: a loyal friend
Eggs: new life
Eye: caution, foresight
Fountain: great happiness
Hat: an upcoming honor, promotion, or raise
House: comfort, home
Kettle: peace in the home
Kite: wishes that will come true

Ladder: success in business
Leaf: a new life
Letters: names of friends or relatives
Man: a visitor, male or female
Numbers: indicate spans of time, like months or years
Owl: good or bad luck ahead
Pig: greed
Snake: an enemy nearby
Spider: reward for work
Square: the need for caution
Star: hope
Sword: warning of future arguments
Tree: health
Triangle: a good omen, good luck
Turtle: criticism
Wolf: jealousy

8. Libanomancy: The Ritual Art of Incense Divination

By Katlyn Breene

Burnt spices flash, and burnt wine hisses,
The breathing flame's mouth curls and kisses
The small dried rows of frankincense
All round the red blossoms smolder,
Flowers colored like fire, but colder,
In a sign of things taken hence…
      (From Algernon Swinburne's "Illicit")

Libanomancy is the art of divination through incense. Signs are read in the flares, pops and crackling sounds as the incense burns upon the coals and also the shapes formed in the rising smoke. Incense containing small seeds (corriander, jesamine, fennel, hemp) or vesta powder (saltpeter) works well when asking a question of the oracle censer. As you ask your question aloud, listen for the answer in the popping of the seeds or the flashing of the powder. For example, one sign for "yes," two in quick secession for "no," silence for "the outcome is unclear." Signs can be read by scrying in the smoke, watching its direction. If it drifts toward you it is a positive omen.

If you are at one with me,
Rise towards me O smoke.
If you are not at one with me,
Rise athwart me O smoke,
Either to the right or to the left…

If the incense ceases to burn prematurely it means that "now is not the time to ask." The ashes can also be read when the burning is complete, finding shapes and symbols in the censer much like reading tea leaves in a cup. Magicians and seers of the 16th and 17th centuries used aromatic seeds in a rite of divination. The seeds were cast into a fiery cauldron and the future interpreted from the shapes assumed by the smoke. Trea-sure-seeking magicians used incense and fire wor-ship to achieve their ends as observed in this old incantation:

Fire, fire, blessed fire,
Unto fortune I aspire.
So I hope that I may see
A fortune that will come to me.

9. Dowsing
© 2004 by Donata Ahern (aqua)

Note: This material is adapted, with permission, from "Letter to Robin" by Walter Woods, a long time dowser, at http://www.lettertorobin.org/ The American Society of Dowsers has more informa-tion at http://www.dowsers.org/

According to the ASD, "dowsing is the active and sys-tematic experiencing of intuition." Dowsing is done with the use of a tool. Dowsing has been used for cen-turies to find water. Water, minerals, and other objects seem to have a natural magnetic, electromagnetic or other energy. The body is sensitive to these energies. Most people can develop a degree of dowsing skill with training, and practice. A dowsing tool makes you more aware of subtle subconscious reactions. A dows-ing tool is simply an interface or communication de-vice that seems to be controlled through or by your subconscious. Most dowsers use some type of dow-Ing tool, the most popular of which is the **Pendulum.**

Four different types of dowsing rods.
Abbe de Villemont, Traite de la Physique Occulte, *1693*

Basic Dowsing Tools

There are many very successful dowsing systems and methods, with or without tools. The most popular in-volve the use of **L Rods, Y Rods**, and the **Pendulum.** Many dowsers have a whole pile of dowsing tools that they have collected or made. Your choices should be determined by what tools feel and work good for you.

L-RODS
(Angle Rod, Swing Rod, Pointing Rod

Shape: With or without a sleeve handle. The top wire can be 4 inches to over 2 feet long. The usual length is around 12 to 16 inches.

Material: Usually wire. A metal coat hanger is a good source. Welding rod is also a very popular mate-rial. You can use use about anything that you can bend into the L shape.

How to Use: Hold loosely in your hand with the top wire tilted slightly downward. When one L Rod is used alone, it acts as a pointer or a swing rod. It can be requested to point towards a target or direction, or to swing sideways when encounter-ing a specified energy field. (i.e. an aura or nox-ious zone.) When using two L Rods, they are nor-mally programmed to point straight forward for the ready position, to cross for the "yes" response or when over a target, and to swing outward for the "no" response.

Advantages: Easy to make, easy to use, very versa-tile and popular. Works well when walking over rough ground. They are generally not affected by mild winds.

Disadvantage: Not as easy to carry or conceal as a pendulum. Although the small 4 - 6 inch ones can be put in your shirt pocket or purse.

Y-ROD (Forked Stick)

Shape: Traditionally it is a forked stick looking like the letter Y. They can be any size, but are usually around 12 to 24 inches in length.

Material: Can be wood, metal or plastic. Plastic is commonly used by modern dowsers, probably be-cause it is easy to store.

How to Use: Hold with pointed end down. Thumbs will be up and palms towards center. Hold tight and spread Y Rod outward while rotating your wrist outward. Your thumbs will now be pointed outward and your palms up. The Y Rod will flip up into a delicate balance. Pointing upward at an angle of around 45 degrees is usually used for the ready position. Swinging down from the ready position to point at a water vein or target. This may also be used for the "yes" response. Swinging up from the ready position is usually used for the no" response.

Advantages: Acts quickly, can point directly towards a water vein or target. Works well while walking over rough ground or in fairly strong winds.

Disadvantage: Not as versatile as other dowsing tools. It only has an up and down motion. You will need to turn your body to find direction.

PENDULUM

Shape: Can be anything that you can hang, on a string or chain. They can be any size, even as small as a paperclip on a thread. The chain or string is usually about 3-4 inches long.

Materials: Anything you can find. Go by your feelings. Crystals, metal, and wood all work well.

How to Use: Hold end of string between thumb and forefinger, with pendulum hanging down. The usual response request is swinging straight forward for "yes," sideways for "no," and at a angle for "ready for question."

Advantages: Easy to make. Easy to use. Very Popular. Small enough to go in your pocket or purse. Quick response. Excellent tool for dowsing charts or maps.

Disadvantage: Some problem in the wind or when walking. This problem can be overcome by requesting (prearranging, programming) the pendulum to spin in a clockwise or counterclockwise direction to indicate the "yes" or "no" response.

Pendulum Dowsing

Learning to use the pendulum:

Find a quiet place where you will have privacy. Hold the pendulum as shown in the picture. You will want to know how your pendulum responds to "yes" and 'no." The most common response is for the pendulum to swing straight forward for "yes," and sideways for "no." You may get sideways for "not at this time" or "maybe." Some pendulums swing clockwise for "yes" and counterclockwise for "no." Feel free to program your dowsing tool to respond any way you like.

Step 1. Relax, and drift into a quiet state.

Step 2. Take your pendulum and hold the end of the string or chain between your thumb and first finger. Next, dangle the pendulum over the center of a chart like this one (right).

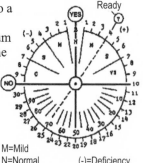

M=Mild
N=Normal   (-)=Deficiency,
B=Balanced   decrease, etc.
S=Strong   (+)=Excess,
VS=Very strong   increase, etc.
C=Critical   Numbers=intensity

Step 3. Move your hand and fingers to make the pendulum start swinging towards the "YES" and ask and expect it to keep swinging on its own without your help. If it stops, start over again, and ask it to keep going. Repeat until the pendulum swings on its own. You will be deliberately starting the pendulum and then asking it to keep swinging with no additional help from you.

S*tep 4.* Do the same thing for the "NO."

Step 5. Once it is swinging by itself to the "NO," ask it to work its way clockwise back to "YES."

Step 6. These are the basic pendulum controls you will need. If you can do the above steps, you are now ready to proceed. If you were not able to accomplish the above in about 15 minutes, try again in about half an hour or the next day. Don't give up.

Do's and Don'ts When Dowsing

1. **Sensing:** When sensing for information, don't attach yourself to it. For example, if you are watching a movie, you are free to react to it in many ways. How you approach the seeking of information is your choice. The advantage of using a pendulum, or other dowsing device is that you don't need to try to physically sense or become part of the energies.

2. **To Protect Yourself**. To avoid absorbing undesirable energies, talk to your pendulum as if it were a person. This will direct the energies to the pendulum and not to you. This keeps your mind on the action of the pendulum and not on the energies.

3. **The Question:** The subconscious mind is very literal in its interpretation of your questions and apparently makes no assumptions. For example if you ask: "Does my car need gas?' The answer is YES. You assumed it knows you were talking about the amount of gasoline in the gas tank, but that was not what you asked. Many seemingly wrong answers are really correct in the literal interpretation of the question. Make the question a definite request for information existing somewhere, and not for an opinion of the past, present or future. Make your question as complete as possible. An example of an incomplete question is: "Do you have enough money?" For what? The answer will be unclear. If instead you ask: "Do you have enough money, in your pocket right now, for a $1 ice cream cone?" You could then give a very definite and accurate answer.

4. **Life's Lessons and Restricted Areas:** It is unethical to interfere with anyone's 'Lessons in Life", their free will choices, their "Karma" or other unknown areas. Always ask your pendulum, May I, Can I, Should I? If the answer is NO, then don't ask the question.

5. **Privacy**: Never dowse a person without their knowledge. Always respect personal privacy.

6. **Karma: Keep in mind the** law of cause and effect, or Karma, that what you send out will return to you.. Always dowse for the best good of others. Never dowse for evil or harmful purposes.

7. **Diagnosing:** Do not diagnose or give medical advice of any kind!! Always advise anyone to get medical advice if they think they have a problem.

8. **Keep it Simple:** Try to keep your dowsing as simple as you can. Be sure to practice and enjoy your dowsing.

9. How to Make Your Own Runes

By Rev. Robert Lee (Skip) Ellison (yellow)

Runes are a valuable tool to help us tell the future and to listen to what our subconscious mind is telling us. For most people, runes work best if they are made by the person using them. Because people's level of skill for making runes varies, this section will be discussing methods that range from very easy to slightly more difficult.

The easiest method is to find some flat discs at a craft store about 1" in diameter and drawn one rune on each with an ultra-fine point Sharpie®. These discs are usually made of hardwood and come 25 to a bag so work perfect for this project. Runes made this way hold up very well over time.

The next method involves the same flat discs but instead of using a pen to draw on the rune, a wood-burning tool will be used to create an older looking depiction of the rune. Using a wood-burning tool takes practice. Before working on your actual rune discs, practice drawing each rune several times on a piece of scrap wood with the tool to get the feel of using it.

A third method using the flat disc involves scribing each rune on it with an awl to get an incised line rendering of each rune and then using a very fine paint brush to fill in each line. This method takes much more practice and time but produces some very beautiful runes. You can color each aett (group of 8 runes) a different color or use one color for all or have each rune a different color.

The next material to work with is stones. The best stones to use for runestones are small stones that have been tumbled in a river to produce smooth surfaces. Bags of these stones can be found in craft stores or for a more personalized set, you can pick them up yourself along a river. Either way, they make very nice looking rune material.

For the runes and their meanings, see the *Grimoire*, pp. 234-235. These runes can be drawn on the stones with the ultra-fine point Sharpie® or, for a more challenging project, they can be engraved with a variable speed Dremel® tool using a small carbide tip. Working with a Dremel® tool takes even more practice than with a wood-burning tool so allow plenty of time and material for the practice!

Once you have decided on your material and method and have practiced so that you can comfortably draw all the runes, it is time to get to the actual work. If you purchased the material, you might want to do a simple cleansing on the discs or stones first. This can

be done by allowing them to sit in the light of the sun and the moon for a twenty-four hour period. The light of the full moon works best for this process. The runes will be used to contact your subconscious mind so it is important to let that part of yourself work in the creation process.

Start by laying all the discs or stones out on a table before you. Think of the name of the rune you will be creating and see it strongly in your mind. Say it aloud and let the name vibrate in the air. Slowly move your hand over the discs or stones while repeating the name until one of the disc or stones 'calls' to you—that it is the one to be used. Take that disc or rune and lightly mark the name of the rune on it with a pencil or place it so that you know which rune goes with it. At this point, all you are doing is picking which stone or disc will be used for each one, not doing the actual work of placing the rune on it. You may need to allow yourself an hour or two for this work.

When all the discs or stones have been associated with individual runes, it is time to start the process of placing the runes. As you are doing the actual work of putting the rune on, by whichever method you choose, keep repeating the name of the rune over and over, vibrating it fully and seeing it fully developed in your mind until it is fully placed and then set it aside. The time you need will depend on the process but if you take 10 minutes for each rune, it will be a total of four hours. So make sure you set enough time aside to do this part.

With the main work done, it is time to bless your runes and prepare them for their work on a higher level. Place them in the bag they will be kept in and make a call to your gods and ancestors to help you in your work with them. In the Druid way, the call would go something like: *"I call now to my ancestors, to the spirits of nature and to the gods I swear by, hear me now! I hold before you this set of runes that have been made by my own hand. I pledge to you this day to always use them in honesty and trust, to interpret them to the best of my ability and preserve the old ways. Mighty Kindreds, hear me and bless my runes!"*

Now that your set is completed, it is time to attune them to you even more. Keep them in a bag and place them near you as you sleep. Also carry them with you whenever possible and during the day, allow your hand to move through them, to become accustom to the feel of them. To do a divination with them, move your hand through them until you feel the one that calls out to you to be picked. Over time, you will gain confidence in your new runes set and will learn that what it tells you is true.

Department VIII: Performance [orange]

These Poems Are Not Very Shy

These poems are not very shy.
My words have spirits of their own –
I give them wings and bid them fly.

I do not have the artist's eye
To paint with ink or carve with bone,
But poems are not very shy.

It does not matter what you try,
For words have spirits of their own

And will not lay them down to die.

They give me wings and bid me fly
Through skies that I have never known
Where moonbeams bow as I go by.

We spread our wings and dare to fly
With words and spirits of our own,
For poets are not very shy.

—Elizabeth Barrette

1. Introduction

ELCOME TO THE WORLD OF Performance Magics! Also called *conjury* or stage magic, performance magic deals with "miraculous" illusions and special effects, which have been used in enhancing the theater of ritual since the first campfire was lit. Various types of performance, such as magic acts, acrobatics, juggling, puppetry, and fire-eating, all came from such rituals. This department also covers the Bardic Arts of music, chanting, poetry, singing, and storytelling.

You may notice that everywhere else in this book, "magick" is spelled with a "k." This convention was established by Aleister Crowley (1875-1947) to distinguish transformational magick from illusions, or conjury. But in this Department, we will, indeed, be exploring the magic of illusion and performance, so here we will spell it without the "k."

This department will teach you the essential skills, both physical and conceptual, to make your performances consistent with magickal and ritual activities. These arts follow the time honored position of getting the audience's attention so that focused magical arts can be effective and memorable.

The color of magick associated with this department is orange, representing pride and courage; heroism and attraction; kinship and prosperity (as in a good harvest). Orange is attuned to warmth, friendship, abundance, spirit, will, principles, theory and alertness. It is also associated with the performance arts and conjury.

2. Archetypes of the Magician

By Jeff "Magnus" McBride (orange)

At Mystery School, we wanted to create a feeling of intimacy, trust, and connection among the participants. I knew it would be important for us to be able to meet in smaller groups, so we created four divisions of people with similar desires, interests, and skills. The theme of each group was one of four aspects of the roles of the magician: the Trickster, the Sorcerer, the Oracle, and the Sage. These four archetypes represent a life cycle, and a learning curve, but of course there are many other possible combinations of magical masks—or personae—that the actor/magician may choose to play.

Tricksters are fast-talking, and quick-thinking. They represent the element of Air. Many magicians get into magic around the age of adolescence. The Trickster teaches us how to use magic to develop our communication skills. Some magicians stay Tricksters and never feel the need to explore the other archetypes. Some modern day Tricksters have developed this style of magic to a high art. Penn and Teller, Dan Harlan, and Robert Neale are all excellent examples of modern performers that exude the Trickster spirit. In the age cycle of the magician, this would represent the earliest phase, and the birth of our fascination with magic.

Sorcerers are skillful, disciplined and put considerable time and energy into their magical work. They evoke the element of Fire. Not only are they interested in their art, they are interested in honing their skills in stage craft and the theatrical arts. Modern-day sorcerers would include Jonathan Pendragon, Siegfried & Roy, and Lance Burton. Many magicians choose to move into the discipline of the Sorcerer after they've explored the archetype of the Trickster to their satisfaction. In the age cycle of the magician, this represents physical mastery and would approximately fall between the ages of twenty through the forties.

The Oracle becomes more interested in matters of insight and intuition. Oracles explore subtle techniques of mentalism and psychology. The elemental correspondence of the Oracle is Water. Exploring the depths of the collective unconscious are modern-day Oracles Max Maven and Alain Nu. This represents the middle stage in the magician's maturity, age forty to sixty.

The Sage is the mentor and master of the art, whose work it is to pass on a lifetime of distilled wisdom to those who would seek to drink from this font.

Sages represent the element of Earth, patience and power. They are interested in the philosophy and history of magic and in teaching what they've learned, keeping the art alive. Eugene Burger and Rene Lavand are two of the important Sages in the world today. The Sage represents the later part of a magician's life, from age sixty and up.

We have contemplated these roles of the archetypal Magician for many years and learned that a well-rounded magician can play any one of them at various times, sometimes in the course of a single performance. But to begin, you can select one to focus on. Which one of the four faces of the Magician will you choose?

3. Bizarre Magik

A magical performance with the emphasis on entertaining rather than just fooling the audience is known among professional conjurers as "Bizarre Magik." Theatrical elements and special effects are added to make the entire journey a magical experience. Props are designed to look like authentic ancient magickal artifacts. Here is what a few noted performers of this art have to say about it:

"Bizarre Magik provides you, the performer, a chance to put wonder and mystery back into magical entertaining. To create the mystery of the old mage, the Merlin of the past, and deal with what your audience would perceive as real magick, not just tricks and illusions, but the real thing. All of this should leave your audience with the feeling that real magic does exist and they have just seen it…The scope is only limited by our imaginations, so free yours and be not just another magical entertainer but a worker of wondrous miracles." —Frank Allen

"First and foremost, Bizarre Magik is Theatre. And when I say that, I mean theatre in every sense and style of the word; dramatic, comedic, suspenseful, emotional, evocative, sensational, spectacle, and spiritual. The theatre, as we know it, originated in the Dionysian religious dramas of Greece—presentations that told the stories of the Gods. These stories strove to give civilization a way of understanding their connection to the Universe, each other, and ultimately

what happens after death. Bizarre Magik does all of this, and uses all of the element of theatre—story and stagecraft—to tell tales, tales that ultimately help us understand our place in the world, our relationship to others, and our relationship to the Universe…Conventional magic suffers from many boundaries and inadequacies—Bizarre Magik does not know of such boundaries. Tthey do not exist." —**Fred Zimmerman**

"It is in the performance of Bizarre Magik that we find the closest living examples of the nearly forgotten Wizards of ancient lore… the true Wise-ards of the past who knew the difference between illusion and Truth; the realists that understood the power of science and words and wonderment and how to bring into our mundane reality an elusive mystery known to us now as MAGICK." —***Craig Browning***

Bizarre Magik
by Don Wildgrube (orange)

I have known for quite a while that the art of "trickery" was a part of religion since religion became organized but I did not understand its usefulness. I had read about the ancient Egyptian temples at Crocodiliopolis that issued a clap of thunder when the doors opened, and mysterious altars on which a person built a sacrificial fire so that, if done right, a statue above it would pour a wine libation on it. I had read about the coffin of Xerxes, King of Persia, that could not be completely filled with oil, and how when food was left for the God Bel, in Babylon, in the evening, it was gone and only empty plates remained in the locked room in the morning.

To quote Walter B. Gibson in *Secrets of Magic*, "In Hero's day, the visitor to a pagan temple was at the mercy of its various optical and acoustical contrivances once he crossed the threshold. Bright lights, even pictured images were projected by burnished metal disks, some shaped like concave mirrors. Echo chambers and whispering galleries produced eerie voices that could be ascribed to any of the countless deities of that pantheistic age."

I also read about the Shamans that gathered bits and pieces of objects to apport (appear to materialize from thin air) when doing healings for others, or the Psychic Surgeons that pulled strange and bloody things out of a non-existent wound. Or even the miracle healings that are done at special places or in tent revivals. I never understood gullible people buying in to all of this.

In Mircea Eliade's book on *Shamanism*, the author says that in his training, he was taught to pick up "things" and put them in his medicine bag to be used later. When doing healing, some of them would be palmed and then shown to show that the healing was effective. Trickery or not, the patient believed that it happened and was cured. Does it really make a difference if trickery was used? In the case of the Psychic Doctor, does it really make a difference if he produces chicken entrails and blood in the non-invasive "operation," as long at the person gets better?

Trickery was used in ancient times and was recorded in the Bible. The Pharaoh's Sorcerers turned staffs into serpents. The staff is actually a snake, the *naja haje,* or the Egyptian cobra, that has the oddity to stretch out rigidly and became temporarily paralyzed by pressure just below the head. When thrown to the ground, it becomes its serpentine self again.

The Middle Ages were rife with other tricksters and charlatans.

To take this a step further and update it, there is a branch of stage magic called "Bizarre Magick." I was fortunate to find some old copies of a newsletter called "The New Invocation." In an issue from February 1989, Eugene Burger defined Bizarre Magick as: "Now bizarre magik is, at the very minimum, an attempt to make magical performance non-trivial." It was further defined by the late Tony Andruzzi (aka Masklyn ye Mage), who said:

"There are a few people intent on taking the special effects out of movies and doing them in the living room." The Goeticists [Tony preferred to use the term Goetic instead of Bizarre] are akin to the Alchemist. They took themselves seriously. They felt that by reciting certain rites and rituals they could control the elements of nature and the cosmos. Pretty grandiose! Bizarre means different. A goeticist uses Ritualistic Magick, to remove them from a suspension of disbelief and journey back, almost gene by gene chronologically to a time when their forefathers believed that those thing existed. It is a grandiose deception that I am playing." I always say in my opening patter, 'What you are about to see is neither religious nor sacrilegious but only a psychodynamic experiment to recreate what the old mages once thought valid. Let us see what validity lies in those beliefs.'"

"There is something soul satisfying in knowing that you've deceived someone thorough the goetic. It is more than doing magic tricks. For a moment you have not suspended disbelief, you have made believers who will later defrock themselves. A goeticist dies on a stage. The moment you put a proscenium arch around a goeticist you add theater."

This may sound confusing and wonder what this has to do with present day Pagans and Witches. If you go to websites about Tony Andruzzi, you will find that he was well regarded as a magician. But what is not written is that Tony was a Pagan and a Sicilian Witch— I met him at the 1972 "Gnosticon." He used his magick to play the role of the ancient priesthood. He used his magick to do more than his "brother" magicians in that he also used it in Ceremonial Magick. He used it to teach.

Now, why an article on Bizarre Magik or Goeta Magick? Because it is time to put some pizazz in our rituals. It is time for some special effects, some pyrotechnics, and who better to learn from than people like Tony Andruzzi?

I got a taste of it with my High Priest. When we put our hopes and wishes, etc. to paper to burn in a candle flame or cauldron, we did not use animal parchment, nor did we use vegetable parchment. We used flash paper. Touching the "spell" to a candle flame gave a quick, blinding flash. The speed of the flash and the duration of the flash would be used to tell how effective the spell was. This brought excitement to our coven gatherings.

He also used "Witch Powder." Witch Powder is powdered Magnesium and Saltpeter mixed in a plastic squeeze bottle with a nozzle. The powder was squirted into a candle flame and the result was a very large, bright flame about a foot wide and about 3 feet long. It too, was impressive and almost fatal. At one meeting we were doing a First Degree Initiation. The postulant was standing at the door to the circle, bound and blindfolded. The High Priestess had the coven sword at his heart and was asking the password for entry. At that time, the High Priest squirted the Witch Powder into the flame and nearly singed the High Priestess's rear, nearly causing her to impale the initiate. Fortunately, she was able to hold the sword in check. Since the initiate was blindfolded, he didn't know what had happened.

When I had a Church of All Worlds Nest in St. Louis in the early 1970s, I used some pyrotechnics in our Yule ritual. I wrote a short play in which the lessons of Winter's barrenness were taught. The ritual took place in my living room, which was changed into a throne room. The King and Queen were sad because summer was gone and the cold was coming on. "Old Father Winter" (played by Oberon) was called and, after a stern lecture, he decided to give the spark of life back to the people to show the return of warm weather. He pointed at a cauldron in the center of a low table and, as he did so, it burst into flame.

When Oberon pointed at the cauldron, an accomplice pushed a button. The concealed wires ran from a battery, across the floor under rugs, up through a hole in the tabletop and cover, through a crack in the cauldron, and finally ended at a model rocket motor starter. This was in a small can filled with paper, cloth and paraffin. The starter was surrounded by match heads and when the starter lit, it ignited the match heads, which set the cloth/paper/paraffin afire. Impressive!

I have chemical recipes for making different colored flames in the fire. Cremora works well to make a fire flare up (Unless you hold it in your hand too long and it absorbs the sweat from your palms.) There are other chemicals that make liquids glow. Morning Glory's recipe for "Intergalactic Gargle Blaster" is a simple one. She made punch from Grapefruit juice and rum, poured it into a clear glass bowl, put some glow sticks in the bottom (the long necklace ones work best) and placed a couple of hunks of dry ice in it.

Now on to some charlatry in the "New Age" movement. Many of you have seen people use "Kinesthesiology" to test people for things that are no good for them. The subject is asked to stand before the tester, hold one arm out to the side very rigidly. The tester then holds the persons shoulder in one hand while testing the strength of the subject. The first time is to gauge the strength. Next an item is placed in the free hand, or a cigarette in the mouth or some such connection. This time when the strength is tested there is no strength in the arm and the tester can easily move the subjects arm down. This may be honest in some cases but I am very skeptical when such tests take place. Look closely at the hand on the shoulder and you will see the tester's thumb placed just in the soft tissue above the collarbone and the neck. The slightest pressure there will render the subject powerless. This is, in fact, the basis of Star Trek's "Vulcan grip."

In another case, there was an article in an old *Fate* magazine about a small, slightly built, young lady that could not be picked up, even by the strongest weight lifter. The photos were a dead give away. The person doing the lifting was to place his hands under the elbows of the girl and lift. The girl rested her hands lightly on the lifters forearm near the inside of his elbow. Again a slight pressure from the thumb in the "crotch" of the arm, renders the most powerful and strong, powerless. I know, it happened to me!

Gypsies know about tricks. I'm not talking about the obvious scams. I am talking about seemingly truthful happenings. As an example, a gypsy horse trader fed a horse a portion of a tobacco leaf daily for months, then sold the horse to an unsuspecting buyer. The next day the horse escaped his "new owner" and made its way back to his "contact."

Another trick that we should be aware of is the use of the Ogham alphabet. There are four sets of five letters. Does this strike a familiar tune? We have five fingers and four knuckles on each hand. By subtle moving of the hand over a pre-arranged object, a message could be sent to another who was in on the trick. In "The White Goddess" by Robert Graves, there is a description of a color, an animal, and more associated with each Ogham symbol. A verbal coded message can be sent that will go over the heads of the uninitiated but well understood by those who are aware.

I say that we need to be more aware of subtle images, movements, talk and more, and we need to be able to use them for our benefit. If we can have these "super powers" we will truly be magicians of the highest caliber. For after all, the goal of Magick is results, whether by waving our actual wands or by waving a wand of another sort.

4. The Magician's Code
By Ken (faucon) Muller (grey)

You will find references to the "Code of Magic" in many myths, stories, books and articles. There is no single documented source or listing on which to call, but all references have certain themes in common. Yet the Code is more than an "unwritten agreement." It represents a personal commitment to the ideas of the preservation and vitality of the performing art. You will meet many people who do not subscribe to such a Code or who, after making a pledge, choose to violate it. However, as an apprentice Wizard you should be aware of the seriousness of the long-reaching effect of what you learn and practice. You will hopefully engage in magic performance, and "tricks" are easy to come by with no commitment whatsoever. As you enter advanced classes and serious practice, though, you will have to achieve a balance between your own personal code of action and ethics and what the mundane world subscribes to.

The art of magic is shrouded in secrecy. There are several reasons for this:

- The historic link with shamanism and magick
- The protection of livelihood (earning a living)
- The element of surprise
- The vitality of misdirection
- The bond of brotherhood among practicing magicians

The Code, then, is more of necessity than of honor. Simply put, if everyone knows what you are about to do, then there is no *magical* experience! Therefore:

1. Never reveal how an effect is done except to other magicians
2. Do not perform effects that you have not practiced
3. Avoid repeating the same effect for the same audience
4. Never admit that what you did (mistakes) was not planned
5. Never claim another's effect to be your own invention

Conjurer's Pledge

Stand in front of a mirror and read these words aloud. You are the only witness, but for a Wizard, that is all that is needed!

> *I, [your name], pledge and avow that I will strive to:*
>
> *Keep confidential and sacred all secrets and methods of conjuring which I learn, making sure that these are never revealed on purpose, or by accident, to those who are not entitled to learn them*
>
> *Never perform an effect without sufficient practice and concern with setting so as to not accidentally reveal any secrets or methods*
>
> *Honor and support the creativity and invention of fellow magicians, and to acknowledge those who have gone before*
>
> *Be appropriate in my selection of effects for a particular setting or audience*
>
> *Never invalidate or embarrass a volunteer from the audience*
>
> *Never use the Arts of Conjury to bilk or defraud others.*
>
> *So mote it be.*

The student who accepts this pledge is no longer a layperson, but rather a fellow member of the magical community.

6. Elemental Magics

By David Birtwell (orange)

If one looks at the Magician card from the Rider-Waite Tarot Deck, you will see the tools of the Wizard (or magician) displayed. Several of these tools represent the Elements.

- The **Wand** held by the magician represents the Element of **Fire** (or, alternatively, **Air**).
- The **Cup** or Chalice on the table represents the Element of **Water.**
- The **Sword** (an Athamé or magickal dagger can be substituted) represents the Element of **Air** (or, alternatively, **Fire**).
- The **Coin**/Pentacle/Disk on the table represents the Element of **Earth.**

THE MAGICIAN.

One of the strongest powers a Wizard can possess is to have control over the Elements. This can be represented through the use of performance magic, or Orange Wizardry. Here I will present some magic effects that will demonstrate the type of control over the Elements a Wizard might have.

Fire – the power of the Wand

The following routine will utilize the Wizard's Wand, which represents the Element of Fire. The Wand is one of the most important tools for the Wizard. It must always be treated with respect.

This effect works best using a smooth wand, perhaps a simple wand made from the branch of a tree (see the *Grimoire for the Apprentice Wizard* for directions on making your own magic Wand), or one of the Harry Potter style wands sold at many gift shops and occult shops. Be sure to get one that is completely smooth. You'll see why later.

Effect:

The Wizard explains that the Wand is a most powerful tool of the Wizard. To demonstrate the power of the Wand, the Wizard asks two people to help.

The Wizard removes two ropes thatare tied around his/her waist and ties them to the Wand. Two bracelets are borrowed from the audience and threaded through the ropes and another knot is tied to further secure them. The helpers hold the ends of the ropes.

The Wizard then repeats a magic spell and removes the Wand from the ropes. The bracelets are now seen to have also been pulled free along with the wand. The ends of the rope are still held by the helpers. The power of the Wand has freed the bracelets!

Setup:

The Wizard needs to have two pieces of rope worn around his waist as a sash. The pieces of rope don't have to be worn around the waist, but it adds to the mystique to use items worn or on the Wizard's person. This gives the impression that everything owned by the Wizard is magical.

These ropes should be about 5 feet in length, but you can use almost any size larger. Smaller lengths of rope tend not to leave much in the way of ends with which to work. Experiment with the rope length until you find a size with which you are comfortable using. I recommend using a soft cotton rope, or sash. It's harder to work with a stiff rope. Clothesline rope is ideal, as is the type of rope sold at performance magicians supply shops.

The Wand should be in an easy to reach location, either in the Wizard's hands, or on the table.

You don't have to borrow the bracelets, but it's good to borrow items from the audience when you can, so long as you take care of the items and return them unharmed. The bracelets should be bangle bracelets, the type that are completely solid and don't have a break or hinge. If you wish to use your own, you can wear the bracelets yourself and simply hand them to one of the helpers. If you don't feel comfortable using bracelets, you can use solid metal rings, which can be found at craft shops. Also, feel free to use more than two rings. I usually use four bracelets or rings myself, but it might be hard to find four appropriate bracelets in the audience.

Arcanum:

The secret to this effect is known as "The Cords of Fantasia" and is described using various items tied to the cords, and can even be done with a pencil, string or shoelaces, and some finger rings. I think this works better using rope and the Wand. Besides, this way you can demonstrate the power of your Wand!

Step 1 – Remove the two ropes from around your waist and hand both to one of the helpers. Ask the other helper to hold the Wand horizontally by holding it with both ends. Each hand will hold a separate end.

Step 2 – Take the two pieces of rope from the holder and place them onto the Wand. Fig. 1 shows the way things would look after completing steps 1 and 2.

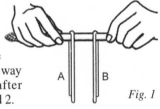

Fig. 1

Step 3 – Tie the two pieces of rope around the Wand using an overhand knot (Fig. 2).

Pull the overhand knot all the way and tighten it against the Wand (Fig. 3 will show how this knot looks).

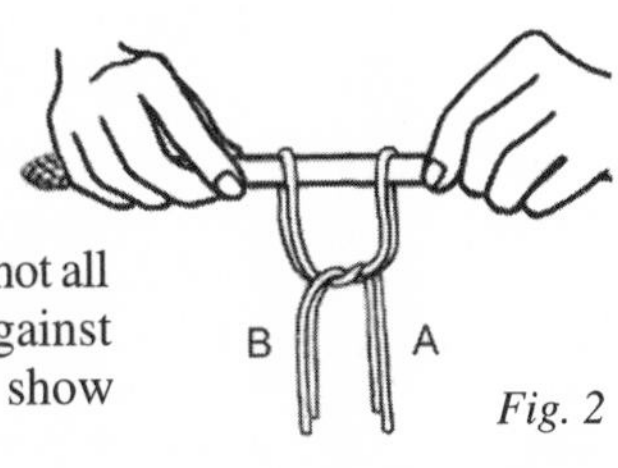

Fig. 2

Step 4 – Give the ends of the rope to the helpers to hold, so the wand is left hanging tied upon the ropes. Each helper will hold a separate set of ends, one helper standing on the right, and one helper standing on the left. (Fig. 3 will show how the ends of the ropes are to be held by the helpers).

Fig. 3

Step 5 - Borrow some bracelets from the audiences (or remove the bracelet from your own

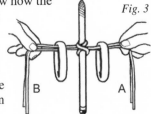

wrists. See Setup for more details). Then thread a bracelet through the rope ends to the left of the Wand and hand the rope ends back to the helper. Then thread another bracelet through the rope ends to the right of the wand and hand the ends back to the second helper. At this point, everything should look like Fig. 3.

Step 6 - Ask one of the helpers holding the ends of the rope to let go of one end of the rope. It doesn't matter which end they let go of, as long as they only let go of one end (and re-

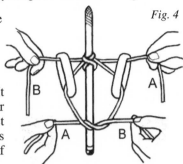

Fig. 4

main holding the other end). Then ask the second helper to let go one of their ends of the rope. Again, it doesn't matter which end of rope they let go of, as long as they only let go of one end. Tie the loose ends in an overhand knot and give the ends back to the helpers. See Fig. 4 for more details.

The final result will be similar to what you see in Fig. 3, except that there will be an additional overhand knot present.

Step 7 - Now announce that it is time for the spell. Look serious and say:

By the power of the Wand and the Element of Fire, I command the bracelets to do as the Wand … and also go free.

As you say the above, slide the bracelets towards the center of the ropes where the Wand is tied and grab hold of them with one hand (let's say the right hand). Then grab hold of the Wand with the other hand (let's say the left hand). Hold the Wand so that one end points down and the other points up. Then pull the Wand so it slides "down" and out of the knot. At the same time you pull the Wand free with your left hand, pull the bracelets free with your right hand. The bracelets don't have to be pulled much, as they will actually fall free of the ropes. This is all done as one simultaneous motion.

Believe me, this will all sound confusing during the first read-though, but this is much easier to understand if you read through the effect with all of the items in your hands. You can place everything on a table to mimic two helpers holding the ropes. During practice, I would tie the ends of the ropes to two chairs when I got to step 7. If you can get two friends to help you practice this effect, all the better.

When pulling the Wand free of the knot, you will notice that the ropes stay still, so the Wand easily slides out of the knot. As I mentioned, the bracelets just fall free. If they are your bracelets, you can choose not to hold onto them and just let them drop to the ground. I don't recommend letting borrowed bracelets drop to the floor, however. You must always treat borrowed items as if they are worth a fortune. These might have much sentimental value to the audience member who owns the bracelets.

This is a wonderful illusion and has been used by many of the great magicians and Wizards of the past and present. Guard the secret and use it well!

Water - the power of the Chalice

Effect:

The Wizard brings forth three Chalices and a small clear pitcher of water. The Wizard then asks one of those present to help with a little game used to demonstrate the power of the Element of Water. The Wizard asks the helper to stand where they are. The Wizard then lines the Chalices in a row, facing horizontally towards the audience. The Wizard then pours water into the center Chalice. The water can be clearly be seen pouring into the Chalice from the pitcher.

The Wizard then mixes the chalices very slowly. After the Wizard is done moving the chalices around, the helper is asked to locate which chalice contains the water ... the one at the left end (the Wizard points to it), the one at the right end (Wizard again points to this chalice), or the one in the middle. No matter which one the helper chooses, it is shown to be empty by turning the Chalice upside down. The Wizard then turns the remaining two Chalices upside down to show that no water pours from these cups either.

Arcanum:

The idea for this effect came during a conversation with my good friend, Adrian Deery. Adrian is a practitioner of Bizarre Magik, or storytelling magik (see above for a discussion of Bizarre Magik). The secret lies in a product known as "slush powder," which can be found at most performance magic shops. Fear not, this product can also be easily obtained from a common item found at the super market. "Slush powder" is found inside disposable diapers. This powder, when it comes in contact with liquid, will create a sort of gel. If placed in the chalice prior to the water being poured, this gel will stay stuck in the cup when it is turned over.

Simply purchase some disposable diapers, or if you have younger siblings, you could use a few of their unused disposable diapers. Place some paper or plastic down on a table to ease with the cleanup, as this might get a little messy. Cut the diaper open with scissors and gather up the powder found inside the diaper. This is the "magic" material we are trying to gather. Also, the cotton material you find between the layers will also contain some of the powder. Place some of the cotton-like material contained between the layers in a large quart-sized zip-lock bag, seal the bag, and

then shake. The powder will gather at the bottom of the bag after shaking for a small amount of time. You will only have to cut open two or three diapers to get enough powder, depending upon the size of each diaper. A tablespoon of this powder is plenty to absorb 8 ounces of water. Also, even though this material is safe (remember, it does come in contact with baby bottoms), it's a good idea not to breathe in the dust. You also will want to be careful not to spill any, especially if you have pets. This stuff gets messy if it comes in contact with liquid.

Required Items:

- The special "slush powder"
- 3 opaque (not see-through)t Chalices
- A small carafe or pitcher
- About 8 ounces of water
- A tablespoon of ordinary table salt

Setup:

Obtain three Chalices, goblets or cups that look like those a Wizard would own. They can be made of any material but must not be see-through. We wouldn't want anyone to see the secret!

In one of these cups, place about a tablespoon of the "slush powder." Experimentation will tell you how much you need to absorb more water, or less than 8 ounces of water. Also get a small clear pitcher or carafe and fill this with the water. Place these items on a table, or some place near your performance area.

Performance:

Step 1 – Bring forth the three Chalices and pitcher full of water, if they are already not on the table.

Step 2 - Ask a member of the audience to help you with the game to display the power of the Water Element. Ask that this audience member remain standing where she is.

Step 3 – Line up the Chalices horizontally in front of you. Place the Chalice containing the "slush powder" in the center.

Step 4 - Simply pour some water into the Chalice containing the "slush powder." The amount of water you pour will depend upon the size of the Chalice and the amount of "slush powder" you added to the Chalice. Then say while waving your Wand above the Chalices:

> By the power of the Element of Water, I command that the water remain hidden from our knowledge.

Step 5 - Slowly move the cups around, mixing them up, but moving slowly enough that the helper can follow what you are doing. Also, the "slush powder" takes some time to completely gel up and this slow movement will waste some time. Practice will let you know how much time it takes and you can tell by the way the water looks when the gelling is completed.

Make sure that the audience is far enough away so that they cannot see into the Chalice and see the secret! Also be aware of tall audience members who may be standing up. I recommend that the audience helper remain seated if tall, or close to the performance area. We don't want the audience or the helper to have a chance to see inside the Chalice!

Step 6 - Ask the helper which chalice she believes the water to be in. It doesn't matter which chalice your helper chooses, but she will probably choose the one containing the slush powder.

Turn the selected one over. Make sure you turn the Chalice over facing AWAY from the audience, or to the right or left. This is important. We don't want them to see that there is anything in the cup. Just turning the cup over will give the illusion that the cup is empty.

Step 7 - After you show that the chosen chalice is empty, make sure you say:

> *Do not feel bad, for I asked the water to remain hidden ... see, it is not found in any of the Chalices! This is the power of the Water Element. It is always around us, but sometimes not seen.*

Then turn over the remaining two chalices the same way you did the Chalice containing the "slush powder" (or the first selection).

Cleanup:

You will not want to pour the gel down the drain as it is, as it might cause clogging over time. There is an easy way to reverse the gelling process. Adding ordinary table salt to the "slush" will break down the gelling. Pour about a tablespoon of ordinary table salt into the Chalice with the gel and let it sit for a while. You don't have to wait for the gelling to completely reverse; a minute or two should do it. You can then stir the solution. Once it has been mixed and partially broken down, you can pour it down the drain while running the water. **DO NOT pour this down the drain until you have added some table salt**.

Air - the power of the Sword

Effect:

The Wizard takes a length of rope and holds it in one hand. The Wizard then removes his/her Sword (or Athamé) from his scabbard and cuts the rope in two pieces. The ends are tied into a knot. The knot is clearly seen on the rope.

The Wizard describes the power of the Sword/Athamé. The Sword/Athamé is then waved over the rope and some magic words are said. The knot is now slid off of one end of the rope. The rope is seen to be fully restored.

Arcanum:

This effect can be accomplished in many ways using what is commonly called the "cut and restored rope.". I will describe what I believe to be one of the simplest methods.

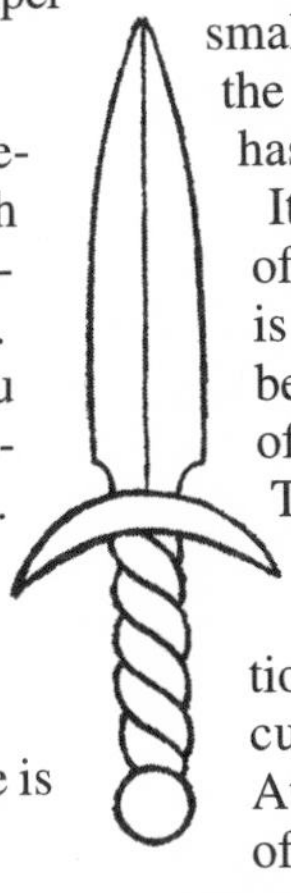

The rope is not actually cut **in the center.** Only a small portion of one of the ends is cut. Because of the way the rope is handled, it appears that the rope has been cut in the center.

It's easiest to follow these directions with a piece of rope in hand. A piece of rope about 4 feet long is a good size. After practice, you might actually be able to use one of the pieces from "The Power of the Wand."

The Sword is actually a short dagger or Athamé the Wizard has as one of his magickal tools. It should be sharp enough to cut the rope. Caution must be used while handling the blade and cutting the rope. Also, make sure the Sword/Athamé is put away when not in use and kept out of reach of children.

> *NOTE: Some Wiccan traditions insist that an athame should be kept dull, and never used for cutting. This opinion is not held in Wizardry! If you're going to have a blade at all, it should be kept functionally sharp—and you should learn how to use it properly and safely!*

Required Items:

- A 4-5 foot piece of soft rope. Soft cotton clothesline rope or "magicians" rope is ideal
- A small sword or knife that is sharp enough to cut the rope

Setup:

The rope can either be one of the pieces used in the "Power of Fire," can be lying on the table, or removed from around the Wizard's waist.

The Sword/Athamé should be in a scabbard and either worn around the Wizard's waist, or set out on the table.

Performance:

The illustrations will be shown from your viewpoint. That is, the palm of the hand will be facing you, while the back of the hand will be facing the audience.

Step 1 - The rope should be held in the left hand, as in Fig. 5, with the ends of the rope at the top and the middle of the rope hanging down.

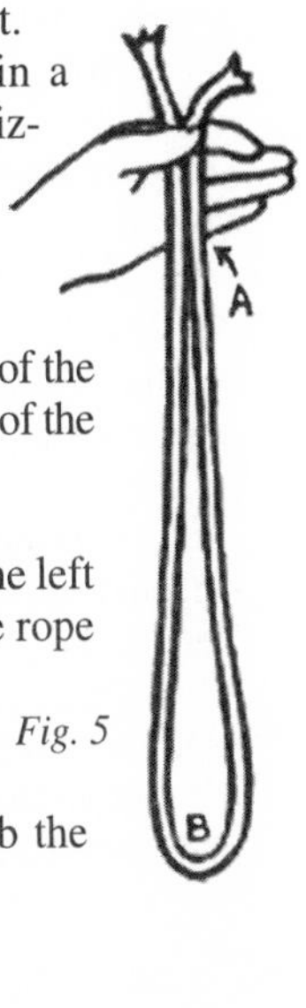

Fig. 5

Step 2 – With your right hand, grab the

middle of the rope (see Fig. 6) with your index finger and the thumb going through the loop formed by the center.

Step 3 - "Lift" the loop towards the top. If you look at Fig. 7, you will see how this is done. Do this slowly the first few times, following the directions.

Fig. 6

Step 4 - As the center of the rope nears the top of your right hand, grab the part of the rope detailed in Fig. 8 with the right hand.

Step 5 – This is the most important part. This is where the secret "move" is done. While pulling up the section you grabbed in step 4, you sort of pull it up and form a second loop (see Fig. 9).

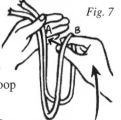

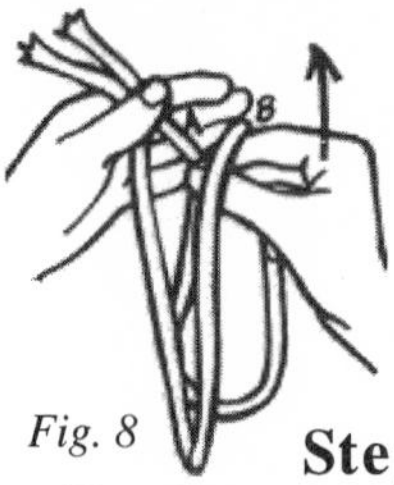

Fig. 7

Step 6 – Continue pulling this second loop up towards the top of the left hand, letting go of the actual middle of the rope (see Fig. 10).

Fig. 8

Step 7 – You will end up with what appears to be the center of the rope poking out of the top of the fingers of the right hand appearing next to the two ends. Hold the ropes in your hand as seen in Fig. 11.

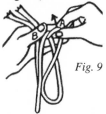

Fig. 9

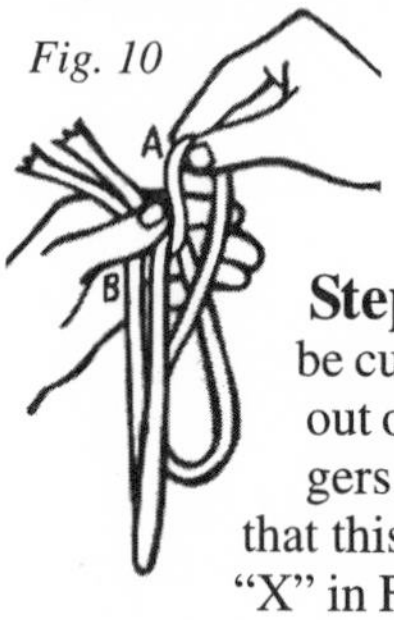

Fig. 10

Fig. 12 shows how the rope actually would appear without the left hand in place.

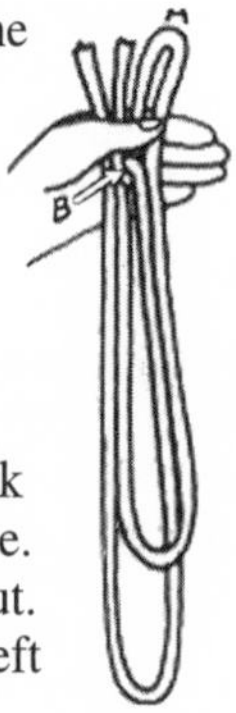

Step 8 – The rope should be cut at the loop appearing out of the top of the left fingers. The audience will think that this is the middle of the rope. "X" in Fig. 12 shows where to cut. Fig. 13 shows what it looks like with the left hand in place.

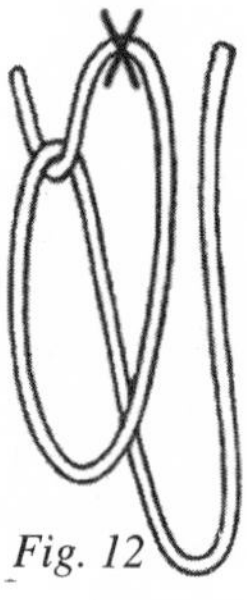

Step 9 – Place the Sword/Athamé down on the table.

You can now let go of the two long ends of the rope (the ones shown to the right in Fig. 14).

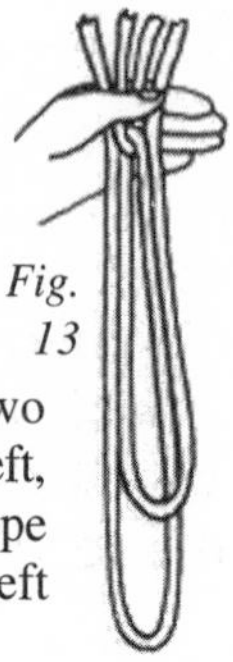

Fig. 13

Now tie together the two short ends of the rope on the left, forming a knot around the rope (see the the arrows in Fig. 14). Again the left

Fig. 12

hand has been removed for clarity.

Step 10 - Now most of the trick is completed. You can freely show the rope, and it appears to be a cut piece of rope, tied in the middle. In reality, it is a long piece of rope with a short piece tied in a knot around the middle of the rope.

Step 11 - Hold the rope in one hand and wave the sword over the knotted area while saying:

By the power of the magickal Sword,
I order the rope to be fully restored!

Step 12 - Now put down the Sword/Athamé. Move the knot along the rope and slid it off of one end of the rope. This can easily be done, as the knot is only a short piece of rope tied around the rest of the rope. The knot can be tossed aside and the rope can be shown to be fully restored.

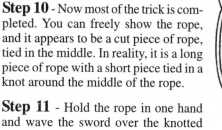

Tie

Fig. 14

> **NOTE:** *Alternatively, you could wrap the rope in your hand, sliding the knot along the rope as you wrap it in your fist, until the knot comes off. You can wave the sword over your fist, say the magic words and pull the rope out of your hand. The knot will be left behind and is hidden, or "palmed" in your hand.*

Earth – the power of the Crystal

Effect:

The Wizard tells of the magical properties of certain rocks, crystals and minerals. The Wizard further tells of the properties of crystals. The Wizard then removes a clear crystal from his/her pouch and says he/she would like to give a demonstration of the power of Crystal.

The Wizard places the Crystal inside the closed fist of a member of the audience and asks the participant to focus on some bad thoughts, or problems he may be having. The Wizard asks the helper to also focus on the Crystal while thinking about these "bad" things.

The Wizard then asks the helper to open his/her hand to see if the power of the Crystal has shown itself. When he opens his hand, it is seen that the Crystal is now dark, or black.

The Wizard tells the person that this demonstrates the power of the Crystal and that some of the pain, bad thoughts, or negativity have been absorbed by the Crystal. This is the symbol that remains.

Arcanum:

The secret to this effect is a little bit of slight of hand called the "Bobo switch. The name comes from a magician to whom the move is attributed, J.B. Bobo.

This sleight is most often used in effects involving coins, but works well for many small items. Once you learn this particular sleight, you can begin making up your own effects using it.

In this particular effect, we will use this little bit of sleight of hand to switch a clear crystal for a darkened, or black crystal.

Don't let the sleight of hand scare you. It's actually easy to do, if you give it some practice. I recommend practicing until you can do the switch without looking. The switch will be described in the performance section.

As described above, there are two crystals. You should purchase two crystals almost the same size and shape. You want the audience to believe that only the clearness of the crystal changes, or that the crystal darkens. Crystals can be purchased quite inexpensively at new age shops, rock shops, or rock and mineral shows. If you cannot find a shop selling real crystals, you can find glass "gems", or marbles at most craft shops. These marbles are often used in the bottom of vases to hold flower arrangements.

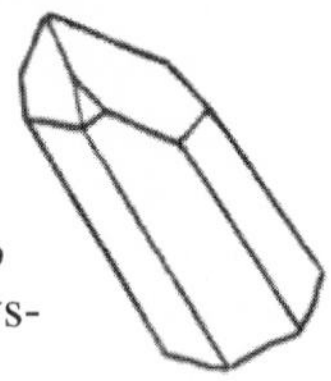

Although quartz crystal "points" (see illustration) look the best, they are a little harder to work with until you are comfortable with the Bobo Switch. I recommend using quartz crystal stones, about the size of a quarter.

Quartz comes in clear crystal and smoky crystal. If you can't find a smoky crystal to match the clear crystal, you can get a piece of obsidian, or "apache tear." These are all quite inexpensive and shouldn't run you more than $1.00 each.

Setup:
- The clear crystal can be in a pouch, a pocket, or on the table
- The "dark" crystal should be in a pocket, or someplace you can quickly get it into "palmed" position (see performance description for more on this)
- You can use a magic wand to add to the magical effect, if you wish

Performance:
Take the dark crystal from a hidden location and put it into finger-palmed position, or you can put it into palmed position (see *Grimoire for the Apprentice Wizard* page 242 for a description and illustration of the palmed position). I will describe the move from the finger-palmed position (Fig. 15).

It is probably best to try this with the actual crystals, as it will make much more sense. If you don't yet have the crystals, you can try this with 2 coins about the size of a quarter. Remember this sleight was actually designed for use with coins in the first place!

Step 1 - As seen in Fig. 15, the dark crystal is gripped in the first two flanges of your right ring and index

finger closest to the palm of your hand. The illustrations below show how the dark crystal would look from your point of view. The audience would not see that this crystal even exists.

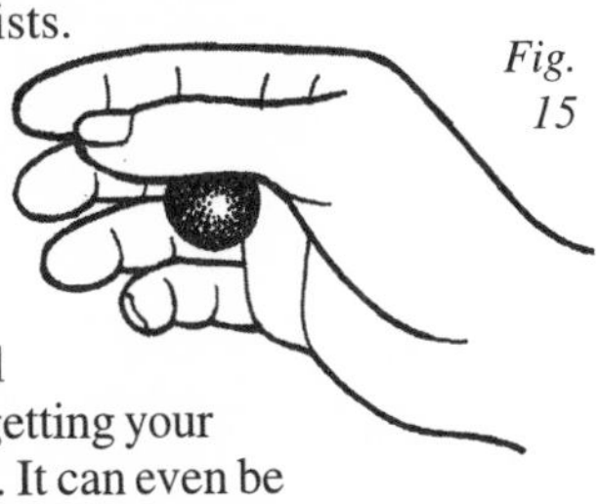

The hand should be held to your side after the dark crystal has been secretly placed in this position. You can get the crystal into this position while getting your wand from within a box. It can even be hidden beneath your table and held into place with the type of putty used to put up posters and pictures on the wall, sometimes called "blue tac." When you are ready, you can secretly grab the dark crystal and get it into the finger-palmed position.

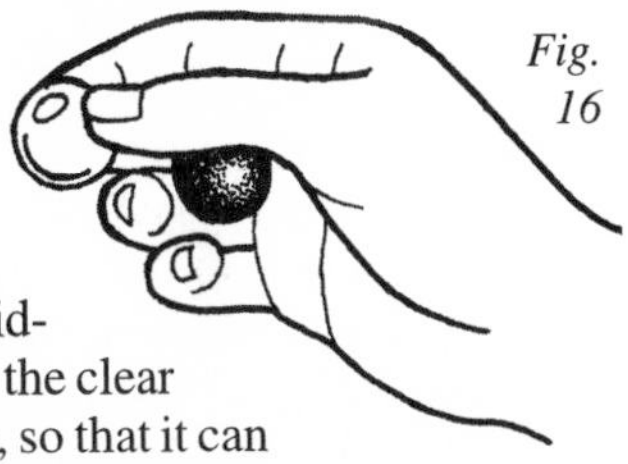

Fig. 15

Step 2 – Take the clear crystal out of a bag, pocket or someplace with your right hand (which is already holding the hidden dark crystal). Hold the clear crystal at the fingertips, so that it can be seen by the audience. Fig. 16 shows how everything looks from your point of view. Notice how the dark crystal can easily be held in "finger palmed" position while the clear crystal is held at the fingertips. From the audience's point of view, it only appears that you are holding the clear crystal at your fingertips.

Fig. 16

Step 3 – Now comes the real secret, or "move" of the effect. You appear to place the clear crystal into your left hand, while actually placing the dark crystal in your left hand. This is done as follows:

(While practicing the first few times, you should try these steps out slowly. As you become more comfortable with this sleight, you will be able to speed things up.)

1) The right hand moves towards the left hand, holding the clear crystal extended at the fingertips
2) While doing this, the right hand does these two steps simultaneously:
   a) pulls back the clear crystal from the fingertips, until it is hidden behind the fingertips (it now can only be seen by you).
   b) releases the dark crystal from the finger-palmed grip, letting it fall into the left hand (Fig. 17).

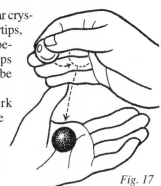

Fig. 17

Step 5 - When the dark crystal drops into the left hand, the left hand closes immediately around it so, the audience doesn't see that it is actually the dark crystal.

The right hand moves down to the right side, continuing to pull back the clear crystal into a finger-palmed position, where the dark crystal was held previously. Until you are comfortable moving the dark crystal into the finger-palmed position, you can just simply hold the dark crystal behind the fingers with the thumb. No one should be looking for any "strange moves" anyway.

> *NOTE: Practice this a few times with only the clear crystal (without the finger-palmed hidden dark crystal) and really put the clear crystal into your left hand. This way you will get the feel of what it is like to really just do what you are making the audience believe you are doing— that is, just moving the clear crystal from your right hand fingertips to your left hand.*
>
> *Also, this, as well as any sleights should be practiced in front of a mirror, until you can get the sleight down without it showing. Leaning this sleight of hand switch, although not too difficult, does require practice. Never perform any effect until you have practices until you feel confident that you can perform the move without looking.*

Step 6 – You have completed the hardest part. Now you ask a helper to take the crystal in her hand. Have herplace one hand face-up and outstretched, like sheis going to receive some change. You then place your closed left hand (containing the dark crystal) and place it on top of her hand. You then instruct the helper to close her hand around yours as you drop the crystal into her hand. This should all be presented as one fluid motion and look as though you are just dropping the crystal—which is what you are doing. You just don't want the audience to see that the crystal is not clear before the "magic" has taken place. If you look the person in the eyes while you are dong this move, you will get more cooperation. You can also stall by removing your hand until your helper has closed her hand. Again, practice will prepare you for doing this as one fluid movement.

Step 6 – You can pick up a magic wand with your right hand, making sure you don't hit the wand with the hidden clear crystal and make a "clicking" sound. This again, becomes easy to do with practice.

Wave your magic Wand over your helper's hand while repeating the magic words or spell:

> *Crystal from Earth, take away pains;*
> *All shall be well, just the symbol remains.*

When you are done, you can get rid of the hidden crystal as you put your Wand away. If you are not comfortable doing this, you can just keep your hand at your side and wait until the effect is over. Then you can put the hidden crystal away while getting something else, or while putting something else away.

Step 7 – You now ask the helper to open her hand to see if the experiment worked. When she opens her hand, act as surprised as she does.

Explain that the experiment was successful and that the crystal took away some of her negative feelings. The darkness of the crystal is the "symbol" about which you spoke with the magic words.

If you can get matching dark crystals cheaply, you might wish to give one to the helper to keep. You can tell the audience that whenever she feels bad, or has a problem, she can take out the darkened crystal to hold, and hopefully, it will absorb some more negativity.

Also, it's always nice to give something away whenever possible, especially if it can bring someone happiness. Think of the magic you can give to someone for only a few cents!

7. Production Boxes
By Oberon (grey)

Production boxes are specially constructed with hidden compartments to allow objects to appear or disappear mysteriously. These can be smaller than a shoebox or as large as a wardrobe cabinet. They can be shown to be completely empty, and yet various items (including rabbits) can be withdrawn from them to the astonishment of your audience. Inthe following section, Jim Fish will show you how to make your own magic production box from a cut-out page in the back of this book.

When you have amazed your friends and family with some of these conjuring illusions, I can guarantee that they will ask you to "Do it again!" And everyone will want you to tell them how you did it. But the special charm of conjuring magic for an audience is in their *not* knowing how it is done. Once the secret of the illusion is out, it loses its mystery. Without that sense of wonder and amazement, no one will be interested in your illusions. So here are two cardinal rules of conjuring: *never* repeat an illusion in the same performance, and *never* tell anyone else how you did it!

Jim's Magic Box
By Jim Fish (orange)

Effect:
Flat pieces of a box are placed on the table. The Wizard assembles them. When the box is opened it is found to magically contain wonderful things.

Or, the box is assembled and objects are placed

into it. The box is taken apart again, and everything inside has vanished.

Or both. You get to design your presentation to suit your needs.

Cautions:

This is a small model of a classic Magician's Production Box that is used today by professional magicians.

Guard its secret very carefully.

It is best used with one person across from you, seated at a table.

This is NOT beginner's magic!

You can't assemble it today and perform it tonight. You will want to put a mirror in the spectator's chair and watch your moves from someone else's point of view. When you can fool yourself, you can try it out on a good friend, one you can trust to keep the secret if you blow the illusion. This is strong magic that must be taken seriously. Take the time to perfect the wonder that it holds.

When you understand it, you can build larger boxes to use on stage or with smaller groups to delight and amaze your audience. I built one that allowed my ten-year-old apprentice to produce a hamster for an audience of about 100 people.

The Magician's Oath:

(Say this in front of the mirror you will use for your practice):

I promise, before I continue, that I will do my utmost to guard the secret of this magic box, both with my silence and with my righteous practice.

Okay, I trust you, and we will continue.

Look in the back of this book and find the tearout page called "MAGIC BOX TEMPLATE." Take this to your local copy center, and print it on card stock with an enlargement of 121%.

Solid lines indicate cuts, and dotted lines indicate folds. Before you cut the pieces out, you need to score along the dotted lines, using a straight edge (such as a ruler), and the back edge of a thin-bladed table knife.

There are four pieces that have to be carefully cut out and glued together. They are:

The Base
The Sides
The Lid
The Secret Chamber

The Base is a rectangle with prongs at each corner. Cut out the Base and slit the prongs, and fold them upwards. (Fig. 1) They will hold the sides in place.

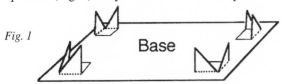

Fig. 1

Base

Cut out the strip that becomes the Sides. Fold up on the dotted lines, and glue the tab to the far end to make a rectangle. (Fig. 2) Practice fitting this rectangle on the base inside the prongs.

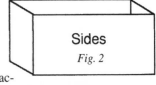

Sides

Fig. 2

Lid

Fig. 3

Fold up

cut this window out

Fold down

Cut out the strip that becomes the Sides.

Cut around the perimeter of the Lid. It has two parts: the solid part on the left, and the window on the right. (Fig. 3) The window has four flaps that fold in. (Fig. 4)

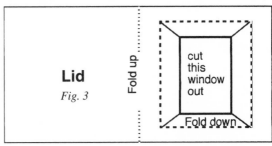

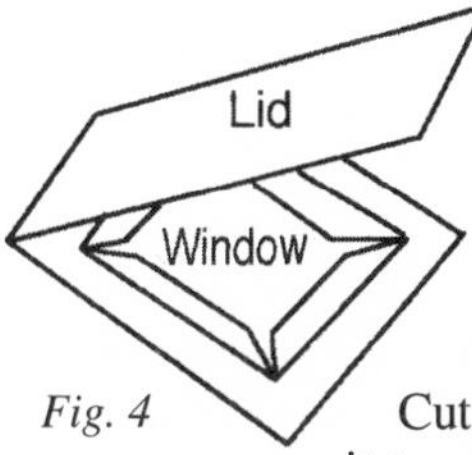

Lid

Window

Fig. 4

Cut out the Secret Chamber, and fold it to make a box with the black sides out. Glue the tabs to the inside of each side. (Fig. 5)

Hang the Secret Chamber from the back of the lid with two lengths of black thread as shown in Fig 6. Glue the top ends of the threads to the back of the window flap closest to the lid, and glue the other ends to the

Fig. 5

Secret chamber

back of the Secret Chamber. The Secret Chamber should hang behind the lid, as shown in Fig. 7.

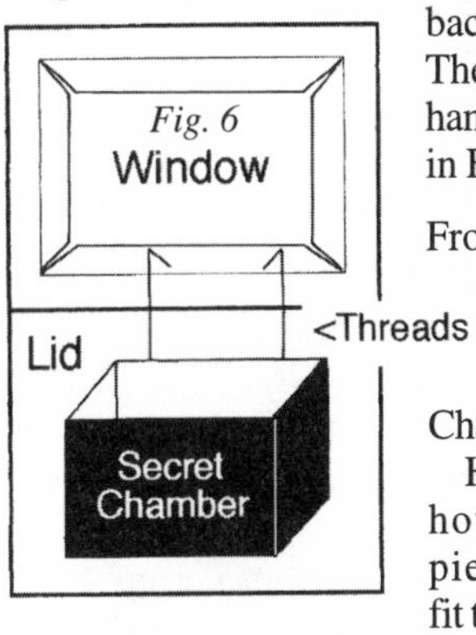

From this point of view, the little flaps inside the window are facing you. The lid hides the Secret Chamber.

Here's how the pieces all fit together

Fig. 6

Window

Lid

<Threads

Secret Chamber

(Fig. 8, next page). The prongs on the base squeeze the sides from outside, while the flaps on the lid window go inside the top of the Secret Chamber, which fits into the sides of the box. The window flaps conceal the top edges of the Secret Chamber.

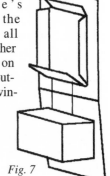

Fig. 7

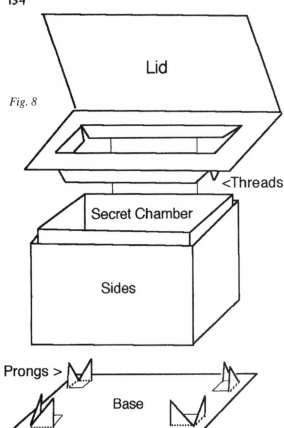

Fig. 8

Lid

Threads >

Secret Chamber

Sides

Prongs >

Base

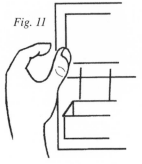

Fig. 11

pieces of my Magic Box, the Secret Chamber loaded with plastic gold coins.

To make such a book-box yourself, first go to a used bookstore and buy a cheap paperback copy of *Treasure Island,* or some other book about Pirates. The cover should be really lurid, with large letters. Carefully remove the cover, and cut it into three parts: front, back, and spine. Get a piece of heavy cardboard and make a "book cover" the same size, only with the spine exactly 1½" thick. Score the fold lines, as above. Glue the front and back of the paperback to the front and back of the cardboard cover, and also glue the spine, centering it along the wider space.

Fig. 12

Then take a piece of heavy corrugated cardboard and cut it into a long strip 1½" wide, with the holes going across the short space. The strip needs to be long enough to be made into the sides of your book box, with the back of the cover glued to the

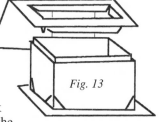

Fig. 13

bottom, and the front acting as the lid. Score the corners, and glue it all together.

To complete the effect, take a long 1½" strip of paper, and using a ruler, draw a lot of thin pencil lines to look like book pages; then glue it around the sides, so the entire box looks just like a book. Put the pieces of your Magic Box inside, and you're ready for showtime!

You will need to create a hidden shelf behind your presentation table (Fig. 9) or display the pieces atop a book (Fig. 10) or keep the pieces hidden and bring them out one at a time as you assemble the box.

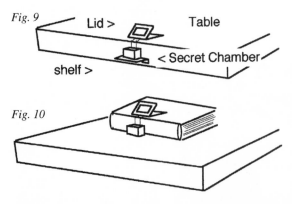

Fig. 9   Lid >   Table

shelf >   < Secret Chamber

Fig. 10

If you grasp the bottom of the window between your thumbs and first fingers, (Fig. 11) your hands and the lid naturally conceal the Secret Chamber from the spectator. (Fig. 12) Let the lid hang down behind the box until you have inserted the Secret Chanber and put the window into place. Then close the lid. (Fig. 13)

Setup—making a book box:

The great magician Jeff McBride gave me a wonderful box that looks just like a book. Inside I keep the

My Presentation:

I talk about the wonders of the imagination and the power of a good book to take us into the land where dreams themselves often seem real. Taking out my book box, I speak to our love of pirate tales, like *Treasure Island,* and the fantasy of discovering a chest of pirate gold. While speaking, I open the book and take out first the Base, then the Sides, and finally the Lid of my Magic Box. I lay the lid on the closed "book," as shown in Fig. 10, hiding the Secret Chamber.

I invite the audience to imagine that what I'm building is a pirate's treasure chest. Once the box is assembled and the lid is closed, I pause and ask the audience to imagine what we would do with a fortune in gold doubloons. Then I turn the box so the front faces the audience, slowly open the lid, and dump out the coins. I let them examine the coins as I put my Magic Box back into the book. Alas, I say, the coins are only plastic, because this is, after all, just the world of the imagination. But I let them keep the coins as a reminder.

Have fun. Create Wonder!

8. Hosting a Bardic

By Oberon (grey)

One of the most popular things to do in magickal gatherings is to hold a *Bardic*—a sharing of songs, stories, poetry, jokes, or even magical illusions. This may be done in a living room, in front of a fireplace, or—best of all—outdoors around a campfire. Morning Glory and I have hosted numerous Bardics, and I'd like to share with you our formula, so you can do this too.

Well ahead of time, in the invitations to the gathering, let everyone know that a Bardic will be held, and that they should bring songs, stories, poetry, etc. to share. These may be original compositions or not. If an offering is to be musical, invite guests to bring appropriate instruments.

When the Bardic is to begin, everyone gathers into a circle, seated comfortably. If this is to be part of a larger ritual, just make sure that there are enough chairs, cushions, benches, sofas, etc. to accommodate everyone. The most important element is a large chalice or drinking horn filled with an appropriate thirst-quencher: water, apple juice, and mead are all popular.

Bardics are often begun, now as in olden times, with an invocation and dedication to Brigit (Irish saint and goddess, matron of all creative endeavors) or the Muses (Greek matrons of the arts and sciences). Here are some examples:

Brigit

Shining Brigit, hear our call;
Join us in your hallowed hall.
Lady of the forge and art,
Lady of the boundless heart,
Healing craft and Bardic laughter,

Teach us now, and ever after!

Orphic Hymn to the Muses

Daughters of Jove, dire-sounding and divine,
Renown'd, Pierian, sweetly speaking Nine;
Clio, and Erato, who charms the sight,
With thee Euterpe minist'ring delight:
Thalia flourishing, Polymnia famed,
Melpomene from skill in music named:
Terpsich ore, Urania heav'nly bright,
With thee who gav'st me to behold the light.
Come, venerable, various, powers divine,
With fav'ring aspect on your mystics shine;
Bring glorious, ardent, lovely, famed desire,

And warm my bosom with your sacred fire.

Begin by explaining the idea of a Bardic:

In ancient times, the Bards dedicated themselves to memorizing the lore of the People in stories, poetry, and song. Thousands of years before there was TV or movies, the best entertainment in the village was a Bardic performance. Through these, children and adults learned the history of their ancestors, the myths of the gods, the adventures of heroes, and the lessons of the legends.

But you don't have to be a professional Bard to participate in a Bardic! Anyone can tell a story or a good joke, or read a favorite poem—even if you can't sing or perform in other ways. A Bardic is a sharing experience, like a potluck, in which everybody gets to contribute something.

Now, it's well known that Barding is thirsty work! So we will pass the horn (or chalice) around the circle. When it comes to you, take a drink, and enter the center to offer your contribution. When you are done, take another drink, and pass it on to the next person. If, when the horn/chalice comes to you, you aren't ready yet, just say "pass" and hand it on to the next in line.

And, as Host, you take a drink and begin with the first offering…and then pass the horn/chalice to the person on your left.

Department IX: Alchemy & Magickal Sciences (red)

The Computer Wizard

Silicon mysteries whisper to me
From the glinting interstices of a crystal cube,
Hinting at vaults of knowledge
That unfurl their secrets like strange flowers.
If I have become something of a hermit,
Adrift in a crystal wilderness,
What of it?
The myriad shimmering wisdoms draw me in,
And I see my face reflected in every facet.
Here I can make magic,
As sure as ever ship or star.

And Merlin? No doubt
They thought him mad as well,
But Camelot fell
For want of him.
Let me spin my crystal spell,
A spider's web in a hidden cave,
Raining questions and answers fine as frost.
Only wait,
And when I call you to the screen,
See what new worlds I've made.

—Elizabeth Barrette

1. Introduction

ELCOME TO THE WORLD OF Alchemy and Magickal Sciences! This department concerns the science of magick and the magick of science, especially transmutation and transformation. The forerunner of modern chemistry, *Alchemy* has roots in Egypt, Greece, and the Middle East. Historically, Alchemists sought to turn base metals into gold, to formulate an "Elixir of Life" that would grant immortality, and to create an artificial man called a *homunculus*. The inner Mysteries of Alchemy concerned the transformation and perfection of the soul. Contemporary aspects of these studies include chemistry, physics, metallurgy, philosophy, metaphysics, life extension studies, genetics and cloning, robotics, cybernetics, and artificial intelligence—in fact, any areas where magick and science overlap through the manipulation of substances or objects.

Modern science was born in the athanors and crucibles of Alchemical laboratories, and those we call scientists today were formerly known as Alchemists—the Red Wizards.

The color of this department is Red, associated with Physical work, as in the healing of people and animals as well as physical passion. Red is the power color. It is associated with command, the planet Mars, Tuesday, the astrological sign of Gemini and the 1st (Root) *Chakra*. Red is the color of fire, inspiration, vitality, pride, anger, bravery, strong emotions, purification, arid places, aggressive music (especially heartbeat-like drumming), and lightning storms. Red is also associated with Alchemy and the magickal arts and sciences of transformation. Red is the best color to ward off danger. Use it for stability, grounding, prosperity and physical health.

2. Alchemical Symbolism
By Nicholas Paranelle (red)

> 'Twas brillig, and the slithy toves
> Did gyre and gymbol in the wabe;
> All mimsy were the borogoves,
> And the momeraths outgrabe.
> ~Lewis Carroll, Jabberwocky

Now, Lewis Carroll wasn't an Alchemist – but you wouldn't know it from his writing. His poem "Jabberwocky" is as cryptic as any Alchemical work ever published!

Why the symbols instead of simple words? Well, symbols have the ability to convey more information per unit than words can – they are "three dimensional."

We've all heard the phrase, "a picture is worth a thousand words." Let's try to describe everything you see in Heinrich Khunrath's "Amphitheatre" on the next page.

Could you describe everything in it in one or two words? Probably not – yet an Alchemist could convey extremely complex thoughts – the entire process for turning lead into gold for example – in just one picture.

The use of symbols provided a degree of secrecy – permitting the Alchemists to hide their methods from the mundanes of their times.

The symbols allowed Alchemists to share thoughts and ideas with others who might not read or write in the same language. So, a Greek Alchemist could describe an Alchemical Sequence to an Alchemist from the Middle East without the inconvenience of a language barrier.

And it may have simply been good fun– a way of fooling others with a deceptively simple game (have you ever written anything in code just to have a bit of fun with someone?)

For example, what do each of these symbols represent?

These are all Alchemical Symbols for the element Gold!

And here is a key to some of the most important symbolic images found in Alchemical art. It is followed by a table of some Alchemical glyphs. You might enjoy using some of these in your Journal and other notes—especially for your experiments!

3. A key to symbolic Alchemical imagery

By Oberon (grey)

Adam = "Prima Materia" (primordial substance)-male aspect
Amorous Birds of Prey = Multiplication process of dissolution and coagulation
Angels = Volatile or spiritualized matter
Amber = Gold
Apollo = Red tincture

Basilisk/Cockatrice = Elixer of transmutation
Beheading = Division of the black matter in the alembic
Black Crow = Black or purifying matter
Black King/Ethiopian = Black matter (nigredo)
Black Raven = Black mixture
Castle/Fortress = Hermetically sealed vessel
Chemical Wedding = Chemical reaction
Child/Infant = The Philosopher's Stone
Cock & Hen = Male and female aspects of matter
Crucified Serpent = Fixation of the volatile
Diana/Artemis = White tincture
Deer/Stag = Mercurius as intermediary uniting body and spirit of the Stone
Dog & Bitch = Male: hot, dry; female: cold, moist
Dove ascending = White sublimate
Eagle = Philosophic mercury; white tincture
Egg = Vessel of transformation to hatch the Philosopher's Stone
Eve = "Prima Materia" (primordial substance)-female aspect
Flowers = Powdery substances
Fountain = Magickal transforming substance
Garden = Secret vessel
Grave/Coffin/Tomb/Prison = Vessel for putrefaction
Green Lion = Raw antimony ore
Grey Wolf = Antimony (lupus metallorum)
Gryphon = Female principle
Head = Vessel for separation and putrefaction (alembic)
Hermaphrodite = Combined male-female principles/ elements
Honey = Philosophical solvent; all-healing Elixer
House = Alchemical vessel
King of the Sea = Philosopher's Stone as it is being created
Labyrinth = The Alchemical Work
Lion = Sulphur
Mercurius/Hermes = Universal agent of transmutation
Mountains = The place where the Prima Materia may be found
Nest = The Alchemical vessel
Peacock's Tail/Rainbow = Transition stage between black and white
Phoenix = The Philosopher's Stone
Red Lion = Red sulphur; male seed of metals
Red King (Sol) = Gold; also sulphur
Red Sea = Mercurial water; prima material
Red Rose = The perfect red (rubedo) Philosopher's Stone
Roots = 4 Elements: Earth, Air, Fire, Water
Salamander = Fiery male seed of metals; sulphur
Saturn = Lead; prima material
Seed = The spark of life within metals
Serpent = Ancient matter at start of process
3 Serpents = 3 Principles (mercury, sulphur, salt)
Ship = Vessel used for dissolution of black matter
Skeleton/Skull = Black matter (nigredo)
6-pointed Star = Antimony; also Mercurius the transformer

Sun = Gold; also masculine principle

Swan = White stage *(albedo);* Elixer that transmutes base metals to silver

Toad/Frog = Swelling matter during putrefaction stage

Tower = Athanor, or furnace

Truncated Tree = Dissolution/dissolution phase

Twins = King/sun/sulphur/gold & Queen/moon/silver

Unicorn = Masculine, penetrating aspect of Mercurius; spirit of the Stone

Uroboros = Circular nature of process of transformation

Venus/Aphrodite = Copper

Virgin's Milk = White mixture; white mercury

Vulcan/Hephaestos = The archetypal Alchemist

Vulture = The entire Alchemical work

Well = Vessel in which various dissolutions and purifications occur

White Lily = The pure white Elixer; a symbol of purity

White Queen (Luna) = Silver; also white elixer

White Rose = The white stage *(albedo)* which comes before final red stage *(rubedo)*

Winged Dragon/Serpent = Volatile principle (mercury)

Winged Lion = Mercury

Wingless Dragon/Serpent = Fixed principle (sulphur)

Womb = Alembic, or vessel in which the Stone is conceived

Worm = Solvent to dissolve corrupt matter

4. Kitchen Alchemy
by Susan Pesznecker (Moonwriter)

Our kitchens are alchemical laboratories. They include machines for heating and cooling, tools for measuring and mixing, and all kinds of raw chemical materials—foods and beverages—including the most important molecule known to humankind: water. In this class you will use the kitchen to explore crystals, the states of matter, physical and chemical change, and non-Newtonian fluids. You'll have a chance to stir up solutions, create colloids, and make magickal ink, crunchy sparks, and more.

> *Important note: Apprentices under age 14 should have a parent help with these experiments*

Why the kitchen?

Our tongues have five different types of sensors (taste buds): sweet, sour, salty, bitter, and *umami,* the taste of mono sodium glutamate, MSG—found in tomatoes, parmesan cheese and soy sauce, etc.

Taste has important survival functions. Thousands of years ago, our forbearers hadn't yet learned to hunt or grow food—they simply ate what they could find. Much of their diet involved things that they found growing. Some of these were poisonous. The sense of taste helped to identify these foods, which were often bitter or caused the mouth or burn or become numb when tiny amounts were tested.

Humans do best with a varied diet. Sugar and carbohydrates are an important source of energy. Salt has an essential role in chemical processes throughout the body. Fats provide energy and are building blocks for hormones. Proteins are the building blocks of enzymes and body tissues.

Every time you use a recipe, you are conducting an experiment. You start by reviewing your procedure and thinking about what might result from it. By thinking about what might happen, you create a hypothesis. You prepare for the experiment setting out the ingredients and tools

Some Alchemical Glyphs

4 Elements
Earth
Air
Fire
Water

7 Primary Metals
Gold
Silver
Iron
Mercury
Tin
Copper
Lead

12 Processes
Oxidation
Crystallization
Stablization
Solution
Digestion
Distillation
Sublimation
Separation
Incineration
Fermentation
Transmutation
Transformation

7 Operations
Filter
Mix
Dissolve
Boil
Distill
Precipitate
Melt or Liquify

3 Principles
(Tria Prima)
Sulphur
(Combustibles)
Mercury *(Metals)*
Salt *(Metalloids)*

4 Intervals of Time
Hour
Day
Week
Month

Other Materials & Processes
Alcohol
Alkali
Alum
Amalgam
Annealing
Anglesite
Antimony
Aquafortis
Arsenic

Bismuth
Bolus
Borax
Brimstone
Essential Oil
Glass
Hematite
Lime
Lye
Magnesium
Minium (Aluminum)
Olive Oil
Orpiment
Platinum
Potassium
Precipitate
Precipitation
Sal Ammoniac
Saltpeter
Steel
Subacetate of Copper
Sublimation
Talc
Tartar
Vinegar
Vitriol (acid)
Water
Wax
White Arsenic
White Lead
Zinc

you'll need to complete it. Finally, you do the experiment, measuring out the ingredients, mixing them together, and testing the results. Depending on how things came out, you'll probably start thinking about what you'd do differently the next time, or how you would modify the experiment.

The process of developing a hypothesis, designing and carrying out an experiment, and evaluating the result is known as the "scientific method." And there's no more fun place to learn it than in the kitchen!

A basic outline of Alchemy

Chemistry and Alchemy originated with the Greeks, who believed that all matter was composed of the four elements: earth, air, fire, and water. Further, each element was a combination of hot/cold and wet/dry. For example, earth was cold and dry, while fire was hot and dry.

The main goal of Alchemy was the identification of the Philosopher's Stone, a substance that would allow base metals to be changed—transmuted—into gold.

The word *alchemy* comes from Arabic: *al* (the) and *khem* (Egypt). Although the exact origins of Alchemy are unknown, many believe that it started in Egypt in or around the 6th century CE.

In the 16th century, the physician Paracelsus redirected Alchemy into a search for medicines, creating a field of study known as *iatrochemistry*. His work incorporated *metallurgy* (the study of the science and technology of metals) into healing.

In the 17th century, the Age of Reason brought a new emphasis to science and saw mystical ideas lose much of their importance. Robert Boyle attacked the "four element theory" and proposed the definition of the chemical elements. Antoine Lavoisier developed

modern quantitative chemistry, followed by John Dalton's work in identifying the atom as the foundation building block of all matter.

Organic chemistry and electrochemistry emerged in the 19th century, as did the creation of the periodic table of elements by Dmitri Mendeleyev. The periodic table organized elements in terms of regular, repeating properties and similarities.

In the 20th century, atomic bonds were identified and explained, synthetic materials were formed, and non-natural elements created in the laboratory.

The search for the Philosopher's Stone goes on. Today, many scientists think that the answer will be found in the field of quantum physics/mechanics, a very strange place where all of matter—living and non-living—are made of the same particles and are thought to posses the same inherent types of energy.

For now, as a beginning student of Alchemy, the kitchen can be put to use to create fun (and tasty!) demonstrations.

Chemistry 101

Atoms are the smallest building blocks of matter. All ordinary matter consists of atoms. An atom is composed of a nucleus and electrons. The nucleus contains one or more positively-charged protons and one or more neutral (non-charged) neutrons. One or more negatively-charged electrons circle around the nucleus, like a tiny moon orbiting a planet.

To get an idea of how small an atom is, take a pinch of sugar, then separate out one sugar crystal. If you were to cut that single crystal into one hundred or more parts, each would be about the size of an atom.

Elements consist of matter that is made of one type of atom. Elements cannot be broken down into other substances. Examples of elements are oxygen, carbon, iron, and sulfur.

The known elements are organized into a chart called the Periodic Table of the Elements. For an amazing interactive visual tour through the Periodic Table, see "A Visual Interpretation of the Table of Elements" at: http://www.chemsoc.org/viselements

There are 92 natural elements, which are elements that occur in nature. There are another 20-plus elements that have been produced in the laboratory. All of these are radioactive.

Molecules are chemical structures that are made by joining elements together. The elements connect through atomic bonds, connections formed between the atoms of different substances.

Common Kitchen Molecules.

One of the most common and important kitchen molecules is H_2O, or water. It is formed of two hydrogen (H) atoms and one oxygen (O) atom. Water is required for all of the chemical processes that occur in the body.

Without water, humans die in about three days.

Another very common molecule is NaCl, or salt, formed of one sodium (Na) atom and one chloride (Cl) atom. In cooking, salt strengthens dough, increases flavor, and acts as a preservative. Our bodies cannot make salt, and so we must get it from our foods. This is why people tend to crave salty foods from time to time.

Sugars are composed of carbon, hydrogen, and oxygen. Sugar provides energy and is essential for the functioning of brain and muscle tissue. In the kitchen, sugar makes food taste sweet and also links proteins together, helping create such tasty foods as meringue and custard.

Fats and oils are composed of carbon and hydrogen. Fats and oils give foods a rich, creamy, feel in the mouth and so are often an important part of "comfort" foods, such as chocolate, macaroni and cheese, and ice cream. Fats are the way the body stores energy for later use. Fats are also necessary for making hormones.

Proteins are composed of chains of amino acids, which are made of carbon, hydrogen, and nitrogen. Our body's biochemical actions are controlled by proteins, so we need lots of protein in our diets. Proteins change their properties when heated or beaten and may react together chemically at high temperatures, making them a unique part of food preparation. Eggs are a good example of this: imagine how heating or beating an egg changes its look and consistency.

Starches are large molecules made by joining many sugar molecules together. Starches don't taste sweet, because the long molecules are too large to reach the sensitive parts of the taste buds on our tongues. In the kitchen, the major sources of starch come from root vegetables (potatoes, carrots, turnips) and cereals and grains (rice, noodles, flour, oatmeal). Starch granules can absorb astonishing amounts of water.

Supplies & materials for the experiments

Salt
Sugar
Flour
Cornstarch
Cotton fabric
Sharp knife
Saucepan
Cookie sheet
Saucers
Sharp knife
Black tea bags
Vinegar
Butter
Cotton string
Masking tape
Bowls- 1 small

Several spoons (the kind you'd eat cereal with)
Sodium bicarbonate (baking soda)
Wintergreen Life Savers candy
Unsoaped steel wool pads
Food coloring (optional)
1 yellow or red onion
Liquid laundry starc
Small cutting board
Hydrogen peroxide
Instant potato flakes
Magnifying glass

States of Matter

All matter is composed of particles—either atoms or molecules. Most matter here on Earth is either a solid, a liquid, a gas, or a combination of those forms. Each form of matter has specific characteristics:

Solids (the Element of Earth)
The particles in solids are held very close together so they can hardly move.

Solids do not flow like liquids—they stay in one place.

Solids keep their shape. They do not take the shape of their container.

Solids always take up the same amount of space. They do not spread out like gases.

Liquids (the Element of Water)
In a liquid the particles are not so tightly packed, so they can move a little.

Liquids flow easily.

Liquids change their shape, and always take the shape of the container they are in.

Liquids always take up the same amount of space. They do not spread out like gases.

Gases (the Element of Air)
In a gas the particles are spread apart and can move easily.

Gases spread out freely. They can take up more or less space, depending on the size of their container.

Gases can be compressed ("squashed"), as in heavy pressurized tanks of oxygen..

A fourth state of matter—**Plasma** (the Element of Fire)—is present under unique conditions and isn't found under normal Earthly conditions. The closest place you're likely to see natural plasma is in the northern lights, the *aurora borealis*. However, small plasma balls, or plasma generators, can be found in many novelty stores.

A fifth state of matter—**Dark Matter**—exists only in the depths of the universe and cannot be seen.

Experiment 1:

Physical changes

You will need a small saucepan, a pie plate, a hot pad, and a tray of ice cubes. Before starting the experiment, fill the bottom of the pie plate with ice cubes and set to one side.

1. Observe the ice cubes. What do you see? What state of matter are they?

Cover the bottom of the saucepan with ice cubes and turn on medium-high heat under the pan.

2. What happens to the ice cubes in the saucepan? What state or states of matter are they in now?

Once steam is rising from the pan, use the hot pad to hold the pie plate about 6 inches above the saucepan. (Be careful that the steam doesn't burn your hand!)

3. What happens to the bottom of the pie plate?

There are two important things happening here.

A. The water is undergoing a chemical change. It changes from solid to liquid to gas and then back to liquid again. If you poured it all back into the ice cube trays, you could freeze it into water once again. Despite moving from solid to liquid to gas, the nature of the water has not changed. These types of changes are physical changes, meaning that there has been a temporary change only in the physical nature of the substance, without actually changing the molecular arrangement of the substance. The actual water hasn't changed.

B. You have also just demonstrated the water/rain cycle here on earth! Water evaporates from rivers and rises into the air. When it encounters cold temperatures in the clouds or upper atmosphere, it condenses into rain and falls back to earth.

Experiment 2: Chemical changes

Place a small skillet on a burner over low-medium heat. Have a glass of ice water ready.
    Measure 2 Tsp sugar. Observe with the magnifying glass, noting the shape of the sugar crystals.

1. What shape are the individual crystals? What state of matter are the crystals in?

Place the sugar into the skillet, watching carefully. Stir it from time to time.

2. What happens? What state of matter is the sugar in now?

Continue cooking until the sugar has melted into a

syrup. Turn the heat off. Take a spoonful of syrup and drip it into the ice water.

3. What happens? What state of matter is the sugar in now?

You should see the syrup solidify into a caramel-like or brittle form (the form will depend on how well cooked the syrup was). You can eat it—it will taste like caramel, or brittle. In fact, many candies are made from cooked or melted sugar.
    Let the pan cool completely. Examine the syrup with a magnifying glass.

4. What do you notice? Can you see crystals now?

Now, add ½ cup water to the cooled pan and stir.

5. What happens?

The sugar has undergone a chemical change, meaning a permanent change in its structure. The molecules of the sugar in the pan have been permanently rearranged, and no longer have a clear crystalline structure.

Experiment 3: Crystals and Solutions

Examine some salt crystals with a strong magnifying glass. What shape are the crystals? Are they the same or different than the sugar crystals were?
    Make a *solution** by dissolving ½ tsp. salt in ½ cup hot water.

*A solution is an evenly mixed *(homogenous)* mixture of two substances. It is created when a *solute* (in this case, salt) is dissolved in a *solvent* (in this case, water).
    Fill a deep saucer or jar lid with the solution. Set it in a place where it will not be disturbed. Watch the saucer over several days, as the water evaporates.

Hypothesis: What do you think will happen to the solution?

1. What eventually happened to the solution?
2. Did you prove your hypothesis?
3. Did the salt undergo a physical or a chemical change?

When you dissolved the salt in the water, you created a salt solution. The salt crystals dissolved into the solution, but when the solution evaporated, the crystals reformed. The crystals are called the *evaporate* of the solution.

4. What do you think would have happened if you had boiled the solution instead of simply letting it evaporate?

Experiment 4:
Colloids and Mixtures

You've already learned about solutions. Example: a solute (e.g., salt) dissolves in a solvent (e.g., water). After dissolving, the solute is no longer visible. If left alone the solution will remain dissolved and will not "settle out."

A *mixture* combines two substances, but both substances retain their original characteristics. Nothing dissolves or changes, and both substances remain visible. If left alone, the two substances will separate and one will "settle out."

A *colloid* is a mixture that does not settle out. In a colloid, one substance is suspended in another substance, but neither substances dissolves. One or both substances may remain visible. Examples: foamy shaving cream, jams and jellies, pudding, soap that floats on water

Materials:

Four quart-size jars with lids
Water
Sand
Kool-Aid (any flavor, 1 packet)
1 packet Jell-O (and flavor)
Vegetable oil
Vinegar

Label the jars A, B, C, and D.

In jar A, place 2 cups water and ¼ cup sand. Cover and shake for 30 seconds.

What do you see happening in the jar? Can you still see the grains of sand? Does anything settle out?

Allow the jar to sit undisturbed for 2 hours.

In jar B, place 2 cups water and the packet of Kool-Aid. Cover and shake for 30 seconds.

What do you see happening in the jar? Can you still see the grains of Kool-Aid? Does anything settle out?

Allow the jar to sit undisturbed for 2 hours.

For Jar C, Add the packet of Jell-O to the empty jar.

Bring 1 cup water to a boil. Pour it carefully into the jar. Stir until the Jell-O dissolves.

Add 1 cup cold water to the jar and stir briskly for 30 seconds.

What do you see happening in the jar? Can you still see the grains of Jell-O? Does anything settle out?

Place this jar, uncovered, into the refrigerator.

Allow the jar to sit undisturbed for 2 hours.

In jar D, put 1cup vinegar and ¼ cup oil. Cover and shake for 30 seconds.

What do you see happening in the jar? Can you still see the oil and/or the vinegar? Does anything settle out?

Allow the jar to sit undisturbed for 2 hours.

**Wait two hours, so that the Jell-O in jar C can become solid. Then answer the following questions.

1. Does jar A hold a solution, mixture, or colloid?
2. Does jar B hold a solution, mixture, or colloid?
3. Does jar C hold a solution, mixture, or colloid?
4. Does jar D hold a solution, mixture, or colloid?
5. Does jar A hold a solid, a liquid, a gas, or a combination of one or more?
6. Does jar B hold a solid, a liquid, a gas, or a combination of one or more?
7. Does jar C hold a solid, a liquid, a gas, or a combination of one or more?
8. Does jar D hold a solid, a liquid, a gas, or a combination of one or more?

NOTES: Add another 2 cups of water to jar B and you'll have drinkable Kool-Aid.

The Jell-O in jar C is edible.

Add ½ tsp. salt and a good shake of pepper to jar D and you'll have a tasty salad dressing. Shake vigorously just before serving.

Experiment 5:
Acids and Bases

Acids and bases are defined by whether they produce hydrogen ions (H+) or hydroxide ions (OH-) when placed in a watery solution. When the solution ends up with a higher amount of H+ ions, it is said to be *acidic*. When it contains more OH- ions, it is said to be *basic*.

Acid-base chemistry is important to all of our bodily functions. The relative "strength" of acids and bases is measured using the pH scale, which ranges from 0-14. The lower the pH, the more acidic the substance. The higher the pH, the more basic the substance. A pH reading of 7 is neutral.

In general, acidic foods taste "sour" while basic foods have a flat taste. Here are some pH values for common foods:

Lemons: 2.1   Apple juice: 4.0
Milk: 6.4   Egg white: 8.0
"Tums": Varies; usually 10 or higher

Hypothesis: What
do you think will happen when you mix an acid and a base?

Materials:
Tall glass
Vinegar
Baking soda
Measuring
    spoons

"Stork" vessel

Food coloring (your choice of color)

In a tall glass, pour ¼ cup vinegar. Stir in a few drops of food coloring.

1. What do you call the mixture of vinegar and food coloring?

Measure 2 Tsp of baking soda. Add it to the vinegar ALL AT ONCE.

3. What happened?
4. What did you see?
5. What did you smell?
6. Was what happened a chemical change or a physical change?
7. Did you prove your hypothesis?
8. Try the experiment again, using different proportions of vinegar and baking soda. What proportions give you the most impressive reaction?

The strong reaction between acid (vinegar) and base (baking soda) caused the response.

For fun: Create a volcano out of non-hardening clay. Build the volcano around a plastic or paper cup where the cone would be. Fill the cone with a quantity of baking soda. Prepare a solution of vinegar and red food coloring. ALL AT ONCE, pour the vinegar solution into the volcano's cone. If your proportions are correct, "hot lava" will fizz up and pour over the sides of your volcano.

Experiment 6: Alchemical ink

This experiment uses chemical changes to create your own alchemical ink. You can use it to write with.

Materials:

Vinegar
Strainer
Small bowl
1 black tea bag
A small saucepan
Unsoaped steel wool
Toothpick or wooden skewer
3% hydrogen peroxide (buy at drug store)

Place the tea bag in a tea cup. Add 1/3 cup boiling water and let steep for 15 minutes. Wring tea bag out and throw away. The tea contains tannic acid.

In a small saucepan, warm ¼ cup vinegar. Use scissors to snip bits of unsoaped steel wool into the hot vinegar (add as much as you can, but make sure the vinegar continued to cover the steel wool). Heat until the steel wool dissolves and/or forms a colored

"Tortoise" vessel

solution (iron sulfate). Allow to cool.

Pour the tea into the small bowl. Strain the iron solution into the tea. This will form black iron tannate. Be very careful: this is indelible and will stain clothes, carpet, or whatever it touches!

Dip a toothpick or skewer into the "ink" and try writing with it. If the ink seems watery, let it sit out for a day or two until enough evaporates to make it slightly thicker.

Store your ink in a tightly capped bottle.

For extra fun: use a bird feather or buy a quill at a craft store. Use a pocket-knife to sharpen the quill, and use the quill as a pen. Just like a real Wizard!

Questions:

1. What did the tea mixture look like?
2. Did the tea mixture represent a chemical change or a physical change?
3. What color was the vinegar and steel wool solution?
4. Did the vinegar and steel wool solution represent a chemical change or a physical change?
5. How did your ink work?

Experiment 7: Alchemical candy

You will need some simple ingredients and some cooking utensils...and a few hungry people to test the honeycomb after you have made it.

Hypothesis: What will happen when you add a mixture of vinegar and baking soda to a candy syrup?

Materials:

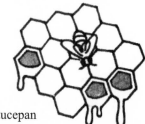

1 cup sugar
1 tsp. butter
¾ cup water
2 Tsp vinegar
A baking tray
¼ tsp. baking soda
A large (4 quart) saucepan

Grease the baking tray with a small amount of butter.

Mix the sugar, butter, and water in a large saucepan. Bring the mixture to the boil, stirring constantly. Once it begins to boil, stop stirring, and continue boiling until it turns golden yellow.

Remove the mixture from the stove, and quickly stir in the baking soda and vinegar. (Have someone help you; one of you should add the substances while the other stirs briskly.) The carbon dioxide produced will cause the mixture to froth up, so be careful it doesn't spill.

Pour the mixture into a baking tray that has been greased with butter. When it is cool, cut or break the honeycomb into pieces to eat.

Questions:

1. How did the boiling syrup look and smell?
2. What happened to the syrup when you added the vinegar and baking soda?
3. Describe the appearance of the finished candy when you broke a piece open?
4. How did the finished candy taste?
5. Did you prove your hypothesis?

In this candy, chemical reactions between acids and bases are responsible for the action. Vinegar reacts with baking soda to produce carbon dioxide gas; the gas fills the candy with thousands of tiny bubbles, creating a honeycombed appearance.

Experiment 8: Crunchy sparks

One of the easiest ways to create your own miniature light show is to munch on wintergreen Lifesavers.

Hypothesis: What do you think you will see when you crunch wintergreen lifesavers before a mirror? (Never mind the table manners—we're doing science here!)

Experiment: Place two wintergreen Lifesavers in your mouth. Stand in a dark room before a mirror and crunch the Lifesavers with your mouth open.

2. What do you see?
3. What color were the sparks?
4. Did you prove your hypothesis?

Wintergreen Lifesavers include *methyl salicylate* (oil of wintergreen). When the sugar crystals in the Life Savers get crushed (by chewing), electrons break loose and are scattered. The electrons "try" to return to return to the sugar crystals they broke free from. The problem is that nitrogen molecules (from the air) have taken their place. When the free sugar electrons crash into the nitrogen electrons, the nitrogen emits a very faint ultraviolet glow (a kind of radiation). The ultraviolet radiation is absorbed by the wintergreen flavoring, methyl salicylate. This then emits a fairly bright light as sparks.

The phenomenon is called *triboluminescence*, light resulting from crushing or tearing. The same phenomenon may account for other mysterious lights observed in nature, such as deep-sea luminescence.

Experiment 9:

Non-Newtonian fluid

We've shown that liquids behave in specific ways.

Non-Newtonian fluids are named for Sir Isaac Newton, who wrote many of the laws of fluid dynamics. Non-Newtonian fluids are liquids that behave in unusual ways.

For one thing, their *viscosity** depends on the force applied. Have you ever played with Silly Putty? Silly Putty is a non-Newtonian fluid. If you pull on it slowly, it stretches out and flows, like a fluid. If you leave it sitting on a hard surface, it eventually flows into a puddle-like shape, again like a fluid. But if you pull it apart abruptly, it snaps and breaks like a solid.

*The term *viscosity* refers to a fluids "stickiness," which causes it to resist flowing.

With cornstarch, you can make and play with your own non-Newtonian fluid.

"Pelican" vessel

Hypothesis: What do you think will happen when you mix cornstarch and water?

Materials:
Cornstarch
Water
A small bowl
An empty wax milk carton or a heavy plastic freezer bag

Place ½ cup cornstarch in the bowl.

Add water, 1 Tsp. at a time, stirring well after each addition.

When the cornstarch mixture begins to thicken, strike it sharply with your finger or with a spoon. When the strike feels like it hits something "solid," your non-Newtonian fluid is ready.

Play with your weird fluid. If you squeeze it in your fist, it feels solid. But relax your hand and it will ooze out and stream over the edges of your hand, like a liquid.

1. What happened?
2. What did the cornstarch look like before you added water? How did it feel?
3. What did the cornstarch look like after you added water? How did it feel?
4. Is the cornstarch substance a fluid or a solid?
5. Did you prove your hypothesis?
6. What did you create in this experiment?

> *IMPORTANT: When done playing with this, dispose of it in a plastic bag or milk carton and throw it in the trash. Do not put it down the drain as it will clog your pipes!*

Experiment 10: Paper towel Chromatography

Chromatography is a technique that is used to separate mixtures of color. In paper chromatography, the colors are separated using a piece of absorbent paper.

As you probably know, most colors actually are formed of combinations of many other colors. For example, yellow and red make orange, yellow and blue make green, and red and blue make purple.

If you could put all of the known colors together, you would get white. If you could remove all color from a place, you'd be left with black.

Hypothesis: What do you think will happen when you mix colored ink and water on a coffee filter?

Materials:
Coffee filters (these work best) or paper towels
Washable (not permanent) colored markers
Water
Eye dropper or a very tiny spoon

Draw a 1 inch circle on a paper towel with one washable color marker.

Add drops of water to the center of the circle, one drop at a time, until the water spreads outside the circle.

Allow the paper towel to sit for 20-30 minutes. Make observations throughout this period.

Repeat this experiment with at least two more colors.

1. What color did you start with?
2. What colors did you see by the end of the experiment?
3. What do you think happened?
4. Did you prove your hypothesis?

The water was drawn out between the fibers in the filter or paper towel by a force known as capillary action.

As the water passed through the ink circle, the different water-soluble dyes in the ink dissolved in the water (went into solution) and were carried out through the paper with the water. As the water moved through the paper towel, it left behind the individual colors that were mixed together in the marker.

Some dyes are made of molecules that are big and heavy, while other colored dyes are made of smaller, lighter molecules. The larger the molecule, the shorter distance it is carried out through the paper. Thus, the dyes separated according to the size of their molecules.

At the end of the experiment you have produced a chromatogram: a visual way to show all the individual dyes and colors present in your colored pen.

Just for fun:
See how many colors you can get to come out of one marker.

See if all brands of markers use the same color combinations.

Plating an iron nail with copper

Materials:
1 iron nail
½ tsp. salt
½ cup vinegar
A small, clean glass jar
Steel wool or abrasive cleanser
10 dull copper pennies (1983 or older)

Mix the vinegar and salt in the glass jar.

Add the dull pennies to the vinegar mixture and leave them there until they look very clean and shiny. Remove them, saving the vinegar mixture.

Clean the iron nail thoroughly with steel wool and/or cleanser.

Place the clean nail into the vinegar mixture and allow to remain in the solution for 10 minutes. The nail will now be covered with a bright solution of copper!

18. Bubble Mixture

Materials:
Clean glass jar
1 cup warm water
2 Tsp liquid dishwashing detergent

Stir the water and detergent gently together. Pour into the jar and allow to stand overnight. Use for blowing bubbles.

NOTE: for extra stability, add a few drops of glycerin (available at your local pharmacy).

Dancing raisins

Materials:
Raisins
Unflavored soda water or
    colorless soda pop (e.g., 7-Up)

Pour a glass of soda or soda water. Add raisins, and watch as the carbon dioxide bubbles cling to the raisins, carrying them up and down!

Did you know....?

If all the salt in the oceans could be removed and spread evenly over the Earth's land surfaces, it would form a layer more than 500 feet thick!

To do your own salt evaporation, dissolve 1 teaspoon of salt in a cup of hot water. Pour the water into a shallow pie plate and leave in the sun or in a sunny window until the water evaporates, leaving the salt behind.

Color-changing liquid

Here's a nifty little experiment in Kitchen Alchemy from Jim Fish. It can also be used in Conjury. It goes like this: a clear glass or pitcher containing a purple liquid is poured into a series of five clear cups. In each cup, the color of the purple liquid changes, until in the final cup, it becomes completely colorless!

The purple juice is created by chopping up some red cabbage, boiling it, filtering out the residue, and diluting it with water to a nice clear purple.

Each of the five cups holds a small amount of clear liquid solution, which will turn the cabbage juice the following colors:

1. **Red:** acid - white vinegar will do.
2. **Blue:** baking soda solution (sodium bicarbonate).
3. **Green:** washing soda solution (sodium carbonate); non-sudsy ammonia solution also works.
4. **Yellow:** a weak Clorox solution.
5. **Clear:** a stronger Clorox solution will turn the liquid clear.

NOTE: *DO NOT drink these liquids!*

It is easy to get these results by pouring the purple juice out of the pitcher into each cup separately. Experiment with the amounts of the liquids already in the cups.

However, it is possible, by balancing the pH, to pour the same liquid from cup to cup, in the above sequence, and cause it to turn each of the colors, as long as you save the bleach for last.

This is a great improvement, but it requires more delicate control. Again, you will need to experiment to determine just how much of the solutions you will need to have in each cup to make the color changes work. In the context of a conjury or ritual, having the same juice go from purple through the colors to clear could be quite powerful.

To incorporate this effect into a ritual, such as at Midsummer (where you could begin your Quarter callings in the South), you could set up the pitcher and 4-5 cups on a central altar. Then, starting with the Element of Fire, you would turn the

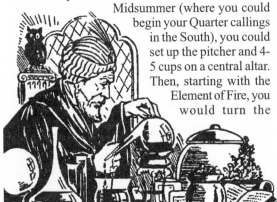

juice red, and place the 1st cup on the South Altar. Next, you would turn a 2nd cup of juice blue for Water, and place it on the West altar. Then turn the 3rd cup green for Earth, to the North; and the 4th one yellow for Air in the East. A 5th cup could be turned clear for Spirit, and placed in the Center. To add to the mystique, go to a party supply store and buy a few boxes of "Kizzy Color Flame Candles." These come five to a set, and burn with flames that match the candle colors: red, orange, green, blue, and violet. If you cannot find them in a store, you can order them from www.kizzycolorflame.com. These can be set in holders on each altar, and lit when the cups are placed with them.

There is much great magick in this experiment because we are working with the actual pigments of flowers, fruit, and autumn leaves and also with the anti-oxidant *licopenes,* which are so life-giving.

The usual explanation for plant pigments is about the symbiosis between flowers and insects, but the truth is that these evolved as the plants crept out of the seas into a hostile atmosphere full of CO_2, which let in all the ultraviolet light which destroys chlorophyl, and pigments developed as protection against the harm. This was long before plants themselves then destroyed the atmosphere with poisonous free oxygen and the mitochondria showed up to eat the oxygen and gave us our animal attributes. Mitochondria block radiation effects, repair DNA, eat the free radical oxygen, and work within us as we eat our veggies.

Strong magic, indeed.

8. Marvelous inventions
By Oberon (grey)

Give me a lever long enough, a fulcrum, and a place to stand, and I will move the world. —Archimedes, 230 BCE

Some famous Wizards were also great inventors. Archimedes of Syracuse (287-211 BCE) invented systems of levers and pulleys to lift and move heavy objects, and he discovered ways to measure a circle and determine the volume of solids. His "Archimedean screw" was an ingenious hand pump that

Archimedean Screw by Fra Gioconda, from 1522 edition of Virtruvius's De Architectura.

could spray water directly from the Nile onto the fields of Egypt. Archimedes used geometry and astronomical observation to accurately determine the circumference of the Earth, and he built a device to measure the angles of the rising sun, enabling him to correctly calculate for the first time the exact length of a year.

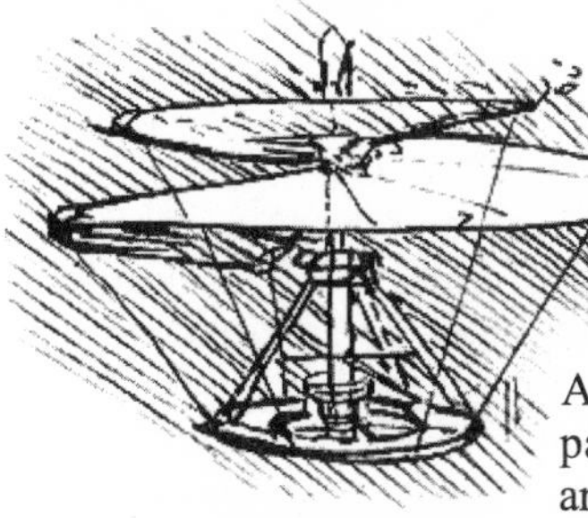

But certainly the most famous Wizard inventor of history was the great genius Leonardo da Vinci (1452-1519). Among the thousands of pages of his notebooks are designs for helicopters *(above)*, armored tanks, submarines, parachutes, drawing machines, drilling rigs…and, most famous of all, a flying machine, or *ornithopter* ("bird-wing"). Unlike Archimedes, however, Leonardo never actually built any of his marvelous inventions! But you can construct a working model of his flying machine using the cutouts in the back of this book.

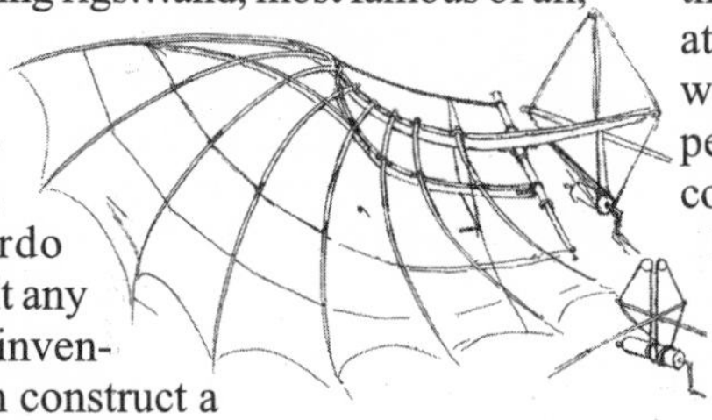

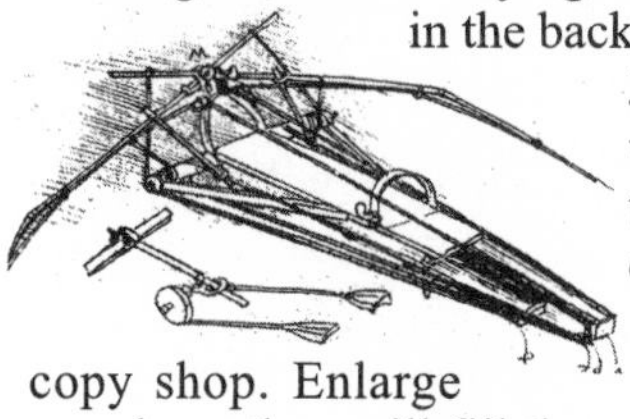

Just take the two pages with the ornithopter pictures and copy them onto a parchment card stock at your nearest copy shop. Enlarge them to 121% when you do, sothey will fill the page. Lay the card stock pages on a hard smooth surface, and score along all the dotted lines with the dull back edge of a table knife, following curves where so indicated. Then cut out the pieces, and fold the creases to make the assemblies. There are two wings, a tail, a fuselage (body section), two braces, and two little washers. (Fig. 1)

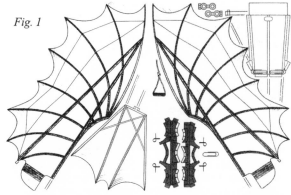

Fig. 1

You will also need a package of 12-inch bamboo skewers, as used for shish-kebobs. You should be able to buy these at any large grocery store. You will also need four small paper clips (see template for exact size), a medium-sized rubber band, and some brown embroidery thread for cables. For tools, you will need scissors, a table knife, a fine wood rasp (an emery board works great), a small bottle of white milk glue (Elmer's is good), needle-nosed pliers, and wire-cutters.

Fig. 2

Follow the directions on the cutout pages. One of the important things is making the curved sections in the wings and tail, with the drawings of struts visible at the peaks of the creases, so these look like dragon-wings. Then glue the skewers along or across these peaks, as shown above (Fig. 2). The outside skewers connecting the fuselage and tail (Fig. 3) will be the full 12 inches long, and so will the front skewers supporting the wings. Others will need to be cut to the indicated lengths, using the wire-cutters.

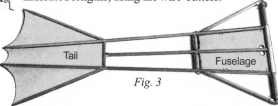

Tail   Fuselage

Fig. 3

Assemble the fuselage and tail first (Fig. 3). Then construct the braces around small cut pieces of skewers, as shown (Fig. 4-5). Cut and bend four pieces of paper clip as shown, and insert one end horizontally into the top corner of each brace (Fig. 5). Then glue the braces onto the fuselage.

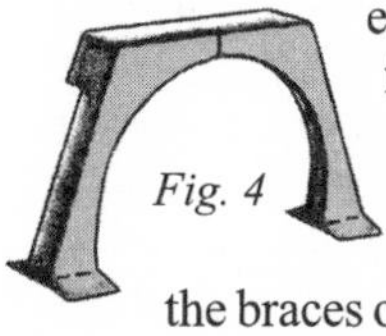

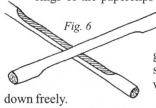

Fig. 4

Next, assemble the wings (Fig. 2). The long exposed parts of the front wing skewers will need to be half-sanded so they can slip past each other to flap the wings. (Fig. 6) Insert the exposed ends of the wing skewers through the rings of the paperclips on the braces,

Fig. 5

2″
Top
Back
R.Side
Front
2″

Fig. 6

and then wrap the flaps around the upper brace struts and glue them to the underside of the wings so the wings can move up and down freely.

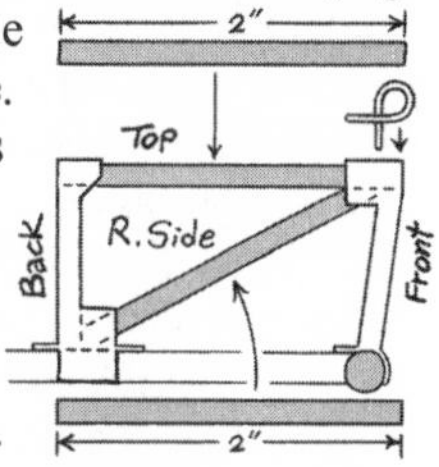

Then you will need to make the foot stirrups and cables, to flap the wings the way it would be done if you were actually flying the ornithopter, by lying on the fuselage platform with your feet in the stirrups and your hands on the long wing levers.

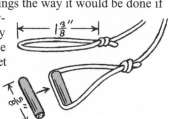

$1\frac{3}{8}″$

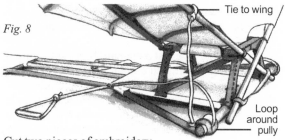

Fig. 8

Tie to wing

Loop around pully

Cut two pieces of embroidery thread to lengths of 12". Then cut two small pieces of skewers to 5/8". Tie a 1-3/8" loop in the thread as shown in the diagram, and glue a stirrup into the loop, as shown in Fig. 7.

Then run the thread through the paperclips at the back of the fuselage, around the front bar through the pulley washers, and tie it to the leading edge of the wing at the indicated point. (Fig. 8)

Fig. 9

Rubber band

Finally, run a rubber band around the end of one of the front wing strut skewers, up and over the hole and skewer in the front of the fuselage, and back out again to wrap around the front strut of the other wing. (Fig. 9) The rubber band will create the same kind of tension to raise the wings as if you were

Fig. 10

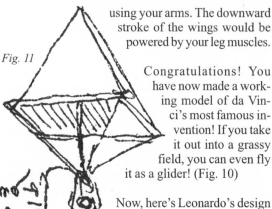

Fig. 11

using your arms. The downward stroke of the wings would be powered by your leg muscles.

Congratulations! You have now made a working model of da Vinci's most famous invention! If you take it out into a grassy field, you can even fly it as a glider! (Fig. 10)

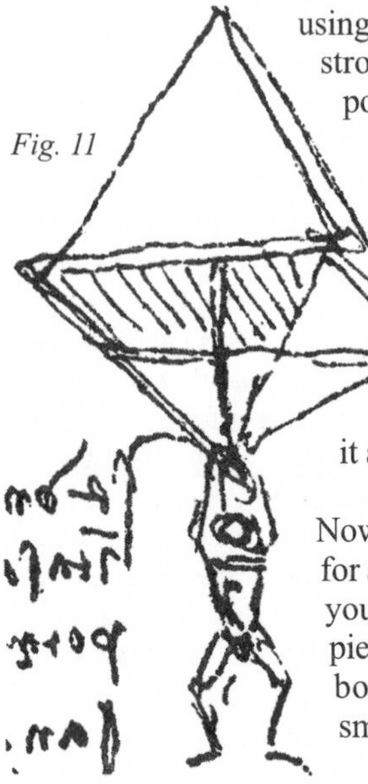

Now, here's Leonardo's design for a parachute (Fig 11). See if you can make a model using a piece of card stock, some bamboo skewers, string, and a small action figure.

9. Technomagick: Explorations in Cyberspace

By Elizabeth Barrette (grey)

Welcome to cyberspace, perhaps the most accessible of metaphysical realms. "Metaphysical" literally means "beyond physical," and what else is cyberspace but a world of ideas rather than objects? Cyberspace exists within a physical computer, but it is so much more than its shell – much the same as your soul exists within your body, but is far more vast and complex and eternal than the flesh housing it. We can manipulate cyberspace. We can enter it with our minds, but never with our bodies. Yet in this space we can create wonders. What could be more magickal than that?

The world inside the crystal

The best description I've ever found of technomagick comes from a song called "The World Inside the Crystal" by Stephen Savitzky, copyright 1985. The most famous rendition is that of Kathy Mar, available on her album *Plus Ça Change*. This song introduces the realm of cyberspace ("the world inside the crystal") and its limitations ("where my body cannot go"). It consistently equates technology and Wizardry, comparing the computer to a "magick crystal mirror." Furthermore, it captures the mingled sense of power and dislocation that characterize people whose talents span the often incompatible fields of magick and science: "Call us hackers, call us wizards, with derision or respect."

The lyrics also lay out the rules of how cyberspace works, such as "the only law is logic." It's defined as magickal because it's a place "where symbols have the power to become the things they name." What could be more mystical than a world in which words – in esoteric symbolic languages, no less! – actually *be-*

come what they describe? You tell a computer, "Take me to this Website," and there you are. How is this different from a Portal or Scrying spell? You describe what you want and it happens, just like that.

Of course this is machinery rather than spellcraft, but there is an old saying by author Arthur C. Clarke: "Sufficiently advanced technology is indistinguishable from magick." On the flip side, sufficiently advanced magick is indistinguishable from technology! The reason the two become indistinguishable in their fullest form is because, at that point, they both function *on the same levels.*

Cyberspace as an out of body experience

Cyberspace is good practice for dealing with other levels of reality. It's special because it has such a tight link to "everyday" reality but it is very different from that. Personal interactions aren't the same here. Some of the skills you gain here will stand you in good stead when dealing with spirits, while traveling other dimensions, and so forth.

The first thing you learn, if you pay attention, is what defines you as "you" – because in cyberspace, you are what you type (or otherwise transmit). You can practice being other people; you can change your gender, age, social class, race, physical description – anything you can pull off the attitude and reality tunnel for online. It makes you think about your definitives. How much can you change and still be recognizably *you?*

Also, cyberspace reveals new aspects of your personality. Some folks come across completely different online than they do in person. This has a downside with people falling in love online and then discovering they can't stand each other face-to-face. For the exact same reason, it also allows people to interact and enjoy each other's company online when they could never do so otherwise.

The atmosphere of cyberspace affects your perceptions, too. You can pick up "danger signals" that steer you away from creepy people online even though you are not in physical proximity. Maybe their phrasing seems too hostile or they try to dig into your personal life more than you want to share. You come to view knowledge as something that yearns to be free; as a medium in its own right, like an ocean in which you can swim; as a means of trade or barter; as a necessary and integral part of life no less essential than oxygen.

Unless you are just a die-hard bigot with a mind like an airtight seal, you quickly shed a lot of prejudices because cyberspace acts as a great equalizer – people don't have to tell you they are black or female or so poor they have to use the access terminal in a public library. You put much more emphasis on intelligence, conversation skills, and personality than you do on irrelevant trivia. Some people don't see this or believe in it, but I have seen it in action and it is truly beautiful.

You also figure out how to navigate without using your body as a vehicle. Just think of that – cyberspace activity is a kind of out-of-body travel! You park your body in a chair and use your hands to type, but your body stays right in that chair while your mind and personality go zipping off to Switzerland or New Guinea or wherever.

This is very much like traveling between the worlds where a thought is a thing and your intent determines your direction. This type of "travel by intent" stands you in good stead in meditation, after death, or in other realities when you do not have a physical body to use as a vehicle. If you already have some experience in moving without one, then you have a much easier time adapting. Thus it's good to practice, as Wizards spend a lot of time working in or with metaphysical dimensions.

This does not obviate the need for physical reality, but it does demonstrate unmistakably that actions taken in a nonphysical reality can have direct and profound effects on physical reality. If you shop online and find a Website selling the perfect wand, you can key in your credit card number (assuming your credit line permits) and that wand will arrive at your door. This kind of profound link between two very different but intricately intertwined realities provides a wonderful example of how things like magick, ritual, and prayer can work. You begin to understand how cyberspace and "meatspace" can exist in the same place, yet without touching, only able to connect through special interfaces. In the same way, we can touch Faery or other spirit worlds only at certain times or in mystical places.

Identity in Cyberspace

You are not your body. Instead, your spirit wears your body much as you wear your favorite clothes. Your hair texture, skin and eye color, size, shape – all these things are temporary. They apply to your current body and life; they are not permanent characteristics of your soul.

A spirit has no size, shape, or color of its own. Much like water, it takes on characteristics from the container it fills. It's difficult to change your body, but easy for your spirit to shift and flow from one seeming to another. Another way to look at this, since we're talking about technomagick here, is that if you were a computer, your body would be the hardware and your spirit would be the software.

When you enter cyberspace with your mind, your options are unlimited. You can choose to present yourself very much as you are – your actual age, gender, body type, etc. This is honest, but not always exciting. It can also be risky to give away too many details, like where you live or work. However, you can instead choose to present yourself as someone quite different. You might create an online persona who is older or younger, taller or shorter, even the opposite sex. Many people go by a "handle" or "screen name," a special nickname they use online—kind of like the magickal names used in the Grey School!

In cyberspace, people only know the part of you that you reveal through your words and actions. They can't see (unless you use a Web camera) your body or what you're doing with it. Instead, they come to know you as a frequent poster or a lurker, a mediator who soothes disputes, or a troll who starts flamewars. They may know you as a Wizard with subtle knowledge of computers, obscure languages, or fascinating lore; they may know you as an ignorant twit with no experience worth hearing. It all depends on the choices you make.

Cyberspace is one of the most readily accessible magick realms. In this place, you can truly be a Wizard. What you do here is up to you. Use the power wisely.

10. A Glossary of Technomagick

By Elizabeth Barrette (grey)

Astral Travel – the ability or techniques of slipping your spirit briefly out of your body and then back in again; aka "astral projection." Also called "out of body experience," or OOBE.

Censorware – any of several programs designed to block, alter, delete, or otherwise tamper with material which the programmer (or more rarely, the controlling user, such as a parent) deems objectionable.

Computer Wizard – a term known even to most mainstream people, indicating a person whose ability to make computers do useful or enchanting things goes so far beyond the mundanely explicable as to seem, or be, magickal; see also **technomage**.

Cyberspace – a dimension bridging reality and imagination, generated within some computer(s), its qualities influenced by machine capacity and programmer skill, but not limited in any physical sense and existing beyond the bounds of any one machine, program, or user.

Definitives – those characteristics of a soul which are innate and consistent through eternity, whereby entities may recognize each other when disembodied or when embodied in forms different from their first meeting.

Emoticons – originally a set of ordinary letters or other symbols intended to convey such things as voice tone or expression to an unseen audience. The first emoticon is believed to be the smiley: :) Many programs now convert those keystrokes to a little picture: ☺ Some even have tiny cartoon faces showing how the user feels.

Facetime – any period which people spend in each other's physical company, as contrasted to time spent interacting in cyberspace.

Filk Music – songs with a science fiction or fantasy theme; this includes many songs about computers, computer Wizards, technomagick, etc.

Handle – a nickname someone uses online; aka "screen name."

Meatspace – the opposite of cyberspace, this is a colorful term for ordinary reality, the world of bodies and objects. I discourage the use of "realspace" for this, as cyberspace can be absolutely real, just not material.

Metaphysical – literally means "beyond physical," relating to matters of magick or spirit.

Multi-User Dimension – a "location" in cyberspace where people or their characters can interact, most often a game setting; aka multi-user domain, multi-user dungeon, or MUD.

Reality Tunnel – a certain way of perceiving the world, such as a political methodology or a religion; see books by Robert Anton Wilson for elaboration of this concept. Instead of one narrow tunnel, a Wizard often inhabits a *matrix* of reality tunnels, like a cave complex with many twists and levels and junctures through which the Wizard can navigate at need.

Spam – unsolicited bulk email, frequently obscene or fraudulent.

Technomage – a more esoteric term for "computer wizard," which implies above-average skill with computers combined with a tendency to incorporate them into magickal workings.

Technomagick – a branch of mystical study which concerns machines, and cannot function if either the machine or the mystical aspect is removed; see also **computer wizard**.

Department X:
Lifeways (pink)

The Friends We Meet Along the Way

What makes life worth the price we pay?
It seems too high, until we greet
The friends we meet along the way.

Our hopes are gold, our flesh is clay;
Our path wears blisters on our feet.
What makes life worth the price we pay?

Who dances with us through the fray?
Who shares the bitter and the sweet?
The friends we meet along the way.

Our dreams are curds, our fears are whey;
Our bellies churn at each defeat.

What makes life worth the
price we pay?

When skins grow slack and
hairs grow grey,
Who swears we are not obsolete?
The friends we meet along the way.

Our time is measured, day by day;
Our tears are slow, our laughter fleet.
What makes life worth the price we pay?
The friends we meet along the way.

—Elizabeth Barrette

1. Introduction

 ELCOME TO THE WORLD OF LIFE-ways! Here is where you will learn applied Wizardry in your personal and everyday life, and in your relationships with your family, friends, and community.

Lifeways is all about human relationships…*your* relationships. Each of you now has, or will later experience, every kind of relationship. You have relationships with your family members, with your friends (peers), with your teachers, your friends' parents, and other adults and authority figures. You even have a relationship with your pets, but that particular relationship will be addressed in the Beast Mastery Department. You have a relationship with your community, the people who live where you live, and the groups you belong to. Your relationship with the Earth (which many believe is also a living being) is one of stewardship. As you get older, you will also be developing romantic relationships. But the most important relationship you have is the one with your SELF. You will be living with your self for the rest of your life. This relationship actually has two parts: your inner self (your mind, feelings, spirit) and your outer self (your body).

It is the mission of this Department to orchestrate the highest degree of personal growth and self-directed learning toward becoming a productive member of humanity. Such learned skills and knowledge are essential to any level of Wizardry, measured in the positive results the apprentice has on others, and in the development of personal awareness and presence. Special knowledge and skills include goal setting, research, organization, record keeping, scheduling, com-

mitment, communications and critical analysis.

The magickal color of this department is Pink. Like copper, pink is also a color of Venus. Copper is related to the agrarian aspects of Venus—plants, fertility and growth are the common associations. Pink is more related to the emotional and spiritual aspects of Venus, particularly the emotional love of oneself and others. Pink is the color for all our relationships with other people—especially those involving family, love, intimacy, and romance.

2. Your Life as a Wizard
By Lilana d'Venus & Linda C. Young (pink)

It is through relationship that changes
[and growth] occur —Dane Rudhyar

Basic Premises

In the Lifeways Department, we are starting from some "Basic Premises." A basic premise is a "fact" that we simply assume to be true, and accept at the start. Here is a list of some of them:

1. Life will present you with choices, now and always. The consequences of your choices will affect your future.
2. You will encounter a few "absolutes" (things you cannot change). Learning what they are and how to deal with them is part of growing up. One strategy for coping with things you can't change is to shift your viewpoint to a new perspective. Look at it a different way or try to see it from another person's point of view.
3. Mistakes can be valuable lessons. If you were already perfect, you would never learn anything. Mis-

takes are opportunities for growth.

4. Adolescence is the tunnel to your future. There IS a light at the end of the tunnel. Hanging in there is worth it!

5. Just when you think you have yourself figured out, you change again. Your "identity" is in transition. The good news here is that if you don't like the person you or other people think you are, you have the opportunity (and power) to do something about it. You need never stop learning, growing, and changing for the better.

You are a Spirit-Being residing in a physical body. Taking this viewpoint makes sense out of a lot of mysteries.

You and your Family

Basic Premise: By law, your parents or guardians are responsible for your care and your behavior until you are 18 years old and "of age" The law also says (for the most part) that the one who bears responsibility also has the right to exercise control, meaning that they can say what you will or won't do.

Families can be fun, even if you are the only magickal person and the rest are not. One way to create fun in a family is to start having family meetings on a regular basis. In family meetings you have an opportunity to communicate with each other. (Communication is an important skill for a Wizard and we will be offering a class in communication skills later.) In your family gatherings you can talk about things that you want to do that would impact the other family members. Discuss problems that affect other people in the family. Ask for help that another family member may be able to give. Perhaps you all have chores that you rotate.

You can accept assignments during your family meeting. You can plan outings that the whole family would enjoy, such as a trip to the zoo. And always end the meeting with a fun activity that involves everyone, a game or a project, or maybe a jam session, if you all play instruments, or sing along if you don't. (Important rule: Turn off the TV during family meetings.)

Assignment:

Write in your Journal about your family. Talk about your feelings and your hopes concerning your family. If your family does not now have family meetings, think about how you might suggest beginning to have them. Ask your friends if any of them have family meetings, and what they do.

You and your Friends

Basic Premise: You need to have like-minded friends. It is no fun to feel like you are all alone in a hostile world. There ARE others like you out there. You just need to know how to find them.

If you were lucky enough to be born into a magickal family, your parents no doubt have magickal friends who may have magickal kids. This is your starting place for a group of like-minded friends.

If not, at school you might look around for kids who wear a pentagram pendant (a five pointed star in a circle). This is a likely clue that they are interested in magick or Wizardry. Once you have befriended one other magickal person, it will be easier to find more. You might even form an after-school club to talk about magickal things with each other and share information you have found.

If you are allowed to go to such things, you will find other magickal people at such gatherings as Renaissance Faires or Pagan festivals. Wear your magickal regalia, or at least a tunic and leggings if you are a boy. Girls might want to browse some thrift shops for long dresses or skirts, all the better if they look Medieval. The *Grimoire for the Apprentice Wizard* (pp. 124-126) will tell   you more about these gatherings.

If you happen to have friends who would like to learn Wizardry but their parents have said "no" to their magickal interests, assure them that being a Wizard begins in your mind, heart, and spirit. You might consider lending them this book, as well as the *Grimoire*. Your other magickal friends may have some other books they can lend you, and these books will give you all kinds of ideas for magickal things to do together.

Assignment:

Write in your Journal about your friends. Think about why you have chosen these people as friends. How do you help each other? How does having these friends make your life better?

You and your Community

Basic Premise: You will challenge authority. How you go about this will make a profound difference in the outcome. Your way of questioning affects the results.

When I was in 2nd grade, the principal's office was at the top of a narrow staircase. School rules forbade going up those stairs unless you were sent. Another school rule forbade sliding down banisters. My seven-year-old brain decided both rules were "stupid," so one afternoon on a dare I broke both rules at once. Consequences were swift. Landing at the bottom was much more abrupt and bruising and painful than I had expected. And of course a teacher caught me and kept me after school to write "I will not... etc." one hundred times. Defying authority on that issue was not worth it in the long run.

My point being, when you decide to challenge authority, save it for the important issues. It is a good idea to have your reasons clearly thought out. When Rosa Parks refused to give up her bus seat in 1955, she sparked a civil rights revolution. Choose your own issues as carefully. Be sure that "right" is on *your* side. (If you would like to know more about Rosa Parks, check her out at Google.com)

Basic Premise: People are not all alike. Members of a group cannot be lumped together and defined with one word or phrase. For instance, it would be very unobservant, unkind and unfair to say all "cheerleaders" are "airheads."

In any group, there will be some people you admire greatly and some you find impossible to like… and many more that fall somewhere in the large space between the two extremes. It is most useful to focus your attention on the good people, the ones you admire. However, if you find yourself having to deal with one or more very unpleasant people (such as a school bully) you may want to try a Wizardly spell that I like to use called "The Chill-Out." I write the person's name on a small piece of paper. Then I get a paper cup and fill it with water. I fold up the piece of paper with the name inside and put it into the water until it gets soaked and drifts to the bottom. Then I put the paper cup in the back of the freezer. As I am doing this I say,

Let this person from now on be,
Unable to do any harm to me,
Chilled and frozen and gone from my mind.
Now I'll attract someone good and kind.

Basic premise: Finding a role model is a worthy goal.

Recently a writer interviewed hundreds of teenagers. One thing many of the kids spoke of was the importance of having a role model as you are growing up. A role model is someone you admire, someone who has qualities that you would like to have, someone people look up to who is worthy of respect and high regard, someone of whom you can say, "I'd like to be like him (or her) when I grow up."

Look for role models among people you know. If you can find more than one role model, so much the better. If there is no one person that you would choose as a role model, look for the qualities you especially admire and desire in several different people and list those qualities in your Journal as a composite of who you want to be more like.

Assignment:

Begin a list of issues that you feel are unfair and worth speaking up about. Spend a few days or weeks looking around for people older than yourself whom you can admire. Name them in your Journal, and tell what it is about them that earns your admiration and respect. If you created a composite list of qualities, your instructor will want to read what those are and why you chose them.

You and your body

The body is a sacred garment. It is what you enter life in and what you depart life from; and it should be treated with honor. —Martha Graham

Basic Premise: Your body will grow and change throughout your life. How you deal with these changes will affect your happiness.

Growth and becoming is what life is all about. Nature will amply demonstrate that nothing stays the same, whether animal, vegetable, or mineral. The one thing you can count on is change. And whether you are a plant, animal, or a human, the best change when you are young is growth. The body changes that begin to happen in adolescence are perplexing, and sometimes embarrassing, but they are all a part of growing into the adult you will eventually be.

Basic Premise: Your body is the only one you have for this life. If you wreck it, you don't get to trade it in for a new one. If you hate it, you *can* trade your attitude for a new one. If you take good care of your body, it will serve you for a long time.

As an apprentice Wizard, you may have many ideas of what you want to do with your life. With a healthy body you will be able to do much for your world, and accomplish more of your Wizardly goals. Wizards value their bodies. They view their bodies as a gift from their Creator (by whatever name you recognize as your Source, Goddess, God, Universe, Great Spirit, Gaia, etc.). Wizards don't trash the gift. They honor it by taking good care of it.

There are several essentials that your body needs to thrive. The most important are: **Air, Water, Nourishment, Cleanliness, Exercise, Rest,** and **Touch.**

Air—The first and most important thing you did the moment you were born was to start breathing. Without air, a person will die very quickly (I have a t-shirt that says, "When you can't breathe, nothing else matters"). Almost as important as having air to breathe is the quality of that air. It needs to be clean and contain enough oxygen. If you live in a city where air quality is poor, try to get out of the city as often as possible, to the countryside, the seashore, or the mountains. As a bare minimum, keep as many houseplants as you can take care of. They put oxygen into your air. You will also want to develop the habit of breathing deeply.

Water—Pure water is a birthright and (I am getting on my soapbox here) modern industry is making it harder and harder to find. If you are not lucky enough to live near an artesian well like I do, the next best alternative is a high-quality faucet filter. If your parents are willing to buy one, ask them to browse some websites on the subject. Even a cheap filter from the drug store is better than no filter at all.

Some co-ops and natural food stores sell water from their own special filters. You can bring bottles and fill them yourself.

Our bodies are said to be 90% water, and we must frequently replenish it (re-supply that which is lost in sweat or urine). The rule of thumb that I was taught is drink "one ounce of water for every 2 pounds of body weight" per day. This means that if you weigh 100 pounds, you should drink 50 ounces of water during a 24-hour period. I measure out mine in bottles in the morning, and sip it every half-hour or so throughout the day.

Nourishment— Every body is different. What works for one person may not work for another. Some people feel a raw food diet is healthier. Others prefer to eat half cooked and half raw. Some people thrive on a vegetarian diet. Others need to eat meat, poultry, and fish. But with all the scary reports we are hearing these days about mass produced food, I am compelled to advise you to please try to eat organic food as much as possible.

The less processing a food goes through, the more wholesome and nourishing it is. My favorite advice is "Eat Close to the Source." This means that the ideal would be to grow your own food and eat it fresh from the garden. Or hunt your own game meat and eat it fresh from the wild. But we do not live in an ideal world and few of us can do this. However, you may be able to find a local organic farmer willing to deliver fresh from the field. Or your dad might hunt venison in the fall and fill the freezer.

With the basic premise that organic is best, I advise eating more fresh fruits and vegetables than anything else. For carbohydrates, choose whole-grain cereals and breads. For proteins, find a co-op or natural food market that provides organically grown meats and dairy products. (My personal preference is goat dairy, which for most people is easier to digest than cow dairy.)

Become informed about fats and oils. (I am including a web link in the resource list that will provide good information.) There are good fats that your body requires called essential fatty acids. The most important of these are the omega 3s and omega 6s. Flaxseed oil and fish oils are the best sources for these.

Keep salt, sugar, and sweets at a minimum. (Learn about reading labels.) Choose honey or maple syrup over table sugar. Try dulse or whole salt (the complete mineral spectrum is left in it) instead of table salt.

You already know that for best results you need to avoid such things as potato chips, sodas, donuts, tobacco, alcohol, and drugs. Try to avoid anything with monosodium glutamate (MSG) in it. Not only are they totally un-nourishing, they cause problems that take you away from your goal.

Throw away all aluminum cookware and eating utensils! Aluminum ions in your system can cause nerve damage later in life. Some researchers believe aluminum cookware is a major factor in the rise of Alzheimer's disease. Also get rid of all Teflon products.

Likewise, avoid toothpaste that has sodium fluoride in it. This is a deadly poison, also used for killing rats! Calcium fluoride or stannous fluoride are OK. But if there's a poison warning label on the tube of toothpaste, don't use it! Tom's of Maine makes toothpaste that doesn't have sodium fluoride.

Cleanliness—You already know all this. Take daily baths or showers. Brush your teeth, preferably after every meal, but never go to bed with un-scrubbed teeth. Keep your hair and scalp clean. Change your sox and underwear every day. If your shoes stink, sprinkle baking-soda in them. Use a natural deodorant for your armpits. Smelling bad is not the way to attract new friends.

Exercise—Your school probably provides gym classes. Take advantage of them. If you can't take a gym class, take walks, ride a bicycle, jog to the store instead of driving. Bodies need to move. Turn off the TV and do something active.

Rest—Some of us are interested in so many things that it is hard to take time out to sleep. But you really DO need 8 hours of sleep at night. If you are not getting enough, your body will not be as strong and energetic. Possibly your grades and moods will suffer too. Try to arrange your schedule to allow adequate time for sleep. If you have to cut something out, TV should be the first to go. Wizards have better things to do than be a tube-zombie. (And by the way, NEVER leave a TV going while you are sleeping; it is *very* unhealthy, both for your body and for your brain.)

Touch—Many years ago, a hospital study discovered that babies left without human touch (they were fed by robots) did not thrive. In fact, many of them sickened and died. Humans need the touch of other humans. People who get lots of hugs are happier and healthier. Get and give hugs every day. If you feel you are not getting enough hugs from the people you know, volunteer at a rest home or a children's hospital to rub lotion on the hands or feet of people who desperately need your touch. This is "reciprocity"—when you give you get.

Plus THIS—A note about risk-taking. Taking risks is a part of being an adolescent. An article in *Prevention* magazine tells about how baffled and distressed adults are by the stupid risks some kids take, often with disastrous and tragic results. Parents ask, "What were you thinking?!" And the answer—researchers have concluded—is, "I wasn't thinking at all."

The same article (there is a link in the reference section) includes descriptions of research that indicates rapid developmental changes in the teenage brain may be responsible for foggy decision-making. So this is (as my grandmother used to say) "a word to the wise" for you. Know that there will be moments when you simply are not thinking. Be on guard for them.

One area of major risk these days is sexually-transmitted diseases. So if you're having sex, use condoms!

Assignment:

Set up a separate Journal or a separate section of your Magickal Journal for body care. Keep track of your daily eating habits. Log your exercise, how much rest you get, how much touch, how much water you drink. If you live in a place with poor air quality, notice any correlations or connections between fluctuations and changes in air quality and how you feel. (Your newspapers or TV weather reports will tell you when the air is bad.)

The Inner You

Basic Premise: Your inner world is your safety zone. Develop it for a sense of balance and a place to go.

As a young child, when things got too intense inside the house, or I felt like I needed to breathe, I would go outside and take a walk down to the creek or the woods. When I was in my early teens, I figured out that when things in my world were just more than I wanted to deal with, I could close my eyes and "go inside." People usually thought I was napping. What I was really doing was thinking. I would mull over a problem till I could make sense of it. Or I might think about a happy memory, or an interesting plan for the future. Later when I learned to meditate, "going inside" meant taking a few moments for a refreshing meditation. See the lessons about meditation in chapter 4. This is a valuable tool for a Wizard.

Basic Premise: Your inner world is where the YOU that is the REAL YOU resides. The real you is the "watcher" who observes… the part of you that can speak of "my brain," or "my hand," knowing that all these parts of you are the body that YOU live in.

So who IS this YOU that lives in your body? One of the tasks of a Wizard is to answer that question. An ancient Greek Wizard, Socrates (469-399 BCE), said, "Know thyself!" This is still good advice.

You will find that your set of values is part of who you are. Values are qualities that you believe are important. You hold your values within your inner world. You will want to consider the values that are characteristic of a Wizard, and work on cultivating those in which you are not yet strong. The Grimoire lists some on page 102. They include: Honor, Loyalty, Integrity, Honesty, Respect, Fairness, Gratitude, Hospitality, Generosity, Reverence, Reciprocity, Responsibility, Resourcefulness, and Interdependence.

Being a Wizard requires extraordinary honesty, dedication, persistence, and a deep commitment to change. Real magick requires a fundamentally balanced personality willing to take on the challenges of accelerated growth, and accepting responsibility for everything you do. As Oberon says, *Being a Wizard is not about power, but about service.*

Classes in the Dept. of Lifeways will explore specific aspects of who you are, and help you determine your personal code of ethics. Meanwhile read pages 98 to 102 in the *Grimoire* for more on the ethics of magick.

Assignment:

Write in your Lifeways Journal about your personal values. What values have you already incorporated into your life, and what do they mean to you?

Resources

Support is always out there. No matter how hopeless a situation may seem, there is someone who cares, and there is help, even when it seems not so. The following is a list of teen resources that was published in 2001. Some of the numbers may have changed. If an 800 number doesn't work, call 800 information at 1-800-555-1212 and give the operator the name of the organization. If any non-800 numbers do not work, try 411.

Teen Help Hot Lines

Al-Anon/Alateen
    800-344-2666
Alcohol Treatment and Referral Hot Line
    800-ALCOHOL
Center for Substance Abuse Treatment
    800-662-HELP
Children of the Night Hot Line (for runaways)
    800-551-1300
Domestic Violence Hot Line
    303-839-1852
Eating Disorders Hot Line
    541-344-1144
Narcotics Anonymous
    818-773-9999
National Child Abuse Hotline
    800-422-4453
National Gay & Lesbian Youth Hot Line
    800-347-TEEN
National Runaway Hot Line
    800-621-4000
Nine Line (for teens in crisis with families or schools)
    800-999-9999
Planned Parenthood
    800-230-PLAN
Rape, Abuse, & Incest National Network
    800-656-HOPE
Safe Alternatives Hot Line
    800-DON'T-CUT
Teen AIDS Hot Line
    800-234-TEEN
Youth Crisis Hot Line
    800-448-4663

3. Secrets of the Inner Circle: simple web-weaving for young Wizards

© 2004 Elizabeth Barrette (grey)

In today's fragmented society, connections often get frayed; many people have a hard time making friends and don't know how to mesh themselves into a group they admire.

Here you will learn some basic techniques and principles that, carefully applied, can improve your personal growth as well as your crowd appeal. Have you ever wondered how to become more popular? The most straightforward way to do it is to make yourself indispensable to the people whose company you seek.

If you have ready access to the magical commu-

nity, that's nice; dive right in if you feel comfortable. If you don't have that kind of access yet, that's okay too. You can start in your regular school, a neighborhood club, or any other social group. The skills you learn are completely portable, and making friends just gets easier with time.

Networking

The first aspect of weaving a Wizard's web is called *networking*. It means forming connections between people and using them to get things done. Here are some principles of networking…

YOU are the community, whether you are a novice or an expert. Teach what you know. Study what you don't know. Get involved. There is no one ultimate authority in this life; there is nothing stopping you but yourself. Community is all about forming bonds, exchanging energy, and celebrating both our unity and our diversity. You get out of it what you put into it.

Decide what you want and then figure out a responsible plan for achieving it. Most skills can be learned if you're willing to put in the necessary time and effort. You probably know somebody who seems to do everything – what would happen if that person couldn't work? Lack of grassroots involvement causes leaders to burn out, and then all the lovely services disappear. So pitch in and do your part.

When networking, offer someone a favor before you ask for a favor. We all have knowledge, skills, contacts, experience, etc. to draw upon and exchange. If you want a friend to help you study for a test, proofread their homework. If you want people to attend your reading of magical poetry, announce on the flyers that you'll be serving tea and cakes there. If you want help with your current project, offer to help the other person with theirs. You get the idea.

Jump right in. You can get terrific results by showing up at a meeting or a festival and saying, "Hi! I'm Danny Oakleaf and this is my first trip here. Can you tell me what's going on?" or the like. People tend to be gregarious and usually try to make sure that novices have a good time. More advanced attendees can help you make the most out of the experience.

Having a hard time finding the right kind of group in your area? Join a national or regional organization instead. They're easy to locate. Many of them are listed in area phonebooks, or advertise in local newspapers. They can often put you in touch with other members who live nearby – and by meeting folks from all around, you increase your chances of stumbling across someone near you, too.

If you want ideas on where to start, many special interests combine well with Wizardry. For history buffs, consider the Society for Creative Anachronism or another historical reenactment group. In addition to science fiction conventions, readers have other genres to choose from – mystery fans sometimes host a live-action "murder" to solve, and so forth. If you like space, the Young Astronauts can teach you all about model rocketry. Anywhere you can find supplies or space for a hobby, you can usually find the hobbyists too. Check your local parks for nature clubs, your library for reading clubs, craft stores for quilting circles, and so forth.

If you can't find a group, consider just starting one of your own, like a mythology study group. You can get the word out by hanging flyers in your local library, bookstore, supermarket, etc. Sometimes a public facility like a library or school will offer you function space to hold meetings. At each meeting, invite people to sign up for a mailing list so you can notify them when the next meeting will be. Don't wait around for somebody else to set up a group – there are probably a bunch of people already waiting for *you* to do it!

Volunteerism

One foolproof way to get involved is through *volunteerism*. This means that you donate your time and energy to accomplish something special, like putting on a school play or holding a food drive for charity. Many organizations run on volunteer power.

Just as an example, I love reading, and that led me to the wonderful world of science fiction conventions. Years ago, I decided that I wanted to present panels and talk about favorite books, while getting to know cool folks in the science fiction community. So I'd show up a convention and volunteer for whatever needed doing that didn't require vast experience. I never got turned down. *Never.* And I met a lot of exciting people while checking badges and emptying trash cans and carrying coffee ... people who were very appreciative of my willingness to spend an hour or two helping, after spending $30 to get into the con.

Now I no longer have to pay my way in; I volunteer for two or three panels instead. Everybody wins. I've networked my way very successfully into what I wanted. It really does work. Whenever someone asks me how to break into a group, I tell them to show up and offer to help.

You want to get involved with an organization you admire? Volunteer at their events and within a year or two, you will have lots of friends and contacts, plus some highly valuable experience. Some events require attendees to help with chores, programming, etc. so be prepared for this – but they too will appreciate it if you do more than required. Want to learn more advanced skills like directing traffic (for parking lots), facilitation (guiding meetings), or cooking for the masses? Just ask! The organizers can probably pair you with a more experienced volunteer, and by the end of the event, why, you'll have that kind of experience too. Of course there are other methods ... but this is one of the best.

Basically it works like this. Find the organizer(s), introduce yourself, list any special skills you have or volunteer for general labor, and tack on a timeframe. If you're at a small event, like a book club meeting, look around for the host(ess) and say something like, "Hi! My name is Carol Meadowlark. I'm new at this and I'd really like to pitch in. Do you need somebody to stay after and help clean up?" If you're at a large event like a festival, the organizers will probably have an office, tent, desk, etc. serving as a central meeting point for logistics. Go there and say something like, "Hi! I want to help make this event a success. I'm new at this but I could spend a couple hours doing fetch and carry, or washing dishes, and by the way I'm good with computers if you need someone in the information booth."

When you see something that needs doing, and you know how to do it, don't wait to see if someone else will notice – just *do* it. This is the mark of the true Wizard. If you see that the bathroom is out of toilet paper and you don't know where it's stocked, ask. If you notice that there's an electrical short making the lights in the main hall blink on and off, and you know nothing about electronics, go find one of the organizers or a janitor or somebody who can handle it and tell them about the problem. If you see garbage lying around, don't step around it, pick it up. Taking care of the world and each other is what Wizardry is all about.

Likewise, when you have a great idea, run with it. Don't let it lie around and die of old age; get it moving, get it growing. If you need help to develop it, then ask people for what you need. Also don't look for someone to take over for you. It's *your* idea – it's your responsibility to make it manifest. That's why the universe gave it to you instead of somebody else.

Do not let limitations stop you. Wizards know how to turn disadvantages into advantages. If you're too small to reach supplies on a high shelf, you're small enough to fit behind the stand and plug in the television. If you ride a wheelchair, maybe you can sit behind a table and help people sign in when they arrive at the event, instead of gathering firewood. If you're susceptible to cold weather, hey, somebody has to look after the fire! Use your imagination. Remind the organizers, if necessary, that just because an attendee can't do *everything* does not mean he or she can't do *anything*.

Influence

This is a subtle kind of magic, but very powerful. *Influence* is the effect you have on other people and events. It's like when you drop a stone into a pond – the ripples go out and move leaves floating on the surface, even though you could not reach out and move those leaves with your fingers from where you stand.

Feedback is crucial. Praise what works. There's nothing like spending three months setting up for a harvest fair, and then on Sunday night after it's rained all weekend having somebody tell you that the indoor storytelling was the best they ever experienced. If you see something that doesn't work, don't just criticize; explain *why* it didn't work and offer any ideas you may have for improvements. Join those fireside conversations where people discuss how a lecture went or what their favorite part of the event was.

Become a thoughtful consumer and donor. Think of your money as a folding vote. Every time you spend a dollar, you vote for the ideals and practices of the company or organization to whom that dollar goes. Once or twice a month, you can skip a McDonald's meal and send that money to your favorite club or charity instead. Even a little at a time adds up. Of course, if you're blessed with abundance, take advantage of the "Law of Returns" and spread it around generously! Remember that it's extremely tacky, and ultimately counterproductive, to mooch off of a group's largesse without returning anything. You go to their meetings, you eat their muffins, you drink their grape juice ... you drop some funds into their donation jar.

Conclusions

It all comes down to a matter of responsibility and connections. Wizardry teaches that you are responsible for your own actions and their consequences, and that we are all connected. So don't expect someone else to do all work for you. Roll up your sleeves and help. My mother, who is a very wise and magical woman, puts it this way: "If you're not responsible, then you're irresponsible, and that's worse."

Once you get started, you'll be amazed at how fast you learn and how much fun it is. Even the ratty chores can bring moments of grace. One of my fondest memories involves crouching on the floor, elbow-to-elbow with several justifiably famous Wizards, as we used credit cards to scrape up spilled candle wax. Everybody at that ritual was an expert in their own right, many accustomed to leading rituals in their own tradition; and instead of leaving the awkward job to just one or two people, almost everyone in the room stopped to take a few swipes at the wax. It cleaned right up – and we were reminded that a little cooperation goes a long way.

That's the real secret of the inner circle.

4. Embracing our maleness: Pan & the Green Man

By Jesse Wolf Hardin (silver)

We envision Gaia as a goddess or "Mother" Earth, but this inspirited planet is a balance of male powers as much as female. And it's this dynamic mixture that fuels the rise of life itself! In this day and age when men and "male energies" are blamed for everything from sexism to war, it's all the more important to understand and utilize the power of our true natural maleness. While we males are born with a higher capacity for aggression, this is also the power that we need to tap when it comes time to defend ourselves and our loved ones from immanent harm. Men and boys' tendency to think more than feel can be a handicap, but our ability to think under pressure also means we should be able to accomplish amazing things in the middle of stress, confusion, flying arrows or raging storms.

For a young man, growing up can seem more difficult and challenging enough without being made to feel guilty for being born a male. In reality, the discovery and embrace of our sacred, natural maleness is essential to our magickal identities, the expression of who we really are, and the gathering and growing of true power. To be responsible wizards, co-creating a magical universe, we need to embody our authentic beings. This means to love, sense and utilize our physical bodies no matter what size or shape, to feel and to responsibly channel our sacred sexual energies, and to embrace not only our gentleness and sensitivity but also our inner drive and forceful wills. It's important to remember even as adults, that we don't need to become something other than what we really are in order to be worthy of life. We are born not "bad" but "good," and through practice we can only get better. For the good of our magick and the good of the world we need to become more ourselves, not less.

One of the models for our maleness is the trickster god Pan, half wild goat and half thoughtful man. He represents the balance I've been telling you about, playful as a child and yet terrifyingly wild to those adults who feared him. He is lustful like an adult creature of the forest, but would also just as soon dance with no audience in the Spring meadow, or play his flute with the birds. Pan literally means "all," everything! He can be found living within all things natural, just as the God/Goddess is said to be "all there is." Pan can express himself through any form, be it wind or willow, sweaty rock & roll singer or shining river rock! He's finds himself home in each and every lifeform, and all the various lifeforms can be found within him. Pan is most often portrayed with the torso of a man, the hoofed legs and twisty horns of a wild goat, and the capricious face of a human. Other times and places he wore elk antlers or rhino horns instead, dancing about the walls of torch-lit caverns with feather and paw, fin and claw. Pan is yet another name for omnipresent Spirit, but he's also the immortal jester, the coyote trickster of the Southwest Indian tribes, and the Norse Loki. He's an impish instigator as well as fierce guardian of the animals and forests and all things wild. At the sound of his pan-pipes all of creation lifts its head, senses alerted, feeling pumped up and fully alive!

Pan is the partner, servant and playmate of the feminine Goddess in all her forms. Together they continue to assert magick and spirit in the face of soul-deadening rationality, regimentation and rules, fears and habits. To promote passion and empathy in spite of the current trend to objectify and be pacified. To inspire connectedness where separation and dogma and borders are the rule. To inspire sensuality in the restrained, and to excite those who are distracted and bored. To make the wounded among us whole.

The second mythic model for our maleness is the archetypal Green Man. You've seen Green Man masks I'm sure, or been to a Beltane ritual where there was someone painted green with twigs and leaves in his hair. Just as Pan represents our animal spirit and creatures we share this Earth with, the Green Man is the

spirit of the plants we eat and the wise trees we sit beneath. He's been honored by different peoples at different times as the Straw Man and Wicker Man, the god of food crops and the symbol of seasonal change. He's embodied in Tolkien's giant tree-creatures, joining in the heroic battle against the agents of death and destruction. He can be found in the sexuality of pollen clouds pollinating wildflowers as well as our corn and wheat, and in the courageous spirits of outlaw dandelion weeds, insistently poking their heads up through the cracks they've made in sidewalk concrete.

As with Pan, the Green Man exists within us as much as around us. We can feel it in the urge to find a home and extend our roots like stabilizing anchors or hungry mouths in the living, breathing ground. In the hidden wisdom inside us, akin to the secret knowledge of the dark and fermenting soil. And in our desire to reach up towards the light.... to blossom in beauty, to be seen, to stretch, to know and to grow. He lives not just in the garden but the conscious gardener, not just in the giant ancient redwood trees but also in those brave logging protesters who climb them to keep them from being cut down.

The power of a wizard as with the power of any woman or man, comes from his most authentic, unrestrained expression. We're informed by the rustling voice of the Green Man, and inspired by the example of Pan. When I was studying with a Taos Indian elder, I learned this Tewa prayer: "Within and around the Earth, within and around the hills, within and around the mountain, your authority returns to you." It's the authority to be wholly ourselves, and everything we can be.

- Find guy friends you can honestly share your feelings and struggles around masculinity with. They don't need to be from your magickal circle, and in some ways it's better if they hold different beliefs. Confront or avoid friends who act like the stereotype of pushy, arrogant or insensitive males.
- Define for yourself the real meaning of "masculine."
- Make a list of those traits, qualities and tendencies in you that you define as largely male (such as assertiveness, strength, will, etc.). Then under each, make room for two columns: one for the ways in which these traits are expressed that you see hurting feelings or causing harm.... another for the ways they're expressed that contribute to our well being and spirits, as well as the well being and spirits of

both the people the natural world around us.

- If you keep an altar, make sure you have something on it to symbolize sacred natural masculinity, whether a carving or drawing of Pan, or a fanciful stick or dried mushroom in the shape of a man's phallus (penis).
- Try making a Green Man mask using wet and formed rawhide, woven reads or a curved sheet of tree bark, embellished with small branches and leaves, and perhaps a shaggy beard of usnea or moss.
- Speak about and write letters, songs or poems that tell the story of sacred maleness.
- Discourage the actions of males who give us guys a bad name, and also stand up for your gender when you hear men labeled as all being a certain negative way.
- Do you best to use every resource you have including your natural male energies, and to represent mankind in a way that is passionate and compassionate, powerful and purposeful, artful and honorable.

5. Boy, Man & Elder: our Rites of Passage

By Jesse Wolf Hardin (silver)

Those of us born male have inherent gifts and traits that we can put to good use, responsibilities we must meet and special opportunities to make the most of. Our journey from boyhood into manhood is marked by ritual moments where we commit to new ways of being and seeing, and pledge to carry a bigger load. We call those moments "rites of passage," some of which are preplanned ceremonies sponsored by our elders, with elaborate tests, special spells and memorized vows. Other rites of passage happen when we least expect it, when life surprises us with huge challenges we have to face and solve. For example, a young man undergoes a rite of passage if he chooses of his own will to get a job to help with the bills, or when a difficult situation arises and he decides for the first time in his own heart what the right thing to do is, instead of simply doing what others say he should do. Going on to college can be a rite when done to answer a need and dream instead of just to please one's parents or to increase the chances of making money.... and even dropping out of school can be a rite of passage, if it leads to a life change that's positive, and results in our full time following of some

Inside every aging Wizard is a playful and curious child, and within the heart of every child is a budding Wizard who just needs to study and practice to be all he can be. Art by Jesse Wolf Hardin.

magical service, mission or dream. Rites can bless our passage into sexual puberty, or our acceptance of our roles as elders once we get old. As with all sacred or magickal acts, in every case the most important ingredient is our conscious and purposeful intent. In this way each level becomes something we voluntarily take on, instead of an obligation that nature or society forces on us.

Most tribal societies have formalized specific ceremonies to mark the pivotal points in a male's growth. Examples include the special tests and dances required by the White Mountain Apaches, the Samoans tattooing their sons' skin with sharks teeth, and the telling of one's personal power story in the middle of a circle of clan men during the age of the Viking. Other cultures from Asia to the Americas isolate a child from the rest of the tribe, teach them the ways of "medicine" and manhood, and then reintroduce them to the tribe. Some tribes have taken that to extremes, teaching the boys in secret underground chambers or ceremonial kivas. Picture being kept in training in the relative dark of a circular room deep in the bosom of Gaia, remaining there day in and day out for months or even years, and then imagine what it would feel like to climb out at an appointed moment to see sunshine and the surface world for the very first time!

In a way, that's how every rite of passage should be for us, seeing the world as something fresh and amazing instead of taking it for granted and looking through the prism of old habits. That's why it's called a passage, an opening from one way of being to another. We are anointed with a sprinkling of sacred river water or covered naked with mud, with a warrior's parrot feathered headdress or the blade of a sword gently laid on our shoulders. We could stay behind, but instead we choose to go forward, to pledge to important assignments, to act in new and powerful ways. These are our portals of promises, and the proof and power of our manhood is in promises kept.

- If you will soon be entering puberty, or if you went through puberty in the last year or two, ask the people who mean most to you to help you create a meaningful rite of passage. If you are not a member of a tribal culture that still practices such things, then the responsibility is on you to initiate it. You can expect ideas and support from adults in your circle, or Pagan or nature spirituality community.
- Remember that a rite of passage should include at

least the five following elements:

- A period of time devoted to your fulfillment of difficult tasks or a special assignment.... and tests of knowledge, strength and awareness. This could include a solo quest where you stay alone, open hearted and focused somewhere out in nature, preferably in a place of power, and with adults designated to ensure your safety.
- A ceremony in which those you love and those who have an influence on you gather to ritually recognize and honor your passage. Ideally your parents or guardians will be there to grant you specific increased freedoms, as well as more say in your own life.... and your friends and magickal allies will attend to support you. I suggest special costumery, appropriate to such an occasion.
- Giving thanks to the source of your developing skills and roles, to the people who created you, to the caring people and harsh experiences that have taught you, and to the Earth and Spirit that provides all.
- A pledge voiced out loud to those attending, and a solemn oath made in silence to self and spirit.... in which you swear as to how you will carry and make use of your evolved abilities and new responsibilities.
- And a celebration befitting an essential and well done event.

Women can be as powerful Wizards as men, and sometimes more so! Kiva Rose honors her destiny by making the hard choices, making use of her inner powerrs, and serving an enchanted canyon where she teaches other young women. Art by Jesse Wolf Hardin.

- Keep in mind that your rites of passage can be difficult or threatening for your parents as well. With each passage you make, you come through the other side a little more their peer and equal, more responsible for your own fate.
- Repeat the elements listed above, at other crucial and pivotal points in your life. Whenever you make a dramatic shift and assume more responsibilities, a rite of passage can guarantee its lasting significance, plus win the support as well as participation of Spirit. When we have witnesses to our passages, they can hold us to our pledges. And those who honor us, can fairly expect us to live up to our positions and awards, capacities, callings and roles.
- Do what you can to encourage others of any age to go through their own rites of passage. The stronger they are in their identities and purpose, and the more recognized and affirmed they feel, the stronger our circles of relationships will be and more powerful our collective magick.

6. Rites of Passage for the woman Wizard: honoring the beauty of our Becoming

By Kiva Rose (Pink)

We don't hear much about women wizards, but that's partly because the myths and tales we live by have mostly been written by men. There have always been women and girls born with a sensitivity so great that they stood out even from the other naturally intuitive women of the tribe. The lives of these curendaras, brujas and priestesses included special transitory times, times of pivotal change in the person or their magickal direction. Rites of passage for we modern female wizards are no less important than for males.

For every life event there are certain events that mark the passage of time. We're born, we grow hair and teeth, we learn to laugh, we take our first steps into the wide world. Later, we bleed at our first moon time, that beautiful beginning of our uniquely female cycles. We conceive, give birth to our own children, we age as our children grow and find their own lives and ways of being. Our bleeding ceases, we pass into the crone time, the time of the wise woman tending herself and her fire. In these miraculous and constant ways we change, both inside and out. We're living beings and our nature is to move, to grow, to change at varying speeds and paces. In order to best recognize and celebrate these transitional times we need to create new forms of rites of passage, rituals that draw on an ancient knowledge of women's cycles but also adapt to our modern and diverse lives.

As women we are instinctual empaths and intuitive thinkers. We're daughters of the Goddess, our bodies perfect expressions and extensions of the natural world. We're able to intimately feel the world around us, both the beauty and the tragedy. This special gift of feeling gives us access to enormous amounts of both joy and pain. During times of transition our emotions will be even more sensitive and opened up than usual. We must take care that we do not allow our capability for incredible sensitivity to lead to emotional imbalance. It is for just this reason that many traditional rites of passage begin with time spent all alone. Each descent into the self is a period of rapid growth, vulnerability, empowerment and knowledge.

Every ritual transition is time to rethink who we are and who we want to become, time for coming to know ourselves more intimately than ever before. Each is an optimum moment to correct imbalances in our lives and add new responsibilities and challenges. This process is symbolized by the descent of the goddess in many cultural myths, most clearly illustrated in the descent of Inanna. She is the Sumerian Queen of Heaven who descended into the underworld, shedding clothing, jewelry, every vanity and every external pretense. In the same way we strip away our image of ourselves and other's images of who we are, as well as all dogma, preconception and illusion until all that's left is our true selves: flesh, spirit, heart and mind. And like Inanna, we each ascend from the underworld more completely who we really are, more vibrant, alive and beautiful. We emerge from each passage better prepared to experience, understand and utilize the challenges and joys of our lives. We will also be better prepared to know and help others when we first know and nurture ourselves.

Whether you are experiencing the first moon cycle of your womanhood or one day preparing for a ceremony of elderhood, you can make good use of your time of passage.

- Envision your ideal life. What new visions have you been having, and what long lasting dreams are there that you haven't found the time to pursue yet? Imagine all the ways in which you can grow closer to that ideal.
- Think about what changes you want to manifest in yourself and your life. What aspects of our life are no longer benefiting you, or have you grown beyond? Which ways of being, which habits and situations should we try to magickly and practically alter or do away with altogether?
- Now work to make those changes. If it's impossible to change your habits with the friends you have, make new ones that can value and support your growth and empowerment. When there are situations or obligations you can't avoid such as having to go to school, you can still sculpt your reality by changing majors or schools, by home schooling or seeking out after-school mentors to teach you what you really need to know to become the wizard that you hope to be.
- Next, consider what qualities, habits or activities you want to manifest in yourself and your life. These could be ways of being, learning, relating, expressing and acting. Or it could mean dreams of going to herb school, joining or starting a clan or coven, starting our own rock band or personal business, beginning a community garden or finding a way to move closer to nature.
- Remember that no dream is realized overnight, and all the changes we make in ourselves and our world happen in an endless series of steps. Take pride in every step you make, in the direction of what you believe in!
- Ritualize and celebrate your transitions not only alone with Sprit, but also with your closest community in special rituals that acknowledge and honor your changing roles and relationships.
- During these celebrations, try wearing clothes bought or made specifically for the occasion, reflective of the new period of life being. If appropriate you might have a sister, mother or close female friend paint your body, hands or face with henna or a similar natural body pain in a way that accentuates your beauty and symbolizes your passage Spirals are a pancultural design that intimates the endlessness of our cycles and lives. Flowers and leaves show our connection to the Earth and the beauty of life. Hearts show the immensity of our love for ourselves, each other and the divine essence of life.
- These are times to spend with our families, closest friends and spiritual partners. Quiet celebration is in order, a time to celebrate the furtherance of ourselves and a time to share your dreams and visions as well as some or all of the commitment made to self and Spirit during your ritual isolation.
- Every flower births, blossoms, fruits and fades… and every life is insistent and willful in its longing for passion and meaning. We become our most beautiful and powerful selves through the cycles of our body and our innate connection to the Earth we were born from and will one day return to. Whenever possible, celebrate outside and eat wild foods to provide a tangible connection to our mother Gaia.
- Remember to celebrate and make sacred every moment of your beautiful lives, not just your rites of passage. You are magickal beings with infinite potential, and every step along your life path is sacred and blessed. Let us honor the beauty of your becoming in every possible way.

7. Activism for the practicing Wizard

By Jesse Wolf Hardin (silver)

Activism means literally "to act," and there's no more important requirement of the wizard than our acting decisively to help co-create our world and our reality. Activism can take the form of resisting a wrong, such as working to halt the clearcutting of the rainforests in British Columbia and the Amazon, some corporation's racist policies or a government's taking away of our individual liberties and rights….or proactively working to create alternative community and healthier ways of living. Whatever we attribute our consciousness, instincts, visions and magickal powers to– such as the Goddess, God or the Great Spirit– we can show our gratitude by acting to right the wrongs that need righting, heal what needs healing, create and spread gifts and beauty. And we can best honor the challenges we've learned from and the mentors who have taught us, by making the most of our wisdom, awareness, abilities and skills.

If we aren't more active we may find we have no sacred groves left to circle in, or that the U.S. Congress has passed laws banning our practices and religions. We're all affected by what goes on in society and local and national politics, and whatever ecological damage is done to planet Gaia impoverishes and endangers us as well. It often seems as if there isn't enough activism among Pagan groups, so it may be up to the willing wizards among us to reverse that trend and start bringing about much needed change.

The most radical environmental activists have often been people who describe themselves as Pagans. When a young environmental activist Julia Butterfly sat in a small platform a hundred feet up in a redwood threatened by logging, the reasons she gave for her months of dedication and risk included her spiritual bond to the tree.

While some Pagans have considered it their duty and their form of activism to serve in the armed forces, others have helped organize against various conflicts overseas. Author and respected witch Starhawk has been active for years protesting not only environmental destruction but also nuclear proliferation, war in the Mideast and the policies of the World Bank. She set an example for us of commitment and versatility, approaching each mythic battle differently. In the campaigns she and her affinity group combine assertive nonviolent public protest with public education, focused drum circles in the offices of their opponents, special incantations, meditations and spells.

- Identify and list any threats to those things you treasure and value most, whether those things be a precious freedom or belief, a family or clan, a certain tree you love or the entire natural world.
- Read books such as Starhawk's *Truth Or Dare* and my own *Gaia Eros*…books that describe the issues and problems in a meaningful way, and others that inspire us to live deeper and act more today!
- Study the issues and the problems, find out who the powerful interests are, and then ponder and meditate on the best ways of approaching them.
- List all the possible ways you might be able to effect and alter a bad or ominous situation. Split the list into two sections, one for those ways you can help to resist injustice or destruction and defend what's under attack. In the second section, list all the positive ways you might be able to improve, help or heal each situation.
  - Legal means of resistance include organizing, petitioning, sending off press releases, giving interviews to the press, participating in protests and demonstrations, and developing public education tools such as guerilla theatre, public concerts and music with lyrics raising awareness about the problem.
  - Civil Disobedience involves protests and actions that break existing laws, but can be effective when nothing else works. "C.D." actions in the past have included tagging with activist graffiti, blockading logging roads, trespassing on Nevada's nuclear testing grounds…and of course the dumping of English tea into the Boston Harbor in the warm up to America's War Of Independence.
  - Research to see if there are any local or regional activist groups or campaigns already in existence that are working on issues you feel strongly about, then decide if you can work with them and the methods they use.
- If you can't find an appropriate group to work with, start your own. The core of any group no matter how large, is the "affinity group" made up of a handful of people who know and trust each other, and who share strong feelings about what needs to be done to better the world.
- Don't wait for assistance and alliance to act. Set an example of assertive conscious action, and other like-hearted folks will join you. It's also true that some of the most powerful activism of all is by nature best done in solitude.
- The wizard assumes full responsibility for the results and consequences of what he or she does.
- The wizard makes sure that every action one undertakes is done out of a sense of vision as well as compassion.
- Magickal spells alone can't be expected to accom-

plish everything you need to…but you can make magick an empowering element of every applied act you do.

8. The Raven Haven Rules
By Oberon

Over several decades of living communally with other people, Morning Glory and I have worked out a basic set of Cardinal Rules that are absolutely essential to living together. We have had these posted on the refrigerator in a number of homes we've lived in, and many people have asked for copies, which have become spread far and wide. Here's a copy for you:

The Raven Haven Rules

1. If you make a mess, clean it up.
2. If you sleep in it, make it up.
3. If you drop it, pick it up.
4. If you spill it, mop it up.
5. If you eat off it, wash it.
6. If you open it, close it.
7. If you get it out, put it away.
8. If you move it, put it back.
9. If you borrow it, return it.
10. If you use it up, replace it.
11. If you break it, fix it.
12. If you can't fix it,
    find someone who can.
13. If it ain't broke, don't fix it!
14. If you don't like it,
    you can't have any.

---

9. Throwing a Wizard-themed party
By Moonwriter (indigo)

Why throw a wizard-themed party?
Your birthday
To celebrate the release of a magickal movie or book
To celebrate completion of magickal studies or schooling (as in the Grey School of Wizardry)
To have a bardic circle, or magickal ritual
Just for fun!

Where to Hold Your Party
If the weather is nice, you may wish to hold it outdoors. Wizards love nature!

Otherwise, hold it indoors. Make sure you have room for all of your guests, a place to set up food, play games, etc.

Invitations
You can buy invitations, but it's also very easy to

make them. You can do this on a computer, or you can fold construction paper and make them by hand. Some ideas:

Roll the invitations like a scroll, tied with a piece of ribbon

Make an invitation in the shape of a castle, or a wizard hat.

Decorations
Use construction paper to make "candles"; suspend them from the ceiling with thin thread or finishing line, for a "Hogwart's ceiling" effect. Or, suspend stars, moons, and planets for a nighttime effect.

Cover the table with purple and silver paper tablecloths, scattered with silver star confetti. Use silver Mylar balloons and strings of clear or colored lights for a nice effect.

Candles add atmosphere, but must be handled safely. One way to display candles safely is to set them inside of glass mason jars. Even if the candle tips over, it won't catch anything on fire, and the jar adds a nice lantern effect.

For the table, use clear plastic plates and cups. Decorate with colored or metallic permanent markers; use astrological signs, runic script, or other magickal symbols.

Encourage your guests to come in costume: capes, wizard hats, etc.

Food
Serve spooky hors d'oeurves. Finger-sized pieces of SPAM with an almond stuck in one end become witch's fingers, while roasted teriyaki chicken wings become bat wings. Cherry tomatoes, hollowed out and filled with cream cheese, are great eyeballs. Sandwiches—filled with tuna, egg salad, etc.—can be cut with a sharp knife into the shape of wizard hats, coffins, etc.

For candy, offer Pop rocks, gummy worms (and other shapes), light-up suckers, and crystalline rock candy. A visit to your local candy store will yield all sorts of interesting and magickal treats!

Use star- and moon-shaped cookie cutters to prepare cosmological sugar cookies. Sprinkle with blue sugar.

Cupcakes are always a hit at parties. Sprinkle with star confetti for a wizardly effect. Or allow your guests to make "wizard cupcakes." Provide already-frosted cupcakes, cone-shaped ice cream cones, cans of frosting, tubes of decorator frosting. and various types of sprinkles. The cones are placed—upside down—on the frosted cupcakes, forming a wizard's cap. The cones are covered with frosting and decorated as desired.

Cones can also be used to make Ice Cream Wizards ahead of time. Use a round scoop of ice cream for the wizard's head; add an ice cream cone for his hat. Return the wizards to the freezer for a couple of hours so that the head and hat harden up. Then, take it back out and use canned and/or tubes of frosting to decorate the wizard's head and hat as desired. Return to freezer until the party.

Instead of cupcakes, you might choose a sheet cake; use frosting and other decors to create a magickal castle, a wizard's hat, or some other magickal motif.

For drinks, serve "magick waters:" Serve cups full of clear, fruit-flavored water. Pour the water into glasses from a pitcher; as you do, wave your magick wand over the pitcher, and say, *Intensum Flavorum!* Then watch your guest's faces as they take a big drink of what they expect to be plain water!

Or, offer drinkable potions! Fill a variety of large jars (Mason jars work well) with a variety of multicolored sports drinks. Furnish clear plastic glasses and allow your guests to mix and match their own "potions." Provide mint leaves for added fun.

Serve punch from a cauldron or hollowed out pumpkin. To chill the punch, fill a rubber glove with water, close with a rubber band, and freeze. At party time, peel the glove off and float the icy hand in the punch!

Canned pumpkin, vanilla ice cream, sugar, and milk make a wonderful pumpkin milkshake. Top with whipped cream. Yum!

Activities

For a gathering activity, **play "Who Am I?"** Before the party, write the name of a magickal creature (e.g., unicorn, hippogriff, gryphon, centaur, dragon, etc.) on enough 5x7 inch index cards to allow 2 for each guest. When each guest arrives, tape a card to their back, but don't let them see it! they must find out who they are by asking the other guests questions. For instance: Do I fly? Do I breathe fire?

Make magick wands: Provide straight dowels (about 16-18" long), brass or copper wire, glitter, glue, Styrofoam balls, metallic ribbon, permanent markers, stickers, acrylic paint, small gems or crystals, a hot glue gun, and anything else that you think might be a fun addition to a wand. Offer a prize for the best one.

Make wizard staffs: Provide broomstick dowels and the same supplies as for wands, above.

Hold a tri-wizard tournament: Come up with three indoor or outdoor tasks to be completed in a certain period of time.

Do face-painting: lightening bolts, stars, and moons are popular wizardly choices.

Play "Pin the Hat on the Wizard."

Hold a trivia game about your favorite Harry Potter book. Have an adult ask questions directly from the book.

Make magickal journals: Provide special papers, hole punches, and colored yarn. Each guest places several pages together, punches holes in the sides, and ties/ binds them with yarn. Furnish feathers and ink and allow your fellow wizards to practice writing in their new journal with their quills. (Note: before the party, use a very sharp knife to slice off the tip end of the quill at an angle; this makes a slanted tip, which becomes the tip of the pen.) Even better, provide examples of Runic or Theban scripts, and have your guests practice using them.

Have potions class! Provide a variety of empty bottles and lids (strange-shaped and colored jars are ideal), spoons, and vials of food coloring. Also provide labeled jar full of potion materials: frog lime (mint jelly), bug eyes (poppy seeds), powdered Unicorn (baking soda), blind cat eyes (cocktail onions), cave worms (cooked spaghetti), mandrake root (pieces of ginger root), pickled beetles (capers), pond water (water to which clean sand or potting soil have been added), dragon tears (vinegar with red food coloring added), etc. use your imagination! And make sure to have a safe working place, where nothing will be damaged if anything spills. Have everyone try different combinations—make sure to mix the powdered Unicorn and dragon tears for an astounding reaction!

Have a Sorcerer's Stone hunt. Wrap goodies in balls of aluminum foil and hide around the house or yard.

Hire a magician to put on a conjuring show!

Read tea leaves *(tasseomancy):* For each guest, place 1 tsp of dried mint leaves into a teacup. Cover with freshly-boiled water and allow to steep for five minutes. Either have your guests drink the tea, or pour the water off carefully, leaving the leaves and a bit of liquid. Each person then covers their cup with their hand and swirls the cup several times. Then, guests should exchange teacups and "read' the leaves. The clumps form the symbols, including shapes, letters or numbers. See 7: 5: "Tasseomancy" for interpretations.

Goodie Bags

Send your guests home with a bag of magickal items: gemstones, a miniature set of tarot cards, vials of sparkly pixy dust, cookie cutters shaped like moons and stars, light sticks, plastic spiders, gummy candies, etc.

Note to Older Youth and Adults

Modify the above suggestions as needed (adults should never be afraid to have fun!), and use them in conjunction with a ritual or bardic circle. In the latter, the guests sit around a fire (or group of candles) and take turns telling stories, singing songs, sharing poems, etc., until either time runs out or everyone is out of stories. The host welcomes the guests at the start of the circle and gives a solemn thank-you at its end. If a fire is used (either in a fireplace or an outdoor fire circle), the fire lighting may also be an important part of the circle. See 8:8: "Hosting a Bardic" for more on this.

Department XI: Beast Mastery (brown)

Mastering the Menagerie

How do you speak to the beasts of the land?
How do you call them all into your hand?

Sing to them softly, in your heart of hearts;
Name them and know them, and that's where it starts.

Bear is the shaman, whose power is dreams;
Salmon the drinker of wisdom in streams.

Cat walks alone, like a shadow with fur;
Skunk has a scent that's more bitter than myrrh.

Wolf is the singer whose tracks mark the sky;
Goose is the herald of seasons gone by.

Deer in the autumn is graced with a crown;
Dog circles three times before he lays down.

Eagle is vision that strikes from above;
Ram is a master of push and of shove.

Elephant towers as tall as the trees;
Mouse eats whatever his wee paws can seize.

Rabbit is fast, but he still knows his place;
Cheetah is fastest of all in a race.

Snake sheds her skin when she needs to renew;
Whale dives and spouts in the ocean so blue.

Peacock is proudest,
*   just look at that tail;*
Kangaroo leaps over
*   river and rail.*

Hummingbird hovers with
*   artistic haste;*
Camel drinks deep, and then crosses the waste.

Horse is the drumming of hooves on the earth;
Caribou stands a few minutes past birth.

Llama climbs calmly on mountainsides sheer;
Penguin survives on the ice so austere.

Bee is the sweetest, but watch for her sting;
Owl flies in silence, she's death on the wing.

Panda eats bamboo and sleeps in the sun;
Hyena laughs – and this list is now done.

The law of the wild is ancient and strange,
And all that is living must pass through its range.

So listen, young Wizard, if you would learn
How you can summon the beasts in your turn.

It's all in the asking, not the command;
All in the knowing, if you understand.

—Elizabeth Barrette

1. Introduction

ELCOME TO THE WORLD OF Beast Mastery! This department concerns everything to do with animals of all kinds—especially animal communication. Beast Masters include "horse whisperers," animal trainers, pet psychics, and all people who seem to have an uncanny ability to communicate and work with animals. Beast Mastery includes knowledge of zoology and the lore of Totems. Beast Masters seek to know the names of all animals, as well as how they evolved, what they eat, their behaviors, lifestyles, mating rituals, and languages. It also includes the Lore of Magickal animals, such as Unicorns and Dragons.

It is the mission of this Department to provide skills in communicating with the animals and other nature spirits while learning to understand the environment that we share, with lessons in animal communication, the lore of animals, magickal animals, Totems, familiars, and more.

The color of magick in this department is Brown, the most common color of fur and feathers, and represents all things soft and fuzzy. Brown Wizards often work in pet stores, animal hospitals, shelters or zoos, or become park rangers or wildlife rescuers. And always they are surrounded by critters—whether pets, farm animals, wild creatures, or other animal companions.

Fur and feather and scale and skin—
Different without, but the same within!
Many of body but one of soul;
Through all creatures are the gods made whole!
—Sable

2. Animal Guides & Totems
By Jesse Wolf Hardin (silver)

Nature is our teacher and example, but just as some people have a more powerful impact on our lives than others, so do some animals better represent our energies and powers. These are what we call our "totems" or "animal spirit guides." They are our allies, not necessarily because they come when we need help, but because they are our most honest mirrors. Their weaknesses are ours, so we can learn from them what needs strengthening, and where to compensate or be extra careful. And their strengths are our potentials. If the hawk is our totem, it is because we have a synergy with them and that includes an ability to see far...but also a problem with up-close intimacy. My wolf totem means I'm loyal to my clan and pack, but also that, like the wolf, I will act true to my nature even if it results in misunderstanding or loneliness, making less money or even making enemies.

Because of this, we don't really get to "pick" our totem, and our major animal guides are seldom our favorite animals. It may in fact be that we are predominantly of elk energy when we might have rather had the bear. Or maybe we wish we didn't have so much snake energy, when snakes get such a bad rap in this society. If we are bear people, we spend a lot of time looking inside ourselves instead of out, just as the bear goes into a cave to hibernate. We may be short-tempered and need to work on developing patience, and be a natural born healer just as the bear once lead human kind to the best places for finding medicinal mushrooms and healing herbs.

You don't discover what totem you have by drawing from an animal card deck, but by learning your innermost qualities, weaknesses and strengths, preferences and needs. When you know your true nature, you then look out at the natural world for those animals, both living and spirits, that resonate with your inner animal powers. They are your primary mirrors and guides, teachers and allies, and they will come to you in real life as well as in your dreams. And they will keep coming whether summoned in circle or not. They are the animal spirits that live in you and through you.

- Make a list of your native traits, the ways you feel when you feel most yourself. What are your fears, hopes, loves? What is most difficult for you, and what things seem to come easiest and most naturally? What environments do you feel most powerful in, and which you could live in (oceanside, mountain top, desert, forest or grasslands)? How do you respond to strangers, affection, misunderstanding, and threats?
- Make two lists of animals. One should be a list of the animals that come into your thoughts and dreams most often, or that keep showing up in real life when

The hawk represents the ability to see far. When we find the medicine of the hawk within us, we feel the ways that we and the wild world are part of the same woven body. Art by Jesse Wolf Hardin

you least expect them. Another should list those animals that have native traits in common with you. Now try to empathize, which means to try and feel what each of the animal feels, to see the world as each of them does. Your allies and guides should be obvious upon close comparison.

- Remember that the little feathered wren is a warrior and anything but insignificant, and that size and glamour don't necessarily mean more power.
- Find ways to strengthen those areas needing work in your totems and thus in you too. Identify and capitalize on your totem's strengths, which are the same strengths that you need to take credit for and put to magickal use yourself.
- Practice recognizing the traits, tendencies and lessons of every animal, and every life form—even those that are most different from your own. Feel all of life not just as your teacher but as a part of your larger Gaian self. Heed what they show us as to how to live, and heed what they have to say.
- Honor your totems with sculptures and offerings on your altar. Construct a mask representing your dominant totem, and wear it to invoke and express its power and energy.
- Remain aware of the animal energies and influences, qualities and powers that speak through you when relating to others. Find and relate to the animal spirits and traits that speak through them. Trust that they are the animal tendencies you find within them, and not necessarily what they want you to see or believe.
- Find a way to connect directly to your totem animals, even if it means visiting them in zoos or taking vacations in their habitat where you can feel their presence, spot their tracks, or even get a chance to encounter one face-to-face in the wild. However, you shouldn't go off in search of certain animals—it isn't wise to be out looking to spend some time alone with a wolf or a bear' nor should you confuse "communing" with an animal totem with encountering one that might be dangerous in the wild.
- When you are learning and gaining help from your totems, you have a responsibility to give back to them. Even if you only engage your guides in the spirit and dream worlds, you owe them some service in real life. If the wolf is your ally like it is mine, we have to find ways to contribute to their continued survival in the

few pockets of wilderness left in this country. Whether we donate money, protest or write letters, we have to do something—it would be dishonorable to summon the wolf spirit to aid us, if we allow the last wild wolves to be put in cages or driven into extinction.

3. Wee Spirits: Totems, history, and evolutionary complexity

By Elizabeth Barrette (grey)

Totem magic is a popular topic, both in its practical and theoretical aspects. People wonder how and why it works. One of my favorite excursions began with a discussion on the "Sisters of Avalon" email list. We had been talking about different totems and people started to work their way down the evolutionary ladder: Do all totems have to be "photogenic megafauna" like Eagle and Bear? Can Mouse be a totem? Can insects be totems? What about something even smaller, like diatoms? We finally summed up the debate like this: Is there a minimum level of complexity and/or awareness required in order for a species to serve as a totem? If so, what is that level and why?

I originally argued that there had to be a lower limit, for a variety of reasons. First, a totem needs enough awareness to exist on the spirit plane as an active entity. Second, a totem must have distinctive traits and/or powers which affect chosen humans; for instance, Hawk brings the gift of keen vision both physical and metaphysical. Third, a totem should be recognized as such by some magickal or spiritual tradition that commonly works with totems. This made a pretty nice presentation and made sense to me.

But then I happened to recount the debate to my partner, who came up with an absolutely brilliant counter-argument, which went something like this: Suppose that Adolf Hitler's totem was Virus. Consider the insidious nature of both, the amount of destruction wreaked, the percentage of deaths, and the tendency to take over another entity and stuff it full of one's own programming. Then consider the fact that long after Hitler's death, his vicious ideas continue to reproduce in small isolated populations with occasional larger-scale outbreaks. Finally consider that a good look at Holocaust history, combined with any kind of rational thought, can serve as a very effective "vaccination" against infection by Nazi memes. Virus as Hitler's totem sounds incredibly apt to me, so much so that I abandoned my earlier stance.

Now, Virus is the bottom rung on the ladder of life; in fact, some scientists still insist that a virus is not even alive, because it can't reproduce on its own but must find a host cell to use as a "factory" for churning

out virus copies. So there can't be anything lower on the ladder than Virus, and thus if Virus can serve as a totem, it stands to reason that evolutionary sophistication alone is not a qualifying/disqualifying factor. One might argue that prions are lower even than viruses, yet again, many scientists do not consider prions a life form at all, but rather a kind of organic poison.

This raises some other fascinating ideas. For instance, totems are typically taken from animals native to and known in a particular region. The pool of totems available has expanded considerably as more of us have a chance to know animals not native to where we happen to live. Now, suppose that part of that knowledge has to do with *awareness,* such that as we developed evermorepowerful microscopes, we also expanded the pool in a different direction. Diatom could not serve as a totem earlier because the physical manifestation isn't visible to the naked eye, so nobody knew Diatom was there. Now that we know, does that make a difference? Some people feel a strong attraction to diatoms, and I've always been rather fascinated by the little gems myself. So Diatom as a totem in contemporary times also sounds reasonable to me.

Historically, it has been possible to recognize the "personality" of various diseases (does anyone question that *Yersinia pestis* / Black Death has a conspicuously vicious and predatory mien?) but nobody knew exactly what caused the disease until recent decades. Might a vile kind of totem spirit, such as Virus, qualify as the "evil spirit" or "black vapour" sometimes described in ancient medical texts? Not all totems are nice, after all; some tribes used to spot troublemakers by noting who Weasel had taken a fancy to, for instance. I think this connection offers a new explanation for such references, though not necessarily the only explanation.

Also, does a totem spirit necessarily fade away when the last physical manifestation dies? Can it survive by using a non-living anchor? I know Mammoth is still around, from very direct and subtly dramatic

personal experience. At Ancient Lifeways Camp there is an old quarry cave decorated in traditional fashion, with red ochre paintings of a Mammoth and a Bison, which I and other campers helped work on.

One night we went up to the cave to sit and listen to stories, and our storyteller happened to recount one about Mammoth. Out of the corner of my eye I saw a sudden blue-white spark hovering in the air, and I thought it was a strange shade for a firefly; my friend sitting next to me also saw this and we watched for the "firefly" to light up again, which never happened. The visual effect was exactly as if the stone wall had suddenly turned transparent and let a single star shine through. (There was no electricity in the cave and no mundane explanation. We checked diligently.) Later when we turned the lanterns back up, I noticed that the spark had appeared precisely where Mammoth's eye was on the cave wall. And then I KNEW: Mammoth had *looked* at us. What a thrill!

Since almost all cave paintings are Spirit paintings imbued with great magical power, it stands to reason that they might make an acceptable vessel/anchor for a totem spirit whose animal form had all died out. Alternatively, there could still be some living mammoths roaming around somewhere, or perhaps fossils or other remains could suffice. This is no excuse to let anything go extinct, but it does raise some intriguing questions about the nature of totem spirits and their magic. Seeing how totems have evolved and changed over the years also makes for interesting study, and leaves me wondering what will turn up next.

4. Observation and collection

By Moonwriter (indigo)

To *observe* is to become aware of something through careful and directed attention. *Observation* means taking that careful attention and using it to notice or record various occurrences or phenomena. If you're *observant,* you're alert and quick to perceive or notice things.

Observation doesn't come naturally to many of us. In our busy everyday lives, we tend to focus on whatever we're concerned with at the moment, and we often don't really notice everything that's going on around us. Fortunately, the skills of observation can be practiced and learned. Good observation skills are important for an aspiring Wizard; they will help you in your magickal studies.

As you study Beast Mastery, you'll learn that good observation is all about two things: *patience* and *repetition.*

If you want to really see what goes on in a natural setting, you must be willing to spend a great deal of time and patience to do so. The best results are often gathered by finding a natural area and sitting motionless and silent, while watching to see and hear what happens around you. As the wildlife become accustomed to your presence, more and more action will appear.

As for repetition, in order to understand animal behavior , you must watch them over and over again. This allows you to observe changes and also will allow you to see their responses to the turning of the great seasonal wheel.

As you practice observation, you'll find yourself looking at the natural world with renewed curiosity and understanding. You'll come to appreciate the magickal qualities of nature, and may find ideas to incorporate into ritual and observances.

Bird Watching or "Birding"

Bird watching—also called "Birding"—is a source of pleasure for many and an easy hobby to indulge. After all, there are millions of birds in the world! Whether you live in the city or the country, cast your eyes skyward and it'll probably only be a matter of seconds before you see or hear a bird.

As with all forms of observation, birding requires patience and repetition. Birds are shy by nature, so your best bird watching will be done at a distance and sitting as quietly as possible. Wear clothing that blends into the surroundings, and know that birds are particularly wary of bright colors, such as red and yellow.

If you become interested in bird watching, you will probably want to invest in a Field Guide of your local birds. These can be obtained very inexpensively in used form from places like Amazon.com and Powells.com. There's also a lot of good field guide information available online.

Feeding Birds

An excellent way to bring birds into your yard for a close-up view is to provide

them with food and water.

The simplest way to feed birds is to scatter bird-seed along a fence, rock wall, or other surface. A disadvantage to this is that it can be messy, especially is the fence or wall is part of a public area. It can also attract mice and rats.

Another simple method of feeding is to place the seed in a tin pie plate, weighted down with a large rock.

Water can also be added to a tin plate, to make a makeshift birdbath. It should be no deeper than 1½ inches, as birds will both drink from and bathe in it. The water should be changed every 1-2 days and the pan washed out as needed. Ideally the birdbath should be at least 2 feet above the ground, to avoid danger from prowling cats.

Speaking of cats…cats today are a terrible threat to songbirds everywhere, killing huge numbers of them. The best way to prevent this is to keep cats indoors. If this isn't possible, they should be "belled" and should be kept inside during peak bird-feeding times of the day (mid-morning and later afternoon).

The type of food that you make available will have a lot to do with the type of birds that visit. Black oil sunflower seed is the best bet, as it is eaten by a wide variety of birds including finches, woodpeckers, sparrows, and chickadees. Millet is preferred by sparrows, while suet is the chosen treat of bushtits, woodpeckers, and flickers.

Make sure to keep the feeders and dishes clean. When birds have to eat and drink from unclean containers, they often become ill.

If you decide to feed birds, please keep in mind that they will come to depend on your food source, meaning that you cannot suddenly stop putting out seed. This is especially true in the cold months, when natural foods are less available. Birds are in particular need of water during the winter; even if you don't feed them, they will appreciate a regular, fresh source of unfrozen water.

Activities for You

There are several ways in which you may "collect" birds:

1. Many birders keep a bird "life list," that is, a detailed list of which birds they've seen, when, where, etc. Many add sketches of the birds or their setting. Some dedicated bird watchers are so intense about this that they will travel hundreds—or even thousands—of miles to have the chance to spot a unique bird.
2. You might develop a collection of bird photographs.
3. You can use recording equipment to capture bird-song. An especially wonderful time to do this is about 1-2 hours before dawn, when birds sing their "dawn chorus." This is especially loud and beautiful in the spring and early summer.
4. You may choose to collect bird "evidence": feathers, eggs, nests, etc. If you do, you are ethically

bound to be sure that the items have been discarded and are not being used by living birds.

Preparing and Mounting Feathers

Many birds are infested with tiny lice. To kill the lice, put the feathers in a plastic bag and put the bags into the deep freeze for 3-4 days. This will kill the lice and their eggs. *(NOTE: if using someone else's freezer, be sure to ask first!)*

If the feather has been "messed up," you may be able to straighten it carefully with an old toothbrush. Use the toothbrush dry, or dip it in a little bit of water.

Let the feather dry if you dampened it.

Arrange the feather on a piece of heavy paper or cardstock ("biology paper" works well for this). Use narrow strips of tape to fasten the feather to the paper.

Label in the lower right corner with the following:

Date feather was gathered
Where it was found
Identification of the bird

If you're good at drawing, add a sketch of the bird to supplement your mounted feather.

Blowing out egg shells

Practice this skill on regular chicken eggs; that way if you ever find a special egg that you want to blow out, you'll know how to do it. You'll need:

A raw egg
A large darning needle

Wash the egg gently with soap and water; dry carefully.

Work over a large bowl Using the needle, poke a hole in the "pointy end" of the egg. Do this carefully so that the eggshell doesn't crack.

Use the needle to poke a similar hole in the egg's "round end." But this time, use the needle to make a larger hole, about the size of a spaghetti strand.

Now, put your lips over the small hole on the egg's "pointy end," and blow gently. The liquid egg should start to slowly drip from the larger hole on the "round end." If it doesn't, make the "round end" hole slightly larger and keep trying.

After you have blown out all of the egg's contents, run clear water gently through the shell until it is entirely cleaned out. Blow the excess water from the egg (in the same way that you blew out the contents). Leave the egg in a sunny window to dry, "round end" up.

Your egg is now ready for display!

Preparing Bones, Teeth, and Shells

If you're lucky enough to find the bones or teeth from dead or decomposed animals, you'll find it easy to add them to your natural history collection.

Step 1: *Cleaning.* Start by donning a pair of latex or rubber gloves. Soak the bones or teeth in hot water, then rinse wash with fresh hot water and dishwashing detergent, scrubbing with an old toothbrush or fingernail brush.

Step 2: *Boiling.* Place the items in a saucepan and cover with 2-3" of water. Simmer on the stovetop for 10 minutes or longer. This will loosen any excess material and will also kill any germs that are present. After boiling, drain and allow to cool. Pour off water and remove bones and teeth very carefully! Small front teeth tend to fall out at this stage, so make sure not to lose them.

Step 3: *Bleaching and disinfecting.* Soak the items in a solution of 1 part bleach and 10 parts water* for 30 minutes. Remove with tongs. Rinse and allow to air-dry.

*Making a bleach solution:

Mix the solution in a bottle or jar with a tight cap.

Set the bottle in the kitchen sink before adding solutions.

Add 10 parts water and 1 part bleach, working slowly so as to avoid splashing on your clothes or skin.

Label the container *"10:1 Bleach Solution"* so everyone will know what it is.

(NOTE: This is POISON. Make sure to put it where small children cannot reach it, and keep it tightly capped so that it cannot spill.)

To use, place the item that needs disinfecting in a small jar or bowl, and pour on enough of your bleach solution to submerge the object.

Save the rest for future use. Store in a dark place, rightly capped.

NOTE: Freshly-gathered seashells may be washed and disinfected in the same way. When collecting shells, please be sure that there is no creature still living in them! If there is, leave them be!

For skulls, carefully glue all teeth into place in jaws with white glue, and then glue lower jaws (mandibles) together at chin. Bind the join with a rubber band until the glue dries. Then mix a thin wash of white glue and water, and brush it over the entire skull, making sure the glue gets into all suture joins.

Allow your freshly-prepared items to dry, then display them in your natural history museum, with little identifying cards. A piece of felt or wool (in your magickal colors, of course!) makes a nice display surface.

You'll also want to record the objects in your nature journal. Include where and when you found them, and what sort of animal they're from.

5. The magick of tracking
By Jesse Wolf Hardin (silver)

Nature isn't something separate from us that we go to "study." Nature is magickal life around us and within us, the very expression of the living planet/goddess Gaia that we're forever a part of. Instead we look to the other animals and to the plants not just as wise elders or even our sisters and brothers, but as extensions of ourselves. By learning their ways we can learn more about what it means to be us.

Tracks all tell stories once we learn to read them, tales written in hoof and claw, pressed into mud or sand. A spot in the snow ruffled by feathers and marked with blood tells of a rabbit killed by a hungry hawk. Other marks speak of curiosity and courtship, and meals of seed and grass. When someone is clueless we sometimes say they are "off-track," an expression dating back to when most boys by the age of 12 were expected to be able to read and identify tracks, and even to hunt and bring back meat for the family pot. But even if you are vegetarian or vegan, you can benefit by the increased awareness and magickal connection to Nature that comes from being able to "read" the ground, raising our awareness of the details and clues of the real world around us.

Close examination, preferably early morning or late evening when the tracks are sidelit, will show us not only what species of animals have been by but also in what direction they were going. The depth of the track indicates weight and size, while the distance between tracks can tell you if they were walking fast or slow. If a deer's tracks are far enough apart and very deep, it's likely they were running and leaping away from a real or imagined threat. With people, the kind of print can tell us if it was a man or woman, professional or athletic, hurried or relaxed.

For our ancient tribal ancestors, this ability to read track could mean the difference between starvation and full meal—between catching something to eat, or ending up as a grizzly bear's meal. Everyone was expected to be hyper-aware, and the most aware of all became the esteemed hunters, spiritual warriors, shamans

As we get deeper and wiser, the wildest tracks of all will be the ones we leave. Art by Jesse Wolf Hardin.

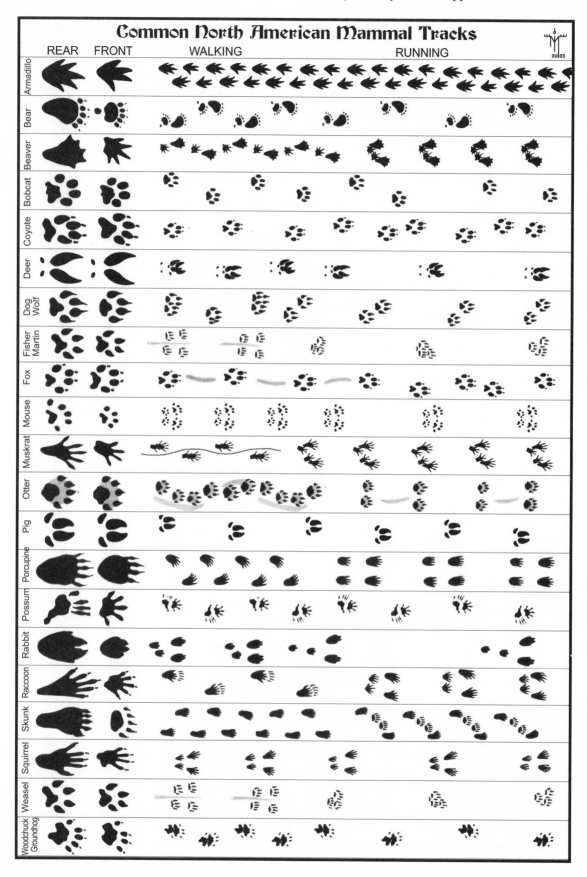

Common North American Mammal Tracks

and magicians.

As you can see, the responsibilities get bigger as our awareness grows, but the rewards increase at the same time. After a magickal day on the trail, we can't help but appreciate how much sweeter recorded music sounds to ears freshened by Nature's song and silence. Eyes taught to notice the tiniest details of sign have an easier time noticing the details of a beautiful painting or the clues in a good movie. Noses stirred by the subtle smells of the forest come back wakened to the aromas of a yummy dinner! Sign is a kind of enchantment or sorcery in that it can help lead us deeper into the experience of Wonderland, and in the process, deeper into our own enchanted beings. When we practice tracking animals, what we really end up finding is our own awakened and empowered selves.

Assignments:

• Go out to the nearest wild place with your track identification guide and see how many different kinds of tracks you can positively identify. Remember that tracks get larger and more rounded as they age or get rained on, sometimes making them look like something they're not.

• If you can't get to a secluded beach, state park or forest to track, find the nearest bare soil or unpaved lot and look for the always present signs of feeding birds, scurrying mice, domestic cats and dogs. You also don't have to leave the city to find signs of the many species of wildlife that venture in or make their homes there. These can include snakes, squirrels, skunks, raccoons, and sometimes even coyotes— although their tracks are mighty hard to distinguish from those of small domestic dog.

• Watch not only for tracks, but for disturbed pine needles, bits of fur stuck on a sticker bush or wire fence, and animal feces. You can tell what animal left the feces by what you find in it, hair in the poop of predators who hunt for their food, nutshells and plant matter in that of rodents and coons.

• Try to determine the direction an animal was going not only by the shape of the print, but by the way the soil around the track is disturbed. Most animals throw some dirt to the rear as they step.

• See if you can figure out how long ago the animal passed by, based on how distinct or fallen-in the tracks are, how much loose leafy material has blown in since it was made, and whether or not it has rained.

• Try pouring and collecting plaster tracks from the more well-defined signs, until you get samples from all or most of the neighboring species.

• Use the skills of awareness, observation, intuition and deduction that you develop reading tracks in order to also "read" the people and situations around you in everyday life. Then you can see at a glance where someone has been, anticipate where they are going, and decide what is your wise and wizardly course of action.

6. Critter Care
By Oberon (grey)

For a Beast Master, few experiences can be more rewarding than caring for and rehabilitating orphaned or injured wild animals until they are able to be released back into the wild. Many communities throughout the world have local Wildlife Rescue Agencies, which I strongly recommend all Brown Wizards to look up and become involved with, as I have done. For general information, see the International Wildlife Rehabilitation Council (IWRC): PO Box 8187, San Jose, CA 95155; phone (408) 271-2685; http://www.iwrc-online.org/ (I designed this logo for them back in 1987!)

An important aspect of Beast Mastery is the care of orphaned baby animals that you may find along country roads after their mother has been run over, or after a natural disaster, such as a forest fire, flood, or hurricane. Should you encounter any of these, and wish to raise them until they are old enough to be released, here is some basic information for various common North American and European mammal species, adapted from materials provided by the Alexander Lindsay Jr. Museum Wildlife Rescue Program in Walnut Creek, Califia. For birds and animals native to other countries, contact the IWRC.

For all of the following, you will, of course, need to obtain bottles and nipples of the appropriate sizes from a vet, pet supply store, or farm feed store. Sterilize these before each use. You will also need to prepare nesting boxes, with blankets and electric heating pads to keep the babies warm.

Keep careful notes of everything you do when raising wild animals, and report these to your local Wildlife Rescue Agency. And it should go without saying that you should *never* release a non-native animal into the wild!

Badgers

FORMULA: Canned *Esbilac* (bitch's milk supplement available at most pet stores and vets).

RAISING: Until eyes are open (at 3-4 weeks old), feed *Esbilac* 5-6 times per day. Once eyes open, switch to a good dogfood diet, cutting back on the *Esbilac*. Add *Vet-Nutri* vitamin/mineral supplement (from vet; follow label). Introduce mice and baby rats when they're onto solids, and get them killing their own at 4-5 weeks. Allow them to dig in the ground, as they are natural burrowers.

RELEASE: Release in a local foothill area near a ground squirrel colony—far away from ranchers or farmers!

Bobcats, Lynx

FORMULA: *Bordon's KMR* canned cat formula (available at most pet stores and vets). Soon introduce Gerber's strained lamb and veal, then graduate to regular canned cat food. If you can't get *KMR*, use *Esbilac* with strained baby meat added, as cats need extra protein.

RAISING: Until eyes are open, feed *Esbilac* six times per day around the clock. Better to feed too little than too much, and burp after each feeding (they are prone to gas). After eyes are open, five feedings will do. Stop feedings when stomach is tight, and cut back if stools are runny. Wash their little rear ends and watch for "diaper rash."

Keep them warm with a heating pad and blanket nest, and give them lots of mothering—caressing, hugging, etc. Wash in warm room and dry quickly. Dust with cat flea powder right after obtaining them, and vaccinate for canine and feline distemper. Vaccinate for rabies at three months.

As soon as eyes are open (at 3 weeks old), begin feeding canned kitten food mixed with *Esbilac* in a dish; start with ¼ tsp. per feeding, and expect a mess.

A week after eyes are open (at 4 weeks old), mash in a little kitty kibble. Go slow and watch for gas or bloating. At 5-6 weeks, switch to a full meat diet of mice, rats, rabbits, etc.

RELEASE: When they can hunt and kill their own prey, release far away from people.

Brush Rabbits, Cottontails

FORMULA: Canned *Esbilac*.

RAISING: If eyes are not yet open, feed with 1 cc eyedropper or tuberculin syringe. Feed 2-3 droppersful every hour, and check stomach. If it's still tight at feeding time, extend length of time between feedings. Keep bunny temperature about 85° F with heating pad and towels.

When its eyes are open (at 8-12 days), feed with eyedropper or little "pet nurser" bottle—3-4 cc, 4-5 times per day. Leave little pieces of lettuce, apple, Cheerios, and baby rabbit pellets (from pet store) in its nesting box. As bunny starts to feed itself, taper off on formula. As it gets older, introduce carrots, apples, corn, and alfalfa pellets.

Tickle its bottom with a Q-tip after each feeding to stimulate elimination, and keep it clean to avoid "diaper rash." If rash occurs, use A&D Ointment (from pharmacy—follow label). Bunnies are very prone to gas problems, so don't overfeed; less is best. If bloated, warm tummy, massage gently with finger, and skip a feeding. If gas problem continues, water down the formula by ¼.

Baby bunnies should be handled carefully—over a bed or soft place—as they will spring from your hands, and can injure themselves in a fall.

RELEASE: When bunny is eating completely on its own, and is kitten-sized, release it in a woodland meadow away from people and dogs.

Deer

FORMULA: Fresh goat's milk is excellent. Or you can make up "Fawn Special Formula" as follows: to 1 quart. homogenized whole cow's milk, and add ½ cup whipping cream. Take 1 quart of this mixture and heat to boiling. Add ½ cup *Calf Mana* (from farm supply store) and blend in blender for 4-5 minutes. Store in refrigerator for up to 3 days; blend again before using.

RAISING: If you find an adorable tiny spotted fawn all curled up in the tall grass away from a road, *leave it alone!* Its mother will be grazing nearby so as not to draw attention to her baby. The fawn is perfectly safe—odorless, well-camouflaged, and invisible to predators. Only if you find a fawn in the vicinity of a dead doe (such as has been hit by a car), should you rescue it.

Deer are very prone to shock, and should be kept warm, dark, and quiet when first brought rescued. Talk softly with them and give them lots of loving hugs, petting, and cuddles. They usually prefer women—but keep them away from dogs!

Feed goat's milk or formula at body temperature (sprinkle a bit on the inside of your forearm to test), using a goat-nipple (from farm supply store). To encourage feeding, cup your hands around its muzzle, or cover its eyes. Older fawns are obstinate feeders, and require patience and perseverance.

For a fawn up to 5 lbs., feed 4 oz. four times a day (i.e. 7:AM, noon, 5:PM, 10:PM). Tickle behind after each feeding to encourage elimination; remember, overfeeding causes diarrhea! If this occurs, use 1 tsp. *Kaopectate* per feeding.

At around 10 lbs., expand feedings to 5 oz. per feeding (max. 20 oz. in 24 hrs.). Introduce alfalfa, dried leaves (esp. pyracanthus), fruit tree branches and leaves, and whole wheat bread. If you let them outside, they'll learn to browse on their own. At 3-4 weeks, begin to cut back on formula and let them browse more. At 2 months, they will need only an AM and PM formula feeding. By 3 months, they should be off formula altogether.

RELEASE: Deer may be released as soon as they are eating fully on their own—usually 3-4 months. Release them in an area with plenty of wild deer, as they will need to join a herd. However, deer imprint on people very strongly, and if a fawn you have raised has learned a name while in your care, it will come to you when called for the rest of its life.

Foxes, Coyotes

FORMULA: Canned *Esbilac.*

RAISING: Until eyes are open (at 3-4 weeks old), feed *Esbilac* 5-6 times per day. Then switch to a good dogfood diet, cutting back on the *Esbilac.* Add *Vet-Nutri* vitamin/mineral supplement (from vet; follow label) as canines need extra calcium. Introduce mice and baby rats when they're onto solids, and get them killing their own at 4-5 weeks. Fox kits also like fruits—try different kinds.

Keep them in a secure pen or on a lease—and away from pet dogs, which they need to fear!

RELEASE: Dust with dog flea powder, and vaccinate for canine distemper and rabies before releasing at 3-4 months—far away from people and chickens!

Jackrabbits

FORMULA: Goat's milk or "Fawn Special Formula" (see Deer)

RAISING: Jackrabbits are hares, not rabbits, and are born full-furred with eyes open. Put lots of towel in their nesting box to burrow into. They are very shy and nervous, and scared by sudden noises. They can injure themselves by suddenly springing in alarm.

Feed as with rabbit bunnies (see above), using an eyedropper or pet nurser bottle. They are prone to suck too much, so don't overfeed. As soon as their bellies feel full, stop. Stimulate their bottom after each feeding, and wash them up with warm water.

Provide a supply of fresh natural food at all times: mustard greens, lettuce, rabbit pellets, Cheerios. They may not eat much, but any nibbling they do is important.

RELEASE: When they are the size of a kitten and eating on their own, release in an open field with trees, away from people and dogs.

Muskrats, Beaver

FORMULA: Canned *Esbilac.*

RAISING: See below for Squirrels, and feed these in the same way. When eyes are open, offer them celery, fruit-tree branches and leaves, rabbit pellets, and Lab Chow (from feed store). As kits get older, allow them to swim in the bathtub daily, or their fur will lose its ability to repel water.

RELEASE: When they are eating entirely on their own, release them by a stream or pond that has year-round water.

Possums

FORMULA: Canned *Esbilac.*

RAISING: You generally find an orphaned possie when it's just left its mama—about 4-6" long (excluding tail), fully-furred, and with beady little eyes open. It won't need a bottle. Mix *Esbilac* with canned dogfood and chopped hardboiled egg. Possums eat on their own very early, and will soon eat virtually anything; it's fun to offer them different treats—like French fries, or popcorn.

They can climb out of anything, so keep the little possie in a latched cage with a big wooly sock for a "sleeping bag," and cover the cage with a towel to keep it dim inside. As much as possible, carry it around with you in a knitted purse hung around your neck and tucked inside your shirt.

RELEASE: When the possum is a foot long, you may release it along a running stream in a local park. North American possums only live a year or so in the wild, and they make charming and loveable pets, which you might wish to consider…

Raccoons, Coatis, Ringtailed Cats

FORMULA: Canned *Esbilac.*

RAISING: Raising a 'coon is like raising a human baby. Better to feed too little than too much, and burp after each feeding (they are prone to gas). Until eyes are open, feed *Esbilac* six times per day around the clock. After eyes are open, five feedings will do. Stop feedings when stomach is tight, and cut back if stools are runny. Wash their little rear ends and watch for "diaper rash."

Keep them warm with a heating pad and blanket nest, and give them lots of mothering—caressing, hugging, etc. Wash in warm room and dry quickly. Dust with cat flea powder right after obtaining them, and vaccinate for canine and feline distemper. Vaccinate for rabies at three months.

As soon as eyes are open (at 3 weeks old), begin feeding Gerber's strained meat and veggies mixed with *Esbilac* in a dish (but avoid beef and green beans); start with ¼ tsp. per feeding, and expect a mess.

A week after eyes are open (at 4 weeks old), mash in a little puppy kibble. Go slow and watch for gas or bloating. At 5-6 weeks, switch to a good dogfood and fruit diet, cutting back on the *Esbilac*. Occasionally include a skinned mouse or fish.

RELEASE: When the little 'coon is able to walk around, take it on short walks along streams, allowing it to explore and find things to eat. Plant small raw fish along the way. At about four months, when it has learned to hunt its own food, it can be released near running water. But be aware that 'coons imprint very strongly on people, and it may not want to go off on its own!

Skunks

NOTE: Do not attempt to handle or raise orphaned wild skunks! They are a major vector of rabies, and the most common reason they become orphaned is because their mother died from this virus! Contact your local Health Department so they can be checked for rabies, and do not allow them to scratch or bite anyone! *Rabies is fatal!*

Squirrels, Ground Squirrels, Chipmunks, Woodchucks (Groundhogs)

FORMULA: Canned *Esbilac*.

RAISING: As with rabbits, all these rodents begin life hairless, with eyes closed. Their eyes open at 14-18 days. They should be kept at 85° F with some humidity. A heating pad wrapped in a towel in the nesting box works well. If possible, it's best to raise several baby squirrels together, to keep each other warm, play, etc.

"Pinkies" should be fed carefully until stomach is just bulging and tight; overfeeding will cause diarrhea. Feed ½-¾ oz. of formula every 24 hrs., about every 90 min., with one feeding in the middle of the night. After each feeding, burp them gently and tickle their bottoms with a Q-tip to stimulate elimination. If they get diarrhea, give them an eyedropper-full of *Kaopectate* 4 times a day until they're better.

When they are furry all over, but eyes still not open, offer ¼ oz. per feeding, every 2-3 hours during the day. Once their eyes are open, they can take ½-¾ oz. per feeding. If their stool gets watery, cut back on the amount of food. Introduce *Gerber's Hi-Protene Dry Cereal* mixed with the *Esbilac* to start them on solids, and start leaving some apple slices, Cheerios, and lettuce in their box to gnaw on (no oranges!).

Continue stimulating their bottoms after each feeding, and wash them with warm water. They'll be able to handle lower temperatures now (75°-80° F), and should be moved into a larger cage. Leave plenty of towels, but remove the heating pad.

As they get older, introduce them to fruits, carrots, seeds and nuts of all kinds—starting with easy-to-open sunflower seeds and peanuts. Also offer fruit-tree branches and leaves (they love the bark).

RELEASE: When they are close to full-sized, and can easily chew through a walnut, release them into a wooded area, or near where you found them.

Weasels (including Stoats, Ferrets, Mink, Fishers)

FORMULA: Canned *Esbilac*.

RAISING: Baby weasels don't open their eyes until they are 30-25 days old. Feed *Esbilac* 5-6 times per day around the clock, ticking their bottoms to stimulate elimination. Stop feedings when stomach is tight, and cut back if stools are runny.

They start raw meat as soon as their eyes open. Leave fresh-killed pinkie mice and rats in with the little weasel, and when it freely eats these, quickly taper off the formula. Soon, introduce live mice, chicks, and young rats and let the weasel kill them.

RELEASE: As soon as the little weasel is killing and eating on its own, release it in an area where there are plenty of rodents. Be careful when handling and releasing, as all wild species of weasels are notoriously nasty biters!

7. More fabulous Beastes

By Oberon (grey)

In the *Grimoire* (pp. 324-330), I presented some the most well-known of fabulous beasts. Now here are some of the more obscure creatures of the mythical menagerie:

Ammut— A terrible monster in the Egyptian underworld, she had the head of a crocodile, a lion's mane, a leopard's spots, and the back end of a hippopotamus. The Egyptians called her "the eater of the dead." In Osiris' Hall of Justice, the hearts of the dead were weighed against the feather of truth, and those who failed to past the test were fed to Ammut.

Amphisbæna— A snake-like reptile with glowing eyes and heads at both ends of its body. Its name means

"goes both ways" in Greek. It gets about, in either direction, by placing one of its heads in the other's mouth and rolling along like a wheel. Wearing a live amphisbæna is said to protect pregnant women, while wearing a dead one cures rheumatism. This is a real animal, a kind of legless burrowing "worm lizard" *(Amphisbænidae)* whose tail is shaped exactly the same as its blind, earless head. They grow up to 20 inches in length, and crawl equally well forwards or backwards (but they don't roll like a hoop!).

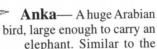

Anka— A huge Arabian bird, large enough to carry an elephant. Similar to the **Phoenix,** it lived 1,700 years, at the end of which time it burned itself to ashes and rose again. Because of its huge size, it has also been associated with the **Roc.**

Barliate— A type of Goose that was believed to begin life as a kind of barnacle growing from trees or attached to driftwood. Based upon actual "goose-neck" barnacles. It is also called *Bernaca, Bernicle,* Barnacle Goose and Tree Goose.

Barometz—Also called the *Tartary, Barbary Lamb,* and *Vegetable Lamb.* In Hebrew legend, the Barbary lamb is a woolbearing sheep-like creature that is half vegetable. They are produced from little gourds, and attached to shrubs by very short stems. Once they have eaten all the grass within reach, they die of starvation. Barometz is considered a delicacy as its meat tastes like fish, and its blood like honey. Its bones are used in rituals to give the power of prophecy. This is actually the cotton bush.

Behemoth—An exaggerated Biblical version of the hippopotamus. The word comes from the plural of the Hebrew *b'hemah,* meaning "beast." Any large, heavy, and otherwise unknown animal can be called a "behemoth." In apocryphal literature and Jewish legend, the Behemoth is a monster of formidable strength. It is commonly depicted in battle with the **Leviathon**, which is a similarly exaggerated version of the ferocious Nile Crocodile.

Benu— An Egyptian version of the **Phoenix,** this heron-like bird is identified with Ra, the sun god. The

word *Benu* in Egyptian means both purple heron and palm tree. Much of the phoenix mythology is based on Egyptian myths of the Benu. This bird was also a symbol of Osiris, resurrecting itself from death.

Bishop-Fish—A sea-creature depicted in 16th century bestiaries as looking somewhat like a Bishop of the Catholic Church. They are described as having a mitered head, a scaly body with two claw-like fins instead of arms, and a fin-like cloak. This is evidently a male ray or skate, taxidermically manipulated as an art form later called "Jenny Hanivers."

Bunyip— A fierce Australian water-monster of Aboriginal legend, said to inhabit *billabongs* (water-holes). Described as looking somewhat like a giant seal, hippo, or dragon, it is greatly feared as a man-eater.

Cameleopard— Supposedly the offspring of a camel and a leopard, it is about the size of a camel, but has the spotted skin of a leopard and two large curving horns. It is clearly identified as the giraffe.

Echeneis— A little fish that can stop a ship under full sail by attaching itself to the hull.

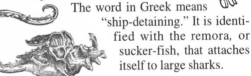

The word in Greek means "ship-detaining." It is identified with the remora, or sucker-fish, that attaches itself to large sharks.

Garm— The blood-spattered four-eyed dog that guarded the gate to Hel in Norse mythology. Very fierce and dangerous, Garm has been compared to **Cerberus**, as both are ferocious dogs that guard the realm of the Underworld in their respective mythologies.

Garuda— A gigantic manlike bird of India who was the mount of the god Vishnu.

Giant Ants— Described as "larger than a fox and smaller than a dog," these lived in the deserts of India, where they dug up gold that men tried to steal. They have been identified as marmots—large mountain rodents living in colonial burrows like prairie dogs.

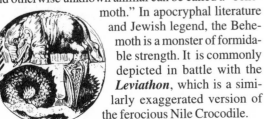

Ho-oo— This is the Japanese *Phoenix,* the Ho being the male and the Oo being the female. It comes to Earth to do good deeds for people, and this appearance heralds the dawn of a new era. The bird then ascends back to heaven to await the next cycle. Much like the Chinese Phoenix the *Feng-Huang*, the Ho-Oo has been adopted as a symbol of the royal family, particularly the Empress. It is supposed to represent the sun, justice, fidelity and obedience.

Hsigo— The Chinese Hsigo are much like the flying monkeys from *The Wizard of Oz.* I think they are probably based on fruit bats, or "flying foxes," of India, Asia, Indonesia and Australia. These monkey-size bats are not related to the other insectivorous bats, but are genetically closer to primates.

Jormangund— Also called the *Midgard Serpent* of Norse myth, it circled Middle-Earth *(Midgard),* the world of humans, with its tail in its mouth. Jormangund was the second of three children of Loki and the giantess Angraboda. The first was the Fenris Wolf, and the third was Hel, Goddess of the Underworld.

Kappa— This is a river-dwelling Japanese creature with the body of a tortoise and the head of a monkey. If treated with courtesy, it is friendly. However, if it is ill-treated, it will eat its tormentor.

Karkadan— A large so-called *"Unicorn"* of Ethiopia and India. Also called *monoceros* ("one-horn"), it is described as having the head of a stag, the body of a horse, the feet of an elephant and the tail of a boar. It is clearly based on the rhinoceros.

Kelpie— A creature 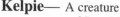 of Scottish legend. Normally it is an ugly black beast, part horse and part bull, with two sharp horns. But it can shape-shift into the form of a beautiful white horse. If anyone mounted this horse, it would gallop into the water and drown the rider, whom it would then devour.

Ki-Lin— A kind of Chinese *Unicorn* with the head of a one-horned dragon, a lion's mane, the body of a stag, and the tail of an ox. The *Ki* is the male,

Ki

Lin

and the *Lin* is the female. Symbolizing wisdom, justice and righteousness, it appears only during the time of an upright ruler, or before the birth or death of a sage. In Japan the same creature is called *Ki-Rin*. Japan also has the *Sin-U* which has leonine features.

Lamassu— Winged lions with human heads that guarded the gates of Assyrian temples and palaces. See also *Shedu*, with which it is paired.

Lindwurm—A winged serpent from Germanic legend. It has a scaly green-gold legless body, and guards treasures. It symbolizes war and pestilence, and eats cattle and people.

Lympago— A man-lion or a man-tiger from Medieval heraldry.

Mermicoleon— The "Ant-Lion." A creature generated by a translator's error. A word meaning "lion among ants" was mistranslated as a ferocious composite of lion and ant. The name is now applied to insects that prey on ants by digging a conical sand-pit, and lying in wait underground for ants to slip in. This was the basis of the "sarlak" pit monster in the Star Wars movie, *Return of the Jedi.*

Monk-Fish—A sea-creature depicted as looking like a cowled and robed monk, with tentacles for arms and legs. From the pictures, it seems that these were simply large squids, artistically arranged and preserved, as "Jenny Hanivers" (see *BishopFish*).

Nuckalavee— An Irish parody of the *Centaur,* it  has a rotten stench, and its breath was said to have brought the plague. It is an ugly amphibious monster with a large, hideous head and froglike webbed feet rather than hooves. Its hairless skin is thin, moist and transparent, giving it a flayed appearance. These vicious creatures despoil their surroundings and kill for pleasure.

Pegasies— Ethiopian birds with ears l 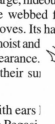 horses. As recorded by Pliny, the Pegasi was a great bird with the head of a horse.

Possibly the Shoebill stork.

Pheng— A bird from Japanese legend which is so gigantic that it eclipses the sun and can carry off and eat a camel. Much like the *Roc* of Arabian myth.

Piasa— A man-eating North American water monster, supposedly painted by Indians on a cliff face above the Mississippi River near Alton, Illinois. It looks like a winged dragon with a human face and deer antlers. It has clawed feet, batlike wings, and a fishtail at the end of a very long tail.

Scolopendra— A sea-monster depicted as a spouting whale-like creature with numerous appendages hanging from its underside. This looks most likely to be a large shark, such as a great white, whale-shark, or basking shark, with many remoras attached to it.

Senmurv— A creature from Persian mythology that combines features of mammal, fish, and bird. It is said to be the union of earth, sea, and sky.

Serra— A huge flying fish, with enormous wing-like fins. Ancient authorities identified it with the sawfish, but it seems more likely to be a fusion of the flying fish and the manta ray, both famed for soaring leaps out of the water.

Shedu— Similar to the *Lamassu,* with which it is paired, this winged beast from Assyrian-Babylonian mythology has a human head and the body of a bull. It guards temples and palaces.

Simmurgh— The spectacular King of the Birds in Arabian legend. Related to the *Roc* and the *Phoenix,* this bird lives for either 1,700 or 2,000 years. Some accounts claim it is immortal, nesting in the Tree of Knowledge. It is so large that it can carry off an elephant or a camel.

Sleipnir—The eight-legged horse of Allfather Odin in Norse mythology. He could run faster than the wind, traveling in the air, on the Earth, and even down into the underworld ruled by the goddess Hel.

Sz— A Malaysian Unicorn which looks like a one-horned water buffalo. It's also called the Sword Ox.

Tarasque—Ferocious river monster of the Rhone Valley in southern France. Larger than an ox, it had six legs, the head of a lion, paws of a bear, and a scaly body with a long serpentine tail ending in a sharp barb. The leathery shell on its back was covered with spikes. It was subdued by St. Martha, who tied her belt around its neck and led it docilely back into the town of Nerlue, where the villagers killed it with stones and spears. Afterwards, the town's name was changed to Tarascon, and annual processions continue to commemorate this event. In depictions, the Tarasque closely resembles an ankylosaur or a glyptodont.

Tengu— Winged creatures of Japanese myth, they are part human and part bird, with large beak-like noses.

Yala— A black bovine the size of a horse, with the tail of an elephant and the jowls of a boar. "It carries outlandishly long horns which are adjusted to move at will," one pointing forward and the other backwards. The Nandi Tribes in Kenya train the horns of their cattle in this way, and these are known as "Kamari cows."

Yeti— A snow-dwelling "man-ape" of the Himalayan mountains in Tibet.

Yowie— An Australian "man-ape," similar to the *Yeti* or *Sasquatch.*

Ziz— Mentioned in the book of Psalms, the ziz is a bird of enormous size, much like the *Roc.* It can block out the sun with its wings and has incredible strength. It is said that it was created to protect all the small birds, and without its protection, these birds would have died a long time ago.

8. Make four nifty Dragon models

By Oberon (grey)

In the back of this book, I have drawn up a couple of pages of cut-outs to make a model of a classic Flying Dragon, based on the historical fact that the first European sailors who reached the island of Madagascar brought back preserved speci-mens of the little rib-winged gliding lizard they called *Draco volens* ("flying dragon"). These were pre-sented as genuine baby dragons, and the imagination of artists projected their anatomy into enormous "adult" versions that formed the basis of all concepts of flying dragons with four legs plus wings—as opposed to Wyverns, which, like birds, bats, and pte-rosaurs, had wings consisting of modified forelimbs.

To assemble your own model, first remove the pages with the Dragon cut-outs and copy them onto colored card stock at your nearest copy shop. Enlarge them to 121% when you do. Use colored pencils and your imagination to embellish these colorfully. Then lay the card stock pages on a hard smooth surface, and score along all the dotted lines with the dull back edge of a table knife, following curves where so indi-cated. Then cut out the pieces, and fold the creases sharply to make the assemblies. There are 10 pieces: two wings, two tail sections, two body sections, two neck sections, and two head pieces.

For tools, you will need scissors, a table knife, spring clothes-pins, a sharpened pencil, and a small bottle of white milk glue (Elmer's is good).

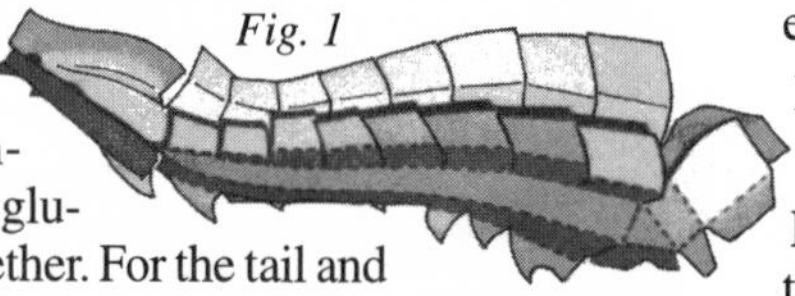

Neck and Tail:
Follow the num-bers for order of glu-ing the pieces together. For the tail and neck, first glue the top crest sections together one at a time, starting at the big end. Clamp each one tightly with clothes-pins, and let it dry before doing the next one. A good way to give time for drying is to work on several pieces at once, taking turns with gluing parts.

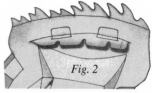

Draco volens

Once the upper crests are all glued for each piece, it's time to glue the scales into place under the throat and tail. These must be glued in an overlapping back-and-forth pattern—follow the numbers carefully. (Fig. 1) Stick the pointy end of the pencil up behind each scale as you glue them to have a surface to press against, and to shape the curved sections.

When making the fin at the end of the tail, glue only the top part together. Leave the bottom unglued, and spread it open to make a triangular triple fin.

Head: Glue the top parts of the head pieces to-gether, and then glue the cheeks into place over the corresponding tabs at the front of the neck. Then glue the under-side of the jaw, and bend the ears outward in a curve.

Wings: First, gently bend the large wing surfaces into a curve. Then insert each wing into the long slot in the side of each body half, and glue the two little tabs in each wing into the inside of the back above the slot.

Fig. 1

(Fig. 2) Then run a bead of glue along the slot on the under-side of each wing.

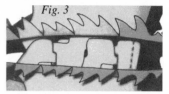

Fig. 2

Body: When the glue on the wings is dry, assemble the two body halves, interlocking the large wing tabs inside to make them stiff. (Fig. 3) Then one section at a time, as with the neck and tail, glue to-gether each section of crest, clamping with clothes-pins un-til the glue is dry.

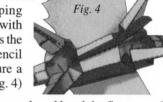

Fig. 3

Tail to Body: Glue the tabs at the top front of the tail into inside of the back rear. Then fold the remaining tail tabs and glue them into place along the backs of the thighs, following the numbers.

Neck to Body: Glue the tabs at the base of the neck into the front body and shoulders in exactly the same way as you did with the tail.

Legs: Make sure the creases connecting the body and legs—behind the upper arms and in front of the thighs—are as sharp as can be. Wrap the sections of each leg all the way around, and glue the last flaps into place as indicated. Finish by gluing the elbow and knee flaps into place.

Belly: Glue the belly scales together in overlapping sections as you did with the neck and tail. Press the pointy end of the pencil on the inside to ensure a good connection. (Fig. 4)

Fig. 4

Feet: Fold the feet forward, and bend the fingers and toes into curved claws. Glue the tab under the heel into place, and adjust all the toes to stand. (Fig. 5)

Your Dragon is now complete!

I have also provided an alternate set of batlike wings, as well as an extra head and parts for an Orien-tal Dragon, so you can make several dragons, with or without wings, in different colors.

Make a Dragon Mobile!

Fig. 5

Department XII: Cosmology & Metaphysics (violet)

Dance of the Wanderers

The Sun, he comes; the Sun, he goes
As each day blooms just like a rose.

The Moon, she goes; the Moon, she comes
The ocean dances to her drums.

Fleet Mercury brings word of all
That passes in the heavens' hall.

Fair Venus, she flies like a dove
The light of beauty and of love.

Red Mars, he makes a fear-
some foe
But fights with honor, even so.

Great Jupiter spills from his hands
A rain of health and wealth and lands.

Dark Saturn takes what others give
But some must die for some to live.

So learn these names, and learn them well
The Wanderers their secrets tell.

—Elizabeth Barrette

1. Introduction

 ELCOME TO THE WORLD OF COSMO-logy and Metaphysics! In this department we will explore the wonders of the Universe. The great bowl of the night sky—the Celestial Sphere—that surrounds our tiny globe has always been a subject of magickal and Wizardly studies. The movements of the sun, moon and planets through the signs of the Zodiac gave us our calendar, our first way of keeping time, and our earliest form of effective Divination. Cosmology is also concerned with the larger questions: How did everything begin? Where are we going? Is there anyone else out there?

The magickal color of this department is Violet, which is associated with power, wealth, and good fortune. Considered the color of royalty, violet (purple) represents judgment, industry, and religious thought, the planet Jupiter, Thursday, the 7th (Crown) Chakra and old age. It is also associated with several astrological signs: Gemini, Virgo, Libra, Sagittarius and Pisces. Violet is the color of spirit, etheric realms, higher esoteric learning, ancient wisdom and the deeper Mysteries of the Cosmos. Use violet as your focus for spiritual centering and meditation, as well as expanded consciousness and cosmic awareness.

Most of this chapter is written by Susan "Moonwriter" Pesznecker, Dean of the Grey School's Dept. of Cosmology and Metaphysics. Other authors are indicated.

2. Naked eye astronomy

By Moonwriter (indigo)

The night sky is full of magick.

Thousands of years ago, Stone Age people looked up into the night sky with the same sense of wonder that we have today. The Ancients believed that Gods ruled the heavens, and looked to heavenly occurrences as having great significance. Archaeoastronomical monuments such as Stonehenge and the *caracol* at Chichén Itzá were observatories, built by so-called "primitive" people to track important celestial events. Many of these alignments had accuracies of plus or minus one degree, and still work perfectly today. Later, the positions of sun and stars were used to guide navigators over land and water. Stargazing may have been the first true science.

And yet, none of these people had telescopes! Their only tools were their eyes, their brains, and a great deal of patience.

An important underlying theme of astronomy is that the Universe is a rational place, with related objects that behave in predictable ways according to known tenets of chemistry, biology, and physics. As with any science, observation is both the foundation and the most important skill. .

How to learn the night sky? Just look up and let curiosity take over. The things that you see will make you start asking questions: Why? Who? When? Where? These questions will lead your study of astronomy. As your skill grows, you'll find yourself looking at the stars as old friends. Whether identifying constellations, locating direction by star position, experiencing a meteor shower, or spotting one of the visible planets, you'll experience great satisfaction while constantly coming up with new challenges.

Learning your way around the night sky begins with your own pair of eyes. Even today—in this era of scientific instrumentation—astronomers recommend that the night sky first be learned "by eye" before it is learned through telescopes or other tools. To step outside, look up into the night sky, and have a sense of what you are seeing never fails to be wondrous. You're about to begin a wonderful adventure.

Your journey through the Universe begins here.

Star Quest

Go outside on a clear night, about two hours after sunset, and look up. For best viewing, go as far from city and other lights as possible. Make sure that you're warm and comfortable; a great way to sky-watch is to lay on a blanket on the ground, which allows you to look straight up.

stay outside for at least 30 minutes. Don't study any star charts or do any preparation ahead of time; just look up at the stars, the moon, bright spots that seem to cross the sky, the Milky Way, and anything else that is apparent. See how many stars or constellations you already know. Think about where the direction "north" is. Imagine that you are a Stone Age person who knows nothing of the science of astronomy. How does this all make you feel?

After your period of observation, come inside and jot down some notes about your observations. You might also wish to make an entry in your magickal journal about the experience.

3. Measurement, Direction, and the Night Sky

By Moonwriter, with contributions by Oberon

The Celestial Sphere

Imagine the sky as the ancients believed it to be— a great, hollow sphere surrounding the Earth. This imaginary sphere is called the *celestial sphere.* Thinking about the sky in this way helps us imagine "directions" when we talk about the position of the stars.

Imagine that you are standing on the north pole of Earth. Now imagine that you draw a line straight up, extending the pole into the heavens. You have just "drawn" the *celestial North Pole.* You could also use Earth's south pole to imagine the celestial South Pole. When we try to locate stars in the night sky, we can use the celestial poles as references points.

What is the celestial equator? Imagine that you are standing on the Earth's equator, the imaginary line that encircles the globe. Now imagine that you extend the entire equator straight up, extending it into the heavens. You have just "drawn" the *celestial equator.*

Circumpolar stars are those that never rise or set, but appear to rotate around the celestial north and south poles. Because of their fixed position in the sky, they can be used to locate other stars and constellations, and can also help find direction.

The current north polar star is *Polaris.* The five constellations that circle Polaris are called the north circumpolar constellations. Circumpolar stars are visible from the northern hemisphere at all times of the year. These are *Ursa Minor* (the little bear), *Ursa Major* (the great bear), *Draco* (the dragon), *Cepheus* (the King) and *Cassiopeia* (the Queen).

There is no real south polar star. The visible star closest to the south celestial pole is the dim *Sigma Octantis,* sometimes called *Polaris Australis.* However, the bright Southern Cross (*Crux*) points towards the south celestial pole.

Because the pole star and circumpolar stars appear to be unchanging, they are said to have magickal properties of stability and dependability. However due to the Earth's *precession*—a slow, conical wobbling of the Earth's rotation—the polar stars change every several thousand years. In 2300 B.C.E. the north pole star was in the constellation Draco. By 12,000 C.E., the star *Vega* in the constellation *Lyra* (the lyre) will be the pole star, and Polaris will simply be a nondescript circumpolar star.

For those in the northern hemisphere, Polaris can be used to find the direction north. First, locate the Big Dipper in the constellation of Ursa Major. To find

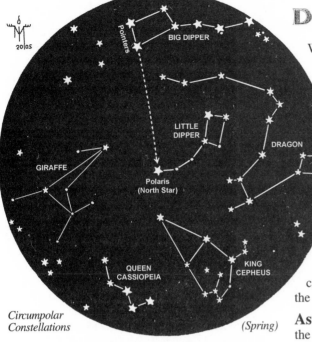

*Circumpolar
Constellations*   *(Spring)*

Polaris, trace an imaginary line through the two "pointer stars" at the end of the Dipper's bowl (see diagram). Once you have found Polaris, stand facing it. You will now be facing north. Ancient mariners used Polaris as an important directional tool in their travels.

The apparent yearly path of the sun through the stars and around the celestial sphere is called the *ecliptic*. This circular path is tilted 23.5 degrees with respect to the celestial equator because the Earth's rotation axis is tilted by 23.5 degrees with respect to its orbital plane.

The ecliptic and celestial equator intersect at two points: the vernal (spring) equinox and autumnal (fall) equinox.

To measure distances on the celestial sphere, astronomers use *degrees* and *angles*.

There are 360 degrees in a full circle and 90 degrees in a right angle. Any object directly overhead is 90 degrees above the horizon. An object "half-way up" in the sky (i.e., an equal distance between the horizon and being directly overhead) is about 45 degrees above the horizon. An object that is directly over the viewer's head is said to be at *zenith*.

The average adult human hand—held at arm's length—provides a good way to estimate angles. A closed fist covers (subtends) an angle of about 10 degrees, while the widest finger is about 1 degree. In other words, two stars that are "one fist" apart are about 10 degrees apart, and if they're about half-way up between the horizon and zenith, they are at about 45 degrees relative to the horizon.

Simple directions like these will help you with star chart and planisphere location/identification of celestial objects.

Distance

While it is not terribly important for naked eye astronomers to be able to use detailed concepts of astronomical distance, these distances are part of the language of astronomy. It's important that you understand the basics of distances, not only so you will have a reference point when studying astronomy, but so that you'll have one more way to feel a true sense of wonder and awe when considering the size of our Universe!

Astronomers use the same conventional measurements that other scientists use: kilometers, miles, meters, inches, pounds, degrees, kilograms, etc. But because of the vast distances between stars, planets, and galaxies, astronomers have also developed their own specialized systems of measurement. Here are some of the more common ones you'll hear about:

Astronomical unit (AU): The AU is equal to the approximate distance between the Earth and the sun. 1 AU = 9.96 million miles. The distance from Earth to Jupiter is approximately 5.2 AU—that's a lot simpler than saying 51.79 million miles!

Light-year: A light-year is the distance that light travels in one year. Since light travels at the speed of 300,000 km/second (186,000 miles/second), one light year equals a distance of some six trillion miles!

Parsec: The parsec is based on the appearance of an angle seen a great distance away. A parsec is a unit of distance that equals 3.26 light years.

Remember how we explained that there are 360 degrees in a full circle? Each degree can be subdivided into 60 *arcminutes,* and each of those into 60 *arcseconds* (arcsec). A *parsec* is the distance required to subtend one arcsec. A *kiloparsec* is one thousand parsecs; a *megaparsec* is one million parsecs.

Brightness and Magnitude

Some heavenly objects are brighter than others: Astronomers use an extension of a system invented in the second century BCE—*magnitude*—to describe this varying brightness.

Magnitude is expressed in two ways:

Absolute magnitude refers to the relative brightness of an object at the specific distance of 10 parsecs (32.6 light years). This measurement is used mostly by working astronomer-scientists.

Apparent magnitude is a more relative description: the brighter an object appears to be in the sky, the lower its apparent magnitude. Apparent magnitude is the more common measurement, and it's the one we'll use here. (Note: If you're reading an astronomy source and it simply refers to "magnitude," it is referring to apparent magnitude.)

In both types of magnitude, the smaller the number, the brighter the object. In other words, a star with a magnitude of two is brighter than one with a magnitude of 10. Very bright objects—like the sun—are so bright that their apparent magnitude is a negative number.

Here are a few examples of apparent magnitude:

The sun: magnitude -27
The full moon: magnitude -12
Venus (at its brightest): magnitude -5
Sirius and Canopus (the two brightest stars):
    magnitude -1
The dimmest objects visible with the naked eye:
    magnitude +6
The dimmest objects visible with binoculars:
    magnitude +10

IMPORTANT SAFETY NOTE: Never look directly at the sun, either with naked eye or through a lens of any kind. To do so may cause permanent eye damage, and even blindness!

Star Quest

Go outside on a clear night. Get comfortable, and stay out long enough to actually see the night sky change. Pick out the moon, a constellation, a bright star, or some other very obvious landmark. Watch it for at least an hour or two. Use what you know about angles, degrees, and directions to make notes about where the object starts and where it ends up.

4. The Mariner's Astrolabe

By Oberon (grey)

In the early days of ocean navigation, there was no known way to determine the east-west *longitude* of a ship at sea. But the north-south *latitude* could be quite easily determined by measuring the angle above the horizon of the sun at noon, or a known star at night, at the moment when it crossed the *meridian*—the line from due south to due north. The sun's or star's known *declination* (the angular distance of a heavenly body north or south of the celestial equator) for the date was then looked up in an almanac. The latitude would be 90° - measured altitude + declination.

To go to a location of known latitude, the ship first sailed to that latitude, and then sailed east or west along the latitude line until it reached its destination.

An *astrolabe* is any instrument used to measure altitudes above the horizon. The **Mariner's Astrolabe**, popular in the late 15th and early 16th centuries, was a device used to determine the latitude of a ship at sea by measuring the noon altitude of the sun, or the meridian altitude of a star of known *declination*. It consisted of a simple ring, marked in degrees, with a rotating *alidade* for sighting the sun or a star. The ring was cast brass, quite heavy, and cut away to keep it from blowing around in the wind. It was not a very good instrument and errors of four or five degrees were common.

You can make your own Mariner's Astrolabe from the cutouts in the back of this book. Copy the page onto card stock, at 121%. Cut out the ring and the alidade, and assemble them according to the instructions on the pages. You can use a brass paper fastener through the hole in the center, or, better, a grommet from a craft store.

To sight the angle of the sun, hold the Astrolabe at eye level, edge on to the sun, and rotate the alidade so that the sunlight is projected straight along the sighting bars. Then read the angle of altitude from the scale on the ring. To get the latitude, make this measurement at noon, and then look up the readings in an almanac of Solar declinations.

5. Seasons, Equinoxes, and Solstices

By Moonwriter (indigo)

Everyone knows that the earth rotates around the sun. Did you also know that the earth isn't "straight up and down?" It's actually tilted 23.5 degrees off-axis. Since the earth is tilted, different parts of the globe are closer to or farther away from the sun at different times of the year.

Seasons

During the portion of the year when the earth's orbit tilts part of it toward the sun, that part of the earth experiences summer, while the part tilted away from the sun experiences winter.

The tilt also explains why seasons in the two hemispheres are opposite, i.e., when it's winter in the northern hemisphere, it's summer in the southern hemisphere, and vice-versa.

Equinoxes

Equinoxes are days in which day and night are of equal (or almost equal) duration. The two yearly equinoxes—spring and autumn—occur when the sun (on its ecliptic) crosses the celestial equator.

The word equinox comes from Latin words meaning "equal night." At the time of the equinoxes, day and night are approximately equal everywhere on Earth.

The Vernal (Spring) Equinox occurs around March 20-22, marking the beginning of spring in the northern hemisphere and the beginning of fall in the southern hemisphere.

The Autumnal (Fall) Equinox occurs around September 20-22, marking the beginning of fall in the northern hemisphere and the beginning of spring in the southern hemisphere.

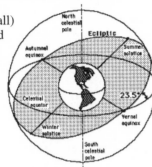

Solstices

The summer and winter solstices represent the northernmost and southernmost (respectively, and relative to the celestial sphere) points on the solar ecliptic. Remember that the Equinoxes occur when the ecliptic *crosses* the celestial equators. At the solstices, the sun is at its *farthest* point north or south of the celestial equator, and the respective hemisphere will either have its longest period of daylight or darkness at that time.

The winter solstice usually occurs on December 21 or 22 and marks the beginning of winter: the shortest day and longest night of the year. At the winter solstice, the sun doesn't get very high in the sky for people living in places north of the equator (e.g., United States, Europe, and China), with the sun above the horizon for 8-9 hours or less.

Since it doesn't climb very high and seems to move slowly, the Solstice sun appears to stand still in the sky. "Solstice" is derived from two Latin words: *sol,* meaning sun, and *sistere,* to cause to stand still, i.e., "sun stands still."

The diagram shows how the sun moves through the sky on the Winter Solstice, from the vantage point of people living in the United States.

The Summer Solstice usually occurs on June 21 or 22 and marks the beginning of summer: the longest day and shortest night of the year.

6. Make your own Sundial

By Oberon (grey)

Long before clocks were invented, people marked the passage of time by the movements of the heavenly bodies—sun, moon, and stars. At night, the turning of the starry sky around the fixed pole star gave a very precise measurement. And during the day, time could be noted by the movement of a shadow cast by the sun. The first sundial was invented when someone stood a stick in the ground, and marked regular divisions of its moving shadow. Over the millennia, countless ingenious varieties of sundials have been designed, and they have remained a popular artform even in these days of digital watches.

In the back of this book you will find a cutout pocket sundial that you can make. This is the common variety with the shadow-casting *gnomen* (the wedge-shaped piece).

Copy the page onto card stock at 121%. Cut it out and assemble according to the instructions. To use it, align so that the "South" and "North" marks line up with the true north-south meridian line of wherever you live. Use a compass to determine this line, and check it by sighting with the North Star at night. Read the time by the position of the shadow or the sunlit strip, and be sure to correct for Daylight Savings!

7. The Moon

By Moonwriter (indigo)

O, swear not by the moon, the fickle moon,
The inconstant moon,
* that monthly changes in her circle orb,*
* Lest that thy love prove likewise variable.*
—Shakespeare, *Romeo and Juliet,* Act 2, scene I

The moon is one of the easiest objects to watch in the night sky, and also one of the most interesting. Geologically, the moon is a dead, inactive world. It makes no light of its own; the moonlight that we see when we gaze at the moon is actually light being reflected by the sun.

The moon orbits the Earth once in approximately every 28 days as it moves through a series of phases. There are eight names for the **phases of the moon,** described in terms of *"waxing"* (growing) and *"waning"* (shrinking):

New moon: This is when the moon is dark, and not visible in the night sky.

Waxing crescent: The first appearance of the growing crescent; ¼ of the moon is lit.

First quarter (or waxing half): ½ of the moon is lit.

Waxing gibbous: The moon approaches being full; ¾ of the moon is lit.

Full moon: The round, bright moon is fully lit.

Waning gibbous: The moon begins to darken; ¾ of the moon is still lit.

Third quarter (or waning half): ½ of the moon is lit.

Waning crescent: Only a crescent is left: ¼ of the moon remains lit.

New moon: Back to the completely dark moon.

The different moon phases always rise and set at about the same times:

New moon	Rises at 6 AM	Sets at 6 PM
Waxing crescent	Rises at 9 AM	Sets at 9 PM
First quarter	Rises at noon	Sets at midnight
Waxing gibbous	Rises at 3 PM	Sets at 3 AM
Full moon	Rises at 6 PM	Sets at 6 AM
Waning gibbous	Rises at 9 PM	Sets at 9 AM
Third quarter	Rises at midnight	Sets at noon
Waning crescent	Rises at 3 AM	Sets at 3 PM

Do you see the pattern? Each phase rises and sets 3 hours later than the one before it (6 PM, 9 PM, midnight, etc.).

Can you see that the moon always rises and sets in a 12-hour cycle (rising at 6 and setting at 6, etc.)?

Once you understand how the phases work, and you memorize at least one moon rise/set time, you can work out the others in your head. The easiest rise/set to memorize is probably the full moon, because it's the one that rises around sunset, is visible through the night, and sets around sunrise.

Magickal Associations

In magickal terms, the different phases of the moon have their own associations:

Waxing: growth, new beginnings. This is an ideal time to start new projects and work with new ideas.

Full moon: A time of greatest power, useful for completion and fruition and the realization of plans and desires.

Waning: A time for winding down, studying, meditating, and making plans.

Dark (new) moon: The best time for banishing work, dealing with psychic attacks, understanding angers and passions, and bringing justice to bear.

Since we sleep at night—the time when the moon is most often seen—many believe that the moon rules the world of dreams.

During a full moon, many wizards leave a chalice of water out all night to charge it with the moon's energy.

8. The Stars
By Moonwriter (indigo)

When you consider that there are billions of galaxies in the known Universe, and that each galaxy contains billions of stars, the number of stars in the Universe becomes incomprehensible.

The unaided human eye can potentially see 6,000 stars in the night sky. However since half of those are below the horizon at any time, we can actually only see about 3,000 of the estimated 100 billion stars in the Milky Way galaxy.

The stars in Earth's sky are further grouped into 88 different constellations. Each constellation is a patch of "sky" that includes specific stars and groups of stars.

The constellation of *Ursa Major* is one of the best known in the northern sky. Ursa Major is a northern circumpolar constellation, i.e., one that appears to revolve around the northern Celestial Pole and that never sets below the horizon. It is best seen during the early evening of April, when it appears large and brilliant in the night sky.

Asterisms are groupings of stars that are found within constellations. For example, the well-known asterism, "The Big Dipper," is found in *Ursa Major*.

If you want to find your way around the sky, the constellations are good starting points. The constellations available in your night sky depend on where you are in the world, the time of day and the time of year.

In the Northern Hemisphere the following are good choices:

> Winter evening or autumn morning: Orion
> Spring evening or winter morning: Big Dipper
> Summer evening or spring morning:
>   Summer Triangle
> Autumn evening or summer morning:
>   Great Square of Pegasus

Once you learn each of these, you can use them as "landmarks"—along with a star chart or planisphere— for locating other stars and/or constellations.

9. Star Charts and Planispheres

By Susan "Moonwriter" Pesznecker (indigo)

To find your way around the night sky, you will want to consult a star chart or planisphere. Astronomy magazines often include **star charts** that are valid for the current month, again showing stars down to about magnitude 4.5. These also include positions of visible planets, as well as information about comets, meteor showers, and eclipses.

The Weather Undergound site (see Resources) has good star charts for all locations. Star charts are also available in various night sky field guides.

The "Starry Night" software (see resources) can print detailed star charts for any location, time, and season.

Star charts may be somewhat confusing at first. While most star charts indicate north as "up," east is usually to the left and west to the right, a mirror image of most land-based maps.

To align a chart to the night sky, start by finding a circumpolar star as a reference. Then orient the chart so that what you see in the sky is also what you see on the chart.

Make your own Planisphere

By Oberon (grey)

A **planisphere** is a simple device that shows the bright stars and constellations and can be adjusted for location, time, and season. Most planispheres show only the brightest stars and constellations and so are good for beginners.

Go to www.asahi-net.or.jp/~zs3t-tk/plani-sphere/planisphere.htm for a wonderful model planisphere you can copy and assemble for yourself. This one has star maps for both Northern and Southern hemispheres.

To make this planisphere, copy the pages onto white card stock, enlarging to fit the paper. First, cut out and assemble the two parts of the outside horizon mask with the cut-out slots. Then cut out the circular disks with the constellations. Insert a constellation disk into the mask, and rotate it to match up the date on the disk with the time on the mask.

To use your planisphere, hold it over your head facing in the directions indicated. The constellations showing will match those in the sky, so you can learn to recognize them.

The edge of the oval star map represents the horizon all around you, as you would see if you were standing in an open field and turned around in a complete circle. The part of the map at the oval's center represents the sky overhead. By turning, you can match the direction you face with that shown on the planisphere.

> NOTE: *When you use a star guide or planisphere while you're stargazing, don't switch on a regular flashlight, as the bright light will destroy your dark-adapted eyes and make it very difficult to see the stars. Instead, cover the end of your flashlight with red cellophane secured with a rubber band to read your guide. The red light will allow you to read while maintaining your night vision.*

You may notice that stars appear to "twinkle." This is because they are very far away, and irregularities in the Earth's atmosphere make them appear to shimmer. Planets never appear to shimmer because they are much closer to us than stars.

10. The Planets

By Moonwriter (indigo)

The term "planet" originally meant "wanderer." Sky watchers long ago observed that certain points of light "wandered" (changed their position) with respect to the background stars. These turned out to be the planets, which always follow the ecliptic through the sky.

In ancient times, before the invention of the telescope and before one understood the present structure of the Solar System, there were thought to be seven such wanderers or planets: Mercury, Venus, Mars, Jupiter, Saturn, the Moon, and the Sun. This list is different in several respects from our modern list of planets:

—The Earth isn't on that list, because the Earth was originally thought to be the center of the Universe; early astronomers didn't realize that the Earth was also moving through space.

—Uranus, Neptune, and Pluto are also missing from the list. They were too small to be seen with the naked eye and weren't discovered until the invention of the telescope.

—While we know that the Moon and the Sun aren't planets, they were called planets in ancient times because they appeared to move through the skies just like the planets did.

Oberon: In the *Grimoire,* p, 265, I mentioned that Pluto's status as a true planet is debatable, and that some astronomers thought there may be another planet yet to be discovered closer to the predicted Titius-Bode distance of 77.2 AU (Astronomical Units).

On Oct. 21, 2003, a new "planet," larger than Pluto, was discovered! Designated 2003 UB313, it has been unofficially code-named "Xena" until a permanent name can be agreed upon. Regrettably, the most obvious names, which everyone wanted--*Proserpina* or *Persephone* (Roman/Greek wife of Pluto/Hades)-- had been appropriated over a century ago for asteroids and are thus unavailable.

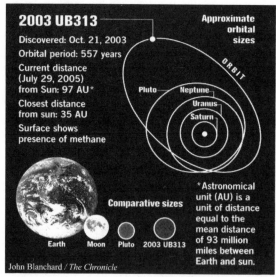

2003 UB313
Discovered: Oct. 21, 2003
Orbital period: 557 years
Current distance (July 29, 2005) from Sun: 97 AU*
Closest distance from sun: 35 AU
Surface shows presence of methane

Approximate orbital sizes

*Astronomical unit (AU) is a unit of distance equal to the mean distance of 93 million miles between Earth and sun.

Comparative sizes
Earth   Moon   Pluto   2003 UB313

John Blanchard / *The Chronicle*

The estimated diameter of the new planet is 1,777 miles. It has two moons, and it orbits the Sun in 560 Earth years. Its orbit takes it as far out as 97 AU, and as close in to the Sun as 35 AU (closer than Pluto's average disrtance), but I have not yet learned its average AU to compare with that predicted 77.2...

Finding the Planets in the Sky

Venus, Mars, Jupiter, and Saturn are easy to observe with the unaided eye. Each planet is visible within a fixed schedule that is well known to astronomers. Over the course of the year, each of these planets will be visible at least part of the time. The planets will appear like stars; it isn't possible to see any detail without a telescope.

Whenever Venus is visible, it is much brighter than anything in the sky other than the sun and moon. Mercury, Mars, Jupiter and Saturn are brighter than anything other than Venus, each other, the sun or moon,

or the two brightest stars (Sirius and Canopus).

Mars goes from bright to dim back to bright every two years. Sometimes it is almost as bright as Venus. When Mars is bright, it is bright red; when it is dim, it is a pale pink and can be difficult to see at all.

To observe Mercury, you must plan ahead. It often is most visible just before sunrise, and rarely rises high in the sky. Therefore it must be observed from a location unobstructed by trees, mountains, or other tall structures on the horizon. Given the right conditions, Mercury is very bright and easy to see with the naked eye.

Magick and the Planets

Like the stars, the known planets in our solar system have magickal correspondences:

☿ Mercury
Named for: Roman messenger god
Influences: Communication, travel, journeys
Magick: Metapsychics (thought projection, telepathy, astral travel, etc.)

♀ Venus
Named for: Roman Goddess of love and beauty
Influences: Females, reactivity and artistic energy, love, abundance
Magick: Harmony, balance, love, relationships

⊕ Earth
Named for: Teutonic Goddess Hertha
Influences: Responsibility, planning, organization
Magick: Grounding and centering, reliability, steadfastness

♂ Mars
Named for: Roman God of war
Influences: Males, strength, power, aggression, fertility
Magick: Assertiveness power, overcoming obstacles

♃ Jupiter
Named for: Roman King of the Gods
Influences: Prosperity, abundance, money, growth and expansion
Magick: Wealth, money, prosperity

♄ Saturn
Named for: Roman God of Time, Death and Harvest
Influences: Karma, education, learning, meeting obligations and responsibilities
Magick: Education, reliability, past and future lives

♅ Uranus
Named for: Roman Lord of the Sky
Influences: Unpredictable events or

happenings, rewards, discoveries
Magick: Innovation, willpower

Neptune
Named for: Roman Lord of the Oceans
Influences: Imagination idealism, the super-natural
Magick: Intuition, emotion, psychic ability

Pluto
Named for: Roman God of the Underworld
Influences: Will power, control, the human shadow, light and dark as opposites
Magick: Change, opposition, opposites of all kinds

11. Comets, Meteors, and Satellites

By Moonwriter (indigo)

Comets

Comets are dusty clumps of rock and ice, formed 4.5 billion years ago from the same material that made the planets and sun. They are celestial fossils!

Comets come in all sizes. The biggest ones are as much as 50 miles wide, with tails millions of miles long. A comet seen in 1843 was said to have a tail 500 million miles long. If this was made into a string, it could wind around the Earth more than 20,000 times!

A comet's orbit is ovoid in shape and takes it far from the sun, where the low temperature of deep space keeps it frozen. When the comet's orbit brings it closer to the sun, it heats up, thaws a little, and emits the gases and dust that reflect light and make it visible from Earth. The liberated gases create a luminous glow, and some of the gases trail behind the comet, creating the visible tail.

There are current-ly two main reservoirs for comet formation: the Kuiper belt and the Oort cloud. The Kuiper belt lies in the ecliptic plane and extends from around Pluto's orbit to very near the sun. The Oort cloud extends from the Kuiper belt to some 50,000 AU from the sun. It does not lie on the ecliptic but is a spherical presence centered on the sun. These two reservoirs contain tens of thousands of *planetesimals* 100 km or larger.

Halley's Comet

Some comets are short-period comets; that is, they return after a set period as short as three years or as long as 200 years. Comets with periods longer than 200 years are not considered to be short-period.

The best known of the short-period comets is Comet Halley, which returns every 76 years. Halley (rhymes with "alley") was named for Sir Edmond Halley, the first astronomer to say that comets were a natural part of the solar system. Halley's comet was last seen in 1986 and is due to return in 2061. How old will you be when Halley returns?

At any point in time, over a dozen comets can be seen through telescopes. Unfortunately, most of these are invisible to the naked eye. For a list of currently visible comets, see the Jet Propulsion Laboratory's Comet Page (Resources).

Comets and Magick

In the past, the appearance of a comet was called an "apparition." Comets were often said to herald the birth of kings, and sometimes were associated with storms, earthquakes, and other phenomena. In 1910, vendors sold "comet pills" for protection again the powers of Halley's Comet.

Even today, many people see comets as being signs or omens. This is particularly true of the periodic (returning) comets. People will examine what happened when the comet last appeared, and will the predict that similar events will happen again. The famous writer Mark Twain was born during a time when Halley's comet was visible, and died 75 years later when it returned.

Meteors, Meteorites, and Meteor Showers

A meteor is a piece of metal, rock, or mineral that falls from the sky. Most meteors burn up when they hit the Earth's atmosphere; if one hits the ground, it is then called a meteorite.

Most meteors are very small. More than 100 million dust-sized meteors enter Earth's atmosphere every day. Over the course of a year, some four million tons of meteoric dust falls to Earth.

Occasionally meteors are very large, even gigantic. The movie *Armageddon* tells a story of what might happen if a Texas-sized meteor were to hit the Earth. A similarly massive meteorite strike—by what is called the KT Meteor—is thought to have caused the extinction of the dinosaurs.

Meteor showers are one of the most spectacular events visible to the naked eye. A meteor shower occurs when Earth passes through an area of dust. When the dust encounters Earth's atmosphere, each piece burns up, creating the classic display of "shooting stars." Even relatively small meteors can create quite a show—while a meteor the size of a walnut can look as bright as the full moon.

Several meteor showers occur at regular times during the year. Each meteor shower has a "radiant," a point in the sky from which the meteors appear to "radiate." During a meteor shower, the number of meteors seen is higher if the radiant is high overhead.

The main annual meteor showers are described

The Great Leonid Meteor Storm of 1833. A woodcut by Adolf Vollmy based upon an original painting by Swiss artist Karl Jauslin.

below (the dates vary slightly from year to year):

Quadrantid (peaks on January 3). The radiant is near the northern border of Bootes, and there are about 40 meteors per hour. Most activity occurs during a 19 hour period.

Perseid (peaks on August 11). The most dependable of the major showers, with 50-150 meteors visible per hour in dark-sky northern hemisphere locations. Perseid meteors can be seen over a three week period. The Perseid meteors come from the rubble left behind from comet Swift-Tuttle's visits to our inner solar system. The Perseids occasionally cause problems with orbiting satellites, and at least one Perseid meteor has poked a hole in the Hubble Space telescope.

Leonid (peaks on November 17). At their best, the Leonids are 100 times as intense as any other shower, but intensity varies from year to year. Leonid activity tends to follow a 33-year cycle; most of the activity occurs during a 5 hour period. The radiant is near the "neck" of the constellation Leo.

Geminid (peaks on December 14). Geminid meteors can be seen December 7 through December 15 and are one of the best showers of the year, with an average of 50-60 meteors per hour. The radiant is north of Castor and Pollux (in Gemini).

Many people have believed meteors to be omens of death or disaster. Others saw them as a time of birth, with the shooting stars representing new souls coming down from heaven.

Artificial Satellites

There are thousands of man-made satellites in orbit around the Earth. While some are too dim to be seen with the unaided eye, others are easy to see if you know when and where to look. The Space Station and Space Shuttle can also be seen. They will look like small stars, moving slowly across the night sky in a straight line.

StarQuest

Find out about the next significant meteor shower that will be in your home viewing area, and arrange to see it. Find a place as far away from city lights as possible, with a wide clear view of the sky. The best viewing will be between the hours of midnight and dawn, when the Earth is turned towards the oncoming shower.

12. Special Effects

Aurorae

Aurorae (singular: aurora) are bright lights visible at night caused by electrons entering the earth's upper atmosphere. Aurorae in the Northern Hemisphere are called Aurorae Borealis or Northern Lights; aurorae in the Southern Hemisphere are called Aurorae Australis or Southern Lights.

Aurorae can appear in several different shapes, but the most common shapes have been described as sheets, curtains and streamers. They can appear in different colors; green is the most common, with red, violet and blue sometimes observed.

Color of stars

The color of stars is easily observed. Color is directly related to the star's temperature and age. The coldest and oldest stars are red; the hottest, youngest stars are blue-white.

In magickal terms, the color of a star also has magickal implications:

White: Cleansings, strength
Blue-white: Peace, banishing of negativity
Blue: Tranquility, healing
Yellow-white: Intelligence, mental growth
Yellow: Mental activity, wisdom
Orange: Creativity, conjury
Red: Passion, power

Note: Many of these colors are not distinguishable with the naked eye, but star color is based on a scientific taxonomy known as spectral type, and color is part of all star classification. Hence, finding the color of any known star just takes a little research.

Green Flash

The "green flash" is a rare phenomenon. Under certain conditions, just as the sun sets or rises, the sky will appear to light up green for a moment. The green flash is best observed if you have a full horizon view of the sunset or sunrise. It is most often observed from a ship at sea.

Moonbows

Just as rainbows are lit by the sun, "moonbows" are lit by the moon. Since the sun is so much brighter than the moon, rainbows are much brighter and more commonly seen than moonbows. Since moonlight is itself reflected sunlight, the colors are nearly the same. Both rainbows and moonbows are created by light that is scattered throughsmall water droplets, typically from a nearby or recent rainfall; each raindrop then acts as a miniature prism, with all the drops creating the picturesque spectrum of colors.

Cumberland Falls State Resort Park is located in the Daniel Boone National Forest. Known as the "Niagara of the South," the waterfall forms a 125-foot wide curtain that plunges 60 feet into the boulder-strewn gorge below. The mist of Cumberland Falls creates the magic of the moonbow, only visible on a clear night during a full moon.

The Night of the Moonbow is an excellent book by Thomas Tryon. Set in a boy's summer camp in the 1950s, the pivotal events take place on a dark night, as a legendary moonbow fills the sky.

A nice image of a moonbow may be seen at: http://antwrp.gsfc.nasa.gov/apod/ap010704.html.

And here is the Cumberland Falls State Resort Park Body Page: http://www. state.ky.us/agencies/parks/i75frames/cumbfal2-body.htm.

Moon Pillars
By Hannegal Skye

Some night you may see a band of faint light across the sky just north of the moon going east to west. This is called a *Moon Pillar.* It's really interesting how moon pillars form—and it's a very rare event. A moon pillar becomes visible when tiny, flat ice flakes float downward in near-windless air, with the flat faces of the ice almost perfectly parallel to the ground.

This usually happens when the moon is just rising or near setting. The part of the pillar above the moon is usually short and sort of stubby. The part of the pillar below the moon can stretch down to the horizon, usually ending in a point. It's even more rare when a lower and upper pillar form simultaneously.

Light pillars can form above and/or below both the moon and the sun. At night, when winds are extremely calm and if the air is fill of these flat ice crystals, you can see these types of light pillars above and/or below street lights and bright yard lights. There has been conjecture that the Biblical "Star of Bethlehem" was a simultaneous lower and upper moon pillar.

A similar event to moon and sun pillars are moon or sun "dogs," where the light pillars appear to emit from the sides of the sun or moon. This is caused by hexagonal ice crystals falling with a flat side parellel to the ground on a windless night, with the light refracted several times over.

If you go to Google images and search for "moon pillar" or "sun pillar," you'll find some truly amazing photographs.

13. Galaxies and Beyond
By Moonwriter (indigo)

Our solar system is part of the Milky Way galaxy, and if you can find a very dark location from which to do your viewing, you can see the Milky Way stretching across the sky like a trail of smoke. What you're seeing is actually the outer rim of the galaxy, much as if you were inside a Frisbee, looking out toward its rim.

Throughout history, aboriginal people have watched the Milky Way, incorporating itinto their mythic traditions and giving it different names. The Cherokees call it "a river in the sky," imagining that it results when Turtle (a creative figure in their tradition) swims along the river bottom, churning up sand. Other Native Americans called it a "ghost trail" or a "river of smoke." The ancient Greeks and Romans believed it to be a river or road of milk, which is how it got its present name.

The sun is one of about 100 billion stars in the Milky Way, which is one of billions of ordinary galaxies in the universe. The Milky Way is a spiral galaxy, shaped like a giant pinwheel with a chubby "bar" in the center. In official terms, it is classified as a "barred galaxy." Our solar system is about halfway out on one of the galaxy's spiral arms, about 26,000 light years from the galactic center, on a little spur off the Perseus Arm called the Orion Arm. In magickal terms, the Milky Way is a trail that connects us with the rest of the Universe.

On the next page is a little diagram of our own Milky Way galaxy, showing the positions and names of the arms.

The Milky Way itself spins around its own center, causing all the stars—including our Solar System—to orbit the center of the galaxy in the same way that the Earth orbits the sun. It takes about 266 million years for our sun to complete one galactic orbit, traveling at about 130-180 miles/second. (These measurements were completed in 1999 using the Very Long Baseline Array, a system of 10 large radio-telescope antennae placed 5,000 miles across the United States, from the U.S. Virgin Islands to Hawaii.)

The universe is composed of billions of galaxies, each containing billions of stars. Since our planet is inside the Milky Way, almost all the objects we see with the unaided eye are within our own Milky Way galaxy. Here are a couple of exceptions:

a. The most distant object easily visible to the unaided eye is M31, the great **Andromeda Galaxy** some two million light-years away. Without a telescope, the immense spiral galaxy appears as an unremarkable, faint, cloud in the constellation Andromeda.

Here is a good image of M31:
http://antwrp.gsfc.nasa.gov/apod/ap040718.html.

b. The Large and Small **Magellanic Clouds** are easy to see, but only from the Southern Hemisphere.

Here's an image of the Large Magellanic Cloud:
http://antwrp.gsfc.nasa.gov/apod/ap040902.html.

Make a model of the Milky Way Galaxy

By Oberon (grey)

In the back of this book you will find a cutout model of the Milky Way Galaxy that you can assemble. You will also need a white Ping-Pong ball. First, copy the two pages onto white card stock at a copy center, enlarging them by 121%. Use white glue to glue the wedge-shaped flaps as shown on both disks. Then position them around the Ping-Pong ball in the center opening and glue the edges together, matching the wedge tab sections with each other. The Ping-Pong ball will comprise the central bulge that in our galaxy surrounds the black hole at its center. When you also assemble the conical stand, you will be able to set up the model so it appears to be floating in space.

14. Time and the Mayans

By Oberon (grey)

The Mayan Indians of the Yucatan Peninsula were obsessed with the cycles of time. 2,300 years ago (around 355 BCE) the Pre-Mayans developed one of the most intricate calendar systems ever invented. According to their reckoning, since the beginning of time there have been six great World Ages, or *Baktuns,* of 5,125.36 years each. Here are the dates of the Baktuns of the Mayan Long Count Calendar:

Baktun	Time Period
6th Baktun	3114 BCE-2012 CE
5th Baktun	8240-3114 BCE
4th Baktun	13,365-8240 BCE
3rd Baktun	18,490-13,365 BCE
2nd Baktun	23,616-18,490 BCE
1st Baktun	28,742-23,616 BCE

Five Baktuns take 26,000 years to complete—a full precessional of the Equinoxes through all 12 Zodiacal Aeons. See pp. 56-57 in the *Grimoire,* and notice how close the 5th Baktun's starting date of 8240 BCE comes to the end of the Ice Age, the beginning of the Neolithic, and the start of the Zodiacal Aeon of Cancer. And note that the 2012 date for the end of the 6th Baktun corresponds with the beginning of the Age of Aquarius!

In 2012 the plane of our Solar System (the *ecliptic*) will line up exactly with the plane of our galaxy, the Milky Way; and on Winter Solstice of that year (Dec. 21), the Galactic Center (in Sagittarius) will rise *heliacally* (i.e. directly in line with the Sun).

With the sun positioned precisely over the center of the Milky Way, and the path of the ecliptic aligned with the galactic equator, the planets (including the Earth) would then all appear to progress against the "dark path" of dust that forms a line from Galactic Center to the North Star.

The Mayans believed that this alignment would thus open a "stargate" to the Afterworld, and all beings will transition over that path to a new phase of spiritual evolution. That's why this date marked the end of their calendar.

And many asrologers today believe this date will also mark the beginning of the Zodiacal Aeon of Aquarius.

15. Mystic Pyramids

By Oberon (grey)

Pyramids have been raised all over the world since before the dawn of history. The earliest known were built in Egypt over 4,800 years ago. They have always represented the essence of Mystery—how they were built, and why, have been questions that have engaged the wise and curious through the ages. There are many who believe in "Pyramid Power"—that the very shape of a pyramid creates a special kind of field within it that mummified the bodies of ancient Egyptian Pharoahs, and can even preserve food and sharpen razor blades in miniature models. Pyramid-shaped hats are even said to stimulate the brain of the wearer into higher consciousness!

With the "all-seeing eye of God" in its capstone, the pyramid became the mystical symbol of the Masonic fraternity as well as its offshoot, the Illuminated Seers of Bavaria. As the Founding Fathers of the American Revolution were Masons and Illuminati, they incorporated this design into the Great Seal of the United States, and so it appears on the back of the US $1 bill.

Build your own Mystic Pyramid

In the back of this book you will find a cut-out model of the Mystic Pyramid, based on the image on the Great Seal. Copy this page onto parchment card stock, and follow the directions to assemble your own miniature pyramid. First, score along the fold lines with the back edge of a table knife, then cut out and glue together as indicated using white glue.

The cutouts also include a little platform that is exactly the right level to position a small object that you may use to conduct your own experiment with "Pyramid Power." Try placing a grape on the platform with the pyramid over it. See if it turns into a mummified raisin!

But what do pyramids have to do with Cosmology?

In 1995, Egyptian engineer Robert Bauval caused a sensation by claiming in his book, *The Orion Mystery,* that "After 4,000 years, the secrets of the pyramids had been solved." Part of that solution was his observation that the three great pyramids on the Giza Plateau were aligned in a pattern that mirrored the pattern of stars in Orion's belt—the constellation associated with Osiris, Egyptian god of the Underworld. Bauval also calculated that the southern airshaft in the burial chamber of the Great Pyramid of Cheops pointed directly to the same star in Orion's belt that would correspond to that pyramid.

The last Pharoah was believed to become the god

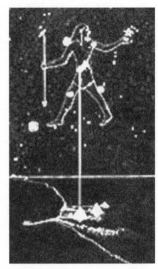

Osiris after his death. Osiris was represented in the heavens by the constellation *Sah,* which is identical to our modern Orion. Bauval concluded that—as in many cultures—the Egyptian Realm of the Dead was located in the sky, and the placement of the pyramids represented the most important stars. The Giza pyramids were a mirror image, the earthly representation of the Belt of Orion, the destination of the dead King. Thus, more than just a tomb, the Great Pyramid of Cheops was the starting point of the Pharoah's journey back to the stars from whence it was believed he came.

© John Legon 1995, 2000

16. What's Next?

By Moonwriter (indigo)

If you've caught the astronomy bug, you might want to expand your naked eye viewing with binoculars or a small telescope.

With a pair of good binoculars, one can see nebulae in our Milky Way Galaxy, as well as distant comets, faint galaxies, and details on the moon. The wide field of view of binoculars helps novice sky watchers to locate objects, particularly if a tripod device is added. With a simple telescope, you can see even more.

You might want to get a copy of "Starry Night" software (see Resources). This will allow you to know what's going on in the night sky all the time, even during inclement weather, full moons, or in the middle of a brightly-lit city.

The Grey School offers additional Cosmology classes, with new ones being uploaded all of the time. You might also want to investigate astrology, and the study of the stellar Zodiac.

"As above, so below." The stars of Orion's belt and the Pyramids of Giza; a perfect match..

Department XIII: Mathemagicks [clear]

The Radicals

There are Wizards who wander
Cartesian plains, contemplating
The progression of sunflower seeds.
This area begins with basic assumptions
And ends with irrational fringes of things
Which are not real and yet still exist.
Who can keep track of such ephemera?
Only those who can coordinate law
With lyric, derive meaning from myth,
And transpose even the root of all evil
Into elementary equations. These are
The ones who know the power of nothing,

And the fleeting functions of
    infinity.
They peer into mysteries
    integral
To life, the symbolic logic of all
    things
Named and numbered. For them, every
Argument has a point, approached
From any angle. They circle around to
Wisdom, mapping the matrix as they go,
Until the universe itself resolves into
The concise elegance of magic squares.

—Elizabeth Barrette

1. Introduction

ELCOME TO THE WORLD OF MATHE-magicks! The Pythagorean Mysteries laid the foundation for all mathematics, particularly arithmetic, geometry and music. Their motto was: "All is Number." According to Pythagoras, everything in the universe is based upon the same fundamental "blueprints" created by geometric patterns that repeat over and over in an endless dance of sound, light and color. These patterns form a matrix of grid energy derived from a central source. They create the entire natural world, and allow us to experience duality, emotions, linear time, and all the reality we apprehend In this department we include sacred geometry, numerology, and chaos theory magicks.

It is the mission of this Department to help students acquire the essential skills, both practical and theoretical, to understand and use number and form in their magickal work, and to comprehend the esoteric mathematical foundations of the universe. Relevant topics include Pythagoreanism, the archetypal numbers, numerology, gematria, sacred geometry, esoteric mathematics, the *I Ching*, chaos magick, and the esoteric *Quadrivium* (arithmetic, geometry, music, astronomy).

The color of magick associated with this department is really a non-color, reflecting the transparency with which all creation is suffused with magickal formulae—underlying everything, but invisible to all but the imagination.

2. Sacred Arithmetic

By Apollonius (White)

Modern science is based on numbers, but the ancient Pythagoreans understood that numbers also have a magickal dimension. Numbers are not just quantities or a way to measure; numbers are fundamental Cosmic Powers and Divine Ideas. Ancient Pythagoreans, Wizards and Magi explored the inner anatomy of numbers and the interconnections with them: "*Omnia vivunt, omnia inter se conexa.*" (Everything is alive, everything is interconnected.)This section is an introduction to the magickal practice of Sacred Arithmetic as taught in Pythagorean traditions. Please read the related sections in the *Grimoire for the Apprentice Wizard* (6.III). to understand this section more easily.

Figured Numbers

Pythagoreans taught the magickal *virtues* (powers) of the numbers by arranging them into specific forms, called figured numbers (we still call numbers "figures"). I have included some examples of these Pythagorean figures. The most common figures are called planar or two-dimensional: triangles, squares, rectangles, pentagons, and so forth. Pythagoreans also arrange numbers in solid or three-dimensional forms, including pyramids, squares, rectangular *parallelopipeds* (box shapes), and others. Numbers may also be arranged in linear or one-dimensional forms, which are useful, but don't reveal their inner structure.

Many ancient scholars—including Pythagoreans—used calculations to explore the mysteries of numbers. They manipulated stones or pebbles (Latin., *calculi*. Today we use written numerals and calculators to get answers more quickly, but working with actual stones is important for imprinting the wizard's mind with an intuitive understanding of the esoteric properties of numbers.

To get the full benefit of this introduction to Sacred Arithmetic, do the exercises here as suggested before trying your own explorations of the numbers. You will need a set of about 50 stones. Any small, rounded objects will do; for traditions sake, I recommend stones or pebbles.

We begin our exploration of Sacred Arithmetic with the number series: 1, 2, 3, etc. Sacred Arithmetic is different from the arithmetic you learn in school. In Pythagorean arithmetic the first number, 1, is not, strictly speaking, a number at all—it"s the "Monad" or "Unity." Monad, the Principle of All Numbers, is the Power, Potency, or Potential (Latin, *Potentia;* Greek, *Dynamis)* of all numbers, which generates them in Actuality (Latin, *Actio;* Greek, *Energeia)*. Number 1 has a special role in Pythagorean Sacred Arithmetic.

The second number, 2, also has some special properties. Pythagoras believed all the numbers have unique characters. In addition to being the ordinary number, 2 (the Dyad), also exists as a Potency, the Indefinite Dyad, the Power of separation, otherness, and multiplicity. It is the Indefinite Dyad that converts the potential of the Monad (1) into the actuality of the other numbers.

According to Pythagorean doctrine, even numbers are female and the odd numbers are male (see illustration figures 2 and 3). Unlike modern mathematicians, Pythagoreans consider the Monad (1) to be unique, neither odd nor even; they call it androgynous (male-female), because it comes before the division of the sexes by the Indefinite Dyad (2), which grow out the Monad (1). As the origin of both sexes, it has the power to change one into the other (adding one to an even number produces an odd number and vice versa).

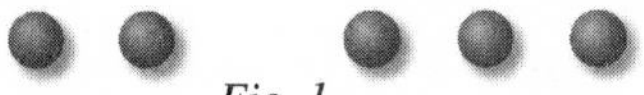

Fig. 1

Exercise:

Explore the maleness and femaleness of numbers with your stones. So long as the number is female (even), division into a multiplicity can continue, but as soon as a male (odd) number is reached, the process is halted by the unit. Male (odd) numbers are associated with the world of spirit or mind, the archetypal ideas are rigid, eternal, unchanging, determinate, and definite. Female (even) numbers are associated with the material world and matter, are infinitely divisible and ever-changing.

Notice that whenyou divide an odd number into two equal groups, you will always have a single stone left over. Divide your stones into two piles of even numbers (place the extra stones aside). Now divide each of these piles into two equal piles. Keep dividing the piles in half until you are stopped by an odd number. Practice halving with different numbers of stones to get an intuitive understanding of the process of halving and how it ends.

The Monad (1) is the principle of identity, unity, termination, finiteness, and definiteness. The Dyad (2) is the principle of otherness, multiplication, infinity,

and indefiniteness. Additional characteristics of the Monad and the Dyad are illustrated in the exercise.

Fig. 2

Triangular numbers can be arranged in an equilateral, or equal-sided,triangle (see Fig. 2). The first triangular number is 1, the second is 3, the third is 6, the fourth is 10, and so on. An important part of Pythagorean numerology is to understand the genesis of the triangular numbers and other series of figures. Monad (1), which is the first triangular number. The second triangle is the total of the first two numbers, 3 = 1 + 2. The third triangle is the total of the first three numbers, 6 = 1 + 2 + 3; the fourth triangle is 10 = 1 + 2 + 3 + 4; etc.

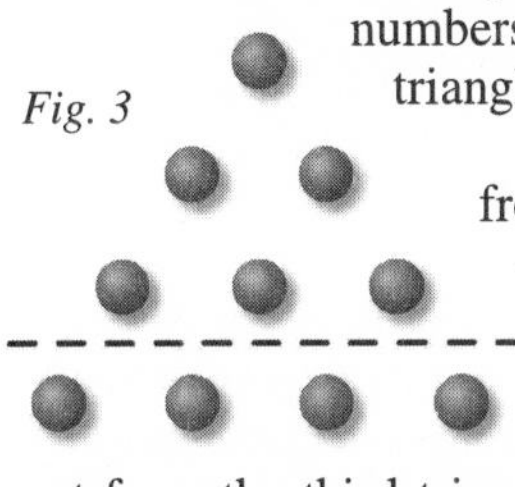

Fig. 3

Triangular numbers come from the number series 1, 2, 3, 4, by accumulation or continuous addition. You can also see how to get from each triangle to the next: to get from the third triangle to the fourth, add 4 (see Fig. 3); to get from the fourth to the fifth, add 5. In general, to get triangle $N + 1$, add the line $N + 1$ to triangle N. The line that transforms each figure into the next is called a *gnômôn* (Grk., rule), as I will discuss later.

Exercise:

Use your stones to construct the series of triangular numbers. You will quickly develop an intuitive understanding of how the triangles arise from the number series by accumulation.

Many triangular numbers are important in magickal lore. The fourth triangular number, 10, is central to Pythagorean Lore; it is called the *Tetractys.* The seventh triangular number is 28, the number of days in a lunar month (four weeks), establishing the connection between 7 and 28, revealing the esoteric structure of the lunar month. The sixth triangular number is 21, the number of cards in the Tarot's Major Arcana (excluding the Fool, a traditionally unnumbered card). The sixth triangular number also gives the number of different rolls of two six-sided dice, evidence of a connection between the tarot and ancient dice divination. The twelfth triangular number is 78, the total number of cards in a Tarot deck, (all Major and Minor Arcana cards). It is also the number of rolls of two twelve-sided "dice" found in the ancient world and some modern games. The twelve-sided dodecahedron is one of the five Platonic solids and is associated with the Quintessence or Fifth Element (*Grimoire*, 6.III.4). See my "Pythagorean Tarot"on pp. 21–6, for more on this connection.

Fig. 4

The Square numbers are those that can be arranged in a square (see Fig. 4), modern mathematicians still call them squares. The 9 is the third square
number, or the square of 3, which is the square number erected on a side of 3. (Similarly, 27 is the third
cubic number, the cube of 3, which is a cube with a
side of 3.) Notice that each square number can be generated from the previous one
by adding an L-shaped border
(also called a *gnômôn*) around
two sides. Fig. 5 shows adding a 7-stone gnômôn to the
third square to produce the
fourth square.

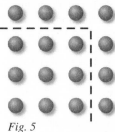

Fig. 5

Exercise:

Arrange stones in a fairly large
square (say 6 by 6). You are going to remove the *gnômonoi* (the L-shapes) until a single unit remains. First
remove the 11 stones of the *gnômôn* from the sixth
square so that the fifth square remains. Put the 11
stones of the *gnômôn* aside in their own pile on your
right. Now take a 9-stone *gnômôn* from the fifth square
so that the fourth remains. Place these 9 stones to the
left of your previous 11-stone *gnômôn*. Continue this
procedure until your square has been reduced to a single stone, and then look at the *gnômonoi* you have
removed. Do you see the pattern? It is the series of
male (odd) numbers.

The Greek word *gnômôn*, which I have translat-
ed as "rule," comes from a verb meaning "to know"
(an English word related to gnômôn), which also gives
gnômê (means of knowing, intelligence, maxim).
Gnômôn is literally "something by which one knows,"
and so it can refer to a carpenter's square (as apparent
in the gnômôn used to construct the square numbers),
a straight-edge (a ruler), the pointer of a sundial, a
code of regulation, a rule of life, or a wise interpreter
or guide. The gnômôn shows the way to reach beyond
the finite toward the infinite.

Exercise:

Can you see how the squares are generated from
the male numbers by continuous addition (accumulation)? Set out the series of male numbers (including
the Monad): 1, 3, 5, 7, 9, … as far as you can. The
unit is the first square number. Add the 3 stones to this
unit to get 4, the second square; then add the 5 stones
to get 9, the third square, and so on.

The square of a female number is female, the
square of a male is male, the square of the androgynous unity is unity. To understand intuitively, think of
a female number in linear
form; it is divisible into two
equal halves. When we
square this number, the result
will be a square divided evenly into four quarters (Fig. 6).
To understand why the square
of a male number is male,
think of a male number as a unit added to a
female number, which can be divided in half.

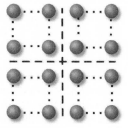

Fig. 6

Therefore, when we square a male number, we a get a
figure with four parts (Fig.
7). We have the smaller, female square (as before) surrounded by a *gnômôn* com-
prising two female lines,
but also an added unit,
which is not divisible.
Therefore, the large square
is male.

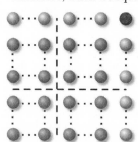

Fig. 7

Exercise:

There is an intimate re-
lation between the triangular
and square numbers. Notice
you can take any square number and separate it into two
parts, above and below the di-
agonal, which are each triangular numbers (in fact, consecutive triangular numbers). For example, Fig. 8
shows that the fourth square comprises the fourth and
third triangles (because 16 = 10 + 6). Try this several
times with your stones until you have intuitive insight
into why it must be so.

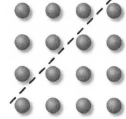

Fig. 8

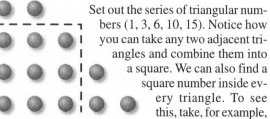

Fig. 9

Exercise:

Set out the series of triangular numbers (1, 3, 6, 10, 15). Notice how
you can take any two adjacent triangles and combine them into
a square. We can also find a
square number inside ev-
ery triangle. To see
this, take, for example,
the fifth triangle, but arrange it as a right triangle rather than an equilateral triangle (Fig. 9). Note that it
contains the third square and two copies of the second
triangle (15 = 9 + 3 + 3). Repeat this decomposition
with several other triangles until you see the pattern.

The continuous addition of the male numbers produces the squares. You may wonder what sort of numbers are produced by continuous addition of the *female* numbers. Start from 2, adding 4, the next female, produces 6; adding the following female, 6, produces 12, and so on. The generated series of numbers
is 2, 6, 12, 20, 30, 42. Can you guess their shape?

Fig. 10

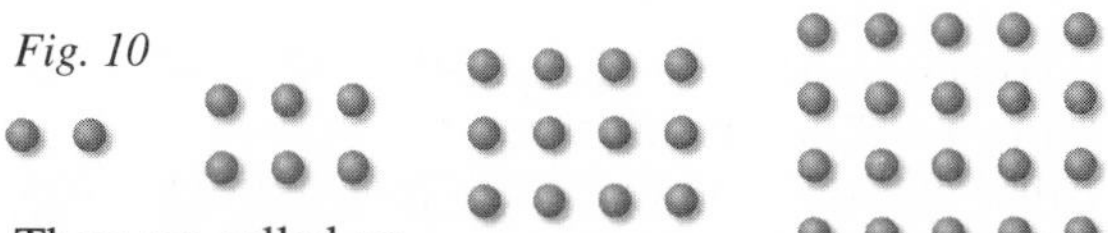

They are called *un-equilateral* (Greek, *heteromêkes*) numbers (or sometimes, less accurately, *oblong* numbers), and they can be arranged in rectangles in which one side is one unit longer than the other side. They are rectangles shaped 1´2, 2´3, 3´4, 4´5, etc. (Fig. 10) Some numbers can be arranged into several figures: for example, 6 can be triangular, unequilateral, or lineal. These are different *qualitative* aspects of the same *quantity* and have different roles in magick.

Exercise:

As you did for the square numbers, explore the genesis of the unequilateral numbers. Discover how you can add a (female) gnômôn to each unequal number to get to the next unequal number.

Notice that an unequilateral number can be divided into two copies of the same triangular number.

Compare the unequilateral rectangles to *equilateral* rectangles (squares). The equilateral numbers are associated with the eternal Archetypal Ideas, the *"Realm of Being,"* because as we proceed through the series the figures do not change shape. In contrast, the unequilateral numbers are associated with the material world of generation, development, and decay, the *"Realm of Becoming,"* because the shapes of the rectangles change as we progress through the series. The equilaterals have a constant *logos* (ratio) between their sides, the unequilaterals have ever-changing *logoi* (ratios).

All unequilateral rectangles are female, because one side is always female. This symbolizes sexual generation in the material world (considered female: Mother Earth or Nature). On the other hand, the square of a male is male and the square of a female, female. So both males and females exist in the *Realm of Being*, but as Archetypal Ideas with the same *logos*.

Pythagoras is credited with discovering the relationship between musical pitch, frequency of vibration, and the lengths of strings He discovered that the unequilateral numbers represent the musical intervals in order of decreasing consonance. Thus 2:1 is the ratio of the octave (e.g., C-c), the most consonant interval (unison is not an interval at all). The next unequilateral is 3:2, a musical fifth (C-G); following it are 4:3, a fourth (C-F); 5:4, a major third (C-E); 6:5, a minor third (C-E♭). A whole tone or major second is given by 9:8 (C-D) or 10:9 (D-E), since in Pythagorean tuning the whole tones are not all the same size; the minor second E-F is 16:15. Pythagoras noted these laws of harmony apply not just to music, but to the music of the spheres, the cosmic harmony by which the Universe operates and which is fundamental to magick.

Means

A central concept in the Pythagorean Tradition, as in many others, is the Mean or Median (Grk. *meson* or *mesotês*): that which conjoins and transcends the opposites.

The Mean is applied in all areas of philosophy, including ethics (the "Golden Mean"), medicine (balancing the temperaments or humours), and art, but also in alchemy and magick. Means are important as the links connecting the planes of reality and for establishing magickal sympathies and correspondences. We can learn about Means from Pythagorean numerology. A Mean may be defined as a relation between three numbers such that the middle one (the Mean) joins the other two (the Extremes) in such a way that the Mean has a similar relation to each of the Extremes (it is equally related to each of them). Pythagoreans distinguish twelve numerical Means.

The simplest Mean is the *arithmetic*, in which the mean is equidistant from each of the extremes. For example, the arithmetic mean of 3 and 7 is 5, because 5 is equidistant between 3 and 7. Notice that there is an arithmetic mean between two numbers only if they differ by an even (female) amount, because otherwise, the mean cannot have the same difference from the two extremes. (In Sacred Arithmetic we do not use fractions, although we do use ratios; see below.) There is an arithmetic mean between 3 and 7 (which differ by 4), but not between 2 and 7 (which differ by 5). To compute the arithmetic mean, set out the two extremes as figures. Move stones from the greater extreme to the lesser until the two figures are the same size; when you are done, both piles are equal to the arithmetic mean. In this way you can see that the arithmetic mean represents balance and equality. Also, during the process of moving the stones you will see a series of pairs of numbers that have the same arithmetic mean.

Exercise:

Compute the arithmetic mean of several pairs of numbers by using this procedure. Observe what happens if the extremes differ by an odd number.

The most important mean, the *geometric mean*, which Plato calls "the most perfect bond," has the same ratio to each of the extremes. For example, 9:6:4 is a geometric progression because the ratio of 9 to 6 is the same as the ratio of 6 to 4 (in both cases the ratio is 3:2).

It's easy to see that there is a geometric mean between any two perfect squares. For example, 9 = 3´3 and 4 = 2´2 have the mean 6 = 3´2. In esoteric terms, one extreme has two parts S (where S is any occult quality) and the other has two parts T (some other occult quality).

Exercise:

Compute the geometric mean between several pairs of perfect squares, so that you understand it intuitively. Simply take the length from one square and the width from the other, and the resulting rectangle will be the geometric mean.

You will see that a geometric mean exists between two extremes only if they are *the same multiples of different squares*. Then the mean is the same multiple of the products of the sides of the two squares. For example, 30 is the geometric mean between 45 and 20. This is because the extremes are $45 = 5´3´3$ and $20 = 5´2´2$ (the same multiple of different squares). Hence, the mean is $5´3´2 = 30$. More generally, if $A = CSS$ and $B = CTT$, then $M = CST$. (Note that either S or T could be 1!) As before, the esoteric interpretation is that hidden in A are the two parts of S and in B are the two parts of T, and therefore the mean replaces one part of S with one part of T.

A geometric mean is connected with its extremes by a combined process of multiplication and division (sometimes multiplying or dividing by 1). For example, consider the geometric progression 9:6:4. In going from 9 to 6, you multiply by 2 and divide by 3, as you do in going from 6 to 4. In general, consider the geometric progression $CSS : CST : CTT$. In going from CST to CTT via the mean you multiply by T and divide by S; in going from CTT to CSS you multiply by S and divide by T.

Exercise:

Consider 9:6:4. Start with the square number 9. Multiply it by 2 by making another copy of it (so you have 18 stones). Now divide this figure in thirds so that you have 3 figures of 6 stones, which is the mean. Now do the same multiplication and division: Duplicate the 6 so that you have 12 stones, then take a third, which is 4 stones. This shows the ratio 9:6 equals the ratio 6:4.

Exercise:

The arithmetic and geometric means reveal another important relationship between the unequilateral and equilateral (square) numbers. Set out in order the series of square and unequilateral numbers. So you will have the figures 1, 2, 4, 6, 9, 12, 16, ... Notice that the *arithmetic* mean between two consecutive *unequilateral* numbers is the *square* between them; for example, the arithmetic mean of 6 and 12 is 9. Conversely, the *geometric* mean between two consecutive *square* numbers is the *unequilateral* number between them; for example, the geometric mean of 4 and 9 is 6. Explore the sequence of figures until you have an intuitive grasp of how they are interconnected. This is easy to understand: between two consecutive squares, SS and $(S + 1)(S + 1)$ the geometric mean is $S(S + 1)$. Likewise, between the consecutive unequilateral numbers $(S – 1)S$ and $S(S + 1)$ is the arithmetic mean SS.

Thus the equilateral and unequilateral numbers form a chain interlinked by arithmetic and geometric means by which the Monad progresses toward Infinity. The process in continuous and connected by means of the shared factors between adjacent terms: $1´1, 1´2, 2´2, 2´3, 3´3, 3´4, 4´4$. Notice the interweaving of male and female powers. Observe also how alternating equilateral and unequilateral numbers repeat their genders in a cycle of 4.

The Tetractys

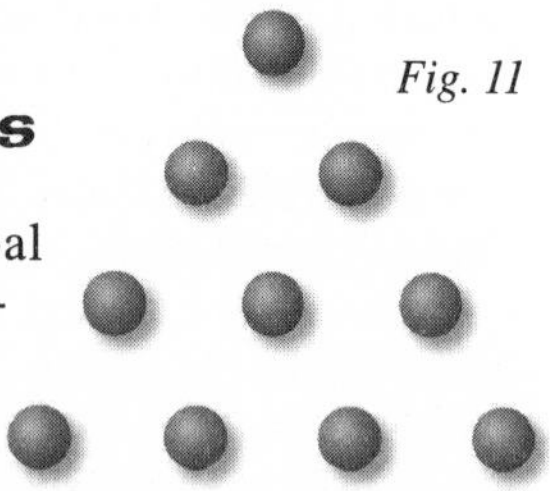

Fig. 11

Among all the archetypal numbers, the most important is the Decad (10), the fourth triangular number (Fig. 11), which they call the *Holy Tetractys* (teh-TRAFig. 1K-tiss). Pythagoras is said to have discovered it. There is not space here to reveal all the esoteric lore that is hidden in this symbol, so I must limit myself to a few of the secrets explained by Sacred Arithmetic.

Pythagoreans say that the Decad encompasses the entire universe, for after 10 the numbers return to their beginning; that is, all the greater numbers are images of the Decad in a plane of greater manifestation. Therefore, all that is, is encompassed in the first 10 numbers. However, the Tetractys shows that the Decad is generated by accumulation from the first four numbers, the Monad, Dyad, Triad, and Tetrad. These represent the most fundamental powers in the universe, which create and govern all the others. I'll explain briefly each of the *levels* or *planes* of the Tetractys.

The Monad at the apex of the Tetractys represents the Ineffable One, which unifies all things and transcends all opposites: male and female, mind and matter, eternal and mortal, being and non-being, and so on. The Monad corresponds to the Tao (*Grimoire*, pp. 132–3, 270).

The second level is the Dyad, which represents Duality, and the distinction of essences that comes at the level of the eternal Archetypal Ideas; it is the realm of Being, the level of the World Mind. The second level is formed when the One proceeds outward from itself, extending in a *line*, to generate the Other. The Dyad corresponds to the Yin-Yang pair and all the opposites (*Grimoire*, pp. 133–4, 270).

The third level is the Triad, representing Conjunction, a joining of the opposites, and all kinds of mediation (*Grimoire*, pp. 134–5, 270). It corresponds to the World Soul, which joins the World Mind to the World Body (material reality) by bringing the eternal Archetypal Ideas into manifestation in space and time in the material world. The three units of the Triad define a plane, which is extended in space but has no thickness. The third level represents existence that has extension, that is, it occupies space, but it has no material substance. It is the level of incorporeal (but time-bound) entities, such as souls and spirits.

The fourth level is the Tetrad, representing the stable Equilibrium of opposed powers as manifest in the four elements of material reality and their opposed qualities: warm/cool, moist/dry (see *Grimoire*, pp. 136, 245, 270). The Tetrad corresponds to the World Body, vitalized and governed by the World Mind through the mediation of the World Soul. In the fourth level, the plane extends into the third dimension to form three-dimensional, solid objects, the plane of material reality. In it, the eternal dance of the opposites leads to the creation, growth, and decay of physical objects in time.

You can use Sacred Arithmetic to deepen your understanding of the Tetractys by beginning with a figure called the *Lambdoma* or Platonic Lambda, which is named for its similarity to the Greek letter lambda L (Fig. 12). The Lambdoma is related to the Tetractys. Plato said that the numbers of the Lambdoma (1, 2, 3, 4, 8, 9, 27) define the boundaries of all numbers. Therefore we need to fill in the missing units in each level in order to bind the Tetractys into a whole, which is accomplished by using geometric means to transcend the gaps.

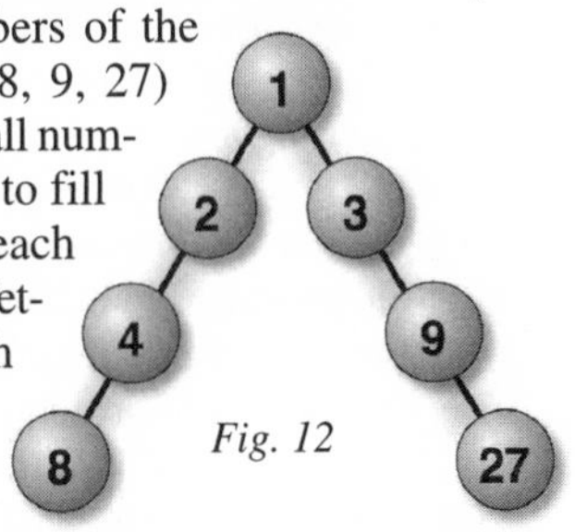

Fig. 12

In this figure we have two axes emanating from the (androgynous) Monad. On the left is the Axis of the Different, generated by the powers of the (female) Dyad: 2, 4, 8, and on the right is the Axis of the Same, generated by the powers of the (male) Triad: 3, 9, 27. On the first level we have the unit; on the second, linear figures (2, 3); on the third, planar squares (4, 9); and on the fourth, solid cubes (8, 27). The left axis, generated from the primary female number (2), is the axis of material manifestation, for all of these numbers are pure powers of the Dyad of separation, creation, and multiplicity. It is the downward path of *evolution* from the One through generation into multiplicity and physical existence. The right axis, generated from the primary male number (3), is the axis of the development of conscious, for all these numbers are pure powers of the Triad of union, mind, and spirit. It is the upward path of *involution* from fragmentation and separation, through integration, back to union with the One.

The first two levels are already complete (Monad and Dyad); there is no geometric mean between the prime powers 2 and 3. The third level is bounded by the square planar numbers 4 and 9; 6 is their geometric mean. Therefore 6 binds, unifies, and completes the Triad of the third level; there must be three

Fig. 13

units on this level (Fig. 13), that is, three parts on the level of soul. The fourth level is bounded by the cubic solid numbers 8 and 27. Euclid has shown that two geometric means are required to unite two cubes. These means are 12 and 18, and so the numbers 8:12:18:27 form a geometric progression, because the ratios 8:12, 12:18, and 18:27 are all equal (2:3). This progression represents a gradual transition from the purely fixed $(2´2´2)$, through the intermediates $(2´2´3, 2´3´3)$, to the purely volatile $(3´3´3)$. According to Plato, this is why there must be two elements, Water and Air, intermediate between the extreme elements Earth and Fire, the foundations of material reality (because they are the essence of tangibility and visibility, respectively). Therefore in the three lower levels we proceed to the right by removing a material factor (2) and including a spiritual factor (3).

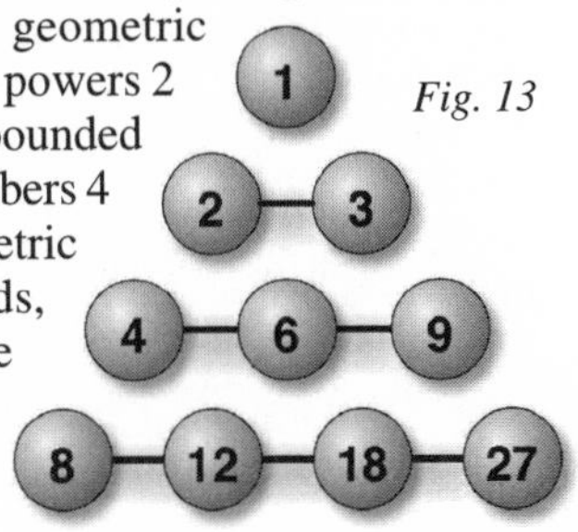

The geometric means bind the third and fourth levels each into a unity, but they also bind the separate levels to each other. Notice that the geometric progressions 1:2:4:8 and 1:3:9:27 unite the boundaries of the Tetractys, and the progressions 2:6:18 and 3:6:12 bind the interior parts.

The entire Tetractys is bound into a whole, as shown in the Alchemical Tetractys (Fig. 14). This symbol is much richer in meaning than I can explain here, but you can explore it on your own by referring to the *Grimoire for the Apprentice Wizard* (p. 245) and my "Pythagorean Tarot" (406–11, 433–8; see References).

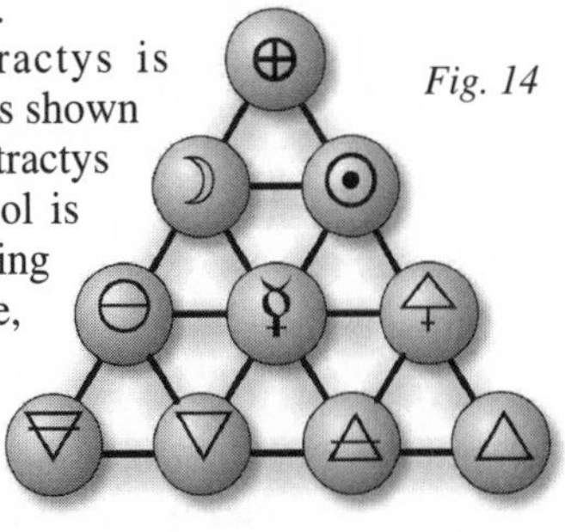

Fig. 14

At the bottom are the Four Elements, from Earth, which is absolutely dense, to relatively dense Water, to relatively volatile Air, to absolutely volatile Fire. On the third level, we have the Tria Prima, the Three Principles of alchemy: Salt, Mercury, Sulphur. On the second level are Luna and Sol (Moon and Sun), the Two Seeds, the female and male principles in the universe. On the first level is the One Fruit, the Philosopher's Stone, which transcends and unifies the opposites. If you use Sacred Arithmetic to explore the relations, horizontal and diagonal, within the Tetractys, you will learn much about these fundamental magickal principles.

4. History of the Number 13
By Moonwriter (indigo)

Have you ever notice how many people are nervous around the number 13? The number has become the focus of so much superstition, that even today, 80% of hotels and tall buildings don't have a 13th floor, instead going directly from 12 to 14, or calling the missing 13th floor something like "12a." Many people avoid traveling or signing legal documents on the 13th. Others refuse to draw a number 13, or to have the 13th place in line. Airports rarely have a 13th gate, while hospitals and hotels regularly skip over room number 13.

What might be at the root of these fears?

13: The bad news

Many people date the fear of 13 to Norse mythology. Loki, one of the most evil of the Norse pantheon, showed up un-invited for a party at Valhalla, the banquet hall of the gods. A party of 12 guests was underway—Loki became the 13th, and ended up causing the death of Balder, the god of light, joy, and reconciliation.

In ancient Rome, witches were reported to gather in groups of 12, with the 13th participant believed to be the Devil.

Christians believe that Friday is unlucky because it was the day of Jesus' crucifixion. Since there were 13 people present at the Last Supper, the number 13—particularly when it fell on a Friday—was considered very unlucky. Also, if both Judas and Matthias are counted, there were thirteen apostles present at the Last Supper.

Superstition against the number 13 grew during the Middle Ages. On Friday, October 13, 1307, King Philip IV of France ordered the arrests of Jacques de Molay, Grand Master of the Knights Templar, and sixty of his senior knights, while also arresting thousands of those loyal to the Templar's cause. Since the Templars had pledged their lives to a holy cause—guarding the location and lore of the Holy Grail—this episode only added to fears of the number 13.

In the 18th century, the ship *HMS Friday* was launched on Friday the 13th. It disappeared soon after and was never heard from again. There are few people more superstitious than those who make their living on or around the sea, and since that episode, ships are almost never launched on either a Friday or on a 13th day.

Interestingly, the 13th falls on a Friday more often than any other day.

It is considered unlucky to have 13 people share a meal, or even a gathering. In renaissance France, socialites known as the *quatorziens* (literally, "fourteeners") made themselves available as 14th guests, to fill out a dinner party and keep it from being limited to an unlucky total of 13 guests.

The number 13 may suffer because of its position following 12. Many numerologists consider 12 to be a "complete" number and one that is nearly perfect and signifies harmony. There are 12 months in a year, 12 signs of the zodiac, 12 gods of Olympus, 12 labors of

Hercules, 12 tribes of Israel, and 12 apostles of Jesus.

13, in contrast, is the number of transgression. In exceeding 12 by 1, 13's association with bad luck may have to do with its thwarting of the sense of completeness, and its creation of imbalance.

13: The good news

Today, many people—especially magickal folk—are re-embracing the number 13. This is particularly true of modern Pagans and Wiccans, who have also publicly reembraced such negatively-perceived symbols as black cats, brooms, and the dark of night.

13 is considered by many—especially Gardnerian Wiccans—to be the ideal size of a coven.

In numerological terms, 13 equates to 1+3, which equals the base number of 4. Four is seen as a highly sacred number to magickal folk, representing the four cardinal directions, four elements, four seasons, four winds, the year's four divisions (2 equinoxes and 2 solstices), etc.

For Jews, 13 is the age of maturity, and the time of Bar or Bat Mitzvah (for boys and girls, respectively). 13 is also the number of the tribes: 11 are the sons of Jacob and 2 more are named after sons of Joseph. 13 is the number of principles of Jewish faith according to Maimonides, and in Jewish tradition, God has 13 attributes of mercy.

In the Sikh religion, the number 13 is considered a special number and is linked to the meaning, "belonging to God."

For some Chinese people, 13 is regarded as a lucky number because it sounds similar to a word which means "must be alive."

In the Tarot's major arcana, the 13th card is "Death." However this is usually interpreted as representing regeneration, rebirth, renewal, or transformation.

And finally, Mathemagicks just happens to be the 13th Department of the Grey School, and the 13th chapter of this book!

5. Moebius Strips
By Moonwriter (indigo)

The Moebius strip is a one-sided surface. It was long thought to have been discovered by A.F. Moebius, and it still bears his name. But recent evidence suggests that the strip was actually discovered two months earlier by German mathematician J. B. Listing.

To understand a Moebius strip, it's more fun to actually *do* it than to read about it!

You will need:

    Strips of white paper- 1in. wide by 24 in. long
    Transparent tape
    Scissors
    A felt marker
    Crayons

Experiment 1: No twists

A. Take one strip of paper. Color one side red (or use the color of your choice). Tape the ends together, forming a circular loop. Now, cut down the middle of the loop, cutting all the way around until you are left with two separate loops. Examine each one. If you cut down the middle, they should be nearly identical, and should each have two obvious sides: one red, one white.

B. Mark an 'x' on the colored side of the strip. Starting at the 'x,' use your finger to follow the strip all the way around its "top" side. What happens to the color under your finger? You will find that your finger traces the colored side all the way back around to the 'x.'

C. Cut the 2 strips apart by cutting open the taped sections. Stretch the 2 strips out and they will each measure 24 inches.

No problem yet, right? Everything's behaving as you figured it would.
　　Just wait….

Experiment 2: Half-Twist

A. Take a new strip of paper. Color one side red (or use the color of your choice). Give the strip a one-half twist; if both hands are holding an end of the strip, the white side will be facing up at one end and the red side now facing up at the other end. Tape the ends together as you did for Experiment #1. Now, cut down the middle of the loop, cutting all the way around until you are left with…what?

B. Mark an 'x' on the colored side. Starting at the 'x,' use your finger to follow the strip all the way around its "top" side. What happens to the color under your finger? At first, your finger traces the strip's colored side, but then suddenly, it changes to white, then to colored, and then to white again before your finger finally comes back to its 'x' starting point. But how can that be? If the paper strip you started with had two sides, how can both colors now be on the *same* side?

The answer? You have created a Moebius strip: a 1-sided surface.

C. Cut your 2A strip apart by cutting open the taped sections. Stretch the strip out and it will measure 24 inches.

D. Repeat Experiment 2A. This time, instead of cutting the strip down its middle, cut 1/3 of the way from the strip's right edge. Cut all the way around the loop again, until your scissors come back to where they started. Now what do you have? Wow!

E. Cut your 2D results apart by cutting open the taped sections. Measure the resulting strip(s).

Experiment 3: Full Twist

A. Take a new strip of paper. Color one side red (or use the color of your choice). Give the strip a full twist. Tape the ends together as you did for Experiment #1. Now, cut down the middle of the loop, cutting all the way around until you are left with…what?

B. Repeat Experiment 3A. This time, instead of cutting the strip down its middle, cut 1/3 of the way from the strip's right edge. Cut all the way around the loop again, until your scissors come back to where they started. Now what do you have?

C. Cut your 3B results apart by cutting open the taped sections. Measure the resulting strip(s).

Experiment 4: One and One-Half Twists

A. Take a new strip of paper. Color one side red (or use the color of your choice). Give the strip one and one-half twists. Tape the ends together as you did for Experiment #1. Now, cut down the middle of the loop, cutting all the way around until you are left with…what?

B. Repeat Experiment 4A. This time, instead of cutting the strip down its middle, cut 1/3 of the way from the strip's right edge. Cut all the way around the loop again, until your scissors come back to where they started. Now what do you have?

C. Cut your 4B results apart by cutting open the taped sections. Measure the resulting strip(s).

More Experiments!

Continue the experiments by adding an extra half twist and repeating the results.

6. The Klein Bottle
By Oberon (grey)

In 1882, Prussian mathematician Felix Klein imagined sewing two Möbius Loops together to create a single-sided bottle with no boundary. Its inside is its outside. It contains itself.

In the *Grimoire* (p. 276), I mentioned the Klein Bottle, with a photograph of one I made out of a couple of clear plastic "donut" rings, such as may be obtained as elements of infant toys.

Several people have asked for clearer images, so as to attempt to make their own. So here on the next page are some diagrams I drew many years ago, showing my "Zell Pretzel" from several different angles. See if you can make one of these!

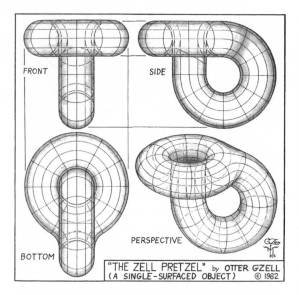

FRONT   SIDE

BOTTOM   PERSPECTIVE

"THE ZELL PRETZEL" by OTTER GZELL
(A SINGLE-SURFACED OBJECT)   © 1982

7. Sacred Geometry

By John "Apollonius" Opsopaus (White)

Sacred Geometry helps us to recognize the hidden patterns and connections in Nature and art. Sacred Geometry studies the esoteric relations among the Archetypal Forms of the World Mind as manifested in the forms and processes of Nature, and applies these relations in art, architecture, and magick. It uses many of the practices of Euclidean geometry, but is sensitive to the symbolic forms and relationships which are ignored in the geometry taught in school. Wizards imprint these patterns on their minds by practicing Sacred Geometry exercises.

Sacred Geometry deals with continuous magnitudes such as lengths, angles, areas, and volumes. Sacred Arithmetic deals with discrete whole numbers. Although modern mundane mathematics muddles these two notions, Sacred Mathematics is clear about their difference. In Sacred Geometry we measure magnitudes, but do not reduce them to numbers. In Sacred Arithmetic we consider the ratios of numbers, but don't use fractions or decimal numbers.

Tools

For these exercises, you will need unlined paper, an ordinary school compass, and a straightedge or ruler (an unmarked straightedge is preferable). Treat your Compass, Rule, and Pencil with respect, they are the magickal tools of Sacred Geometry. You will want to consecrate these tools if you continue to practice.

The Rosicrucian sage Robert Fludd (1547–1637) describes the symbolism of the Mystical Compass (Fig. 1). The hinge represents the unity of all things in the One. The fixed leg, (placed in the center of the circle), represents the Pivot, the realm of invariable Archetyp-

al Ideas. The moving leg (carrying the pencil) travels around the circumference, circumscribes the phenomena of the mundane world as they evolve from the Ideas. The curved part that connects the legs is the bond of love and justice. When we stand the Compass on the Paper it symbolizes the World Axis connecting the One to the Earthly Plane. Opening the Compass represents divine love emanating outward from the Center into the world of manifestation, the central act of creation.

Fig. 1

Empedocles (*Grimoire*, 67), an ancient Pythagorean taught that two forces govern all change in the Universe, Love and Strife, the powers of union and separation. So also, the Compass cannot create unless its legs are separated but remain united by love. The Compass is a symbol of the radiant Heavens and Celestial Realm which move in circles.

Because the drawing of a circle represents the evolution of a complete Unity from the Divine Center, Schneider recommends the use of only complete circles drawn in a single motion in the constructions of Sacred Geometry (illustrations use partial circles for clarity and space).

Circular motion is characteristic of the Heavens. Rectilinear (straight-line) motion is characteristic of the Earth and everything in the material world Your Straightedge Rule is a symbol of the fruitful Earth. Straight lines show the direction of energy and motion; draw your lines with confidence in one stroke. In the mundane world all things are mortal, with a beginning and end, like a line segment. In the Heavens change is cyclic and eternal. The circle and the line symbolize heavenly perfection and earthly limitation. The Compass and Straightedge represent the spiritual and material aspects of Nature and Life.

The ancient Greek word for "straight-edge," *Kanôn*, also refers to a Rule in general, a standard, model, a canon, or philosophical principle, etc.; the *Kanôn*, the Rule, shows us the Way. The Compass is called *Diabêtês* in Greek because it stands astride or steps across (diabainô), bridging the realms of Being and Becoming, the archetypal and material worlds.

The Compass and Rule construct formal relationships between Circular Lines (male), the Straight Lines, (female), and Points (androgynous) at the intersection of lines. These formal relationships exist only as Archetypal Ideas. To experience them, they must be manifested in material reality using a pencil and paper (ancients used Stick and Earth). The Pencil, Compass, and Rule are the Three Tools of Sacred Geometry, which correspond to the threefold Divine Emanation of the One. Paper is the Space where manifestation occurs, the alchemical Prime Matter and Matrix (Womb) of Creation. Always make your Sacred Geometry exercise an active contemplative meditation. When you draw a figure, understand it as a Magickal Act, a work of materialization, an emulation and living symbol of Divine Creation.

Finally, I recommend that you don't erase mistakes; instead, continue with the correct construction. It is crucial to understand that our creations can never match the perfection of the eternal Archetypal Forms, and it's hubris to think they can (recall the ancient Greek myth of Arachne?). In our Sacred Geometry, as in our Magick, it is important to be aware that we cannot undo what we have done, although we can act again in order to restore harmony and come closer to our goal. (See Quatrain LI in the first version of Fitzgerald's Rubáiyát of Omar Khayyám, LXXI in the fifth.)

Basic Techniques

Sacred geometry uses traditional Euclidean geometry techniques. I'll illustrate some basic procedures that you will need for exploring the Golden Mean. We will begin by constructing a square on a given line segment using paper, compass and straightedge..

Exercise 1 (Constructing a Square):

We will construct a square on a given line segment AB (Fig. 2). Begin by extending the line in both directions to at least three times its original length (think of this baseline as the Earth). Our first goal is to erect perpendicular lines at points A and B. To do this, first set your compass to radius AB. Then swing arc CFB around center A, and swing arc AGC¢ around center B. Next, adjust your compass to CB. Then swing arc DB with center C, and swing arc CD with center B. Draw a line from A through D, the point where these arcs intersect; this line is perpendicular to AB (the spiritual Compass is used to ascend from the Earth). The point F is where the perpendicular AD intersects the arc CFB. Next, use corresponding procedures to find the point G: using the same radius, swing arc AE with center C¢, and swing arc EC¢ with center A. The line BE is perpendicular to AB; note its intersection G with arc AGC¢. Draw the line FG to complete the square ABGF.

*If you had drawn lines AH and BH you would have constructed the equilateral triangle, the first planar figure born of the line.

Fig. 2

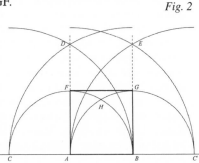

The Golden Section

The magickal implications and applications of Ratios are ignored in mundane geometry. From studying the Grimoire for the Apprentice Wizard (3.VI) you know the importance of correspondences and analogies in magick. In Sacred Geometry these relationships are expressed in means of ratios of magnitudes (ie: lengths or areas). Ratios establish correspondences, analogies and bind phenomena together and are useful in the practice of magick.

In the simplest case, two ratios may be equal. For example, let A, B, C, and D be four magnitudes. If the ratio of A to B is the same as the ratio of C to D, then we write A:B :: C:D, this is a (Discontinuous Geometric) Proportion (Grk. analogia). If we have two different circles, then the ratio of their diameters is the same as the ratio of their circumferences. If d and D are the diameters of the smaller and larger circles, respectively, and c and C are their circumferences, then d:D :: c:C. The magickal significance of Proportions is that they show a correspondence. If A:B :: C:D then the relation between A and B is parallel, or analogous, to that between C and D; the relations correspond. Similarly, the relation between A and C is parallel to that between B and D. In the Discontinuous Proportion the four terms are all distinct, and so the ratios are completely external to each other. This Proportion is especially appropriate for correspondences and analogies in the realm of physical manifestation and of distinct objects. Although the Discrete Proportion involves four magnitudes, only three are independent, because the fourth can be determined from any three.

Discontinuous Proportion establishes a relationship between four magnitudes, that is, corresponding relationships between two pairs, which may be otherwise unrelated. For magickal purposes we often want a tighter relationship, and this is established by a Geometric Mean, which creates a relationship among three magnitudes A, M, and B. In a Continuous Proportion the ratio of A to M (the Mean) is the same as the ratio of M to B, that is, A:M :: M:B, which we may write A:M:B to emphasize that this is a relation among three magnitudes. (A and B are called the Extremes relative to the Mean M).

As an example of a Geometric Mean, suppose we have two circles and that the area A of the larger is nine times the area B of the smaller. The Geometric Mean is a circle with an area M that is three times that of the small circle. You can see, we have a Continuous Proportion A:M:B because the ratios A:M and M:B are the same, that is, three to one. Although the Continuous Proportion involves three magnitudes, only two are independent, the third is determined by the other two. As with all Proportions, we have corresponding relationships A:M and M:B, but because the Mean M is common to both, they are intimately connected, not parallel.

In esoteric mathematics Geometric Means are used as the links between the Planes of Reality. They allow us to go beyond working in corresponding systems by providing a path from one system to another; it is the Proportion of magickal connection and influence. Continuous Proportions often represent the emanation of higher principles into lower ones and show their interconnection. They are especially connected with the Triadic principles that structure the higher realms and with the World Soul, which mediates between the World Mind and Nature. (See "Sacred Arithmetic Exercises" for more on esoteric use of Geometric Means and Proportions.)

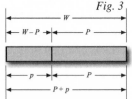

Fig. 3

The tightest sort of connection would involve only two magnitudes, but interrelated in some way by a Continuous Proportion. This is accomplished by dividing a magnitude in "mean and extreme ratio," that is, by dividing a magnitude into two parts so that the ratio of the whole to the larger part is the same as the ratio of the larger part to the smaller. In mathematical terms, we are given a magnitude W, the whole, and we want to find a part P of it so that the ratio W:P is the same as P:p, where p is the remainder, p = W–P. More briefly, we want P to be a Geometric Mean between the whole and the smaller part, W : P: W–P (Fig. 3). This is called the Golden Section (or Division) of W, and P is called the Golden Mean. This relationship involves only two magnitudes, W and P. Using different names for the same magnitudes, note W = P+p, we can write this relationship P+p : P : p. The ratio of P to p, is the same as the ratio of P+p to P, is called the Golden Ratio.

Although the Golden Ratio involves two magnitudes, only one of them is independent, because once we have chosen the whole, there is only one way to divide it in mean and extreme ratio, its Golden Section is unique. Esoterically, the Golden Section is implicit in Original Unity. It is the Duality, inherent in Unity, by which the One divides itself in the most self-harmonious way possible (the Golden Ratio (Khruseos Logos). According to Pythagorean philosophy, it shows the natural and inevitable emanation of the One into Two, which begins the division into Ideal Multiplicity. Division into the Archetypal Ideas in the World Mind, and ultimately into process, change, energy, and matter, from which arise our world. It is an ideal topic to explore through Sacred Geometry.

The Golden Ratio might be considered no more than a mathematical oddity, but its significance is demonstrated by its widespread occurrence in Nature. It is a reflection of the eternal, archetypal Forms or Ideas according to Pythagorean philosophy. Artworks making use of the Golden Ratio are considered the most beautiful since they embody these Ideal Forms. This is an enormous topic, a mere mention must suffice here;

see the books by Lawlor and Schneider (Resources and References), and others, for more information.

Exercise 2 (Golden Section):

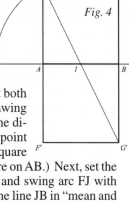

Fig. 4

Construct a square ABGF on line segment AB, as you did in Exercise 1. Construct another square ABG¢F¢ on the other side of AB (Fig. 4). If you pay attention, you will see that you can construct both squares at the same time by drawing complete circles. Next draw the diagonal line FIG¢, I being the point where it intersects AB (the square on FIG¢ is five times the square on AB.) Next, set the radius of your compass to IF and swing arc FJ with center I. The point A divides the line JB in "mean and extreme ratio," that is, it divides it according to the Golden Section. The ratio of the whole line JB to its larger part AB is the same as the ratio of the larger part AB to the smaller JA, that is, JB:AB :: AB: JA.

Exercise 3 (Golden Rectangle):

Since ancient times, the Golden Rectangle has been considered the most aesthetically pleasing rectangle, and has been used frequently in architecture, art and design.

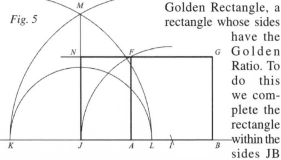

Fig. 5

We will construct a Golden Rectangle, a rectangle whose sides have the Golden Ratio. To do this we complete the rectangle within the sides JB and BG (Fig. 5.). Construct a perpendicular to JB at point J using the same procedure as before. First, pick a convenient point L between A and I. Set your compass to radius JL and swing the arc KL. Next set your compass to KL and swing arcs with centers K and L, intersecting in point M. JM is then perpendicular to JB. Extend GF until it intersects JM at point N. JBGN is your Golden Rectangle.

Because JAB is a Golden Section, JB:AB:JA. Therefore, JB:JN:JA. That is, just as the sides of the larger rectangle JBGN are in the Golden Ratio (a Golden Rectangle), the sides of the smaller rectangle JAFN are also in the Golden Ratio, it too is a Golden Rectangle. The Golden Rectangle JAFN is contained in the Golden Rectangle JBGN, and we get it by subtracting square ABGF. This process also may be turned outward, extending each Golden Rectangle in a larger one.

Exercise 4 (Gnomic Evolution):

Begin with your Golden Rectangle JBGN (Exercise 3). We will construct a square on NG (Fig. 6). First, extend the lines BG and JN upward. Set the radius of your compass to GN and swing arcs NT around center G and GU around center N. The points T and U are where these arcs intersect the upward extensions of BG and JN, respectively. Connect points T and U to complete square NGTU. You can see that BGT is divided in Golden Section, and JBTU is a larger Golden Rectangle containing the original Golden Rectangle JBGN.

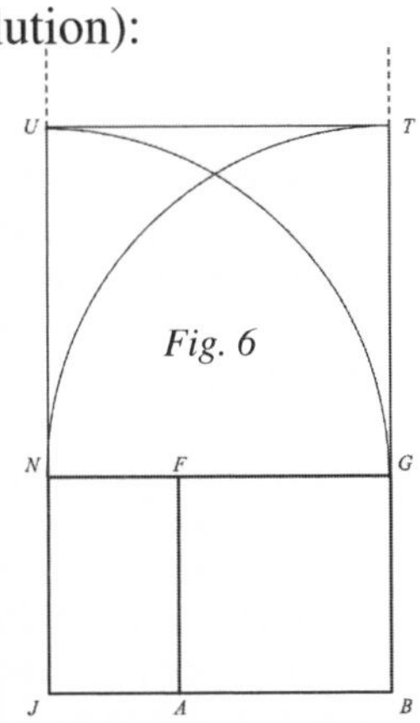

Fig. 6

This process of Gnomic Evolution can be continued forever, in each case constructing a square on the longer side of the previous Golden Rectangle in order to create a larger Golden Rectangle (Fig. 7). By drawing the quarter circles in each square we can see that this evolution defines a perfect spiral called the Golden Spiral, because it evolves from the unity of the Golden Ratio. (Latin evolvo means to roll out or unfold). It appears many places in nature, and is closely connected with the Fibonacci Numbers (*Grimoire*, 6.III.5).

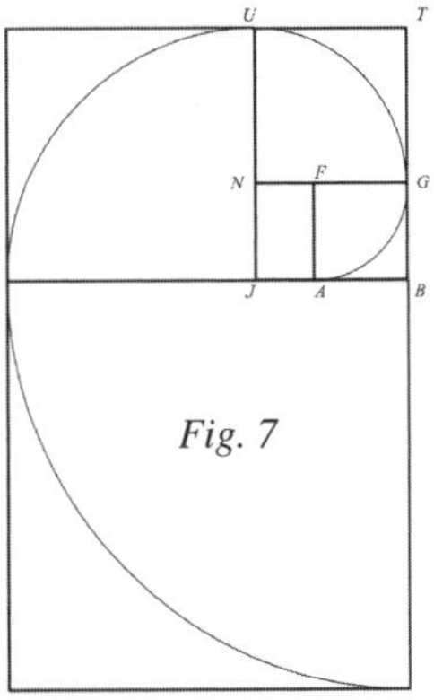

Fig. 7

This growth process is called Gnomic Evolution because each new rectangle is constructed by adding the same Gnômôn (a square, in this case) to the old rectangle (see *gnômôn* in "Sacred Arithmetic Exercises"). There is a similar process of Gnomic Involution by which the Golden Rectangles spirals inward toward the infinity within (Latin *involvo* means to roll in, wrap up, or envelop).

Exercise 5 (Gnomic Involution):

Begin with the Golden Rectangle JBGN (Exercise 3). Within the smaller Golden Rectangle JAFN construct a square as follows (Fig. 8). With your compass set to radius JA, swing arc AR with center J, and swing arc JS with center A. The points R and S are where these arcs intersect the lines JN and AF, respectively. By construction JASR is a square and it is easy to see that JRN is divided in a Golden Section and RSFN is an even smaller Golden Rectangle.

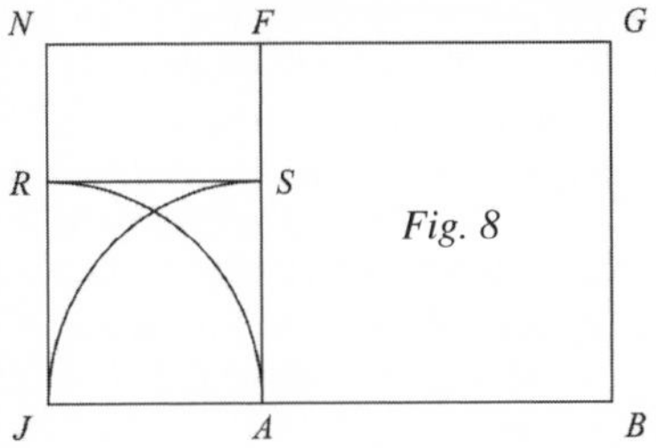

Fig. 8

This process can be continued ad infinitum, constructing ever-smaller Golden Rectangles within your first rectangle (Fig. 9); the divided Golden Rectangles are self-similar. This is the process of Gnomic Involution, by which a finite object spirals inward toward unity, but never reaches it. In the figure I have inscribed quarter circles in the squares to construct a decreasing Golden Spiral. Evolution and Involution can be combined into one universal Golden Spiral, which spins outward into space and spins inward into the depths, uniting outer and inner infinity by the one Golden Ratio.

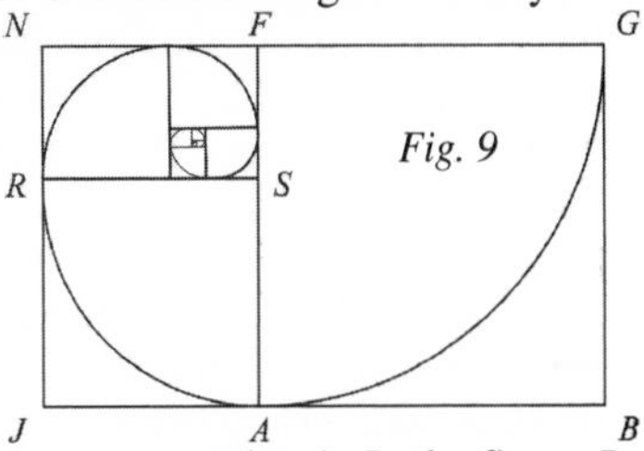

Fig. 9

The Pentagram

Exercise 6 (Pentagon):

There is a close connection between the Golden Ratio and the Pentagon (and Pentagram). Construct the Golden Section as you did in Exercise 2 (Fig 10). Set the radius of your compass to BJ and swing arc JPO around center B. With the same radius swing arc J¢P¢O around center A. The point O is where the two arcs intersect; it will be the apex of your Pentagon. Set your compass radius to AF and swing arc FPQ around center A; point P is where arc FPQ and JPO intersect. Swing arc GPQ¢ around center B to determine point P¢. Your Pentagon is completed by connecting points OPABP¢O.

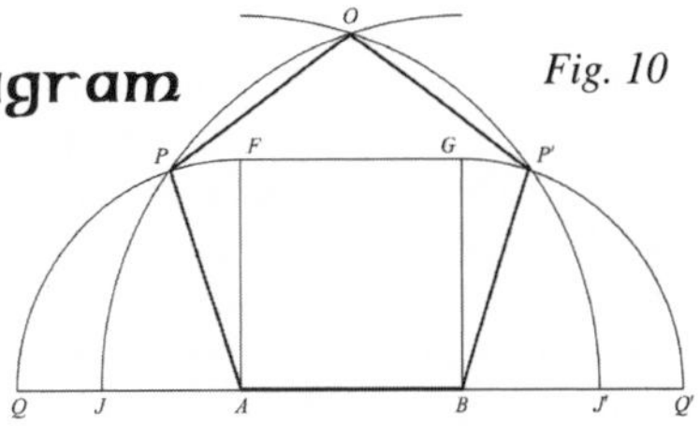

Fig. 10

Exercise 7 (Involution of Pentagram):

A Pentagram can be constructed by connecting the points OPABP¢ of the Pentagon (Fig. 11). As you can see, this Pentagram contains a smaller Pentagon in its heart, and so the gnomic involution of the Pentagram/Pentagon may be continued ad infinitum.

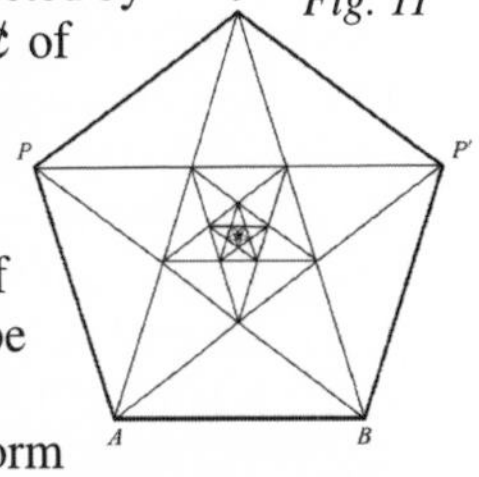

Fig. 11

It is easy to see that the form of the Pentagram arises from the Golden Ratio. From the construction of the Pentagon (Exercise 6) you know that PB and AB are in Golden Ratio. Therefore, because of the self-similarity of the Golden Section, many other lines, and parts of lines, in the Pentagram are also in Golden Ratio. A good exercise is to see how many of them you can find.

Exercise 8 (Evolution of Pentagram):

Similarly, the points OP-ABP¢ of the original Pentagon can be extended outward to form the points of a surrounding Pentagram (Fig. 12). By connecting the points of this Pentagram to form a larger, surrounding Pentagon, the gnomic evolution of the Pentagon/Pentagram may be continued ad infinitum.

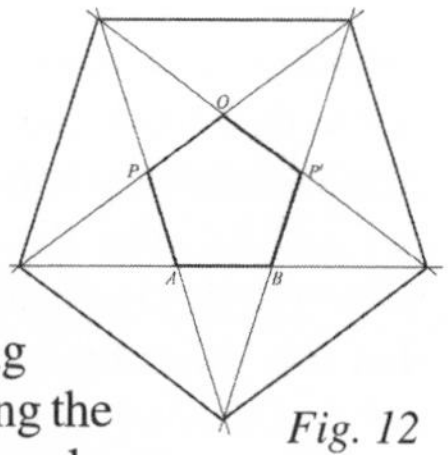

Fig. 12

Golden Mean Calipers

Many objects in Nature have forms obeying the Golden Mean, and many beautiful objects have been designed, consciously or unconsciously, in accord with it. For discovering Golden Ratios in the world around you, Michael Schneider suggests using Golden Mean Calipers, similar to those used by ancient architects and other practitioners of Sacred Geometry.

Project:

We will begin with simple calipers. Fig. 13 shows how the Pentagram determines the calipers' proportions (the Pentagram is not part of the calipers; it is just used to measure the sizes of the two "legs"). Draw a fairly large Pentagram so that you can measure Golden Sections of many sizes. The legs can be made of cardboard or other

Fig. 13

stiff material (e.g., thin wood, sheet metal). The hinge allows the legs to be spread apart or closed up to measure Golden Ratios of different sizes. You can use a nut and bolt, a wing-tip brass paper-fastener, or other hardware to hold the legs together, but it should be loose enough to allow adjustment without slipping too easily. ("Wing nuts" allow the calipers to be adjusted easily.) For accurate measurement, it is important that the ends of the legs be aligned with the points of the Pentagram and that the hinge be accurately aligned with the intersection of the Pentagram's lines. The calipers can be used to compare any two lengths to see if they are in the Golden Ratio. For example, if the short ends of the legs are adjusted to the short side of a Golden Rectangle, then the long ends will give the size of the long side of that Golden Rectangle.

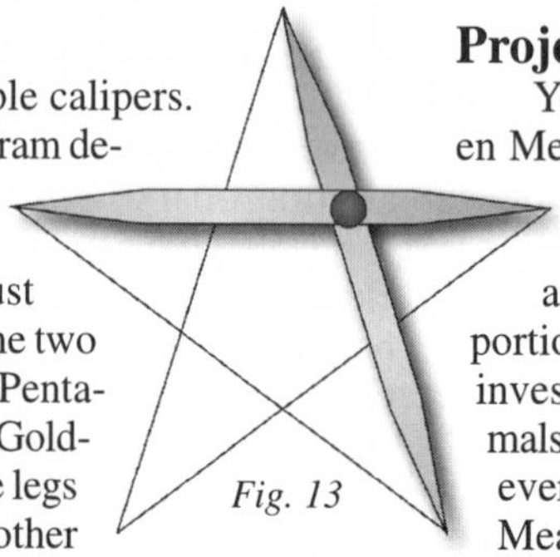

It's easy to see how the calipers work. The angle between the long ends of the legs is always equal to the angle between the short ends. The triangle formed by the long ends is similar to (the same shape as) that formed by the short ends. The ratio of the length of the long end to the length of the short end that is the Golden Ratio, is equal to the ratio of the distance between the tips of the long ends to the distance between the tips of the short ends.

Project:

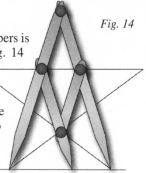

Fig. 14

The second set of calipers is a kind of pantograph. Fig. 14 shows how the Pentagram determines its proportions. The four hinges allow the legs to be spread apart or closed up to measure Golden Sections of different sizes. For accurate measurement, it is important that the lower (pointed) ends of the legs be aligned with the baseline and that the hinges be accurately aligned with the intersections of the Pentagram (the rounded ends of the legs can project outside of the Pentagram, as shown in Fig. 14). As with the simple calipers, draw a fairly large Pentagram so that you can measure Golden Sections of many sizes. For you convenience I have provided a template for the simple calipers and the pantograph.

Project:

You can use these calipers to check for the Golden Mean in many different natural and artificial objects; Schneider's book contains many suggestions. Check the proportions of your own and other people's hands and faces, check proportions in photos of famous buildings and artwork, investigate natural objects (flowers, sea shells, animals). Soon you will be discovering the Golden Mean everywhere! Record the occurrences of the Golden Mean you have found in your journal.

We have only scratched the surface of Sacred Geometry. There are many books from which you can continue your study and practice. See the **Resources and References** in the Appendix of this book.

8. Make Models of the Five Platonic Solids
By Apollonius (white)

In Pythagorean lore, the creation of the material world is understood in terms of the extension of the infinitely thin two-dimensional plane, which is therefore incorporeal, into the third dimension, giving thickness, volume, and substance. Therefore the ancient Pythagoreans studied all the possible ways that a volume could be enclosed by identical regular planar figures, that is, by flat figures with equal sides and angles all around. As you know from reading the *Grimoire for the Apprentice Wizard* (6.III.4), there are only five such *Perfect Bodies*. They are also called *Platonic Solids* because Plato explained in the *Timaeus* (53c–56c), his most Pythagorean dialogue, how these Perfect Bodies define the essence of the Five Elements (which he called the *Primary Bodies*).

The Emanation of the Primary Bodies

A point has no dimensions, but two points determine a line, which has one dimension; three points determine a plane, which has two dimensions, and the simplest and most perfect planar figure is an equilateral triangle. Four points define a volume in space, which has three dimensions, and therefore the most perfect three-dimensional figure is a Tetrahedron, composed of four equilateral triangles. Since planar figures have no thickness, they have no substance, and so they correspond to the incorporeal spiritual realm, and the first material emanation corresponds to the first Perfect Body, the **Tetrahedron.** Since the four Material Elements emanate in order, from most subtle to most gross, the Tetrahedron corresponds to the subtlest element, Fire.

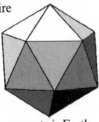

The next two elements in order of density, Air and Water, correspond to the next two Perfect Bodies made from equilateral triangles, the **Octahedron** (8 triangular faces) and **Icosahedron** (20 triangular faces). These three elements (Fire, Air, Water) are similar to each other (and different from Earth) in that they don't remain within their own bounds. Fire spreads upward, Water spreads downward, and Air spreads outward, and the mobility of these elements corresponds to the sharpness of the triangles; they are governed by the Triad (the number 3, *Grimoire*, 6.III.2).

The fourth Material Element to emanate is Earth, which is the grossest element and corresponds to the **Cube,** the faces of which are squares, not triangles. Therefore Earth is governed by the Tetrad (the number 4), which gives it stability and permanence, corresponding to the right angles of the square. This is why Earth is the Material Element that remains within its own bounds, giving shape to physical objects. However, as Plato shows us, the square can be divided into two isosceles right triangles; they have only two sides equal, so they are a step away from the unity of the equilateral triangle, which has all its sides equal. Thus Earth is the Material Element furthest removed from the Inexpressible One, from which all things emanate and which unifies everything. Also, the right angles in these isosceles triangles limit the mobility of Earth.

The fifth Perfect Body, the **Dodecahedron,** cor-

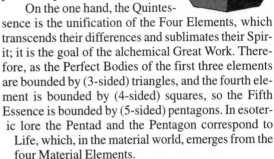

responds to *Aether*, the Fifth Element, the *Quintessence* (the Fifth Essence), a non-material element belonging both before and after the four Material Elements (which shows that this emanation is an eternal process, not one that took place at a particular time).

On the one hand, the Quintessence is the unification of the Four Elements, which transcends their differences and sublimates their Spirit; it is the goal of the alchemical Great Work. Therefore, as the Perfect Bodies of the first three elements are bounded by (3-sided) triangles, and the fourth element is bounded by (4-sided) squares, so the Fifth Essence is bounded by (5-sided) pentagons. In esoteric lore the Pentad and the Pentagon correspond to Life, which, in the material world, emerges from the four Material Elements.

Plato (*Tim.* 55c) says that the Demiurge (the Platonic creator God) used the Fifth Perfect Body "for the Whole, making a pattern of animal figures thereon." That is, the Dodecahedron comprehends all the Material Elements, and so it corresponds to the Cosmos or the Celestial Sphere. Most likely the "animal figures" are the signs of the Zodiac (from Greek *zôion* = living being), corresponding to the twelve faces of the Dodecahedron, but they also allude to the Quintessence as the element associated with life and the soul. According to Aristotle, the Material Elements move by rectilinear (straight-line) motion, which has a beginning and end, but the Celestial Bodies move by circular motion, and therefore they are eternal, as is the soul, which is of the same substance (see "Sacred Geometry Exercises" for more).

On the other hand, Aether, as the immaterial substance of the soul and the stars, is the subtlest element (*pneuma*, *prana*), and so it precedes the Material Elements, which are "crystallizations" or materializations of it: Aether, Fire, Air, Water, Earth. Therefore, of the Perfect Bodies, the Dodecahedron is nearest in shape to the Sphere, which corresponds to the Inexpressible One, and it is the Perfect Body most capable of circular motion, the motion characteristic of the soul.

According to Homer (*Iliad* XV.189), the three brothers Zeus, Poseidon, and Hades divided Their sovereignty as follows: the Heavens (Olympus) and the Earth (corresponding to the most and least subtle elements) they hold in common with all the Gods; of the three intermediate elements, Zeus rules the Air, Poseidon rules the Waters, and Hades rules Fire, for He governs the Underworld, the region of the Central Fire, according to Pythagoreans (for more on the correspondence between these Gods and the Elements, see my *Ancient Greek Esoteric Doctrine of the Elements*, cited under Websites in the Appendix under **Resources and References**).

Constructing the Platonic Solids

In the back of this book you will find templates to create models of the five Perfect Bodies. These make neat things to have on your shelves in your Sanctum Sanctorum. Copy the pages at 121% onto stiff card stock of appropriate colors: green for the Cube; blue for the Icosahedron; yellow for the Octahedron; red for the Tetrahedron; and lavender for the Dodecahedron. (You can get single sheets of colored card stock at any Copy Shop.).

Cut out the figures and bend them inward along the solid lines. The grey, curved parts are tabs to help you glue or tape the solids together; they go inside the solids. If you are using glue, you will want to assemble the solids step by step, gluing one or two tabs at a time and letting them dry before going on.

9. Sacred Geometry in Nature

By Oberon (grey)

Many natural forms and even living plants and animals are constructed according to the principles of Sacred Geometry. For example, the Tetrahedron, Cube, and Octahedron appear in the structures of various mineral crystals. Seashells form according to the principles of the Golden Spiral, often sectioned proportionately according to the Golden Phi Ratio. Many other natural forms adhere to these proportions, as in these lovely examples.

Starfish and other echinoderms have a radial symmetry based on pentagons and pentagrams. The numbers of petals on many flowers are found on the Fibonacci Sequence.

The noted 19th-century German biologist and philosopher Ernst Haeckel (1834-1919) was fascinating with the beauty and symmetry of living organisms—particularly the infinitely varied miscroscopic marine organisms called *radiolarians*. He drew and published 100 plates of exquisite renderings

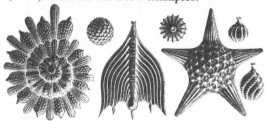

of the organisms he studied, titled *Artforms in Nature* (1904). Here are but a few examples:

10. How to measure the height of a tree or tall building

By Lady Ravenweed (indigo)

Sometimes it's necessary for a Wizard to have a good idea of how tall something really is. To measure the height of a tree or a tall building (H), go out on a fairly sunny day. You'll need to bring a long measuring tape. Find a nice straight stick of an even number of feet tall (a Wizard's Staff can make a perfect measuring stick). Stand the stick up vertically (or stick it in the ground so it's exactly an even number of feet high) and measure its shadow. Then measure the shadow of the tree or building.

You'll need these measurements:

The height of the stick (in feet) = A

The length of the stick's shadow (in feet) = B

The length of the shadow of the tree or building (in feet) = C

To get your answer, you'll have to do a small amount of basic calculation.

1. Multiply the height of the stick times the length of the tree's or building's shadow: A x C = X
2. Divide the answer by the length of the stick's shadow: X/B = H (height)

This approxi-mate height in feet of the tree or building you are measuring.

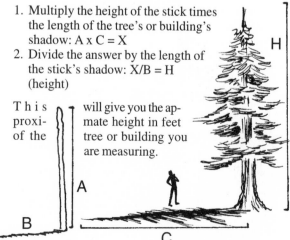

Department XIV: Ceremonial Magick [white]

The Rite Way

Broidered robes and silken stole
Veil the power with control
Pour the herbs into the bowl

Scribe the chalk upon the ground
Mark the circle three times 'round
Strike the bell, a magic sound

Earth and Water, Air and Flame
Call the Elements by name
Shape their forces in this frame

Read the book and chant the spell
Will it shrink or will it swell?
Only time and skill can tell.

—Elizabeth Barrette

1. Introduction

ELCOME TO THE WORLD OF CERE-monial Magick! Originating in the 17th and 18th Centuries within se-cret magickal orders, Ceremonial Magick is based upon both the Qabalah and the Hermetica, along with Neo-Platonism and Oriental doctrines. In its highest sense, Ceremonial Magick is a transcendental experience that takes the magician into mystical realms and into communication with the High-er Self. It awakens the magician to the Divinity within.

Our mission here is to help the student acquire the essential skills, both practical and theoretical, to conduct effective Ceremonial Magick and to achieve the personal spiritual development afforded by these magickal systems. Classes in this area depend on many of the concepts and techniques taught in other Grey School departments, and the Ceremonial Magick De-partment, in return, teaches the lore and art of the great magickal orders.

The color of magick for this department is White, used for all types of ceremonies, rites, and rituals. The color of purity, white represents friendship, the moon, Monday, infancy and the sign of Aries. Crystal white is the color of sincerity, divinity, transformation and singular focused sounds such as a gong or bell. White is also the color of the Goddess, and so is used in all forms of blessings.

2. Creating Personal Ceremony

By Donata Ahern (aqua)

Why do you use ceremony? What is your purpose? Some common reasons are to celebrate some growth, accomplishment, or positive change within yourself or your life, to celebrate a transition such as graduation, or to honor both yourself and Spirit. Through the cre-ativity and discipline of ceremony you can develop self-empowerment or self-mastery to create a richer, more meaningful life. Ultimately, ceremonies are used to cre-ate and increase positive change and energies and to balance existing energies in yourself and your envi-ronment. Always keep in mind the intention that what you do is for your Higher Good, and with the free will of all concerned.

You have three parts, or 'Selves,' within yourself. You are most aware of your logical active self, or the Conscious Self, that is in charge most of the time. Your next self is your intuitive Inner Self. You need some-thing to distract your Conscious Self so you can listen to your Inner Self. This can be done with meditation and with ceremony. Your third self is your Higher Self, which connects you to Spirit, or to the Divine, and gives you inspiration and guidance. You can only communi-cate with the Higher Self through your Inner Self. Cere-mony opens the communication between your Selves.

In ceremony you focus your energy through the strength of your *intention* and *desire* – that is, the force of your *Will* – to celebrate, to honor, and to produce positive results and changes in your life. Everything is *energy.* Everything begins with an *idea,* or in other words, *in your mind.* Your Will is your personal ener-gy focused on the outcome you desire. This is a very strong force when you learn to use it! Remember to use the power of your Will for good, with no harm to others.

Attention and intention are the main ingredi-ents needed to create a ceremony. As you drink a glass of water, you can create a ceremony by your attention and intention. You may drink in gratitude for this gift of pure water. You might say, "May I never thirst," or, "May I be purified." You might choose to pour some onto a plant in thanks for the sharing of life energy.

All ceremony depends on **intention** and **desire.** Your intention creates the meaning and symbolism, and can transform the simplest and most ordinary action into a sacred, affirming, transforming ceremony.

There are four elements commonly recognized in Western practice: **Air, Fire, Water** and **Earth.**

- **Air** in the **East** represents mind, thought, inspira-tion, beginnings, dawn, spring, planning, and youth.
- **Fire** in the **South** represents creativity, passion, and

romantic love. It is the time of noon, summer, adult-hood, working on projects and growing crops.
- **Wate**r in the **West** represents the emotions, intu-ition, sunset, autumn, maturity, harvest, and com-pletion of projects.
- **Earth** in the **North** represents the body and all material things. North is the place of abundance, material gain, money, practical matters. It is the time of winter, midnight, old age, wisdom, and rest.

When you set up your Circle, you can place objects that represent the Elements at the Quarters, or Cardi-nal directions, or you might choose to place a 'point' candle at each direction, or point of the directions. You may prefer to include both a symbol and a candle.

In the **East,** the place of Air, you couldplace a feather. East is the place to put your incense, since the smoke of the incense represents visible air. At the start of a ceremony, it's good to use incense to purify yourself and anyone present. This clears negativity in yourself and the general area and helps to set the atmosphere.

In the **South,** the place of Fire, you couldplace a candle. You can bless the circle area with it as you create, or cast, your Circle.

In the **West,** the place of Water, place a seashell and a cup or bowl with water in it. Bless yourself with the water. Purify the circle area with it as you create, or cast, your Circle.

In the **North,** the place of Earth, you might have a dish of herbs or salt. Add a sprinkle of the herbs or salt to your water before you bless yourself.

Your Inner Self responds to symbolism. This is aid in your ceremony. Symbols represent the energy or power behind their representation. For example, a candle represents the element of Fire, which includes the qualities associated with fire. The symbol speaks to your Inner Self, and in a sense, *becomes* what it represents. The symbol gives you a focus for your own energy. This increases the power of your ceremony.

If you are working to manifest something in partic-ular, you might draw or find a picture of the object and place that for focus on your altar. Remember always that the deepest and most important purpose of any magick is your personal transformation and growth.

A ceremony can be very simple, and can be some act that you normally perform during your day, but which is transformed into a ceremony by your in-tention. In this way, if you bless your food with grati-tude for its abundance, and the life of the plants and animals who contributed to your meal, you make your meal a ceremony. A ceremony can also be more com-plex. A discussion of the parts, or elements, of cere-mony follows in the lessons below.

Grounding, Centering, and Running Energy

You hear these terms often. What do they mean? And how do you do them? When you "center" your ener-gy, you are focusing it on one area of the body, usually the lower abdomen, just below the navel. When the energy is focused and collected there you will feel peaceful and at ease.

How do you do this? It's largely a process of visualization. Energy fol-lows thought and intention. When we focus our minds on our en-ergy gathering at this spot, it will.

Methods to aid you in cen-tering are meditation, visual-ization, breath work, yoga and tai chi or chi kung. People who work with healing methods, such as Reiki, will be able to center easily. Chanting is a form of focused meditation that is help-ful for many. The Tree Exercise giv-en below is also an excellent way to ground and center your energy. When you prac-tice any of these methods, you automatically clear any blockages in the even flow of energy in your physical body and in your etheric body. The etheric body is also called the "aura."

The aura is an energy field made up of your per-sonal energy vibrations, which change depending on your mood or your own energy level. When you are joyful and happy, the aura can extend several feet around you in an ovoid shape. When you are ill or depressed, it may shrink to a couple of inches around you. Your etheric body mirrors your physical body, so illness or stress will show up there before it manifests in your physical body. Energy work can help to keep you physically healthy. It also increases your sensitivity and psychic ability, which is important if you are to be successful in both your magickal and mundane efforts.

Grounding

Grounding your own energy can be compared to a lightening rod that grounds excess lightening energy so it isn't harmful. In the same way, when you work with energy and fill your body with it, you can have so much that you can feel distracted, light-headed or diz-zy, and 'spacey,' not able to focus and concentrate. Obviously this isn't what you want! Grounding your energy is a very simple process of sending any excess energy in your body down into the earth. This extra energy will aid the earth and is never harmful. The most complete method to ground your energy is to get on your hands and knees and consciously send any excess energy down into the earth. Take a few deep breaths and visualize the extra energy flowing down into the earth as you exhale. Do this a few times, until you feel the difference. You should feel peaceful and energetic, with a stable energy.

Another simple way to ground your energy, when getting down on your hands and knees isn't practical, is to point your hands down at the earth and send excess energy down as you exhale. You can also wash your hands and shake off the drops of water visualizing them as the excess energy. You can use either of these methods quickly, wherever you are. Ground whenever you feel upset or distracted. You cannot ground too much! This is always safe and beneficial.

These methods will remind you that you do in a very real way create your environment, and that you can control your responses to what is happening around you. When someone upsets you, it can tell you more about yourself than about the other person! Why does this upset you? Your meditations and energy exercises will help you to be more objective about the normal upsets and stresses in your life.

Centering

The Tree Exercise is an excellent way to fill your body with energy, and to center the energy you raised.

To do the Tree Exercise:

Breathe deeply a few times, releasing tension as you breathe out. Imagine that you are a tree. Now sink deep roots into the Earth, either from the soles of your feet if you are standing or sitting in a chair, or from the base of your spine if you are sitting down. Let your roots reach down through the Earth layer, the stone layer, down through the water level, deep into the fiery center of the earth. Breathe up the energy of the earth. Do this several times. Allow the Earth energy to rest in your heart center.

Now reach your branches up high into the sky. As you breathe in, pull down sky energy, sun, moon, and stars. Do this several times. Allow this energy to gather in your heart center. Now let the Earth and sky energy in your heart center mingle as one energy. Sense this mingled energy flowing from your heart center to all parts of your body. See it as light as it flows into all parts of your body. As the light flows through your body, your arms and legs become filled with pure light. Your torso and head become filled with pure light. All parts of your body are filled with pure light. You are a Being of Light!

Enjoy this feeling for a few moments. Let the Light flow beyond the physical boundaries of your body, to fill your aura. Feel yourself surrounded by Light. Slightly harden the edges of your aura so that it is like an eggshell to create a protective shell that keeps out negative or distracting energy. It lets in all positive harmonious energy. Negative energy will simply slip off the edge of your aura and sinks harmlessly into the Earth where it becomes mulch for the Earth. Make the intention that the Light will remain in your body and aura, with the protective shell, all day.

As a last step, fold your hands over your heart center and then open them to send your Light and energy to the entire planet. After a moment you may sense this energy returning to you as it spreads around the planet. When you do, accept it, and fold your hands over your heart center once again. To finish: consciously ground, and send any excess energy within your body and aura into the earth. If you wish, get on your hands and knees as you do this.

This may seem to be a long meditation. When you get used to it, it can take less than five minutes. You may take longer as you come to enjoy the peace and joy meditation gives you.

As you gather your energy into your heart center, you are centering, or collecting all your energy that might otherwise be scattered and distracting, into one place in your body. You may choose your heart center as the resting place for your energy, or you may prefer the area just below your navel. This is called the Dan Tien in Eastern practices such as Tai Chi, and is considered an area of great strength and stability. Experiment to find your own natural center.

Running Energy

To do this, visualize a ball of energy, like a glowing sun, centered in your heart. When you feel this strongly, visualize or imagine that the ball of light is flowing down below your feet, up your back, and down the front of your body. Do this three times. Now bring the ball of light up your right side, and down your left side three times. Gather the energy ball again in your heart. This time, let the ball of light flow down to your feet, and then up into your body, filling it, and then flowing out the top of your head like a fountain. Do this three times. Follow this with Grounding and Centering.

Ceremony during the day

NOTE: *Please feel free to adapt or create your own ceremonies. These are given as examples of ceremonies only. Start each day as a renewal or rebirth; end each day by releasing stress and tension. As you awaken, give thanks for the gift of a new day, for the gift of life.*

The bath or shower as a ritual of purification and renewal

NOTE: *This works equally well if you take your shower or bath at the start or the end of the day.*

a) **Pour water seven times** (or once) over yourself, with the intention of removing all negativity, and purifying the spirit as well as the body. You may visualize the water that runs off of you as dirty and gray, and as you continue to splash it over yourself, you sense that it becomes clearer. This symbolizes inner purification and a rebirth for the new day. Say, "I purify my body and spirit. I am reborn and renewed." Finish by blessing your feet, knees, genitals, heart center, hands, lips, eyes, and head with water for the day. Include in your self- blessing gratitude and love for your body and appreciation for the work of each part. At the end of your bath or shower, feel your body emerging from the water sparkling with energy and health. (This is adapted from a Cherokee ritual).

b) **Washing the hair:** The Yoruba people of West Africa believe that the hair is a protective shield that catches and traps any negative energy. You can wash your hair with the intention of cleansing it of any negative influence it holds and prepare it to protect you all day.

c) **Drying:** Briskly towel yourself, and say, "My body is healthy and strong."

d) **Deodorant/Cologne:** As you apply, say, "May my day be pleasant and sweet."

e) Talculm Powder: As you sprinkle it on, say, "May my day be easy and smooth."

f) **Brushing your hair:** As you brush, think of your hair as a shield to catch or deflect negative energy. Many cultures consider hair the reservoir of personal power (as with the biblical Sampson). As you brush your hair, sense the energy and power flowing through it.

g) **Face, Teeth, and Hands:** As you brush your teeth or wash your hands and face throughout the day, have a similar intention of purification and protection. You can also shake your hands briskly to shake off any stress.

Morning/Evening Ceremony or Meditation

Have a special place, permanent if possible, for ceremony. This may be a mantle, a table, or a shelf. Place articles of meaning to yourself in this special place. You may choose to have representations of the four Elements. You may create a kinship altar, with something to represent family members, friends, and your beloved dead. Include statues or pictures, if you wish, of spiritual meaning to you. Your sacred space may be as elaborate or as simple as you choose. For example, a simple wheel may be set up with five stones at the cardinal points and one in the center. This can represent the universe, with yourself at the center. Flowers or plants add the energy of life and beauty. Crystals enhance the energy, and are beautiful. Your altar may change with the seasons or with your purpose for ceremony.

Do your best to allow 5-10 minutes each morning and evening to be in sacred space for meditation, ceremony, or a combination. This is a perfect time to ground and run energy. The Tree Exercise is excellent as a morning practice to create a protective and energized aura shield of protection for the day, and energize the chakras within the body. You may choose to direct light into each of your chakras along the spine, to energize and clear them. It will happen anyway but consciously directing light to them will increase it for you. In the same way, you may choose to send light to any part of your body you feel may need it, such as your nervous system, lungs, liver, pancreas, etc.

Sacred Space at School or Work

You spend many of your waking hours at school or work, and it is helpful to establish your own sacred space there. Set up a focus. This may be one stone or a dish of stones, a plant or crystals that sit on your desk. If you don't have a permanent desk, you can carry an object that is important and meaningful to you in your pocket. If you have more than one important object, you can create a Mojo bag, or small Mesa. Mojo and Mesa are terms for a portable altar you can carry with you. Use a small leather pouch or coin purse as your Mojo or Mesa. It's your intent that makes any space sacred. If there is no way to do anything that's obvious, your own *intention* will suffice. A simple thing to do, which increases your own awareness, is to just turn around sunwise at your desk , and affirm to yourself that you are creating sacred space that will surround you all day. You will find that this simple action will make a difference in your day. During the day wash your hands frequently with the intention that you are clearing and purifying yourself on all levels, not just the physical. If you feel stress, ground and center.

Cycles of the Day and the Month

1) Cycle of the Day:

You get up in the morning, work until you eat at noon, rest in the afternoon, and go to bed in the evening. These are four natural times of the day that you can make into brief ceremonies.

Greet the sun each morning, even it it's not visible. Here is a simple morning ceremony given to me by an Objibwe Elder. Bless tobacco (chemical free if possible) and take a pinch in your hand. Step outdoors. Hold the tobacco up to Father Sky and say, "Thank you." Hold it down to Mother Earth and say, "Thank you." Place the tobacco on the Earth as an offering and gift. That's all you need to do.

At lunchtime, take a moment to notice that your day is about half over. Think briefly of what you already did today, and what you plan to do for the rest of the day. Center and ground by taking a few breaths in and out, with intention.

When you get home, wash your hands, change your clothes (at least your shoes), and take a few minutes to center and ground. Shake your hands to release any stress or worry you brought home with you. Greet your family/pets with a smile, and without complaints! Set a cheerful mood for yourself and others. Enjoy your evening meal.

It's recommended that you do not watch the news as you eat, or just before you go to bed. These images promote stress and prevent the relaxation you need at this time of day.

Before you go to bed take a few minutes to review your day, to give thanks, and to meditate. As you prepare for sleep, mentally or actually draw a circle of light about your bed as a protection against nightmares and other disturbances and to bring peace. If you wish, make the intention that you will remember your helpful dreams. Again, ground and center!

THE PLANETARY DAYS

This is another way to go through the day with awareness. Each day is dedicated to one of the seven visible planets, including the Sun and the Moon.

The simplest way to deal with the energy and influence of the planets is to work with them daily.

In this system, Sunday is 'ruled' or influenced by the Sun, Monday is influenced by the Moon, Tuesday is influenced by Mars, Wednesday is influenced by Mercury, Thursday is influenced by Jupiter, Friday is influenced by Venus, and Saturday is influenced by Saturn.

Each hour of the 24 hour day is also influenced by a planet in addition to the daily one. See chapter 3:6, "Make a Planetary Calculator." The following correspondences work very well for the hours as well as the days..

Sun – success, happiness

Moon – development of intuition. Waxing Moon good for increase, bringing in what you want. Waning Moon good for overcoming obstacles to what you want, and to release or remove anything – habits, relationships, etc. Moon also influences illusion.

Mars – courage, determination – also, anger and destructiveness.

Mercury – mental activity, communication especially writing, gaining knowledge, commerce.

Jupiter – wealth, expansion, fame, good fortune, power.

Venus – Love, friendship, pleasure, appreciation of the arts and luxury, generosity, fertility.

Saturn – overcoming obstacles, learning through experience, long life, safety, protection, completion. Also, destruction.

BLESSING THE ELEMENTS

Based on Wiccan practice, this is useful as a daily ceremony. While this may look complicated, it only takes three or four minutes once you learn it.

Place water in a bowl. Point your hand into the water and say, "Blessed be, creature of Water. May I be purified this day." Take a moment to focus on the qualities of Water you wish for the day.

Take a few grains of salt or a few herbs in your left hand. Point your right hand at them and say, "Blessed be, creature of Earth. May you aid me this day." Take a moment to focus on the qualities of Earth that you wish for the day. Touch a drop of the blessed water to your forehead (third eye) and say, "Bless me Mother/Father/Spirit this day."

Light a candle. Point your hand at the

candle and say, "Blessed be, creature of Fire. May you may aid me to do my best in all I do this day." Focus on the qualities of Fire that you wish for the day.

Take incense (stick, loose, cone). Hold it up and say, "Blessed be, creature of Air. May you carry my prayers and praise on high." Light it. Focus on the qualities of Air that you wish for the day. The incense is the union of fire and air. Visualize the smoke carrying your intentions to God/dess/Spirit. Smudge yourself with the lighted incense to clear and bless your aura. You may also smudge your altar.

As you end, put out your candle. Don't blow it out with your breath. Breath is sacred to life. Use a snuffer or your fingers, but be careful not to get burnt!

2) Cycles of the Moon

Each month the Moon cycles through four phases as it waxes from New to Full, and then wanes from Full to Dark. The Moon has a strong influence over the watery and airy elements. Although women, and the waters of the Earth, are the most obviously influenced by the Moon, everything and every creature responds to some degree. Water has a notable tide, but even rocks must move in response, even if only by nanometers. Thus, very actually, changes in hormones, in the blood, etc., happen to everyone, and these changes cause responses in the brain which come out, for one example, as changes in emotions.

The time leading up to the Full Moon is the best time to work on manifestation of anything you want in your life. It is a good time to work on positive habits, such as study or work habits. It is a good time to start a project. Bring in the light and energy of the Waxing Moon to add to your own energy and efforts in your practical methods to gain what you want. This is also a good time to do work for more healthy energy and vitality in your life.

Full Moon is the time of greatest energy, when all the energy of the waxing time is stored up and is ready to be released. Do your ceremony at this time to release this positive energy for your intention.

The Waning Moon, from Full to Dark, is a good time to work to overcome obstacles. It is also a good time to release what you no longer need in your life. This includes letting go of anger or resentment against

anyone, and forgiving them. Forgiveness is simply knowing that what happened is in the past, it's over. It doesn't mean that you will let it happen again! If you want to change a bad habit, this is a good time to work on that and do ceremony to aid you. As the Moon phase comes close to the Dark Moon this isn't a good time to start something new. It's a better time to finish up something you started earlier.

During the Dark Moon you may notice you have more dreams, and that your intuition is more active and accurate. This is a good time to develop your intuition and psychic ability. In ceremony, this is a good time for deep meditation intended to help you change and transform.

Dark Moon is immediately followed by New Moon. Now you are starting the monthly cycle again! This is a time to start something new, to make plans, and to be more active.

Your ceremonies may reflect this. You can focus on what you want to bring into reality in the next two weeks.

Cycles of the Year

There are many examples of rituals that celebrate the Wheel of the Year. The most easily observed spokes of this wheel are the Solstices and Equinoxes, which form an equal armed cross within the circle that represents the year. These are dates that are recognized in the mundane world as the start of the seasons of Spring, Summer, Autumn, and Winter. These are the hinges of the year. The hinges are the change points and are marked easily by these stations of the Sun. In between each hinge, the power of that tide of energy rises and gains in power to the midpoint, and then wanes until the next hinge. The power points are at the cross-quarter points. In Pagan spirituality the hinges and power points are celebrated as Eight Festivals. Briefly, Pagans celebrate the seasons, as follows:

The *Greater Sabbats,* or Fire Festivals, are Samhain, Imbolc, Beltane, and Lammas.

These are the Cross Quarter days—the times of greatest power. The Solstices and Equinoxes are the *Lesser Sabbats*. These are the hinges at the turning of the Wheel of the Year.

Spring Equinox/Ostara: on or near March 21:

This is a moment of perfect balance between day and night, dark and light. We seek balance and harmony in our own lives. This is the time of celebration of renewal and resurrection in many other religions. Easter and Passover are at this time of year.

Beltaine: Eve of May 1.We celebrate the sacred

marriage of the God and Goddess. We dance the Maypole & jump the Bonfire! We laugh and love, play and feast! Maypoles are common in mainstream culture and signal a time of play and laughter. In the US, Memorial weekend at the end of May is typically the start of summer, and outdoor activities.

Summer Solstice/Litha: on or near June 21:

Crops are planted, and flowers are in bloom. The Sun is at its height of power, and now begins to wane. The Oak King gives way to the Holly King. We celebrate with picnics and outdoor barbecues. In older times, this was the feast of St. John.

Lughnasadh/Lammas: Eve of August 1. First

Harvest, of grain. We give thanks for the harvest. We mourn the death of Lugh, God of grain, the Green God. We know he will rise again in the springtime, and we rejoice. Many state or county fairs are held at this time.

Autumn Equinox/Mabon: on or near September 21. A time of balance between dark

and light, day and night. Dark begins to overcome light - we look within. We celebrate the Second Harvest, of fruits and berries. Before the equinox, in early September, the US celebrates Labor Day, to mark the end of Summer and recognize the work we do.

Samhain: Eve of November 1, or Hallowe'en. We

honor the Ancestors of the land on which we live, the Ancestors of our spiritual tradition, and the Ancestors of our blood lineage. We remember our Beloved Dead. The Hallowe'en tradition of ghosts and goblins reminds us of older celebrations in honor of the Ancestors.

Winter Solstice/Yule: on or near December 21.We

celebrate the birth of the Sun and the return of Light! We recognize the ever-returning cycles in our own lives. This is a time of holidays of light and rebirth around the world, in all religions, including Christmas and Hanukah.

Imbolg/Oimelc: Eve of February 2. We sense the

early stirrings of the spring to come. This is the festival of the great Celtic Triple Goddess, Brighid—Goddess of Poetry, Healing and Smithcraft. This is the time of the Christian Feast of Candlemas, also a celebration of returning light. In the Catholic church this is called the Purification of the Virgin Mary, when the church celebrates her motherhood of Jesus. The mainstream celebration of Ground Hog's Day also recognizes that spring is coming.

3. Some basic ritual procedures

by Estara T'shirai (black)

Cord cutting

This practice enables you to detach yourself from draining persons or situations. It is a good thing to try when you are feeling inexplicably drained or obsessed, or when you are conscious of wanting to "cut ties" with a particular person.

Simple Method:
Center yourself, then relax. Imagine that you are studying yourself, with eyes open or closed, whichever makes it easier for you to "see" astrally. Notice whether there are any colored strands of energy attached to your body. They will most commonly attach to chakras if they are present. Some strands may lead to friends rather than enemies, and these will look and feel benign. If you notice that any strands are unusually thick, dark-colored, or simply feel bad, you may decide to cut them. To do this, simply imagine yourself taking up a knife or a pair of scissors and severing the cord close to your body. Imagine the cut searing, making it impossible to reconnect. Your short end is reabsorbed into your body, and the long end fades away into nothing. Do this as unemotionally as you can, since a strong reaction only serves to reinforce the connection.

Variations:
With practice, this can also be done for other people. You can also learn to move your consciousness along a cord to see who or what is at the other end.

Clearing a Space

This should be done before shielding an area (or casting a circle, which is after all only a variant of shielding), for the same reason that you should cleanse yourself before shielding yourself. A banishing (a gung-ho version of clearing space) is often sufficient in itself without a shielding, though it never hurts to put up a shield if you want negative energies to stay away.

Simple Methods:

Some of the same things work for space as for individuals—you may move around the area with a smudge stick or incense, or sprinkle consecrated water if you know how to make it, or shake a rattle or bang a drum. The general practice is to move clockwise as a general rule, but for banishing there is also a case to be made for moving counterclockwise. Experiment (at a non-crucial moment) to see which feels better.

Banishing:

Below is the Lesser Banishing Ritual of the Pentagram, an essential of Ceremonialist practice. A CM (ceremonial magician) will tend to do this ritual at the least provocation, whereas Wiccans, when they know the practice at all, tend to save it for emergencies. Note that the standard CM version is Qabalistic, utilizing Judeo-Christian names for God and angels. For those who are not comfortable with this, there follows an explanation of what each part does and how it can be altered.

> *Preliminary notes: as you draw figures in the air, imagine that energy (of your personal color) is flowing down your arm, through your fingers or Athamé (ritual knife), and actually creating the desired picture in the air.*

The Banishing Pentagram mentioned is that of Earth. To draw it, start at the lower left corner of the star, move to the top point, and so on. Ceremonialism has a different Banishing Pentagram for each Element, but this one will do for a start.

1. The Qabalistic Cross

This establishes your association with God and the center of the universe. In Cabalism, "Atoh" is the Crown, or God as total potential; "Malkuth" is the Kingdom, or the physical realm; "Gedurah" is the Pillar of Severity, "Gebulah" is the Pillar of Mercy, and "Le-Olam" is the center of harmony. (In Biblical terms, "Thine is the Kingdom, the Power, and the Glory, Forever.") If your path gives you some way of identifying yourself with Godhead or the center of the universe, it can be put here in the place of the Cross.

Touching the forehead, say *"Atoh."* (*AH-tow*)
Touching the chest, say *"Malkuth."* (*MAL-kuth*)
Touching the right shoulder, say *"Ve-Gedurah."* (*VAY-ge-DOO-rah*)
Touching the left shoulder, say *"Ve-Geburah."* (*VAY-ge-BOO-rah*)

Clasp hands at the heart and say *"Le-Olam. Amen."* (*LAY-o-LOM, ah-MEN*)

2. The Pentagrams

If you hate pentagrams, you can replace them with another symbol of protection (Thor's hammer is the other popular choice). The Names of God (the words you say as you thrust) can be replaced with the names of deities that you associate with the directions or Elements.

Facing East, point with fingers or athame and draw the Banishing Pentagram. Thrust into the heart of it, saying, *"Yod He au He!"* (*YOD hay AW hay*) Turn toward the South, continuing to draw a circle as you do.

Facing South, draw the Banishing Pentagram and thrust into it saying, *"Adonai!"* (*AA-do-NYE*) Turn toward the West, continuing to draw the circle.

Facing West, draw the Banishing Pentagram and thrust into it saying, *"Eheieh!"* (*eh-HAY-yeh*) Turn toward the North, continuing to draw the circle.

Facing North, draw the Banishing Pentagram and thrust into it saying, *"Agla!"* (*AG-lah*) Turn toward the East, completing the circle.

3. The Archangels

The Archangels serve as protectors. They can be replaced with other protective entities: some people use more gods here, but it seems more appropriate to use demigods, heroes, totems, or some other mid-level beings. The *"About me flames..."* statement is basically an affirmation that the banishing is successful.

Facing East, stand with your arms stretched outward in a T, and say:

> *Before me, Raphael!*
> *Behind me, Gabriel!*
> *At my right hand, Michael!*
> *At my left hand, Auriel!*
> *About me flames the Penta*
> *And in the column shines the Six-Rayed Star.*

4. Repeat the Cabalistic Cross

4. Introduction to Theurgy
By Apollonius (White)

Theurgy may be defined as a collection of magickal practices by which one may have congress with Gods and Daemons in order to communicate with Them, to enter into liaisons ("pacts"), and even to experience deification through unification with Them. I will often use the terms "Divinities" and "Spirits" to refer to Gods and Daemons together, but who are these beings?

I will explain Theurgy from a polytheistic perspective (that is, referring to multiple Gods) for several reasons. First, Theurgy arose in the polytheistic cultures of antiquity, and so it is easiest to understand it in its original context. Second, these ideas, once understood, are easily transferred to monotheism. Thus, there have been in the past — and still are today — Jewish, Christian, and Moslem Theurgists. So, if you are a monotheist, you can think of the Gods and Daemons as Angels of various ranks. Indeed, there is even a perspective from which non-believers can understand these spirits without reference to any religious framework, as aspects of Universal Law, related to particular phenomena in the universe, and especially to particular experiences of human life.

"Theurgy" is the English form of the Ancient Greek word *theourgia*, which comes from two roots. "*The-*," of course, refers to Divinity, as in "theology" and "polytheism." The other root is related to words such as *ergon*, which means "work." Therefore the literal meaning of "theurgy" is "God-work," and thus it is contrasted with "theology," which means "God-talk" (from *logos* = word, verbal account, etc.). Or, to put is differently, while in theology we *discuss* the Gods, in theurgy we *work* directly with Them. "Theurgy" is pronounced THEE-er-jee, with a soft "th" as in "theology."

Several important kinds of Theurgy were practiced in ancient times, including (1) Dream Incubation, (2) *Telestikê*, (3) Binding and Release, (4) Liaison, and (5) Ascent. *Telestikê* (tell-less-tih-KAY) refers to the "ensouling" of a statue or other image with a Divine Spirit; *Binding and Release* refers to the evocation (calling up) of a Spirit to possess another person; *Liaison* refers to communication and pacts with Spirits; and *Ascent* refers to the spiritual elevation and deification of the Theurgist.

Why would you want these interactions with Gods and Daemons? It's certainly not an activity you can mention in polite company! The fundamental reason is that the Gods and Daemons have an enormous influence on our lives. Although we do not recognize it, we are almost always under the influence of one God

or Daemon or another. Therefore one goal of Theurgy is to become better aware of the Divinities who have such an impact on our lives. However, Theurgy provides much more than a simple awareness of Their influence, for it allows us to enter into a dialogue with these Spirits, to understand Their plans for us, and to seek Their aid in our magickal work and in our lives.

5. The Lunar Calendar: Magickal Ways to Spend Each Full Moon

By Katlyn Breene (orange)

There are 13 Lunar months, the full moon being the mid-point of the month. These full moons may not always fall with in the month given here, for the first new moon of the Lunar Year may not coincide with the first day of the first month. Check a calendar to find the correct date and time for each full moon.

The Wolf Moon (January) The first full moon of the year is a time of silence and sitting by the home fire. As the wild winter howls, appreciate the warmth of home and family. Now is the time to go within and plan the changes you will make in the spring. Consider now what you will plant. Start a moon journal to record your lunar tides and write down your spring dreams.

The Storm Moon (February) With this moon, begin your spring cleaning. Think about what needs to be released and let go of in your life and in your home. Burn white candles and purifying incense, sweep out the cobwebs and prepare for the new growth of Spring.

The Chaste Moon (March) This is the moon of the maiden and Faery folk. Gather the seeds of inspiration and imagine what they can grow into. Build an altar to the moon and bless your garden in the moonlight. Prepare the earth for planting and yourself for change.

The Seed Moon (April) At the Seed Moon, plant your seeds of magick, whether it be in a garden, in a pot by the window or simply in your heart. Fill your home with light and flowers, create colorful eggs to decorate it and bring fertility and joy. On the full moon, plant herbs. Sing in the rain.

The Hare Moon (May) Now is the time to celebrate life and love. Renew and affirm your sensuality, kindle the fire of romance. Dance and make love by the light of a bonfire, the glow of red candles, or just the full moon's radiance. Free your wild nature.

The Dyad Moon (June) See how things are growing! The old has died away to make room for the new. Create an altar of roses and honor the beauty of Nature. Send flowers to your mother. Hike to the top of a mountain.

The Mead Moon (July) Bask in the warmth of summer and take time for yourself, relax. Perhaps a moonlit walk by the sea to gather sacred seashells. Make an ocean amulet necklace for one you love.

The Corn Moon (August) This is a time to harvest the gifts you have nurtured and give to those who are in need. Collect and store fresh herbs for the coming winter. Bake special breads to honor the God and Goddess of grain and growing things; share them with your family and friends, but save some to offer the Earth.

The Wine or Harvest Moon (September) Drink a toast to Dionysos, the god of wine and ecstasy—the son of the Moon! Gather with friends to celebrate the vine with a bottle of good wine and good cheer. Catch the moon's reflection in your cup, and raise it up in salutation! Now drink in Her essence and feel the presence of the Gods.

The Blood Moon (October) In the past this was the time of hunting and storing. The Wheel of the Year turns like the cycle of life and death. At this moon the veil is thin; make an altar to honor your ancestors and ask them to guide and protect you. Carve pumpkins and place candles within to light their way.

The Snow Moon (November) Winter's cold descends and outward growth slows. Make this a time for inner growth. Learn a new craft or study the arts of divination. When the moon is full, do a reading for yourself or your friends. Develop your psychic talents.

The Oak Moon (December) The time of the Sun's return approaches and the Moon awaits Her lover. Make wreaths of holly, pine, oak, cedar or ivy; on the Full Oak Moon burn them as an offering. Create a sacred moon ornament to hang on the boughs of your Yule tree.

The Blue Moon - This is the second full moon that falls within a single month. When it occurs will vary each year. When the Blue Moon occurs, plan to do something strange, something you have never done before. Write letters to folks you have not seen for years, or plan a surprise for someone you love. Howl at the moon!

6. Drawing Down the Moon

By Moonwriter (indigo)

In the world of magick, the moon is considered to have a feminine correspondence, and is thus an important part of Goddess-related magickal practices.

The ritual known as "Drawing Down the Moon" is extremely important to many Pagan and Wiccan traditions. During the ritual, the Goddess—symbolized by the full moon—is invoked and becomes present, a powerful force that touches all attendees and blesses them with Her spiritual powers.

The origins of the ceremony go back to classical times, when Witches were felt to be able to control the moon. An ancient Thessalian tract said,

If I command the moon, it will come down.
If I wish to withhold the day, the night will linger
*   over my head.*
If I wish to embark on the sea, I need no ship.
If I wish to fly through the air, I am free of my
*   weight.*

This idea of the moon coming down in response to one's command may be at the root of the concept of "drawing down" the moon. As for the feminine connotations, the moon's cycles are closely attuned to women's menstrual cycles. In fact, many women who follow Earth-based traditions are able to synchronize

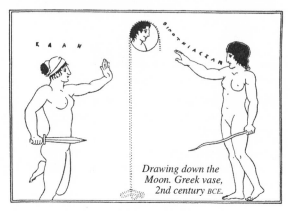

Drawing down the Moon. Greek vase, 2nd century BCE.

their menstrual periods with the moon's cycles.

In the classic form of the Drawing Down the Moon ritual, the circle is cast and the "Charge of the Goddess" is spoken. The coven's High Priestess then extends her arms skyward, beckoning to the moon and drawing down its energy. If a High Priest is also present, he assists in drawing the Goddess into the High Priestess. The High Priestess enters a trance-state and becomes a vessel for the Goddess, a transformation that allows the energy of the Goddess to affect everyone in the circle.

The Charge of the Goddess is a lyrical address written by Doreen Valiente, a High Priestess of Gardnerian Wicca. The Charge has undergone some variations over time, but retains its poignant beauty in all of its iterations. This version includes elements from Apulius' *The Golden Ass*, and Leland's *Aradia* .

Listen to the words of the Great Mother, who of old was called Artemis, Astarte, Dione, Melusine, Aphrodite, Cerridwen, Diana, Arienrhod, Brigid, and by many other names:

Whenever you have need of anything, once in the month, and better it be when the moon is full, you shall assemble in some secret place and adore the spirit of Me who is Queen of all Witches.

There shall you assemble, who have not yet won my deepest secrets and are fain to learn all sorceries. To these shall I teach that which is yet unknown.

You shall be free from slavery, and as a sign that you be free you shall be naked in your rites.

Sing, feast, dance, make music and love, all in My presence, for Mine is the ecstasy of the spirit and Mine also is joy on earth.

For My law is love unto all beings.

Mine is the secret that opens upon the door of youth, and Mine is the cup of wine of life that is the Cauldron of Cerridwen that is the holy grail of immortality.

I am the Gracious Goddess who gives the gift of youth unto the heart of mankind.

I give the knowledge of the spirit eternal and beyond death I give peace and freedom and reunion with those that have gone before.

Nor do I demand aught of sacrifice, for behold, I am the mother of all things and My love is poured upon the earth.

Hear the words of the Star Goddess, the dust of whose feet are the hosts of heaven, whose body encircles the universe:

I who am the beauty of the green earth and the white moon among the stars and the mysteries of the waters,

I call upon your soul to arise and come unto Me. For I am the soul of nature that gives life to the universe. From Me all things proceed and unto Me they must return.

Let My worship be in the heart that rejoices, for behold — all acts of love and pleasure are My rituals. Let there be beauty and strength, power and compassion, honor and humility, mirth and reverence within you.

And you who seek to know Me, know that your seeking and yearning will avail you not, unless you know the Mystery: for if that which you seek, you find not within yourself, you will never find it without.

For behold, I have been with you from the beginning, and I am that which is attained at the end of desire.

The ritual begins within a Circle, which becomes a sacred place through its casting, a place between worlds. The Circle is held outdoors at the full moon—an Esbat—and usually in a private location. Within the Circle the participants use music, chanting, and dancing to raise what is called a "cone of power."

After the power is raised, the actual "drawing down" begins. Once evoked, the lunar energy can be further directed toward a particular purpose, such as healing, or those present can simply bask in the energy until the ritual ends.

Communing with the Moon

Although Drawing Down the Moon is traditionally done with a group, you can conduct your own version all by yourself, or with one or two others.

Purify yourself by bathing or showering (a bar of Frankincense soap is a nice touch for purification), then don clean clothing. If you have magickal robes or garb—particularly if they are silver or white—these are ideal attire. You may also wish to wear magickal jewelry, particularly anything that includes moons or moonstones. You might also wish to purify yourself by some other means, such as smudging.

Your Moon ritual should take place outdoors on a night when the Moon is full. Ground and center yourself, then spend some time meditating on what it is that you plan to do. You may wish to play soft background music on a portable CD player—drumming, soft chants, Celtic harp music, Native American flutes, etc.

Set up your altar as desired, then cleanse and consecrate your space and cast a magick Circle. Call the quarters and invite the presence of the God and Goddess.

Now, stand at the center of your circle and raise your arms above your head, facing the full moon. Speak to the Goddess that is the Moon, asking her to fill you. Feel the energy as it flows down your arms and fills your soul. Many report feeling a tingling sensation, or a feeling of warmth. Most people feel very emotional at this time, and may laugh or weep.

After drawing down the Moon's energy, you may wish to dance, or simply even to walk the inside perimeter of your circle in a deosil (clockwise) fashion. If you choose to direct the energy towards another purpose, this is the time to do it. Otherwise, simply enjoy feeling the energy move through you, and be aware of being blessed and enriched by its presence.

When you're ready, release the quarters, close the circle, then kneel and place your hands on the Earth, sending the excess energy back to the Mother.

While still under the full Moon, celebrate with "wine and cakes," or some variation thereof. Finally, spend some time meditating on what you have accomplished. (Later on, record the entire ritual and its effects in your magickal journal).

Yet another way to benefit from the full Moon's energies is to place your magickal tools out overnight to charge under the Moon. A chalice full of rainwater or spring water can also be left under the full Moon to charge; save the water for ritual purposes.

7. A Full Moon Dedication Ritual

By Adella DragonStar

This is to be done on the night of the full Moon. Open the Circle by starting at East, working clockwise. Stand in the middle of the Circle, representing the center of all things. Say:

> *Mother Earth and Father Sky, I call to you.*
> *I ask the aid of the four Arts.*
> *By the light and power of the Full Moon,*
> *May you hear my words.*

With Athamé in one hand and wand in the other, raise hands and follow the corners.

(Face East)

> *I call to the East,*
> *Ruler of the sylphs and zephyrs.*
> *Color of yellow and element of Air.*
> *Heading to the suit of the Wands,*
> *For protection against all evils.*
> *May you hear my call.*

(Face South)
> *I call to the South,*
> *Ruler of salamanders and firedrakes,*
> *Color of red and element of Fire.*
> *Heading to the suit of the Swords,*
> *To battle enemies with pride.*
> *May you hear my call.*

(Face West)
> *I call to the West,*
> *Ruler of nymphs, undines and merpeople.*
> *Color of blue and element of Water.*
> *Heading to the suit of the Cups,*
> *To drink from in celebration of the Ancients.*
> *May you hear my call.*

(Face North)
> *I call to the North,*
> *Ruler of gnomes, dwarfs and trolls.*
> *Color of green and element of Earth.*
> *Heading to the suit of the Pentacles,*
> *For strength against all odds.*
> *May you hear my call.*

(In the Center)
> *I am one with the power of Spirit, my dedication and appreciation of my studies growing with each passing moon phase. May all the powers that be work with me to make me grow strong and wise, helpful and giving, gentle and loving to all beings. May I learn more about the Earth and her marvelous powers by the day, indulging in the night. May I understand and be able to help those in need of me, as long as their need not interrupt the Wiccan Rede. Hear me, oh wise ones of the earth and sky, moon and sea. May I truly live to my ultimate potential in all things possible to me.*

At this point, you may wish to dedicate your magickal tools, or your own creative work. Perhaps drink from

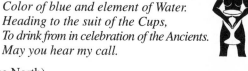

the chalice. Take a moment to meditate and commune with Spirit. Finally, when you feel the rite is completed, end by dismissing the quarters as usual, and opening the Circle (see *Grimoire*, p. 180).

8. Computer Mirror Protection Spell

By Donata Ahern (aqua)

Visualization:

This computer mirror protection spell is visualization with intent, which is done in a state of light trance, after casting your personal Circle or Sacred Space. See yourself creating a Shield of Light around your home/car, etc. The Shield always has firm boundaries to define what you are protecting. It can be extended to the Internet by visualizing your computer screen, and the computer screens of any who would seek to do you or your computer any harm.

In the visualization, see yourself forming a Shield of Light that creates protection around yourself and your home. The light for the shield may be generated by a Body of Light meditation, as follows.

Start by visualizing Light coming down into your head from a point above the head, and filling your entire body until you are a glowing body of Light. Then extend the Light beyond the physical edges of your body to fill your aura, which is about 6-8 inches all around you in an ovoid or egg shape. Harden the edges of this ovoid and place outward facing mirrors all over it. This is your Shield of Light. You may include your home, computer, etc., within the protection of this Shield. Design your mirrors, that is, have the intention, so that they allow positive energy to enter inside your Shield, and to strongly deflect back any negative energy either to its source, or harmlessly into the earth. The computer screens of the Internet can be visualized as forming a continuous Shield on the web, adding to your protection.

In an extreme situation you may have the intention in your visualization that the mirrors of your Shield will make whatever they protect invisible to a seeker. This can be useful in case of a possible hacker. The Shield becomes your personal firewall!

Ceremony: (to set up the Shield of Light):

Cast your Circle, or create Sacred Space in your usual way (see *Grimoire*, pp. 175-177).

Call on your choice of divinity to aid you and say:

I, [your name], am a living soul and a body of Light. I ask help from [name of deity] to protect me, and aid me in all my needs and rightful desires.

I am in need of protection. I call on you to aid me in establishing my Shield of Light of protection, which shall remain in place after this ceremony. I ask you to aid me in creating a Shield of Light that will reflect all negativity and evil that comes towards me through my computer, and to deflect all such negativity and evil that would harm, use or misuse my computer. I further ask that my shields reflect any evil or negative energy away from me to return it to its source, or to send it into the earth.

I place this Shield of Light around myself, my home, and my possessions. I extend this Shield of protection to my computer, and to any aspects of myself—my pictures, web site, posts, any other information, etc.— that are on the Internet.

It is my firm intention that the computer screens throughout the Internet will form a mirror shield to protect me and mine. Any evil intent to use, misuse, or manipulate any picture, web site, posts, or other information of mine will be deflected away from me to return to the sender. The computer screens of any enemy will be the focus for this shield, which will return their own energy to them in its full force and power, to stop them and prevent further harm.

I ask to be protected from all negative, evil, and harmful forces, regardless of their origins. I (your name) now manifest this Shield of Light. It will remain in place after this ceremony. I thank you, (name of deity) for your aid in establishing this Shield of Light of protection. It is so!

Close Circle or Sacred Space in your usual way (see *Grimoire*, p. 180).

Daily:

Now that you have set up your Shield of Light, it only takes a few moments, with seven deep breaths, to reinforce your Shield daily.

First breath; bring up the light of the Earth.

Second breath; bring down the light of the sky.

Third breath; sense the mingling of these energies in your heart center.

Fourth breath; send the Light throughout your body.

Fifth breath; let the Light fill your aura.

Sixth breath; harden the edges of your aura, and visualize your mirrors.

Seventh breath; thank your Deity and release excess energy into the earth.

Blessed Be! So Mote it Be!

Department XV: Lore (grey)

Waveforms

Myth is not
Something you can
Put in a bottle and take down
When you want a little drink before bed.

It is something potent and faintly dangerous,
Not tame, but a tidal force that rises and
Falls before you quite catch
Hold of it.

It tells stories
Ancient and strange,
Blurring the lines between light and dark,
Like the grey ocean that mirrors an overcast sky.

Myth seethes and whispers, casts
Its seeds on careless shores,
Dares us to dream and
Dive deep.

Myth is water
Dancing with the moon
Starlight on restless waves,
Writing words no waking eye can read.

It belongs to the part of ourselves
That is older than all language
And more magical than
Meaning.

It is not
Solid, not something
You can touch and hold,
Less a product than a
    process.

Myth is a waveform flowing through
Waters so wide that they span
Day and night at opposite
Edges.

Myth soaks
Through your bones
In those moments when your eye's
Attention is all on the surface of things.

It is a slap in the face, a tickle in the back
Of the mind, cold mermaid fingers
Closing around an ankle
In the shallows.

It's deeper
Thank you think.
Be careful if you swim out
Past the dropoff, over your head.

Myth is slippery, sinuous, a sleek serpentine
Spiral spilling gems from its scales, so
Beware of this sea! For here
There be dragons.

—Elizabeth Barrette

1. Introduction

ELCOME TO THE WORLD OF LORE! *Lore* means "teachings," and Lore Mastery is all about knowing *arcane* (hidden) secrets and esoteric mysteries known to very few others. It is said that "knowledge is power," and much of a Wizard's true power comes from his vast knowledge. Lore particularly concerns myths and legends; a Lore-Master is also a storyteller who can always come up with a tale to make any point.

It is the mission of this Department to help the student develop the ability to access, synthesize, and critically evaluate arcane knowledge from a variety of magickal cultures. Such knowledge is crucial to the Wizard in practice as well as development and includes, but is not limited to: world mythology, world history, hidden realms, wizardly fiction, and cultural pantheons.

The color of magick associated with this department is Grey, representing knowledge, lore and wisdom. Like Indigo, Grey is particularly associated with Wizardry, as it is neither black nor white, and indeed encompasses all colors without being any one of them.

2. Lost Continents and Civilizations

By Oberon (grey)

The great majority of human history (or rather, prehistory) occurred in a world very different from the one we now inhabit. Up until only 10,500 years ago, much of North America and Northern Europe was covered in mile-thick sheets of ice, and the sea levels were hundreds of feet lower than they are today—exposing the vast areas of the continental shelves. This was the period of the Würm Glaciation, and it lasted for 59,500 years! Early on in this period—about 60,000 years ago—a massive volcanic eruption in what is now Sumatra reduced the entire worldwide human population to only a few thousand people. Because of this narrow bottleneck in the human journey, today the entire human race has less genetic diversity than the members of a single troop of chimpanzees!

The choice locations for human settlements have always been at the places where rivers empty into the sea. Along with fresh water from the rivers, and the abundance of seafood, there are also easy means of transportation—upriver, and along the coastline.

When the last ice age ended about 10,500 years ago—with a large comet or asteroid impact in the Bahamas—the melting ice raised the sea levels 400 feet, and the new coastlines moved hundreds of miles inland. Since all coastal communities were thus drowned, those few people who had survived in the uplands passed down tales of lost civilizations.

Some of these may have been quite significant. Submerged megalithic ruins are being discovered in several places that were once dry land. These include such structures as the still-debated "Bimini Wall," a large apparent "temple" complex off Japan, and other rectangular and pyramidal remnants in various offshore locations. A few mysterious ancient monuments—such as the great Sphinx of Egypt's Giza Plateau—are now being re-evaluated as far older than previously thought, extending their origins back farther than 10,500 years ago.

Atlantis

By far the most famous of all legendary "Lost Civilizations" was the fabled island of Atlantis. Its historical existence and location have been debated for over two thousand years, but have never been confirmed. It was first mentioned by the Greek philosopher Plato (427-347 BCE), who claimed the story had been passed down in his family from his great-grandfather, who knew Solon (638-558 BCE), a Greek statesman who had learned the account from the priests when he visited Egypt in 560 BCE Plato wrote down Solon's story around 360 BCE in his dialogues *Timaeus* and *Critias,* stating that Atlantis had been destroyed by volcano, earthquake, and/or tsunami about 9,000 years prior to Solon's time, or 9,600 BCE. Here is a brief summation:

The Story of Atlantis

The paradise island of Atlantis (meaning "Land of the Pillar") was the home of Poseidon, god of the sea. He fell in love with a mortal woman, Cleito, and built a palace for her on a hill near the middle of the island, so surrounding her with protective rings of water and land.

Cleito bore five sets of twin boys who became the first rulers of Atlantis. The island was divided among the brothers with the eldest, Atlas, becoming the first King of Atlantis. At the top of the hill, a temple was built to Poseidon. Here the rulers met to discuss laws, pass judgments, and honor Poseidon.

To facilitate travel and trade, a canal was cut through of the rings of land and water running south

for 5.5 miles to the sea. The populous city of Atlantis extended in an 11-mile circle around the outer ring of water. Beyond the city lay a fertile plain 330 miles long and 110 miles wide, surrounded by another canal to bring in water from the mountains.

Soaring mountains dotted with villages, lakes, rivers, and meadows surrounded the plain to the north. The mild climate allowed two harvests each year. Many varieties of herbs, fruits, and nuts grew in abundance. Large herds of animals, including elephants, roamed the island.

For generations the Atlanteans lived simple, virtuous lives, but eventually they became corrupted by greed and power. Angered by their immorality, Zeus convened the other gods to determine a suitable punishment. Soon, in one violent cataclysm, Atlantis, its people, and its memory were swallowed by the sea.

Map of Atlantis based on Plato's description, published in The New York American, *Oct. 20, 1912.*

Where was Atlantis?

Several different "Atlantises" and locales have been proposed over the years.

Plato said that Atlantis had been located "beyond the Pillars of Heracles," an ancient name for the Straits of Gibraltar. If true this would place Atlantis out in the Atlantic Ocean—most likely around the Azores Islands, about 900 miles west of the Portugese coast. Some people believe the islands are the mountaintops of the sunken continent of Atlantis. These rise from a larger foundation called the Azores Plateau, or, by mariners, "Dolphin Ridge." This Spain-sized region is a discrete block encircled like a plug by the Mid-Atlantic Rift, and the entire plateau would have been above water during the Ice Age, until the last opening of the surrounding Rift evacuated the underlying magma and dropped the island into the hole. This happened around 8,500 BCE, close to Plato's date.

A comet or asteroid crossed North America, its debris leaving the oval-shaped craters known as the carolina Bays, and crashed into the ocean. The impact site is known as the Nares Abyssal Plain. Its proximity

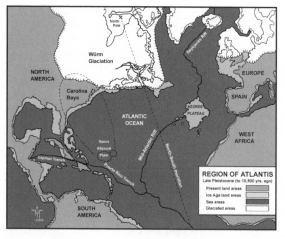

REGION OF ATLANTIS
Late Pleistocene (to 10,500 yrs. ago)
Present land areas
Ice Age land areas
Sea areas
Glaciated areas

to the Puetro Rico Trench triggered the opening of the Mid-Atlantic Rift.

As a result of the impact, the Earth's axis was shifted—the North Pole, which had been in Hudson Bay, was shifted to its present location in the middle of the Arctic Ocean (the magnetic pole is still catching up…).

During the Ice Age, large portions of Antarctica were ice-free and temperate, and some serious researchers place Atlantis there.

Still other researchers believe Atlantis was in South America, and point to certain geophysical features that match Plato's description, as well as the ruins of Tiahuanoco in Bolivia—an ancient city on the shore of Lake Titicaca. Salt deposits indicate this lake was once part of a vast inland sea that filled the entire Amazon Basin during the Ice Age, and that Tiajuanoco was then a seaport. But after the impact, the entire continent of South America was tipped. The Eastern side sank, while the west coast rose thousands of feet (the "Andean Upheaval"), spilling the sea out into the Atlantic and raising Tiahuanoco over 2 miles above present sea level. See: http://www.thule.org/tiahuanaco.html for more info on this—my own personal favorite claimant.

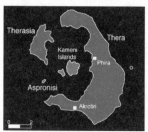

On the other hand, many feel that Plato's description of the Atlantean civilization and its cataclysmic destruction seemed more like that of Bronze-Age "Minoan" Crete, located in the Aegean Sea. Just north of Crete is a circular volcanic island called Thera. In 1628 BCE an enormous volcanic explosion obliterated the entire central area of the island and devastated the magnificent Minoan civilization. Some settlements on Thera were buried under as much as 100 feet of ash. This event was recorded in the *Book of Exodus;* the Biblical "ten plagues" that beset Egypt— and even the parting of the Red Sea—were all aspects

of it. Huge tsunamis drowned coastal Greece, Syria and Egypt, and the volcano below the horizon was visible for hundreds of miles as a "pillar of smoke by day, and fire by night." (Exodus 13:21)

It has been argued that Solon may have confused the Egyptian glyphs for "hundred" and "thousand," and that the destruction of Atlantis should have been read as having occurred 900 years earlier, rather than 9,000. If so, then the proper date would have been 1,600 BCE–– the time of the Thera eruption. Reducing the figures of thousands to hundreds also brings the dimensions of Atlantis into line with those of Thera.

The controversy begun by Plato continues unabated to the present day. Various modern writers have argued convincingly for the location of Atlantis in Peru, Ireland, the North Sea, the Bahamas, Indonesia, the Black Sea, or Antarctica. As many of these areas were in fact submerged at the end of the Ice Age, drowning any settlements that may have existed there, it may be that all locations are valid, and the original legend of lost Atlantis may be based upon memories of a global maritime civilization whose coastal communities were all destroyed when the sea levels suddenly rose 400 feet.

I believe that the truly ancient legend was simply grafted onto the later similar destruction of Thera, just as America was called "The New Atlantis" (1627) by Francis Bacon (1561-1626).

Lemuria

Lemuria is the name of a submerged land that was hypothesized to have extended from Madagascar through India and throughout Indonesia. The name was coined in 1864 by geologist Philip Sclater to account for the existence of lemurs only in these now widely-separated areas. While no "lost continent" ever filled the Indian Ocean basin, it is true that many islands of this region were originally part of a contiguous land mass during the Ice Ages, when sea levels were far lower and the continental shelves were exposed. Although Madagascar was still an island during the Pleistocene, the modern islands of Indonesia were once mountains of the vast area now called *Sunderland,* which extended almost to Australia.

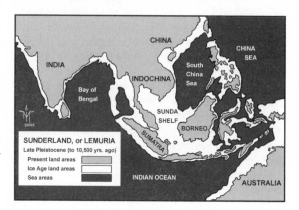

SUNDERLAND, or LEMURIA
Late Pleistocene (to 10,500 yrs. ago)
Present land areas
Ice Age land areas
Sea areas

The idea of a "lost continent" in the Indian (or Pacific) Ocean was picked up by some occult writers, who made it the home of various imagined races and creatures. In the 1880s, Madame Helena Blavatsky (1831-1891), founder of Theosophy, asserted that Lemuria was sunk by the gods to destroy its sub-human inhabitants. In 1894, Frederick Spencer Oliver published *A Dweller on Two Planets*, which claimed that surviving Lemurians were living in a complex of caves and tunnels beneath NorCalifia's Mount Shasta, and were occasionally seen walking on the mountain in white robes. This belief remains a popular local legend.

Mu

Mu is the name of another vast land mass imagined to have once existed in the Pacific Ocean, the remnants of which are New Zealand and Polynesia. This idea was first proposed by Augustus Le Plongeon (1825-1908), who claimed that his fabricated "translations" of ancient Mayan writings told of a drowned land whose survivors became the Mayan Indians of the Yucatan Peninsula. *The Lost Continent of Mu* was later popularized by James Churchward (1852-1936) in a series of rather preposterous books with that title.

3. This Age of Heroes
By Jesse Wolf Hardin (silver)

> *If you want to read the mystic story*
> *Written in your future,*
> *You better start to write it now!*
> ("Secret of the Crossroads Devil," by Gaia Consort)

From out of the mythic, mist-draped past, a host of heroes and heras beckon us to hear and heed, urge us forward to our own opportunities for heartful heroism. The stories of brave Ulysses and Queen Boudica, the wise Merlin and indominable Sparticus, are not meant to merely entertain us. Nor did our ancestral wizards and warriors intend to spare us our own great struggles, enlightening challenges and soul-satisfying victories! They acted and sacrificed, succeeded and excelled in order to meet the unique threats and critical needs of their people, their lives and times. Our own day and age is no less perilous or in need of able champions than was theirs, and plenty of events arise in our contemporary lives that demand an assertive and valiant response.

If you look in your dictionary you'll notice that "hero" is one of the few English nouns without a synonym that can substitute for it, there being no other word in our language that conveys the same powerful meaning. Similarly, nothing can substitute for personal heroism when immanent danger or an urgent purpose arise. You can deny your heroism to others out of a sense of duty or humility if it makes you feel bet-

ter, but any time you give yourself fully to a mission on which much depends, you're a hero or hera, simple as that!

One defining element of being a hero is being willing to drop our schedules, abandon comfort and certainty, face our fears, and take genuine risks. It can be heroic just to resist the pressure to fit in at school, because there is a very real risk that we'll be shunned and dissed if we're authentic, exposing our real feelings and spiritual or magickal beliefs. There's some heroism involved with majoring in creative writing when everyone else is focused on math or business classes, listening to bardic or ambient-trance music if the popular trend is towards commercial country tunes or gangsta rap, or studying to be a wizard when most people no longer believe in personal integrity, the living Earth, Spirit or magick.

The most heroic acts of all are those committed not just for ourselves but for the protection and betterment of our loved ones, our communities and clans, Gaia's endangered species and threatened forests. A time when governments are waging wars against each other and their own people, when personal liberty is being surrendered in hopes of increased safety, when the natural world is rapidly being destroyed, is truly the golden age of heroes. The challenges we face today offer us more chances than ever to use our skills and demonstrate our worth in knightly magickal service. All around us today are examples of nature being trampled for profits, women and children being mistreated, entire countries being plundered and cultures stripped of their diversity and dignity.

The hero in us is called forth into the light, whenever and wherever we encounter ignorance, prejudice,

cruelty, injustice or greed… called to act whenever there's a clear and vital need. To be heroes can mean to heal or create with love, rather than to fight and bleed. The measure of any hero lies in our compassion and the strength of our intent. And in the form and fact of our deeds.

• The work of the Wizard is inherently heroic, and all heroism benefits from the skills of the wizard.

• Both wizards and heroes grow to serve compassionate missions, but neither bend to serve either institutions or men.

• Develop and write up your own heroic code of honor, including:

1) the sort of things you pledge never to do, such as betraying an ally or cause, denying even the most painful truths, or giving up when the going gets rough

2) ways of acting that are clearly inappropriate for a wizard and a potential hero, such as being petty, arrogant or cowardly

3) the various types of indignities and threats you pledge to confront, resist and transform when and where they arise

4) the kinds of people, other life forms, natural areas and sacred places of power, liberties and rights that you can promise to protect and nourish, further and celebrate

• Develop a plan to deal with each situation as it comes up, intensely focusing your wits as well as your magickal energies. Then be prepared to set your plans aside as the threats morph and the situations change.

• Maximize your knowledge and abilities in preparation for heroic events, but know that no matter how powerful you are, you need not depend on yourself alone. Enlist human allies and aides, tap the ancient wisdom that still resides in your bones, call on the spirits of place for help, and invoke the Great Spirit or Goddess by whatever name.

• It is the purpose of wizards and heroes to attempt the impossible.

• Always set out to exceed your imagined limitations. Nothing is wholly impossible, regardless of the odds stacked against us.

• The greater the odds against us, the more important our deeds and the greater any accomplishments.

• Not all heroic acts are completely successful as intended. What makes you a hero is how hard you try…. plus your noble reasons why.

• Live a heroic life, and future generations will tell your story as you have read and retold the stories of those courageous ones who came before.

4. Amazons and Warrior Women

By Trina Robbins (grey)

The Amazons that the ancient Greeks wrote about were a tribe of warrior women who lived in Themiscyra, which was probably located near the Black Sea in Southern Russia or Georgia. It's obvious from their writings that the Greeks admired and were fascinated by the Amazons, but, because Greece was a patriarchy (a male-dominated society), in their stories, the Greek heroes always won over the Amazon warriors. Thus, Heracles successfully stole the golden belt of Amazon Queen Hippolyta, and Theseus successfully carried off Queen Antiope, whom he married. According to Greek legend, when Antiope's Amazons invaded Athens in an attempt to get their queen back, she actually fought against them at her husband's side! (I choose not to believe this.) Fifty years after Theseus captured Antiope, Queen Petheselia led her warriors into the Trojan War, joining the Trojans in their battle against the Greek invaders. According to Greek legend, Pentheselia slew many Greek warriors before finally being slain herself by the Greek hero, Achilles. When Achilles removed his dead enemy's helmet, he was so struck by her beauty that he regretted having killed her, and mourned her death.

Many people today claim that stories of tribes of warrior women are nothing but legend. Recent archaeological discoveries prove them wrong. In 1995, ancient burial mounds near the Russian town of Pokrovka, on the border of Manchuria, yielded up skeletons of horseback-riding women buried with armor and weapons. The women were all exceptionally tall for those days, averaging 5'6". One young woman was buried with a quiver and forty Bronze-tipped arrows. Another had an arrowhead lodged in her ribcage; evidence that she died in combat. Burials of male warriors and of priestesses were also found at the site. Obviously the tribes buried there, the Sarmatians, or Sauromatians, were not a total matriarchy (female-dominated), but treated both sexes equally, had high regard for women, and even worshipped a goddess.

Warrior women have existed all over the world. In Africa, the King of Dahomey had an army of women warriors. In photographs taken in the late 19th century, the Dahomey Amazons proudly surround their king, carrying spears. They wear elaborately beaded breastplates and are adorned with necklaces, bracelets, and jeweled belts.

Crouching Tiger, Hidden Dragon was not merely a beautiful movie, and Disney's Mulan was not just a pretty cartoon for kids. China has a long history of women warriors ranging from Fa MuLan, who really existed about 1,500 years ago, to Lai Choi San, the pirate queen of Macau, who ruled the South China seas during the 1920s and 1930s. Japan also had its share of women warriors, Samurai women who fought with the naginata sword, and they didn't have to disguise themselves as men. The most famous of these was Itagaki, a leader of her clan in the 13th century.

From the mythic Queen Maeve, who may or may not have existed, to the historic Briton Queen Boudica, who fought successfully against the Roman invaders, to the famed Irish pirate queen Grania O'Malley, the Celtic lands have a history of women warriors. Ancient Roman writers Plutarch and Ammianus Marcellinus wrote that the Celtic women fought beside their men in battle, and often were stronger and fiercer than the men.

The Valkyries of Norse mythology were beautiful, armored maidens who rode through the sky on winged horses, carrying off to Valhalla the souls of brave warriors who died in battle. They may have been only legendary, but ancient records are full of tales of northern European women warriors, like Thyra, Queen of Denmark, who led an army against invaders in the 9th century, or the Lady of Mercia, daughter of Alfred the Great, who led troops against the Vikings in the 10th century. Archaeologists have uncovered Anglo-Saxon graves from the 5th and 6th centuries that yielded skeletons of women buried with weapons and shields.

Even the state of California is named for a legendary Amazon queen—and her image appears on the State Seal! In the year 1510, 18 years after Columbus discovered the New World, Spanish novelist Garcia de Montalvo wrote a book called Las Sergas de Esplandian (The Deeds of Esplandian). In his book, he described a tribe of Amazons who lived on an island located "close to Paradise" and named California. These beautiful warrior women rode Gryphons and wore golden armor studded with precious gems. Their queen was a woman named Califia. Many people who read Montalvo's book accepted it as truth rather than fiction. In 1542, when the Spanish explorer Juan Rodriguez Cabrillo anchored his ship off the coast of what is now San Diego, he must have believed it was the mystic island of Amazons, because he wrote in his journal, "I have found California."

5. More myths & legends

OZ: In the Grimoire, I provided brief synopses of a few of my favorite Classical myths and legends—stories I felt that all Wizards should know. I would like to continue these "Campfire Tales" with a few more—this time told not just by me, but also by other students and teachers at the Grey School of Wizardry. So pull up a log to sit on, and join me around the fire as we pass the drinking horn to the next storyteller...

Phaethon & the Sun-Chariot
By Morgan Felidae (brown)

Many believe the god Apollo to be the master of the Sun (in Greek mythology) but that is not quite true. Apollo was the god of Light, but the object that brightened up the daytime sky was said to be driven by Helios, son of the Titan Hyperion (which means "he who goes before the sun" in Greek) and the Titaness Theia. Helios also had two sisters: Selene, the moon, and Eos, the dawn. Every morning, after Selene had driven her silver chariot home and Eos, with her rosy fingers, opened the gates of Heaven, Helios would drive his fiery-footed steeds across the sky with a firm hand and his chariot would shine its light upon the world.

Helios had many daughters and two sons, Aeetes & Phaethon. Unlike Aeetes, Phaethon was the son of Helios by a mortal woman, Clymene. She told him of his parentage and he went to the palace of the Sun to seek the truth. When Helios revealed that the lad was correct, he offered to prove it to the lad. He swore by the river Styx (a sacred oath unbreakable by the gods) to grant him anything he requested. The boy, in awe of his mighty father, instantly cried that he wished he might drive the golden chariot for one day. Reluctantly, Helios agreed, after attempting to warn his son of the dangers and seeing the youth was not to be dissuaded.

The next morning, Helios attended his son's departure. At first, things were calm and Phaethon felt a few ecstatic moments of being Lord of the Sky. Then the horses felt the light grip at their reins and the lighter weight in the chariot and knew it was not their master behind them, and took control. The horses ran to and fro and every which way they so desired, setting the lands and seas ablaze and drying up the waters. Frightened, Gaia let up a cry which reached the ears of the gods. They looked down from Olympus and saw that quick action was required, so Zeus let fly his mighty thunderbolt at the rash driver. Phaethon was struck dead and the chariot shattered, the maddened horses sent running into the sea. Phaethon's body was retrieved by the naiads of the river Eridanus and they buried him in a tomb to be remembered and grieved for his arrogance.

Cupid & Psyche
By Onyx Ravenclaw (violet)

A certain king and queen had three daughters. Psyche, the youngest, was the fairest of all, and people came from far and wide to look upon her with amazement, paying her that homage due only to Venus herself. This gave great offense to jealous Venus, who called upon her son, Cupid, to punish the girl. But when Cupid saw Psyche, he fell in love with her, and determined to make her his wife in secret from his mother.

The king took Psyche to the oracle because her sisters had married princes while Psyche remained single. The oracle said that she would be married not to a man, but to one living on a mountain, whom no one can stand. This dreadful decree filled all the people with dismay. But Psyche said, "Why, my dear parents, do you now lament me? You should rather have grieved when the people showered upon me undeserved honors, and called me a Venus. Lead me to that mountain to which my unhappy fate has destined me."

As Psyche stood on the ridge of the mountain, quaking with fear, gentle Zephyr (the breeze) raised her up and bore her to a flowery dale, where she laid down on the grass and slept. When she awoke, she beheld a magnificent palace. Cupid came in the hours of darkness, and made Psyche his wife. But he instructed her not to look upon him, because he wanted her to love him as an equal. Then he fled before the dawn's light.

At length Psyche missed her family. With Cupid's permission, she visited her sisters. They asked what sort of a man her husband was, and she confessed that she had never seen him. The sisters reminded her of the oracle and advised her to kill her husband if indeed

he be a monster, and regain her freedom. Psyche resisted these persuasions, but they nagged her mind. So, as instructed by her sisters, she prepared a lamp and a sharp knife, and hid them out of sight of her husband.

When Cupid had fallen asleep, Psyche silently rose, and uncovering her lamp, saw not a hideous monster, but the most beautiful of the immortals. As she leaned over for a nearer view of his face, a drop of burning oil fell on the shoulder of the god. Startled awake, Cupid opened his eyes and fixed them full upon her. Then he spread his wings and flew out of the window, admonishing her as he flew away for breaking her vow.

When Psyche looked around, the palace and gardens had vanished, and she found herself in a field near where her sisters dwelt. She told them what happened, at which, pretending to grieve, those spiteful sisters inwardly rejoiced. "For now," said they, "he will perhaps choose one of us." Each of them secretly arose early the next morning and ascended the mountain, where she called upon Zephyr to bear her to Cupid. Then leaping up, unsustained by Zephyr, each fell down the precipice and was dashed to pieces.

Meanwhile, Venus found out about Cupid and Psyche and became incensed, so she devised several trials for Psyche to prove herself worthy of her son. Venus was hoping for her to fail, but Psyche always managed to succeed through the help of others. This only angered Venus more and more, and each task became more difficult.

Finally, Venus sent Psyche to the Underworld to obtain some of the "beauty" of Proserpina, Queen of Erebus. Guided by a mysterious voice, Psyche passed by three-headed Cerberus, and prevailed upon Charon to ferry her over the black river and return. But the voice warned, "When Proserpine has given you the box, filled with her beauty, you must never open or look into the box!" Thus Psyche passed safely into the realm of Pluto and Proserpina, who silently filled the box with the precious substance, and returned it to her.

But as Psyche emerged into the light of day, she could not restrain herself from opening the box, just to take a tiny bit of this beauty for herself, in order to make herself more appealing to her husband. Alas, the "beauty" of Proserpina is a serene and peaceful death, and Psyche was immediately stricken lifeless.

But Cupid, unable to bear the absence of his beloved, flew to the spot where Psyche lay, and gathering up the sleep from her body closed it again in the box, and awoke Psyche with a light touch of one of his arrows. "Again," said he, "hast thou almost perished by the same curiosity. But now perform exactly the task imposed on you by my mother, and I will take care of the rest."

Then Cupid presented himself before Jupiter with his supplication. Jupiter lent a favoring ear, and pleaded the cause of the lovers so earnestly with Venus that he won her consent. On this he sent Mercury to bring Psyche up to Olympus, and when she arrived, handing her a cup of ambrosia, he said, "Drink this, Psyche, and be immortal; nor shall Cupid ever break away from the knot in which he is tied, but these nuptials shall be perpetual."

Thus Psyche was reunited with Cupid, and in due time they had a daughter whose name was Pleasure (Voluptas).

Cupid is the Roman name for the primal force of love, called Eros *in Greek. The Greek word for a butterfly is* Psyche, *which also means "soul." There is no metaphor of the immortality of the soul so apt as the butterfly, bursting on brilliant wings from the mummy-wrapped cocoon in which it has lain, after a life as a lowly cater-pillar, to flutter in the blaze of day and feed on the fragrant flowers of Spring. Psyche, then, is the human soul, purified by sufferings and misfortunes, which is thus prepared for true happiness when wedded to Love. And this tale is an allegory of how the human soul gains immortality through love.*

The story of Cupid and Psyche first appears in the works of the Roman mystic Apuleius (c.124-172CE). A much later version became the story of "Beauty and the Beast."

Arachne & Athena

By Oberon & Morgan Felidae (brown)

Arachne was the daughter of Idmon of Colophon, a famous dyer in the much-prized Lydian purple. Arachne herself excelled in the art of weaving, and was justly proud of her skills. Not only were her creations beautiful, but the act of her weaving itself was enough to cause nymphs to cease their frolicking and watch breathlessly. Her works were so remarkable that someone commented she must have been trained by Athena herself, the goddess of weaving. Scornfully, Arachne declared that not even Athena could surpass her. This was a fatal mistake.

Angered, Athena came to Earth and challenged Arachne to a weaving contest. Arachne accepted, agreeing to suffer whatever punishment the goddess decided if she lost. The looms were set up, and the pair began. Athena wove a tapestry depicting her contest with Poseidon for the city of Athens. Arachne wove a scene depicting the many love affairs and infidelities of Zeus. The two finished at the same time and Athena was incensed to discover that no one, including herself, could judge Arachne's work inferior.

Athena was outraged—by the effrontery of the challenge itself, the scandalous choice of subject matter, and the mortal's victory. In a jealous fit, Athena

tore Arachne's tapestry to shreds and broke the loom over the woman's head. Burning with shame and humiliation, Arache hanged herself.

When she calmed down, Athena realized that she had been a bit harsh, and that Arachne hadn't deserved to die for her justifiable pride in her work. Athena cut Arache down and restored her to life. But to punish Arachne for daring to challenge a goddess, Athena sprinkled her with the magical juices of aconite (which we call "monkshood" today), transforming the woman into a spider, and the rope into the webbing that Arachne and her myriad descendants would spin and weave henceforth for all eternity.

And this is why the estimated 120,000 species of spiders are called "Arachnids."

Daedalus & Icarus

By Crow Dragontree (grey)

Daedalus squinted his eyes against the salt spray as he stared out of his tower window. Although extremely high, his tower was precariously perched over the shore. The huge swells of water cast droplets in the air, which were in turn caught by the warm upward breezes to his vantage point. He turned from the window and began to pace across the stone floor.

"Dad, what's wrong?" asked Icarus, reading the worry on his father's brow.

Daedalus looked at his son, bemused. Did the boy not understand their situation? He smiled grimly and returned his gaze out of the window, looking away from the child playing with some unidentified objects on the stone floor before him. He took a deep breath.

"Remember how I was asked to build a special room for the Minos?" He began.

"The king?" Although Icarus had heard this story many times before, he was fond of listening to Daedalus tell of his dealings with the King of Crete. He was intensely proud of his clever, well-connected father.

"Yes, he wanted a place to hide his Minotaur, a place where the monster could enter, but never escape."

"And you built the Labyrinth for him!" His son couldn't resist exclaiming his father's accomplishment.

"Yes, I made a huge maze that consisted of nothing but meandering tunnels, never ending or beginning, but simply turning upon each other." For a moment, Daedalus stared unseeing at the crashing waves below, his eyes glazed over with proud memory. Quickly, he shook himself back to the present.

"Anyway," he continued, "Minos was quite happy with what I had built. So pleased, in fact, that he used my creation as a death trap!" His hands, rested upon the grey stone sill of the window, curled into white-knuckled fists. "Our dear King began sending people—children, really—into the Labyrinth to be fed to the Minotaur. He called it 'tribute,' and demanded that Athens send their youths to die in my Labyrinth." His teeth gritted. "*My* Labyrinth!"

"When Princess Ariadne," Daedalus continued as his son's head snapped up at the name of the king's daughter, "begged me to help her new boyfriend, Theseus get in and out of the Labyrinth to slay that confounded beast, of course I helped." It was as if Daedalus was pleading his case to a very young judge. "I gave her the thread to tie to the entrance. Theseus unwound the other end as he walked through and followed it back out." Daedalus paused, wondering why Theseus hadn't thought of doing that himself.

"Simple, really."

Icarus shrugged.

"So, that's why we're stuck here in this prison. Minos not only lost his Man-Bull, but his daughter ran off with Theseus back to Athens. We're imprisoned here as my punishment for helping them."

Although explaining the situation aloud, hearing his own words as he spoke them somehow helped him feel a bit better, Icarus seemed to have been paying more attention to the small, fluttery objects that he had collected on the floor. As if sensing that his father's tale was at an end, he shrugged.

"So, why don't we leave?"

Exasperated, Daedalus restrained himself from shouting. "We can't!" He flung up his arms in despair. "Minos not only controls this whole island, but the waters as well!" He pointed down at the violent tide. "See how the waves crash up and get larger and louder whenever we even think of nearing the shore?"

As if seeing his son for the first time, Daedalus stared down at his son as he played with a small cluster of feathers that he must have collected from the seabirds on the beach. His voice became suddenly soft and almost distant as he picked up a small, downy feather, turning it over between his fingers in amazement.

"The only thing he doesn't control around here is the air…"

***

Icarus thoroughly enjoyed the task his father set him over the next few weeks. Although the tower was high and guarded, they were frequently allowed to walk together along the beach. Icarus was given the task of finding and collecting as many feathers as he could. This task, Daedalus assured him, was of the utmost importance.

Icarus performed well. He provided his father with large, strong feathers, small fluffy feathers that seemed to hover in midair and all of the sizes and types in between. In the meantime, Daedalus worked tirelessly, using thread and wax to form four large, gently curved wings, complete with leather straps into which a person's arms might fit quite comfortably. Entering his father's room in the tower with an armload of feathers, Icarus regarded his father's creation with raised eyebrows.

"Icarus," said Daedalus, as he knelt in front of his son, staring into his eyes, "how would you like to fly?"

Icarus smiled broadly and nodded. If any other man had offered such an opportunity, Icarus would have thought him mad, but if anyone could fly, it would indeed be his father.

"Okay," said Daedalus, sliding a pair of wings onto his son's arms. "I'm going to jump out of the window first. Do exactly as I do, and follow me closely. While we're flying, do not fly too high or too low. The heat from the sun and the moisture from the water might hurt your wings."

"Sure," shrugged Icarus. It was clear that he would agree to anything for the opportunity to fly.

"Right," Dedlaus let out a long exhale as he drew himself back to his full height. He pulled on his wings and stood before the tower window. He turned toward his son and, winking, jumped.

Icarus watched in horror and disbelief as his father plummeted straight down. He was quite sure that anything his father built would work perfectly, but these wings were clearly defective. Sure that he was destined to be an orphan, tears began streaming down Icarus' face. About midway to the point of imact with the ground, however, Daedalus was suddenly no longer heading straight down, but had actually leveled off and was flying toward the sea.

Tears still wet on his face, Icarus laughed and, without any hint of hesitation or fear, leaped from the tower window. There was an intense moment of gut-dropping fear as he dipped, but it was as if he was weightless the moment he left solid ground. He had not plummeted as his father had, but immediately caught a warm current of air, sweeping him into his fathers' wake.

"Lower!" Commanded Daedalus, looking over his shoulder at his flying son. Tiny fishermen against a rolling blue backdrop pointed from their miniscule boats, waving and cheering. Icarus saluted them by performing a sweeping dive that skimmed the tops of their sails.

"No! Higher!" Daedalus screamed at his son.

For miles across the sea, Daedalus and Icarus flew. Icarus, laughing and singing at his newfound gift of flight climbed as high as he could upon the currents of air, then plummeted down to just above the water's surface, screaming with joy as his father cried out reprimands and warnings.

Either ignoring his father's words, or unable to hear over the roar of the sea and rush of the air combined with his own shrieks of excitement, Icarus continued this climb-and-swoop pattern, growing every closer to the hot, wax-melting sun and the damp, heavy sea. He never noticed the first, tiny feather float on the air away from his wing, no longer held in place by the liquefying wax.

Looking back, Daedalus screamed. His son's silhouette hovered, several yards above him, surrounded by a swarm of feathers, resembling moths dancing about a child-shaped frame. This image hung for a few seconds, then began their descent.

This was not Icarus' well-practiced graceful swoop, but a screaming, terrified, and uncrontrolled plunge. Staring in horror and agony, Daedalus watched his son crash into the wall of water below.

His vision blurred with tears, Daedalus made out a small island in the distance. Landing, he waited on the beach for his son to return to him. After the small body washed up against the shore, Daedalus prepared a grave for him. Naming the island *Icaria* in honor of his child, Daedalus eventually sailed off toward Sicily.

_____

The story of Daedalus and Icarus is truly a Wizardly tale. Daedalus was an extremely clever Wizard who was credited with the invention of the Labyrinth—which is frequently used as a symbol and tool of Magick. In addition, Daedalus was the only one smart enough to solve the challenge of passing a length of thread through a seashell (he tied it to an ant) and, as we see in this story, he seems to have invented an early form of hang gliding. For all of his cleverness, however, this tragic story illustrates not only the consequences of not heeding the advise of the wise, but the price one may pay for great heights without proper preparation and the sorrow a clever Wizard may face when pushing people to do things for which they may not be ready.

Baucis & Philemon
By Oberon (grey)

Once Zeus and Hermes—messenger of the Gods—decided to see how people were getting along on the Earth. They disguised themselves as poor travelers and visited Phrygia.

They were treated rudely and turned away at every door they knocked on, until they came to a small thatched cottage, where Baucis, a pious woman, and her husband Philemon, married when young, had grown old together. The old couple welcomed the strangers hospitably, and gave them food and lodging.

Zeus flooded the inhospitable country, but spared the kindly couple, transforming their humble hut into a magnificent temple, and making them its Priest and Priestess. When he offered to grant them any wish, they asked only that they be allowed to die at the same moment so that neither would have to bear the grief of losing the other.

When death finally came, Zeus transformed them both into trees, an oak and a linden, which grew and flourished side-by-side, their branches intertwining. For many years thereafter, visitors to the temple would be shown those trees and told this story.

_____

The virtue of hospitality is such an important tribal value that tales such as this have been told in many different cultures. An almost identical version among the Norse featured Odin and Loki as the disguised gods.

6. The Mabinogion: The wizardry of Welsh mythology
By Crow Dragontree (grey)

In general, Wizards are constant storytellers. The stories they choose, however, go far beyond mere entertainment. Wizardly stories tell about virtues, values, and consequences. They offer ideas as to how to solve problems and they preserve the spirit of a people that may have passed this way centuries ago. In sum, Wizardly stories teach while pretending to entertain. In this lesson, we will explore a story selected from the Mabinogion. The Mabinogion is perhaps the most important series of stories of the ancient Welsh Wizards and is believed by some to be the precursors for many of the King Arthur legends. If you find yourself interested in further exploring this fascinating piece of Celtic lore, I highly recommend that you take the course *The Mabinogion* at the Department of Lore in the Grey School for Wizardry. This story represents a very small portion of what is offered in that class.

It is important to note that ancient stories such as this weren't written down until very recently by monks who had some idea of the importance of the culture they were preserving. Whenever stories are retold, however, the teller changes them in some subtle way, reflecting a tiny piece of the storytelling Wizard's essence.

This is the way it should be, and in this spirit, I must warn you that my retelling of the Mabinogion is by no means a faithful translation of the original texts written by the monks of whom I speak. It is, instead, a retelling of a story in as close to the oral tradition of the Wizards of old as I can accomplish—with a bit of commentary added to point out the particularly interesting tidbits! If, however, you are interested in a faithful translation—and I applaud that decision—I heartily recommend reading one or both of the translations that you'll find in the reference section below.

In this portion of the *Companion*, I will briefly present and discuss a story from the fourth "branch" of the Mabinogion. This branch is somewhat different than the others in that it concerns the *Sons of Don* (thought to be synonymous with the Irish *Tuatha De Dannan*). These are said to be the Faery folk of the Otherworld. In fact, it is sometimes argued that, while the other branches are told from the viewpoint of the mundane world looking into the Otherworld, this branch is told from the point of view of the denizens of the Otherworld as they venture into Mundania.

In this branch, shapeshifting takes on a highly significant role, as does the importance of music in the Celtic conceptualization of magick. Here we are introduced to the role of the Bard in Celtic society and the concept of the song-spell. Emphasis is also placed on Gwydion's ability to play tricks in these stories, but there is a lesson here that mischief should not be created for its own end. Justice will, eventually, be meted out.

The fire before you blazes up and dies down in a rhythmic pattern, punctuated with the crackling and hissing of burning wood. A combination of the warmth from the flames and heady aroma of wood fills your head and the amber glow the fire casts upon your friends and trees around you seem to intensify. All eyes are fixed upon a figure seated close to the fire, wrapped in a grey cloak and wearing a wide-brimmed hat.

He picks up a stick lying near him and pokes the fire's coals. Flames leap up and the smoke begins to drift into tight spirals, taking on recognizable shapes and patterns. Through the silence, the Wizard speaks...

How to Start a War over Pigs

King Math was one of the more unusual rulers in Wales. It's not certain exactly how old he was, but it was rumored that he was immortal. Perhaps the key to his longevity was his insistence upon sitting in his throne room with his feet propped up in the lap of a maiden. In addition to being quite old and peculiar about his choice of footrests, he was recognized as an extremely wise man. He had an uncanny ability to see the truth of a matter in ways that others could not. His intuition and insight led people to believe that anything said in secret between two individuals was carried to Math in the form of whispers on the wind. In essence, Math was a true Wizard; he *saw* what others merely looked at.

It's also important to note Math's nephews, Gwydion and his brother, Gilfaethwy (Gil-FIGH-thooee). Gwydion was also something of an accomplished Wizard, and had a particular knack for shapeshifting. He could not only transform himself to look like other people or animal, but he could transform others as well. In fact, it was a favorite pastime of Gwydion's to roam the countryside in disguise, often as a Bard, to learn the latest news of the various courts and kingdoms. Gilfaethwy, however, also had one particular gift: desire.

Poor, lovesick Gilfaethwy had gotten so deeply infatuated with Math's footmaiden that he was convinced that he was going to die without her. As a rather charming fellow, however, he was quite certain that he could woo the young lady without much difficulty if only he could be alone with her for a few moments. However, every time he saw the woman of his dreams, she was most certainly not alone, but instead had a rather large and old pair of feet in her lap. Gilfaethwy was becoming quite frustrated with this predicament, and had lapsed into a rather deep depression.

"Don't worry, my brother!" said Gwyidon heartily, slapping him on the back, "I'll get you alone with her. I've got a plan!"

Indeed he did. Gwydion immediately took on the disguise as a traveling bard and set out on the road south to Dyfed. He had heard that their king, Pryderi, was in possession of a small herd of marvelous beasts called *pigs* and he had to go see them. After all, they were crucial to his plan to aid his brother. Upon seeing these fantastic creatures, he immediately asked for one or more of the pigs.

Pryderi winced. "I'm sorry, friend, I promised Arawn that I wouldn't give them away until I've bred enough to have twice as many as I do now. They're quite rare, you see." He lowered his voice into a conspiratorial tone. "They came to me from Annwfn."

Disappointed, Gwydion went for a stroll that evening in the forest, gathering a variety of very interesting-looking mushrooms. Returning to the castle with an armload of edible fungi, he worked a bit of magick. The next phase of his plan was nearly complete.

The following night, Gwydion leaned over toward Pryderi over dinner and said in his most casual voice, "You said last night that you couldn't give away any of your pigs." Gwydion paused for a moment for dramatic effect. "I wonder, could you possibly *trade* them?"

Gwydion nodded toward an open window, through which Pryderi could see two dozen of the most beautiful animals humans have seen. Twelve horses and twelve hunting dogs, with golden leashes, saddles, collars and bridles glittered in the moonlight. Gwidion raised his eyebrows as if asking "Well, how about it?" Within minutes the trade was made.

***

The next morning, Pryderi rose early and rushed to the stables, excited at the prospect of seeing his new animals in full sunlight. Once he arrived, however, he stopped and stood stock still, surrounded by stablehands who were equally immobilized by shock and staring at empty stalls. Where there should have been a beautiful horse or fine, gilded, dog, there was instead a small, rather ordinary mushroom. He had been duped.

Meanwhile, Gwydion had left during the night and was fleeing cross-country with all of Pryderi's prized pigs. He stopped to build a pen for his newly-acquired pigs in which to hide them before meeting with King Math and his army.

"What's going on?" asked Gwydion, noting that the king and his soldiers were preparing for war.

"King Pryderi has gotten his army together and is coming to attack us." Math said grimly. He gave Gwydion a significant look. "There appears to be a problem with a trade he made with you involving pigs."

Gwydion nodded, and tried to look as grim as King Math. Inwardly, however, he felt the smug sensation that one gains when a carefully laid plan comes together. As long as King Math was out at war, he was not at his castle with his feet in his footmaiden's lap, and Gilfaethwy was guaranteed some alone time with her.

The price for Gilfaethwy's desire, however, was much heavier than Gwydion had expected. Pryderi's attacks were strong and difficult to repel. Many soldiers from both kingdoms were killed or were severely wounded in combat. In the meantime, Math's footmaiden insistently refused Gilfaethwy's advances and, in his rage, he assaulted her.

In an effort to finally put this fiasco to an end, Pryderi, Math, and Gwydion agreed to end the war with a fight between to two men whom this conflict concerned.

Pryderi was a very skilled fighter, but Gwydion had the advantage of magick and, after a spectacular battle, Gwydion finally slew Pryderi. Deeply affected by the losses on both sides, the armies began their somber marches toward their homes. Once back at his own castle, Math was confronted with the news of the attack upon his footmaiden. It was all suddenly clear to him what Gwydion and Gilfaethwy had done.

Enraged, King Math rounded on them.

"I cannot begin to express how angry this makes me!" He bellowed. "You have cost this woman more than any of us can know, you have caused the deaths of countless innocent men, and you have—in essence—cheated and then murdered a neighboring king!"

Gwydion gasped slightly as he saw Math's hand move for his wand.

"There is no way that you or I can undo this damage, but you will pay," the blaze in Math's eyes intensified, "at least in some small way!" Math leveled his wand upon Gilfaethwy and he transformed into a large hind. In a state of blind panic, Gwydion began to run. As fast and clever as he was, however, Gwydion could not outrun Math's magick. Before he even reached the door, he had been transformed into a magnificent stag. King Math smiled bitterly.

"You two like to plot together, so let's see you become mates in the animal kingdom for a while. This year, Gilfaethwy, you're the female, next year it will be Gwydion and so forth. Each spring, bring your offspring to me. When you do that, I'll transform you into your next animal form. This year it's deer, obviously, but next year you'll be pigs," he inclined his head toward Gwydion, "and the third year—wolves, I think."

He eyed them both intensely, turning his wand end over end in his fingers.

"Now get out of my sight."

***

You stare at the image in the dying fire transfixed. The amber forms of two frightened deer flee within the forest of lightly glowing logs. You stare transfixed by the fading image, not daring to look away. You hear the Wizard move and look up.

The embers provide a dim illumination to him from below as he stands, leaning on his staff. His slightest movements reflected by the flow and sway of his cloak.

"These stories are not just mine. They are yours now. Upon hearing them, stories such as these become a part of you, connecting you with the storyteller and become your history. Yes," he assures, noting a look of incredulity, "no matter what culture from which you hail, these stories are the history of all people."

"Your own stories are of the utmost importance." He continues, "They connect you with all people as well as nature. Tell your stories to others, and learn theirs."

The Wizard winks and turns his back to the fire, raising his staff slightly and taking a step away, he disappears. It is almost as if the night between the trees engulfed him. Words drift across the dying glow of the fire pit from the darkness.

"The rest, of course, is completely up to you."

7. Magickal Artifacts
By Oberon (grey)

Magickal lore includes not just places, stories, and characters, but also wonderful magickal objects, commonly called Artifacts. There are as many of these as there are stories; some of them really existed, and may still be found in museums.

The Holy Grail
By Oberon & Morgan Felidae (brown)

There have been many references to Grails (or *Graals*) in various mythologies, and the most famous artifact in Western tradition is undoubtedly the Holy Grail. This was supposed to have been the cup that Jesus drank from at the Last Supper. He passed it full of wine around to his apostles, saying: "Drink this, for it is my blood." (Oddly, however, it does not appear in Leonardo da Vinci's famous painting of that scene.)

It was also claimed that the same cup was later used by Joseph of Arimathea to catch the blood of Jesus at the crucifixion, when he was stabbed by the spear of a Roman soldier—reportedly a centurion named Gaius Cassius Longinus (John 19:34). It is this continuous association with blood that has given it the name *Sangrail,* a close spelling of the combination *sang-real* or "royal blood."

Following Christ's death, the Holy Grail began to collect stories of having miraculous healing powers. It was said that Joseph brought the Grail to the island of Avalon, the future site of Glastonbury. After that, it passed into the hands of secret Grail-keepers in a hidden castle.

The Holy Grail became a major theme in the legend of King Arthur, as his Knights of the Round Table were sent throughout Europe in quest of it. It attained a mystical significance which linked it to the feminine mysteries of the Chalice and the Blade, the Cauldron of Cerridwen, and the Lady of the Land. In the stories, it was either Sir Galahad the Pure or Sir Percival who saw the Grail for the last time before it disappeared into the mists of legend.

OZ: A number of cups have been claimed over the centuries to be the Holy Grail, and I know of one whose documented history I find convincing. But I am pledged not to reveal more...

The Holy Lance
The Spear of Longinus also became a religious relic, known as the Holy Lance. It is said to have been unearthed by St. Helena at the same time and place as the Holy Nails and the True Cross.

Helena's son, Constantine (285-387 C.E.), became the first Christian Emperor of Rome. So a legend grew that whoever possessed the Lance would rule the world. It was said to have been wielded by Emperor Theodosius, Alaric the Goth (who sacked Rome in 410), Atilla the Hun, Charles Martel (who defeated the Moslems in 733), Charlemagne, and Frederick Barbarossa.

After serving the Holy Roman Emperors, the Spear was put on display in the Hofburg Palace in Austria. In 1912 a young Adolf Hitler visited the Museum and learned of the Lance and its reputation. In 1938, after he had risen to power as the Chancellor of Germany, Hitler annexed Austria and seized the spear. After Hitler's defeat, the Holy Lance was returned to the Hofburg Museum, where it resides today.

Excalibur
The legendary sword of King Arthur was said to have been given to him by Viviane, the Lady of the Lake. One version has it that a hand holding the sword rose from the water to offer it. After wielding Excalibur successfully in many battles, Arthur finally fell to the rebel forces of his bastard son, Modred. As he lay dying on the battlefield, Arthur commanded his most trusted knight, Sir Bedivere, to hurl the sword into the lake—whereupon, so goes the story, a hand arose from the water to seize it.

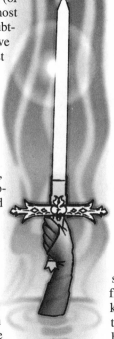

The lake in question once surrounded the mystic Isle of Avalon, now known as Glastonbury Tor. The lake has long since been drained. Perhaps someday the legendary sword Excalibur shall be exhumed in its vicinity.

Magickal Jewelry

Jewelry has always been a popular repository of magickal power—especially rings, such as in J.R.R. Tolkien's epic *Lord of the Rings*:

> *Three Rings for the Elven-kings under the sky,*
> *Seven for the Dwarf-lords in their halls of stone,*
> *Nine for Mortal Men doomed to die,*
> *One for the Dark Lord on his dark throne.*
> *In the Land of Mordor where the Shadows lie.*
> *One Ring to rule them all,*
> *One Ring to find them,*
> *One Ring to bring them all*
> *And in the darkness bind them!*
> *In the Land of Mordor where the Shadows lie.*
> —J.R.R. Tolkien, *The Fellowship of the Ring*

Solomon's Ring
By Solaris (aqua)

One of the most influential Wizards of history, King Solomon (970–928 BCE) possessed a magickal signet ring. According to legend, heaven gave Solomon the ring, on which the secret "Most Great Name of God" (JHVH—the Tetragramaton) was engraved. The ring was made with two metals—brass and iron. The brass side had Solomon's written commands to the good genii. The iron side has his commands to the bad genii. The ring bore the Seal of Solomon, which is the Star of David inside a circle with dots or other symbols filling in the gaps. Solomon set four jewels, given to him by four different angels, in the magickal ring.

With his ring, Solomon was very powerful. The ring gave him healing powers, knowledge of anything Solomon wanted to know, the ability to communicate with animals, and control over demons (*djinn*) and the four elements.

According to one Arabic story, the demon Sakhr tricked one of Solomon's wives into giving him the ring. For forty days Sakhr ruled while Solomon wandered the country as a poor man. Sakhr eventually threw the ring into the sea, where it was eaten by a fish. This fish was caught by a fisherman, who cut open the fish, found the ring and gave it back to Solomon. When Solomon returned to power, he made Sakhr build him a great mosque.

The Nibelungen Ring
By Rainmaker (red)

In the great Germanic Saga, *The Song of the Nibelung,* the Nibelungen Ring is fashioned by the *Nibelung* (meaning "dwarf") Alberich from the *Rheingold,* a magickal treasure in the river Rhine that was guarded by the three Rhinemaidens. The ring will let its bearer rule the World, but only one who renounces love completely can fashion the ring. Alberich curses love, seizes the treasure and fashions the ring. The trickster Loki steals the ring from Alberich, who is crushed by his loss, and lays a curse on the Ring: until it returns to him, whoever does not possess it will desire it, and whoever possesses it will receive unhappiness and death.

The ring is later used, together with the *Tarnhelm* (see below), to ransom Freyja from the giants Fafner and Fasolt. Odin schemes to regain the ring with a plot that spans several generations, setting up his grandson Siegfried to gain the ring from the giant Fafnir, who has turned himself into a dragon with the help of the *Tarnhelm.* However, Alberich's brother Mime is plotting to gain the ring for himself and has raised Siegfried to kill Fafner for him. Siegfried kills Fafner and takes both the ring and the *Tarnhelm* from the dragon's hoard. He discovers that Mime intends to poison him and kills the dwarf.

On his return trip Siegfried discovers the Vakyrie Brünnhilde and awakes her from a magic sleep. Brünnhilde is won over by Siegfried's love and renounces the world of the gods to stay with him. She urges Siegfried to seek more adventures and he leaves with her the Nibelungen Ring as a pledge of fidelity. However, he is tricked by the Gibichung siblings Gunther and Gudrun, into drinking a potion that makes him lose his memory of Brünnhilde and fall in love with Gudrun. He pledges to help Gunther gain the love of Brünnhilde. With the help of the *Tarnhelm,* Siegfried disguises himself as Gunther and gains Brünnhilde as Gunther's wife, but Siegfried cannot resist taking the Nibelungen Ring off Brünnhilde's finger and placing it on his own.

When Gunther leads Brünnhilde into the castle, she sees Siegfried wearing the Nibelungen Ring, and realizes that she has been betrayed. She seeks revenge and ultimately Siegfried is killed during a hunting party. Brünnhilde takes charge of the funeral preparations and orders a huge pyre built on the banks of the Rhine river. She takes the ring and tells the Rhinemaidens to claim it from the ashes of the pyre once the fire has cleansed it of the curse. Once the pyre is lit, Brünnhilde rides her horse into the fire and vanishes. As the fire burns, the Rhine river overflows and the Rhinemaidens reclaim the ring, bringing about the "Doom of the Gods."

Draupnir
By Rainmaker (red)

Draupnir, the golden arm ring of Odin, was forged by the dwarves Brokk and Sindri. It was a source of endless wealth as each ninth morning it created eight more golden rings just like itself, although without the ability to multiply. Odin placed the ring on the funeral pyre of his son Baldur. Another of Odin's sons, Hermod, later retrieved the ring from Baldur in the Underworld. The ring was also used by Freyr's servant Skirnir in the wooing of Freyr's future wife, the giantess Gerd.

Brisingamen
By Rainmaker (red)

Brisingamen is the mostly gold (other sources say amber) necklace of the Norse goddess Freya. It was forged by the Brisings, four dwarves named Davlin, Allfrigg, Berling and Grer. In order to get the necklace from the dwarves, Freyja had to sleep with each of the dwarves for a night.

When Freyja wore the necklace, mostly in the springtime, no man or god could withstand her charms. This seriously upset the other goddesses. The necklace also gave support to any army which Freyja favored on the battlefield.

Well, it wasn't only the goddesses who envied Freyja her possession, but the gods, as well. In one of the more humorous stories of Norse mythology, Thor's hammer was stolen by the giant, Trym. Trym's demand for the return of the hammer was to marry Freyja. Well, the gods/goddesses, especially Freyja, didn't think too highly of this idea and recommended that Thor trick Trym by disguising as Freyja. The story of this is somewhat long and involved, but ultimately Thor, dressed up as Freyja and identified by the necklace Brisingamen, succeeded in regaining his hammer.

On another occasion, the necklace was stolen by Loki, the trickster god, while Freyja slept. When she awoke to find her necklace missing, she harnessed her cats to her wagon and went out to find it. Heimdall helped in her search and eventually they found the thief, Loki, who had transformed himself into a seal. Heimdall also transformed into a seal and fought Loki. After a lengthy battle, Heimdall won and returned Brisingamen to Freyja.

Other Magickal Objects

The Tarnhelm
By Rainmaker (red)

The *Tarnhelm* (German for "Helmet of disguise") was fashioned by the Nibelung (dwarf) Mime, who is the brother of Alberich, the creator of the Nibelungen Ring. The helmet does not render the wearer invisible, but instead allows the wearer to appear in a different form, such as an animal or a different person. Alberich used the helmet to turn himself into a snake and a toad in order to impress the trickster Loki. The giant Fafner used it turn himself into the dragon that was ultimately slain by Siegfried, and Siegfried in turn used it to disguise himself as Gunther in order to claim Brünnhilde as Gunther's wife. It is not clear what happens to the helmet in the end…so it may still be out there!

The Philosopher's Stone
By Solaris (aqua)

The "Holy Grail" of any medieval alchemist was to discover the Philosopher's Stone. The Philosopher's Stone, believed to be made of *carmot,* is a magickal stone from which a powder was derived, and the powder was turned into the Elixir of Life. Originally, this elixir was not supposed to stop death, but simply delay it. It cleansed out the impurities in the body, restored youth, and prolonged life. It wasn't until years later that the Philosopher's Stone was considered the key to immortality and turning inexpensive metals into gold, which according to the alchemy's philosophy is the purest metal. It was Zosimos the Theban (c.250-300 C.E.) that claimed the stone held the secret of life and health and contained spiritual importance. Its immense range of powers increased until the 13th century. Only a very small portion was needed to complete the transformation.

The quest for the stone, also called the "Great Work" or "Magnum Opus," was detailed in a seven-step formula described by the *Emerald Tablet of Hermes.* These seven steps included calcination, dissolution, separation, conjunction, fermentation, distillation, and coagulation. The first four steps took place in the realm of matter; while the remaining steps took place in the realm of mind and creative imagination.

The origin of the stone began with the theories of Geber, an eighth century alchemist. According to Geber, every metal was the co mbination of the four qualities: hot, cold, dry, and moist. Geber originated started ed the idea that every metal could be transformed by rearranging its basic qualities. This change was caused by a substance called *elixir.*

Nicolas Flamel (1330-1418 C.E.) was the only person to ever hold the key to making the Philosopher's Stone—the mysterious *Book of Abraham the Jew.* Flamel was wealthy, which most historians believe came from investments. In a period when no one lived beyond the age of 35, Flamel died at the age of 88. After his death the mysterious book vanished, and it has not been found since.

Throughout history, fortunes were invested to find the Philosopher's Stone, and those fortunes were lost. The closest anyone in recorded history has come to turning lead into gold was to put a gold-plated layer on the metal, which some people did. Now since modern science has taken the forefront, the Philosopher's Stone has become a metaphor for man's attempt to escape death.

Department XVI: Dark Arts (black)

Ebony Edifices

It is the shade that shields us from the sun
And keeps us safe – for light, untempered, slays.
Without the nights, we could not stand the days;
Nor know the light, if darkness were undone.
Behold the sword that cuts, the cord that binds!
Yes, we are Wizards too, who take such pains.
Can't hold your horses? We will catch the reins,
And help to harness what bright magic finds.
Here is the counter for the spell, the lock

That binds the door to
all things trouble-
some.
We serve the greater
good with what we call
And build our shadowed
castles, rock by rock.
Be certain that sometime a day will come
When you, too, will be grateful for the wall.

—Elizabeth Barrette

1. Introduction

ELCOME TO THE WORLD OF THE Dark Arts! The simplest form of Low Magick is *sorcery,* in which a physical act is performed to achieve a result. Sorcery forms the bulk of folk magick, and is often referred to as "Black Magick" or "the Dark Arts."

Unfortunately, when people today talk about "Black Magick," they are generally referring to magick used for selfish purposes rather than altruistic ones. In particular: dominating and manipulating people against their will; compelling people to do things they do not wish to do; working against the best interests of others, intentionally threatening or inflicting harm on others—all these are considered practices of the Dark Arts …and of Sorcerers. However, a very important aspect of traditional sorcery is magickal defense against all ills and evils, so this chapter contains techniques for "Defense against the Dark Arts."

Also included in this chapter are "Children of the Night," those monsters that haunt our nightmares and scary movies, on the borderlands between the living and the dead—Ghosts, Demons, Vampires, Werewolves, Zombies, and Ghouls—as well as unexplained "Mystery Monsters," such as Mothman and the Jersey Devil. These have one foot in our reality and the other in the worlds beyond.

The color of magick associated with this department is Black, relating to constricting, binding and Saturn energies. As the color of night, black represents foreboding, fortitude, and consistency because of the need to "make it through the darkness." Black is sometimes used as a protective color for magickal tools—especially handles and wrappings. It is also used when trying to banish a bad habit, turn negativity, or make dras-tic life changes. Black is also, of course, the traditional color of Sorcery and the Dark Arts.

2. Wizardry and the Shadow

By Apollonius (white)

We all come in contact with the Dark Side, whether we wish to or not. No matter how hard we try to avoid it, Wizards need to understand the Dark Side, even if they do not specialize in the Dark Arts. As you know, true Wizardry is grounded in wisdom, and Wizards agree that there is much in common among all the great wisdom traditions. Wisdom helps us to understand the foundations of *right thinking*, *right speech*, and *right action*, which are important for all people, but especially for Wizards, who have unique duties in the cosmic community. Further, wisdom-practices, including Wizardry itself, help us to live in accord with this understanding.

Ethics, in the broad sense, is one of the fundamental components of wisdom (and hence of Wizardry), and that is one reason ethics is required in the Grey School curriculum and addressed in several classes. Although we might debate details, there is broad agreement on fundamental ethical principles, that is, about what is good, and what is evil. Although we focus on the good, an essential part of wisdom is knowing, understanding, confronting, and coming to an accommodation with the Dark Side. I can express this most easily in terms of Jungian psychology, where it is called the "Shadow." The Shadow exists on many levels: *collective* (i.e., common to all humans), *cultural*, and *personal*. Psychologically, It resides in the collective (biological) layers, the cultural layers, and the personal layers of the unconscious mind.

The Shadow comprises everything that we have rejected, consciously or unconsciously, as a species, culture, or individual. Therefore, the Shadow constitutes Evil as it exists for each us. "Satan" is the name that Christians and Moslems apply to their Shadow (which exists primarily at the cultural level). Although the faces of our personal Shadows may differ somewhat, many Wizards have similar Shadows, for our Shadows tend to be egotistical, power-hungry, intolerant, exploitive, sexist, racist, aggressive, violent, vindictive, selfish, lying, thieving, manipulative, greedy, sloppy, irresponsible, lazy, passive, weak, indecisive, argumentative, ill-tempered, ignorant, shallow, materialist, consumerist, etc. Quite a litany of evils, and I'm sure I've left many out, but you get the idea. You want to see the face of *your* Shadow? Imagine the person — real or not —whom you are least able to tolerate!

Psychologist Carl Jung taught two important lessons about the Shadow. The first is that the Shadow cannot be banished, and to the extent we think we have done so, we will be Its unwilling pawn. Denying or ignoring the Shadow's power over our lives is the surest way to expand that power. Further, if we do not recognize the Shadow, we will blame our misfortune or misbehavior on bad luck or on other people ("projecting the Shadow"), which may lead to scapegoating. Jung remarked that the brighter the Light, the darker the Shadow it casts. Therefore it is no accident that the religions and spiritual traditions with the strictest moral codes and ascetic orientations are also those with the most formidable Shadows. And it is no accident that some of the most diabolical attitudes and actions that we observe in the world today arise from groups that pride themselves on their purity and goodness.

The other lesson that Jung taught is that the Shadow is a fount of enormous power and creativity. By the very fact that it has been rejected, it can give us what we lack. Most, if not all, of the Shadow's qualities can have some beneficial effect in the appropriate circumstances. These are powers that should be reclaimed as we strive to become more integrated and whole, to achieve full integrity. This is essential to the character development of all true Wizards, who strive to unify the aspects of their psyches and harmonize them with the cosmos. Therefore, it is valuable for all people — but especially for us Wizards, who channel hidden sources of power—to become acquainted with the Shad-

ow and negotiate a "pact" by which we may obtain this power in return for satisfying the Shadow's demands *in a manner consistent with our ethics*. Obviously this is completely different from abandoning your moral autonomy and enslaving yourself to the Shadow. Doing that would be "selling your soul to the Devil" or "going over to the Dark Side."

In conclusion, it is essential that Wizards have firm ethical standards. We cannot be neutral on all issues; that would not be wise, and wisdom is our foundation. On the other hand, that very wisdom teaches that we should acknowledge the Shadow, and, further, that we should interact and even cooperate with It, conformingly with the ethical convictions born of this wisdom. So, get to know your Shadow and negotiate with It!

3. Monsters
By LeopardDancer (grey)

The word "monster" comes from the Latin *monstum,* or "that which is revealed." While this definition may seem to have nothing to do with the common usage of the word as something frightening, scary and often mythical, appearances may be deceiving. Yes, monsters are strange and often scary, and yes, they are grounded in the realm of myth. However, these denizens of the darker parts do have things to reveal to us, if only we pay attention. They challenge the boundaries of the impossible and show us that things are not always as they seem, or as we would like them to be.

To the Greeks and Romans, the appearance of any mythic beast was a message from the hidden realms of existence. But the Scientific Revolution changed the way that people viewed the world around them. Suddenly, everything could be explained and things that defied explanation were just ignored. The lore of past ages was considered to be of no consequence, and "Creatures of the Night" were relegated to folklore.

Magic and Monsters

Most magickal traditions include detailed information about various types of monstrous beings and how to deal with them. Magickal theory also speaks of various realms of being which are present all the time and are connected to one another.

The physical level is that which we normally see with our eyes and have contact with using our other senses. This is the ordinary body of flesh and blood. The etheric level is next. This is life-force, and it shows itself in an auric form. Next is the astral level, the realm of normal mental activity, of dreams and of the imagination. People have an astral body that can, when one trains properly, be used for astral travel and out of body experiences. After that is the mental level, which is the origin of abstract thought. This is the realm of timeless and spaceless meaning. To connect with this level is to begin to become one with the One, the Eternal Dancer. Last is the spiritual level. This realm is one of primal unity and that from which all other realms originate.

All of these levels are equally important in dealing with monstrous beings, but the etheric may be the most important. Etheric energy is closest to physical and as such, can attain a certain degree of solidity. Tactile sense can pick etheric energy up. It can exert pressure and sometimes be mistaken for a full solid object. When diffused however, etheric energy is invisible and intangible unless certain magickal skills have been mastered. The astral level is the next most important. The astral shapes the etheric just as the etheric shapes the physical. Something changed or created with enough force on the astral level will tend to subtly reshape the etheric which in turn reshapes the physical. Familiarity with the other levels of being will help when dealing with these denizens of the dark.

Ghouls
By Oberon & LeopardDancer (grey)

In the "Dark Arts" chapter in the *Grimoire*, Oberon included a section on "The Dead and the Undead," with short entries on Ghosts, Vampires, Zombies, and Werewolves. Because of space limitations, Ghouls were omitted. So we would like to include them here.

Legends of ghouls originated with the Arabic *Thousand and One Nights.* It is believed that stories of their existence are derived from evidence of wild animal disturbances to graves at night. Ghouls are eaters of human corpses. They dwell in graveyards and burial places throughout the world, and are often confused with Vampires. But Vampires have class and style, whereas Ghouls are just plain disgusting. If clothed at all, they just wear clotted and stained rags, while Vampires go for the elegant evening-wear look. Ghouls are not blood-drinkers, but rather they much prefer human carrion to any other diet,

seldom preying upon the living.

During the Middle Ages—especially in the time of the Plague—Ghouls were not uncommon, scavenging battlefields and the charnel-heaps of often-unburied plague victims. They are still reported in some remote countries where health care and burial practices remain primitive for many. But the development of embalming and cremation in modern mortuary practice has virtually eliminated the Ghoul from modern civilization—unlike Vampires, who thrive in modern cities.

The traditional Ghoul is humanoid in form, with big lantern eyes, long claws and rows of sharp teeth. They appear diseased and desiccated, with cracked lips, chapped knees, and fingers caked with disgusting remnants of their meals. They have little true intelligence, with no speech and only limited knowledge of simple tools. Ghouls may even be eyeless and blind, but their sense of smell is highly developed—useful for finding their prey.

Unlike Vampires, Ghouls are not harmed by sunlight, but they still prefer to work at night when they are less likely to be caught at their grave-robbing activities. Wiley and elusive, they are seldom caught in the act. The only sign of their presence may be the discovery of untidily-opened graves, and the mutilated remains of the deceased.

Ghouls are impervious to pain, are immune to poisons, and have amazing regenerative powers. Weapons will hurt them, but usually not kill them. They are not any stronger than the average human, but are far more agile and swift. Ghouls are cowardly and will only fight if they have an advantage, otherwise they will flee.

Since Ghouls are nocturnal creatures, sunlight or artificial light is your best friend when dealing with them. They will be slowed down when exposed to light, making them easier to deal with. The best way to kill a Ghoul is with fire. These beasties are highly flammable. Electrocution and decapitation also work well, as with any other creature!

4. Monsters of Mystery
By Oberon (grey)

"Monsters" can be sorted into several different categories. There are "freaks of nature," resulting from birth defects, mutations, or other deformities and abnormalities.

There are the legendary creatures of the "Mythic Menagerie" and the classic Bestiaries. These are often made-up hybrids—such as the Centaur, Sphinx, or Gryphon; or they may be exaggerated versions of little-known real animals, such as the Kraken.

There are the "Cryptids" investigated by cryptozoologists—living animals reported by many and often photographed, but not yet captured and conclusively identified. Such creatures include Bigfoot, the

Loch Ness Monster, the Yeti, and the Mokele-Mbem-be of Africa.

Then there are those anomalies that completely defy categorization. These are bizarre and generally unique creatures that are reported from time to time. They are usually a local phenomenon, witnessed late at night in strange encounters. They seem utterly alien from anything known to this world. Perhaps they do come from somewhere else. We can only call them "Mystery Monsters." Here are a few...

Chupacabra

The name of this contempo-rary mystery monster means "goat sucker," as it is said to prey on livestock such as chickens, sheep and goats. It is most commonly reported in Mexico and Pu-erto Rico but has also been sighted throughout Central America, where most of the reports have come from farmers.

Descriptions vary so much from person to person that it is impossible to draw a consistent image of these creatures. They may walk on their hind legs or on all four clawed feet. They have red or black eyes and are sometimes said to have a long tail, sometimes even bat-like wings. They have been reported as being 3-5 feet tall (standing on hind legs), sometimes with hair or spines on their backs, but are more often described as having smooth or scaly skin.

Unfortunately, no photos or other concrete evidence of these bizarre creatures have been obtained. Various people believe that the Chupacabra may be a new species, an interdimensional being, or perhaps some sort of secret government experiment. Some even think it may be extraterrestrial. But for now, it is anyone's guess as to what this creature could be.

The Dover Demon

The "Dover Demon" was first reported on April 22, 1977 in Dover, a suburb of Boston, Massachusetts. Three 17 year-old boys were driving home around ten-thirty at night when the driver, Bill Bartlette, saw in

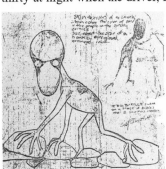

his headlights a bizarre creature crawling along a rock wall off the roadside. He said that it had a head like a watermelon and no features other than two large orange eyes. Its body was thin with long limbs and fingers that grasped the rocks. It was about 4 feet tall with peach-colored, smooth skin.

Bartlette's friends were talking and saw nothing. They returned to the spot, but nothing was there. Once home, Bartlette made a drawing of what he'd seen.

Two hours after that encounter, and about a mile away, 15 year-old John Baxter was walking home from his girlfriend's house when he saw a figure walking towards him on the road. Thinking it was a boy he knew, Baxter called out his name but got no answer. The creature ran off the road and up a bank.

Following it, Baxter got a good look at the creature. He said it had a large head, a thin body, and long limbs and fingers. The hairless skin seemed to have a rough texture, like sandpaper. Baxter stood and watched it for a minute before retreating in fear. He also drew pictures of it. Comparing Bartlette's and Baxter's drawings, it is obvious that they had seen the exact same creature.

The day after these sightings occurred, Bartlette told his friend Will Taintor about what he had seen. That evening at midnight, Taintor was driving his girl-friend Abby Brabham home when Brabham saw a hair-less monkeylike creature crouching on all fours on the side of the road as they drove past. Even though she had not heard of what the others had encountered, her description matched theirs, except that she said its eyes were green. Taintor said he also caught a glimpse of it.

There have been no more sightings since, and the mystery of the Dover Demon remains unsolved.

The Jersey Devil

Philadelphia
Evening Bulletin

The "Jersey Devil" is one of the most famous American "Mystery Monsters." Since its first appear-ances in the early 19th century, it has been seen by over 2,000 people in and around the state of New Jersey. Several dif-ferent origin stories have been told, each in-volving a different woman giving birth to a hideous "devil-child."

"In the early 19th century, Commodore Stephen Decatur, a naval hero, was testing cannonballs on the firing range when he saw a strange creature flying across the sky. He fired and hit the creature but it kept right on flying across the field. Joseph Bonaparte, former king of Spain and brother of Napoleon, saw the Jersey Devil in Bordentown, New Jersey, between 1816 and 1839 while he was hunting. In 1840-41 many sheep and chickens were killed by a creature with a piercing scream and strange tracks. Between 1859 and

1894, the Jersey Devil was seen numerous times and reportedly carried off anything that moved." (—Dave Juliano, *The Shadowlands*)

50 years later, during the week of January 16-23, 1909, the Jersey Devil was seen by over 1,000 people, leaving its odd tracks in the snow all over South Jersey and Philadelphia. It was described as a bird-like, flying creature with glowing eyes, a horse's head, and a piercing scream. Garbage left in yards was eaten. The strange hoof prints were found in almost every yard in Burlington. They went up trees, leapt from roof to roof, and disappeared in the middle of roads and open fields. Dogs refused to follow the tracks, which hunters pursued for over 20 miles, over 5 foot fences and under 8 inch spaces

At 2:30 AM on January 19, Mr. and Mrs. Nelson Evans of Gloucester watched the Devil from their window for 10 minutes. Mr. Evans described the creature thus:

"It was about three feet and a half high, with a head like a collie dog and a face like a horse. It had a long neck, wings about two feet long, and its back legs were like those of a crane, and it had horse's hooves. It walked on its back legs and held up two short front legs with paws on them. It didn't use the front legs at all while we were watching. My wife and I were scared, I tell you, but I managed to open the window and say, 'Shoo,' and it turned around, barked at me, and flew away." (—James F. McGloy and Ray Miller, "The Jersey Devil," *The Middle Atlantic Press,* Wallingford, PA, 1976, p.45)

Many people saw the creature clearly and close up, and described it identically. Some said it barked at them before flying off. One woman heard a commotion in her yard and opened her door to find the Devil standing there holding her dog. She beat at the thing with a broom until it dropped her dog and flew away. The West Collingswood Fire Department turned their hose on the Devil, which initially retreated, but then charged, flying away at the last second.

Although they have tapered off over the past century, sightings of the Jersey Devil—and its attacks on people and livestock—have continued to the present day. There have been many speculations as to what it could be. These have included the rare sandhill crane, a prehistoric pterodactyl, or a supernatural demon. None of these, however, account for all the features and behaviors described. But there is an uncanny resemblance to reports of the Chupacabra.

Sandhill Crane

(The primary source for this entry is Dave Juliano at The Shadowlands: djuliano@theshadowlands.net)

The Loveland Frog

The story of the "Loveland Frog" began in May of 1955, when a man driving through Loveland, Ohio, at 3:30 AM, saw three frog-like reptilian creatures standing upright by the side of the road. The man pulled over and watched them for a few minutes. One of them held up a wand, with sparks shooting out of its tip.

The witness reported this incident to the local police, but nothing more was seen of the creatures until March of 1972, when a Loveland policeman driving down Riverside Road at 1:00 AM spotted a crouching animal on the side of the road. When the headlights fell upon it, the creature rose up on its hind legs, revealing itself to be 3-4 feet tall, with a reptilian or frog-like head and leathery green skin. With a glance at the officer, the Frog leaped over the guardrail into the Little Miami River.

A similar incident was reported two weeks later by another police officer, in which the creature appeared to have been injured as it limped from the road into the river.

The Loveland Frog has not been seen again, and no one knows what it could have been.

Mothman

The "Mothman" was first seen in the fall of 1966 by two couples driving past an old generator plant in Point Pleasant, West Virginia, at 11:30 PM. The door of the plant had been ripped from its hinges and a 7 foot monster with huge glowing red eyes and great folded wings stood in the doorway. As the driver hit the accelerator, the creature shot straight up into the air and began pursuing them at up to 100 mph. At the city limits, it veered off and disappeared.

Over the next few days there were a number of similar sightings and reports of a giant flying creature

that attacked people, stole dogs, and mutilated animals. Its presence also seemed to interfere with radio and TV reception. On November 16, a press conference was held at which the creature was dubbed "Mothman," after the popular "Batman" TV series. Within a year of the first sighting, over 100 reports were recorded.

On October 16, 1967, the Silver Bridge over the Ohio River collapsed in rush-hour traffic, dropping 46 cars into the river. It was the biggest disaster to ever hit Point Pleasant, and many people wondered if there was a connection with Mothman. Since then, there have been no further sightings, and only scattered rumors of Mothman.

5. Demons

By LeopardDancer (grey)

Of all the creatures we cover in this chapter you will probably find the demonic the most frightening. Even religious people admit to the existence of demons, even as they scoff at the existence of Vampires and the Were. Most people shudder at the mere mention of the demonic. It evokes images of cold, malign presences watching us just out of our ability to "see" them. On a different side of the coin though, some deny the existence of the demonic, believing it to be a purely Christian concept. Or that "evil," such as it is, belongs purely to the material world; that once one moves beyond the material realm then all is pure and good.

Demon lore, however, was around long before Christianity, and it plays a very large role in most spiritual traditions worldwide. Many of these have full-blown demonology traditions that list the strengths, weaknesses, nature, powers and names of various demonic entities in great detail. Christianity of the Middle Ages had Demonology as a branch of Angelology, since demons were said to be fallen angels.

Demonic behavior is much better understood than the demons themselves. When demons interact with humans the forms they take are very diverse and confusing, but they are all odd. Weird with a capital W. Ba'al appears as a man with three heads: a man's, a toad's and a cat's. Valefor looks like a sphinx, with a lion body and a man's head. Some have many eyes, some many limbs. Some are a crazy quilt of animal parts, as if Dr. Moreau had gone crazy. Those shown here are from *Dictionaire Infernal* by Collin de Plancy (1863), llus. by L. Breton.

A demon's favorite pastime is possessing or compelling gullible hu-

Astaroth,
demon of sex and fertility.

Azazel, guardian of goats.

mans. Full-scale demonic possession is actually a rare occurrence, Demonic obsession, assault and hauntings are far more common. Demonic assault consists of a supernatural "evil" presence that wants to harm or hurt the individual. Demonic haunting is similar to ghost hauntings, but much more localized and specific—and more likely to happen in places that have been used for regular practice of black magic or demonic summonings.

It is a common point of almost all demon lore that demonic possession and obsession are *voluntary* states. In order for a demon to possess someone or to interact with someone, that person has to forge some kind of link between here and the demon's plane. Demons cannot force their way uninvited. This is where the modern lore of Vampires gets its rule that a Vampire cannot enter a house uninvited. A demon must seduce us, flatter us, or cajole us into forging the link. They cannot do it themselves. The beginning of an episode usually starts with the person brooding over thoughts/feelings of a destructive nature (anger, jealousy, greed). This is followed by feelings of chills, feverishness, and drowsiness, which marks the demon's entrance.

At this point one skilled at reading energy or seeing auras may notice disruptions at the back of the head and base of the skull. Healing magick applied here can help

Belphegor, demon of
discoveries and ingenious
inventions.

the person stave off the demonic influence but the key is in getting them to turn their thoughts away from those that allowed the demon entrance to begin with. Using ritual, meditation and prayer to connect with the higher self will drive off the entity in question. Courage and perseverance alone can overcome demons, but when these are combined with the above methods driving the demon away is a done deal. If, however, the possessed/obsessed person faces the crisis in a passive manner then they will be lost. It takes personal effort to drive demons away.

One must always be sure to eliminate all other possibilities before settling on a demonic one. Could it be the work of another type of spirit or being? Could it be mental illness? Or might it be a hoax? Key things that may point to demonic activity are: one or more witnesses describing a series of events that fit the basic pattern of an assault, haunting, obsession or possession, and the victim shows no signs of other psychological disorders that account for this behavior. If an assault is considered, then Ghosts, Vampires, Fey folk and other spirits have been eliminated; if haunting, then the place shows evidence of black magic being practiced there and ghostly activity is ruled out; if obsession, then the characteristics of it are clear and present; if possession, then the characteristics of it are clear and present, protective/banishing methods bring short-term relief, and other medical/psychological/criminological explanations have been eliminated. All of these must be present before demonic activity can even be considered.

Melchom, paymaster of civil servants in Hell.

When dealing with demons, a priest, shaman or magician should be consulted, as they are usually better equipped to offer advice or counsel. The best defense, though, is a person's own strength and determined force of will. If you find yourself dealing with a full-blown obsession or possession, then calling in a specialist is the best bet. But, again, success depends on the attitude of the victim. If they aren't willing to fight, no amount of help is going to be of any use to them. If you find yourself becoming the victim of an obsession then immediately start trying to block the obsessive thoughts. Massage, energy work and rituals of blessings and healing work wonders (if you believe they will!). Psychological counseling isn't a bad idea either, if only to help ground you in reality.

Nightmares
By Oberon (grey)

> *"The Hour of the Wolf is the time between night and dawn, the hour when most people die, when sleep is deepest, when nightmares are most palatable, the hour when the sleepless are pursued by their sharpest anxieties, when ghosts and demons hold sway. The Hour of the Wolf is also the hour when most children are born."*
> —Ingmar Bergman, "The Hour of the Wolf"

The word *nightmare* is recorded as far back as 1290. The "mare" part has nothing to do with horses, as is commonly supposed. Rather, *mare* is an Old English term for a demon. It derives from the Indo-European root *mer-*, meaning "to rub away or to harm." This is also the root of *mur*der and *mor*tal.

Specifically, a mare was a demon—an *incubus* (male) or *succubus* (female)—that descended upon sleeping victims, paralyzing and suffocating them while having sex with them. So a *nightmare* is a terrifying demon that visits you at night. Over the centuries the meaning became generalized to signify any frightening dream. Another term for this well-documented phenomenon is *night hag*.

In a visitation by a night hag, some people experience a sensation of paralysis, including difficulty breathing, along with a sensation of being visited by other beings. In our modern technological mythos, it is extraterrestrials, not demons, that abduct people at night and conduct strange sexual experiments on them. The phenomenon is still with us—only our interpretation has changed.

6. Great Cthulhu & The Necronomicon
By Oberon & Estara T'shirai (black)

> *"That is not dead which can eternal lie,*
> *And with strange aeons even death may die."*
> —Abd al-Azrad: *Kitab Al-Azif*

The *Necronomicon* ("Book of Dead Names") is a creation that was introduced in the works of H.P. Lovecraft (1890-1937), one of the writers who invented the horror genre as we know it today. In his "Cthulhu Mythos," Lovecraft conceived a secret world beneath our own, inhabited by dark "elder beings" and alien races. All the races and lesser deities of the Mythos acknowledge the Elder Gods, and many worship them.

Under the Elder Gods in power, though not in importance, are the beings known as the Great Old Ones, which are immensely powerful alien beings. Each of the Great Old Ones is independent of the others, and many seem to be temporarily imprisoned in some way. It is said that "when the stars are right" the Great Old Ones can plunge from world to world, but when the stars are not right they cannot live. "Cannot live" does not necessarily mean death for one of this group.

Lovecraft's most famous creation is a Great Old One, Cthulhu, who dwells in the corpse-city of black R'lyeh, sunken deep beneath the surface of the Pacific Ocean. Cthulhu exists in a sort of living death; but someday the city will rise, freeing him to ravish and slay across the world. In the city are also entombed other members of Cthulhu's race ("the Spawn of Cthulhu"). Cthulhu is high priest and ruler of them all and is by far the most potent.

Cthulhu's cult is the most widespread and popular cult of all the Great Old Ones on Earth. The cult doctrines are as follows: Cthulhu plunged from the stars with his kin and built a great prehistoric city at R'lyeh, ruling the world. When the stars changed and their continent sank beneath the sea, the city and its inhabitants fell into a death-sleep where they await their reawaking by members of Cthulhu's cult. When R'lyeh rises above the waves, members of the cult will be required to come to it and open the vast black door behind which Cthulhu waits, when he will awaken and rise to revel across the world in wild abandon with the faithful.

In Lovecraft's stories, the *Necronomicon* was the product of such a cult. It is supposed to be a translation of an earlier manuscript, the *Kitab al-Azif,* written in 730 CE by the "mad Arab," Abd al-Azrad, "Worshipper of the Great Devourer."

Many have insisted that the *Necronomicon* is real, and elaborate and convincing histories of it have been compiled. Over the years, several books purporting to be the actual *Necronomicon* have even been published. The most accessible is the Avon edition published in 1980. It is a fascinating, but often incomprehensible, "Grimoire" of materials largely based on Assyrian and Babylonian sources.

The *Necronomicon* is often dismissed as fiction, and therefore irrelevant. Nonetheless, it is right to be cautious about it. Curious and reckless people have been pouring energy and belief into these stories—and these rituals—for nearly a century, and where there is enough energy something does tend to develop. The rituals themselves were given a sort of trap design: they were put together by people who understood how such rituals should work, and built vaguely on a framework based on what was known about Babylonian and other ancient magical styles at the time. But many of the normal safety valves, including "How to Banish It," are not in place. It was specifically designed as a way for dabblers to get themselves into trouble. At this, it succeeds admirably. Estara is a Defense Against Dark Arts specialist, and there have been times—particularly when she lived on a college campus!—when she had to clean up after things like this. Once, she was even invited to a live-action role playing game built around this stuff, and there were enough people with a little bit of talent there that as time wore on, energy did start to build and strange things did start to happen.

We can't say whether the rituals ever become safe for those who know enough to fill in the safety measures correctly, because to be honest, we've never met someone who had succeeded at that. But even for those interested in flirting with the summoning of the darker powers, there are older, safer, and more reliable systems for doing so than this one.

7. The Evil Eye
by Luna

A famous song talks about strangers in the night exchanging glances. At the delicate borderline between romance/friendship is discomfort/fear. A peripheral glance lasting just a few moments too long can result in the defense mechanisms of the other person engaging. The structure for communication barriers begins, the possibility of a meaningful, new relationship ends. In other days, more significance was given to an untimely look.

What is the Evil Eye?

Praise or admiration, offered in the most generous of terms, can be construed as a malicious or jealous gesture followed by bad luck and/or health to the complimented person. The *Dictionary of Idioms* defines the Evil Eye as "being struck negatively by enthusiastic or jealous looks of others which are believed to do evil or bring bad luck." *Encyclopedia Britannica* would identify the Evil Eye as a "glance believed to have the ability to cause injury or death to those on whom it falls." Common references to this concept are described in terms such as "a sharp glance, a cutting look, a piercing stare, if looks could kill," etc. To generalize, the Evil Eye is a sort of disease caused by someone who might inadvertently show envy or jealousy through their praise. Their gaze has remained longer than appropriate on a given person, animal, tree, etc.

The negative consequences of the Evil Eye include crying and sickening of infants and children. They might become listless, vomit or show other such symptoms. Milk-bearing animals could dry up. Fruit trees might not bear fruit. Men could experience impotence.

Other names for the Evil Eye include invidious eye, envious eye, *ayin ha'ra* (Hebrew for the Evil Eye*), ayin horh* (Yiddish), *mal occhio* (Italian for the bad eye), *mal ojo* (Spanish for the bad eye), *jettatore* (Sicilian for the projection from the eye) and *bla band* (Farsi for the eye of evil).

The History of the Evil Eye

According to Professor Alan Dundes, University of California at Berkeley, the Evil Eye spread in a radius, geographically, from its origin in ancient Sumer. Its influence extended to India in the east, Spain/Portugal in the west, Scandanavia/Britain to the north and North Africa to the south. Evil Eye concepts were unknown in the Pacific Islands, Asia, Americas or Sub-Saharan Africa until the introduction of European cultures.

Dundes' contribution suggests that water equates to life, and dryness equates to death. Thus, the ancients feared that their nursing mothers, milking animals and fruit trees would dry up if subjected to the Evil Eye. He surmises that the Evil Eye dries up liquids, whether they be male or female. The prescriptions, then, derive from maintaining fluids. Fluid deprivation is the bottom line on this approach to the Evil Eye.

The concept of the Evil Eye is clearly discussed in many traditions such as Jewish, Islamic, Buddhist, Hindu, folk cultures and preliterate societies.

The Jewish tradition holds that fish are immune to the Evil Eye because they are immersed in water. Averting the Evil Eye has resulted in some safeguards within the Hebrew community such as allowing coins to be counted rather than people for taxing purposes and disallowing father/son succession in the reading of the Torah unless it is during the time of the fish. In other religions, the Turks, for example, would not allow their newborns to be presented publicly until they were 40 days old. Some Asian societies would paint the faces of their children black to avoid the Evil Eye. Some cultures also were suspect of blue-eyed people as the perpetrators of the Evil Eye.

Protections Against the Evil Eye

Prevention is better than dealing with the sickness and the cure. One could refuse to accept praise on behalf of the child. Parents might also smudge the

child with dirt or spit to detract from their appeal. Formulaic phrases and protective hand gestures could also be preventive. The *mano fico,* or "fig hand," was a gesture that involved inserting the thumb be-

Mano fico

tween the index and

middle finger. The other popular hand gesture to offend the Evil Eye is known as the *Mano cornuto,* a gesture in which the middle and ring fingers are held down by the little and index fingers are extended outwards like horns.

Mano cornuto

Moslems will perform a ritual that is both preventive and curative if their child has been exposed to strangers. The parents light a charcoal disc on top of Aspand seeds and direct the smoke around the child. Frankincense seeds and other herbs can be added to increase the fragrance and potency of this practice.

Other preventions against the Evil Eye include eye-agate amulets or jewelry, cat's-eye shells, blue beads, mirror charms, red thread, red coral, red horns or twigs, Buckle of Isis amulets, horseshoes and crescent-shaped objects.

The best prevention of Evil Eye from the inadvertent perpetrator aspect is to be aware of your non-verbal communication. According to some communication researchers, 93% of all communication is non-verbal. This includes eye contact, appearance, gestures, facial expressions, etc. It has been established that the spatial boundary for comfortable contact is about two feet. If you are within that circumference, you are violating that person's space unless you have an intimate relationship of some sort with that person. The timing of a glance is less precise.

Knowing what you do now, beware the Evil Eye!

8. Shielding
By Estara T'shirai (black)

Shielding, the practice of forming a protective energy layer around yourself, isn't just about blocking psychic attacks of the flashy sort that we all tend to think of, although of course it's vital for that. But shielding also protects you from day-to-day wear in the form of unfriendly environments and annoying people.

Natural Protection

Everyone has a certain amount of natural shielding, to keep them from being completely at the mercy of all the energies that are always around us. If we didn't, we couldn't have the experience of being separate creatures that is so much a part of our physical reality! Actually, the very fact that we have our own energetic field is a big part of our natural shields: there is a border between "me" and "not-me" at the edge of that field, where our own energy naturally repels other energies from its field. Because of this, a foreign energy generally has to be very strong or well-focused to get through very far into "our" field of energy.

There are things we can do to maximize the strength of our own energetic field, which in turn strengthens this natural shielding effect. These are the sorts of things that we learn in health classes, and yes, I'm going to go through them here, because they are a powerful part of your shielding arsenal. **PLEASE understand that I am not a medical professional, and that you should consult with your doctor when contemplating a change in health strategy.**

• **Exercise:** Exercise, depending on its type, improves your over all health, improves your response to stress, and makes you stronger and more limber. Try to get a mixture of aerobic exercise (walking, running, swimming, biking, etc.), strength training (weights, machines, sit-ups, etc.), and stretching and slow exercises like yoga or tai chi. If you haven't exercised for a long time, consult a doctor or trainer before you start, and build up gently.

• **Diet:** A normal diet should consist mostly of grains, fruits and vegetables, with moderate amounts of meat and/or dairy according to your principles and preferences. Try to limit sugar, salt, and artificial ingredients. Also be aware that if you have a special health concern, like diabetes, this may affect what the right diet is for you - again, consult a doctor in this case.

• **Drink:** Six to eight glasses of water or other clear, caffeine-free drinks a day will help your body work more efficiently. Caffeine is okay in moderation, but has a mild drying effect, so compensate with more clear drinks.

• **Smoking:** Don't. Although there are certain traditions that use tobacco in a sacred capacity, any consistent personal use carries tremendous risk of various types of cancer, as well as other types of damage to the brain, heart, lungs, and throat.

• **Meditation:** A daily practice of meditation reduces stress and helps concentration. Although we usually think of meditation as meaning sitting cross-legged and chanting, there are other ways of doing it. Tai chi and yoga can also be used as meditations, for example.

It's also important, and also helpful to your natural shields, to learn how to replenish yourself when you're stressed or tired. While you're not busy, think about what you enjoy, what makes you feel replenished. Extra naps? A nice bath? Chocolate? Make a list if you don't think you'll remember, or if writing helps you think. It doesn't matter how indulgent it is, if it is within your means and harms none. Wizardry is not a path of self-negation.

When you start showing signs of fatigue, stop what you're doing and go to that list. Signs of fatigue include disruption of sleep and eating patterns, mood swings, inability to concentrate, and clumsiness. Anything that is not immediately life-threatening can wait until you've restored your energy levels. Also check your basic self-care to make sure you're not fatiguing yourself because you're getting inadequate nutrition, water, exercise, or sleep. Also remember to *ground* and *center* yourself (see page 68)

Now that we have made the most of our natural protection, we can start to explore shields that we can add on deliberately.

Physical and Emotional Self-Defense

While Wizardly astral shielding is all well and good, I want to instill in you the idea that learning to protect yourself on the more mundane levels is also a very good idea. The best energetic shield in the world won't stop a fist: and although it may protect you against some of the effects of name-calling, teasing, passive-aggressive behavior and so on, you can do more.

There's a famous book called *The Gentle Art of Verbal Self Defense* by Suzette Haden Elgin, which I recommend. It will show you how to recognize certain patterns of verbal abuse, and how to counter them effectively. You can find a number of other such works, including several by the same author, but this is the "classic."

On the physical level, I suggest learning some form of martial art. Tae kwan do is a Korean style that is now widely taught, and there are many other styles

that you can choose from according to what's available near you and what styles you like best. If you can't take a full course in the martial arts, you can probably at least find a basic self-defense course at a local gym. Martial arts not only provide you with a way to protect yourself physically, but they also increase your physical endurance and your concentration. They make an excellent adjunct to any magickal training.

Finally, if you should ever encounter physical, sexual, or serious verbal abuse from another person, I urge you to tell an adult you trust in order to get help, to make you safe and guide you through any process (like reporting to the police) that needs to happen from there. If the first adult you tell can't or won't help, tell another one.

The Basic Bubble Shield

This is the classic shield: it is almost always taught first among shielding techniques, and in many places the only technique that is taught at all.

Sit and center yourself. As you sit, think about your own energetic field, your aura. Feel where the edge of that is—where you stop and the world starts. (This isn't right at your skin, where you stop physically, this is where your energy stops, or at least dissipates. Depending on how you're feeling this could be a few inches, a few feet, or even a couple of yards out from your body.)

Right around the edge where you feel your energy stop, imagine a bubble of crackling blue-white, sort of the way that lightning or electrical-based spells and weapons tend to look in video games. This bubble goes all the way around you in an egg-like shape.

Let me stop and emphasize that, because it's a crucial point: *all the way around you.* I have known at least one self-taught witch who had learned to make a very good shield...but only made a dome over things without giving her shields a floor! Anything that figured this out only had to send energy up through the ground, and her shields were useless.

So, this is the basic bubble shield. The blue-white crackling energy is protective: it keeps things out. In normal mundane life, this very easy, low-maintenance shield is almost always enough.

Mirror Shields

This is what most people seem to imagine when they start learning about shields. In fact, one of the early bubble variations often taught is literally called the "Mirror Shield," and it is imagined as something that is reflective around the outside, like a mirror ball. The intent of a mirror shield is to bounce the negative energy away from you.

First of all, it's very important to make sure that a mirror shield includes the intent that the energy bounces back to the sender, because you don't want it just bouncing in some random direction and hitting an innocent bystander. Second, be aware that if the sender is someone who knows enough to have their own shields up, the energy you bounce back may be deflected from them and hit someone else. Third, some people's ethics make even sending back someone else's harmful energies count as doing harm yourself. Yours may vary. Think this through before you try mirror shields.

Transference Shields

Scott Cunningham offered a short charm for a transference shield:

> Thrice around the circle's bound:
> Evil sink into the ground.

The intent here is that the negative energy, when it fails to break through the shield, will be pulled down into the Earth and converted into something more useful. This has the advantage that no one gets hurt, and something good can even come of it. The disadvantage is that it doesn't satisfy one's taste for justice (or vengeance, depending on your point of view!) and doesn't necessarily stop the sender from trying again. Again, something to think about.

Conversion Shields

A more complicated form of a transference shield is to have the shield itself convert the energy and give it directly to you. To do this, start by imagining two different shields. On the outside, form a shield whose color or form represents the energy you want blocked and converted; on the inside, make another shield whose color or form represents the energy you want to receive instead. (One of my favorites is a hedge of thorns on the outside and roses on the inside.) Between these, imagine a sort of filter that changes the energy from one to the other. So, for example, if the outside is pink (because, I don't know, you're one of those people who hates pink…this is just an example) and the inside is green, between the two imagine energy shifting away from pink and toward green.

What's particularly amusing about this kind of shield is that if you build it well, the more someone attacks you the better your life becomes. This is infuriating to people who are actually trying to hurt you, which makes it fun. Another name you may hear for it is a *transmutation shield*.

9. The Mirror Shield

By Oberon (grey)

Here is a classic protective mirror shield I have been using, with appropriate variations, for decades. I have found it to be quite effective.

I recommend creating your protective circle not with a blade, but with a hand-held round mirror. Ideal for this would be one with a handle. Use lipstick or dry-erase marker to draw a protective pentagram (one point up) upon the face of the mirror. Do this right away—at night, when the Moon has risen and you can capture moonlight in your mirror. If you cannot see the moon from any of your windows, take the mirror outside and catch moonlight reflected in it to charge it. Do this by holding the mirror in such a way that you can see the moon in it, and chant:

> Silv'ry Moon, reflected light,
> Flow into my mirror bright.
> In the darkness of the night,
> Protection grant by magick's might.

Then face the mirror outward and walk around a circle to encompass your space as you visualize a reflective circle forming around your space (best if you can walk around the outside of your entire building, but if you only want to protect your own apartment, then walk around the inside of each room, facing the mirror towards the outside walls. Move your hands, palms flattened and fingers spread wide, up, down, and all around your body at arms' length, while visualizing that you are shaping and pressing against the inside of a "Teflon-coated" shell all around your space. Expand the reflective circle upwards and downwards in your visualization until it becomes a mirrored band, and finally a sphere or bubble completely surrounding your entire apartment, strengthening it into an impenetrable shell, mirrored on the outside, reflecting and deflecting all negative energy back to its source.

As you create your protective circle, chant:

> I cast the Circle round about,
> A world within, a world without.
> Let all within the aerie wheel
> Bear witness to the mystic seal.
> Let all without be turned about
> And hostile forces turned to rout.

After you have created your mirrored bubble of protection, you should purge the interior of this space of all negativity. Make up a bowl of salt water (best is sea salt, available at any grocery store), and use a sprig of sage, basil, bay leaves, or cedar (whichever is easiest for you to obtain) to sprinkle the salt water around the edges and corners of your rooms. As you do this, chant:

> Water and salt, where you are cast,
> No spell or adverse purpose last
> That is not in accord with me.
> As I do will, so mote it be!

And finally, tape small round mirrors or circles of aluminum foil to the insides of your windows, reflecting side out (draw pentagrams on these). Conclude your rite with:

The Circle's cast; the boundaries sealed.
All ills at last may now be healed.
By all the might of Moon and Sea,
As I do will, so mote it be!

10. Shadow Casting

The powerful art of manipulating and
controlling the energy of darkness.
By Marco Collins (black)

A common misconception of darkness is that it is evil. Because people fear what they don't know or understand, they put labels on things that are strange to them. Well, it can be used for evil, or it can be used for good. It's up to you. But use common sense, so you don't create more problems for yourself and others.

Stirring The Shadows Within

Be in a dark room or outside at night and look at the darkness and shadows in the air and in the corners and kind of "blend" with it. Feel the Darkness; feel the Shadow. Know in your mind that it is there and there is no light. It takes a little concept-grasping to get it. Once you feel it, establish a connection with it, and feel as if you love the darkness. Love it like you loved your little puppy or your mother when you were a child.

Now begin to "soak up" the Dark. Bring it into your body and let it mix with your *ki* or any other type of energy you use most. It helps if the Shadow you bring in is the majority of the energy in your body. Once the Shadow has filled your body, let it start to fill your aura. Do this as long as you feel right. If you have auric sight, your aura will be black when you're finished with this absorption. You should feel relaxed and calm when you are done.

Shadow Balls

A Shadow Ball is a collection of Dark Energy that can be manipulated, programmed, and a variety of other things. With practice, you will be able to see the energy collecting, as a solid tangible object.

Creating a Shadow Ball

Stir the Shadow in your body by any visualization you use, then cup your hands and let the Shadow flow to the spot right between them. Just keep on visualizing it flowing there and becoming more solid. You can make it hot, cold, or electrical so it zaps someone when they touch it…or pretty much anything you can think of. Any shape, any size, any color (I prefer black because it's shadow manipulation, not rainbow manipulation!). You just need a strong visualization of what

you want. You don't have to keep it in your hands; you can let it float in the air or sit on a table. As you advance, you can form the ball into any shape, maybe a paper airplane that you can control to fly around the room, or whatever you desire!

With shadow balls, anything is possible. You can make it suck energy from your enemy, and then have it bring that energy back to you for absorption. You can gather thoughts from people: create one shadow ball, split it in half, and send one to the person you want to listen in on. Attach the shadow ball to them and command it to dissipate when you have gathered the information you want. Then attach the first ball to yourself, perhaps over your third eye, and command the ball attached to the other person to send information to the ball on you. Visualize a link between the two. But this it takes *a lot* of practice, and patience. But what you can do with this is unlimited… you can do all the techniques that practitioners of ki and other energy manipulation can do. Be Creative!

You can also affect electric things like lights and TV with this. Once I created a shadow shield around myself and walked under a row of fluorescent office lights and they all went out as I walked under them. Pretty cool.

Invisibility

If you need to go unnoticed, stir the darkness in your body, and let it flow. Then bring it out in your aura, and as you do so, just visualize your body fading into the shadow of you aura. Pretty easy, right? Well, that's for just going unnoticed. With practice, you may just be able to vanish entirely!

Enhance your night vision

Sit in a dark room or outside at night and feel the darkness pulsing around you. Just stare into the blackness. Become one with the Dark. Then when you're ready, concentrate on your eyeballs. Feel them as the stare into the dark, and see the darkness pouring into your eyes through the retina, and then close your eyes when you feel enough of it is inside your eyes. With your eyes still closed, remember how the setting looked when you first sat down; how it was dark and hard to see five feet in front of you. Keep that image strong, and then in your mind see the setting getting clearer and sharper. Visualize this over and over, then open your eyes and look around. You should see a little better the first time you do this. Just meditate on this, and do the technique over and over, until you can see clear as day in the dark. I strongly advise not to go into a bright room or look at a bright light right after doing this technique, because you could over-stimulate your cones and rods, which could lead to temporary blindness! Gradually expose yourself to light again after doing this by lighting a candle for a little bit, and then maybe using a dim lamp, so you don't stress your eyes too much.

Incorporating into Magickal Work

Create a circle you can see that surrounds you

Stir the shadow energy inside of your body, and let it flow within you. Then go about casting your circle as you normally would, but when you trace the perimeter of your circle, visualize the darkness inside you, coming out of you athame and making a glowing trail of darkness.

When you are on the final steps of casting your circle, stir the shadow energy within your body and make if flow through your veins. Then visualize the shadow being concentrated somewhere in your body, like in your gut or lower chest. I like to concentrate it in my solar plexus. Keep visualizing the darkness going to that spot, and make the ball of darkness get bigger and bigger, until you feel it is hard to breathe. Then squeeze all the muscles in your body really hard, and visualize the shadow exploding out of you and stopping at the edge of your circle, so you are enclosed in darkness. Make the "explosion" forceful! Then you can go about your magickal business. Sometimes it may look transparent, and if it does, just go back and concentrate your energy again, and make it explode. This can be very helpful if you are doing magick during the day and you want a more dimly-lit atmosphere.

Defense

At some point in every aspiring young Witch or Wizard's life, they will have a need to defend and/or protect themselves from harm. So if you are at a comfortable stage in your ability of Shadow Casting, defending yourself will be a snap. Simply stir the Shadow within, and make it as solid as possible inside your arm. Then thrust your arm out at the harmful person, visualizing the dark energy exploding out of your arm and going through the other person. You can visualize the projection of energy like a spell from Harry Potter. And if you are able to see your energy, then this little attack will look spectacular when performed.

Warning

As you advance in Shadow Casting, you may begin to notice changes in your body and other powers.

With prolonged practice of Shadow Casting, side effects will manifest, such as paling and graying of the skin, dark circles around the eyes, increased sensitivity to the light, eye and hair color change, and increased empathic sensitivity. Be warned.

11. Weather Magick

By Elizabeth Barrette (grey)

All practical magicks directed at manipulating the physical world are categorized as "low magick," or *sorcery*. For country Wizards, village Witches, shamans and cunning folk, these usually involved workings to benefit the needs of farmers, such as encouraging the growth of the crops and ensuring a rich harvest, or aiding the birth of lambs and calves. One of the most important uses for traditional sorcery has always been Weather Magick—bringing rain to end a drought, or stopping the rain to dry up a flood; clearing the skies to have a sunny day, or re-routing the path of a storm.

To learn weather magick, study meteorology and the climate in your area. You need to know what is normal and what is not, and how the atmosphere works.

Small changes are relatively easy, like summoning a breeze on a hot day. Creating a brief pause in a rain shower is not much harder. A little more challenging is drawing the rain to or away from a particular place, on a day when conditions are right for scattered showers. Banishing rain completely, lessening a severe storm, or bringing rain when the conditions are unfavorable—those are really tough.

You can work weather magic directly if you have the talent for it, by pushing the atmosphere around with your mind. That's the intuitive method; it's not a common talent but it works. Air and water are heavy, so it's not easy to push them around.

Another option is spellcraft, from folk charms (washing your car is a surprisingly effective means of "probability enhancement") to elaborate ceremonies. Yet another way is to beseech the sky or clouds or some higher power to get the result you desire. One of the most beautiful examples of this is the Native American "jingle dress," which was granted in a vision as a means to relieve drought. A good jingle dress dancer can summon rain by wearing a dress decorated with metal cones, and dancing the ceremony to invoke the storm spirits. (The pow-wow version of the dance is a little different, for display without making it rain.) So there are quite a variety of weather magick methods.

Appendix A. Contributors

(NOTE: "GSW" stands for Grey School of Wizardry)

Donata Ahern, M.S.W. (aqua)— Grey Council member and GSW Professor of Nature Studies and Metapsychics. She is a Druid and Bard Tutor in OBOD, a Wiccan Elder, and Priestess of the Mayan Temple of the Deer. She studied Lakota and Mayan Medicine Wheels for over 20 years, developing a personal synthesis and Oracle card set. She led student Circles at SUNYAB for 4 years, forming Silverweb, a cyber training coven. She is an online counselor, a hypnotherapist, and a regular presenter at Pagan Festivals.

Elizabeth Barrette (grey)— GSW Dean of Studies. She has been involved with the Pagan community for more than 17 years, and is Managing Editor of *PanGaia*. She writes for the Llewellyn almanacs and other annuals. Her work includes nonfiction, fiction, and poetry. Besides Wizardry, her other writing fields include speculative fiction and gender studies. She lives in central Illinois, where she enjoys magical gardening and hoarding books.

David Birtwell (Orange) has been studying the magickal arts for most of his life. He has sought out and attended numerous workshops and gatherings in his quest for the understanding of the strange, the unusual and the magickal. David currently resides a stone's throw away from Salem Massachusetts, one of the world's hotbeds of magickal activity. He is the creator of The Modern Wizard's School of Enchantment, which was crafted to provide young people with a unique, interactive magickal experience. More information about this can be found at http://www.SalemWizard.com.

Katlyn Breene (orange)— Grey Council member and GSW Professor of Performance and Lore, she has been creating sacred art, dance and ritual for 30 years. She has written and illustrated many books on spiritual arts and Folklore, and her art can be seen in places of worship around the world. She is also the Co-founder/creator of an initiatory and transformational retreat based on the Mysteries of Ancient Greece at Eleusis. She holds degrees in several different magickal traditions and is the founder and Priestess of Desert Moon Circle—a spiritual community based the Mysteries of the Sacred Wheel. www.HeartMagic.com

Marcus Collins (black)— Young aspiring witch in the Black Arts. Founder of Shadow Casting, and is still in High School. He is a student in all he undertakes such as wortcunning, mythology, magickal lore, and studies of Dark Magick. Student in Media Production in his mundane life, and he is interested in creative writing, photography, art, reading, Goth clubs, and being with his friends.

Francesca De Grandis founded The Third Road® tradition of Wicca, and has been a pivotal influence in the contemporary Goddess Spirituality movement, known for her poetry and innovative magical techniques. She is the author of *Be A Teen Goddess!*, *Goddess Initiation*, *Be a Goddess!*, and *The Modern Goddess' Guide to Life*. Her *Pick the Apple from the Tree* was cited as one of the top 13 Pagan albums of all time. She teaches Faerie Shamanism through international teleseminars and provides down-to-Earth spiritual counseling by telephone for people all over the world: (814)-337-2490. www.well.com/user/zthirdrd/WiccanMiscellany.html

Ash "LeopardDancer" DeKirk, BA (grey)— GSW Dean of Divination. She is a university graduate with extensive knowledge of myth and folklore around the world, specializing in dragon lore and Asiatic/ Native American myth. She holds a BA in anthropology and is working towards a BA in psychology. Her hobbies and pastimes include: reading (all the time!), writing, and games of all sorts. She is in the process of writing a fantasy novel, a Grey School book on *Dragonlore,* and a modern translation of the Chinese folk legend 'Journey to the West.'

Crow Dragontree, PhD (grey)— GSW Dean of Lore. He continues to serve as professional Tarot reader and instructor, Diviner, Priest, Herbalist, Healer, and Magickian. He is the coordinator of The Grove of Dana, an online college of Druidry. He holds a Ph.D. in Psychology and has the fortune to serve as a scientist, mental health therapist, and teacher—roles which he attempts to fulfill simultaneously. It's a good thing he also juggles! www.dragontreemagick.com

Lilana d'Venus, BA.Ed (pink)— GSW Professor of Lifeways and Healing. Her teaching experience has included full-time elementary levels, substituting all levels, and instructing business people in relationship skills at Bellevue Community College. Graduate work in psychology and counseling led to private work with individuals in cultivating relationship skills. Other training includes massage therapy, vibrational (light, color, sound) therapy, chakra energy healing, and Reiki. Hobbies include numerology, reading, writing, and relationships. As an ordained minister, she enjoys officiating weddings and conducting pet funerals.

Robert Lee "Skip" Ellison (yellow)— GSW Professor of Beast Mastery. Initiated into a Celtic Traditional Wiccan coven in 1982, he joined Ár nDraíocht Féin, A Druid Fellowship (ADF) in 1990. He is currently ADF's Archdruid and is a Past Chief of the Magician's Guild. A retired Industrial Electrician, he now works at tending his land and gardens, learning more about history and traveling throughout the world visiting ADF Groves. He has created a magical training system based on the trees of the forest and has authored four books. www.dragonskeepfarm.com

Robert Elm (silver)— GSW Professor of Nature Studies, Metapsychics, Magickal Practices, Dark Arts. He was catapulted into the magickal life in much the same manner as a man who, dying of thirst in the desert, accidentally falls into the clear waters of an oasis. After discovering various exercises to aid others in attaining the experiences he achieved by accident, he has acted as mentor to several aspiring magicians, and has moderated an active online community of Pagan philosophers dedicated to discovering the source of myth within the minds of each individual.

Morgan Felidae, BA (grey)

— GSW Dean of Faculty; dean of Metapsychics; Dean of Beast Mastery; Professor of Wizardry, Practice, Divination, Lifeways, and Lore. She found her way into magick and Witchcraft while attending a Catholic private school and she feels this has enabled her to maintain a strong interest and respect for all religions and systems of faith. Her most important advice to young Wizards is: "Don't judge others for their beliefs unless you want to be judged for yours." She has experimented with many different Pagan paths, including Shamanism, Wicca, Druidry, and Discordianism; and currently identifies with the Feri path.

Jim Fish (clear)

— Grey Council member; GSW Dean of Performance Magic; Professor of Mathemagicks, Alchemy and Magickal Sciences. He studied with Buckminster Fuller, and says: "I like to do the Wizard's work of healing, nurturing and creating. I believe that we belong to the Earth, and that we are here to solve problems and to make things work. I didn't claim the title of Wizard, but was given it by my friends, and now I have surrendered to it and embrace their wisdom. I live in awe of the continuous ongoing miracle that surrounds us and that we ourselves manifest."

Jesse Wolf Hardin (silver)

is a Gaian wizard, founding member of the Grey Council, and teacher of Earth-centered spirituality....living seven river crossings from a road on an ancient place of power. His many works include *Gaia Eros: Connecting with the Magic & Spirit of Nature*, acclaimed by Starhawk as "a must-read," as well as over 500 magazine articles. His CD, "The Enchantment" by GaiaTribe (www.cdbaby.com/gaiatribe), is a cauldron of world music and powerful invocation. Wolf personally welcomes the most intent seekers of all ages for magickal vision quests and advanced training, at their wondrous wilderness sanctuary in S.W. New Mexico www.earthenspirituality.org.

Ellen Evert Hopman, MA.Ed. (green)

— Grey Council member and GSW Professor. She is a Master Herbalist and lay Homeopath with an M.Ed. in Mental Health Counseling. She was Vice President of The Henge Of Keltria, an international Druid Fellowship, for nine years. She is founder of the Whiteoak internet mailing list, and co-founder of The Order of the Whiteoak (Ord Na Darach Gile). She has been a teacher of Herbalism since 1983 and of Druidism since 1990, and is the author of *A Druid's Herbal, Tree Medicine-Tree Magic, Being a Pagan,* and *Walking the World in Wonder—A Children's Herbal.* www.geocities.com/gaias_song/willow.html

Nikki "Solaris" Kirby, BA (aqua)

— GSW Professor of Metapsychics, she was born and raised in a haunted house, and has been involved in magick all her life. She has studied several Martial Arts, and lives by a strict moral code. She is a member of the ADF and the Correllian Nativist Church International. She has experience in several forms of divination and healing. A lover of Dragons, she is a practitioner of Dragon Magick. Her interest and hobbies include learning foreign languages, reading, writing, and teaching.

Frederic Emmanuel Lamond, MA (blue)

— Grey Council member; GSW Professor of Healing and Cosmology. A lifelong pantheist, he was initiated in 1957 into Gardnerian Witchcraft. He is also a member of the Fellowship of Isis, CAW, and Children of Artemis, and is on the Council of the Pagan Federation. He has worked as an independent consultant in the computer industry since 1975. After 40 years in and around London, he has lived in Austria since 1994. He is active in interfaith work and attended the Parliaments of World Religions in Chicago in 1993 and Cape Town in 1999.

Luna, BS & MS

is a GSW student who serves as a foodwriter for *Grey Matters,* the GSW school newspaper. She was the adult winner of the 1st annual GSW Poetry Challenge and is an active member of the GSW Stones Lodge. Recently identifying a magickal path, Luna is also doing her year and a day studies. Luna's mundane roles as full-time wife, mom and insurance agent are complimented by her community service as a Cubmaster, den leader and PTA member.

Jeff "Magnus" McBride (orange)

— A member of the Grey Council, he has been seen on many TV specials, including ABC's *Champions of Magic*, NBC's *Worlds Greatest Magic,* and PBS' *The Art of Magic,* and also on the Discovery Channel's *Mysteries of Magic,* where he served as a consultant on shamanism and ritual magic. He was voted Magician of the Year by Hollywood's Magic Castle. He is also founder of The Mystery School of Magic, a yearly conference for advanced study of magical arts. He has been facilitating Ritual theater events at Festivals throughout the world for the past decade. www.McBridemagic.com

Lady MoonDance

was fascinated with folk magic at a very young age, leading to her discovery of candle and gem magic in 7th grade. She has been spell-crafting for over 25 years and has been active in many Pagan groups for over a decade, as well as leading her own community rituals and events. She is pursuing a Master's Degree in Women's Spirituality from New College of California, but returned to her home near Raleigh, NC, in 2004. She is a contributor to *Llewellyn's 2006 Witches' Spell-A-Day Almanac* and has been published in *Sage-Woman, newWitch* and other magazines.

Ken "faucon" Muller, BA, MS.Ed. (grey)

has been performing magic for 45 years and is a worldwide expert in medieval magic. While not practicing 'arcane' magick, he is proficient in several forms of divination, and has studied fraudulent imitations of 'magick' through conjuring, slight of hand and claimed 'abilities'. Yet he recognizes the value of 'magic' as a prelude to shamanism and 'magick.' He writes profusely on Pagan, Christian, spiritual and Bardic arts themes, with many published books on eclectic themes. His premise is that wizardry is more of 'being' than 'doing.'

John "Apollonius" Opsopaus, BS, MS, PhD

(white)— Grey Council member and GSW Dean of Ceremonial Magick. His writings have been published in over 30 Magickal and NeoPagan magazines. He designed the *Pythagorean Tarot* and wrote the comprehensive *Guide to the Pythagorean Tarot*. He founded the Omphalos, a networking organization for Graeco-Roman Neopagans, and his *Biblioteca Arcana* website has won numerous awards. He is a member of Hellenion, ADF, PEN, and Coordinator of the CAW Scholars Guild. He is listed under "Who's Who in the Wiccan Community" in Gerina Dunwich's *Wicca Source Book.*

Nicholas Paranelle (red)—

GSW Professor of Alchemy and Magical Sciences. Born dead and rebuilt by medical science, he has survived fatal diseases and crushing accidents. His love for and expertise in magick is born out of his experiences. Tutored in the hard sciences, he found that science could not answer all of life's questions. A chance meeting with renowned magician Irv Weiner set him on his current path—understanding the truths of the world through magick. As an Alchemist he combines science and mystery into something greater. Something sought for by Kings and Paupers. And found by very, very few…

Susan "Moonwriter" Pesznecker, RN, AA

(indigo)— GSW Dean of Students; Dean of Nature Studies. Moonwriter is a child of the natural world in all of its concrete and magickal guises. Conceived at Beltane, her magickal roots include the vampire lore of Europe's Carpathian Mountains and a Czech grandmother schooled in traditional healing. A practitioner of Earth-based spirituality for more than a decade, Moonwriter defines herself as a 'Hearth Pagan' and is currently undertaking mentored apprenticeships in Druidry and herbalism.

Onyx Ravenclaw, AS (violet)—

GSW Dean of Cosmology & Metaphysics. She was born and raised in Philadelphia, Pennsylvania, and graduated from college in 2003 with an A.S. in Astronomy. She studied Wicca for one year online, though she has been solitary for over 20 years. She enjoys folklore, learning new twists on old ways, teaching, and helping others.

Holly Ravenweed, BA (indigo)—

GSW Dean of Wizardry. An ordained High Priestess in the Gardnerian tradition, she has studied and practiced Witchcraft for more than 30 years. She has founded eight covens and is currently High Priestess of Clan Ravyn Myst, founded in 1988. Her expertise lies in community outreach, interfaith counseling and networking, coven ritual, and spell crafting.

Trina Robbins (grey)—

GSW Instructor of Lore. She drew the first ever comic about the Goddess in 1970. She writes, lectures, draws comics, and writes books about the Goddess, heroines, Amazons, and women who break the rules. Author of: *Wild Irish Roses: Tales of Brigits, Kathleens, and Warrior Queens*; *The Great Women Cartoonists*; *From Girls to Grrlz : A History of Women's Comics from Teens to Zines*; and *A Century of Women Cartoonists.*

Kiva Rose

is an intuitive and challenging counsel, student of wild plant magic, impassioned lover over of the land, and codirector of The Earthen Spirituality Project & Sweet Medicine Women's Center. Her work has appeared in SageWoman, Beltane Papers, and numerous regional publications and literary journals. She shares a home in the Sweet Medicine Sanctuary, an enchanted river canyon in the Gila wildlands where she hosts the most focused and intent women for Gaian teachings, wilderness quests, the annual Wild Women's Gathering, retreats and resident internships: www.earthenspirituality.org

Athena Schaffer aka The Crowgrrl

is a journalist/author/artist and hereditary Witch. (She is currently High Priestess of the Sherwood Coven, which was handed down through her family.). She originated the "Ferret Familiars" sub-group with the International Ferret Association, and put out the group's newsletter. She has also worked with the Witches' Anti-Discrimination Lobby (WADL) when Dr. Leo Louis Martello headed the organization, shortly thereafter serving as co-tri-state regional director for Maryland, DC, and Virginia. She is currently collecting legends worldwide about ravens and crows for an upcoming book.

Estara T'shirai, BA (black)—

GSW Dean of Dark Arts. She is founder of the Treebridge tradition of Witchcraft, an Archpriestess in the Fellowship of Isis and a former local officer in the Covenant of the Goddess. Her articles have appeared in *Green Egg*, *PanGaia*, and *NewWitch* magazines. She is Co-Editor, *Isis-Seshat Magazine*; and Contributing author of *The Complete Guide to Writing Fantasy.*

Donald A. Wildgrube

became involved in Paganism upon meeting OberonZell-Ravenheart in 1971. He was ordained as a Priest in the CAW in 1973. He took training in the Craft from High Priest Asgarth and eventually took over the Coven. He has founded several Covens and had many hive off. He has recently moved back to the St. Louis area where he is continuing studying and teaching Paganism and the Craft. He is now affiliated with the Grok Fellowship and the international CAW, never forgetting the basic teachings of Oberon and CAW.

Abby Willowroot (gold)—

Grey Council member; founder and director of the Goddess 2000 Project and Spiral Goddess Grove, online Goddess Temple. Her work focuses on creating universal visual symbols and translating cultural concepts into easily understood forms. She is a contemporary folk-artist, reflecting many diverse artistic influences. The Smithsonian Institution has nine of her pieces in their permanent collection; her Goddess Art has been featured in books and museum shows, her writings have been published by Llewellyn; and she was a contributor to the *Grimoire for the Apprentice Wizard.*

Appendix B. Resources & References

Dept. 1. Wizardry (indigo)
BOOKS:

Brandreth, Gyles, et al, *Classic Optical Illusions*. Main Street, 2003.

Jennings, Terry, *101 Amazing Optical Illusions: Fantastic Visual Tricks*. Sterling Publishing, 1998.

Kay, Keith, *The Little Giant Book of Optical Illusions*. Sterling Publishing, 1997.

Paraquin, Charles H., *The World's Best Optical Illusions*. Sterling, 1987.

Seckel, Al, *The Great Book of Optical Illusions*. Firefly Books Ltd., 2005.

Seckel, Al, *SuperVisions: Action Optical Illusions*, Sterling Publishing, 2005.

Simon, Seymour, *Now You See It, Now You Don't: The Amazing World of Optical Illusions*. HarperCollins, 1998.

Thing Enterprises, N.E., *Magic Eye: A New Way of Looking at the World*. Andrews McMeel Publishing, 1993.

WEBSITES:

There are a number of websites that feature delightful examples of perceptual illusions and animated "Philosophical Toys." I would like to recommend the following in particular:

A great many optical illusions—quite a few of them in full color—may be seen at the "Amazing Art" website: http://members.lycos.nl/amazingart

You can build your own working model of a Zoetrope from print-out instructions and templates at: www.groeg.de/puzzles/zoetrope.html

Flipbooks are another simple form of animation, in which images on separate pages are bound together into little books. View some examples at: www.randommotion.com/html/flip.html

Animated examples of the various "philosophical toys" may be viewed at: http://web.inter.nl.net/users/anima/optical/phena/index.htm

And also the "Bill Douglas Centre for the History of Cinema and Popular Culture." www.ex.ac.uk/bill.douglas/Schools/animation/animation1.htm

More animated Phenakistiscope discs may be viewed at: www.mhsgent.ugent.be/engl-plat5.html

Dept. 2. Nature (silver)
BOOKS:

The literature is full of prose and poetry about the natural world. The insights of some of these folks may add to your enjoyment of the outdoors, or may lead you to mundane or magickal connections that you wouldn't otherwise have considered. The following writers are highly recommended:

Henry David Thoreau *(Walden, Walking)*

John Muir *(Nature Writings, Wild Muir)*

Terry Tempest Williams *(Red: Passion and Patience in the Desert)*

Barry Lopez *(Arctic Dreams, The Grace Note of the Canyon Wren, Of Wolves and Men)*

Anderton, Stephen, *Urban Sanctuaries: Peaceful Havens for the City Gardener*. Timber Press, 2000. Instructions on gardening in small spaces.

Boy Scout Handbook and *Boy Scout Fieldbook*. Boy Scouts of America, (www.scoutstuff.org)

Brown, Joseph Epes, *Animals of the Soul: Sacred Animals of the Oglala Sioux*. Element Books, 1992. A look at Native American totems from the animal realm.

Burton, Roberts, and others, *The Audubon Backyard Birdwatcher: Birdfeeders and Bird Gardens*. Thunder Bay Press, 1999. Explains how to attract birds.

Courtier, Jane, *The No-Garden Gardener: Creating Gardens on Patios, Balconies, Terraces, and in Other Small Spaces*. Reader's Digest Association, Inc, 1999. Making the best of container gardening.

Cowan Eliot, *Plant Spirit Medicine*. Swan-Raven & Company, 1995. Spirit guides from the vegetable realm.

Durrell, Gerald, *A Practical Guide for the Amateur Naturalist*. Knopf; reprint, 1989. A marvelous resource, full of splendid pictures and detailed instructions.

Landry, Sarah; illustrated by Roger Tory Peterson, *Peterson First Guide to Urban Wildlife*. Houghton Mifflin, 1994. An introduction to city plants and animals.

Leslie, Clare Walker, *Keeping a Nature Journal: Discover a Whole New Way of Seeing the World Around You*. Storey Publishing, 2000. If you really get excited about Nature journaling, this is an excellent resource.

Mosley, Ivo, ed. *Earth Poems*. Harpercollins, 1996. A compendium of poems from around the world, all honoring the Earth.

Symes, R. F. and Keates, Colin, *Eyewitness: Rocks & Minerals*. DK Chlidren, 2004. If you want to learn more about rocks, this is a wonderful resource.

Zim, Herbert, *Golden Nature Guides*. Golden Press, Simon & Schuster, 1950s-1960s.

WEBSITES:

"Creating the Urban Forest" – *A planting guide for city dwellers:* wwwhortcornelledu/department/faculty/bassuk/uhi/outreach/pdfs/barerootpdf

"Discover Your Animal Totem" – Helpful questions to identify which it is: wwwspiritualnetworknet/totems/discover_your_animal_totemshtm

"How Plant Essences Illuminate Your Soul's Journey" – *Connecting with plants*: wwwwisewayscom/fpahtml

"Medicine-Totem Animals" – *Alphabetical listing of animal guides*: wwwdreamers-worldcom/animalhtml

"Plant Totems" – *Discussion and alphabetical list of plant guides*: http://spiritbytescom/totem/plantshtm

"Urban Habitat" – *A comprehensive guide to city environments, plants and animals* wwwhamilton Natureorg/habitats/urban/urban_plantshtm

"Winter Birdfeeding" – *Tips on attracting birds in the city:* http://wdfwwagov/wlm/urban/winter_feedhtm

Dept. 3. Practice (gold)
BOOKS:

Agrippa, Henry Cornelius, tr. by J. Freake, ed. by D. Tyson, *Three Books of Occult Philosophy*. Llewellyn, 1993

Bonewitz, Ronald L., *Hieroglyphics*. Teach Yourself Books, 2001. Good introduction with a few errors. Also includes a little on Mayan hieroglyphics.

Buckland, Raymond, *Practical Candleburning Rituals* and *Advanced Candle Magick*. Practical Magick Series, Llewellyn, 2002. The first widely regarded book on candle magic, and its sequel. Wiccans may be surprised to find that some of the rituals in Buckland's classic do not follow the Rede regarding magic that affects or controls others. The second book goes beyond candle magic into details of ritual preparation, such as making a robe.

Collier, Mark, & Manley, Bill, *How to Read Egyptian Hieroglyphics*. University of California Press, 1998. An excellent introduction to hieroglyphic writing and Egyptian vocabulary and grammar, oriented toward reading ancient inscriptions.

Conway, D.J., *A Little Book of Candle Magic*. Crossing Press, 2000. All the basic traditional info and a nice assortment of rituals in a small, inexpensive gift book. It also includes info on Asian and Native American color correspondences.

Haislip, Barbara, *Stars, Spells, Secrets, and Sorcery: A Do-It-Yourself Book of the Occult*. Little Brown & Co.

Pajeon, Kala and Ketz, *The Candle Magick Workbook,* Citadel Press, 1991. The workbook format goes beyond your usual candle magic book.

Rosean, Lexa. *The Supermarket Sorceress*. St. Martin's Press, 1996.

Wilkinson, Richard H., *Symbol & Magic in Egyptian Art*. Thames & Hudson, 1994. Chapter 7, on hieroglyphs, is especially informative.

Websites

"Complete Sun and Moon Data for One Day." http://aa.usno.navy.mil/data/docs/RS_OneDay.html. Provides sunrise and sunset time for any date and location. You can also get a table for an entire year.

Dept. 4. Metapsychics (aqua)
BOOKS:

Allrich, Karri, *A Witch's Book of Dreams: Understanding the Power of Dreams & Symbols*. Llewellyn Publications, 2001. Covers archetypes and symbols, shadow work and nightmares, techniques of dream work, and a dream dictionary with magical angles.

Belanger, Michelle, *The Psychic Vampire Codex,* Red Wheel/Weiser, LLC., 2004.

Elgin, Suzette Haden, *The Gentle Art of Verbal Self-Defense*. Dorset House, 1985.

Fontana, David, *Teach Yourself to Dream: A Practical Guide*. Chronicle Books, 1997. Explains the dream world and its potential uses, the art of dream control, interpretation, and the subconscious; a splendid balance between the mystical and the scientific.

Parker, Alice Ann,*Understand Your Dreams*. New World Library, 1991, 2001. Includes a simple and a more complex method for dream interpretation; most useful for the extensive three-step interpretation guide which includes suggested questions to ask yourself when certain symbols appear in your dreams.

Peters, Maggie, *Dreamwork: Using Your Dreams as a Way to Self-Discovery and Personal Development*. Journey Editions, 2001.

WEBSITES:

"How to Remember Your Dreams" by Carine Rudman. Soul Future, http://www.soulfuture.com/dreams/dream_recall.aspOffers suggestions on boosting your dream recall.

"True Silence" by Dr. Karl R. Wolfe, Ph.D. Karl R. Wolfe http://www.karlrwolfe.com/dream-analysis-terms.html. Describes the basics of dreaming and dream skills.

"Scientists Say Everyone Can Read Minds" By Ker Than.

Special to *LiveScience,* 27 April 2005. www.livescience.com/humanbiology/050427_mind_readers.html

"The Makings of Metaphysical Kinship" by Alexzandria Baker (aka Peristera de Magdalene) © 2004, http://articles.solarphallic-cult.org/kin.html

Dept. 5. Healing (blue)
BOOKS:

Thompson, Gerry Maguire, *Atlas of the New Age: The Origins and Development of the World's Spiritual and Mystical Traditions*. Quantum Books, London, 2002.

Dept. 6. Wortcunning (green)
BOOKS:

Bremness, Lesley, *Herbs*. New York: Dorling Kindersley Limited, 1990; 1994.

Brinker, Francis. *Herb Contraindications & Drug Interactions: With Appendices Addressing Certain Conditions & Medicines*. Eclectic Medical Publications, 2001.

Cunningham, Scott, *Cunningham's Encyclopedia of Magical Herbs* (2nd Ed.). Llewellyn, 2005.

Foster, Steven, & Hobbs, Christopher, Houghton/Mifflin, 2002.

Foster, Steven, & Duke, James, *A Field Guide to Medicinal Plants and Herbs: Of Eastern and Central North America*. Houghton/Mifflin, 1999.

Hopman, Ellen Evert, *A Druid's Herbal for the Sacred Year*. Destiny, 1995.

Hopman, Ellen Evert, *Tree Medicine-Tree Magic*. Phoenix Publishing Inc. 1992

Hopman, Ellen Evert, *Walking in the World in Wonder. A Children's Herbal*. Healing Arts Press, 2000.

National Audubon Society Field Guide to North American Mushrooms, Alfred A. Knopf, 1981; 1995.

Ody, Penelope, *The Complete Medicinal Herbal*. DK, 1993.

The Llewellyn Herbal Almanacs. Published annually by Llewellyn Publishing, St. Paul, MN.

Richard, Philip B., *Herbal-Drug Interactions and Adverse Effects*. McGraw-Hill, 2004

Wild, Russell, *The Complete Book of Natural and Medicinal Cures*. Rodale, 1994.

WEBSITES:

"The Boston Tea Party." www.pbs.org/ktca/liberty/chronicle_boston1774.html

"Aunt Bunny's Top 10 Magickal Herbs": www.lehigh.edu/~jahb/herbs/magick_herbs.html

Grieves, M. "A Modern herbal." Missouri Botanical Gardens. www.botanical.com/botanical/mgmh/comindx.html. 2003.

"Herbal Medicine Schools Q&A." Natural Healers. www.naturalhealers.com/qa/herbal.html. 2004.

"Mermade's Sacred Smoke Incense" is a combination precious resins, herbs, minerals, the finest oils, and aromatic woods. All are blended by hand in small batches to insure quality. Mermaid Magickal Arts. http://crystalsandsonline.com/mermade.html

"Mushrooms." California Poison Control System. www.calpoison.org/public/mushrooms.html. 2003.

Old sea routes and land routes used to transport herbs and spices- "History of Horticulture," Purdue University: www.hort.purdue.edu/newcrop/history/lecture26/lec26.html

Dept. 7. Divination (yellow)
BOOKS:

Peschel, Lisa, *A Practical Guide to the Runes.* Llewellyn, 1995

The Fortune Tellers. Black Watch, 1974

WEBSITES:

"Letter to Robin" by Walter Woods, a long time dowser, at www.lettertorobin.org/

The American Society of Dowsers has more information at www.dowsers.org/

Dept. 8. Performance (orange)
BOOKS:

Bobo, J.B., *Modern Coin Magic.* Dover, 1982. Considered a classic book on magic tricks using coins, this is often referred to as *Bobo's Coin Magic.*

Burger, Eugene, & McBride, Jeff, *Mystery School.* The Miracle Factory, 2003

Gilbert, George & Rydell, Wendy, *Great Tricks of the Master Magicians.* Golden Press, 1976. This is my favorite book on Conjury, with 150 tricks explained and illustrated in a large format.

Hay, Henry, *The Amateur Magician's Handbook.* Signet, 1950; 1972. This was one of the first magic books I ever purchased. My 1972 paperback version cost just $1.95.

Karr, Todd, *Backyard Magic.* Scholastic Inc., 1996. This is a perfect "starter book" of Conjury for the young Apprentice Wizard. 15 really neat and easy tricks beautifully illustrated in color.

Nelms, Henning, *Magic and Showmanship: A Handbook for Conjurers.* Dover, 2000. Jeff McBride recommends this book in his Master Classes.

Tarr, Bill, *Now You See It, Now You Don't: Lessons in Sleight of Hand.* Random House, 1976. When it comes to describing and illustrating basic sleights, including palming, this book is the best. Ideal for teens and pre-teens.

Wilson, Mark, *Mark Wilson's Complete Course in Magic.* Running Press, 1991.

MUSIC: Magickal/Wizardly music is generally listed as "Pagan Music," which you can find by Googling for it. I particularly recommend "Gaia Circvles" by Gaia Consort! For the songs of the HOME Tradition, get Gwydiion's CD's, "Songs for the Old Religion" and "Faerie Shaman."

WEBSITES:

Here's a performance magic video dealing with "Pottermania." Andrew Mayne video: http://www.wizard-school.com/

"DragonSkull." This is a great website devoted to Bizarre Magik, including arcane effects and supplies: http://www.dragonskull.co.uk/

Jeff McBride's Magical Wisdom site: "The Miracle Factory:" www.miraclefactory.org

http://www.yourmagic.com This is a good source for magic books and supplies. They feature a great deal on Jeff McBride, David Parr, and Eugene Burger.

Dept. 9. Alchemy & Magickal Sciences (red)
BOOKS:

Anderson, Maxine, *Amazing Leonardo Da Vinci Inventions You can Build Yourself.* Nomad Press, 2006.

Hewitt, Barbara, *Blueprints on Fabric: Innovative Uses for Cyanotype.* Interweave Press, 1995. Includes: History, Chemistry Formulas, Design Sources and Ideas, Blueprinting with Children, etc.

James, Christopher. *The Book of Alternative Photographic Processes,* Delmar Thomson Learning, 2001.

Peterson, Robert. *Out of Body Experiences: How to Have Them and What to Expect.* Hampton Roads, 1997. A good basic guide to the theory and practice of astral travel.

Pinker, Steven. *The Language Instinct: How the Mind Creates Language.* A look at how humans think and speak, also useful in studying computer languages.

Samonek Michael, *The Amazing and Incredible Special effects Cookbook.* M E S/F X Publishing,1992.

WEBSITES:

A number of different Chemistry sets are listed at "Discover This." http://www.discoverthis.com/chemistry.html

An excellent distiller by Gary Stadler is at: www.HeartMagic.com/EssentialDistiller.html

"The Alchemy Website." Adan McClean is perhaps the most informed scholar on the western Alchemical mandala. His book, *The Alchemical Mandala,* is still in print, and a great source of how to meditate with these archaic images. www.levity.com/alchemy

Malin Fabbri, England: Alternative Photography: www.alternativephotography.com/process_cyanotype.html

Make a photo print with a plant leaf! http://www.grand-illusions.com/roman.htm

"New Alchemy and Green Center Archives" in Falmouth, MA http://www.fuzzylu.com/greencenter/home.htm

"Alchemy Lab" by Dennis William Hauck, author of *The Emerald Tablet—alchemical formulas for transformation.* www.Alchemylab.com

"Magick, Technomancy and Witchcraft" – a brief but thoughtful essay on what technomagick is and how it works. www.thecyberwarlock.com/technomagick.html

"An Atlas of Cyberspace" – describes the 'territories' of this virtual dimension. www.cybergeography.org/atlas/atlas.html

"The Censorware Project: Exposing the Secrets of Censorware Since 1997" – everything you wanted to know about censorware and were afraid to discover. http://censorware.net

"The Gender Genie" – a fascinating program which guesses your gender, inspired by the work of Moshe Koppel and Shlomo Argamon. www.bookblog.net/gender/genie.html

"Your Computer Is Made Out of Magick" by James Paige. A hilarious look at the magick theory behind computers. http://hamsterrepublic.com/james/technomancy

For an amazing interactive visual tour through the Periodic Table of chemical elements, go to "A Visual Interpretation of the Table of Elements" at: www.chemsoc.org/viselements

"The Crucible Catalog" offers spiritual products for people engaged in the Great Work of personal and global transformation. All the products are alchemical in nature and range from meditation tapes and posters to actual laboratory equipment used in making tinctures and elixirs. www.crucible.org/index.htm

"The Emerald Tablet Exchange (ETX)" is an international organization devoted to applying the principles of the Emerald Tablet in the modern world. www.alchemylab.com/emerald_tablet_exchange.htm

Dept. 10. Lifeways (pink)
BOOKS:

Brilhart, John, & Galanes, Gloria, *Effective Group Discussion.* WCB Group, 1992. An actual textbook on how people relate to each other in small groups.

Ellis, Susan J., *The Volunteer Recruitment (and Membership Development) Book.* Energize, Inc., 1996. A detailed look at what volunteerism is, how it works, and what people get out of it.

Hardin, Jesse Wolf, *Gaia Eros.* New Page/Career Press, 2004. Beautiful art and inspired essays on Gaia.

Johnson, Victoria Ann, *Johnson's Emotional First Aid: How to Increase Your Happiness, Peace, and Joy.* Blue Dolphin, 1997. Practical techniques for coping with troublesome feelings and promoting positive ones.

Kaner, Sam, *Facilitator's Guide to Participatory Decision-Making.* New Society Publishers, 1996. Read this for an idea of healthy leadership and member participation.

Kimball, Gayle, PhD and over 1500 young people, *The Teen Trip-the Complete Resource Guide,* Equality Press, 1997.

McCoy, Edain, *Inside a Witches' Coven.* Llewellyn Publications, 1999. Most of the information on how to start and nurture a small group is just as applicable to magical groups as spiritual ones.

Starhawk, *Truth Or Dare.* Harper-SanFrancisco, 1989

Zell-Ravenheart, Oberon, *Grimoire for the Apprentice Wizard.* New Page Books, 2004. Plenty of information on magic and Wizards in general.

WEBSITES:

"The Advanced Bonewits' Cult Danger Evaluation Frame" One of the earliest systems for determining how safe and sane a group is. http://www.neopagan.net/ABCDEF.html

"Bill of Rights for Pagan Students and Teachers." Concepts relevant to most learning situations, especially outside a regular school. http://www.wyrdweavers.org/files/bor.html

"The Coven Abuse Self-Help Index" – Another good evaluation system for deciding whether a group is one you want to network with, or avoid. www.wyrdweavers.org/files/cashi.html

"Dr. Andrew Weil's Self Healing." www.drweilselfhealing.com/

"Eat Right 4 Your Type: The Blood Type Diet Online." http://www.dadamo.com/

"Essential Fatty Acids, Flax Seed Oil, Udo's Choice Products FAQ - Frequently Asked Questions!" www.udoerasmus.com/FAQ.htm

"Has Hogwarts Changed the Muggle World?" – A fascinating exploration of how the magical and nonmagical cultures interact in today's world. http://paganwiccan.about.com/gi/dynamic/

"Natural Health: Chet Day's Huge Collection of Healthy Eating Recipes and Natural Health Articles." http://chetday.com/index.html

"Organize a Pagan Moot" – These ideas on how to start a Pagan socializing group would also work for a magical group. http://paganwiccan.about.com/cs/regional/a/aamoot.htm

"Shepherd's Dream, natural wool-filled bedding to enhance better sleep and health." http://shepherdsdream.com/

"Teen Ink Community Service" – Lists volunteer opportunities. http://teenink.com/Resources/CommunityR.html

"Volunteer Resources" – Offers tips for successful volunteer experiences. http://www.serviceleader.org/new/volunteers/index.php

"Why Teenagers Act Weird" http://www.prevention.com/cda/feature2002/0,2479,s1-6704,00.html

Dept. 11. Beast Mastery (brown)
BOOKS:

Costello, Peter, *The Magic Zoo,* St Martin's Press, 1979.

Keel, John A., *The Complete Guide to Mysterious Beings,* Doubleday, 1970; 1994.

Nigg, Joseph, *The Book of Dragons & Other Mythical Beasts,* Barrons Educational Series, 2002.
— *The Book of Fabulous Beasts: A Treasury of Writings from Ancient Times to the Present,* Oxford University Press, 1999.
— *A Guide to the Imaginary Birds of the World,* Apple-Wood Books, 1984.
— *Wonder Beasts: Tales and Lore of the Phoenix, the Griffin, the Unicorn and the Dragon,* Libraries Unlimited, 1995.

White, T. H., *The Book of Beasts,* Dover, 1954; 1984.

WEBSITES:

"Beartracker's Animals Tracks Den." http://www.beartracker.com/ Excellent information on tracking all kinds of North American wild animals.

"International Wildlife Rehabilitation Council (IWRC)" http://www.iwrc-online.org/ Best resource for wildlife rescue programs throughout the world.

"Gareth Long's Encyclopedia of Monsters, Mythical Creatures and Fabulous Beasts (or, the Encyclopedia of Monsters etc.)" http://webhome.idirect.com/~donlong/monsters/monsters.htm Detailed illustrate entries on just about every fabled beast and being imaginable!

List of species in folklore and mythology (from "Wikipedia, the free encyclopedia)" http://en.wikipedia.org/wiki/List_of_species_in_folklore_and_mythology Detailed listings arranged both alphabetically and by categories. Many intrernal links for further info.

"The Medieval Bestiary." http://bestiary.ca/ The beast list includes all of the beasts found in Bestiaries and the *Physiologus,* as well as some from other sources.

Dept. 12. Cosmology & Metaphysics (violet)
BOOKS:

Adzema, Robert, & Jones, Mablen. *The Great Sundial Cutout Book.* Hawthorn Books, Inc. City: 1978.

Bauval, Robert, & Gilbert, Adrian. *The Orion Mystery: Unlocking the Secrets of the Pyramids.* Three Rivers Press. City:1995

Jenkins, John Major. "The How and Why of the Mayan End Date in 2012," *Mountain Astrologer,* Dec-Jan. 1995.

Sky & Telescope Magazine has a section on "Backyard Astronomy: Tips on Observing the Universe". A regular feature of the magazine, Backyard Astronomy, has articles designed to help beginners get oriented.

DAILY WEBSITES:

Phillips. Tony. "Space Weather." Space Weather.com. www.spaceweather.com/. Feb. 23, 2005.

"Moon Calculator." www.calculatorcat.com/moon_phases/moon_phases.phtml. (A web page that gives real-time information about moon phases.)

"Sky and Telescope." http://skyandtelescope.com/.

AS-NEEDED WEBSITES:
Look through each of these at least once, so that you'll know what's there. Then use them as needed. Not all of these are "naked eye" sites, but all are either useful or really cool.

"Earth's Seasons. Zoom Astronomy." www.allaboutspace.com/subjects/astronomy/planets/earth/Seasons.shtml.

"Weather Underground." www.wunderground.com. Has star charts, twilight times, moon phases, and more.

"Astronomy Picture of the Day." http://antwrp.gsfc.nasa.gov/apod/astropix.html. This splendid site offers a new outer space-related picture every day, along with detailed explanations and great links.

"Comet Observation Home Page." http://encke.jpl.nasa.gov/

"Publication Quality Skymaps and Star Charts." www.skymaps.com/downloads.html.

OTHER WEBSITES:
"Astronomy Magazine's Web Site." www.astronomy.com

"Moon Tools." This puts a small box on your computer desktop and shows the moon phase on a real-time basis. Clicking the image opens a box of more detailed information. Macintosh version: www.perkins-observatory.org/software.html Pentium version: www.fourmilab.ch/moontoolw/

"Moon Phase Calendar." Star Date Online. University of Texas. www.stardate.org/nightsky/moon/. 2005.

"Astronomy Dictionary." http://users.skynet.be/sky03361/dictionary/dictionary.html.

Starry Night software is a wonderful, easy-to-use set of CDs that turns your computer into an astronomical observatory and helps you find anything in the night sky. You can download a free, absolutely no strings attached trial version at http://www.starrynight.com/digitaldownload/trial_download.php.

Dept. 13. Mathemagicks (clear)
BOOKS:
Cornford, Francis MacDonald, *Plato's Cosmology: The* Timaeus *of Plato.* Routledge & Kegan Paul, 1937. See especially pp. 210–24 on the Elements and the Platonic Solids.

Haeckel, Ernst Heinrich, *Artforms in Nature.* Dover Publications, 1974.

Hopper, Vincent F., *Medieval Number Symbolism.* Dover, 2000. See especially chs. III, VI.

Lawlor, Robert, *Sacred Geometry: Philosophy and Practice*, Thames & Hudson, 1982. An excellent introduction, with many practical exercises.

Mann, A.T., *Sacred Architecture*, Element, 1993.

Nicomachus of Gerasa, transl. by M. L. D'Ooge, *Introduction to Arithmetic*, in *Great Books of the Western World*, vol. II, ed. by R. M. Hutchins, Encyclopedia Britannica, 1952.

Opsopaus, John, *Guide to the Pythagorean Tarot.* Llewellyn, 2001. For the Tetractys, see pp. 406–11, 433–8. For the symbolic meaning of the numbers of the Decad, see the discussion of the pip cards, pp. 295–353.

Rawles, Bruce A., *Sacred Geometry Design Sourcebook: Universal Dimensional Patterns.* Elysian Publishing, ISBN# 0-9656405-8-2 Contains 27 3-D "fold-up" patterns to create exquisite shapes. Order from http://

www.intent.com/elysian/sgds.html

Schneider, Michael S., *A Beginner's Guide to Constructing the Universe: The Mathematical Archetypes of Nature, Art, and Science*, HarperPerennial, 1995. Although the emphasis is on geometry, arithmetic is also covered. Chapters 4 and 5 discuss the Platonic Solids.

Taylor, Thomas, *The Theoretic Arithmetic of the Pythagoreans*, Weiser, 1983. A comprehensive introduction.

Theon of Smyrna, transl. by R. & D. Lawlor, *Mathematics Useful for Understanding Plato*, Wizards Bookshelf, 1979. Books I & II are the most relevant.

WEBSITES:
The Ancient Greek Esoteric Doctrine of the Elements http://omphalos.org/BA/AGEDE. A discussion of the Elements from the perspective of ancient Pythagorean philosophy.

The Pythagorean Tarot by John Opsopaus http://omphalos.org/BA/PT.

Summary of Pythagorean Theology http://omphalos.org/BA/OTP. Discusses the mythological background of Pythagorean cosmology.

Dept. 14. Ceremonial Magick (white)
BOOKS:
Theurgy and the Soul: The Neoplatonism of Iamblichus by Gregory Shaw. Pennsylvania State University Press, 1995. Good, scholarly introduction to the principles underlying the practice of Theurgy.

WEBSITES:
A Summary of Pythagorean Theology by John Opsopaus www.omphalos.org/BA/ETP. Provides the cosmological background of Theurgy and some additional information on the practice.

Dept. 15. Lore (grey)
BOOKS:
Apuleius, Lucius, *The Transformations of Lucius: The Golden Ass* (trans. Robert Graves). Farrar, Straus and Giroux, 1998.

Beathm, George. *Fact, Fiction, and Folklore in Harry Potter's World An Unofficial Guide.* Hampton Roads Publishing Company, Inc. 2005.

Berlitz, Charles, *Mystery of Atlantis.* Avon, 1977.

Bulfinch, Thomas, *Bulfinch's Greek and Roman Mythology: The Age of Fable,* Dover Publications, 2000

Donnelly, Ignatius, *Atlantis: The Antediluvian World* (1882), Dover Publications, 1976

Ford, Patrick K, *The Maginogi and Other Medieval Welsch Tales*, University of California Press, 1977

Gaimon, Neil, *The Sandman* (comic book series), DC/Vertigo Comics, 1989-1996

Galanopoulos, A.G., and Bacon, Edward; *Atlantis: The Truth Behind the Legend,* Bobbs-Merrill Co., 1969

Guest, Lady Charlotte (translator), *The Mabinogion,* 1877

Plato, *The Atlantis Dialogue: Plato's Original Story of the Lost City, Continent, Empire,* Shepard Publications, 2001

Spence, Lewis, *The Problem of Atlantis* (1924). Kessinger Publishing; Reprint edition, 1942

Robinson, Herbert Spencer, & Wilson, Knox, *Myths & Legends of All Nations.* Littlefield, Adams & Co, 1978

WEBSITES:
"Lia Fail." www.themystica.org/mystica/articles/l/lia_fail.html

"The Mysterious & Unexplaine." www.activemind.com/
    Mysterious/Topics/Atlantis/story.html
"Wikipedia Free Encyclopedia." http://en.wikipedia.org/wiki
"World Mysteries.co" http://www.world-mysteries.com/
    awr_alchemy.htm

Dept. 16. Dark Arts (black)

BOOKS:
Byfield, Barbara Ninde, *The Glass Harmonica: A Lexicon
    of the Fantastical.* MacMillan Co., 1967.
Elgin, Suzette Haden, *The Gentle Art of Verbal Self
    Defense.* Dorset House Publishing Co Inc., 1985.
Johnson, Robert, *Owning Your Own Shadow: Understand-
    ing the Dark Side of the Psyche.* HarperSanFrancisco, 1991.
Keel, John A., *The Complete Guide to Mysterious Beings.*

Doubleday, 1970; 1994.
Petersen, Sandy, *Call of Cthulhu.* Chaosium Inc., 1989.
WEBSITES:
A very extensive exposition on the nature and history of the
    Necronomicon may be found at "The Necronomicon Ati-
    FAQ." www.digital-brilliance.com/necron/necron.htm
"The Evil Eye." www.luckymojo.com, www.ilyasoglu.com
    and www.discovery.com.
"The Shadowlands." djuliano@theshadowlands.net. This
    site by Dave Juliano is the best resource for information
    on The Jersey Devil.
www.Unexplained-Mysteries.com "Your Gateway to the
    Paranormal"
www.WordOrigins.org. This site is devoted to etymology
    (the origins of words and phrases).

Appendix C. Art Credits

Aldrovandus (1640): 176
John Baxter (1977): 239
William Blake (1825): 176
John Blanchard: 187
Katlyn Breene: 60, 85, 118, 119, 135,
    213, 214
L Breton (1863): 241, 242
Joe Butt: 39, 40, 83, 89, 90, 91, 172,
    173, 174, 175, 177, 207, 209,
    210, 216, 218, 220, 224, 225,
    229, 233, 237, 238, 239, 240,
    242, 243 244, 245, 247
James C. Christiansen: viii
Sandy "Xander" Carruthers: 226, 227,
    228, 230, 232
N.J. Crowley: 118
Jim Fish: 133, 134, 273
G.H. Fisher: 17
Scott Fray: 149
Fra Gioconda (1522): 146
Jesse Wolf Hardin: 16, 24, 97, 159, 160,
    166, 170
Ernst Haeckel (1904): 207

J.G. Heck (1851): 32, 179
William Hogarth (1754): 17
Scott Hollander: 59, 119, 214
Heinrich Khunrath (1595): 137
John Legon: 192
Matthaus Merian (1718): 176, 177, 178
Jean William Naumann: iii, 257
John "Apollonius" Opsopaus: 48, 50,
    194, 195, 196, 197, 198, 202,
    203, 204, 205, 269, 270, 284,
    285, 286
Trina Robbins: 287, 288
Theophilius Scheighart (1604): 109
Roger Shepard: 17, 18
J. Sluper (1572): 176, 177
Pamela Coleman Smith (1909): 126
G. Elliot Smith (1918): 178
Daniel Blair Stewart: 70
Julia Star: 42
Moria Starbuck: 41, 152, 156
Tracy Swangler: 44, 45, 52, 53, 55, 56,
    57, 58, 61, 62, 63, 64, 66, 68, 72,
    76, 78, 81, 96, 107, 118, 121, 142,

    161, 162, 173, 174, 216
Abbe de Villemont (1693): 119
Leonardo da Vinci (1542-1519): 147,
    148
Abby Willowroot: 45, 51
Oberon Zell-Ravenheart: x, 12, 13, 18,
    19, 20, 25, 26, 29, 30, 31, 33, 34,
    35, 36, 37, 38, 40, 43, 45, 46, 47,
    54, 55, 57, 59, 60, 67, 80, 82, 84,
    87, 91, 95, 96, 107, 108, 112, 113,
    119, 120, 122, 127, 128. 129, 131,
    135, 136, 141, 143, 145, 147,
    148, 150, 165, 169, 171, 172,
    177, 178, 179, 180, 182, 183,
    191, 193, 201, 206, 208, 211, 215,
    219, 221, 223, 234, 236, 265,
    266, 267, 268, 271, 272, 274,
    275, 276, 277, 278, 279, 280,
    281, 282, 283
*(NOTE: If any of the artwork printed
    here anonymously can be attrib-
    uted, please inform author for
    credit in future editions.)*

Appendix D. Index

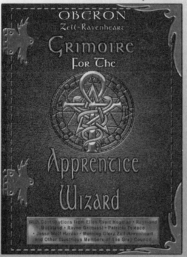

About the Author

Oberon Zell-Ravenheart (1942-) is a renowned Wizard and Elder in the worldwide magickal community. He received his BA (Psychology, Sociology, Anthropology and Pre-Med) from Westminster College in 1965, attended graduate school at Washington University on a USPHS scholarship in Clinical Psychology, and earned his Teacher's Certificate from Harris Teacher's College in 1968. He has worked professionally as a teacher and counselor in public and private schools, from Headstart to High School, and was also Director of Services for the Human Development Corporation. Oberon is an initiate in several magickal Traditions, and has been involved in many interfaith projects, including the founding of several major groups and alliances. Through his publication of the award-winning *Green Egg* magazine (1968-2000), he was instrumental in the coalescence of the modern magickal community. Oberon lives in NorCalifia with his beloved lifemate Morning Glory (married 1974). They have two grown children. He is also Founder and Headmaster of the online Grey School of Wizardry: www.GreySchool.com

Watchbird Watching You!

by Oberon Zell-Ravenheart (See pp. 18-19)

Copy onto card stock; color as you wish. Score on dotted lines, cut out and follow instructions.

Completed Assembly
(back view)

Position Watchbird with eyes perpendicular to yours. To see the effect, close one eye and move your head back and forth. The Watchbird will turn its head to follow you!

This Watchbird illusion by Oberon Zell-Ravenheart is based on a similar concept originally designed by Jerry Andrus and Simon Powell of Binary Arts, Alexandria, Virginia

Place the Watchbird inside of a globular fishbowl to enhance the effect...

This is the Watchbird watching YOU!

Thaumatropes & Fantascopes
by Oberon
(see pp.19-21)

THAUMATROPE
1-Magick

IMPORTANT:
Glue Thaumatrope
disks together
upside-down
to each
other.

COVER for
FANTASCOPE
Cut out and fold back
two pie-shaped doors.

THAUMATROPE
2-Canary

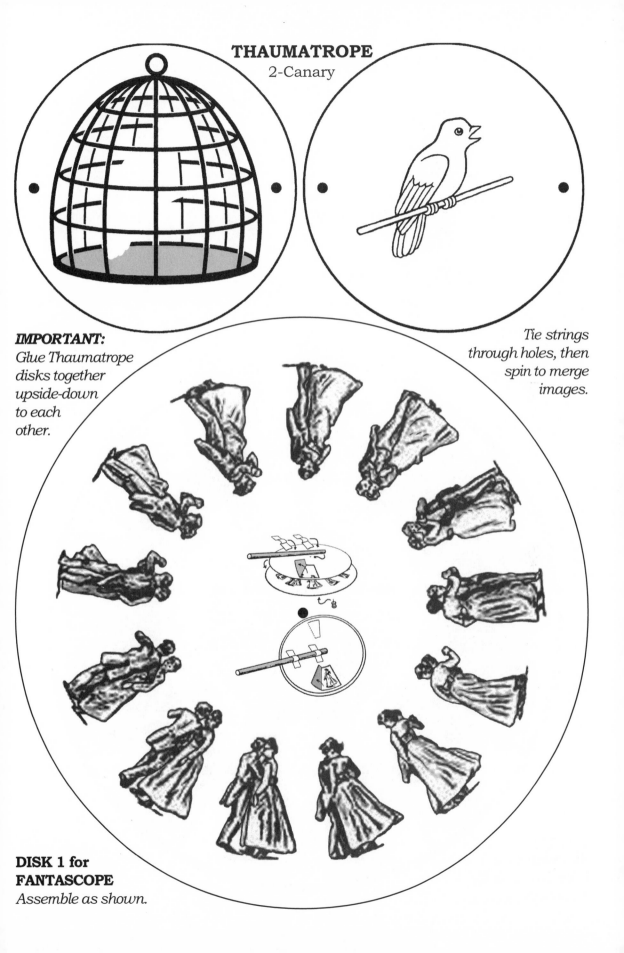

IMPORTANT:
Glue Thaumatrope disks together upside-down to each other.

Tie strings through holes, then spin to merge images.

DISK 1 for FANTASCOPE
Assemble as shown.

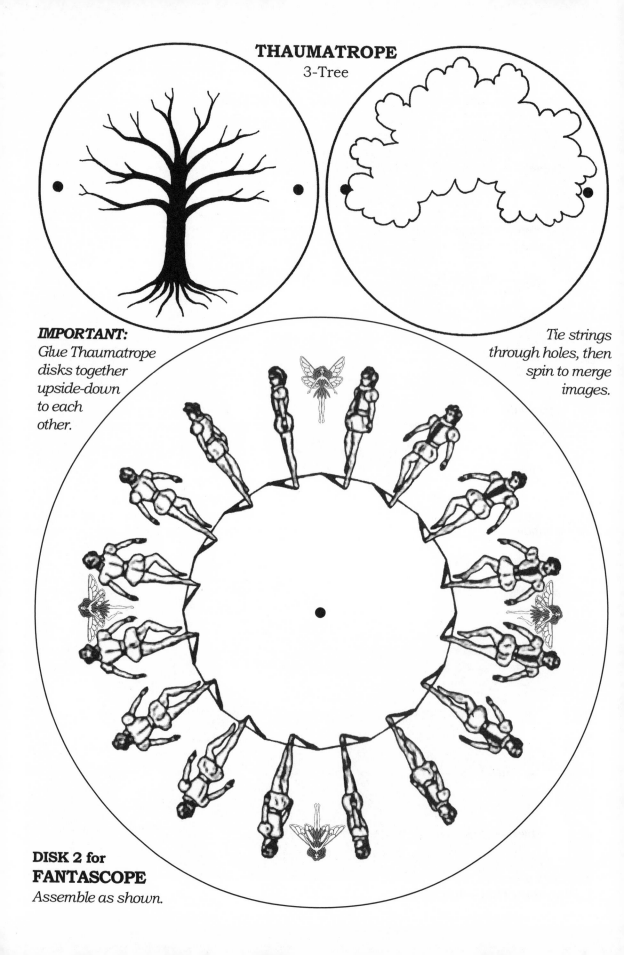

THAUMATROPE
3-Tree

IMPORTANT:
Glue Thaumatrope disks together upside-down to each other.

Tie strings through holes, then spin to merge images.

DISK 2 for FANTASCOPE
Assemble as shown.

Planetary Hour Calculator

by John "Apollonius" Opsopaus (See pp. 47-50)

Planetary Hour
Calculator

•

©2005, John Opsopaus

1. Planetary Dial -- backplate

There are two parts to the Planetary Hour Calculator, the *Planetary Dial* and the *Hour Divider*, which I'll discuss in order. The Planetary Dial has two parts: the *back-plate*, which is engraved with cherubs and the numbers 1 to 12 in two rings, and the *dial*, which is engraved with a *heptagram* (seven-pointed star) and the signs of the planets. Copy these two pages onto card stock and carefully cut out the back-plate and dial. Next you will have to mount the dial on the back-plate so that the dial turns freely. The easiest way to do this is with one of those two-winged brass paper fasteners you can find in stationary stores. Carefully punch holes in the centers of the dial and the back-plate and enlarge them until they're big enough for the "wings" of the fastener. Push the fastener through the dial and back-plate and bend the wings out flat. An even better way is to use a grommet, which you can buy in a fabric store.

3. Hour Divider: Hour Grid

2. Planetary Dial

The second half of the Calculator is the Hour Divider. It has two parts, the Hour Grid (which has many lines marked with three columns of numbers) and Hour Ruler (which has the numbers 1 to 12 from left to right). Cut these out and use them as per the instuctions on page 48.

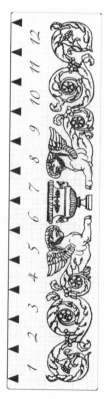

4. Hour Divider: Hour Ruler

Telepathy Cards

by Oberon Zell-Ravenheart (See p. 272)

Psychokinesis Spinners

by Oberon

(See p. 272)

Cut spiral to center.

Cut and glue head and bend lower jaw under to make head 3-D.

Mount Spinners by inserting needle into bottle cork, point up. Practice moving them by psychokinesis.

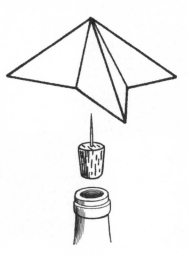

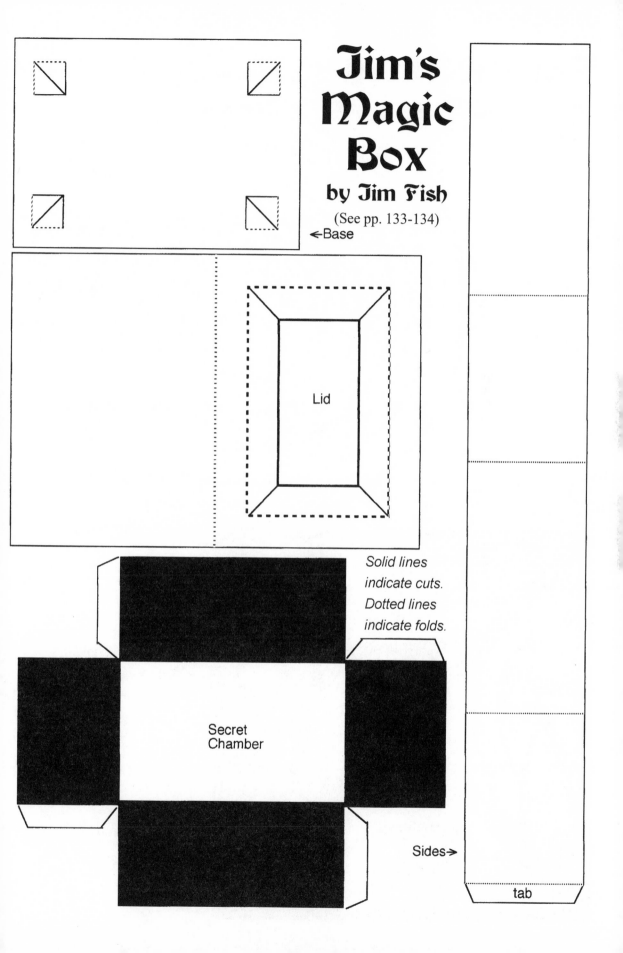

Jim's Magic Box

by Jim Fish

(See pp. 133-134)

←Base

Lid

*Solid lines
indicate cuts.
Dotted lines
indicate folds.*

Secret
Chamber

Sides→

tab

Leonardo da Vinci Ornithopter
by OberonZell-Ravenheart (See pp. 147-148)

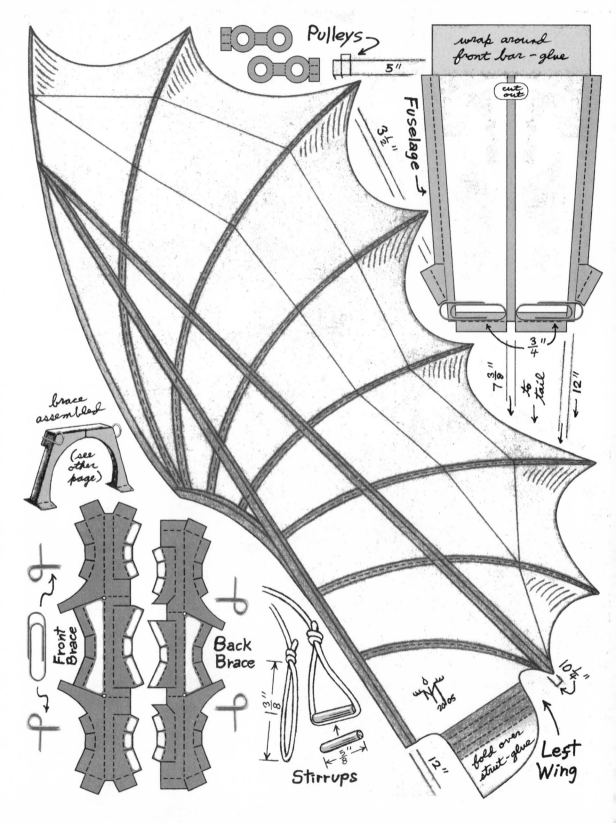

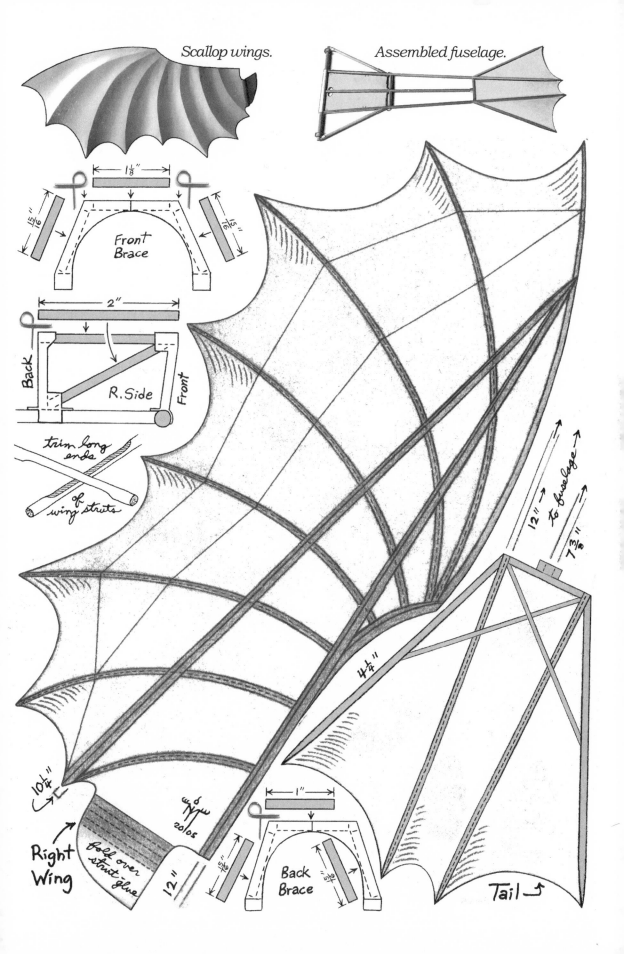

Scallop wings.

Assembled fuselage.

Front Brace

$1\frac{1}{8}''$

$\frac{15}{16}''$

$\frac{15}{16}''$

Back

$2''$

R. Side

Front

trim long ends

of wing struts

$12''$ To fuselage $7\frac{3}{8}''$

$4\frac{1}{4}''$

$10\frac{1}{4}''$

Right Wing

fold over strut glue

$12''$

$\frac{5}{16}''$ 6 20/05

$\frac{5}{16}''$

Back Brace

$1''$

$\frac{5}{16}''$

Tail

4 Nifty Dragons

by Oberon Zell-Ravenheart (See p. 179)

Using the cutouts on these three pages, you can assemble four different types of Dragons:
1. *Ancient-Medieval Western (wingless)*   2. *Renaisasance Western (fin-wings)*
3. *Modern Western (bat-wings)*   4. *Oriental (wingless, with flames on legs and head)*

Copy onto colored card stock, enlarge by 121%. Score on all dotted lines for folding. Cut out and glue together.

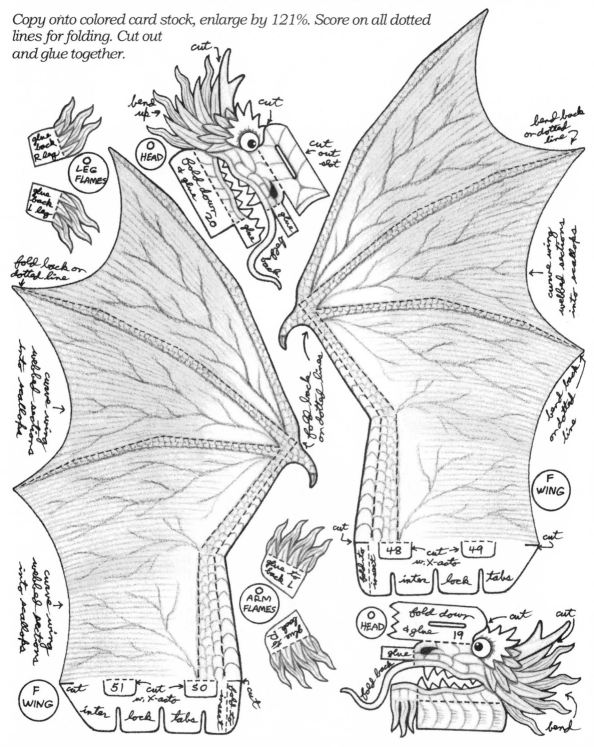

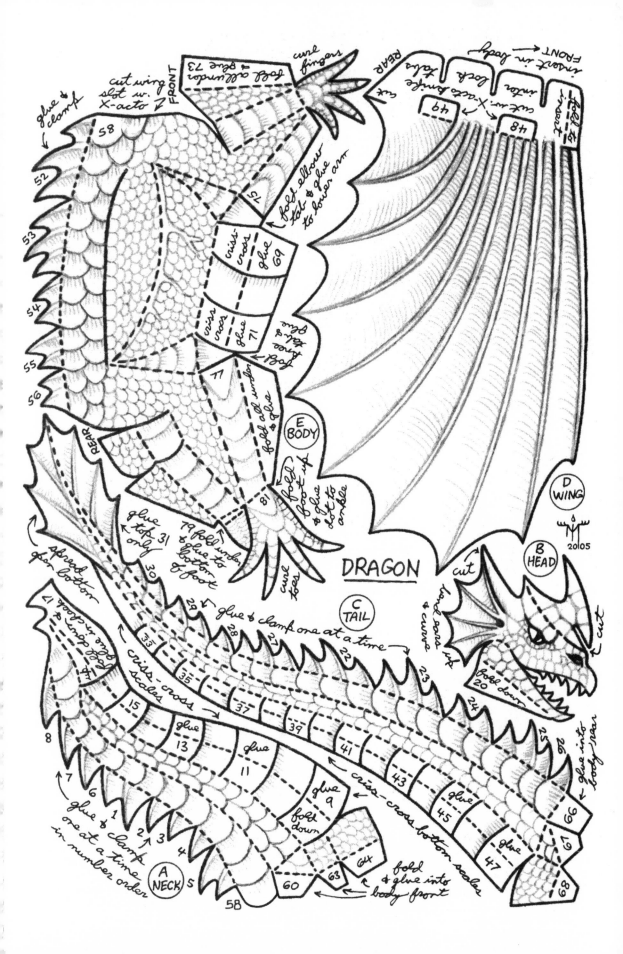

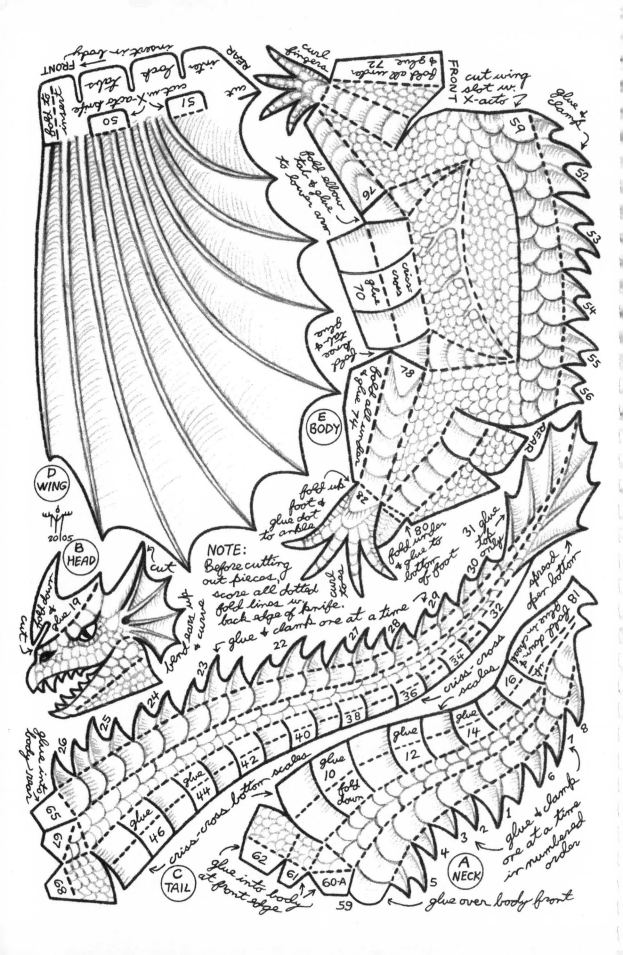

Mariner's Astrolabe

by Oberon Zell-Ravenheart (See p. 183)

(Cut out and remove four quarter sections with instructions.)

insert large paper clip or split ring through hole to suspend.

To determine latitude, you must frst sight the angle of the sun at noon. Suspend the Astrolabe from the finger ring at eye level,

edge on to the sun, and rotate the alidade so that the sunlight is projected straight along the sighting bars. Read the angle

of altitude from the scale along the outer edge of the ring. Then look up the latitude for that angle in an almanac of Solar declinations.

fasten alidade to ring with paper fasteners or grommet through center holes.

RING

ALIDADE

fold up along dotted lines — both sides

Pocket Sundial
by Oberon Zell-Ravenheart (See p. 184)

Copy onto card stock, then cut out along thick outer lines. Fold so it looks like the little picture below. Glue together the triangular sections marked with degrees of latitude into a vertical fin. This part is called the gnomon.
After glue is dry, determine your local latitude, and cut the gnomon off at that line.

Cut off at your own latitude line ———

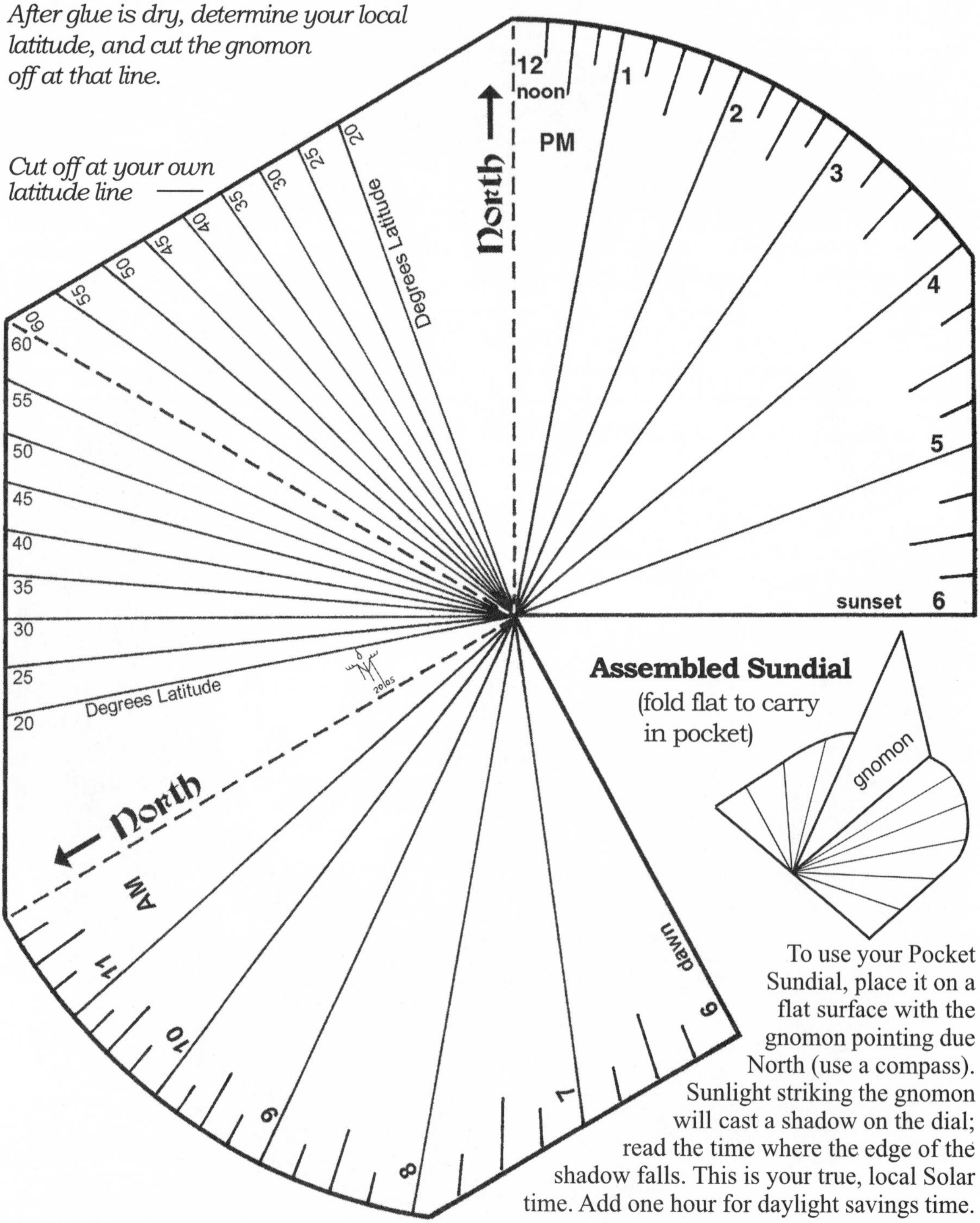

North →

12 noon
PM
1
2
3
4
5
sunset 6

Degrees Latitude

20 25 30 35 40 45 50 55 60

60 55 50 45 40 35 30 25 20

Degrees Latitude

← North

AM

11
10
9
8
7
dawn
6

Assembled Sundial
(fold flat to carry in pocket)

gnomon

To use your Pocket Sundial, place it on a flat surface with the gnomon pointing due North (use a compass). Sunlight striking the gnomon will cast a shadow on the dial; read the time where the edge of the shadow falls. This is your true, local Solar time. Add one hour for daylight savings time.

The Milky Way Galaxy

by Oberon Zell-Ravenheart (See p. 191)

Our galaxy, the Milky Way, is about 13 billion years old, and contains 400 billion stars. At its center is a gigantic black hole, called Sagittarius A. The main galactic disk is 100,000 light-years in diameter, with a central bulge 16,000 light-years thick. However, it is believed that an outer ring of ancient stars may extend the Milky Way's full diameter to 200,000 light-years.

The Milky Way's structure is called a "barred spiral." There are four main spiral arms, named Perseus, Carina-Sagittarius, Crux-Scutum, and Norma. Our Solar system is located 26,000 light-years from galactic center, between the outer Perseus Arm and the next inward Sagittarius Arm, on a secondary spur of stars we call the Orion Arm. In our region, the galactic disk is only 3,000 light-years thick, and we are 20 light years above the galactic plane. It takes about 266 million years for our sun to complete one galactic orbit, traveling at about 130-180 miles/second. We cover about a million miles each day!

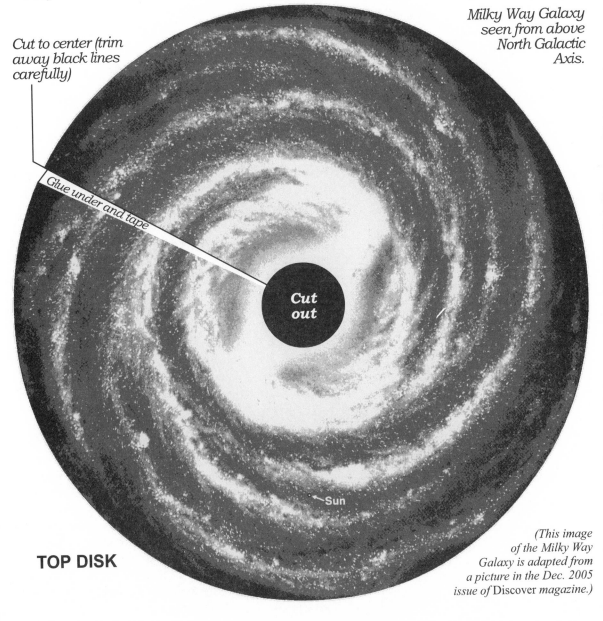

Milky Way Galaxy seen from above North Galactic Axis.

Cut to center (trim away black lines carefully)

Glue under and tape

Cut out

→ Sun

TOP DISK

(This image of the Milky Way Galaxy is adapted from a picture in the Dec. 2005 issue of Discover *magazine.)*

The Milky Way Galaxy

The Milky Way is one of two giant spiral galaxies in the Local Group, a cluster of three large and over thirty small galaxies, and is the second largest (after the Andromeda Galaxy M31. But with a mass between 750 billion and one trillion solar masses, the Milky Way is perhaps the most massive member of this group.

The Local Group lies on the fringe of the much larger Virgo Cluster, which contains 2,000 galaxies!

To assemble your model of the Milky way Galaxy, copy onto white card stock at 121% and cut out both disks, including the center holes. Glue and tape the wedge as shown. Insert a 1½" styrofoam ball (available at craft stores) in the center, and then glue the edges of both disks together, matching them up at the cuts.

Top Disk —

1½" styrofoam ball —

Bottom disk —

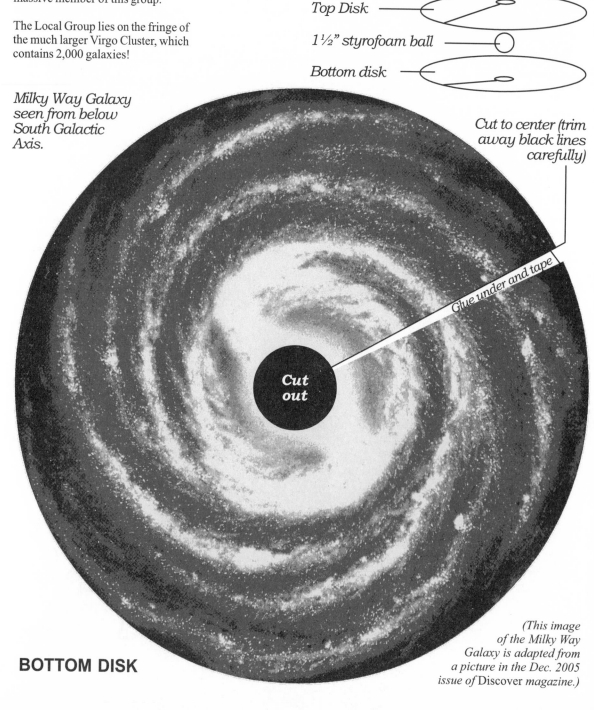

Milky Way Galaxy seen from below South Galactic Axis.

Cut to center (trim away black lines carefully)

Glue under and tape

Cut out

BOTTOM DISK

(This image of the Milky Way Galaxy is adapted from a picture in the Dec. 2005 issue of Discover magazine.)

The Mystic Pyramid
by Oberon Zell-Ravenheart (see p. 192)

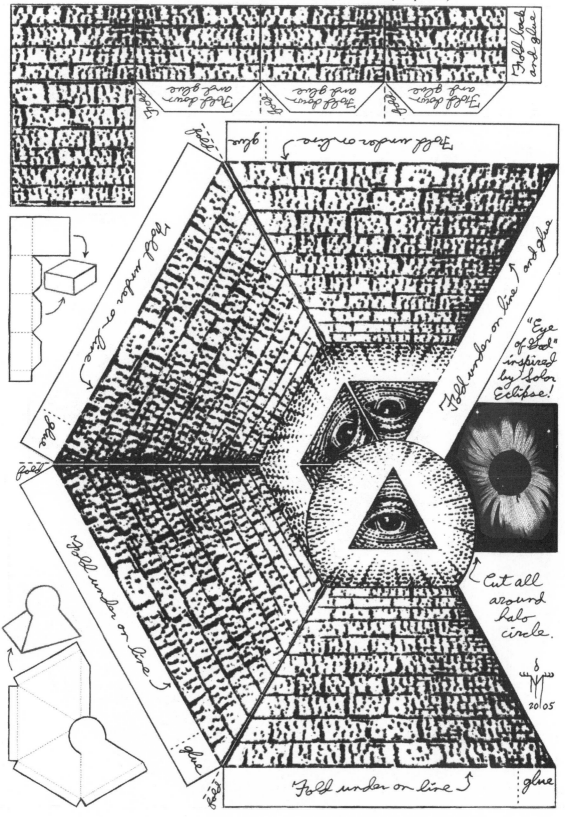

Golden Mean Calipers

by John "Apollonius" Opsopaus (See p. 285)

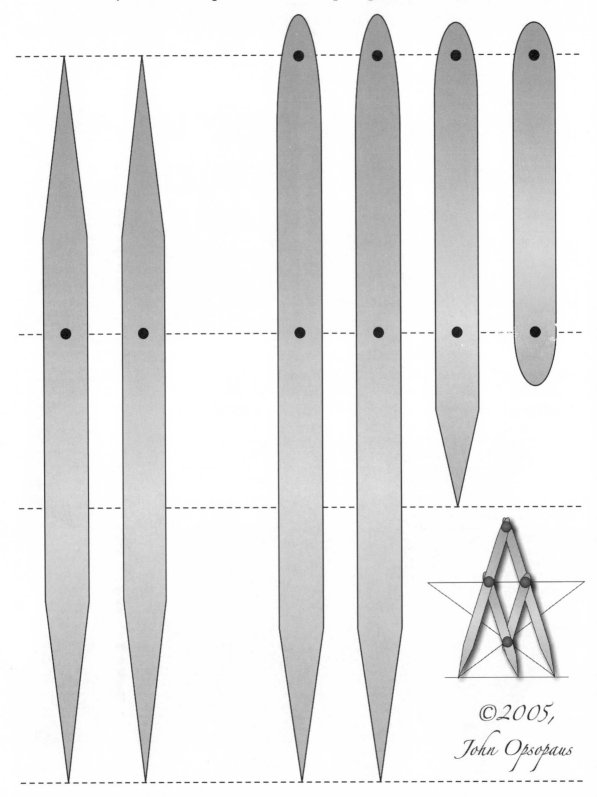

The 5 Platonic Solids

by Apollonius & Oberon (See pp. 205-206)

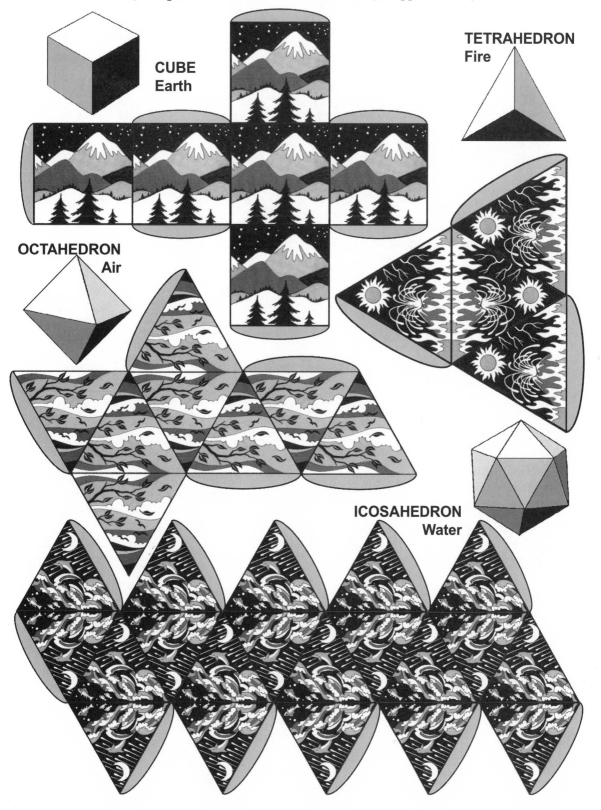

CUBE
Earth

TETRAHEDRON
Fire

OCTAHEDRON
Air

ICOSAHEDRON
Water

The 5 Platonic Solids

by Apollonius & Oberon

(See pp. 205-206)

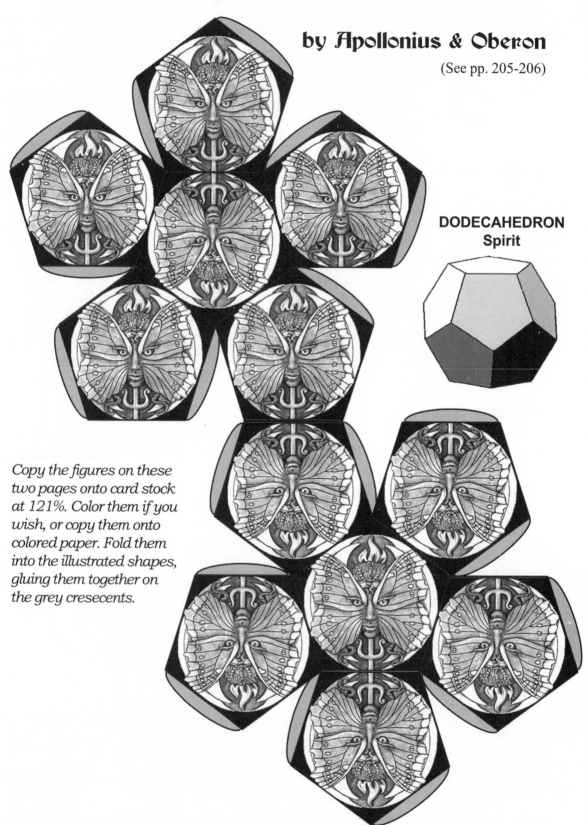

DODECAHEDRON
Spirit

Copy the figures on these two pages onto card stock at 121%. Color them if you wish, or copy them onto colored paper. Fold them into the illustrated shapes, gluing them together on the grey cresecents.

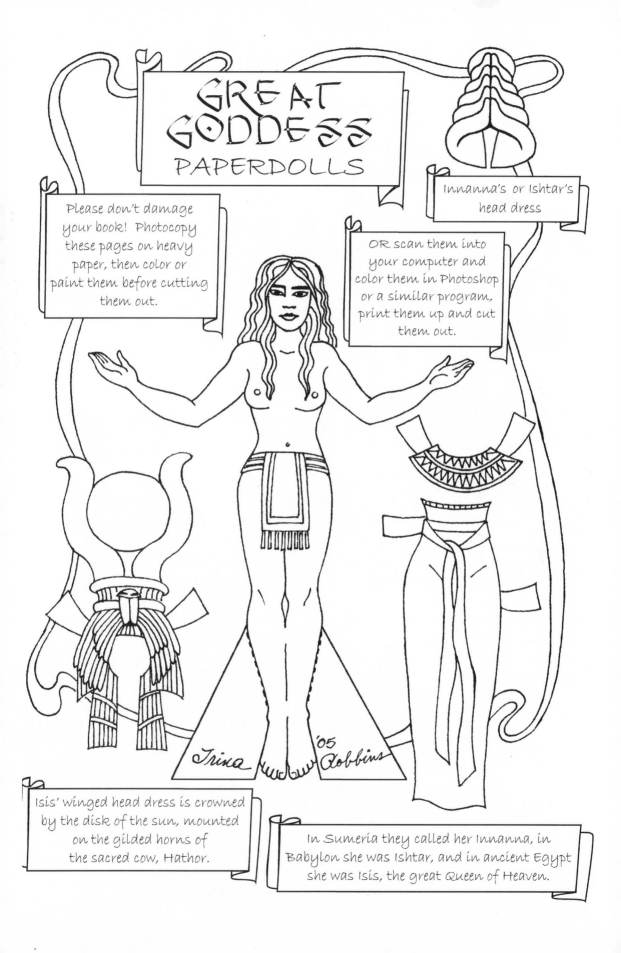

GREAT GODDESS PAPERDOLLS

Please don't damage your book! Photocopy these pages on heavy paper, then color or paint them before cutting them out.

Innanna's or Ishtar's head dress

OR scan them into your computer and color them in Photoshop or a similar program, print them up and cut them out.

Isis' winged head dress is crowned by the disk of the sun, mounted on the gilded horns of the sacred cow, Hathor.

In Sumeria they called her Innanna, in Babylon she was Ishtar, and in ancient Egypt she was Isis, the great Queen of Heaven.

Trina '05 Robbins